Cases in MARKETING MANAGEMENT

Cases in
MARKETING
MANAGEMENT

Kenneth L. Bernhardt
College of Business Administration
Georgia State University

Thomas C. Kinnear
Graduate School of Business Administration
The University of Michigan

1978

BUSINESS PUBLICATIONS, INC. Dallas, Texas 75243
Irwin-Dorsey Limited Georgetown, Ontario L7G 4B3

ISBN 0-256-02081-7
Library of Congress Catalog Card No. 77–90479

Printed in the United States of America

1 2 3 4 5 6 7 8 9 0 K 5 4 3 2 1 0 9 8

To Kathy and Connie

Preface

Marketing is an exciting and dynamic discipline. Unfortunately much of the excitement is hidden among the definitions and descriptions of concepts that are a necessary part of basic marketing textbooks. We believe that one way to make the study of marketing exciting and dynamic is to use cases. Cases allow the student to work on real marketing problems, to develop an appreciation for the types of problems that exist in the real world of marketing, and to develop the skills of analysis and decision making so necessary for success in marketing and other areas of business. Cases represent as close an approximation of the realities of actually working in marketing as is possible without taking a job in the field.

Your task as a user of this casebook is to work hard to develop well reasoned solutions to the problems confronting the decision maker in each of the cases. A framework to assist you in developing solutions is presented in Part I of this book. Basically you will be using this, or some other framework suggested by your instructor, to analyze the cases in this book. By applying this framework to each case that you are assigned, you will develop your analytic skills. Like all skills, you will find this difficult at first. However, as you practice, you will get better, until it will become second nature to you. This is exactly the same way one develops athletic or musical skills.

The cases in this book represent a broad range of marketing problems. The book contains consumer and industrial cases, profit and nonprofit cases, social marketing cases, specific marketing mix area cases, and general cases, plus cases on marketing and public policy. Each case is designed to fit into a specific section of a course in marketing management. The cases are long and complex enough to require good analysis, but not so long and complex to be overly burdensome.

This book contains 41 cases and 2 case-related exercises. Twenty-four of the cases and both exercises were written by the authors of this book. In some instances we had a coauthor and we have noted the names of the coauthors on the title pages of the cases concerned. We wish to thank these coauthors for their assistance and for allowing us to use the cases: William Bohan, Duncan LaBay, Peggy Lipsey, Cynthia Rice, and John Wright. Also, we owe a special thank you to Bonnie Reece and Sherri McIntyre for their assistance on a number of cases.

We would also like to thank the executives of the companies who allowed us to develop cases about their problems, and who have released these cases for use in this book.

The remaining 17 cases were written by many distinguished marketing casewriters. We appreciate their allowing us to reproduce their cases here. The names of each of these persons are noted on the title pages of the cases concerned: Gerald Crawford, Kenneth Hardy, Robert Hartley, Subhash Jain, C. B. Johnston, Fred Kniffin, Robert Kaiser, Zarrel Lambert, T. Levitt, Iqbal Mathur, John Murphy, Robert Nourse, Lonnie Ostrom, Charles Patti, C. P. Rao, William Rief, Adrian Ryans, Donald Scotton, R. Sorenson, Jose de la Torre, David Weinstein, and U. Wiechman.

We are also indebted to Charles Gebhard, former Director of the Intercollegiate Case Clearing House, for his assistance in gaining releases for two cases.

In writing some of the cases, we were assisted by graduate student casewriters. We appreciate their efforts. They were: Cheryl Allen on the Samahaiku case, Steven Becker on the Consolidated Bathurst Pulp and Paper case, Stephen Field on the Sears, Roebuck and Company and the FTC case, G. Ludwig Laudisi on the Amtrak case, Terry Murphy on the League of Catholic Women and the *Michiganensian* cases, William O. Adcock on the Rich's Department Store case, and Marty Schwartz on the League of Catholic Women case.

We should like to thank our colleagues at Georgia State University, the University of Michigan, and the Southern Case Research Association for their helpful comments on early versions of some of the cases. We would specifically like to thank C. Merle Crawford, Claude Martin, James Taylor,

Martin Warshaw, and John Wright. We would also like to thank James Scott for his direction on the Da-Roche Laboratories, Dutch Foods (A), and Wolverine World Wide cases.

Finally, we would like to thank Brenda Hemperley, Judy Kindig, and Pamela Brown for their dedication in typing this manuscript, often under adverse conditions. Theirs was the truly hard work.

February 1978   KENNETH L. BERNHARDT
                                                          THOMAS C. KINNEAR

Contents

PART III.   MARKETING RESEARCH, 81

PART IV.   PRODUCT DECISIONS, 135

PART V. DISTRIBUTION DECISIONS, 211

PART VI. PROMOTION DECISIONS, 255

PART IX. MARKETING PROGRAMS, 479

PART I

AN ORIENTATION TO THE CASE METHOD

CHAPTER 1

Note to the student on the case method

The case method is different from other methods of teaching, and requires that students take an active role rather than a passive one. The case method places the student in a simulated business environment, and substitutes the student in the place of the business manager required to make a set of decisions. To define it, a case is:

> typically a record of a business issue which actually has been faced by business executives, together with surrounding facts, opinions, and prejudices upon which the executives had to depend. These real and particularized cases are presented to students for considered analysis, open discussion, and final decision as to the type of action which should be taken.[1]

With the case method the process of arriving at an answer is what is important. The instructor's expectation is that the student will develop an ability to make decisions, to support those decisions with appropriate analysis, and to learn to communicate ideas both orally and in writing. The student is required to determine the problem as well as the solution. This method of teaching thus shifts much

---

[1] Charles I. Gragg, "Because Wisdom Can't Be Told," *Harvard Alumni Bulletin,* October 19, 1940.

of the responsibility to the student, and a great deal of time is required on the part of the student.

The case method often causes a great deal of insecurity on the part of students who are required to make decisions often with very little information and limited time. There is no single right answer to any of the cases in this book, an additional source of insecurity. The goal is not to develop a set of right answers, but to learn to reason well with the data available. This process is truly learning by doing.

Studying under the case method will result in the development of skills in critical thinking. The student will learn how to effectively reason when dealing with specific problems. The development of communication skills is also important, and students will learn to present their analysis in a cogent and convincing manner. They must defend their analysis and plan of action against the criticism of others in the class. In the class discussion, individual students may find that the opinions of other members of the class differ from their own. In some cases this will be because the individual has overlooked certain important points or that some factors have been weighted more heavily compared to the weighting used by other students. The process of presenting and defending conflicting points of view causes individual members of the class to reconsider the views they had of the case before the discussion began. This leads to a clearer perception of problems, a recognition of the many and often conflicting interpretations of the facts and events in the case, and a greater awareness of the complexities with which management decisions are reached.

In preparing for class using the case method, the student should first read the case quickly. The goal is to gain a feel for the type of problem presented in the case, the type of organization involved, and so on. Next, the student should read the case thoroughly to learn all the key facts in the case. The student should not blindly accept all the data presented, as not all information is equally reliable or relevant. As part of the process of mastering the facts, it frequently will be desirable to utilize the numerical data presented in the case to make any possible calculations and comparisons that will help analyze the problems involved in the case. The case will have to be read a number of times before the analysis is completed.

The student must add to the facts by making reasonable assumptions regarding many aspects of the situation. Business decision making is rarely based on perfect information. All of the cases in this book are actual business cases and the student is provided with all the information that the executives involved had at their disposal. Often students cannot believe the low level of information available for decision making, but this is often the case. What is required in those situations is the making of reasonable assumptions and learning to make decisions under uncertainty. There is often a strong reluctance on the part of the student to do this, but the ability to make decisions based on well-reasoned assumptions is a skill that must be developed for a manager to be truly effective.

Once the student has mastered the facts in the case, the next step is to identify and specify the issues and problems toward which the executive involved should be directing his or her attention. Often the issues may be very obscure. Learning to separate problems from symptoms is an important skill to learn. Often there will be a number of subissues involved and it will be necessary to break the problem down into component parts.

The next step in the student's case preparation is to identify alternative courses of action. Usually there are a number of possible solutions to the problems in the case, and the student should be careful not to lock in on only one alternative before several possible alternatives have been thoroughly evaluated.

The next step is to evaluate each of the alternative plans of action. It is at this stage of the analysis that the student is required to marshall and analyze all the facts for each alternative program. The assumptions the student is required to make are very important here, and the student must apply all the analytical skills possible, including both qualitative and quantitative.

After all the alternatives have been thoroughly analyzed, the student must make a decision concerning the specific course of action to take. It should be recognized that several of the alternatives may "work," and that there are a number of different ways of resolving the issues in the case. The important consideration is that the plan of action actually decided upon has been thoroughly analyzed from all angles, is internally consistent, and has a high probability of meeting the manager's objectives.

Once an overall strategy has been determined, it is important that consideration be given to the implementation of that strategy. At this stage, the student must determine who is to do what, when, and how. A professor may start out a class by asking the question, "What should Mr. Jones do tomorrow?" Unless the students have given some thought to the implementation of the strategy decided upon, they will be unprepared for such a question. Improper implementation of an excellent strategy may doom it to failure, so it is important to follow through with appropriate analysis at this stage.

During the class discussion the instructor will act more as a moderator than a lecturer, guiding the discussion and calling on students for their opinions. A significant amount of learning will take place by participating in the discussion. The goal is for the students to integrate all their ideas, relating them to the goals of the company, the strengths and weaknesses of the company and its competition, the way consumers buy, and the resources available. A suggested framework for the integration of these ideas is presented in the next chapter of this book in the Appendix entitled "Outline for case analysis."

The student's classroom discussion should avoid the rehashing, without analysis, of case facts. Students should recognize that the professor and all the other students in the class have thoroughly read the case and are familiar with the facts. The objective therefore is to interpret the facts and use them to support the proposed plan of action. The case method obviously requires a great deal of preparation time by the student. The payoff is that after spending this time adequately preparing each of the steps described, the student will have developed the ability to make sound marketing management decisions.

CHAPTER 2

*Introduction
to marketing
decision making*

In Chapter 1, you were introduced to your role in the execution of an effective case course in marketing. In summary, the primary task is to complete a competent analysis of the cases assigned to you. If you have never undertaken the analysis of a marketing case before, you are probably wondering just how you should go about doing this. Is there some framework that is appropriate for this task? Indeed, there arc a number of such frameworks. The purpose of this chapter is to present one such framework to you. We think you will find it useful in analyzing the cases in this book.

AN OUTLINE FOR CASE ANALYSIS

The Appendix to this chapter is the summary document for the approach we believe that you should use for case analysis. We suggest that you apply the types of questions listed there in your analysis. Figure 2–1 provides an overview of this outline. Basically, we are suggesting that you begin by doing a complete analysis of the *situation* facing the organization in the case. This *situation analysis* includes an assessment of (1) the nature of demand for the product, (2) the extent of demand, (3) the nature of competition, (4) the environmental climate,

(5) the stage of the life cycle for the product, (6) the skills of the firm, (7) the financial resources of the firm, and (8) the distribution structure. In some cases legal aspects may also form part of a good situation analysis. The premise here is that one cannot begin to make decisions until a thorough understanding of the situation at hand is obtained.

Once a detailed situation analysis is prepared, one is in a position to summarize the *problems* and *opportunities* that arise out of the situation analysis. This in turn should lead to the generation of a set of *alternatives* that are worthy of being considered as solutions to the problems and actualizers of the opportunities.

These alternatives are then *evaluated* using arguments generated from (1) the detailed situation analysis, (2) the summary statement of problems and opportunities, and (3) relevant financial analysis (break-even points, market shares, and so on). The use of financial analysis is discussed in Chapter 3. The point here is that we use the situation analysis to generate and evaluate alternative programs. The pros and cons of each alternative are weighed as part of this evaluation and a *decision* is then reached.

A GOOD CASE ANALYSIS

The question naturally arises: In applying the outline in the Appendix to a case, how do I know when I have done a good analysis? The purpose

FIGURE 2–1

Overview of a framework for case analysis

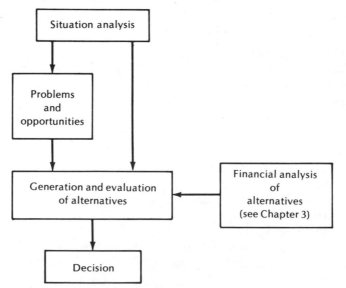

of this section is to raise some points that are often used by instructors to evaluate either an oral or written analysis.

1. Be complete. It is imperative that the case analysis be complete. By this is meant that each area of the situation analysis must be discussed, problems and opportunities must be identified, alternatives must be presented and evaluated using the situation analysis and relevant financial analysis, and a decision must be made. An analysis that omits parts of the situation analysis, or only recognizes one alternative, and so forth is not a good analysis.

2. Avoid rehashing case facts. Every case has a lot of factual information. A good analysis uses facts that are relevant to the situation at hand to make summary points of analysis. A poor analysis just restates or rehashes these facts without making relevant summary comments. Consider the use of a set of financial facts that might appear in a case:

Rehash: The current ratio is 1.5:1, cash on hand is $15,000, retained earnings are $50,000.

Analysis: Because of a very weak financial position, as demonstrated by a poor cash position and current ratio, the firm will be constrained in the activities it can undertake to ones requiring little immediate cash outlay.

3. Make reasonable assumptions. Every case is incomplete in terms of some piece of information that you would like to have. We would, of course, like to have all the necessary information presented to us in each case. This is not possible for two reasons. First, it would make the cases far too long to be capable of being analyzed in a reasonable period of time. Second, and more important, incomplete information is an accurate reflection of the real world. All marketing decisions are made on the basis of incomplete information. Often, it just costs too much or takes too long to collect the desired information.

A good case analysis must make realistic assumptions to fill in the gaps of information in the case. For example, the case may not describe the purchase decision process for the product of interest. A poor analysis would either omit mentioning this or just state that no information is available. A good analysis would attempt to present this purchase decision process, by classifying the product (a shopping good?), and drawing on the student's real-life experience. Could you not describe the purchase decision process for carpeting, even though you have never read a research report about it?

The reasonableness of your assumptions will be challenged by your fellow students and instructor. This is one of the things that makes case discussions exciting. The point is that it is better to make your assumptions explicit and incorporate them in your analysis than to use them implicitly or not make them at all. If we make explicit assumptions we can later come back and see if our assumptions were correct or not.

4. Don't confuse symptoms with problems.   In summarizing a firm's problems a poor analysis confuses the symptoms with real problems. For example, one might list two problems as (1) sales are down, (2) sales force turnover is high. This would not be correct. These are symptoms. The real problem is identified by answering the question: Why are sales down or why is sales force turnover high? For example, sales force turnover may be high due to inadequate sales training. But this may not yet be the root problem. You still need to ask: Why is sales training inadequate? It may be that the sales manager has ignored this area through his or her lack of knowledge of how to train people. What you do is keep asking "why" until you are satisfied that you have identified the root problem.

5. Deal with objectives realistically.   Most cases present a statement from management about their objectives. For example, it might say they want a sales growth rate of 25 percent per year. Good analysis critically evaluates statements of objectives and revises them if necessary. Then it uses these revised objectives as part of the argument about which alternative to select. Poor analysis either ignores the stated objectives or accepts them at face value.

6. Recognize alternatives.   A good analysis explicitly recognizes and discusses alternative action plans. In some cases, these alternatives are stated in the case. In other cases, the student must develop alternatives beyond those stated in the case. A poor analysis explicitly recognizes only one or two alternatives or only takes the ones explicitly stated in the case.

7. Don't be assertive.   In some case analyses, the decision that was made is clear to the reader or listener in about the first sentence of the situation analysis. The whole rest of the analysis is then a justification of the desired solution. This type of analysis is very poor. It in effect has asserted an answer before completing a situation analysis. Usually, other alternatives are ignored or treated as all bad, and the desired solution is treated as all good. You must do your situation analysis, and recognize alternatives, before evaluating them and reaching a decision.

8. Discuss the pros and cons of each alternative.   Every alternative always has pros and cons. A good analysis explicitly discusses these. In a poor analysis there is no explicit discussion of the pros and cons of each alternative.

9. Make effective use of financial and other quantitative information. Financial data (break-even points, and so on) and information derived from other quantitative analyses can add a great deal to a good case analysis. Totally ignoring these aspects or handling them improperly results in a poor case analysis. This analysis should be presented in detail in a written appendix or in class if asked for. However, in the body of a paper or in an oral discussion only present the summary conclusions out of the analysis. Say: "The break-even point is 220,000 units," and be prepared to present the detail if asked.

10. Reach a clear decision.   You must reach a clear decision. You might like to hedge your bets and say "maybe this, maybe that." However, part of the skill of decision making is to be forced to reach a decision under ambiguous circumstances, and then be prepared to defend this decision. This does not mean that you do not recognize limitations of your position or positive aspects of other positions. It just means that despite all that, you have reached a particular decision.

11. Make good use of evidence developed in your situation analysis. In reaching a decision, a good analysis reaches a decision that is logically consistent with the situation analysis that was done. This is the ultimate test of an analysis. Other students may disagree with your situation analysis and thus your resultant conclusion, but they should not be able to fault the logical connection between your situation analysis and decision. If they can you have a poor case analysis.

The "Outline for case analysis" contained in the Appendix is designed to assist you in doing case analysis. You should keep the points stressed in this section in mind when you apply this outline.

OVERVIEW OF ANALYSIS STRUCTURE

Outline for case analysis*

I. Situation analysis
   A. Nature of demand.
   B. Extent of demand.
   C. Nature of competition.
   D. Environmental climate.
   E. Stage of product life cycle.
   F. Cost structure of the industry.
   G. Skills of the firm.
   H. Financial resources of the firm.
   I. Distribution structure.
II. Problems and opportunities
   A. Key problem areas.
   B. Key opportunities.
   C. On balance, the situation is.
III. Generation and evaluation of alternative marketing programs
   A. Objectives defined.
   B. Marketing mix/program decisions.
IV. Decision

DETAILS OF ANALYSIS STRUCTURE

I. SITUATION ANALYSIS

A. Nature of demand

   The purpose of this section is to make *explicit* your beliefs and assumptions regarding the nature of the purchase decision process (consumer or industrial) for the goods or services under investigation. In case analysis we are concerned primarily with developing your *skills* of analysis to identify areas of problems and opportunities and in developing well-supported marketing program recommendations. Conflicting student beliefs and assumptions should lead to interesting and enlightening class dis-

---

* This outline is adapted from an unpublished note by Professor James R. Taylor of the University of Michigan. Used with permission.

cussion regarding the nature of the purchase decision process and its implication for marketing programs. We hope that through this type of class discussion, you will increase your sensitivity to, and understanding of buyers and their behavior. Again, the value of this type of analysis concerns its application to better *reasoned* and *supported* marketing program decisions. Hopefully, the development of your skills in this area has value in improving your *judgment capabilities* and in increasing your understanding of marketing decision making.

Analysis areas and questions

1. How do buyers (consumer and industrial) *currently* go about buying existing products or services? Describe the main types of behavior patterns and attitudes.

    a. Number of stores shopped or industrial sources considered.
    b. Degree of overt information seeking.
    c. Degree of brand awareness and loyalty.
    d. Location of product category decision—home or point of sale.
    e. Location of brand decision—home or point of sale.
    f. Sources of product information and current awareness and knowledge levels.
    g. Who makes the purchase decision—male, female, adult, child, purchasing agent, buying committee, so on?
    h. Who influences the decision maker?
    i. Individual or group decision (computers versus candy bar).
    j. Duration of the decision process (repeat, infrequent or new purchase situation).
    k. Buyer's interest, personal involvement or excitement regarding the purchase (hairpins versus trip to Caribbean).
    l. Risk or uncertainty of negative purchase outcome—high, medium or low (specialized machinery versus hacksaw blades) (pencil versus hair coloring).
    m. Functional versus psychosocial considerations (electric drill versus new dress).
    n. Time of consumption (gum versus dining room furniture).

    Basically, we are attempting to determine the *who, what, where, when, why,* and *how* of the purchase decision.

    Note: The key to using the above analysis is to ask what are the implications for marketing programs? For example, if the purchase (brand) decision is made in the store and branding is not important to the buyers, what implication does this have for national TV advertising versus in-store display? Do you see how you might *use* this information to support a recommendation for intensive distribution and point-of-purchase promotion and display?

2. Can the market be meaningfully segmented or broken into several homogeneous groups with respect to "what they want" and "how they buy"?
    Criteria:
    a. Age.
    b. Family life cycle.
    c. Geographic location.
    d. Heavy versus light users.
    e. Nature of the buying process.
    f. Product usage.

> *Note:* For each case situation, you should determine whether a more effective marketing program could be developed for each segment versus having an overall program for all segments. The real issue is whether tailoring your program to a segment will give you a competitive advantage. Of course, there may be negatives to this strategy in terms of volume and cost considerations.

B. Extent of demand

The purpose of this section is to evaluate demand in an aggregate and quantitative sense. We are basically concerned with the actual or potential size of the overall market and developing sound estimates of company sales potential.

Analysis areas and questions
1. What is the size of the market (units and dollars) now and what will the future hold?
2. What are the current market shares and what are the selective demand trends (units and dollars)?
3. Is it best to analyze the market on an aggregate or on a segmented basis?

> *Note:* We are basically concerned with making *explicit* assumptions regarding primary and selective demand trends. These estimates are critical to determining the profit (loss) potential of alternative marketing programs.

C. Nature of competition

The purpose of this section is to evaluate the present and future structure of competition. The key is to understand how the

buyer evaluates alternative products or services relative to his
or her needs.

Analysis areas and questions

1. What is the present and future structure of competition?
   a. Number of competitors (5 versus 2,000).
   b. Market shares.
   c. Financial resources.
   d. Marketing resources and skills.
   e. Production resources and skills.
2. What are the current marking programs of established competitors?
   Why are they successful or unsuccessful?
3. Is there an opportunity for another competitor? Why?
4. What are the anticipated retaliatory moves of competitors? Can they
   neutralize different marketing programs we might develop?

> *Note:* Failure to correctly evaluate demand and competition is one
> common reason for unprofitable marketing programs. Also,
> Sections A, B, and C are analysis areas particularly important
> in making decisions concerning "positioning" your product
> and developing the marketing program to support your posi-
> tioning strategy.

D. Environmental climate

It's not hard to identify current marketing programs that have
been highly disrupted by a changing environmental climate. The
energy crisis together with pollution, safety, and consumerism
concerns, can bring many such examples to mind. We are sure
you can identify firms who have benefited from the energy crisis
The point is that the environment is constantly changing and
those organizations which can adapt to change are the ones
which enjoy long-run success.

Analysis areas and questions

1. What are the relevant social, political, economic, and technological
   trends?
2. How do you evaluate these trends? Do they represent opportunities
   or problems?

E. Stage of product life cycle

The purpose of this section is to make explicit assumptions
about where a product is in its life cycle. This is important because the effectiveness of particular marketing variables may
vary by stages of the life cycle.

Analysis areas and questions
1. In what stage of the life cycle is the product category?
    a. What is the chronological age of the product category? (Younger more favorable than older?)
    b. What is the state of the consumers' knowledge of the product category? (More complete the knowledge—more unfavorable?)
2. What market characteristics support your stage of life cycle evaluation?

   F. Cost structure of the industry
        Here we are concerned with the amount and composition of the marginal or additional cost of supplying increased output. It can be argued that the lower these costs, the easier it may be to cover the costs of developing an effective marketing program (see accompanying table).

	Marginal costs	
	High*	*Low†*
Selling price per unit.........................	$1.00	$1.00
Variable costs per unit......................	0.80	0.10
Contribution per unit........................	$0.20	$0.90

* Such as the garment and auto industries.
† Such as the hotel and telephone industries.

   G. Skills of the firm
        The purpose of this section is to critically evaluate the organization making the decision. Here, we effectively place limits on what they are capable of accomplishing.

Analysis areas and questions
1. Do we have the skills and experience to perform the functions necessary to be in this business?
    a. Marketing skills.
    b. Production skills.
    c. Management skills.
    d. Financial skills.
    e. R&D skills.
2. How do our skills compare to competitors?
    a. Production fit.
    b. Marketing fit.
    c. Etc.

H. Financial resources of the firm

Analysis areas and questions
1. Do we have the funds to support an effective marketing program?
2. Where are the funds coming from and when will they be available?

I. Distribution structure

The purpose of this area is to identify and evaluate the availability of channels of distribution.

Analysis areas and questions
1. What channels exist and can we gain access to the channels?
2. Cost versus revenue from different channels?
3. Feasibility of using multiple channels?
4. Nature and degree of within and between channel competition?
5. Trends in channel structure?
6. Requirements of different channels for promotion and margin?
7. Will it be profitable for particular channels to handle my product?

II. PROBLEMS AND OPPORTUNITIES

Here we prepare a definite listing of *key* problems and opportunities identified from the situation analysis which relate to the specific issues or decision questions faced by management.

A. Key problem areas
B. Key opportunities
C. On balance, the situation is:
   a. Very favorable.
   b. Somewhat favorable.
   c. Neutral.
   d. Somewhat unfavorable.
   e. Very unfavorable.

Note: At this point, the critical issue is whether a profitable marketing program can be formulated or whether a current marketing program needs to be changed in order to overcome the problem areas and/or take advantage of opportunities.

III. EVALUATION OF ALTERNATIVE MARKETING PROGRAMS

A marketing program consists of a series of marketing mix decisions which represent an integrated and consistent "action plan" for achieving predetermined goals. Different marketing programs may be required for various target segments. For a given target segment, alternative programs should be formulated and evaluated as to the effectiveness of each in achieving predetermined goals.

A. Objectives defined
1.   Target market segments identified.
2.   Volume to be sold (dollars or units).
3.   Profit analysis (contribution analysis, break-even analysis, ROI, etc.).

B. Marketing mix/program decisions
1.   Product decisions
     a.   Develop new product(s).
     b.   Change current product(s).
     c.   Add or drop product from line.
     d.   Product positioning.
     e.   Branding (national, private, secondary).
2.   Distribution decisions
     a.   Intensity of distribution (intensive to exclusive).
     b.   Multiple channels.
     c.   Types of wholesalers and retailers (discounters, so on).
     d.   Degree of channel directness.
3.   Promotion decisions
     a.   Mix of personal selling, advertising, dealer incentives, and sales promotion.
     b.   Branding—family versus individual.
     c.   Budget.
     d.   Message.
     e.   Media.
4.   Price decisions
     a.   Price level (above, same or below).
     b.   Price variation (discount structure, geographic).
     c.   Margins.
     d.   Administration of price level.
     e.   Price leadership.

   Note: The above four decision areas involve specific strategy issues which together form a marketing program.

   The key to effective marketing decision making is to evaluate alternative marketing programs using information from the situation analysis. The pros and cons for each alternative should be presented and discussed.

IV. DECISION

The outcome of the evaluation of alternatives is a decision. You must make a decision. Case analysis is designed to develop your skills in making well-supported and reasoned marketing decisions. The quality of your reasoning is much more important than reaching any particular decision. Generally, if your situation analysis is different (you perceive the facts differently and have made different assumptions) from someone else, you should reach different decisions.

CHAPTER 3

Financial analysis for marketing decision making

In Chapter 2, we laid out an approach to marketing decision making. The "Outline for case analysis" summarized this approach. There is, however, one more important aspect of a competent case analysis that was not presented in that outline. This is the financial analysis of the alternatives, presented in a case.

The ultimate goals of all marketing activities are usually expressed in financial terms. The company has a particular return on investment in mind, or growth in earnings per share. Proposed marketing activities must thus be evaluated for their financial implications. Can you imagine asking your boss for $1 million for a new distribution center or an advertising program without having to present the financial implications of such a request? It does not happen in the real marketing world, nor should it happen in a good case analysis.

Financial analysis can be complex. Our purpose here is to present some simple financial calculations that can be useful in case analysis. More sophisticated financial techniques are left to courses in financial management. Basically, the advanced techniques add little to the understanding of the cases in this book, and take too much time and effort for the reader to implement.

It should clearly be understood that

financial considerations are only one aspect in the evaluation of marketing alternatives. Marketing alternatives cannot be reduced to a set of numbers. Qualitative aspects derived from the situation analysis are also relevant. Sometimes the qualitative aspects are consistent in terms of pointing to an alternative to select. In other cases, they may point to different alternatives. The task of the student is to formulate both types of arguments for each alternative, and to select an alternative based upon which arguments the student thinks should carry the most weight.

This chapter assumes that the student is familiar with elementary financial accounting concepts. What we will present here are some useful concepts not usually presented in basic accounting courses.

CONTRIBUTION

Contribution per unit is defined as the difference between the selling price of an item and the variable costs of producing and selling that item. It is in essence the amount of money per unit available to the marketer to cover fixed production costs, corporate overhead and having done that, to yield a profit. So, if a manufacturer sells an item for \$12.00, and the variable costs are \$8.40, then

$$\begin{aligned}
\text{Contribution per unit} &= \text{Selling price} - \text{Variable costs} \\
&= \$12.00 \qquad - \$8.40 \\
&= \$\ 3.60
\end{aligned}$$

Each unit this company sells gives it \$3.60 to cover fixed costs.

Total contribution is the contribution per unit times the number of units sold. So, if this firm sold 20,000 units:

$$\begin{aligned}
\text{Total contribution} &= \text{Contribution per unit} \times \text{Units sold} \\
&= \$\ 3.60 \times 20,000 \\
&= \$72,000
\end{aligned}$$

If the total relevant fixed costs of this product were \$42,000, the *profit* earned by this product would be:

$$\begin{aligned}
\text{Profit} &= \text{Total contribution} - \text{Fixed costs} \\
&= \$72,000 \qquad\qquad - \$42,000 \\
&= \$30,000
\end{aligned}$$

COSTS

In determining contributions and profit we used the terms variable cost and fixed cost. At this point we want to define them more formally. Variable costs are those costs that are fixed *per unit* and therefore, vary in their total amount depending upon the number of units produced and sold. That is, it takes a certain amount of raw materials and labor to produce a unit of product. The more we produce the more total variable costs are.

Fixed costs are costs that remain constant in *total amount* despite changes in the volume of production or sales. These costs would thus vary per unit depending upon the number of units produced or sold.

Sorting out which costs are variable and fixed is important in good case analysis. The rule to apply is: if it varies in *total* as volume changes, it is a variable cost. Thus, labor, raw materials, packaging, salesperson's commissions would be variable costs. Note that all marketing costs except commissions would be considered fixed costs. Don't be fooled if a marketing cost or other fixed cost is presented in a per unit form. It may look like a variable cost, but it is not. It is only that much per unit at one given volume. For example, if we are told that advertising cost per unit will be $1, what this means is that at the end of the year when we divide total sales into advertising expenditures the result is expected to be $1 per unit. What we must be told is at what volume advertising is expected to be $1 per unit. If the expected volume level is 300,000 units, we then know that the firm intends to spend $300,000 ($1 × 300,000 units) on advertising. This $300,000 is a fixed cost. Note that if they sold less than 300,000 units, the cost per unit would exceed $1 and vice versa. So beware of fixed costs that are allocated to units and presented in a per unit form.

BREAK EVEN

A solid perspective on many marketing alternatives can often be obtained by determining the unit or dollar sales necessary to cover all relevant fixed costs. This sales level is called the break-even point. We define

1. Break-even point in units $= \dfrac{\text{Total fixed costs}}{\text{Contribution per unit}}$

2. Break-even point in dollars $= \dfrac{\text{Total fixed costs}}{1 - \dfrac{\text{Variable cost per unit}}{\text{Selling price per unit}}}$

or

$$= \text{Break-even point in units} \times \text{Selling price per unit}$$

Let's illustrate these definitions. Suppose that (1) direct labor is $7.50 per unit, (2) raw materials are $2 per unit, (3) selling price is $22 per unit, (4) advertising and sales force costs are $400,000, and (5) other relevant fixed costs are $100,000.

$$\text{Contribution per unit} = \text{Selling price} - \text{Variable costs}$$
$$\text{Contribution per unit} = \$22.00 - (7.50 + \$2.00)$$
$$= \$22.00 - \$9.50$$
$$= \$12.50$$

$$\text{Break-even point in units} = \frac{\text{Total fixed costs}}{\text{Contribution per unit}}$$
$$= \frac{\$400,000 + \$100,000}{\$12.50}$$
$$= 40,000 \text{ units}$$

$$\text{Break-even point in dollars} = \frac{\$500,000}{1 - \dfrac{\$9.50}{\$22.00}}$$
$$= \frac{\$500,000}{1 - 0.4318181} = \$880,000$$

Alternatively

$$\text{Break-even point in dollars} = 40,000 \times \$22.00 \text{ per unit}$$
$$= \$880,000$$

PROFIT TARGETS

Breaking even is not as much fun as making a profit. Thus, we often want to incorporate a profit target level into our calculations. Basically, we are answering the question: at what volume do we earn X profits? Covering a profit target is just like covering a fixed cost. So in the previous example, if we set $60,000 as our profit target we would have to sell an additional number of units equal to:

$$\text{Units to cover profit target} = \frac{\text{Profit target}}{\text{Contribution per unit}}$$
$$= \frac{\$60,000}{\$12.50} = 4,800 \text{ units}$$

Total units to reach this target is

$$40,000 + 4,800 = 44,800 \text{ or } \frac{\$500,000 + \$60,000}{\$12.50} = 44,800$$

Break-even analysis is a useful tool for comparing alternative marketing programs. It tells us how many units must be sold, but does not help us with the critical question of how many units will be sold.

MARKET SHARE

$$\text{Market share} = \frac{\text{Company sales level}}{\text{Total market sales}}$$

This calculation adds perspective to proposed action plans. Suppose that the total market sales are 290,000 units and our sales level needed to break even is 40,000 units. Thus, the required market share to break even is:

$$\frac{40,000}{290,000} = 13.8\%$$

The question then to ask is whether this market share can be obtained with the proposed marketing program.

CAPITAL EXPENDITURES

Often a particular marketing program proposes expenditures for capital equipment. These would be fixed costs associated with the proposed program. Typically, they should not be all charged to the relevant fixed cost for that proposal. For example, suppose that $5 million are to be expended for equipment that will last ten years. If we charge all this to the break-even calculation in year one, it will be very high. Further, for years two through ten, the break-even point will fall substantially. It is better to allocate this $5 million equally over the ten years. Thus $500,000 would be a relevant fixed cost in each year associated with the equipment. What one needs to do is to make some reasonable assumption about the useful life of capital assets and divide the total cost over this time period.

RELEVANT COSTS

The issue often arises as to what fixed costs are relevant to a particular proposal. The rule to use is: a fixed cost is relevant if the expenditure varies due to the acceptance of that proposal. Thus, new equipment, new research and development, and so on, are relevant. Last year's advertising or previous research and development dollars, for example, do not vary with the current decision and thus are not a relevant cost of the proposed program. Past expenditures are referred to as *sunk costs*. They should not enter into current decisions. Decisions are future oriented.

Corporate overhead presents a special problem. Generally, it does not vary with a particular decision. We don't fire the president in selecting between marketing programs. However, in some instances, some overhead may be directly attributable to a particular decision. In this instance it would be a relevant cost. We should recognize that to stay in business a firm must cover all its costs in the long run. Also, from a financial accounting point of view all costs are relevant. This type of accounting is concerned with preparing income statements and balance sheets for reporting to investors. In marketing decision making we are interested in managerial, not financial, accounting. Managerial accounting is concerned with providing relevant information for decision making. It, therefore, only presents costs that are relevant to the decision being considered. Such things as allocated overhead or amortized research and development costs only serve to confuse future-oriented decisions.

MARGINS

Often a case will present us with a retail selling price, when what we really want to know is the manufacturer's selling price. To be able to work back to get the manufacturer's selling price, we must understand how channel margins work.

When firms buy a product at a particular price and attempt to sell it at a higher price, the difference between the cost price and the selling price is called margin or markup or mark-on. Thus,

$$\text{Selling price} = \text{Cost price} + \text{Margin}$$

An example could be:

$$\$1.00 = \$0.80 \quad + \$0.20$$

So a company has bought a product for $0.80, added on a $0.20 margin and is charging $1.00 for the product.

Margins are usually expressed as percentages. This raises the question as to the base on which the margin percentage should be expressed: the cost price or the selling price. Here, if the $0.20 margin is expressed as a percentage of selling price the margin is $0.20/$1.00 = 20 percent. If it were expressed as a percentage of cost price, the margin is $0.20/$0.80 = 25 percent. The most common practice in marketing is to express margins as a percentage of selling price. Margins expressed in this fashion are easier to work with, especially in a multilevel channel situation. Unless explicitly stated otherwise, you may assume that all margins in the cases in this book use selling price as the relevant base.

A number of different types of margin related problems arise. They include:

1. Determining the selling price, given you know the cost price and the percentage margin on selling price. Suppose that a retailer buys an appliance for $15, and wants to obtain a margin on selling price of 40 percent. What selling price must be charged? The answer $21 is not correct because this margin ($6 = \$15 \times 0.4$) would be on cost price. To answer this question we must remember one fundamental relationship. This is that

$$\text{Selling price} = \text{Cost price} + \text{Margin}$$

Here we are taking selling price as the base equal to 100 percent, so we can write

$$100\% = \$15 + 40\%$$

That is, the cost price plus the margin must add to 100 percent. Clearly the $15 must then be 60 percent of the desired selling price. Thus,

$$\text{Derived selling price} = \$15/60\%$$
$$= \$25$$

The dollar margin is then $10 which is $\$10/\$25 = 40$ percent of selling price.

The general rule then is to divide one minus the percentage margin expressed as a decimal on selling price, into the cost price. For example, if cost price is $105 and the margin on selling price is 22.5 percent, then the desired selling price is $\$105/(1 - 0.225) = \$105/0.775 = \$135.48$.

2. Conversion of margin bases.   Sometimes a margin is given on a cost price basis, and we wish to convert it to a selling price base or vice versa. How do we make the conversion? Suppose that a product costs $4.50 and sells for $6.00. The margin is $1.50. On a selling price basis the margin is $\$1.50/\$6.00 = 25$ percent. On a cost price basis the margin is $\$1.50/\$4.50 = 33.33$ percent. The conversion from 1 percentage margin to the other is easy if we remember that selling price is composed of two parts: margin and cost.

For selling price base.

$$\begin{aligned} \text{Selling price} &= \text{Margin} + \text{Cost} \\ \$6.00 \quad &= \quad \$1.50 \ + \ \$4.50 \end{aligned}$$

or more importantly

$$100\% \quad = \ 25\% \quad + 75\%$$

For cost price base.

$$\begin{aligned} \text{Selling price} &= \text{Margin} + \text{Cost} \\ \$6.00 \quad &= \quad \$1.50 \ + \ \$4.50 \end{aligned}$$

but here the cost is the 100 percent base, so

$$\$6.00 \quad = \ \$1.50 \ + 100\%$$

or

$$133.33\% = 33.33\% + 100\%$$

That is the selling price should be thought of as 133.33 percent of the cost price.

Conversion from selling price to cost price base.

$$\text{Selling price} = \text{Margin} + \text{Cost}$$
$$100\% = 25\% + 75\%$$

So if we want to convert the 25 percent margin to a cost price basis, the 75 percent that is the cost becomes the relevant base and

$$\text{Margin as a percentage of cost price} = \frac{25\%}{75\%} = 33.33\%$$

Note that this is exactly the same as dividing $1.50 by $4.50.

A simple formula for making this conversion is

$$\text{Percentage margin on cost price} = \frac{\text{Percentage margin on selling price}}{100\% - \text{Percentage margin on selling price}}$$

In our example this is

$$\frac{25\%}{100\% - 25\%} = \frac{25\%}{75\%} = 33.33\%$$

Note that the only piece of information that we need to make this conversion is the margin percentage on selling price.

Conversion from cost price to selling price base.

$$\text{Selling price} = \text{Margin} + \text{Cost}$$
$$133.33\% = 33.33\% + 100\%$$

The margin is 33.33 percent and the relevant selling price base is 133.33 percent, so

$$\text{Margin as a percentage of selling price} = \frac{33.33\%}{133.33\%} = 25\%$$

Note that this is exactly the same as dividing $1.50 by $6.00.

A simple formula for making this conversion is

$$\text{Percentage margin on selling price} = \frac{\text{Percentage margin on cost price}}{100\% + \text{Percentage margin on cost price}}$$

In our example this is

$$\frac{33.33\%}{100\% + 33.33\%} = \frac{33.33\%}{133.33\%} = 25\%$$

Note that the only piece of information that we need to make this conversion is the margin percentage on cost price.

MULTIPLE MARGINS

Often a manufacturer gives a suggested retail selling price and suggested retail and wholesale margins. For example, the suggested retail price may be $7.50 with a retail margin of 20 percent and a wholesale margin of 15 percent. To determine the manufacturer's selling price in this situation we simply take the appropriate margins off one at a time. Thus

Retail selling price......................................	$7.50
Less retail margin (20% of $7.50)........................	1.50
Equals retail cost price or wholesale selling price.......	$6.00
Less wholesale margin (15% of $6.00)...................	0.90
Equals wholesale cost price or manufacturer's selling	
price...	$5.10

No matter how many levels there are in the channel, the approach is the same. We simply take the margins off one at a time. Note that we cannot just add up the margins and subtract this amount. Here 20% + 15% = 35%, and 35% of $7.50 is $2.63, making the manufacturer's selling price $7.50 − $2.63 = $4.87. This is not correct.

This chapter has outlined some financial concepts that add greatly to our abilities to make sound marketing decisions. These concepts should be applied where needed in the cases in this book.

PART II

INTRODUCTION TO MARKETING DECISION MAKING

In Part I of this book you have studied how marketing decisions should be made. The cases in this section are designed to let you begin to apply this approach in decision making. These cases should be viewed as an opportunity to practice your skills on some broad issue marketing cases, before we go to other sections of this book where we study cases that are more specifically tied to product or distribution, and so on.

CASE

1

Da-Roche Laboratories, Inc.

In December, the officers of Da-Roche Laboratories, Inc., met to discuss the company's sales and advertising plans to re-launch their new product, Dapper-Diaper. The focus of the meeting was the strategy to be used in the marketing of the new product which had recently been approved by the Food and Drug Administration (FDA). They were particularly interested in the possible methods of promoting the product and in the channels of distribution to be used in distributing Dapper-Diaper.

BACKGROUND

Da-Roche Laboratories, Inc., was established in Jackson, Michigan, to develop and market a new antibiotic baby product, Dapper-Diaper. Dapper-Diaper was composed of an aqueous solution of the antibiotic neomycin sulfate which was placed in a ten-ounce aerosol can. Neomycin inhibited odors in the animal kingdom, and Mr. Roy Crutchfield thought that the antibiotic could be used to eliminate odors from baby diapers. Dapper-Diaper kills bacteria which cause the decomposition of urea and thereby prevents ammonia from forming in diapers.

Da-Roche Laboratories convinced selected doctors to do some initial testing of its new product and the results were very encouraging. Doctors discovered that when sprayed on diapers in the diaper pail, it solved the odor problem. In addition, if sprayed on a clean diaper before it was worn by the baby it appeared to stop or prevent diaper rash on the baby.

GAINING FDA APPROVAL

With a great deal of encouragement from the doctors involved in the initial testing of their new antibiotic product, Mr. D. R. Wiley, then president and general manager of Da-Roche Laboratories, along with Mr. Crutchfield and Dr. John B. Holst, the company's consulting M.D., went to Washington and informed the FDA that they had discovered a new gift to mothers which they wished to begin marketing immediately. The FDA did not agree and told the Da-Roche personnel that they would have to do studies to show that the product actually did what it claimed to do, and at the same time show that there were no harmful side effects from using the antibiotic product.

Thus, while they thought they could go through the Food and Drug Administration (FDA) for approval of a new cosmetic-type product, the Da-Roche executives discovered that they had actually created what was termed a new drug which had to be approved by the New Drug Division of the FDA.

Although the one active ingredient in "Dapper-Diaper" was neomycin sulfate which had been known and widely used for about 15 years as one of a number of antibiotic products, the ingredient had never been mixed with water and other chemicals and placed in a pressurized spray can for sale over the counter. It appeared that it was due to the packaging and marketing plans for the new product, rather than its active ingredient, that it was declared a new drug, subject to FDA jurisdiction.

Consequently, what started out to be a new cosmetic product which would not have had to prove that it did any good as long as it did not do any harm, ended up being a new drug under FDA regulations. Consequently, both the efficacy of the product and the absence of any harmful effects had to be proven to the satisfaction of the FDA committee of doctors. This effort required approximately four years and the expenditure of nearly $500,000 in testing costs alone.

Three basic steps had to be taken to get the required certification by the federal Food and Drug Administration. First, research of all the available literature was undertaken to see what kinds of problems should be researched in experimental situations. Animal testing (toxicity) was next conducted, including autopsy reports of white mice to be sure there were no harmful effects from continued use of the new product. The third step in the testing procedure involved clinical tests on infants using a placebo (the product minus the active ingredient) with double blind and double blind crossover techniques whereby aerosol spray cans labeled X and Y were tested both for safety and for efficiency. The doctors and nurses involved in these clinical observation studies did not know which cans contained the aqueous solution of neomycin sulfate and which contained the placebo, in order to ensure their objectivity throughout the duration of the study. Culture studies of diapers and the babies' skin were made and it was found that the bacteria which produced odor and diaper rash were gradually eradicated in the diaper with no effect on the resident flora (normal balance of bacteria) of the babies' skin.

Finally, at the end of four years, and after 30 visits to Washington and 25 label changes, the FDA approved Dapper-Diaper for over-the-counter sale. Since the machinery for producing the new antibiotic had been purchased and inspected about one and one-half years before the FDA approval had been received, Da-Roche was now able to begin production immediately.

DISTRIBUTION

The original plan was to obtain distribution in Michigan and then use the capital generated by sales in this area to expand into adjacent markets. This plan was to be repeated until Dapper-Diaper was distributed throughout the United States. To obtain regional distribution as fast as possible, Da-Roche hired a broker's broker. This man had formerly sold to brokers and he was well acquainted with the food and drug brokers in Michigan and knew what it would take to get them to handle the company's product. The brokers, in turn, sold to large wholesale drug companies such as McKesson-Robbins and Hazeltine-Perkins, and to large grocers such as A&P, Kroger, Food Fair, and even to smaller "Mom and Pop" stores in some areas. The brokers also sold to some discount chains such as K-Mart. It was felt that established brokers would be much more effective in bargaining with large accounts than salesmen from a new, unfamiliar company.

By March 1, the new product was on the market in many of these retail outlets, and a concerted effort was being made to get every drugstore in Michigan to carry the product as well. This objective was pursued by sending a free sample can of Dapper-Diaper to every major druggist in the state of Michigan. While this plan entailed giving away free more than 2,000 full-size cans of Dapper-Diaper, it also allowed Da-Roche to claim that its product could be found in every major drugstore in the state of Michigan. At the same time, it acquainted all of Michigan's druggists with the new product. By June, brokers had managed to obtain distribution in 80 percent of the stores in eastern Michigan but distribution in the western part of the state was much slower with only about 20 percent of the stores stocking Dapper-Diaper.

PRICING

It was estimated that if the same amount of neomycin as was contained in one, ten-ounce can of Dapper-Diaper were to be bought by prescription, it would cost from $5 to $8. After talking with retailers, brokers, and doctors, it was decided that the "suggested retail price" of Dapper-Diaper would be $1.98. The Da-Roche executives, however, expected that it would sell for between $1.60 and $1.70 within four to six weeks after introduction. And, in fact, it was selling for $1.69 in Kroger and other supermarkets as of April 1. The product sold as low as $1.39 in some stores, and the average retail price was about $1.80.

COST

The average retail price allowed the company enough margin to promote the product properly. The average retail price was about six times the cost of goods sold, which was normal for the drug industry. After discounts and allowances to wholesalers and retailers, the proceeds to the company were about $1 per can. Administrative and overhead costs were $100,000 per year exclusive of marketing costs.

MARKET POTENTIAL

In determining the size of the total market for Dapper-Diaper, Da-Roche executives first found out that there were approximately 8 million babies in diapers in the United States. (There were 350,000 babies in the company's initial marketing area.) A ten-ounce can of Dapper-Diaper was expected to last one month. Da-Roche executives reasoned that they would be able to get 10 percent of the total market to use Dapper-Diaper, resulting in sales of 9.6 million cans per year.

USE OF PERSONAL SELLING THROUGH ETHICAL CHANNELS TO GET INTENSIVE DISTRIBUTION

The original strategy called for personal selling through five detail men. These men were to call on people in all medical professions to explain the benefits of the new product, how it was used, and where it could be obtained. In addition, small-size free samples were left with the doctor so he could recommend the product to a patient and be able to give her a ten-day supply of Dapper-Diaper as well.

Da-Roche's executives were immediately faced with the problem of how to get the detail men in to see a doctor, especially since they represented a new company with only one product. To solve this problem, the five detail men were each given an hourglass which was timed for three minutes. The detail men then went into the doctor's office and started the sand in motion, asking for three minutes of the doctor's time. Only the essential facts were given to the doctor in the three minutes, after which some free samples were distributed and the detail men attempted to leave. At this point, Da-Roche executives declared nine out of ten doctors asked for more information about Dapper-Diaper before the detail man could leave. The following points were made about the new baby product: It is certified by the federal Food and Drug Administration; it is an antibiotic; its active ingredient is neomycin; it is sold over the counter (no prescription needed); it is safe, because it is made from one of the most nearly perfect drugs known; and it is time saving, economical, easy to use, and it really works.

The use of detail men was selected over consumer advertising for the initial promotional job, because the Da-Roche executives believed that if the product was recommended by doctors, women would surely use Dapper-Diaper and tell their friends about it, too. This would give the new product the most desirable kind of promotion possible—word of mouth.

Another consideration which favored personal selling over consumer advertising, was the fact that during the first week of February, when promotion of Dapper-Diaper by the company's detail men was first begun, distribution of the product was just beginning too. If consumer advertising had come in at the same time, the Da-Roche executives believed that much of it would have been wasted because the product was not yet available. It was felt that by April 1, this problem would be remedied and a consumer advertising campaign could be launched at that time. With only a limited amount of money available for advertising, it was important that distribution be achieved before the advertising commenced, in order that the advertising would not be wasted.

Dapper-Diaper consumer advertising campaign

To be consistent with their intensive distribution policy within the introductory selling regions, the Da-Roche executives had planned a consumer advertising campaign which was to begin April 1. They believed that by waiting until April 1, they could be sure that Dapper-Diaper could be readily available to most stores by the time the consumer advertising campaign would begin. Discussion with brokers, people in the trade, and Da-Roche's agency, the La Vanway agency in Jackson, Michigan, resulted in an advertising budget of $50,000 for the first 13 weeks. After that time, advertising would be budgeted at 25 percent of net sales. It was decided that to get maximum reach and frequency, the company should use half- and whole-minute radio spots, with some ten-second IDs; IDs and whole minutes on television, with some advertising in trade journals and newspapers.

In anticipation of the FDA's approval of the new use for Dapper-

Diaper which was expected in the near future, the company's advertising was based largely on the diaper and not exclusively on the narrower diaper pail use for which the product was currently certified by the FDA. A baby wearing a top hat, which appeared on the can, became known as "The Happy Baby" and was used in the company's introductory advertising campaign. All advertising carried the line, "Do your baby a favor, ask your baby's doctor."

PROTECTION FROM COMPETITION

It was hoped that eventually Dapper-Diaper would become almost a generic name, since it would be the first on the market and likely enjoy the status of being the only such product for at least one more year. This protection, it was felt, would be afforded by the patent which was pending on the new product, the trademark and copyrighted Dapper-Diaper name, and the fact than any competitor would have to do extensive testing of the type that took Da-Roche four years, in order to get its product approved by the FDA as a new drug.

PURSUING NEW USES

While Da-Roche was still in the process of introducing Dapper-Diaper into its first region which included all of Michigan and part of Ohio and Indiana, it was also engaged in more clinical testing. The product had received FDA approval only as a diaper pail spray. Knowing that it had no harmful effects on babies and that it would inhibit bacteria growth which caused ammonia burn or diaper rash, Da-Roche was seeking FDA approval to promote Dapper-Diaper as a diaper spray as well. For this new purpose the product would be sprayed on a clean diaper before it was to be worn by the baby. Much of the extensive testing which had already been conducted by Da-Roche, indicated that when diapers were sprayed in the diaper pail, the diapers became clinically clean prior to washing and helped inhibit the growth of ammonia-producing bacteria, preventing odor and diaper rash.

Dr. J. D. Holst, M.D., Da-Roche's medical liaison with the FDA, explained that with the tests that had already been done, it would only require about six months of tests to return to the FDA requesting permission to use a broader label describing Dapper-Diaper as a diaper spray as well a diaper pail spray. This additional use for the product could then be promoted by the company's detail men in talking to doctors and in the company's consumer advertising. Thus, while at the time of introduction Dapper-Diaper was only an antibiotic diaper pail spray which would limit the number of bacteria to control odor, its rash-prevention benefit was a by-product which the Da-Roche executives believed might soon become an equally important use for the new product.

Beyond the new use of Dapper-Diaper in controlling ammonia burn, the nature of the product itself and the way in which it worked suggested a variety of entirely new uses for which the new product might be equally well suited. The active ingredient, neomycin, was extremely effective in reducing or completely eliminating bacterial odor, and for this reason it might be used for eliminating all odors caused by organic decomposition. Examples would include a garbage pail or pet spray.

CONSIDERATION OF A FULL BABY PRODUCT LINE

Da-Roche executives also considered introducing companion products, such as baby powder and paper diapers, which would help better entrench the company as a producer of a more complete line of baby products and perhaps speed the translation of the brand name Dapper-Diaper into almost a generic concept. Another advantage would be that these companion products, as they were developed, could be promoted along with the Dapper-Diaper spray by the company's detail men as they called on doctors and left free samples and literature.

RESULTS, APRIL–DECEMBER

The company ran into significant problems as Dapper Diaper was being introduced. A batch of 180,000 three-ounce cans to be used as samples and distributed to doctors was not approved by the FDA. A change in the can design had resulted in valves which did not fit properly. The company therefore had to use trade cans for samples to distribute to the doctors and, due to the greater cost of the full-size cans, a smaller number of samples was distributed.

After the product had been distributed to the retailers and had been on the shelf for a short period of time, problems with the full-size can became evident. Some of the ingredients in the product were interacting with the can, causing the can to rust. As the can rusted, the pressure in the aerosol leaked out, making it impossible to get the product out of the aerosol can. The company replaced bad cans, as they were found, with good ones, but then even the good ones turned bad. Finally, the source of the problem was discovered and a change in Dapper-Diaper's formulation had to be developed. Da-Roche then had to get FDA approval on the new formulation and on the new can. In effect, the company had to start all over.

THE PRESENT SITUATION

In December, the company finally received approval from the FDA to again begin marketing Dapper-Diaper. Da-Roche executives were now considering several alternative ways of marketing the product. First, they could follow exactly the same strategy that they followed with the initial launching of the product. This would entail both detail men and consumer advertising with distribution through drugstores, supermarkets, and discount stores.

A second alternative was to take a marketing approach similar to that used for ethical drugs. Thus, the company could use established outlets that do not require the high cost of familiarizing people with the product. Instead, detail men would be used to encourage doctors to recommend the product, and people would therefore become familiar with the product through their doctor's recommendation. This would eliminate the need for a significant amount of consumer advertising required to support a product which is to be distributed through supermarkets and discount stores.

Da-Roche's executives came upon a third alternative after reading an article in *Time* magazine. The article quoted the president of The American Diaper Service Association describing the smell of the diaper pail as diaper services' biggest single problem. The urea content of a new baby's urine is not very heavy, but as the baby gets older, the urea gets heavier. Therefore, after the baby becomes about three months old, the smell in the diaper pail significantly increases. Diaper services supply pails with neoprene bags, and therefore the diapers cannot be soaked. The diapers are usually picked up only once a week so there are 50 to 100 by that time. Mothers, therefore, began to buy diapers and wash them themselves three to four times per week.

The Associated Diaper Services of America and the other trade organization, The National Institute for Diaper Services, have members who make 83 million contacts per year where money changes hands. With the help of these two associations, Dapper-Diaper could be made known to millions of women through diaper service distributors. Da-Roche executives felt that either of the diaper services could sell 2 million cans per year with a minimum of effort. The company executives stated that Da-Roche would be very profitable at that volume.

Da-Roche executives had also made contact with a manufacturer of institutional clothing. This company sold very high quality sleeping garments for babies and mentally retarded children in hospitals and training schools, and other garments for hospitals, penitentiaries, and other institutions. The manufacturer would distribute Dapper-Diaper along with his other products. As the institutions have a large problem with odor, Da-

Roche's executives thought that this method of distribution would yield a large market.

Da-Roche executives were also considering one further alternative. A cosmetic broker—the best known in the country—with offices in Dallas, New York, and Chicago, had become interested in Dapper-Diaper. This broker employed over 100 people and distributed products of such well-known companies as Schick, Alberto-Culver, Revlon, and Tampax. The broker told Da-Roche's executives that if they could give him $1 million for advertising, he could guarantee them $3 million in sales with the company's present label (Dapper-Diaper had still not been approved for anything except use as a diaper pail spray).

CASE

2

League of Catholic Women

During the summer of 1975, Mary Lynn Landis, the president of the League of Catholic Women, faced a tightening financial situation. In this period of inflation the League's troubles were compounded by the increased number of Detroiters who needed the League's assistance and by the increased administrative complexity of the social service programs established to administer aid. While the League's budget was approaching $1.5 million annually, most support was in the form of federal or foundation grants earmarked for particular social service programs. In the past, membership contributions had been relied upon to defray administrative expenses, but presently membership in the League was on a sharp decline. Mrs. Landis faced the problem of developing a marketing plan to increase membership without appreciably increasing costs by the beginning of the next membership drive in March of 1976.

FOUNDING, PHILOSOPHY, HISTORY

In 1906 a small group of Catholic women formed the Weinman Center to teach English and religion to foreign-born persons who had settled in Detroit, Michigan. The Weinman Center also functioned as a day nursery and became the first Michigan organization to assist immigrants in establishing themselves. This group of women became the Catholic Settlement Association of Detroit in 1911.

The League of Catholic Women was incorporated out of the Catholic Settlement Association of Detroit in 1915. The League's purpose as originally stated was: "To unite Catholic women for the promotion of religious, intellectual, and charitable work." The charitable work continued

40

the settlement work including family visiting, health care, religious instruction, and maintaining a representative at the juvenile court. The services were directed at women, in particular adolescent and minority adult women, rather than toward families. At the time of incorporation the Weinman Center's program was expanded to include classes in domestic science, sewing, dramatics, dance, manual training, Girl Scouts, athletics, kindergarten, and social clubs. All these classes were taught by volunteers. The Weinman Center program became a model for other League community centers established in 1919 and 1920 in other Detroit neighborhoods.

In the early days of the League's existence there was no ongoing fundraising mechanism. It was then, and remains today, independent of the Catholic Church and as such received no direct aid from the Archdiocese of Detroit. Activities were supported by the personal financing of its members. An example of this financing is the sale of a $30,000 bond issue in 1916 to League members.

The proceeds of that first bond issue established the Watson Street Club House, a residence for homeless girls. In 1925 the League expanded its residence home program by opening the Madeleine Sophie Training Home for Girls. It served primarily delinquent girls and is still operating today as Barat House. The Watson Street Club and the Madeleine Sophie Home created the League's first payroll obligations. While they were staffed primarily by volunteers they had professional social and child care workers on their staffs.

As the League's programs expanded the women began to plan for a headquarters building to house many activities and to provide ample residence rooms for working women and girls living away from their families. The first organized membership drive, held in the early 1920s, netted $11,771.47. This first drive was the kickoff for the Building Fund which resulted in the completion of Casgrain Hall by January of 1928. Casgrain Hall, which still serves as the League's headquarters, was heavily mortgaged and faced foreclosure in its first year. To rescue their building, League members "bought" bricks in the building and avoided foreclosure. The building was paid off by 1940.

In the 1940s the League expanded its services to provide day-care facilities and recreational programs to the black and Latin communities of Detroit. The 1950s and early 1960s saw little change in the League's activities. In the late 1960s the League moved into a new area of rehabilitation programs for women convicts.

PRESENT

Today the League of Catholic Women is the oldest and largest volunteer social service organization operating in Detroit. It is now administered by a 48-member board of trustees, a president (Mrs. Landis), two vice presidents, a secretary and a treasurer elected annually by the general membership. All officers and board members serve without pay. The League administration is no longer involved in day-to-day operations of social services. In the past ten years an agency structure (see Exhibit 1) has been created whereby each League agency has responsibility for a particular area of social service (see Exhibit 2). Each agency has a paid professional executive director and staff, responsibility for planning and executing its own budget, and an autonomous board of directors. The agency boards are chaired by a person appointed by the president of the League of Catholic Women but operate independent of League control. Persons selected to fill agency boards are usually concerned citizens from the neighborhood the agency serves, or professional persons with expertise in social work, health care, or administration. All agency board members serve without pay.

The League is in effect the umbrella administration for the agencies. The agencies operate independently, with supervision from the League board

EXHIBIT 1
Administrative structure

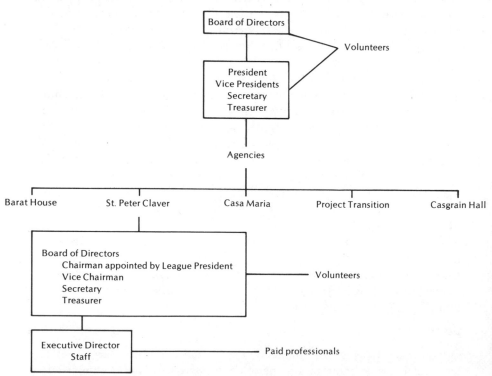

EXHIBIT 2
Synopsis of agency services and funding sources

BARAT HOUSE

An "open" residence treatment center for up to 20 emotionally disturbed teenage girls, offering psychiatric treatment and educational development. Funded by the United Foundation and the State Department of Social Services.

CASA MARIA

Community Center in Tiger Stadium area, serving Latinos, blacks, Maltese, and Appalachian whites. It incorporates a nursery school, recreation, crafts and counseling for youngsters, and adult community programs. Funded by Archdiocese Development Fund and federal grants through the Juvenile Facilities Network.

ST. PETER CLAVER

Community center on the lower east side, serving predominately blacks. It incorporates a Day Care Center, recreation, crafts and counseling for youngsters, and adult community programs. Funded by the United Foundation.

PROJECT TRANSITION

Job training, residence, counseling, and employment assistance for 25 women from the Detroit House of Corrections and other disadvantaged backgrounds. A pilot program initiated by the League in 1971 aimed at offering total rehabilitation for women offenders; it is housed on the fourth floor of Casgrain Hall. Funded by state and federal grants and the Board of Education of the city of Detroit, with some assistance from the League.

CASGRAIN HALL

Eight-story League building near Wayne State University which provides low-cost residence for women of all ages; offers meeting rooms, ballroom and conference facilities for community activities; and serves as League administration headquarters. Funded by rent receipts; currently carrying a large deficit.

---

only in areas of general policy and fiscal matters. The League bookkeeping office handles all bookkeeping for the agencies. All federal, state, and foundation grants for agency programs are channeled through the League office and all payables the agencies incur are billed directly to the League.

Casgrain Hall is the one agency that is handled differently. While it has its own board of directors, it is included in the League budget because it does not receive outside aid. In an effort to maintain low-cost housing in the face of rising operating costs, Casgrain Hall has incurred a deficit each of the past four years. This past year it approached $80,000. The problem has been compounded by an environment that has changed drastically since the widespread civil disturbances of 1967. Since then, the 194-room residence hall has experienced an occupancy rate rarely above 60 percent.

The Casgrain Hall deficit consumes more of the League's surplus funds each year. In the past three years the League has been unable to provide any direct financial aid to its other agencies because of the Casgrain drain. The only money that could be applied to the deficit was the unrestricted public support (see Exhibits 3 and 4). The survival of the League seemed to depend on increasing the unrestricted public support.

MEMBERSHIP

In the early days of the League activity, membership was a loosely defined concept. Any Catholic woman who was in sympathy with League goals and volunteered some of her time to settlement work was considered a member. It wasn't until the early 1920s that membership lists were compiled and an annual dues of $1 were instituted. Early membership rosters indicate that members were drawn primarily from Detroit's upper socioeconomic strata. The lists contain many names from families prominent in the blossoming auto and auto-related industry.

It is evident from records of financial contributions that the early members were not important for their $1 membership dues but for the larger personal resources they could bring to bear on the League's projects. For many years the League operated in a social service sphere in which its programs could be financed almost solely by its members' wealth. This situation changed in the 1930s and 1940s when League programs became more vigorous and the tax laws were changed to place social service more squarely in government hands. Today, large contributions by individual members are rare. The largest component of membership support is now the annual dues.

Today, membership is open to any woman in sympathy with the object of the League. Membership is offered in five classes. Dues are payable annually, charged as follows:

Sustaining	$ 10
Contributing	5
General	2
Life	100
Memorial	100

EXHIBIT 3
LEAGUE OF CATHOLIC WOMEN OF DETROIT, MICHIGAN
Balance Sheets
December 31, 1974
with Comparative Figures for 1973

	1974	1973
Assets		
Cash......	$ 26,020	$ 55,582
Short-term commercial notes...........	54.945	—
Accounts receivable:		
Residence (less allowance for doubtful accounts of $1,200		
in 1974 and $500 in 1973)...........	6,199	2,414
Sponsored agencies..........	9,729	8,222
Related nonprofit corporation........	1,544	3,304
Other........	117	199
	$ 17,589	$ 14,139
Accrued interest receivable........	$ 847	$ 151
Prepaid expense........	5,255	7,174
Due from restricted fund........	8,955	22,693
Total........	$ 113,611	$ 104,739
Cash........	—	$ 22,340
Grants receivable........	216,633	78,629
Total........	$ 216,633	$ 100,969
Land, Buildings, and Equipment Fund:		
Land, buildings, and equipment........	$1,927,586	$1,926,413
Less accumulated depreciation........	237,296	$ 665,278
Total........	$1,690,290	$1,261,135

	1974	1973
Liabilities and fund balances		
Current Funds		
Unrestricted:		
Accounts payable........	$ 5,631	$ 11,633
Advance rentals and security........	3,098	2,641
Withheld from employees........	1,827	2,004
Loan payable........	26,000	—
Total Liabilities........	$ 35,556	$ 16,278
Fund balance........	78,024	88,441
Total........	$ 113,580	$ 104,739
Restricted:		
Due to unrestricted fund........	$ 8,935	$ 27,693
Deferred support........	202,629	50,434
Total liabilities and deferred support........	$ 211,564	$ 76,629
Fund balance........	5,049	22,340
Total........	$ 216,633	$ 100,969
Land, Buildings, and Equipment Fund:		
Fund balance........	$1,190,290	$1,261,135
Total........	$1,190,290	$1,261,135

EXHIBIT 4
LEAGUE OF CATHOLIC WOMEN OF DETROIT, MICHIGAN
Statement of Support, Revenue, and Expenses,
and Changes in Fund Balances
Year Ended December 31, 1974
with Comparative Totals for 1973

	1974				
	Current funds		Land, build-ings, and equipment fund	Total all funds	
	Unre-stricted	Re-stricted		1974	1973
Public support and revenue:					
Public support:					
Contributions.........................	$ 16,884	$ 7,220	—	$ 24,104	$ 63,811
Memberships and fund raising........	29,749	—	—	29,749	27,781
Grants................................		91,889	—	91,889	61,674
Total public support..............	46,633	$ 99,109	—	$145,742	$153,266
Revenue:					
Residence rents.......................	$171,430	—	—	$171,430	$163,876
Bargain counter sales..................	56,505	—	—	56,505	49,086
Nursery service fees...................	96,632	—	—	96,632	96,200
Activities and cafeteria rentals..........	8,609	—	—	8,609	7,345
Investment income....................	5,497	—	—	5,497	4,397
Miscellaneous........................	5,034	—	—	5,034	8,354
Total revenue....................	$343,707	—	—	$343,707	$329,258
Total public support and revenue..	$390,340	$ 99,109	—	$489,449	$482,524
Expenses:					
Program services:					
Residence...........................	$255,725	$ 2,697	$ 42,509	$300,931	$288,067
Nursery.............................	97,426	—	5,409	102,835	112,089
Project transition 1973–1974...........	171	53,866	2,270	56,307	50,725
Project transition 1974–1975...........	109	50,019	2,270	52,398	35,993
Contributions to sponsored agencies..	10,000	—	—	10,000	—
Depreciation of facilities used by sponsored agency and related non-profit corporation...................	—	—	17,018	17,018	17,018
Total program service............	$363,431	$106,582	$ 69,476	$539,489	$503,892
Supporting services:					
Management and general.............	$ 16,584	—	$ 3,249	$ 19,833	$ 20,740
Membership and communication.....	6,669	—	168	6,837	8,917
Bargain counters......................	21,803	—	—	21,803	15,541
Total supporting services.........	$ 45,056	—	$ 3,417	$ 48,473	$ 45,198
Total expenses...................	$408,487	$106,582	$ 72,893	$587,962	$549,090
Excess (deficiency) of public sup-port and revenue over expense.	(18,147)	(7,473)	(72,893)		
Other changes in fund balance:					
Current funds used for the purchase of equipment......................	(1,130)	(918)	$ 2,048		
Transfer—donor release of restriction..	$ 8,900	(8,900)	—		
Fund balances, January 1, 1974..........	88,441	$ 22,340	1,261,135		
Fund balances, December 31, 1974......	$ 78,064	$ 5,049	$1,190,290		

The bylaws of the League make no distinction between membership classes as to privileges or obligations. Exhibit 5 shows the costs incurred in connection with membership. The League bookkeeping office has always separated these costs into "Membership" and "Communication." Membership consists of those costs incurred in communicating solely with members. Communication costs are primarily the cost of quarterly newsletters.

MEMBERSHIP DRIVE STRUCTURE

Membership drives at the League of Catholic Women are conducted on an annual basis during the designated membership month of March. The drives are coordinated by a central committee consisting of a membership chairwoman and up to 17 membership coordinators (see Exhibit 6). Each coordinator directs the activities in a geographical region called a vicariate. Vicariates are composed of groups of individual churches or parishes in approximately the same geographical area (see Exhibit 7). Vicariates were formed in the Archdiocese of Detroit to foster closer ties and better communication among the member parishes and the central Archdiocese offices. Thus, it became a set of natural regions within which the League could conduct the annual membership drive.

EXHIBIT 5
Costs associated with membership

Membership:	
Salaries.................................	$1,933.30
FICA taxes..............................	113.04
Employment tax.........................	21.03
Worker's Compensation..................	16.93
Equipment and maintenance.............	29.94
Office supplies...........................	965.62
Postage.................................	518.53
Telephone..............................	130.00
Mileage.................................	15.72
Printing.................................	588.00
Administrative expense..................	1,921.07
	$6,253.18
Communications:	
Salaries.................................	$1,933.30
FICA taxes..............................	113.04
Employment tax.........................	21.03
Worker's Compensation..................	16.93
Equipment and maintenance.............	29.93
Office supplies...........................	87.49
Postage.................................	34.95
Printing.................................	95.00
Administrative expense..................	1,097.76
	$3,429.43

EXHIBIT 6
Membership drive structure

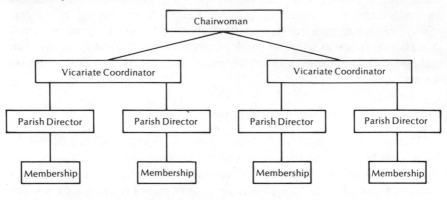

Under each vicariate coordinator in the structure are the parish membership directors (see Exhibit 6). These directors formed the backbone of the general membership structure. It is at this level that much of the major work of the membership drive was conducted. Each parish director had the responsibility for conducting the drive at her own parish in a manner that she deemed appropriate for her parish. Because each parish differed in important characteristics like physical age, and location of the neighborhood, racial and ethnic composition, and accessibility to members, many different methods were employed during the membership drive. The League did not discourage this heterogeneity of technique but in fact encouraged each director to pursue the most appropriate method that the parish director felt would be the most successful during the membership drive.

For the past few years the League has held a luncheon at Casgrain Hall in February for parish directors as a kickoff for the membership drive. This luncheon has been poorly attended in the past. The League officers believe poor attendance is attributable to the fact that suburban directors fear Casgrain's neighborhood or find the distance prohibitive.

After the kickoff luncheon and during the activities each March the League supplied each parish director with materials to be used to accomplish the membership objectives. These materials included the preprinted membership envelopes containing a blank membership card and a preprinted "Dear Parishioner" letter signed by the respective parish director. These letters detailed the activities of the League and contained other facts and information which would be of interest to prospective League members. In addition to the above, postage paid envelopes addressed to the League and an information brochure suitable for inserting into the parish newspaper were available. These materials are made accessible to the

EXHIBIT 7
Map of vicariates

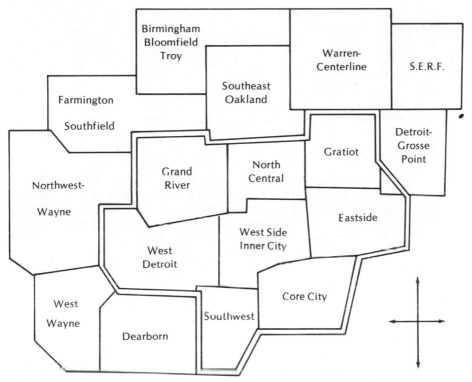

Area enclosed by double line represents city of Detroit limits—outside area: suburbs.

parish directors if they use the convenient order form the League sends to them. Exhibit 8 is an example of League promotional material.

At the beginning of the membership drive each director is issued this publicity information along with a listing of members in her parish from the previous year which are for renewals and a report form used to tabulate the results of the membership drive. Names, addresses, dollar amounts of the donations, and summary totals are the responsibility of each director on the report forms.

Parish directors forward their results and problems to the vicariate coordinators so that the central membership committee is advised of the results. In addition to overseeing the parish directors, the vicariate coordinators are responsible for ensuring that each parish of the vicariate has a director to conduct the membership drive. In the areas of the Archdiocese of Detroit in which the League is active there are 17 vicariates. Contained in these vicariates are 218 parishes of various sizes.

EXHIBIT 8
Sample promotional materials

Dear Parishioner,

A distraught teenage girl acting out her frustrations; a Chicano preschooler learning the alphabet; families being given emergency food supplies; a black grandmother taking sewing lessons; a lonely woman finding a pleasant residence and meals; a woman parolee being counseled in employment skills—these are some of the people you would meet every day in the agencies operated by the League of Catholic Women.

Christ has told us that when we offer food, clothing, refuge, and counseling in His name to His needy ones, we offer it to Him. Since 1906, the League has sought to offer immediate help and a brighter tomorrow to those who have been caught up in the web of poverty, misfortune, or despair—and always in the name of Christ and His Blessed Mother Mary. At the same time it has offered the opportunity for thousands of women across the Archdiocese to unite their hands and prayers in this service.

Yes, membership in the League of Catholic Women makes you a personal participant in these countless daily acts of love and service, as well as a participant in the monthly Mass said for all League members.

The annual drive for memberships is now in progress. Will you join with me and with fellow parishioners in giving your moral and financial support so that the League can continue being a very visible sign of Christian Service and an extension of your hands to the needy?

Most sincerely yours,

Helen Garbo
League Parish Director, St. Johns

MEMBERSHIP PROBLEM

In the summer of 1975 shortly after the conclusion of the March membership drive the League studied the results comparing them to those of previous campaigns. In June of 1975 the League had 10,145 members

EXHIBIT 8 (*continued*)

DID YOU KNOW THAT . . .

. . . the League is the oldest and largest social service agency in Detroit?

. . . Membership does not require regular meetings or volunteer work?

. . . the League agencies and operations are financed by over $1.5 million annually from memberships, government grants, United Fund giving, private donations, and rental receipts?

. . . last year, each dollar given through membership was magnified by $50 from the larger funding sources?

. . . the League is dedicated to services to those in need, regardless of race, color, or creed? You don't have to be Catholic to belong or to be served?

---

that contributed $26,530. But this was a decline of 43 percent from the 1970 total of 17,913 and a decline of 51 percent from the 1965 total of 21,000. Faced with the alarming decline in membership over a ten-year period, a closer examination was conducted. Exhibit 9 presents membership data by vicariates used in examining the problem.

In summary the results showed that 74 of the 218 parishes did not include at least one member of the League and that the vicariate coordinators had solicited a total of 108 parish directors leaving 124 parishes without directors, in 1975. In addition in 1975, 2,508 members from 1974 did not renew their membership, a total of 25 percent of all the previous year's members.

EXECUTIVE REACTION

Faced with the data on membership an executive committee consisting of Mary Lynn Landis (president), Marie Mathers (treasurer), and Christine Viceroy (membership chairwoman), discussed the situation in an attempt to rectify it as soon as possible.

During the discussion each executive felt that the major difficulty was finding women to work at the parish level and that the major reason revolved around the notion that these women were mostly employed and unable to devote their energy faithfully to the membership drives. In the same vein the executive committee also hypothesized that the large decline in membership in the last ten years and especially in the last five years has occurred concurrently with the "white flight" from the city to the suburbs.

EXHIBIT 9
Membership statistics

Vicariate	Number in parish	Number without members	Number of directors	Number of 1975 members	Percent change during 1970–75	Percent change during 1974–75	Number not renewed in 1975
Birmingham–Bloomfield–Troy..................	9	1	7	754	+571%	+10%	178
Warren-Centerline.......	12	2	4	62	− 50	−15	14
S.E.R.F....................	15	10	5	155	− 58	−36	120
Farmington-Southfield...	13	2	10	508	− 9	−18	87
Southeast Oakland......	11	3	6	555	− 27	−16	217
Northwest Wayne........	16	4	6	377	− 44	−24	149
West Wayne.............	16	10	3	44	n.a.	+25	9
Dearborn.................	15	3	11	1,091	− 12	+ 4	177
Detroit–Grosse Pointe....	11	0	9	2,168	− 29	−12	585
Core City–Downtown.....	19	6	7	598	− 9	+ 7	111
East Side................	16	10	5	151	− 78	−20	36
Grand River.............	15	0	7	1,159	− 72	+ 4	260
Gratiot..................	15	2	9	1,578	− 51	− 8	294
North Central............	16	13	2	49	− 82	−49	38
Southwest................	13	7	6	210	+ 14	+14	54
West Detroit.............	12	1	7	445	− 59	+ 4	111
West Side Inner City.....	8	0	4	241	− 64	−33	68
	232	74	108	10,145			2,508

n.a. = not available.

They felt that with the decline of certain inner Detroit neighborhoods along with the threat of court ordered busing looming in the city, Catholic families had moved to the suburbs where League activity was not well established. They believed that the decline of the once strong city vicariates would be counterbalanced by the increase in the membership roles of the suburban vicariates.

They reasoned that the number of city Catholics had decreased a great deal and that the remaining numbers would be attributed to Catholics in the older age brackets who found it financially impossible to move. (see Exhibit 10). In conjunction with changing neighborhoods, League officers noted that as the neighborhoods in the city changed composition from predominately white to racially mixed and as the crime rate increased in the city much personal contact was lost, personal contact which was extremely necessary for soliciting memberships for the League.

Additionally the three officers cited a continuing problem of handling the membership renewal. Often communication among the parish directors, the vicariate coordinators, and central office was inadequate. Lag time between reports had increased which invariably led to duplication of efforts

EXHIBIT 10
Total population shifts, 1970–1974

	1970	1974	Percent change
City vicariates:			
Core City—Downtown			
East Side			
Grand River			
Gratiot			
North Central	1,586,383	1,428,250	− 9.9%
Southwest			
West Detroit			
West Side Inner City			
Suburban vicariates:			
Birmingham–Bloomfield–Troy...............	112,049	127,060	+13.4
Dearborn.................................	184,268	173,600	− 5.7
Detroit–Grosse Pointe.....................	68,657	64,710	− 6.0
Farmington-Southfield.....................	128,321	141,000	+ 9.8
Northwest Wayne..........................	213,728	211,575	− 1.0
S.E.R.F.................................	206,410	201,500	− 2.3
Southeast Oakland........................	274,580	253,850	− 7.5
Warren-Centerline........................	189,639	183,800	− 3.0
Western Wayne...........................	213,547	223,600	+ 4.7
Total...............................	1,591,199	1,580,695	

Note: Catholic population is estimated at 32 percent of aggregate totals.
Source: Figures obtained from U.S. Census figures, U.S. Department of Commerce, Detroit office.

and burdensome bookkeeping errors. The errors were admittedly dis
turbing to workers at all levels but caused the greatest consternation at the
membership level. This generated a good deal of ill will from the members
that was directed toward the central membership office.

Last, Landis, Mathers, and Viceroy felt that the League had become
increasingly confused with an organization called the Council of Catholic
Women (CCW). The CCW is an umbrella federation which encompasses
all women's groups and is funded by the Archdiocese of Detroit. They
stated that the League is the oldest and largest participant of the CCW
and that many Catholic women were under the mistaken impression that
being a member of the CCW automatically included membership in the
League. They thought this confusion had hurt the membership drive in the
past.

At this point the officers felt that further study of the membership situation was required in order to reshape and restructure their marketing
strategy to increase the number of League members. To do this they desired to know more about the population shifts and more about the
women who conducted the membership drives at the parish level.

RESEARCH RESULTS

Obtaining reliable information on just where the Catholic population was located was a major source of concern since it was vitally important to know where the major market centered. The League discovered that the 1970 census did not include a question on religious preference; therefore, it would have to get reliable estimates from a different source.

Turning to the central offices of the Archdiocese of Detroit the League hoped that individual parish censuses had been tabulated but it quickly found out that the only centralized population data was collected in 1970 and had been discarded as incomplete and useless.

The director of financial planning at the Archdiocese, Harvey Crane, indicated that the Archdiocese used a reasonably accurate estimate for its financial planning. He told the League that historically the percentage of Catholics within its boundaries was approximately 32 percent of total population in the area. Through sample testing the percentage had been found to change little in recent years and was considered reliable by the financial planners.

So assuming that any population shifts retained the characteristic 32 percent Catholic identity (that is, for every 100 people to move, 32 would be Catholic) the League felt that census data on the changing population might prove helpful to see if the increases and declines in area memberships occurred concurrently and in the same proportion as the changes in population. Exhibit 10 represents this tabulated data. It shows that the vicariates with the greatest shifts in population were Birmingham-Bloomfield-Troy with an increase of 13.4 percent and the city of Detroit with a decrease of 9.9 percent.

In addition to the census information a telephone survey of 47 parish directors was taken in order to study several aspects of the membership drive to determine the importance of their performance on the success of the drive. (The questions and tabulated results are presented in Exhibit 11.)

Close examination of the results reveals several trends. As expected the League learned that the parish directors pursued a wide variety of methods during the membership drive with suitability dependent on the particular parish. But in the area of problems, parish directors indicated largely that lack of response and understanding of the League appeal had become a major difficulty. Many parish directors felt that the market for charitable donations had become increasingly more competitive. More groups were appealing to their parish communities for aid. Directors felt that the number of groups seeking help severely restricted their appeal. There was also a tendency on the part of their parish priests to channel charitable dollars to only their own parish projects. In addition many directors noted that it seemed that Catholics were indeed moving out of their parishes. And last

EXHIBIT 11
Survey of parish directors (47 respondents)

1. What is your method of operation during the drive?
   a. Use church bulletin................................... 33
   b. Announcements at Mass............................... 9
   c. Appeal after Mass at church......................... 10
   d. Use membership envelopes in church................. 4
   e. Solicit at Ladies' Clubs............................. 26
   f. Use personal contact................................ 11
   g. Go door to door...................................... 9
   h. Corps of helpers used............................... 14
   i. Send out letters..................................... 18
   j. Phone calls.. 20
   k. Invite members to luncheon.......................... 1
   l. Use League speaker................................... 1
   m. File system of parish women.......................... 1

2. What problems do you encounter during the drive?
   a. No support from parish priest........................ 10
   b. No response to appeal................................ 13
   c. Lack of publicity.................................... 9
   d. Lack of knowledge of League activities............... 7
   e. Catholics moving out................................. 13
   f. Young women not interested........................... 9
   g. Retirement... 3
   h. Competition with other charities..................... 7
   i. No helpers... 7
   j. Lack of coordination with League office.............. 5
   k. Director has conflict with other activity............ 1
   l. Director no longer wishes to serve................... 10
   m. No longer serves as director......................... 4
   n. Director is no longer a member....................... 4
   o. Membership implies duties............................ 0
   p. Membership cards..................................... 2
   q. Cannot go door to door............................... 5
   r. Unemployment... 7

3. Do you incur personal expenses?
   a. No... 26
   b. Postage.. 18
   c. Use of car... 5
   d. Printing... 1
   e. Phone.. 4
   f. Luncheon... 1
   g. Pay for some members................................. 2

4. Do you believe new membership can be increased?
   a. Possible... 24
   b. Impossible... 19
   c. Will only decline.................................... 1
   d. Don't know... 4

5. Do you think you are successful?
   a. Yes.. 29
   b. No... 14
   c. Don't know... 4

6. What are the ages of your members?
   a. 20–30.. 0
   b. 30–40.. 6

EXHIBIT 11 (*continued*)

   c. 40–50... 13
   d. 50–60... 32
   e. 60 +.. 35
   f. Mixed.. 9

7. What amount of time do you spend on new memberships?
   a. Equal.. 7
   b. Mostly on new... 7
   c. Mostly on old.. 32
   d. Don't know... 7
   e. Neither... 2

8. What information are you able to provide?
   a. League pamphlets..................................... 37
   b. Personal knowledge................................... 10

9. Is there a best time of day to solicit memberships?
   a. Morning... 12
   b. Afternoon... 8
   c. Dinner.. 5
   d. Evening... 10
   e. Anytime... 8

10. Are you employed?
   a. Yes... 7
   b. No.. 40

Note: Many questions may total more than 47 because multiple responses were recorded to most questions.

the most startling of the tabulations showed that of the 47 directors interviewed, 18 of them no longer served or wished to serve the League as a director while at the same time 29 felt that they were successful as directors.

The League also found through the survey that the membership roles were predominated by members who were over 50 years of age, that it was very possible to increase new membership in future drives, that very little time was in fact delegated to obtaining new members, and that very few of the directors were employed which could have hindered their effect at the parish level.

While conducting the phone survey the researchers discovered another critical problem. The most current list of 1975 parish directors contained many inaccuracies. It appeared that the League would have great difficulty in communicating with its parish directors. This was particularly alarming to the officers because parish directors are the only League salespersons who directly contact the membership. Also this list may possibly reflect the present condition of the membership list. Exhibit 12 displays the results of the attempt to contact parish directors by telephone.

After reviewing this information the League directors were searching

EXHIBIT 12
Telephone survey statistics

Parish directors..................................	108
Surveys completed..............................	47
No answer.......................................	30
Not home..	6
On vacation.....................................	5
No longer director..............................	7
Wrong phone number...........................	9
Disconnected phone............................	5
No phone number listed........................	8
Director with no members......................	3

for solid solutions to the problems they faced. They wondered how to increase memberships without increasing costs appreciably and what changes in procedure and strategy were needed to accomplish the goal. In effect they pondered what changes in their marketing plan were necessary in light of their present information.

CASE

3

Crow, Pope, and Land Enterprises*

In early August 1973, Mr. Dan Thatcher, vice president of CPL Condominium Enterprises, a subsidiary of Crow, Pope, and Land Enterprises, was planning his strategy for a new condominium project in Jacksonville, Florida. The project was an important one, since it was the company's first attempt to diversify out of the Atlanta area with nonresort condominiums. Earlier in the year, Mr. Thatcher had arranged the purchase of an option on a 40-acre tract just outside the city limits of Jacksonville, and the company had to renew the option in the next week or they would lose their earnest money. Before the senior officers of the firm would approve the final purchase of the land for approximately $700,000, Mr. Thatcher had to prepare a report discussing the proposed marketing strategy for the condominiums to be built there. His report was to include discussions of the target market, the specifications of the units to be built, the price range of the condominiums, and the promotional strategy to be used in marketing the units.

COMPANY BACKGROUND

Crow, Pope, and Land Enterprises, Inc., is a developer of residential, commercial, and motel/hotel real estate property, with projects located throughout the world. Headquartered in Atlanta, Georgia, the company was incorporated on January 14, 1967 under the name Lincoln Construction Company. Trammell Crow of Dallas, Ewell Pope of Atlanta, and

* This case was co-authored by John S. Wright, Professor of Marketing, Georgia State University.

Frank Carter of Atlanta were the shareholders of the company. Mr. Pope and Mr. Carter had been partners in the real estate brokerage firm, Pope and Carter Company, which had acted as the leasing agent for several of Trammell Crow's developments; namely, Chattahoochee Industrial Park and Greenbriar Shopping Center. These two adventures had proved so successful that the three men decided to strengthen their association and form Lincoln Construction Company.

In June 1972, Mr. Pope and Mr. Carter decided to establish separate organizations, both of which were formed in association with Mr. Crow. Crow and Carter started Crow, Carter, and Associates, Inc., and Crow and Pope, in association with A. J. Land, Jr., became owners of the continuing company, Crow, Pope, and Land Enterprises, Inc.

The company is organized on a project-management basis, with a managing partner who oversees and is responsible for every phase of the development assigned to each project. The manager of each project acts very much like the president of a small company, with the exception that he has the resources of a much larger corporation to draw upon when it is felt that added expertise would be of assistance. Most of the project managers, including Mr. Thatcher, are young, aggressive M.B.A. graduates from leading schools of business administration.

The projects in which the company is involved range from the development of apartment complexes, condominium complexes, office parks, and shopping centers, to "total community" complexes complete with apartments, condominiums, single-family houses, retail outlets, parks, schools, office buildings, and recreational facilities. The firm has recently become active in the development of urban community centers containing a mixture of such features as commercial high-rise office buildings, luxury hotels, retail shopping facilities, and other pedestrian conveniences designed for high architectural impact in downtown environments. Examples of some of the company's projects include the $100 million Atlanta Center project (a large Hilton Hotel together with office buildings and shopping areas in downtown Atlanta), the $40 million Sheraton Hong Kong Hotel and shopping mall complex, and the Cumberland, Fairington, and Northlake total community complexes in Atlanta. Cumberland, a $65 million joint venture development with the Metropolitan Life Insurance Company, will, upon its completion in 1978, include a 1 million square foot enclosed shopping center, 750,000 square feet of office space, 1,800 apartments and condominiums situated around a 17-acre lake, an indoor tennis center, and hotel/motel facilities.

Crow, Pope, and Land has built a number of condominium and apartment complexes in Atlanta, and has built more condominiums than any other developer in the area. Among the projects currently being sold in the Atlanta area are projects oriented toward retired couples, young swingers, sports-minded couples and families, and couples who want to own their own residence but cannot afford single-family detached housing. The company also has several resort projects in Florida.

BACKGROUND ON THE JACKSONVILLE PROJECT

The original idea for the Jacksonville project came out of a meeting Mr. Thatcher had in early 1973 with Lindsay Freeman, another vice president of CPL Condominium Enterprises. In discussing the future goals and directions for the subsidiary, they decided that a high priority should be placed on reducing their dependence on the Atlanta condominium market where all nine of their projects were located. Since different geographic areas often were at different stages of the business cycle, they felt expansion into new geographical areas would provide a hedge against economic downturns as well as opening up profitable new markets for their products.

The first decision made was that they should concentrate on the Southeast, within a 400 mile radius of Atlanta, allowing greater control from the Atlanta headquarters. Also, projections of housing market demand indicated that this region of the country would experience rapid growth in the coming few years.

A number of cities, including Memphis, Louisville, Chattanooga, Mobile, and Birmingham, were investigated as possible sites for a condominium project. Several criteria were established. The area had to have several condominium projects already in existence since they did not want to be the first project in the area. Their experience had shown that the pioneers had to undertake a large educational effort, which usually took two years and a lot of money. The city should have a population of at least 250,000 so that it would absorb a large number of condominiums if the company decided to add other projects at a later date. Lastly, the area should have a large number of residents in the target market for condominiums—young married couples and "empty nesters," couples whose children are grown and have moved out of the home.

Using census data, information obtained from Chambers of Commerce, and other real estate research sources, Thatcher narrowed the choice to Charlotte, North Carolina, and Jacksonville, Florida. In both places, condominiums had been marketed for two to three years, and a number of developments were being built. In Charlotte, however, the only land that was available for immediate development was not particularly well suited for multifamily building. It had been decided that land that had been zoned for condominium development, with utilities easily accessible would be favored to avoid the normal two-year period to get undeveloped raw land ready for development. Therefore, it was without reservation that Thatcher made the decision to expand into the Jacksonville market.

BACKGROUND ON THE JACKSONVILLE AREA

Jacksonville is the most populated city in Florida and ranks second in the Southeast and 23d in the United States. In October of 1968, the city adopted a new charter which consolidated the city and county governments. All of Duval County is now operated as one government, and the consolidation made the new city of Jacksonville the largest city in the continental United States with 840 square miles (537,664 acres). To put the figures into comparative terms, the city is two thirds the size of the state of Rhode Island.

Recent growth has brought many young people to the Jacksonville area. In 1970, the median age of the population was 26 years, compared to 32.3 years for the state of Florida and 28.3 years for the total United States. Duval County has a large, rapidly growing economy, with a balanced employment profile and a rather diversified economic base. This diversification has produced a stable economy by minimizing its sensitivity to both industrial and national business cycles.

For a distance of approximately 100 miles in all directions, the area surrounding the city is predominantly rural in character. With over 500,000 residents, Jacksonville is the commercial and cultural center of northeast Florida and southeast Georgia. It is one of the principal distribution, insurance, and convention centers in the Southeast.

One of the major impacts on the city's economy is the presence of three large military installations in the area, particularly the Jacksonville Naval Air Station located in the southern part of the county on the St. Johns River just north of the city of Orange Park. This facility is one of the largest naval air bases in the United States. It is supported by a smaller air station, Cecil Field, located in the western part of the county, where several air squadrons operate in preparation for air carrier qualifications. The third facility, the Mayport Carrier Basin east of Jacksonville, has berthing capacity for three of the country's largest aircraft carriers. The military installations employ approximately 34,000 people including some 5,000 civilians, 9,000 shore-based military personnel, and 20,000 mobile/afloat military. Another 5,000 military employees are expected to be transferred to these facilities in the next year or two.

Extensive bedroom areas are forming just outside Duval County, reflecting lower tax rates, lower land prices, an absence of restrictive zoning ordinances and a preference for suburban living. Also, the city of Jacksonville was busing children to achieve racial integration in the schools, and many residents were moving to Orange Park and other areas of Clay County (just south of Duval County) where there was no busing of students. The impact of all these factors made Clay County, and the Orange Park area in particular, a rapidly growing area.

The city of Orange Park lies adjacent to and south of the Duval County line, and is approximately 15 miles from the central business district of Jacksonville. Exhibit 1 presents a map of the area showing the location of Orange Park in relation to the naval air station, Cecil Field, and the business district of Jacksonville.

After talking with many real estate people in the area, and after reviewing the statistics presented in Exhibit 2, Mr. Thatcher decided to obtain an option on a 40-acre tract of land just west of the city limits of Orange Park. As shown in the exhibit, the residents of Orange Park had an above average median family income for the area, and were better educated than Duval County residents. Also, over half the population in the area worked outside the county (principally in Duval County). Thatcher thought the higher income, better educated people would be receptive to condo-

EXHIBIT 1
Map of Jacksonville and Orange Park area

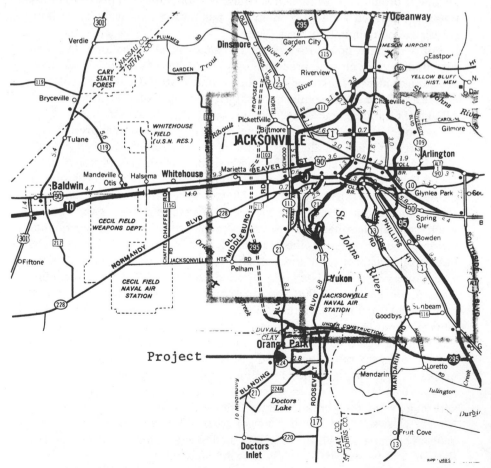

EXHIBIT 2
Selected statistics for Orange Park, Clay County, and Duval County/Jacksonville

	City of Orange Park	Clay County	Duval County/ Jacksonville
Total population, 1970......................	7,677	32,059	528,865
Median family income, 1970.................	$10,021	$8,430	$8,671
Median school years completed— 1970, adults..............................	12.5	12.1	12.0
Percent of residents who work outside the county....................................	—	53.5%	2.6%
Percent of residents who have lived in the same area for five years or more, 1970.....	30.0%	45.6%	67.1%

miniums. Also, he felt that the close proximity to Duval County would be attractive to many potential purchasers.

Access to the site is off Blanding Boulevard (State Road 21 on the map), a heavily traveled two-lane thoroughfare with development, for the most part, consisting of commercial and single-family residential development. Within the past year a considerable amount of multifamily development had occurred, but it was mainly concentrated further northeast in the vicinity of U.S. Highway 17.

Within one mile of the site to the north is a minor shopping center with a Winn-Dixie supermarket as the cornerstone tenant. Two and one half miles north, a 1 million square foot regional shopping center is being developed and is scheduled to open in 1975. The school system in the area is rated excellent, and several elementary schools as well as junior and senior high schools are in close proximity to the site. Churches of all denominations and hospital and recreation facilities are all well represented in the area.

The current housing market in the Orange Park area is composed substantially of single-family houses, with prices of these units beginning at $32,000. Apartments in the vicinity of the site have achieved 100 percent occupancy, with many of the apartments renting for between $150 and $200 per month. There are a number of condominium projects in the area, as shown in Exhibit 3, although almost all of them are situated much farther north. The price range on these condominium projects typically begins in the low $30,000 range and goes up to almost $60,000.

MARKETING STRATEGY

The first question Thatcher had to resolve concerned the target market for the condominiums. There were three basic strategies he had been considering: (a) a specialty type product with a large amenity package oriented toward active, young "swinging" couples; (b) a project oriented

EXHIBIT 3
Condominium projects in the Orange Park area

Project	Rooms	Square feet	Price range
Bay Meadows..............	2BR,2B –3BR,3B	1,350–2,243	$34,850–$48,300
Solano Grove..............	1BR,1B –3BR,3B	874–2,006	26,100– 58,200
Regency Woods............	2BR,2B –4BR,2½B	1,456–2,102	35,500– 45,900
Sutton Place...............	2BR,2½B–4BR,2½B	1,366–1,842	31,500– 38,000
Baytree...................	2BR,1½B–4BR,3½B	1,404–2,214	32,000– 46,750
The Lakes.................	2BR,2B –3BR,2½B	1,330–2,050	37,500– 59,400
Oxford Forest.............	2BR,1½B–3BR,2½B	1,282–1,622	28,500– 35,500

toward the retiree market; or (*c*) a project oriented toward families who wanted to purchase their residence but could not afford a single-family house. Crow, Pope, and Land had considerable experience in building all three types of condominiums in the Atlanta area, and Thatcher was reluctant to consider other types of condominiums that the company had not had experience with. He reasoned that taking a product that had worked elsewhere would reduce some of the risk of entering a new, relatively unknown market. Also, use of a product that the company had built in Atlanta would save the cost of architect's fees, and he would be in a better position to negotiate with a contractor to build the units because he would know in advance what the costs should be (building costs in the Jacksonville area were virtually the same as costs in Atlanta).

Thatcher had located a site along the St. Johns River that would be suitable for the specialty, high-amenity product. There might be some environmental problems with the Army Corp of Engineers who had jurisdiction over the site, but he thought these could be worked out. The Orange Park site under option would not be suitable for this type of project, which Thatcher thought should be built around a body of water. With the high land cost for an appropriate site, and with the high cost for all the recreational amenities, the company would have to price the condominiums under this strategy at about $40,000 (the same price charged for the comparable Riverbend Condominiums in Atlanta).

The optioned site was also not acceptable for the second alternative, a project oriented toward the retirees' market. Experience in Atlanta had shown that retired couples preferred to purchase condominiums with a golf course on site, and the present site was not suited for development of a golf course. Thatcher had located several possible sites suitable for this alternative several miles south of the property under option. Because of the very large investment involved in building a golf course, he felt that a project oriented toward this market would have to be a large one to support the high fixed cost of the golf course.

If the company decided to purchase the property under option, about

12 units per acre could be constructed, or about 480 in total. As they did with almost all their projects, the units would be built in several phases, with phase I consisting of 50 units. Thatcher had determined that units built in the Fairgrounds project in Atlanta could be built and sold profitably in Orange Park for $24,900 for a 1,040 square foot, two-bedroom unit, and $29,900 for a 1,265 square foot, three-bedroom unit. The price per square foot was comparable to the other condominium projects in the area, and the total price was well below most of them because of the smaller size. In addition to the difference in square footage and price, the Fairgrounds models also had different exteriors than the typical ones sold in the Jacksonville area; the Fairgrounds units used brick and aluminum siding, whereas most of the others had a stucco exterior. Although he basically believed that the Jacksonville condominium prospect was very similar to the Atlanta prospect, he wondered whether he should incorporate some stucco treatment into the exterior of the units if he should decide to follow through with this strategy.

Another issue he had not resolved concerned the extent to which the strategy should be oriented toward the large (and growing) military market. If he did define his target market as the military market, what impact would this have on the physical product and on his promotional strategy which was still to be determined? Close to half of the residents of Orange Park worked at one of the three military installations in the area, and both the naval air station and Cecil Field were within seven miles of the proposed site. He was aware of the large word of mouth influence in the Navy—an apartment project not far from the site which was just beginning to lease new units had gone from 5 percent Navy to 30 percent Navy in less than two months.

Another question which concerned Thatcher was the low sales rate of the other condominiums in the area. He thought the reason was the relatively high prices which caused them to compete directly against single-family housing. Also, he had shopped all the projects and found the onsite salesmen to be very uninformed and disinterested in selling the condominiums. He felt certain that this was hurting sales, but was still not sure that the consumers in the Jacksonville/Orange Park area would buy condominiums, even in the price range he was proposing.

The senior officers of Crow, Pope, and Land would also expect a detailed promotional strategy as part of his report. In working with budget figures, he had determined that he could afford to spend $22,000 for promotion (1.5 percent of sales) for the first 50 units, which would be about 12 months projected sales. Brochures, signs, business cards for salesmen, and other miscellaneous items would cost about $2,000, leaving $20,000 for media and production costs.

Crow, Pope, and Land used a small local advertising agency for all their apartment and condominium advertising in Atlanta. Thatcher was uncertain about the role he wanted the agency to play in this project, and was worried that the agency was not attuned to the Jacksonville market. He wondered whether he should try to hire a Jacksonville agency, but was afraid that the account was too small for anyone to pay much attention to it. Also, he felt that the retainer that any decent agency would want to handle the account, about $3,000, could be better spent on media. He had studied advertising and promotion in courses in college, and thought he should consider creating the advertising himself.

There were really only two alternatives for media strategy in the Jacksonville area—radio and newspaper. There were nine AM radio stations and four FM stations. The rates for the four largest stations were all about the same, between $25 and $30 for a one-minute spot during drive time (6:00–10:00 A.M. and 3:00–7:00 P.M.) and about 20 percent cheaper at other times, assuming 12 spots per week for 13 weeks. There were two daily newspapers in Jacksonville, a morning paper with 210,000 circulation, and an evening paper with 148,000 circulation. As a result of common ownership, there was a combination rate available which was only 10 percent higher than the $13.16 per column inch rate for the morning paper alone. The morning paper had a Sunday edition, with a circulation of 182,000 and a cost per column inch of $13.72.

Mr. Thatcher was also concerned about what message to use in his promotional campaign. He was uncertain to what extent they should mention the fact that there was no busing to schools, an important advantage for many potential buyers. He was worried that other people might be upset with the implied racism in such a campaign. He was also concerned with the implications for the advertising creative strategy as a result of the target market decision concerning whether or not to concentrate on the military market. Another advertising issue was the extent to which the copy should promote the fact that Crow, Pope, and Land was a large Atlanta developer, and that this was their first North Florida project.

The one decision Thatcher had made was that there was much opportunity for the company in the Jacksonville market, and, therefore, much opportunity for him personally to expand his responsibilities in the company. As a result, he wanted to make a recommendation that the company definitely enter the market; the only uncertainty was the strategy to be followed. The company had paid $1,000 for the initial option on the Orange Park property. Next week they had to either pay $20,000 to renew the option for 90 days or lose their $1,000 investment. If they decided to renew the option, this would give them time to arrange for the financing of the project and to arrange a production schedule with the contractors. They had to begin this planning immediately since it usually took at least six months to build condominiums, and that meant that they would have to act fast if they wanted to be selling condominiums by the height of the selling season in June. As he sat down to write the report containing his recommendations, Thatcher realized that a decision to renew the option would be a commitment to actually build the units he recommended.

CASE

4

Paul Finney Takes up Tennis*

When Paul Finney started his new job teaching economics at Fanshawe State College in Greenfield, he vowed to himself that he was going to make more time available for sports and other recreational activities. Paul, who was 25, viewed himself as a person who had always been interested in sports and for many years had participated actively in various kinds of athletics. As an undergraduate at Dartmouth, he had been a member of the varsity basketball team as well as playing on intramural squads in volleyball, water polo, and touch football. After graduating from Dartmouth, Paul had spent two years doing postgraduate studies at The University of Chicago. There, the pressure of studies had been too intense to allow much free time. Consequently, he had done almost nothing in the way of sports activities. He often complained to his wife of feeling lethargic through lack of exercise. However, Paul now had a new job in a new city. To him, it was clearly time to resume active participation in sports.

During the fall and winter months, Paul Finney lived up to his self-made promise. He took up badminton—a game that he used to play before going to Chicago. Quite a few of the faculty at Fanshawe played badminton at noon in the gym, and there was never any trouble in finding a partner for a game. True, Paul did not play as often as he had intended but, after all, it was his first year of teaching in a new environment. Besides, it was a substantial improvement over doing nothing at all.

Around February, Paul began to think ahead to the coming summer

---

* This case was written by Robert E. M. Nourse, Vice President of Venturetek International Limited. Used with permission of the author and the University of Western Ontario.

months. Badminton was best played indoors. Paul suspected that most of
his associates at the college gave up the game over the summer in favor of
outdoor activities. He often had heard his friends express their interest
in the arrival of warm weather. By the way they spoke, most of these
people seemed to be looking forward to the opportunity to play one of
two sports: golf or tennis.

Paul had played golf before, but he had never joined a golf club or
played with any degree of regularity. Four years previously, while still a
student at Dartmouth, he and several classmates had taken summer jobs
with the New Hampshire Industrial Department in Concord. Using borrowed or rented clubs, they would occasionally drive to a nearby golf club
and play nine holes in the early evening. Paul probably played golf a
dozen times that summer but had played on only three or four other
scattered occasions during his life. Both of his parents were avid golfers
and had encouraged him to take up the game so frequently and forcefully
that Paul sometimes wondered if he hadn't rebelled against the whole idea.
Golf just didn't seem to be his bag. For one thing, he reasoned, it was
far too time-consuming—at least three hours to play a decent round.
He had never "broken 50" for nine holes and had been told by someone
(he couldn't remember who) that the only way to improve was to play
at least three times a week. At the same time, Paul had the impression
that golf courses were always crowded and he invariably had the feeling
of being rushed.

Tennis might well be different. Paul had never played a game of tennis,
but he had watched Davis Cup matches on television. He reasoned that
he could surely play a recreational game of tennis in an hour or less. This
would allow lots of time in the day for other work. Furthermore, there
were several tennis courts right on the campus at Fanshawe. Quite a few
of his associates at the college seemed to be tennis players and, given
his experiences with badminton, there would probably be no trouble in
lining up a game at any time on a moment's notice. Paul began to think
seriously about taking up tennis in the coming summer.

One night in March, he was sitting in his living room after supper
checking through the day's mail. A sale catalog had arrived from Alden's.
Paul picked it up to browse through. He enjoyed looking through mail-
order catalogs—particularly those advertising a sale—even if he had no
specific purchase in mind. Sure enough, just a couple of pages from the
back, he spotted a tennis racket. It seemed to be a pretty good bargain—
a Dunlop, regularly $17.95, on sale for $10.95. He decided to keep it in
mind.

It was early April before the issue of a tennis racket arose again. Paul
was visiting the home of Dave Babcock, a fellow teacher at Fanshawe, and
recalled having heard that Dave was an active tennis player. He decided

to ask Dave about the racket in the catalog. "I've been meaning to ask you about something," he led off. "I've been thinking about taking up tennis this summer, but I've never played before and haven't any idea of what kind of racket to get. I saw one on sale the other day in an Alden's catalog, but I just haven't any basis for evaluating whether the thing's any good or not. Have you any suggestions as to what I should be looking for in a racket?"

"It's really been some years since I bought a racket," Dave replied. "I'm not so sure that I'm the right person to ask. I don't really know what to tell you. The man you'd be best to ask is Bill Englander in the Math Department. He's played a lot of tennis and was the Junior Champion of Michigan a few years ago."

The next day Paul attended a faculty meeting at Fanshawe. Arriving a little early, he noticed Bill Englander and thought to ask about the tennis racket. Paul had met Bill before and had spoken with him on numerous occasions during the year. It was not difficult, therefore, to broach the tennis racket question in much the same manner as he had with Dave Babcock the night before.

"I have to admit that I'm not too keen on Dunlop rackets," Bill offered. "I've seen a lot of people break them too easily. So I probably wouldn't be too enthusiastic about the racket you saw in the Alden's catalog. That is, not unless it happened to be a Dunlop Max-Ply. For some reason, the Max-Ply is way ahead of the other rackets Dunlop puts out and, in fact, is really a first-class racket. I rather doubt, however, that the one you saw was a Max-Ply. I think they run somewhat more expensive than $17.95, and aren't the kind of racket that's likely to go on sale."

Bill's remark came as somewhat of a disappointment to Paul because he had become quite interested in the Dunlop racket in the catalog. Then, the thought crossed his mind that the racket was reduced to almost half price at a time when the tennis season was just coming up. "Why," he asked himself, "would there be such a large price reduction unless something was wrong with it?"

"A lot of people I know use Slazengers," Bill continued, "but I personally don't like them too well." He proceeded to explain what he didn't like about Slazenger rackets, but Paul was beginning to lose track of the conversation. He wondered to himself if Bill wasn't leading up to recommending a racket that would suit his own needs more than those of a beginner. At the same time, Paul sensed a definite tone of authority and expertise in Bill's remarks. There was little doubt that the fellow could be trusted to recommend a good racket—the only problem was that it might be *too* good.

Although nothing was said, Bill seemed suddenly to sense the hesitations that were running through Paul's mind. He paused for a moment, then began to speak again in a slower and more deliberate voice. "There are several good rackets on the market, but my choice for someone starting to play for the first time would be a Spalding. The reason I say this is that Spalding started making their rackets in Belgium about two years ago. At that time, they really lowered their prices. I think that you'd get better value in a Spalding racket than in anything else. After you've been playing for a while, you'll find that you develop fairly distinct ideas about what you want in a racket—a certain type of grip, the weight, or any one of a number of things. But you have to play for some time before you find this out. If you're just starting, I don't think you could go far wrong with a Spalding."

Paul had begun to listen more intently again. "If I bought a Spalding," he asked, "what would be a reasonable price to pay for it?"

"Well, I would think that somewhere between $12 and $15 would buy you a decent racket. Of course, you'd also have to pay to have it strung. That would cost anywhere from $5 to $15 depending on what kind of stringing you get."

"Do you have any advice on that? I don't know the first thing about having a racket strung."

"For a starter, you should probably get braided nylon. Don't get the plain nylon—it's the cheapest and won't last very long before it breaks. The braided nylon is made up of a lot of strands of thin nylon fiber braided together. That gives it a lot of strength, but at the same time isn't too expensive. They'll probably also ask you what tension you want it strung at—the more tension you have, the more 'zip' there is to the racket when you hit the ball. I'd say about 50 pounds would be fine. If you get the tension much higher than that, it becomes quite difficult to control the ball when you hit it."

When he got home that night, Paul checked the Alden's sale catalog again. As Bill had suspected, the Dunlop racket that was on sale was not a Max-Ply.

For the next three or four weeks, Paul made no further move to buy a tennis racket, but he did think about it a lot. He mentioned to Bob Foulkes, a frequent badminton partner, that he was going to take up the game of tennis and was in the market for a racket. He also followed closely the newspaper accounts of upcoming Davis Cup matches between the United States and Australia. The Americans were supposed to have a good chance of winning but someone must have been too optimistic because they lost ignominiously in five straight matches.

In a casual conversation with a neighbor, Tom Norton, Paul discovered that Tom was also a tennis player. Tom mentioned that he had bought a new Dunlop Max-Ply the previous summer. He offered to sell Paul his old racket, which was not a Max-Ply, at a good price. Paul didn't encourage the idea and the matter of buying a used racket never developed further. Paul frequently met Bill Englander in the course of his work at Fanshawe, and Bill never failed to ask if Paul had bought a tennis racket yet. Each time, Paul replied negatively, always adding that he certainly was going to in the near future.

On the morning of April 28, Paul slept in. He had no classes to teach until 11:30 that morning, so decided to visit Tom Munro Sports on his way into work. Munro's was one of two sporting goods stores in the city of Greenfield. Of the two, it seemed to be the one that most of Paul's friends talked about patronizing. Paul himself had bought badminton shuttles at Munro's on several occasions. Knowing the approximate layout of the store, he quickly spotted the tennis racket section upon entering and started to walk toward it. He was the only customer in Munro's at the time and was intercepted by a youthful-looking salesclerk even before reaching the tennis rackets.

"May I help you, sir?" asked the clerk.

"Yes, I'm interested in buying a tennis racket," Paul began. "I particularly like the Spalding—you do string them right here in the store, I assume?"

"Uh . . . yes sir, we do, but . . ."

"Good. You have the braided nylon?"

"Yes indeed. But I'm sorry to say that we don't have any Spaldings. We dropped their line about a year ago."

"Oh . . . why did you do that?"

The clerk slowly began to walk the remaining short distance toward the tennis racket section. Paul followed as the young man continued to talk. "Well, about two years ago, they dropped the prices on all of their rackets by a really significant amount. They started making their rackets overseas somewhere—Formosa I think—they're not made in North America anymore, you know."

"No, they're made in Belgium."

"Is that it? . . . Well, anyhow, what happened to us is that one day we were selling a Spalding racket for, say, $17.95. All of a sudden, we had the same racket being sold for about $7.95. Pretty soon, some of the people who had paid $17.95 began to notice this. Needless to say, they didn't like it one bit. We'd explain that it was Spalding who had reduced the price, but people were still pretty hostile. Eventually, we found that the only way to avoid this kind of situation was to drop the line altogether."

"No kidding!"

"That's exactly what happened . . . Do you mind me asking if you're new to the city, sir?"

"Well, yes I am—I just moved here last summer."

"I thought so because I was really surprised when you asked specifically for a Spalding. I don't recall ever having anyone ask me for a Spalding before. They just aren't that popular with tennis players around here. . . . Did it have to be a Spalding, or could I show you something else?"

"Well, I'm not sure. I certainly had planned to buy a Spalding. What other lines do you carry?"

"Well, here in Greenfield, all the good tennis players use Dunlop Max-Ply. It's truly an excellent racket. The good players all swear by it."

"What does it run?"

"It's $26.95. Terrific value for a racket of that quality." The clerk removed a Max-Ply from the rack and held it loosely in his hand. Paul did not move to take it from him.

"I'd like to think about it for a while. I don't need the racket right away. What I really came in for was a pair of white shorts, size 36."

"By all means." Without looking further at tennis rackets, the two walked to a nearby counter containing the shorts. There was only one style of white shorts available. They were wrapped in a clear polyethylene bag.

Paul noted the price of $4.95 marked on the outside of the bag, but did not bother to remove the shorts. "I'll take a pair in size 36," he said. Immediately after paying for the shorts, he left the store.

During the next week, Paul was out of town on business. Soon after returning he happened to pass by College Sports, the only other sporting goods store of significant size in the city. He went in and walked over to the selection of tennis rackets. College Sports carried Slazenger, Wilson, and Dunlop rackets, but there were no Spaldings. Paul didn't bother to examine the rackets closely or to remove any from the rack. He left the store almost immediately before a salesclerk had a chance to approach him.

Later in the week, Paul was shopping in Wellington Square Mall, an indoor shopping center in the downtown area. Remembering that he had seen a small sporting goods department on the main floor of Slover's Department Store there, he decided to see if they had any tennis rackets. There was only a limited selection. All except one of the rackets were prestrung and there were no Spaldings. Again, he didn't bother to examine any closely, and left the store quickly.

At about this time, Paul began to wonder if the whole business of buying a tennis racket wasn't taking up too much of his time. He tried to think of any other store in Greenfield that might have a large selection of rackets, but none came to his mind. He had visited three stores and had not found a Spalding racket in any of them. Paul began to think that he'd have to settle for some other kind of racket, but wasn't at all sure what it should be. He could feel himself getting quite confused.

On June 1, Paul took his young son to the Mayfield department store in Greenfield to buy a new pair of running shoes. On entering the store, he realized that it would be relatively convenient to walk by the sporting goods department on the way toward getting his son's shoes. "They probably don't have any more of a selection than Slover's," he thought to himself, "but there's nothing to lose by taking a look anyhow."

While still some distance away from the sporting goods department, Paul could see quite a large number of tennis rackets displayed on a vertical rack sitting upright on an island counter. This rather surprised him. He walked up to the rack and looked more closely. All of the rackets were of a single brand, Jelinek, which Paul had never heard mentioned before. Altogether, there were about 25 rackets displayed in various models of the Jelinek line; they ranged in price from $3.95 to $10.95. Looking more closely, Paul noticed from the label on one racket that the Jelinek brand was manufactured in Japan.

Paul walked slowly around to the other side of the island counter. There, he discovered a display of about two dozen additional rackets that he had not been able to see from his previous position. Most of them were Spaldings, although there were a few Dunlop Max-Ply rackets at one end. All were prestrung except the Max-Ply. Stapled beneath each racket's position on the rack was a small white card indicating the name of the racket, its price and the kind of material with which it was strung. Paul read each of the cards carefully, noticing at the same time that most of the rackets were not hung in the correct position corresponding to their card. One card identified the Max-Ply at $26.95, unstrung. Another indicated a Wilson racket at $16.95, but the store was apparently out of stock because Paul couldn't see any Wilson rackets at all. Of the remaining four cards, all identified various models of Spaldings. Three of the four were identified as being strung with twisted nylon; they were priced at $7.95, $9.95, and $12.95. The remaining Spalding racket was a Fred Stolle model at $15.95, strung with braided nylon.

Removing the Fred Stolle racket from the rack, Paul was surprised to note how heavy and clumsy it felt in comparison to a badminton racket. The grip was much thicker and the whole racket much heavier. He swung is through the air a couple of times.

Holding the Fred Stolle racket in his hand, Paul looked over the remaining ones still hanging on the rack. He re-read the white cards beneath each one and, as he was doing so, a salesclerk approached him. The clerk said nothing. Finally, Paul pointed to the cards on the rack and asked the clerk to explain the difference between twisted nylon and braided nylon.

"I'm sorry sir, but I don't know very much about tennis rackets," the clerk replied.

". . . Well, that's all right. . . . I'm pretty sure this is what I'm look-ing for, anyhow." Paul handed the clerk the Spalding Fred Stolle racket that he'd been holding.

While the clerk rang up the sale, Paul decided to look at tennis balls. The majority of the tennis balls stocked by Mayfield were various price lines of the Jelinek brand. Somehow Paul decided that he didn't want to start out by buying Japanese tennis balls. The only alternative was a large cellophane bag of 12 tennis balls for about $1.99. It was apparent to Paul that these were real "cheapies." Not only were they priced far below the other tennis balls, but they were also not packed in a vacuum cannister. Paul wasn't sure why tennis balls should be packed in a vacuum cannister, but the only ones he could ever recollect seeing had been in a container of that kind. He decided not to buy any tennis balls at this time.

However, after looking at the tennis balls, Paul remembered that he had intended to get a cover for his racket. No one had specifically sug-gested that he should have a cover. In fact, he had never kept his bad-minton racket in a cover. But Paul recalled having seen players walking to or from tennis courts at various times in the past. Most of them had a wooden press or cloth cover protecting their racket when it was not in use. Paul had ruled out the idea of a press, saying to himself that a press was heavy and that he'd never bother to take the thing on and off each time he played. Mayfield had several covers displayed on a counter near the tennis rackets. The first to catch Paul's eye was a white simulated leather cover with black trim and the word "Spalding" boldly emblazoned across each side. It was $3.95. A less expensive cover at $2.95 was avail-able in several different colors, but it had "Wilson" written across each side. Finally, there was a plain blue nylon cover priced at $1.49 with nothing written on each side. He picked up the Spalding cover and the plain blue one, examining each. A small label sewn inside the blue cover indicated that it was made in Japan. After a moment's hesitation, he decided to buy the plain blue cover.

A couple of days after buying the racket, Paul had commented on its purchase to Jack Bailey, a fellow member of the teaching staff at Fanshawe.

"Have you used it yet?" asked Jack.

"Hell, no—I just bought it and haven't played a game of tennis in my life!"

"Then it's about time you started. What are you doing right now?"

"Not a great deal. But are you willing to waste your time with a duffer like me?"

"Sure—I'll show you what little I know of the game. The only problem is that I don't have any tennis balls with me."

"I haven't bought any yet myself, but I'm willing to do so right now."

"Good enough. We can drive down to Munro's and pick some up. Then we'll drop back here and have a game."

The two drove to Munro's in Paul's car. There were no convenient parking places near the store, so Paul double-parked while Jack went into the store. He bought a cannister of three Slazenger balls for $2.59 on Paul's behalf.

Paul enjoyed his first game of tennis, although it was hardly a game in the true sense of the word. Paul quickly realized that he had a lot to learn yet and felt rather awkward at his seeming inability to hit the ball with any degree of accuracy. He noticed that Jack also had a Spalding racket, although not a Fred Stolle model.

During the weeks that followed, Paul noticed that he came to think and talk about tennis quite a bit. For example he told John Lowery, a teacher of economics at Fanshawe, of his initial experience at Tom Munro Sports. Paul raised the question as to whether the store's logic in dropping the Spalding line was sound business practice and whether Spalding's own decision to reduce prices on its rackets so drastically was a good one.

Paul had dinner with a former Dartmouth classmate, Peter Doubless, and learned that Peter was thinking about taking up tennis. Peter said that he thought he'd invest about $5 in a racket. Paul then explained how carefully he'd considered the matter of a tennis racket purchase and why he decided to start out by spending around $15. Peter's response was that he hadn't really thought about it that way, but that he probably should reconsider and spend more than he had initially planned.

Paul also showed his new racket to his neighbor, Tom Norton, and explained the difficulty he had encountered in finding a local merchant who stocked the Spalding line. Tom replied that he wished he had known Paul was looking for a Spalding because he knew that Super-Save, a local discount house, carried that brand. Paul didn't say anything, but the next time he was near Super-Save, he went into the store and looked at their tennis rackets. He noted that there were two Spalding models, but that they were cheaper rackets priced at $3.95 and $5.95.

On one occasion, Paul showed his new racket to Bob Foulkes. Bob apparently played very little tennis, but was very keen on badminton. During the winter months, it had been Bob with whom Paul had played badminton most frequently. Noting that Paul's tennis racket was a Spalding, Bob asked if his badminton racket was also a Spalding.

"I really don't know," Paul replied. "Let me think for a moment . . . about all I can remember is that it's called a 'Viceroy.' But I don't think that's a manufacturer's name. It's just the name given to my particular model of badminton racket. I don't remember ever looking to see who the manufacturer was. I've had the racket for about six years now. It was given to me secondhand by an old fellow named Gord who used to run the locker room in the field house at Dartmouth."

Paul's curiosity was sufficiently aroused by this question that, later in the same day, he made a point of looking closely at his badminton racket. The model name was not "Viceroy," as he had previously reported to Bob Foulkes. Rather, it was a "Varsity" model. The racket had been manufactured by Spalding.

5

Exercise on Financial Analysis for Marketing Decision Making

An important part of the analysis of alternatives facing marketing decision makers is the financial analysis of these alternatives. This exercise is designed to give students experience in handling the types of financial calculations that arise in marketing cases. If you can do the calculations in this exercise, you should be able to handle the financial calculations necessary to properly do the cases in this book.

1. You have just been appointed the product manager for the "Flexo" brand of electric razors in a large consumer products company. As part of your new job, you want to develop an understanding of the financial situation for your product. Your brand assistant has provided you with the following facts:

a.	Retail selling price............................	$30 per unit
b.	Retailer's margin.............................	20%
c.	Jobber's margin..............................	20%
d.	Wholesaler's * margin	15%
e.	Direct factory labor...........................	$2 per unit
f.	Raw materials................................	$1 per unit
g.	All factory and administrative overheads.....	$1 per unit (at a 100,000 unit volume level)
h.	Salesperson's commissions..................	10% of manufacturer's selling price
i.	Sales force travel costs......................	$200,000
j.	Advertising..................................	$500,000
k.	Total market for razors.......................	1 million units
l.	Current yearly sales of Flexo.................	210,000 units

* An agent who sells to the jobbers, who in turn sell to the retailers.

QUESTIONS

1. What is the contribution per unit for the Flexo brand?
2 What is the break-even volume in units and in dollars?
3. What market share does the Flexo brand need to break even?
4. What is the current total contribution?
5. What is the current before tax profit of the Flexo brand?
6. What market share must Flexo obtain to contribute a before tax profit of $2 million?

2. One of the first decisions you have to make as the brand manager for Flexo is whether or not to add a new line of razors, the "Super Flexo" line. This line would be marketed in addition to the original Flexo line. Your brand assistant has provided you with the following facts:

a.	Retail selling price...............................	$40 per unit
b.	All margins the same as before..................	
c.	Direct factory labor..............................	$ 3 per unit
d.	Raw materials.....................................	$ 2 per unit
e.	All factory and administrative overheads........	$ 2 per unit (at a 50,000 unit volume level)
f.	Salesperson's commissions the same percent as before	
g.	Incremental sales force travel cost..............	$ 50,000
h.	Advertising for Super Flexo.....................	$600,000
i.	New equipment needed........................	$500,000 (to be depreciated over ten years)
j.	Research and development spent up to now.....	$200,000
k.	Research and development to be spent this year to commercialize the product....................	$500,000 (to be amortized over five years)

QUESTIONS

1. What is the contribution per unit for the Super Flex brand?
2. What is the break-even volume in units and in dollars?
3. What is the sales volume in units necessary for Super Flexo to yield, in the first year, a 20 percent return on the equipment to be invested in the project?

3. The $40 per unit selling price for Super Flexo seems high to you. You thought you might lower the price to $37 per unit and raise retail margin to 25 percent.

QUESTION

What is the break-even volume in units?

PART III

MARKETING RESEARCH

The need for good information is pervasive of all marketing decision making. Most cases in this book present some information provided by marketing research. However, they also leave many points of uncertainty. The skill of marketing decision making is the use of the information that is available, along with explicit assumptions about uncertain points to make good decisions. The suggestion that we do marketing research has usually not been allowed in other parts of this text. In this section we turn to the undertaking of marketing research activity.

First, let us define marketing research. It is the systematic gathering, recording, and analyzing of data about problems relating to the marketing of goods and services. There are three kinds of marketing research: (1) exploratory, (2) conclusive, and (3) performance monitoring. Exploratory research is useful for identifying situations calling for a decision and for identifying alternative courses of action. Conclusive research is useful for evaluating alternative courses of action and selecting a course of action. Performance monitoring research is designed to provide the control function over marketing programs.

The marketing research process may be thought of as being composed of the following steps:

1. Establish the need for information.
2. Specify the research objectives and information needs.
3. Determine the sources of data.
4. Develop data collection forms.

5. Design a sample.
6. Collect the data.
7. Process the data.
8. Analyze the data.
9. Present research findings.

The responsibility for the execution of these stages is shared by the marketing manager and the marketing researcher. They both must be sure that the problem has been defined properly, that the objectives make sense, and so on. The researcher holds primary responsibility for the technical details of the study. However, he or she must always be prepared to explain these aspects to the manager in nontechnical terms.

Marketing research costs money. Before it is undertaken, it must be ascertained that the value of the information provided justifies the cost. Also, before research is undertaken, the use to which that research will be made should be clearly understood. A specific decision should be the target of the research and the way the new information will be used in helping make the decision should be clearly understood.

This note and the cases in this section focus on the managerial aspects of marketing research. The technical details are mostly left for more advanced texts.

6

The Stereo Shop*

In early May 1976, Mr. Angelo Lorelli was reviewing data he had gathered on the feasibility of establishing a new stereo component retail outlet in Ann Arbor, Michigan. To date, a variety of information had been collected covering such topics as the stereo component industry, the potential market in Ann Arbor, existing competition, supply sources, and projected capital requirements and operating costs. At this point, it was Mr. Lorelli's responsibility to recommend whether he and his two partners should proceed with the proposed venture and, if so, on what basis.

A young man, Mr. Lorelli had recently graduated from a well-known midwestern business school. As his graduation neared, he had realized that he was not enthusiastic about working for a large corporation. Forming his own business was an alternative Angelo had seriously pondered and stereo components, his principal hobby, was a natural area to consider.

With a promise of family financial support, Mr. Lorelli had entered into an agreement with two friends to form a company to retail stereo components. Their plan was to open an outlet that would specialize only in stereo components, and only those of better quality. Mr. Lorelli, who would have a controlling interest in the firm, would be the only equity holder active in its operations. The plan called for him to prepare a feasibility study by no later than May 15, at which time a final go/no-go decision would be rendered.

---

* This case was written by Robert E. M. Nourse, Vice President of Venturetek International Limited. Used with permission of the author and the University of Western Ontario.

THE STEREO COMPONENT INDUSTRY

Statistics on stereo components for the U.S. market were available. These data indicated that the U.S. industry was in a period of substantial growth. Retail sales per year in 1975 were estimated at over $500 million, up from $300 million in 1967. Industry experts were anticipating a $2 billion market within the next few years.

The average price paid for a stereo component system was $500–$600 as compared to $300–$400 in 1967. The increase was thought to be due to increased popularity of better quality components, since price levels of comparable equipment had remained almost stable during this period. An estimated 27 percent of all component sales were replacement, trade-up, or add-on purchases.

In part, growth of the component industry had come at the expense of console sales, in which all components of the stereo system were built into a single piece of furniture, a "console." In 1972, console sales totaled $296 million at retail, compared to $437 million in 1967. Average retail price paid for a console in 1972 was $310, an increase of approximately 6 percent over 1967. Replacements of existing consoles accounted for 28 percent of 1972 sales.

Stereo components were sold in a wide variety of outlets. Specialty stereo shops were the strongest single class of outlet, but appliance stores, radio and TV outlets, department stores, discount stores and mail-order houses also accounted for significant proportions. With the industry experiencing rapid growth, mass merchandising outlets had been particularly active in giving added emphasis to stocking, displaying, and promoting components.

THE ANN ARBOR MARKET FOR STEREO COMPONENTS

The city of Ann Arbor was located about 50 miles due west of Detroit, Michigan. The population of Ann Arbor was about 105,000 in 1975 with per capita income and retail sales equal to $5,325 and $2,612, respectively. Both per capita income and sales in Ann Arbor were among the highest in Michigan. Ann Arbor was located in Washtenaw County which had a 1975 population of 250,000 and per capita retail sales of $1,770. Technically oriented companies dominated the Ann Arbor economy along with the University of Michigan. The student population was over 35,000 which was in addition to the permanent resident population noted previously.

Data on stereo component sales for Ann Arbor were not available. Census statistics were available, however, indicating 1970 *total* sales of the following classes of retail establishments in Washtenaw County:

1. *Furniture, television, radio and appliance stores,* defined as those in which no one of the four lines exceeded 50 percent of total sales.
2. *Household appliance stores,* defined as those in which appliances exceeded 50 percent of total sales.
3. *Television, radio and hi-fi stores,* in which these three lines accounted for over 50 percent of total store sales.

Mr. Lorelli used his own judgment to estimate that stereo (component and console) accounted for 20 percent, 15 percent, and 35 percent of total sales of the respective store classes. On this basis, he arrived at an estimate of $3.3 million for 1970 Washtenaw County total stereo retail sales. Next, using available data on past U.S. experience, Mr. Lorelli developed a simple regression equation to represent industry growth trends. Applying the equation to Washtenaw County, the 1970 figure of $3.3 million was projected to a comparable 1976 total of $5.7 million.

Competition for stereo sales came from a number of sources. The 1975 Ann Arbor telephone directory, for example, listed over 38 retailers under the "High Fidelity and Stereophonic Equipment" section of its yellow pages. Further, these listings did not include either of the city's three major department stores, nor the suburban outlets of major variety chains such as Woolco and K-Mart.

In Mr. Lorelli's opinion, however, many of the existing outlets did not represent direct competition for his proposed store. Their lines were of a cheaper quality and lower price. Others carried stereo components only as a minor sideline to a principal emphasis on television sets and/or consoles. On this basis, only four stores were judged to be direct competitors: Big George's Home Appliance Mart, Lafayette, Mr. Music, and Audioland.

All four direct competitors carried well-known, quality brands in the component industry, and in some instances had exclusive territorial rights to these brands. Display at both Big George's and Lafayette was arranged so that a customer could listen to any speaker from any set in the store. All four offered a listening room where the set could be heard free of other noise distractions. In Mr. Lorelli's view, however, the attractiveness of display and listening room features in all four stores was not what it could be. All four stores were aggressive advertisers.

THE CONSUMER SURVEY

Because of the limited available information, Mr. Lorelli felt it would be appropriate to conduct a consumer survey. Budget was limited, so it was decided that a telephone survey would be most appropriate. The questionnaire shown in Exhibit 1 was designed by Mr. Lorelli for this purpose.

A random sample of 216 names was drawn from the Ann Arbor telephone directory. Because university students were thought to be a prime market for quality stereo components, a further 108 names were drawn randomly from the University of Michigan's Student Directory. Execution of the survey resulted in 167 usable responses from the city population, 81 from the student population. Selected results from the survey are reproduced in Exhibit 2.

OPERATING COSTS FOR A PROPOSED OUTLET

The stereo components industry was characterized by a large number of potential suppliers. Thus, while some well-known lines were held by competitors on an exclusive basis, Mr. Lorelli contemplated no difficulty in obtaining a line of products suitable to his requirement of selling only quality components. Gross margins of manufacturers varied widely, and competitive pressures frequently forced retailers to sell at less than recommended list prices. After allowing for these factors, Mr. Lorelli anticipated that realized gross margin would average approximately 30 percent.

Capital requirements were estimated at $150,000. This sum included an inventory requirement of $70,000, working capital needs, and the necessary store fixtures for a rented outlet capable of projecting a quality image.

Rent for a store of 3,000 square feet would amount to $18,000 per year for a noncentral location, or as high as $25,000–$30,000 per year for a downtown location. Other annual operating expenses would include wages ($35,000), insurance ($6,000), delivery expenses ($2,500), bad debt allowances ($3,000), and telephone, supplies, and miscellaneous ($7,000). Interest on borrowed capital would be charged at a 10 percent rate. An initial projection of $27,000 per annum for advertising was assumed.

THE DECISION

Mr. Lorelli was all too aware of the time pressures he faced in making a decision. With the pressures in mind, he sat down with all the data he had collected with the intention of making the right decision for him.

EXHIBIT 1
Questionnaire used in telephone survey

1. Do you own a stereo? What brand is it?
2. Is it a component or a console set?
3. Are you considering a purchase (repurchase)?
   When?
   a. Within one year.
   b. From two to three years.
   c. From four to five years.
   d. Longer than five years.
   Price range?
   a. $100–$399.
   b. $400–$599.
   c. $600–$799.
   d. $800–$999.
   e. Over $1,000.
4. What type of store would you go to to make this purchase?
   a. Furniture.
   b. Appliance.
   c. TV store.
   d. Specialty store.
   e. Department store.
5. What was (is) important to you in purchasing a stereo?
6. Would you return to the same store for a repurchase?
7. How important is brand name?
   a. Very important.
   b. Moderately important.
   c. Not important at all.
8. Do you know the service arrangement that you have with the store at which you made your purchase?
9. If you made a repurchase, would you trade up to higher price and quality?
10. Would you consider a trade-in service an important feature of a retail stereo shop?
11. What is your age?
    a. Under 25.
    b. 26–34.
    c. 35–50.
    d. over 50.
12. Are you married?

EXHIBIT 2
Selected results of telephone survey

	City population	Students	Total
1. Ownership of stereo:			
Own a console..............................	46%	32%	41%
Own a component set.......................	32	47	37
Don't own a stereo..........................	22	21	22
Total................................	100%	100%	100%
	(n = 167)	(n = 81)	(n = 248)
2. Plan to purchase or repurchase a stereo:			
Within 1 year...............................	17%	12%	16%
In 2–3 years................................	24	45	30
In 4–5 years................................	11	11	11
In more than 5 years........................	7	16	10
Do not plan to purchase....................	41	16	33
Total................................	100%	100%	100%
	(n = 167)	(n = 81)	(n = 248)
3. Price prospective purchasers expect to pay:			
Less than $400..............................	25%	20%	23%
$400–$599...................................	27	38	31
$600–$799...................................	26	20	24
$800–$999...................................	13	9	11
$1,000 or more..............................	9	13	11
Total................................	100%	100%	100%
	(n = 116)	(n = 69)	(n = 185)
4. Type of store respondent would go to for stereo purchase:			
Furniture....................................	23%	12%	20%
Appliance...................................	13	14	13
TV..	16	15	15
Specialty....................................	23	47	31
Department.................................	14	9	12
Don't know/no answer......................	11	3	9
Total................................	100%	100%	100%
	(n = 167)	(n = 81)	(n = 248)
5. Factor(s) regarded as most important in purchasing a stereo:			
Sound.......................................	27%	40%	32%
Style..	11	12	11
Construction................................	11	7	10
Price..	11	9	10
Brand name.................................	2	1	2
Style and price..............................	9	0	6
Sound and price.............................	8	20	12
Style and quality............................	4	5	4
Don't know/no answer......................	17	6	13
Total................................	100%	100%	100%
	(n = 167)	(n = 81)	(n = 248)

EXHIBIT 2 (continued)

	City population	Students	Total
6. Knowledge of service arrangement (for stereo owners only):			
Know service arrangement..................	49%	75%	59%
Don't know service arrangement............	51	25	41
Total............................	100%	100%	100%
	(n = 108)	(n = 64)	(n = 172)
7. Age and marital status of respondents:			
Age:			
25 or less................................	27%	67%	40%
26–34....................................	35	19	29
35–50....................................	17	4	13
Over 50..................................	11	1	8
No answer...............................	10	9	10
Total............................	100%	100%	100%
	(n = 167)	(n = 81)	(n = 248)
Marital status:			
Single...................................	19%	76%	38%
Married..................................	58	21	46
Other....................................	10	1	7
No answer...............................	13	2	9
Total............................	100%	100%	100%
	(n = 167)	(n = 81)	(n = 248)

CASE

7

Bay-Madison, Inc.*

In January 1976, Mr. George Roberts, research director of Bay-Madison, Inc., a large advertising agency, was faced with the problem of how best to conduct a study on Rill, a product of the Ellis Company, one of the agency's clients.

Rill, a powdered cleanser, was first introduced by the Ellis Company in 1923. Its original use was as a heavy-duty cleansing agent for removing dirt and stains from porcelain, metal, and ceramic tile surfaces. A unique bleaching property of the product eliminated the necessity for scrubbing and it contained no abrasive material. In 1936, the company's research department developed and added to the product an ingredient which imparted a light, fluffy texture to textile products washed in a mild solution of Rill. Recognizing the problem of keeping such articles as baby clothes, towels, and blankets soft through repeated washings, the company had promoted Rill both as a cleanser and as a laundry wash water additive since 1937. Over the years, about 50 percent of the company's advertising had featured the product solely as a cleanser, 30 percent as a laundry additive and 20 percent as a dual-purpose product.

Rill was nationally distributed in a concentrated form in three can sizes —4 ounces, 8 ounces, and 1 pound. Six other nationally distributed cleansers and two nationally distributed laundry additives posed formidable competition.

The product had sold well during the earlier years, but during the past five years unit sales had declined considerably apparently because of com-

---

* This case was written by C. B. Johnston, Associate Dean and Professor of Marketing, University of Western Ontario. Used with permission.

petition, although dollar volume over this period had remained fairly constant.

Company and agency personnel were in basic disagreement as to whether the product should be promoted as a cleanser, a laundry additive or a dual-purpose product. In order to formulate marketing and advertising strategy for the coming year, the agency personnel believed it was necessary to supplement the quantitative information they had on unit sales, outlets, margins, and distribution with information of a more qualitative nature on consumer attitudes toward the product, usage patterns, and opinions on different product characteristics such as strength or concentration, odor, and package size.

In November 1975, Mr. Roberts and his staff had drawn up a research proposal which they had forwarded to six marketing research firms for detailed information regarding the following:

1. An appraisal of the proposal and suggestions for any changes.
2. A price quotation on the project (*a*) as outlined and (*b*) including any suggested changes
3. A brief description of the staff who would handle the project.
4. Time required for preparation, implementation, tabulation, and final presentation.
5. Pilot testing suggested.
6. Detailed explanation of suggested sample size.
7. Information on the firm's executive personnel, interviewing staff, and the projects handled over the preceding two years.

The research proposal contained a description of the product's marketing problems, the objectives of the proposed research, broad suggestions regarding research methodology, and a proposed questionnaire.

In his proposal, Mr. Roberts outlined the major marketing problems as follows:

1. We really want to know how many people would buy Rill because (*a*) it is a cleanser, (*b*) it is a laundry additive, or (*c*) it is a dual-purpose product.
2. How do people buy products like Rill? Is it better to have a strong product or a weaker one? What size package should we have? Should it smell like soap or like perfume? At what price should it be retailing?
3. Do people see Rill as being a good, average, or poor product? What do they like about it? What don't they like about it?
4. Do people want a one-use product or a multiuse product?

By early in January, Mr. Roberts had received the submissions of all six marketing research firms requested to bid on the job.

Three of these firms were eliminated after preliminary consideration of their submissions revealed either inadequate staffs, superficial recommendations, or excessively high costs.

In considering the three remaining firms, Mr. Roberts felt he was hampered by his lack of knowledge of the techniques proposed by two of the firms and his inability to decide whether it was reasonable to expect that a detailed plan could be drawn up from the information he had provided in his proposal.

Two of the firms under consideration, National Research Associates and The Progressive Research Group, had outlined quite comprehensive plans for the research. The third, H. J. Clifford Research, had merely stated that they would not attempt to formulate any research plans from what they considered inadequate information. They believed the only way a detailed plan could be formulated was "through a continuing cooperation, based on mutual confidence, between the research firm, the advertising agency and the client."

Mr. Roberts knew that many marketing research executives considered the third firm to be the outstanding marketing research company in the country and because of this, he did not believe they could be overlooked.

SUBMISSION OF NATIONAL RESEARCH ASSOCIATES

INTRODUCTION

The present research proposal is based upon the assumption that it is crucial to obtain answers to the following marketing problems:

1. Is it advisable to continue to promote Rill as a multipurpose product?
2. If it is, should its various uses be promoted simultaneously or separately and what are the promotional approaches which would be most effective?
3. If it is not advisable to continue its promotion as a multipurpose product, for what uses could Rill be most successfully promoted?
4. What would be the most effective promotional approaches for the uses decided upon?
5. Would it be advisable to launch another product, or possibly the same product under a different name, for either of its uses?
6. What are the ways in which Rill distribution, packaging, pricing, and merchandising could be improved?

RESEARCH OBJECTIVES

To be able to plan a sound and effective marketing policy for Rill it will be essential to know:

1. The present market position of Rill in relation to its competitors in each of the fields in which it is used.

2. The reasons why Rill is in its present position in each of these markets.

I. Consumer habits and practices

The study will provide as complete a description as possible of the cleanser and laundry additive markets. Data will be provided in regard to (1) users and nonusers, (2) brand usage, (3) purchasing habits, and (4) usage habits.

This information will be cross-analyzed by age, socioeconomic status, community size, and level of education of the respondent.

II. Consumer attitudes, opinions, and motivations

The study will thoroughly explore the underlying reasons for the market strengths and weaknesses of Rill in each of the usage categories as completely as possible under the broad headings of:

1. The underlying attractions or resistances to using any product for each of the purposes with which Rill is concerned.
2. The comparative strength of attractions to using Rill and to using competing brands for each of these purposes.
3. The comparative strength of resistances to using Rill relative to competing brands.

Some of the specific topics which will be investigated under these general headings are discussed below:

1. The perceived uses of Rill and its major competitors.
2. Factors affecting the perception of Rill; i.e., confusion regarding usage, incompatibility of uses, one use more efficient than the other, and where the attitudes toward the product originated.
3. Attributes of the most desirable product for each of the uses.
4. Common knowledge of the attributes of various brands now on the market.
5. Associations evoked by the brand name Rill and the brand names of competing products.

III. Consumer knowledge of and attitudes toward relevant advertising

1. How far the terms and phrases currently used in promoting Rill and competing brands are seen as (a) meaningful, and (b) appropriate to the product and its uses?
2. What copy points and adjectives might be most effective for the promotion of each use?

IV. An evaluation of the advertising themes and approaches used by Rill

The research will attempt to determine whether the themes and approaches used in past and present Rill advertising are likely to operate toward overcoming resistances to Rill and capitalizing on sources of attraction.

V. An assessment of the Rill packages

The Rill package will be tested to determine:

1. Its visual effectiveness as evidenced by its attention-getting ability, its legibility, its memorability, its apparent size.
2. Its psychological effect on the consumer's perception of the brand.

METHODOLOGY

Market survey. Face-to-face interviews will be conducted with 2,275 homemakers who will be asked to give factual information about the products they use for each purpose. This survey will show the competitive position of Rill, but will not attempt to provide "reasons why."

Intensive interview study. The "reasons why" Rill is in its present position will be explored in 600 one-and-one-half to two-hour depth interviews which will attempt to discover attitudes, perceptions, and feelings toward the product and its uses.

The depth interview is designed to prompt the revelation of true attitudes and reasons for them by employing projective techniques which, instead of emphasizing personal behavior, invite comment on the behavior of others.

In-depth interviewing takes place in a relaxed, informal atmosphere. Interviews are usually conducted in the respondent's home and her verbatim responses to questions are noted.

The interview schedule contains a large number of open-ended and close-ended queries.

In addition, it employs a variety of techniques, most of which are taken from or patterned after standard psychological tests. A description of some of these techniques is given below.

1. The Personification Test. This is essentially an extension of the projective technique employed in psychological testing. It involves an attempt on the part of the respondent to describe certain products in human terms. Such an approach provides an opportunity for the expression of attitudes and opinions not otherwise easily obtainable.

2. The Thematic Apperception Test (TAT). Like the Personification Test, this test is similar to the TAT in psychological projective testing. It consists of presenting to the respondent an unstructured drawing of a particular situation and asking him to "make up a story" of what is happening.

3. Word Association Tests. Respondents are asked to relate what comes to mind when a given word or phrase is read to them. This technique aids in throwing light on areas which may warrant fuller investigation.

4. The Semantic Differential Test. This method, developed by us, has been designed to provide insights and information in regard to the perception of company and product attributes.

Fundamentally, the test consists of having the respondent rate a series of products on specially designed scales. The scales are so designed as to provide an extremely sensitive measure in regard to many dimensions as applied to the various products.

The manner in which these data (along with the data obtained through the use of other techniques) are analyzed makes it possible to determine:

A. The extent to which a given product's image is correlated with the perceived "ideal" product.
B. The desirable direction of change in the perceived product attributes, if such change is found necessary.

Other techniques which may be employed include: (*a*) rank-ordering tests, (*b*) sentence completion tests, (*c*) forced choice tests, (*d*) paired comparison tests, and (*e*) true-false tests.

Laboratory study. Our visual laboratory is equipped to evaluate the relative effectiveness of various merchandising and advertising stimuli. By means of specially designed instruments it will be possible to evaluate the relative effectiveness of the Rill package and label in comparison with those of major competitors.

The various tests which will be conducted include:

1. Attention-getting tests.
2. Product recognition tests.
3. Brand identification tests.
4. Visibility and legibility tests.
5. Memorability tests.
6. Apparent size tests.
7. Color preference and association tests.

SAMPLE

Market survey. For the purposes of economy it is suggested that a quota-controlled, weighted, national sample of 2,275 housewives be employed. The accompanying table presents an unweighted sample in proportion to household figures and the proposed weighted sample.

The unweighted sample exceeds the number of interviews necessary to ensure reasonable reliability.

However, to allow for a cross analysis of white and black and urban

	Rural				Urban		Total	
	Farm		Nonfarm					
	Unweighted	Weighted	Unweighted	Weighted	Unweighted	Weighted	Unweighted	Weighted
Southeast.........	44	44	76	76	132	132	252	252
Northeast.........	101	101	110	110	614	614	825	825
Midwest..........	126	63	139	70	837	436	1,102	569
West.............	179	90	107	53	324	162	610	305
South Central.....	22	22	60	60	242	242	324	324
Total...........	472	320	492	369	2,149	1,586	3,113	2,275

and rural respondents, a total of 3,113 interviews would be required. The weighted sample cuts by 50 percent the number of interviews in the Midwest and the West. The data from these areas will be mathematically converted to representative proportions in the final tabulation.

Intensive study.   Quota-controlled samples of 450 white and 150 black homemakers will be used.

Laboratory study.   The number of respondents varies from test to test, but the samples will be designed to ensure statistical reliability.

FIELD STAFF

Market survey.   Our field staff of 455 interviewers located across the country will conduct the interviews and will be specially briefed and trained for this survey.

Intensive study.   Our staff of 88 university-trained depth interviewers will conduct an average of seven interviews each.

BRIEF DESCRIPTION OF FIRM

National Research Associates has conducted almost 400 separate and varied research projects since its establishment in 1954. The success of the organization is portrayed by its rapid growth from a small unknown company to a recognized leader in the field in the United States. Further attestation has been the establishment of "continuing relationships" with many clients. The company is an "official training ground" for graduate students in the Department of Social Psychology at a prominent university.

The following individuals will be involved in this project:

R. J. Morrison, Ph.D., research coordinator and major client and agency contact; academic training—B.Sc., M.Sc., and Ph.D., 1944 to 1959, major universities; research experience—wide experience in research as study director, consultant and research associate in four U.S. universities from 1944 to 1956; teaching experience— seven years of lecturing in psychology at two American universities.

A. Milton, study director; graduate in economics with ten years' experience in the research field including three years with a prominent United Kingdom research firm and a number of years with other English companies.

H. W. Rolland, associate study director; senior staff psychologist who will coordinate the intensive study phases of the research. M.Sc. working on Ph.D.

R. W. Brown, associate study director; university graduate in sociology and statistics—ten years' experience in research—will handle tabulation and statistical analysis.

(Four additional staff members were listed, all of whom were university graduates.)

TIME AND COST ESTIMATES

The research can be completed in 12 weeks after finalization of the research design. The cost is estimated at $52,000, 50 percent payable upon initiation of the study and 50 percent upon completion.

SUBMISSION OF THE PROGRESSIVE RESEARCH GROUP

NATURE OF THE PROBLEM

It is possible that the two major uses of Rill may, in combination, affect the market negatively. Women may think of it primarily in one sense or the other and those who regard it as a cleanser may not be willing to use it as a laundry additive, or vice versa.

In addition to this possible overall problem, there are certain marketing specifics which may also be important.

1. Is the product right?
2. What about its physical characteristics (strength or concentration, odor, physical form)?
3. What about its psychological connotations?
4. What about the packaging (size of package, nature of package, labeling, and package)?

We propose a consumer study covering the major areas of behavior and attitude including:

1. Brand personality and image for each of several cleansers (including Rill).
2. Brand personality and image for each of several laundry additive products (including Rill).
3. Habit pattern on home cleaning (including products used).
4. Habit pattern on laundry additives (including products used).

SCOPE OF THE STUDY

We see this as a national study as it is entirely possible that varying areas may display differing habits and attitudes.

The section of this proposal dealing with the sample will show the reasons underlying our recommendations. We suggest a total of 750 interviews in this consumer study and the sample will be of a "tight" nature.

THE SAMPLE

Type of sample.   The sample will be of such a nature that it properly represents the homemaker population in terms of region, socioeconomic group, urban-rural, and the like.

The sample design will be a known probability sample. Primary sampling units will be selected proportionately across the country, and randomly selected starting points will be chosen from which a predetermined path of interviewing will be followed.

Size of sample. We recommend a total sample of 750 housewives.

There are several reasons. The first concerns our belief that no subsample on which results are based should have fewer than 150 cases.

The other reason concerns overall accuracy with a sample of 750 cases. Better than nine times out of ten, results based on this total sample should be accurate within some 2.4 percent; this level of sampling accuracy on an overall basis seems highly acceptable for the purposes of this particular study.

Numerical distribution of interviews is indicated in the accompanying table.

	Natural proportional distribution of sample	Proposed sample distribution	Weighting factor	Weighted cases
Southeast....................	77	125	2	250
Northeast..................	211	211	3	633
Midwest....................	265	177	5	885
West.......................	130	130	3	390
South Central..............	67	107	2	214
	750	750		2,372

FIELDWORK

Our field staff is of highest quality. It has been built over a ten-year period, and we spend a sizable amount of money each year on maintenance and development of this staff.

The field staff totals 723 workers, and all states and community sizes are represented.

SUPERVISION

We maintain a staff of 20 salaried regional supervisors across the country. With the exception of a few small, remote areas, this means that every interviewer works under the direct control of a regional supervisor.

QUALIFICATIONS OF INTERVIEWERS

The average interviewer on our staff has been working for the firm for approximately four years. For our consumer work, we make use of women who, on the average, have the following characteristics: (1) they fall between the upper middle and lower middle socioeconomic group, (2) they have completed some or all of high school, (3) they are extroverted, and (4) they are above the average in intelligence.

THE QUESTIONNAIRE

It is difficult to evaluate your questionnaire without considerable field testing. In the present case, there has been no effort at all to do so. We would save our "criticism" for (a) detailed discussion with the agency, and (b) considerable field testing.

We have conducted a group interview with the subject matter pretty much in its present sequence, though the questions asked were more of an open-minded variety than contained in the questionnaire draft submitted with your specifications.

We do know that the sequence of questions will work. We also know that women can and will answer these questions, despite their nature, if the right approach is used. We further know that while the questionnaire form is quite lengthy, it is still feasible in terms of its length. So it is not as if we know nothing about feasibility of the instrument.

FIELD TESTING

As a result of the group interview, it will be possible—though we have not taken the time to utilize it in such a manner—to study the consumer response to the interview so carefully as to make sure that the phrasings used in the questionnaire follow the words and phrases used in the consumer's actual thinking. The group interview thus means that we are that much further ahead in the phrasings of this questionnaire, even though it so far has not been utilized for such a purpose.

We plan a field test—or perhaps several—with a total of 100 home-makers distributed among people of varying socioeconomic groups, largely concentrated (for efficiency of handling) in the Chicago Metropolitan Area to make sure that the sequence and phrasing are of such a nature as to be understandable, to get cooperation, and to obtain unbiased replies.

DESCRIPTION OF THE FIRM

The Progressive Research Group began operations in 1948 and, as such, is one of the oldest marketing research companies. Over the years the company has handled a large number of projects and has among its clients many of the largest consumer goods manufacturers.

The company possesses the most advanced computer equipment in the country and constant improvements are being adopted to speed up and make more economical, complete, and detailed client reports.

The following persons will direct the project:

A. W. Willis, B.A., overall project coordinator; president of The Progressive Research Group and a graduate in economics from a large university.

B. K. *Walker,* M.B.A., project director and client contact; vice-president and a graduate in business administration from a major university.

R. C. *Moffatt,* Ph.D., project adviser; major in sociology—five years' research experience as project director with large U.S. advertising agency before joining The Progressive Research Group in 1957. Three years spent as lecturer and consultant at two large American universities.

TIME AND COST

Our report should be available 12 weeks after the finalizing of the project details. Our estimate of the cost of this project is $23,900 plus or minus 10 percent. It is our practice to bill one half of the estimated cost at the time of authorization with the final half billed on delivery of the report.

In discussing these proposals with his assistant, Mr. Jacks, Mr. Roberts wondered whether his own staff could not answer some of the questions if a thorough study of past Consumer Panel reports were conducted. For some ten years Bay Madison had received full reports from an independent research company which ran a consumer panel, but these had only been used for day-to-day planning. Never, for instance, had a long-term, thorough study of the trends in Rill sales been compared with the various advertising and promotional campaigns the company had used or to the various price levels that had existed from time to time. Mr. Jacks was particularly enthusiastic about the idea as he had long maintained that the agency was not getting full value from the panel data. He said that he would personally like to work on such a project.

Mr. Roberts, in considering the idea further, estimated that such an analysis could be done for approximately $9,000. He had checked with the research company and found that all past reports were kept on automatic data processing cards. The company was most interested in the idea as an experiment and estimated that all the data required by the agency could be compiled for about $2,500. Mr. Roberts thought he could release Mr. Jacks from his other duties for a period of two months and that the cost of Mr. Jacks' salary, statistical and secretarial help, and other expenses would not exceed $5,500.

It was at this point that Mr. Roberts found himself in January 1976. He knew a decision had to be made quickly as the client was very anxious to get the Rill situation straightened away.

CASE

8

The Atlanta Journal and Constitution (A)

Mr. Ferguson Rood, research and marketing director for *The Atlanta Journal* and the *Atlanta Constitution,* was still perspiring from the three-block walk in the hot August sun back to his office from the meeting he had just been to at Rich's Department Store. At the meeting, he had been told that Rich's, the newspaper's largest advertiser, wanted to test the effectiveness of TV and radio advertising versus newspaper advertising for their upcoming Harvest Sale. He had promised to make his suggestions for the research plan in 48 hours, and felt he had much work to do in that short time. He wondered what recommendations he should make for the study, and was concerned that the research design and questionnaire be developed so that the study would represent fairly the effectiveness of *The Atlanta Journal* and the *Atlanta Constitution.* As he began to review his notes from the meeting, he picked up the phone to call his wife and tell her he would be home very late that evening.

BACKGROUND

The Atlanta Journal and the *Atlanta Constitution* are a union of two of the largest circulation newspapers in the South. The *Atlanta Constitution,* winner of four Pulitzer Prizes for its efforts in the area of social reform, was founded June 16, 1868. *The Atlanta Journal,* founded February 24, 1883, became the largest daily newspaper in Georgia by 1889. Also a winner of the Pulitzer Prize, *The Journal* is the Southeast's largest afternoon newspaper.

In 1950, *The Atlanta Journal* and the *Atlanta Constitution* were combined into Atlanta Newspapers, Inc., a privately held company. The two newspapers maintained independent editorial staffs, and there was very little overlap of readers. Exhibits 1 through 4 present data concerning the

EXHIBIT 1
Gross readership impressions, reach, and frequency of *The Atlanta Journal* and *Constitution*

Gross reader impressions

delivered by *The Atlanta Journal* and *Constitution* in 15-County Metro Atlanta:

> During any five weekdays, 864,500 adults read *The Atlanta Journal* or *Constitution* an average of 3.5 times for a total of 3,025,800 week- day gross reader impressions.

> During any four Sundays, 907,600 adults read *The Atlanta Journal* and *Constitution* for an average of 3.4 times for a total of 3,085,800 Sun- day gross reader impressions.

> These newspapers deliver 3,933,400 adult gross reader impressions when one Sunday is added to five weekdays.

Reach and frequency of newspaper reading

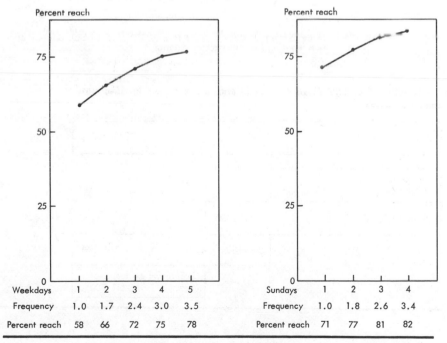

Weekdays	1	2	3	4	5
Frequency	1.0	1.7	2.4	3.0	3.5
Percent reach	58	66	72	75	78

Sundays	1	2	3	4
Frequency	1.0	1.8	2.6	3.4
Percent reach	71	77	81	82

EXHIBIT 2
The Atlanta Journal and *Constitution* readership information

---

644,400 adult readers

Of all metro
Atlanta adults,
644,400 read *The
Atlanta Journal* or
Constitution on
the average week-
day. Of this total,
412,700 read *The
Journal* and
366,100 read the
Constitution.
134,400 adults
read both. On the
average Sunday
782,200 metro
Atlanta adults read
*The Atlanta
Journal* and *Con-
stitution.*

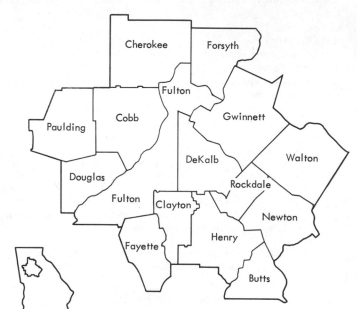

15–county metro Atlanta

78 percent of all daily circulation and 66 percent of all Sunday circulation is within 15-county metro Atlanta.

**Adult readers of *The Atlanta Journal* and *Constitution* in 15-county
metro Atlanta**

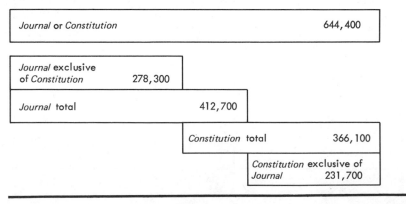

Journal or *Constitution*	644,400

Journal exclusive of *Constitution*	278,300
Journal total	412,700
Constitution total	366,100
Constitution exclusive of *Journal*	231,700

EXHIBIT 3

Readership of *The Atlanta Journal* and *Constitution* over five weekdays

644,400 or 58 percent of all metro Atlanta adults read *The Atlanta Journal* or *Constitution* on the average weekday. Over five weekdays these newspapers deliver 864,900 or 78 percent of all metro-area adults with an average frequency of 3.5 days.

	Total metro area adults	Average 1-day readership		Cumulative 5-weekday readership		Frequency
		Number	Percent	Number	Percent	
Total adults..............	1 105,500	644,400	58	864,900	78	3.5
Sex						
Female..............	588,500	331,700	56	447,600	76	3.5
Male..............	517,000	312,700	61	416,800	81	3.5
Household income						
$25,000 and over..............	104,200	85,900	82	102,700	99	4.2
$15,000–24,999..............	195,300	146,400	75	181,900	93	4.0
$10,000–14,999..............	241,920	152,800	63	203,900	84	3.7
$5,000–9,999..............	334,200	170,600	51	241,800	72	3.5
Under $5,000..............	229,900	88,500	39	133,000	58	3.3
Age						
18–34..............	470,500	234,500	50	345,200	73	3.4
35–49..............	305,600	197,200	65	250,300	82	3.9
50–64..............	211,900	145,800	59	184,600	87	3.9
65 and over..............	116,500	66,700	57	84,700	73	3.9
Race						
White..............	872,800	528,800	61	685,100	78	3.9
Nonwhite..............	232,700	115,600	50	180,100	77	3.2
Education						
College graduate..............	173,500	138,000	80	172,600	99	4.0
Part college..............	194,700	137,600	71	174,100	89	4.0
High school graduate..............	360,500	225,000	62	302,900	84	3.7
Part high school or less..............	365,600	137,000	38	202,200	55	3.4

EXHIBIT 4
Readership of *The Atlanta Journal* and *Constitution* over four Sundays

782,200 or 71 percent of all metro Atlanta adults read *The Atlanta Journal* and *Constitution* on the average Sunday. Over four Sundays these newspapers deliver 907,300 or 82 percent of all metro-area adults with an average frequency of 3.4 Sundays.

	Total metro area adults	Average 1-Sunday readership	Cumulative 4-Sunday readership	Number of Sundays frequency
Total adults.....................	1,105,500	782,200	907,300	3.4
Sex				
Female......................	588,500	418,800	477,800	3.5
Male.......................	517,000	363,400	429,500	3.4
Household income				
$25,000 and over..............	104,200	89,100	97,200	3.7
$15,000–24,999.................	195,300	168,800	180,700	3.7
$10,000–14,999.................	241,900	190,100	216,400	3.5
$5,000–9,999...................	334,400	215,600	267,300	3.2
Under $5,000..................	229,900	118,500	145,600	3.3
Age				
18–34.........................	470,500	313,000	390,000	3.2
35–49.........................	305,600	221,300	248,500	3.6
50–64.........................	211,900	167,000	179,900	3.7
65 and over..................	116,500	80,600	88,500	3.6
Race				
White........................	872,800	633,100	727,900	3.5
Nonwhite....................	232,700	149,100	179,100	3.3
Education				
College graduate..............	173,500	150,200	163,700	3.7
Part college..................	194,700	157,300	180,200	3.5
High school graduate.........	360,500	273,900	313,500	3.5
Part high school or less.......	365,600	192,300	240,000	3.2

adult readership of the newspapers, the gross reader impressions, reach and frequency, and readership over five weekdays and four Sundays.

To provide the advertisers and potential advertisers with information necessary to help them make their advertising media decisions, the newspaper does a considerable amount of research, often approaching $25,000 in a year. Most of the research is designed to be used in selling advertising to a wide range of advertisers, and includes data on retail trading areas, shopping patterns, product usage, and newspaper coverage patterns. In addition to Mr. Rood, the research department had two other trained market researchers and one secretary.

Although there are nine daily newspapers in the Atlanta trading area, all but *The Journal* and the *Constitution* have very small circulations. The principal competition for large advertisers is with radio and TV stations. Exhibit 5 presents information on the circulation of the print media in the Atlanta area. Exhibit 6 contains information on the broadcast media in

EXHIBIT 5
Circulation of print media in Atlanta

Metro Atlanta newspapers	Edition	Total circulation
Dailies		
Atlanta Constitution.....................	Morning	216,624
Atlanta Journal..........................	Evening	259,721
Journal-Constitution....................	Sunday	585,532
Gwinnett Daily News....................	Evening (except Sat.)	10,111
Gwinnett Daily News....................	Sunday	10,100
Marietta Daily Journal..................	Evening (except Sat.)	24,750
Marietta Daily Journal..................	Sunday	25,456
Fulton County Daily Report..............	Evening (Mon.–Fri.)	1,600
Atlanta Daily World.....................	Morning	19,000
Atlanta Daily World.....................	Sunday	22,000
Wall Street Journal.....................	Morning (Mon.–Fri.)	16,180
Jonesboro News Daily....................	Evening (Mon.–Fri.)	9,100
North Fulton Today.....................	Evening (Mon.–Fri.)	2,300
South Cobb Today......................	Evening (Mon.–Fri.)	2,400
New York Times........................	Morning (Mon.–Sat.)	500
New York Times........................	Sunday	3,100
Weekly newspapers		
Atlanta Inquirer...		30,000
Atlanta Voice...		37,500
DeKalb New Era...		16,400
Atlanta's Suburban Reporter..		3,900
Lithonia Observer...		2,765
Northside News...		8,000
Georgia Business News...		4,900
Southern Israelite..		4,300
Decatur-DeKalb News..		73,000
Southside Sun (East Point)...		37,700
Tucker Star..		10,000
Alpharetta, Roswell Neighbor...		6,800
Austell, Mableton, Powder Springs Neighbor.............................		12,123
Acworth, Kennesaw-Woodstock Neighbor.................................		3,242
Northside, Sandy Springs, Vinings Neighbor.............................		20,836
Smyrna Neighbor...		6,872
College Park, East Point, Hapeville, South Side, West End Neighbor..		18,813
Chamblee, Doraville, Dunwoody, North Atlanta Neighbor..................		14,963
Clarkston, Stone Mountain, Tucker Neighbor.............................		15,074
The Journal of Labor (Atlanta)...		17,500
Austell Enterprise..		1,911
The Cherokee Tribune (Canton)...		7,100
Rockdale Citizen..		6,031
The Covington News...		6,000
The Forsyth County News...		4,800
Dallas New Era...		4,075
Douglas County Sentinel...		7,350
South Fulton Recorder (Fairburn).......................................		4,000
Fayette County News...		4,500
Jackson Progress Argus..		2,635
The Weekly Advertiser (McDonough).....................................		5,650
The Walton Tribune (Monroe)...		5,102
Lilburn Recorder..		5,000

EXHIBIT 5 (*continued*)

Metro Atlanta newspapers	Total circula-tion
Lawrenceville Home Weekly...	2,000
Weekly newspapers	
The Great Speckled Bird (Atlanta).......................................	7,925
The Georgia Bulletin.......................................	14,000
The Covington News (Tues. & Thurs.).......................	6,200
Creative Loafing in Atlanta...............................	30,000
Atlanta area newspapers*	
Cobb...	28,000
North Fulton...	36,000
North DeKalb-Gwinnett.......................................	45,000
South DeKalb...	44,000
South Fulton-Clayton.......................................	53,000
Major magazines in Georgia	
American Home...	70,485
Better Homes and Gardens...................................	145,962
Good Housekeeping.......................................	114,045
McCall's...	139,728
Ladies' Home Journal.......................................	128,331
Family Circle...	106,245
Woman's Day...	100,566
Redbook...	86,354
National Geographic.......................................	103,941
Reader's Digest...	331,240
Newsweek...	41,070
Time...	60,438
U.S. News & World Report.......................................	40,417
TV Guide...	345,871
Playboy...	98,389
Sports Illustrated.......................................	38,263
Outdoor Life...	25,918
True......................:.......................................	18,244
Southern Living.......................................	95,000
Progressive Farmer.......................................	70,000
Cosmopolitan...	25,075
Calendar Atlanta.......................................	50,000

* These are supplements to *The Atlanta Journal*, and circulation is to *The Atlanta Journal* subscribers only.
Source: WSB Research Department.

Atlanta. Although there were 40 radio stations, 28 AM and 12 FM, and 6 TV stations, WSB Radio and TV dominated the market. WSB Radio, for example, was consistently rated among the top six stations in the nation, and had a greater Atlanta audience than the next four stations combined. WSB-TV and WSB Radio, both affiliated with the NBC Network, were owned by Cox Broadcasting Corporation, which also owns television stations in Charlotte, Dayton, Pittsburgh, and San Francisco and radio stations in Charlotte, Dayton, and Miami. Cox Broadcasting and WSB-TV and Radio stations shared corporate headquarters in Atlanta.

WSB Radio was founded in 1922 by *The Atlanta Journal* newspaper.

In 1939, former Democratic presidential nominee and Governor of Ohio James M. Cox acquired the newspaper-radio combine. In 1948, WSB-TV was founded, and two years later the newspapers and broadcast media were separated when Atlanta Newspapers, Inc., was established. Today, there is no relationship between the newspapers and WSB Radio and TV.

Rich's Department Store was the largest advertiser for *The Journal* and the *Constitution,* accounting for almost 5 percent of their advertising revenue, and was WSB's largest local advertiser. Founded in 1867, Rich's by 1970 had grown to a company with seven stores distributed throughout Atlanta as shown in Exhibit 7. Sales were approximately $200 million per year with earnings after taxes of almost 5 percent of sales. The company was classified as a general merchandise retailer, and carried a very wide line of products including clothing, furniture, appliances, housewares, and items for the home. Rich's dominated the Atlanta market, with close to 40 percent of department store sales and approximately 25 percent of all the sales of general merchandise. The merchandising highlight of the year was the annual Harvest Sale, first held in October 1925. The sale typically ran for two weeks, and had become a yearly tradition at Rich's.

BACKGROUND ON THE MEDIA EFFECTIVENESS STUDY

Before preparing his proposal to Rich's for the media effectiveness study, Mr. Rood reflected upon the events of the past 24 hours. The day before, he had received a phone call from the vice president and sales promotion director from Rich's, inviting him to the meeting at Rich's the next day. Having been told that Rich's research director and the research director of WSB-TV and Radio would also be there, Mr. Rood had been a little apprehensive before going. At the start of the meeting he was asked if the Atlanta newspapers would be interested in participating in a cooperative research study aimed at measuring the effectiveness of various advertising media during Rich's September Harvest Sale, their largest annual sales event. It became immediately apparent that the research director from WSB, Jim Landon, had met with the Rich's people the week before, and was undoubtedly the source of the idea to conduct the study. A document was then passed out that had been prepared by WSB and was entitled "Suggestions for Rich's Media Research." This document is included in the Appendix, and outlines the objectives of the study, a suggested methodology, together with a questionnaire.

The suggested objectives for the project were: (1) to measure the ability of TV, radio, and newspapers to sell specific items of merchandise in Rich's seven Atlanta stores; (2) to determine how each advertising medium complements the others in terms of additional units sold to various segments of the customer population (age, sex, charge account ownership,

EXHIBIT 6

Broadcast media in Atlanta

Location	Station/network	Established	Frequency	Power	Channel	Network
Metro Atlanta AM radio stations						
Atlanta..........	WSB (NBC)	1922	750 khz	50 kw		
	WAOK	1954	1380 khz	5 kw		
	WGKA (ABC)	1955	1190 khz	1 kw day		
	WGST (ABC-E)	1922	920 khz	5 kw day / 1 kw night		
	WIGO (ABC-C)	1946	1340 khz	1 kw day / 250 w night		
	WIIN (MBS)	1949	970 khz	5 kw day		
	WPLO	1937	590 khz	5 kw		
	WQXI	1948	790 khz	5 kw day / 1 kw night		
Decatur..........	WXAP	1948	860 khz	1 kw		
	WYZE (MBS)	1956	1480 khz	5 kw day		
	WAVO	1958	1420 khz	1 kw day		
	WGUN	1947	1010 khz	50 kw day		
	WQAK	1964	1310 khz	500 w		
N. Atlanta.......	WRNG (CBS)	1967	680 khz	25 kw day		
Morrow..........	WSSA	1959	1570 khz	1 kw day		
East Point.......	WTJH	1949	1260 khz	5 kw day		
Smyrna..........	WYNX	1962	1550 khz	10 kw day		
Buford..........	WDYX	1956	1460 khz	5 kw day		
Austell..........	WACX	1968	1600 khz	1 kw		
Lawrenceville.....	WLAW	1959	1360 khz	1 kw		
Marietta.........	WCOB	1955	1080 khz	10 kw day		
	WFOM	1946	1230 khz	1 kw day / 250 w night		
Canton..........	WCHK (GA)	1957	1290 khz	1 kw day		
Covington........	WGFS	1953	1430 khz	1 kw day		
Cumming.........	WSNE	1961	1170 khz	1 kw		

Douglasville................	WDGL	1964	1527 khz	1 kw	
Jackson....................	WJGA	1967	1540 khz	1 kw day	
Monroe....................	WMRE	1954	1490 khz	1 kw	

Metro Atlanta FM radio stations

WSB-FM	1934	98.5 mhz	100 kw
WPLO-FM	1948	103.3 mhz	50 kw
WZGC-FM	1955	92.9 mhz	100 kw
WKLS-FM	1960	96.1 mhz	100 kw
WQXI-FM	1962	94.1 mhz	100 kw
WBIE-FM	1959	101.5 mhz	100 kw
WLTA-FM	1963	99.7 mhz	100 kw
WJGA-FM	1968	92.1 mhz	3 kw
WCHK-FM	1964	105.5 mhz	3 kw
WGCO-FM	1969	102.3 mhz	100 kw
WABE-FM	1948	90.0 mhz	10.5 kw
WREK-FM	1968	91.1 mhz	40 kw

Metro Atlanta television stations

WSB-TV	9/29/48	2	NBC
WAGA-TV	3/8/49	5	CBS
WXIA-TV	9/30/51	11	ABC
WTCG-TV	9/1/67	17	IND
WETV	1958	30	NET
WGTV	1960	8	NET

Source: WSB Research Department.

and so on); (3) to determine what each advertising medium contributed in regard to additional store traffic. Mr. Rood's broadcasting counterpart stated at the meeting that "If Rich's is interested in conducting research to measure the effectiveness of various advertising media, WSB-TV and WSB Radio will be happy to assist." Rood had no choice, so he volunteered the support of the newspapers to the study.

The Rich's research manager then asked if the media would participate financially in the study. Mr. Rood suggested that each of the three media

EXHIBIT 7
Map of Atlanta and seven Rich's stores

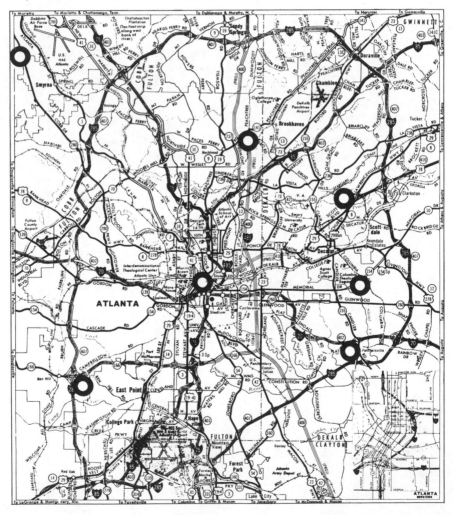

participate equally, and committed the newspapers to $500 for a study that he figured should cost between $2,500 and $3,000 for interviewing. Mr. Landon indicated that Cox Broadcasting would be willing to put in $500 each for TV and radio.

They then discussed how the research could be conducted. The WSB proposal suggested in-store surveys, with a separate survey conducted for each item of merchandise tested. The survey would be conducted by Rich's employees working overtime in appropriate store locations during the peak shopping hours. The tabulation of the results could be handled by the broadcast station's computer. Care was to be taken to ensure that the TV, radio, or newspaper advertising for the individual items not be "stacked" in favor of one particular medium. The questions in the proposed questionnaire (see the Appendix) included questions on how the respondents happened to buy the merchandise at Rich's, if they recalled seeing TV, newspaper or radio advertising, and if they bought anything else. Questions were also asked concerning age and ownership of a Rich's charge account.

Mr. Landon stated that WSB was not trying to take business away from the newspapers, and that Rood had nothing to fear. His recommendation was that Rich's not take anything away from the newspaper advertising budget. He suggested that the amount of space purchased in the newspapers be the same as the previous year, with additional monies being committed to the broadcast media. The Rich's sales promotion director then discussed some of his thoughts concerning the study. He indicated that Rich's had been sending 400,000 direct mail pieces to announce the Harvest Sale; this year they would send 200,000, diverting the other money to broadcast. This would make $7,600 available for broadcast, and another $12,000 to $15,000 would be made available to purchase broadcast time.

The Harvest Sale was to open with courtesy days on Monday and Tuesday, September 21–22, with the sale beginning the evening of the 22nd and running for 13 days. While decisions concerning which sales items were to be included in the study and the media schedules to be used were not yet available, some progress had been made. Approximately ten items were to be researched, and the newspaper ads on Sunday, September 20, would include all or most of the ten items. Newspaper ads for the items would be repeated Monday and Tuesday with emphasis on *The Journal*. The interviews were to be conducted Monday through Wednesday.

On Sunday and Monday, with a possible spillover to Tuesday due to availability, Rich's would run 120, 30-second TV commercials on all commercial stations except Channel 17. During the same time they would run 120 radio 30-second commercials on a list of stations which had not yet been determined. With both TV and radio, WSB was to get the lion's share if availability could be arranged. Mr. Rood felt certain in view of the client and the research that WSB would manage to come up with several prime-time commercial openings even if it meant bumping some high paying national advertisers.

Eleven items were mentioned as possible subjects for the research. The ten final items selected would come mostly from this list, although one or two other items might be chosen. The items mentioned included (1) color TV console at $499; (2) custom-made draperies; (3) Sterns & Foster mattress at $44; (4) carpeting at $6.99 per square yard; (5) Gant shirts at $5; (6) Van Heusen shirts and Arrow shirts at two for $11; (7) women's handbags at $9.99; (8) Johannsen's shoes; (9) pants suits; (10) Hoover upright vacuum cleaner; and (11) GE refrigerator.

Mr. Rood, who had not said very much at the meeting, then asked for 48 hours to review the proposal. Everyone agreed to this, and Mr. Rood promised to present a counterproposal at that time.

Even though it had been rather obvious who initiated the idea for the study and that he at first felt that newspapers were being "set up" by WSB, it had been basically a friendly and relaxed meeting among friends. Mr. Landon and Mr. Rood had worked together in the Atlanta Chapter of the American Marketing Association and had a great deal of mutual respect. Mr. Rood thought Landon was a tough competitor, and understood that he had been successful using awareness type studies in Cox Broadcastings' other markets to gain additional advertising for broadcast.

When he returned to his office, Rood pulled out some of his files on Rich's. He noticed that the amount of advertising had been fairly constant, approximately 40 pages over the two-week period, during the past three Harvest Sales, and that basically the same products had been promoted. A typical Harvest Sale ad is included in Exhibit 8. He also pulled from the files rate schedules for *The Atlanta Journal* and *Constitution* and WSB (see Exhibits 9 and 10), even though he realized that the exact media schedule would be developed by Rich's advertising agency. Approximately $100,000 would be spent promoting the Harvest Sale, with perhaps a third of this amount being devoted to the sale items.

Mr. Rood decided that he would have to assume confidence in the effectiveness of the newspapers. He felt if the study were done right he would get his share of media exposure and influence. The other decision he quickly made was that in preparing his comments on the proposed research, he would take Rich's point of view rather than that of *The Atlanta Journal* and *Constitution*. He then began to review the events of the day and the WSB proposal in light of what he felt Rich's needed to know. He also knew that whatever he proposed would have to be acceptable to Mr. Landon. Noting the lateness in the day, he began work on the counterproposal.

EXHIBIT 8
Typical Rich's Harvest ad

EXHIBIT 9
The Atlanta Journal and the *Atlanta Constitution* retail display rates

Open rate per column inch:
    Constitution.. $8.15
    Journal... $11.27
    Combination... $14.83
    Sunday.. $15.56

Note: There are 8 columns by 21 inches or 168 column inches on a full page.

Yearly bulk space rates:

Inches per year per inch	Constitution	Journal	Combined	Sunday
100..........	$6.21	$8.43	$11.09	$11.65
250..........	6.16	8.35	11.00	11.55
500..........	6.10	8.28	10.90	11.45
1,000..........	6.05	8.21	10.81	11.35
2,500..........	5.99	8.13	10.70	11.24
5,000..........	5.93	8.05	10.59	11.12
7,500..........	5.90	8.01	10.54	11.07
10,000..........	5.87	7.97	10.48	11.01
12,500..........	5.85	7.93	10.43	10.96
15,000..........	5.82	7.89	10.38	10.90
25,000..........	5.70	7.73	10.17	10.68
50,000..........	5.61	7.69	10.05	10.61
75,000..........	5.51	7.65	9.93	10.53
100;000..........	5.41	7.61	9.81	10.46
150,000..........	5.21	7.51	9.56	10.31
200,000..........	5.01	7.41	9.32	10.15
250,000..........	4.81	7.31	9.08	9.99

EXHIBIT 10
WSB radio and TV advertising rates

	One minute	20/30 seconds	10 seconds
WSB-AM radio: Spot announcements— package plans*			
12 per week............................	$40.00	$34.00	$24.00
18 per week.:..........................	38.00	30.00	21.00
24 per week............................	32.00	26.00	19.00
30 per week............................	28.00	24.00	17.00
48 per week............................	26.00	20.00	15.00

WSB-FM radio: Package plan—52 weeks†

1 minute..........................	$16.00
20/30 seconds....................	14.00

WSB-TV
  Daytime rates
    60 seconds............... $ 75–235   depending on program
    30 seconds...............   40–140   depending on program
  Prime-time rates
    60 seconds‡.............. $540–660   depending on program
    30 seconds............... 390–725   depending on program

---

* Available 5:00–6:00 a.m., 10:00 a.m.–3:30 p.m., and 7:30 p.m.–midnight, Monday–Saturday; and 5:00 a.m.–midnight, Sunday. Best available positions in applicable times—no guaranteed placement.
† Quantity discounts available. For example, 18 times per week for 52 weeks is one half the above rates.
‡ Very few available.

APPENDIX

SUGGESTIONS FOR RICH'S MEDIA RESEARCH

OBJECTIVES

If Rich's is interested in conducting research to measure the effectiveness of various advertising media, WSB-TV and WSB–Radio will be happy to assist. As a basis for discussion, here are suggested objectives for this project:

1. Measure the ability of TV, radio, and newspapers to sell specific items of merchandise in Rich's seven Atlanta metro stores.
2. Determine how each advertising medium complements the others in terms of additional units sold to various segments of the customer population (age, sex, charge account ownership, etc.).
3. Determine what each advertising medium contributes in regard to additional store traffic.

HOW THE RESEARCH COULD BE CONDUCTED

The project could consist of a series of in-store surveys. A separate survey would be conducted for each item of merchandise tested. The more items tested, the more reliable the results of the overall research project.

If possible, all seven Rich's stores in the Atlanta metro area should participate in the research.

Each survey could be conducted by placing interviewers (Rich's personnel working overtime) in appropriate store locations during "peak" shopping hours with instructions to complete *brief* questionnaires with customers purchasing the item being tested. (See accompanying questionnaire.)

The interview could cover how the customer got the idea to buy the item, other planned purchases in the store during the same visit, charge account ownership, and any other pertinent data. Each interview would last less than a minute and would not bother the customers.

The sample size would vary, depending upon the number of stores participating, the type of merchandise and the sales volume. Interviewers would strive to include all customers purchasing the items during peak hours. Tabulation of the results could be handled by the WSB computer.

CAREFUL ATTENTION TO ITEMS AND MEDIA SCHEDULES

In order to make the research valid and meaningful, the items to be tested must be selected carefully. In addition, care should be taken to ensure that the TV, radio, or newspaper advertising for these items is not "stacked" in favor of one particular medium. Close attention to the items being tested and the media schedule for each is necessary.

QUESTIONNAIRE

The proposed questionnaire follows:

(All customers purchasing the item advertised are interviewed.)

1. *How* did you happen to buy this merchandise at Rich's?

Saw on TV	( )
Heard on radio	( )
Saw in newspaper	( )
TV and radio	( )
TV and newspaper	( )

TV, radio, and newspaper   ( )
Saw on display   ( )
Other: _____ ( )

ASKED OF CUSTOMERS NOT MENTIONING A MEDIUM: (2, 3, 4)

2. Do you recall seeing this merchandise advertised on the TV?
   Yes   ( )
   No   ( )

3. Do you recall seeing this merchandise advertised in the news-
   paper?
   Yes   ( )
   No   ( )

4. Do you recall hearing this merchandise advertised on the radio?
   Yes   ( )
   No   ( )

5. Are you buying *anything* else at Rich's today?
   Yes   ( )
   No   ( )
   Maybe   ( )
   Don't know   ( )

6. Do you have a charge account at *Rich's?*
   Yes   ( )
   No   ( )

7. In which group does your age fall?
   Under 25   ( )
   25–34   ( )
   35–49   ( )
   50 and over ( )

Store _____

Time of Interview _____

9

White Electric, Inc.*

Mr. Jack Heinen, vice president of WEI's international division, walked into Charlie Gessel's office on a late Friday afternoon in November 1971. He was returning from a staff meeting called by Mr. Robert Griffith, White's executive vice president for operations, regarding the launching of WEI's new microwave oven. The company was gearing up to meet supply commitments for its pre-Christmas introduction of the product. In this connection, Mr. Heinen had been asked to attend the meeting to represent any interest White International might have in the matter.

After sitting down and lighting an excellent Havana that he had picked up on his last trip back from London, Mr. Heinen told Charlie that International had been asked to prepare a quick but reliable estimate on the microwave oven's potential in overseas markets. The urgency of the matter was such that a preliminary report had to be ready for next Wednesday's staff meeting at which production and marketing budgets for 1972 were going to be revised. Jack Heinen left the room leaving behind a thin trail of blue smoke. Charlie reached for the phone, called his wife, and asked her to cancel any engagements for the following week. It looked like a dandy!

COMPANY BACKGROUND

White Electric, Inc., was a medium-sized manufacturer of household appliances, aerospace components, power systems, and other related elec-

---

* This case was written by Jose de la Torre, Associate Professor of Business Administration, INSEAD. Used with permission.

tric machinery. The company had had 1970 sales of $350 million of which $105 million were overseas (excluding Canada). Total profits were $21.5 million.

The domestic appliance market accounted for almost 40 percent of WEI's U.S. sales, or $95 million. This figure represented less than 2 percent of the total home appliance market in the United States, which had exceeded, at retail prices, the $14 billion mark in 1970. Each of the industry giants—Sunbeam, General Electric, General Motors, Singer, Westinghouse, American Motors, Arvin Industries, Ford, and others—had annual sales of household appliances in excess of $200 million to $500 million in the U.S. market. In addition to these, there were approximately 80 manufacturers in the industry which were considered medium to large in size.

White Electric had three other divisions which did various amounts of business. The Aerospace Products Division did mostly subcontract work in government-related business and had declined in pace with the recent general slowdown in that sector. Sales of aerospace products dropped to less than $40 million in 1970. Of this amount slightly more than 5 percent were export sales. All foreign sales were handled by the division's staff in accordance with foreign supply provisions written into their various contractual obligations with defense and commercial establishments abroad. The high degree of technical sophistication involved as well as strict national security restrictions precluded any other division from handling these sales.

The Machinery Division had been acquired in the late 1930s and incorporated into White's growing business during that period. A strong competitor both nationally and internationally, the division had reached a plateau in sales since the mid-1960s. Increased competition at home and abroad were principally responsible for this state of affairs. Sales in 1970 were approximately $60 million in the United States. In addition, White International handled the Machinery Division's export sales on a commission basis through their foreign affiliates and distributors. These exports amounted to over $10 million in 1970.

The fourth division, Power Systems, manufactured generators, motors, and similar equipment for a wide array of customers. However, 80 percent of the division's business was done with large utilities throughout the United States and abroad. Total 1970 sales were $57 million of which nearly $5 million were export sales generated and handled by the division's own staff.

The international division, White International, in addition to acting as an export agent for the Machinery Division, controlled manufacturing, assembly, and sales operations of household appliances throughout the world. It had consolidated sales (exclusive of machinery) in excess of $88 million and profits of $4.5 million in 1970.

WEI had been founded in the early 1920s by Bill White, an aggressive ex-GI who loved to tinker with electricity. He began by manufacturing electric fans and toasters, and was soon into vacuum cleaners, refrigerators, and electric ranges. In 1938, Mr. White acquired the nearly bankrupt Coleman Electric Works and transformed it into the electric machinery division of White Electric, Inc. His brother-in-law, Mr. Robert Wassle, took charge of the new division. Fueled by wartime orders both the division and the company grew dramatically through 1945.

The company took good advantage of the postwar surge in consumer demand adding new lines to its household division. Among these, washing machines and home freezers were particularly successful. During the same period the company diversified further into the aerospace and power fields. This diversification stemmed from the experience gained as a war contractor.

Following Mr. White's death in 1953 and a brief period of reorganization, Mr. Wassle assumed the chairmanship of the board. A public offering in 1955 greatly diluted the controlling interests of the White and Wassle families, but provided much needed capital for expansion.

Mr. Wassle's young and dynamic son, Bill, had played a key role in the firm's development throughout this period. As vice president of the Household Products Division he had moved the firm into the fields of convenience household items, such as air conditioners and dishwashers, items that soon experienced rising demand as income levels grew in the 1960s. Simultaneously, he had launched WEI into the international arena. The first foreign investment was made in 1955 in Canada. This was soon followed by moves into the United Kingdom, Mexico, Germany and Italy. By 1961, a new international division, White International, was formed to coordinate all foreign operations.[1] Mr. Robert Griffith, a marketing professor at a leading U.S. business school, was hired for the job.

In 1966, Mr. Bill Wassle assumed the presidency of WEI and Mr. Griffith became executive vice president for operations. Jack Heinen, former manager of White International's United Kingdom subsidiary and later European regional director, was named to head the international division. Two years later Charlie Gessel joined the division. At 32, he had four years of experience in consumer durables and had recently acquired an M.B.A. with major concentrations in marketing and international business.

Exhibits 1 and 2 provide financial information on WEI and its various divisions. Exhibits 3 and 4 detail the organization of the firm and its international activities.

---

[1] The export activities of the power and aerospace divisions were not assimilated in the new division due to very special technical and sensitive problems.

EXHIBIT 1
WHITE ELECTRIC, INC.
Summary of Consolidated Financial Statements*
(in $ millions)

	1970	1969	1968	1967
Net sales......................	$349.7	$321.7	$305.6	$261.4
Cost of goods sold..............	257.8	231.2	221.7	187.0
Operating profit...............	$ 91.9	$ 90.5	$ 83.9	$ 74.4
Sales and administrative				
expenses....................	29.2	26.8	24.2	21.4
R&D expenses.................	15.3	15.7	12.5	11.3
Other expenses................	1.7	1.6	1.8	1.8
Before-tax profit...............	$ 45.7	$ 46.4	$ 45.4	$ 39.9
Income tax....................	24.2	24.5	23.9	21.1
Net profit.....................	$ 21.5	$ 21.9	$ 21.5	$ 18.8
Cash and securities............	$ 16.7	$ 13.2	$ 11.8	$ 10.2
Other current assets...........	99.4	92.7	87.0	72.9
Net fixed assets...............	38.4	35.1	33.7	25.8
Total assets..............	$154.5	$141.0	$132.5	$108.9
Current liabilities..............	$ 32.1	$ 30.1	$ 30.3	$ 25.2
Long-term debt................	10.3	8.3	14.5	10.5
Equity........................	112.1	102.6	87.7	73.2
Total.....................	$154.5	$141.0	$132.5	$108.9

* Includes all subsidiaries, foreign and domestic, owned 50 percent or more, and a proportionate amount of the accounts of minority owned subsidiaries.

EXHIBIT 2
Divisional performance, 1967–1970 (in $ millions)*

	1970		1969		1968		1967	
	Dollars	Percent	Dollars	Percent	Dollars	Percent	Dollars	Percent
Corporate sales (consolidated)	$349.7	100.0%	$321.7	100.0%	$305.6	100.0%	$261.4	100.0%
Aerospace Products Division	$ 39.2	11.2%	$ 41.1	12.8%	$ 45.3	14.8%	$ 38.3	14.7%
Power Systems Division	57.4	16.4	52.4	16.3	47.2	15.4	39.6	15.1
Machinery Division	70.2	20.1	67.3	20.9	67.7	22.2	64.5	24.7
Household Appliance Division	94.8	27.1	87.2	27.1	81.8	26.8	70.3	26.9
International Division	88.1	25.2	73.7	22.9	63.6	20.8	48.7	18.6
Corporate profits (consolidated)	21.5	100.0	21.9	100.0	21.5	100.0	18.6	100.0%
Aerospace Products Division	$ (1.1)	(5.1)%	$ 1.6	7.3%	$ 4.3	20.0%	$ 3.5	18.8%
Power Systems Division	6.0	27.9	5.6	25.6	5.0	23.3	4.5	24.2
Machinery Division	6.7	31.2	6.6	30.1	6.6	30.7	6.0	32.3
Household Appliance Division	4.3	20.0	4.0	18.3	3.7	17.2	3.0	16.1
International Division	5.6	26.0	4.1	18.7	1.9	8.8	1.6	8.6
Corporate profitability (percent of sales)								
WEI	6.1%		6.8%		7.0%		7.1%	
Aerospace Products Division	(2.8)		3.9		9.5		9.1	
Power Systems Division	10.5		10.7		10.6		11.4	
Machinery Division	9.5		9.8		9.7		9.3	
Household Appliance Division	4.5		4.6		4.5		4.3	
International Division	6.3		5.6		3.0		3.3	

* Sales and profit figures for the Aerospace, Power Systems, and Machinery divisions include both foreign and domestic activities. Figures for the Household Appliance Division include only the United States and Canada. The International Division accounts for the remaining corporate activity outside of North America.

EXHIBIT 3
Organizational structure

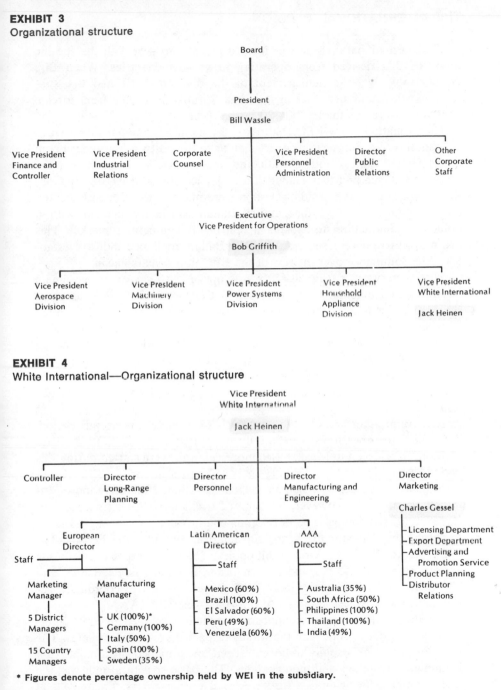

EXHIBIT 4
White International—Organizational structure

* Figures denote percentage ownership held by WEI in the subsidiary.

THE INTERNATIONAL DIVISION

The international division was formed in 1961 to deal with the specific problems that derived from operating in various countries. When Bob Griffith took over the management of the division, WEI had five subsidiaries with combined sales of less than $6 million. Profits from foreign operations were less than $200,000 in that year.

The formation of the EEC (European Economic Community) provided the stimulus to a European recovery similar to the postwar consumer boom in the United States. Both Griffith and Wassle agreed that this was the market to pursue and they launched a major expansion drive on the Continent. Major capital expenditures soon were made in the United Kingdom and Germany. In 1963 the smaller Italian subsidiary merged with a domestic manufacturer to expand in that highly competitive market. This last move proved very successful as the Italian appliance industry established its dominance over the rest of the EEC in the years ahead.

That same year, a regional office was opened in Geneva to coordinate all selling and manufacturing activities in Europe. Jack Heinen assumed the post of European director from his previous job of heading the United Kingdom subsidiary. In the next two years sales activities expanded to every country in Western Europe. Manufacturing facilities were also added in Spain and Sweden to cover two important markets outside of the EEC. Total European sales, including imports of household appliances from the U.S. division but excluding other corporate exports to Europe, reached $25 million in 1965.

Activity in other areas of the world was fairly quiet during this period. The Canadian operations were totally integrated with the United States division. In addition to Mexico, two more ventures were started during this period: a wholly owned subsidiary in Brazil and a minority (35 percent) investment in Australia. When Jack Heinen assumed the direction of International in 1966, however, he initiated a change of policies which included increased emphasis on developing countries.

During the following five years, subsidiaries were added in El Salvador, Peru, Venezuela, South Africa, Philippines, Thailand, and India; licensing agreements were also concluded with firms in Japan, Israel, Chile, and Columbia; and two new regional directors were named to coordinate activities in Latin America and in Africa-Asia-Australia (AAA).

A rather complex organizational structure had developed at White International in order to cope with the widely dispersed system of affiliates. The basic corporate philosophy of decentralized units applied in principle, but with many exceptions and modifications. The basic structural unit was the division management and its three regional profit centers. Each regional director had lone responsibility over the various sales and manufacturing subsidiaries in his region and was accountable for overall performance and profitability. But the patterns differed at this level. The European office, for example, had separate management for the marketing and manufacturing functions. This region was characterized by extensive integration of operations and close centralized control at the regional level. A fairly large staff in Geneva assisted the director in carrying out his duties in this connection. The AAA region was the opposite. Its director resided at corporate headquarters and traveled extensively. He had only two assistants on his staff and each country manager was responsible for all operations in his country. The third region, Latin America, consisted of a mixed pattern with some centralized control and functions, but with a large degree of independence at the country level.

The divisional staff provided a series of services to all regions and subsidiaries. The most active group was the marketing group under Charlie Gessel. In addition to coordinating all export and licensing activities, Charlie's staff provided technical assistance and served as a means of communication in matters pertaining to three major areas: advertising and promotion, product planning and R&D, and distributor relations. Three groups provided these services. The first group was responsible to answer any request for assistance as well as to keep all marketing personnel at the regional and subsidiary level informed on what the United States and each other were doing to promote their products. The second group's principal function was to serve as liaison between the R&D department of the U.S. household division and the various subsidiaries. New product development information, requests for design changes, and product line planning were some of the typical concerns at this level. The distributor relations group kept distributors happy throughout the globe with conventions, technical assistance, management seminars, contests, prices, and the like.

In performing their various functions, members of the division's staff could and did, in fact, rely to a large extent on their counterparts in the domestic division. The greatest dependency was in the product area. While some subsidiaries did some product development work, most of it was performed by the domestic division.

THE MICROWAVE OVEN

The R&D department of the Household Appliance Division had been working on a design for a home-use microwave oven since 1965. A first model was test marketed in mid-1969, but was judged to be unsatisfactory. Very high costs (over $500 at retail level) and other technical problems resulted in its demise.

By 1971, the company had reached what they considered an extraordinary commercial design for a microwave oven. Production costs were such that, given traditional channel markups, the retail price would fall in the vicinity of $350, or 20 percent below the cheapest competitor then in the market. The management of the domestic division agreed to launch the product in time for the seasonal peaks at Thanksgiving and Christmas. The following strategy was agreed upon.

Product. The design would be conventional and portable. It would feature a side opening door with black glass, and two dials, the top indicating time in seconds up to 5 minutes and the bottom calibrated in minutes up to 30. It was compact (20 × 14 × 15 inches) and could be built into a wall or cabinet, or set on a counter top.

Microwave cooking operates through high-frequency radio energy which sets the food molecules vibrating. This generates heat which "cooks" the food from within. Any nonfood and nonmetallic material is not affected; e.g., dinnerware, glass, plastic, and paper. The method is very fast as evidenced in the following cooking times: hamburger in 1 minute, a 12-pound turkey in 90 minutes, frozen lobster tails in 5½ minutes, a 4-pound rolled rib roast in 23 minutes, defrost a 12-ounce steak in 90 seconds, and bake a cake in 5 minutes.

The company was planning to add a microwave oven to one of its standard ranges in 1972. Also under consideration had been the addition of a browning unit that would allow meats to be browned either before or after cooking. This had been dropped for the moment given the need to go into production and the desire for lower costs.

Price. Variable production costs had been estimated at approximately $150 per unit. A margin of $100 per unit would allow a 40 percent markup for the trade and still keep the retail price below $350. Most competing units sold for around $400–$450 with some going as high as $1,000.

Distribution. WEI was planning to hold distribution to certain channels such as company distributors, department stores, and selected appliance dealers. After much debate it was agreed that discounters would not be given the line in 1971. Once the results of the coming season were clear that decision would be reevaluated.

Promotion. A budget of $250,000 had been set for the six-month period July–December 1971. Heavy emphasis was placed on magazines, principally of the type of *Better Homes and Gardens* and *Good Housekeeping,* supplemented with some coverage in *Time, Life,* and other popular women's magazines. A second category of expenditure was point-of-purchase and promotional literature. These had been distributed to all agents and dealers. Finally, some newspaper advertising was carried out selectively in a few communities.

The approach was highbrow, although the price factor was prominently displayed. The copy emphasized time-saving and modernity. Ads focused on the good looks of the cabinets occasionally accompanied by an elegantly dressed woman. The words "speed," "reliable," "modern," and "safe" were highlighted. Sample cooking times were provided for a range of foods.

Back at his desk on Monday morning Charlie Gessel was getting ready to tackle his assignment. He had gathered all the information he needed on the U.S. campaign (summarized above). He also learned that sales of WEI's oven had reached 1,000 units during the first month in the market; that is, from October 15 through November 15. Management was hoping for a total of 3,000 units by the end of the year. Also, that week's *Business Week* carried a brief note on the new product and the tone seemed optimistic (Exhibit 5).

EXHIBIT 5

MICROWAVE OVENS HEAT UP AGAIN

Microwave ovens, those fast-cooking wonders whose glowing sales were doused a few years ago by a flood of safety criticism, are hot once again. In 1968, when the ovens were first catching on, sales of home units leaped from a scant 3,000 to nearly 20,000. But growth soon sagged after a spate of adverse safety reports. Now, boosted by heavy pre-Christmas promotion, sales may top 100,000 —a 75% jump over 1970's total.

"This is the year," beams Robert I. Bruder, president of the Atherton Div. of Litton Industries, Inc., which claims 40% of the market. "We're selling a product whose time has come." Bruder says that one of the chief reasons for the strong performance is that all safety problems have been resolved. "Safety was a great concern to consumers a year and a half ago," he recalls, "but we and other responsible manufacturers have met the new federal safety requirements." Still, safety crusaders find the sudden resurgence disquieting, since many of the ovens rushed to stores for Christmas did not bear the new federal certification seal.

While microwave ovens now coming off the production line must indeed meet more stringent standards, the fact remains that the units currently available for purchase fall into two categories: safe and less safe. Under the Radiation Control for Health & Safety Act, ovens manufactured after Oct. 6, 1971, cannot leak microwave emissions in excess of 1 milliwatt per square centimeter of oven surface at the time they are sold. The units must also be designed so that leakage will not exceed five times that level at any time during their "useful" life. The Bureau of Radiological Health is charged with policing these standards. But before the mandatory federal ruling, the voluntary industry standard was 10 milliwatt/cm^2—and a lot of ovens made prior to the Oct. 6 cut-off date are still sitting on the shelves.

EXHIBIT 5 (*continued*)

No guarantee. "The risk is small from ovens that meet the voluntary industry standard," assures Herbert Klein, assistant to the director of the Bureau's Div. of Electronic Products. "But we cannot say absolutely that no public health hazard exists." However, the radiation expert adds: "I personally would feel confident to purchase one of them."

Manufacturers face other hurdles before they can meet the 75% jump in sales predicted for next year. Consumers remain shy of the hefty prices, generally around $400 but sometimes as high as $1,300. And despite the cleanliness and speed (16 minutes for a 5-lb. roast), homeowners question how useful a microwave oven is.

For one thing, microwaves cannot brown, so everything from chicken to chops turns out an unappetizing gray. (Commercial food operations, which are expected to buy 25,000 units this year, usually brown microwaved meat in regular ovens before serving.) Size is also a problem. "You can't cook a big turkey in many of them," admits Anthony A. Celio, sales vice-president at Norris Industries' Thermador Div. The industry hopes to sidestep such shortcomings by pushing the units as auxiliary cookers or building them into conventional ovens. Litton estimates that by 1975, one of every four ranges sold will include a microwave unit.

Price cut. As for price, the higher volume has already begun to shrink costs. Despite the additional expense of special sealing devices, safety interlocks, and safer viewing screens "prices dropped 20% in the last 12 months," says Litton's Bruder. "We're looking for another 10% in the first half of 1972, and possibly 10% more in the last half."

Retailers agree with the manufacturers that sales will continue to climb sharply. Noting the crowds flocking in for demonstrations over the holiday season, Herman Platt, merchandising manager for the May Co. in Los Angeles declared confidently: "The public used to diddle around. But now the market is really starting to jell."

Source: *Business Week*, November 1971.

A trip to the division's library yielded some comparative information on various countries (Exhibits 6 and 7). Given the need for a quick first reaction, Charlie realized that there would be no time to contact the various subsidiaries and regional offices for additional information. This, of course, would have to be done at a later time.

Other information obtained on short notice included shipping costs and likely tariff schedules. The oven weighed approximately 30 pounds and occupied a volume of nearly 3 cubic feet. On this basis it was estimated

EXHIBIT 6
Selected demographic data

Country	Population (millions) 1968	GNP per capita (dollars) 1958	Electric consumption (kwh per capita) 1964	People per auto 1969	Instruments (per 000 population) Phones 1968	TV 1969	Radios 1969
United States	201.1	$3,980	5,200	1.9	519	392*	1,431*
Canada	20.8	2,460	6,290	2.7	419	294	679
Argentina	23.6	820	529	11	65.4	381	106
Brazil	88.2	250	302	28	16.7		
Chile	9.4	480	631	33	32.4		
Colombia	20.0	310	268	79	26.1	111*	19*
Mexico	47.6	530	333	30	22.1	255	45
Peru	12.8	380	274	39	11.9		23
Venezuela	9.7	950	797	15	37.7	174*	72*
Belgium	9.6	1,810	1,643	4.2		197	107
Denmark	4.9	2,070	1,517	3.8	122	131	182
France	49.9	2,130	1,823	3.7	149	192	302
Germany (West)	60.2	1,970	2,441	4.1	116	117	88
Italy	52.8	1,230	1,308	5.4	188	163	250
Netherlands	12.7	1,620	1,677	5.1	71	23	85
Spain	32.6	730	713	12	456	270	378
Sweden	7.9	2,620	5,141	3.4	102	246	487
United Kingdom	55.3	1,790	2,895	4.0			
Australia	12.0	2,070	2,414	2.7			
India	523.9	100	59	545			
Israel	2.7	1,360	1,251	16			
Japan	101.1	1,190	1,631	6.8			
South Africa	19.8	650	1,575	11			
Thailand	33.7	150	30	126			

*1966 Data

* = 1966 data.

EXHIBIT 7

Saturation rates for selected appliances in selected markets (percentage of households owning the product)

Product	United States			EEC	U.K.	Japan		France	Germany	Italy
	1961	1966	1970	1963	1963	1963	1968	1968	1968	1968
Television	90.2%	94.6%*	95.0%	34%	82%	85%	96.4%†	64%	80%‡	66%
Radio	96.6	97.4	99	79	76	83	72	n.a.	69	n.a.
Record player	50.1	58.8	n.a.	28	39	n.a.	24	n.a.	43	n.a.
Refrigerator	98.4	99.3	99.8	40	30	40	78	73	79	68
Vacuum cleaner	73.5	76.4	n.a.	42	72	—	54	51	80	19
Electric mixer	67.0	69.5	n.a.	21	5	n.a.	n.a.	n.a.	55	n.a.
Dishwasher	5.1	10.8	23.7	—	—	n.a.	n.a.	n.a.	2	3
Electric iron	96.8	97.4	99	81	91	95	n.a.	n.a.	n.a.	n.a.
Washing machine	74.8	72.9	91.9	n.a.	n.a.	65	85	50	61	40
Range	98.8	98.1§	99	n.a.	n.a.	n.a.	n.a.	3‖	53‖	n.a.
Clothes dryer	19	31.1	40.3	n.a.	n.a.	n.a.	n.a.	n.a.	n.a.	n.a.
Freezer	19.4	26.4	29.6	n.a.	n.a.	n.a.	n.a.	n.a.	11	n.a.
Air conditioner	10.5	20.0	36.7	n.a.	n.a.	n.a.	4	n.a.	n.a.	n.a.

n.a. = not available.
* Color, 14.7 percent; black and white, 79.9 percent.
† Color, 5.4 percent; black and white, 91 percent.
‡ Color, 3 percent; black and white, 77 percent.
§ Electric, 40 percent; gas 58.1 percent.
‖ Electric range only, gas not available.

that shipping costs would range between $5 and $20 per unit depending on distance and mode of transportation. Tariff duties varied widely with the EEC countries averaging 10 percent of CIF value, and some Latin American countries going as high as 100 percent of CIF value.

Having reviewed this information, Charlie prepared to write a three-part report that would deal with:

a. A preliminary assessment of the worldwide potential for WEI's new microwave oven. This would include estimates on the market potential of various countries based on a general knowledge of the business and those areas. It would include also a detailed description of the principal factors considered in reaching conclusions about each market's potential.

b. A preliminary assessment of the applicability of the U.S. marketing strategy to those markets of the world considered to have some potential for the product. Included here would be some tentative suggestions about whatever appropriate modifications would be necessary in these various markets. Also included would be a proposal as to how to supply these markets over the next 12 months.

c. An indication of the type of information required from the various areas under consideration. This section of the report would consist primarily of a plan and budget proposal to conduct whatever necessary marketing research activities in the following weeks in order to verify the tentative conclusions above. The results of this research would allow WEI to make a firm recommendation for action to the company's management and take the necessary steps to meet production and marketing requirements for selected foreign markets. It would be highly desirable to have this information on hand and processed by the end of the year.

PART IV

PRODUCT DECISIONS

The six cases concerned with product strategy decisions in this section involve a number of different kinds of decisions. Many marketers believe that product decisions are the most critical of the marketing mix variables because of their importance to consumers in their decision-making process, and because product decisions, once made, are not quickly or easily reversed or changed. Promotion and pricing changes, for example, can be made much more quickly and with greater ease. Furthermore, most product changes usually require changes in the rest of the marketing strategy—changes in promotion, pricing, and sometimes distribution.

Before examining the various issues in the product strategy area, the concept of what a product is should first be understood. A product is "anything that can be offered to a market for attention, acquisition, or consumption; it includes physical objects, services, personalities, places, organizations, and ideas."[1] A product is thus much more than its physical properties and is everything a consumer buys when he or she makes a purchase. It is a set of want-satisfying attributes. It is important to understand this definition because what the consumer is buying is not necessarily what the company thought it was marketing. So mar-

---

[1] Philip Kotler, *Marketing Management: Analysis Planning and Control,* 3d ed. (Englewood Cliffs, N.J.: Prentice-Hall, Inc. 1976), p. 183.

keters must be aware of consumer attitudes, values, needs, and wants with respect to their products.

The major decisions related to product strategy are:

1. What new products should be developed?
2. What changes are needed in current products?
3. What products should be added or dropped?
4. What positioning should the product occupy?
5. What should the branding strategy be?

A brief discussion of some of the concepts related to each of these decisions follows.

NEW PRODUCT DEVELOPMENT

The sales and profits of a product category tend to change over time. The pattern a product category typically follows is called the product life cycle. It is defined to have the introductory, growth, maturity, and decline stages. Because most products reach the maturity and decline stages eventually, a marketer must continually seek out new products which can go through the introductory and growth stages in order to maintain and increase the total profits of the firm. But what new products should be introduced?

To answer this question, a marketer must consider the objectives of the firm, the resources available, the target markets the firm is trying to satisfy, and how the new product would fit in with other products offered by the company and the competition.

To successfully develop new products, the organization will have to set up formalized strategies for generating new product ideas, means for screening these ideas, product and market testing procedures, and finally commercialization. The objective is to obtain products which are differentiated from those of its competitors and which meet the needs of a large enough segment of the market to be profitable.

CHANGES IN CURRENT PRODUCTS

The needs, wants, attitudes, and behavior of consumers change over time, and a company must change its products also or risk losing these consumers to a competitor who more quickly responds to these changes in the marketplace.

Should new features be added to the product? Should the warranty be extended? Should the packaging be changed? Should new services be offered? The marketer must continually monitor its target market and the competition to be able to answer such questions.

WHAT PRODUCTS SHOULD BE ADDED OR DROPPED

A marketer must make decisions concerning the product mix or composite of products the firm will offer for sale. This requires decisions concerning the width and depth of products. Width refers to the number of product lines marketed by the firm. For example, General Electric has many lines while Kellogg's has concentrated on breakfast foods. The depth of the product mix is the number of items offered for sale within each product line. Kelloggs, for example, would have a very deep product line with many different alternatives offered for sale.

Whether a product line should be extended or reduced depends on a number of factors, including financial criteria, market factors, production considerations, and organizational factors. The marketer in making these decisions must examine the potential profit contributions, return on investment, impact on market share, fit with consumers' needs, fit with the needs of the channels of distribution, and the expected reactions of competitors. The production and organizational considerations include impact on capacity for other products, and on the goals and objectives of the firm, both in the short and long run.

PRODUCT POSITIONING

Product positioning is defined as that idea that is put into the consumers' minds by telling them how our product differs from its competitors. The position we strive to occupy will depend on the different market segments available, the attributes of our product compared to the needs of each segment, and the positions occupied by our competitors against each market segment.

BRANDING STRATEGY

The basic decisions here are whether or not to put brand names on the organization's products, whether the brands should be manufacturers' or distributors' brands, and whether individual or family brands should be used.

These decisions depend on the company's resources, objectives, the competition, and consumer choice behavior. For example, a small firm with little resources and much competition in a product category where consumers perceived small differences in the brands available, would probably choose to market its product using private distributors' brands. Family brands such as General Electric and Campbell's are used when the marketer wants the consumer to generalize to the new products all those attributes he associates with the family brand name. The time and money required to establish the brand's name is much lower with this strategy but it does not allow the marketer to establish a separate image for the new product.

CASE

10

Dillon Company, Inc.*

Early in 1976, Mr. J. A. Greene, marketing manager of Dillon Company Inc., began to explore the possibility of offering Dillon's chemical expertise and specialized chemical products to the consumer market. While Dillon Company had confined their marketing to industrial products, Mr. Greene believed that the excess productive capacity of their plant might be profitably utilized by exploiting consumer applications for the same basic products. He further believed that sales potential in the industrial markets was limited with the present product mix and that consumer applications could provide substantially increased sales with the addition of no extra staff or production facilities.

COMPANY BACKGROUND

Dillon operations began in 1911 to serve the railway business. Until the early 1940s almost all business was in providing chemicals for steam-driven locomotives and other steam-driven vessels. At about that time, emphasis was redirected to industrial boiler water treatment where Dillon Company innovated a number of chemical feed systems that continued to keep the company in a position of dominance in that market.[1] In the late 1940s, further diversification brought fuel oil conditioners and industrial cleaners into the product mix. The company became a leader in fuel oil treatment.

---

* This case was written by Kenneth G. Hardy, Associate Professor of Business Administration, University of Western Ontario. Used with permission.

[1] Chemical feed systems are the mechanical equipment necessary to inject chemicals into an operating system at the prescribed times in the correct quantities.

EXHIBIT 1

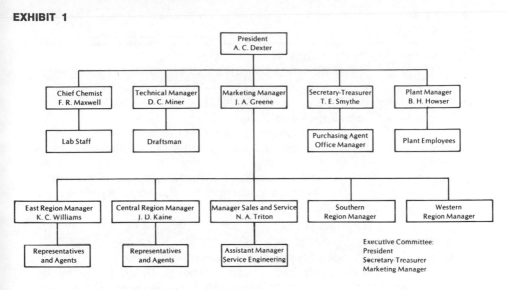

Although considerable effort was made during the 1950s to get market penetration in the industrial cleaner market, the line dwindled to a position of minor importance.

Dillon Company had two major studies of the organization done by management consultants. In 1965, management was decentralized with the appointment of three regional managers. In 1969, a marketing manager was appointed and the position of Western Regional Manager was abolished. Exhibit 1 is an organization chart for Dillon Company as of 1976 and Exhibit 2 provides brief biographies of each of the key managers within the organization.

PRODUCTS AND SERVICES

The products and services offered for steam boilers and cooling water systems applied to a wide variety of industrial and commercial uses. Any firm which generated steam or required cooling for any purpose was a potential customer for Dillon Company. Industrial applications included the pulp and paper industry, petroleum, chemical, mining, rubber, and general manufacturing industries. Typical commercial customers were hospitals, schools and universities, office buildings, and any other commercial building that used steam or hot water heat.

All Dillon Company products and services were geared to the industrial and commercial trade. The promotional budget for industrial products was $600,000. No Dillon Company products or services had ever been offered

EXHIBIT 2
Key managers

A. C. Dexter	President, age 58. Civil engineering background. Started with the company as a field engineer. Later became district manager, general manager, vice president and president in 1958.
T. E. Smythe	Secretary-treasurer, age 56. Spent 13 years with the Bank of California at posts up to assistant accountant. Spent ten years with Dominion Textile as office manager, cost accountant and in planning, production and control. Has been with the Dillon Company for 14 years as comptroller and secretary-treasurer.
F. R. Maxwell	Chief chemist, age 46. Graduate chemist, 1947. Employed as a chemist with Dillon Company until 1964 when he became chief chemist.
D. C. Miner	Manager, Technical Department, age 56. Engineering background. Came to Dillon Company in 1938 as a technical salesman. Became technical manager during the 1940s.
J. A. Greene	Marketing manager, age 37. B.Sc. Chemistry. Ten years with Texaco in industrial sales and supervision of retail operations. Field engineer with Dillon Company for three and one-half years. Appointed marketing manager in 1973.
B. H. Howser	Plant manager, age 61. Began with Dillon Company as a production worker. Subsequently promoted to production foreman and became plant manager in 1969.
N. A. Triton	Manager sales and service, age 60. Began with Dillon Company as a clerk in 1940. Promoted to field sales and became manager of sales services in the 1950s.
K. C. Williams	Manager, Eastern Region, age 55. Chemist. Started in 1941 as a lab chemist. Progressed to sales engineer, district manager, and assistant manager industrial department. Became regional manager in 1965.
J. D. Kaine	Vice president, manager Central Region, age 55. Started with Dillon Company in 1942. Became district manager at Chicago in 1946. Became manager railway sales in the early 1950s. Appointed regional manager in 1956 and vice president in 1958.

---

to the consumer market. Total sales for 1976 were estimated at $22.1 million, broken down as shown in the accompanying table.

Product area	Percent sales
Steam boiler treatment	48%
Cooling waters and closed water systems	7
Fuel oil conditioners	8
Chemical feed equipment	16
Railway sales	12
Test equipment	6
Miscellaneous	3
Total	100%

1. Steam boiler treatment

Dillon Company steam boiler treatment included deposit control, corrosion control, and system cleaning. Deposit control was the prevention of deposit formation-scale much like that found in a tea kettle. This scale could clog pipes and valves with a corresponding decrease in operating efficiency. Corrosion control was the removal and prevention of corrosion or rust within a boiler system. This treatment took the form of rust inhibitors or other neutralizing chemicals. Foam control was simply the prevention of bubble formation through the use of special antifoams.

A complete line of chemicals for the cleaning of new and in-service equipment was available from Dillon Company. Special formulations removed oils, greases, mill scale, and other extraneous matter from new boiler units. Acids and neutralizers were used to clean operating equipment and then water treatment chemicals were used to keep the equipment clean.

For existing plants, steam plant and/or mechanical superintendents invariably had a major voice in the choice of supplier. The plant engineers quite often became involved in such decisions but the purchasing department usually had little or no influence.

Steam boiler treatment chemicals was a mature market which was heavily solicited. There were 30 water treatment companies in the United States and the growth rate in this category was extremely low, perhaps 1 to 3 percent per year. Even this growth largely represented price increases.

2. Cooling waters and closed water systems

Chemicals for the treating of cooling waters represented a rapidly expanding market. The chemicals were used to prevent corrosion, scale formation, fouling by suspended matter, and prevention of microbiological growth. Cleaning chemicals for both new and in-service cold water systems were part of the Dillon Company line. Where cooling waters were involved, they were an integral part of a production process and production personnel had a substantial interest in the purchase.

There were growing pressures to recycle cooling waters. Over the next decade it was anticipated that aqueous cooling systems would be installed at double the rate of the gross national product. Furthermore, ecological considerations would contribute to even higher consumption in the future.

There were similar aspects in the buying process for steam boiler and cooling water chemicals. Members of the decision-making team often would be substantially influenced by users who were located nearby, or by other firms in their industry who were buying from Dillon Company. This stemmed from the fact that the business was essentially one of technical know-how and technical service.

The chemicals themselves were no secret and, indeed, quite a number of accounts purchased chemicals on the open market and engaged Dillon Company or competitors on a fee basis for technical services. In such circumstances, the services of one company were engaged and their materials were purchased as a separate package.

Chemicals served as a vehicle for selling Dillon Company services. In the case of new facilities to be constructed, the combination of consulting engineers, contractors, and competitive bid prices played a major role in the selection of a supplier.

3.   Fuel oil conditioners

Bunker fuel oil conditioners, used at the rate of about one quart per thousand gallons of bunker oil, prevented tank and line sludge deposits, promoted more complete combustion, cut down corrosion and reduced soot, acid, smoke, and other emissions. These conditioners were sold as part of a water treatment package because exactly the same personnel were involved with them.

Mr. Greene thought that fuel oil conditioners presented a mixed picture in that a recent addition to the line of conditioners was catching on very well, but at the same time there were many conversions from heavy oil to gas which were diminishing the usage of fuel oil conditioners. However, he believed that total volume of heavy oil would increase and its usage would be concentrated in higher volumes to fewer plants.

4.   Chemical feed equipment

In addition to chemical products, the company supplied a wide variety of chemical feed equipment. This equipment was for use in almost all areas for which chemicals were supplied. The equipment ranged from fully automatic to manually operated systems and included pumps, tanks, switches, meters, valves, and various other controls. Most of the mechanical equipment was manufactured to specification for Dillon Company. The company held patents on and manufactured some specialized pieces of chemical feed equipment.

Sales of chemical feed equipment rose and fell with new construction. While the total market would grow as new construction expanded, Dillon Company concentrated on capturing a larger share of the existing market.

5. Railway sales

The maintenance of a product sales area under the name Railway Sales was a carry-over from earlier years when the bulk of all sales in the water treatment area had been for steam locomotive maintenance. With the advent of the diesel, railway sales diminished drastically. Fuel oil conditioners, chemical feed equipment and miscellaneous other products were purchased by the railways but only boiler and cooling water treatment were included in the category of Railway Sales. No significant changes in sales were anticipated in this category.

6. Test equipment

Test benches, pH meters along with test solutions and powders were all sold by Dillon Company.[2] The monitoring and test equipment was used to ensure optimum operational level in any system. Laboratory test supplies were available to Dillon Company customers so that they could test results and check on the acceptability of treated aqueous systems. Growth in sales of test equipment depended largely on sales of steam boiler treatment chemicals.

7. Miscellaneous products and services

A variety of other chemicals and compounds were available from the company. Ion exchange resins and other compounds for dealkalizing, deionizing, water softening, organic removal, filtering, odor removal, and color removal were sold to municipalities, industry, and government agencies for the treatment of both primary and waste water.

Dillon Company technicians and engineers were prepared to design complete chemical treatment systems for boiler feedwater, cooling water, hot water, domestic water, and waste or process water. Their brochure

---

[2] pH is a measure of the acidity level of a solution.

outlined a complete range of manual, semiautomatic, and fully automatic systems.

Raw water treatment systems were designed to use the most efficient chemical or mechanical treatment or a combination of both to meet the necessary criteria for the desired final water.[3] This service was particularly applicable to plants contemplating a new source of raw water. The company also offered a surveillance service and would conduct studies to determine levels of operating efficiency.

GENERAL BUYING INFLUENCES FOR INDUSTRIAL PRODUCTS

Mr. Greene reviewed the customer's purchasing patterns in the following words:

> For all product categories except chemical feed equipment and a small portion of the test equipment, the factors which influence a purchasing decision in order of importance are: technical know-how and service, product quality, delivery, and price. Our industry is characterized by many accounts purchasing materials and services at excessive costs. A high degree of faith in an existing supplier can often increase buying resistance to a new supplier.
>
> Of course, there is a segment of the market which is cost sensitive but this segment is about as large as you would expect in a service-oriented industry. The order of importance for the influencing factor in new or bid work is quite different. Price, technical service, delivery, and product quality would be the sequence I would apply to this phase of our business. Product quality may seem unduly low, but specifications can be quite explicit and there isn't all that much room to maneuver.

PLANT FACILITIES

The Dillon Company plant had an estimated annual output of 50 million pounds. This figure represented chemical output only and was exclusive of any machinery or other equipment sold by them for use in chemical feed or control systems. The plant was operating at about 30 percent of capacity.

Chemical formulations were produced in both dry and liquid forms. For dry powders an assortment of containers was used, ranging upward from 50 pounds, although powders had been packaged in ten-, five- and half-pound containers.

Liquid formulations were held in storage tanks for the filling of con-

---

[3] Raw water is the liquid taken into a system before treatment to make it suitable for a particular use.

tainers which held five gallons or more. Smaller containers were filled by hand. There was pill and bottling equipment in the plant.

SALES FORCE AND SELLING JOB

Dillon Company's sales force consisted of a marketing manager, four regional managers and 40 direct sales agents. One of the regional managers was located in New York, one in Atlanta, one in San Francisco, and the other in Chicago. In addition, the company had seven agents who covered the less populated Central States. The majority of the field force held university degrees in chemistry or engineering, and the remainder had direct or closely related experience in water conditioning prior to joining the company.

The majority of sales were made in the U.S. market. Sales leads came from a variety of sources. Requests for technical assistance provided many sales opportunities, as did requests for competitive bids on equipment and chemicals. Notices of new construction or plant expansion in local papers were watched by the salesmen.

Sales were made on a bid basis and through personal selling on the part of company representatives. Regardless of the manner in which the sale was made, management believed that the expertise and service of Dillon Company was at least as responsible for the sale as was the physical product.

All new sales and many of the repeat orders required a large number of calls by the representative and the utilization of many of the developmental and analytical abilities of the company as a whole. In most cases, considerable time and expense was involved before a sale was made. Salary and expenses for each salesman amounted to $18,000 per year.

Management had a policy which established that every sales dollar was capable of supporting a certain amount of service. A customer was therefore charged for service only if that customer's purchases or potential purchases were not sufficient to support the amount of service which was required. The high level of service required by most customers necessitated margins on equipment of 40 percent and contributions on other products of 50 to 55 percent.

COMPETITION

Dillon Company was the second or third largest water treatment specialist in the United States. The largest competitor was Ace Chemical which competed line for line with Dillon Company. As of 1974, Ace was believed to have sales of $33.5 million or an average of 40 percent of the markets in which they competed with Dillon Company. The next largest competitor was Dale Chemicals with sales of $22.5 million. Ace concentrated on large accounts, apparently because the marketing costs per unit of volume were lower. Mr. Greene added:

> Furthermore, at many of the larger accounts for water treatment chemicals, the decision makers quite often feel they have specialized problems and definitely do take comfort in dealing with a supplier who has handled other large accounts.
>
> We have considered the alternative of putting more promotional effort behind industrial products. Our current promotional budget is about $600,000. We could add salespeople, add sales training programs, perform more demonstrations, entertain more clients, develop new sales literature, send more direct mail pieces and even cut prices as a promotional device. My colleagues and I believe that $50,000 or $100,000 applied in an intelligent combination of the above items would yield increased sales of industrial products as shown.

Promotional expenditure

Cumulative probability	Sales increase with $50,000	Cumulative probability	Sales increase with $100,000
0.05	$104,000	0.05	$171,000
0.20	85,000	0.20	141,000
0.70	66,000	0.70	111,000
0.90	47,000	0.90	81,000
1.00	28,000	1.00	51,000

CONSUMER MARKET ENTRY

Company management believed that every effort had to be made to utilize the excess plant capacity and it was for this reason they were considering expansion into the manufacture of consumer products. Management philosophy was that they would take advantage of existing channels of distribution and expect only a manufacturing profit. It was not their intention to become involved in the consumer market beyond the point of acting as a supplier to various distributors. Management expected that the consumer products could be handled by one or two people from head office or by the regional managers. If sales developed to such a point that this arrangement became unwieldy, then additional talent could be found and consumer products could be a separate division of the company.

Many of the products handled by Dillon Company had potential applications in consumer markets. Management was considering a few for initial market entry, and based on the success of the first products, more lines could be introduced later.

ALCO PUR

Management felt that one of the better possibilities for consumer market entry was Alco Pur. This resin was capable of removing aldehydes and ketones from any aqueous solution. Aldehydes and ketones were the materials which caused the harsh taste of some of the cheaper brands of wine and liquor. By exposing such liquor or wine to this resin for a short period of time (about 30 minutes), much of the harshness was removed and the color of the liquid was lightened. Normally, the aldehydes and ketones were removed through the aging process. Therefore, Alco Pur was capable of saving a considerable amount of time required for the natural aging of wines and liquors.

For the purposes of home use, the resin was packaged in a 20-ounce plastic squeeze bottle with a push-pull stopper. The stopper contained a fine mesh screen which allowed the liquid to pass over the resin and yet prevented the resin from escaping when the liquid was emptied. The resin had been declared safe under the Food and Drug Act and was not harmful if accidentally swallowed.

Preliminary examination of the potential market yielded an estimate of wine consumption in the United States of some 340 million gallons. This did not include any of the homemade wines which would add at least another 50 percent or 170 million gallons to the total consumption figure. The liquor market was estimated at over 400 million gallons annually. In 1976, Dillon Company had a number of qualitative tests on Alco Pur in progress. The tests were being conducted by a local winemaking supply house in an effort to gauge the effectiveness of the resin in various situations and to determine consumer reaction to its packaging. The supply house management suggested that the 20-ounce unit should sell for $2 or less at retail. The retailer would expect a 100 percent markup on their cost. It was expected that the resin would cost about 10 cents per unit while the containers and labeling would cost about 35 cents per unit. Labor and shipping would add another 10 cents per unit.

RESIKLEER

The second alternative was Resikleer which had much the same effect on water as activated charcoal, in that it could remove off-flavor and color from water. For experimental purposes Resikleer was packaged in a 20-ounce plastic bottle with a rubber hose for attachment to a faucet. It was possible to package Resikleer in the form of a tea bag or small cannister for complete immersion in water. Campers and sportsmen were the likely buyers for Resikleer.

The only products which performed the same function were filter units which could be attached to water taps and sold for as much as $20. The small plastic bottle in which Resikleer was packaged had one fifth the life of the $20 units. Resikleer could process about 250 ounces of water and had a working life of six months. A 20-ounce unit of Resikleer could be sold at retail for about $5. Wholesale margin would be 25 percent and retail margin would be 100 percent, both on cost. It was expected that per unit product, labor, and shipping costs would be about the same as for Alco Pur. Container costs would be about 50 cents per unit.

The removal of sulfur or iron was also possible with the use of other ion exchange resins and while this had been done commercially, it had not been done for drinking water. Technical personnel at Dillon Company said that deionized water was purer than distilled water.

The estimated investments and fixed expenses for the two resin products are shown in the accompanying table. The company would amortize any investment over a five-year period.

	Alco Pur	Resikleer
Investment:		
One-month inventory..............................	$13,000	$60,000
Packaging designs................................	4,000	2,000
Packaging art....................................	3,000	3,000
Equipment.......................................	10,000	nil
Fixed Expenses:		
Sales literature..................................	5,000	8,000
Advertising......................................	3,000	6,000
One salesperson.................................	9,000	9,000

Mr. Greene believed that second year sales would reach 300,000 units for Alco Pur and 500,000 units for Resikleer. He planned to assign one, or at most two, salespeople from Head Office to call on distributors.

HOME APPLIANCE DESCALERS

Management felt that company expertise in the water treatment area provided an excellent background for entry into other consumer markets. Chemicals to remove scale from household appliances such as steam irons and electric kettles were already on the market, but were often ineffective. Already some appliance manufacturers were packaging citric acid tablets with new appliances, but scale formation was still a major complaint from customers. The chemicals available from Dillon Company were capable of doing a much better job of scale removal and corrosion prevention than existing chemicals on the market.

In 1976, two firms were marketing descaling materials for home steam equipment. Their products were marketed through distributors to hardware and grocery stores. Distributor markup was at least 15 percent and retail markup was 30 percent to 50 percent on selling price.

It was estimated that the current market for steam equipment descalers was about 4,500,000 units annually. Cost and resultant contribution were estimated as shown in the accompanying table.

Manufacturing sale price per unit*.....................	$0.49
Cost of materials (resin and packaging)..............	0.32
Additional costs (delivery, etc.)......................	0.07
Contribution.....................................	$0.10 per unit
Selling price to consumer............................	$0.98

* One unit contains sufficient chemical to treat 250 ounces of solution.

Investment and fixed expense for this line would be identical to Alco Pur. Although the per volume contribution expected from consumer products was not nearly as large as from industrial sales, management believed that far fewer sales calls would be necessary and that technical assistance costs would be considerably less. Therefore, a much smaller contribution would be acceptable.

In December of 1975, Mr. Greene wrote,

> Within the next two weeks we will have finished our research into appropriate products to prevent scaling, corrosion, and promote conductivity. We will then forward formulations to various manufacturers for technical and cost acceptance. This area should be rather interesting to explore because of the degree of interest shown by the various manufacturers and also because these possibilities have been exploited to an extremely limited extent.
>
> If we are successful in our efforts with the above-noted products, we feel we definitely can expand the consumer product line into perhaps furnace humidifiers, swimming pool chemicals, and even get into items which we can handle from a manufacturing point of view.

Before making his final report to management, Mr. Greene wanted to be completely sure that entry into the consumer market was in the best interests of the company. He also had to decide which products were the best for initial entry and appropriate marketing strategies for each new product entry.

Wolverine World Wide, Inc.: Hush Puppies

During the spring of 1968, the director of marketing for Hush Puppies at Wolverine World Wide, Inc., was reviewing past marketing strategies as an aid to formulating marketing plans for 1969. Increased competition, rising raw material costs, and a stabilized demand in the past two years made him wonder what changes, if any, might be appropriate in the Hush Puppies marketing program.

Wolverine World Wide, Inc., first started in 1883 as the partnership of Hirth and Krause, a wholesaler of hides, shoes, and leather supplies. Shoemaking and tanning operations were first begun in 1903. Wolverine, for many years, specialized in the tanning of unusual leathers, enabling the company to occupy a niche for itself in the competitive cowhide field. The firm's main product from the 1920s through the 1950s, when it was called Wolverine Shoe and Tanning Company, was shell horsehide. This was an extraordinarily stiff and strong leather in which the company had a competitive advantage due to the special triple-tanning process which the company had developed. This tannage was highly acid resistant, which was a significant advantage around the farm where there were lactic and other acids. Shell horsehide, a natural leather, dried soft, stayed soft, and was the second toughest leather in the world after kangaroo leather. The company considered itself as selling leather and not just work shoes.

In the late 1930s, the company became concerned about their raw material supply. Horses were becoming more and more scarce (there were 26 million horses in the United States in 1910 and only 4 million in 1950), and the company realized that they could not make shoes out of tractors.

Further, the company believed that its success would be linked to the development of other unusual leathers.

It was about this time that a new opportunity presented itself to the company with the introduction, by the meat-packing houses, of prepackaged sliced bacon. Previously, bacon was sold with the skin on it. After hand-skinning the bacon, people just threw away the rind. The prepackaging made available large quantities of bacon rind from which the company was able to develop a suede pigskin leather suitable for a line of work gloves. This was the beginning of Wolverine's entry into the pigskin business. The company soon turned its attention from smoked bacon rinds to large-scale processing of "green" (unsmoked) pigskin.

Pigskin possesses certain outstanding qualities. It wears exceptionally well and is highly resistant to deterioration from perspiration. It cannot be damaged by moisture and humidity. Another important characteristic is the fact that pigskins are available in large quantities, as some 70 million pigs are slaughtered each year in the United States alone. Of course, not all this pigskin is acceptable for tanning purposes by shoe manufacturers.

Unfortunately, however, the pig is not easy to skin. With horses and cows, the skin fits loosely, like a coat, and is very easy to remove, much as a banana is peeled. On the other hand, skinning a hog is somewhat like peeling an apple; the hide is bound tightly to the animal by a layer of fat. A highly trained worker requires more than a half hour to "slay" or skin a hog. This is an obvious production bottleneck, when large packing houses process 600 or more animals each hour.

During World War II, the War Production Board encouraged packers to develop new ways to produce pigskin as a leather source. Wolverine, due to its experience in tanning unusual leathers, was selected to process this pigskin output into work shoes.

Following the war, the pork packers returned to producing bacon. Wolverine, confronted with a diminishing supply of horsehides, bought several units of a wartime mechanical pigskinner and set out to perfect a new pigskinner that satisfied the requirements of both shoemakers and packers. After seven years of research and upwards of $2 million in expenditures, the company developed a unique and highly efficient machine for effectively skinning pigs at the packing plant without damaging the skins. Twenty packers were induced to install the perfected skinning machines in their pork processing operation. Wolverine now had the first and only volume pigskinner.

The company could now produce a skin uniform in size and about 2 feet square from each side of the animal. The machines, which were owned by Wolverine and cost $15,000 to $18,000 each, could remove pig hides at the rate of about 460 an hour. Another equally expensive unit called a flushing machine removes all excess fat remaining on the skin.

However, the company still had a problem. The only shoes that Wolverine was making at the time were work shoes, and while pigskin made very comfortable footware, its lightness worked against it in the work shoe field. In appraising markets, Wolverine decided that the greatest potential lay in easy-to-care-for leisure shoes. Leisure shoes look attractive with a brushed finish, the best finish for pigskin. Brushing pigskin eliminates surface marks and permits distinctive colors. It also leaves the tiny bristle holes in the leather unblocked, giving the shoes natural ventilation.

In 1957, Wolverine had 30,000 pairs of men's shoes made in the new pigskin leather. The soles were cemented to the uppers, not sewn, as was the practice with most shoes. There was one basic pattern in 11 different colors including scarlet, canary yellow, and kelly green. These shoes were offered to the trade to retail for $7.95, and were distributed nationally through the work shoe salesmen who generally sold in small rural towns.

A big turning point came in 1958, when Wolverine changed advertising agencies and employed MacManus, John, and Adams, Inc. The agency had done no shoe advertising previously, and Wolverine thought that the new agency would therefore be willing to take new approaches and try new ideas in promoting this brand-new product. The first thing the new agency did was to set up a market test. One hundred pairs of shoes were given to consumers, with a follow-up study being done eight weeks later. At the end of the study the researcher told the consumers that the company needed the shoes back, but if they wanted to keep them, they could upon payment of $5. Overwhelmingly, the consumers wanted to keep the shoes. Of course, the company let them keep them without paying the $5.

With strong encouragement from the consumer test, the agency then attacked the problem of what to call the shoes. The only "Hush Puppies" that people had ever heard of at the time was a corn fritter which people in some southern states threw to their barking dogs with the command, "Hush, puppies." Several of Wolverine's executives liked the name and thought it appropriate to give this name to a comfortable shoe that is kind to the feet and hushes that special kind of "barking dog," one's tired feet.

An outside marketing research firm was commissioned to conduct the name study. Interviews were held with 300 people in Los Angeles and Chicago testing six potential names: Swash Bucks, Lazers, Breathers, Slow Pokes, Ho-Hums, and Hush Puppies. Swash Bucks and Lazers were the best liked names. The Hush Puppies name had a high association with food and dogs and was the least desirable name. The agency wanted the company to change the name, but the Wolverine sales manager was insistent that Hush Puppies was the name that should be used, and he won out. To go along with the name, a logo was prepared to help create an image for the shoes. A sad-eyed, droopy-eared basset hound was created for this purpose.

The agency and company then set out to reintroduce the new men's leisure-time shoes. Up until this time Wolverine had sold only 30,000 pairs of the Hush Puppies, an extremely small proportion of the total men's shoe market of 200 million pairs per year. This market was, at the time, a relatively stable market, with the men buying an average of only 1.3 pairs of shoes per year and owning an average wardrobe of only 2.5 to 3 pairs of shoes. Research has indicated that men dislike shopping for shoes and feel little need for owning several pairs, which helps explain the lack of growth in the industry.

INITIAL MARKETING STRATEGY

Wolverine's problem of introducing Hush Puppies was also intensified by the company distribution network in 1958. The company had 57 salesmen who had been selling shell horsehide work shoes and boots, calling on outlets in the small towns and villages of the United States—rarely, if ever, setting foot in the big cities or the growing suburbs. The work shoes and boots were sold primarily to farmers—a main copy point was their stout resistance to "barnyard acid"—whereas the market for Hush Puppies was in the cities and suburbs. A plan to gain new distribution was then worked out.

The company's sales manager was told that the board of directors would approve an advertising budget of 17 percent of anticipated sales, if the sales manager could open 600 new accounts in 35 cities in six weeks. The 35-city plan resulted from an idea to advertise in the 35 cities in which the *This Week* Sunday supplement to newspapers was distributed. This was a large amount of advertising, relative to the industry average of 1.5 percent of sales, and the sales manager accepted the challenge. So in August 1958, all of the company's salesmen were pulled in, literally "transferred" for at least a month, and sent to the 35 cities for a concerted sales drive on Hush Puppies.

It was decided to spend the entire advertising budget in one full-page, four-color advertisement in *This Week* magazine, distributed in 35 leading cities of the country. The extra incentive for the retail stores was that their name would be prominently listed in the Sunday supplement newspaper ad if they ordered the minimum specified assortment of Hush Puppies shoes.

The salesmen were trained by the sales manager on the sales pitch to be used. Each salesman got the highlights of the consumer acceptance study. He carried samples of the shoes in all 11 colors. He used a demonstration kit showing how the "Breathin' Brushed Pigskin" leather resisted soil, rain, and stains, and carried a preproof of the color ad showing how the store's name would be handled.

The Wolverine salesmen received orders from 600 major retail accounts —all new—in three weeks, and the ad was run at the end of August. The copy in the ad was unusual compared with normal shoe industry advertising. The shoes were shown on people's feet, and both feet were shown. Previously, most shoe ads had shown just one shoe, so it could be pictured as big as possible, usually against a solid colored velvet or other elegant background.

The ad ran on Sunday, and most retailers sold out their complete stock in a few days. One hundred twenty thousand pairs of Hush Puppies were sold at a retail price of $7.95. Another ad was immediately authorized for the Christmas gift season, again with the dual objectives of (1) selling the concept of leisure shoes, and (2) using dealer listing to gain better distribution in the large markets. It was felt that *This Week* supplement could best satisfy these objectives because of its high impact and penetration into a large number of homes in each city. The Christmas ad was even more successful than the initial ad in August.

CHANGES IN MARKETING STRATEGY, 1959–1963

For 1959, the strategy continued, but expanded into over 50 additional markets covered by *Parade* magazine. The advertising was scheduled for late spring to give the Hush Puppies salesmen time to cover their newly expanded territories, opening up more new retail accounts. Another men's style was added and sales tripled. Promotion effort and sales results both continued to grow. *Family Weekly* Sunday newspaper supplement was later added plus the *Sunday Group* and independent newspapers. By 1961, Hush Puppies was the most heavily promoted brand of shoes in the United States. The advertising budget, by this time, had leveled off at 7 percent of sales, which was four times the industry average. Demand continued to be greater than capacity, but Wolverine kept on advertising and adding new dealers through the listings. The Sunday supplement promotions were run four times per year: at Easter, at the end of May, in August, and in December. The salesmen would send in a report by telegram on Monday and would file a full report on the promotion's success on Friday of the same week.

The company followed a selective distribution strategy, protecting their dealers so that a proper amount of inventory would be stocked. The price was increased to $9.95 as Wolverine needed a larger margin to support plant expansion and other growth programs, including the largest advertising expenditure for a single brand in the shoe industry. Also, dealers would be more interested in adding the Hush Puppies line if higher margins were offered. All outlets maintained the suggested retail price.

During this period, Wolverine expanded its product line. In 1960, golf

EXHIBIT 1
Pairs of Hush Puppies sold (in 000)

1957..	30
1958..	301
1959..	1,000
1960..	1,500
1961..	2,600
1962..	4,900

shoes were introduced. The total golf shoe market had been about 100,000 pairs per year, but in its first year 94,000 pairs of Hush Puppies golf shoes were sold. In 1961, women's shoes were designed and, by 1963, Hush Puppies were available in styles for the entire family and age spectrum from five years old up.

Until 1963, Wolverine continued to sell Hush Puppies shoes faster than they could ship them, with pairage volume showing great increases (see Exhibit 1). Total company sales increased from a plateau of $11 million to $33 million during this period, with profits increasing by an even greater percentage. Selected financial statistics are in Exhibit 2.

Up to this point, no one in the company knew the real consumer marketing reasons why sales were increasing this rapidly. The main problems executives had been concerned with centered around how to get more pigskin, more tanning, and more production out of the factories, which were working three shifts a day. There had been no time to think about who was buying Hush Puppies or for what reason. The marketing executives thought that the buyers were from the lower middle class, with emphasis among those people, such as service station attendants, who were on their feet much of the day.

EXHIBIT 2
Selected financial information

	Sales (000)	Profits (000)	Percent of profits	Assets (000)	Share-holders' equity (000)	Earnings per share
1956..............	$11,313	$ 251	2.2%	$ 6,394	$4,750	$0.09
1957..............	10,925	125	1.1	6,692	4,200	0.05
1958..............	11,376	341	2.9	6,496	4,387	0.13
1959..............	15,264	591	3.9	8,025	4,742	0.24
1960..............	17,929	658	3.7	9,895	6,159	0.22
1961..............	23,992	1,218	5.1	12,428	7,069	0.40
1962..............	33,231	1,945	5.9	14,375	8,561	0.64

Source: Wolverine World Wide, Inc. *Annual Report,* 1968.

In 1963, the company, in conjunction with its advertising agency, designed a consumer research study to find out more about Hush Puppies' consumers, and about what people's experience with Hush Puppies had been. Twenty thousand screening interviews were conducted, followed by 1,000 in-depth interviews. Some of the results are shown in Exhibits 3 and 4. The study showed that 61 percent of the adult population was aware of Hush Puppies, but only 10 percent of the population had bought a pair. The buyers had higher than average income and education, and their occupation generally was as a professional or skilled worker. The com-

EXHIBIT 3

1963 consumer research on Hush Puppies' buyers

	Percent in United States	Percent of Hush Puppies' buyers
Sex		
Men...	48%	43%*
Women...	52	57*
	100%	100%
Household income		
Under $3,000...	20	7
$3,000–5,000...	19	13
$5,000–7,500...	22	31
$7,500–10,000...	21	28
Over $10,000...	18	21
	100%	100%
Occupation (head of household)		
Professional/technical/merchants/ official/proprietor...	19	30
Skilled/foreman/craftsman...	15	20
Sales-clerical...	10	20
Unskilled/operatives...	20	11
Farmer...	6	1
Service...	5	6
Others...	25	12
	100%	100%
Education (head of household)		
Grade school...	33	8
High school...	46	52
College...	21	40
	100%	100%
Age 18 years and older		
Under 25 years...	14	9
25–34 years...	20	25
35–44 years...	21	34
45–54 years...	18	21
55 and over...	27	11
	100%	100%

* Many of these were purchased for others. (See Exhibit 4.)

EXHIBIT 4
Person for whom Hush Puppies were purchased by men versus women

	Percent of total buyers	Percent of men buyers	Percent of women buyers
For self only......................	46%	66%	32%
For self and others...............	18	12	22 .
For others only..................	36	22	46
	100%	100%	100%

pany, for the first time, really knew who was buying Hush Puppies. When they asked these people why they bought Hush Puppies, comfort kept coming back, followed by light weight and long wear. The company could now plan marketing strategy based on knowledge of both buyers and non-buyers.

MARKETING STRATEGY, 1963–1966

Armed with the information about the consumer, the company was now better able to plan its marketing strategy. To increase the reach and frequency against the new target market, the company began using television in 1964. The "Today" and "Tonight" programs, whose viewers closely matched Hush Puppies' new target market, were tested and subsequently added. This was designed to increase brand awareness and emphasize the comfort theme. It also gave the advertising program some continuity, instead of only the four "waves" per year provided by the Sunday supplement advertisements. Specific advertising objectives were set, and progress was measured. Magazines were added to the media plan to even more effectively reach the newly defined target audience. The following is a list of magazines which were used: *Good Housekeeping, Parents', Jack and Jill, Esquire, Playboy, True, Mademoiselle, Glamour, Redbook, Seventeen, Ebony, Sports Illustrated,* and *Family Circle.*

The company continued to use *Family Weekly, This Week, Parade,* and other Sunday supplements at the beginning of each season to introduce the new styles and to provide a promotional peak for retail tie-in advertising.

The consumer study also resulted in a change in Hush Puppies' copy strategy. The 1964 ads stressed the comfort of Hush Puppies, and in 1965 the theme, "Hush Puppies make the sidewalks softer," was created and used to illustrate and communicate this comfort.

The company's distribution structure now included 15,000 retail accounts consisting of 60 percent shoe stores and 40 percent department stores (which did 60 percent of the Hush Puppies volume). The company maintained its selective distribution policy which was somewhat unusual in the shoe industry, where it was common for a company to have several different labels for their shoes, giving each retailer an exclusive franchise for one of the labels. Another unusual aspect of Hush Puppies' distribution strategy was that some of their biggest competitors were also their biggest customers, through their retail store subsidiaries.

Wolverine had maintained the same $9.95 price from 1959 until 1965. At that time, rising costs forced an increase to $11.95. It was not felt that this increase would hurt sales as the company still had no strong competition in the quality, lower priced, leisure shoe market.

The company's strategy continued to be successful. Sales grew from $39 million in 1963 to $55.4 million in 1965. Profits nearly doubled. The company had gone from 63d in the industry in 1958 to 6th in the industry at the end of 1965. Eighty-four percent of the adult population was now aware of the brand name and 22 percent of them had now purchased at least one pair.

PRESENT SITUATION

By the beginning of 1968, things had changed considerably. Hush Puppies' sales were down from the 1966 level, and total company profits were down 40 percent. Selected financial information for this period is included in Exhibit 5. Increased competition and rising raw material costs were

EXHIBIT 5
Selected financial information

	Sales (000)	Profits (000)	Percent of profits	Assets (000)	Share-holders' equity (000)	Earnings per share
1963	$39,021	$2,527	6.5%	$19,180	$10,424	$0.84
1964	49,083	4,148	8.5	25,080	13,690	1.37
1965	55,357	4,797	8.7	28,266	17,280	1.59
1966	55,813	3,796	6.8	35,393	19,567	1.26
1967	54,839	2,857	5.2	38,295	20,916	0.95

Source: Wolverine World Wide, Inc. *Annual Report,* 1968.

known contributors to the present financial situation. The management reviewed recent research to find other causes of the leveling off of sales and to find ways to change the marketing strategy to renew the company's growth.

By early 1967, 88 percent of the adult population was aware of the Hush Puppies name and 40 percent had purchased at least one pair (see Exhibit 6). Thus, the percentage of the population which had purchased

EXHIBIT 6

	Percent 1967	Percent 1965	Percent 1964	Percent 1963
Awareness of Hush Puppies brand name (total unaided and aided)				
Have heard of Hush Puppies............................	88%	84%	67%	61%
Have not heard of Hush Puppies............................	12	16	33	39
Base: Total respondents..............	(1,234)	(17,685)	(70,420)	(68,409)
Prior purchase of Hush Puppies (1967 compared with prior years)				
Have purchased Hush Puppies............................	40	22	15	10
Have never purchased Hush Puppies.....................	60	78	85	90
Base: Total respondents..............	(1,234)	(14,855)	(47,181)	(41,729)

at least one pair of Hush Puppies had increased sharply in the past few years, and the company management and the advertising agency were concerned with market saturation and what marketing strategy to use to expand sales and profits.

Exhibit 7 revealed another related problem. Fewer former buyers were

EXHIBIT 7
Composition of total franchise (by new, repeat, and former customers)

	Percent in 1967	Percent in 1965	Percent in 1964
New buyers in past year......................	21%	30%	33%
Former buyers, bought in past year..........	16	34	34
Former buyers, prior years but not in past year...................................	63	36	33
	100	100	100
Base: Total buyers.........................	(492)	(3,850)	(10,789)

continuing to buy new pairs. Exhibit 8 showed one possible reason why. Previous buyers who had their Hush Puppies for over one year were not wearing them for as many or as dressy occasions as new buyers. One of the product's advantages, its resistance to wearing out, was apparently hurting repeat buying. The older pairs were being used for painting, mowing the lawn, and so on. The shoes were being downgraded in their usage. However, because the shoes were not worn out, the owners were not buying new pairs.

EXHIBIT 8

Occasions or purposes for which Hush Puppies are worn (1967 new buyers in past years versus other buyers in 1967 study, in percent)

Occasions	Men buyers			Women buyers		
	New in past year	All others	Differ- ence	New in past year	All others	Differ- ence
Grocery shopping..................	90	54	36	85	66	19
In-town shopping..................	81	48	33	71	44	27
Evening out at friends.............	78	47	31	51	38	13
A PTA meeting.....................	52	29	23	43	27	16
At regular work...................	51	33	18	57	41	16
Church............................	35	19	16	25	12	13
A wedding.........................	13	8	5	6	4	2
Don't know/no answer..............	4	28	24	1	27	26
Base: Total buyers................	(83)	(126)		(79)	(204)	

The executives also reviewed the reasons why people purchased and did not purchase Hush Puppies. This information is in Exhibits 9 and 10. Comfort continued to be the outstanding reason for purchase, but dislike of style was the most important reason for not purchasing Hush Puppies.

After reviewing this information, the executives were trying to find good solutions to the problems they faced. They wondered if they should change the copy approach from the present "comfort" appeal. Should the media

EXHIBIT 9

Hush Puppies' product image—February 1967 (men only)

Why purchased: (major reasons)

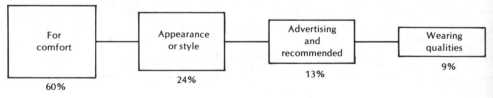

For comfort	Appearance or style	Advertising and recommended	Wearing qualities
60%	24%	13%	9%

Why not purchased: (major reasons)

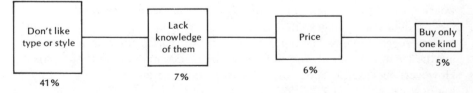

Don't like type or style	Lack knowledge of them	Price	Buy only one kind
41%	7%	6%	5%

EXHIBIT 10
Hush Puppies' product image—February 1967 (women only)

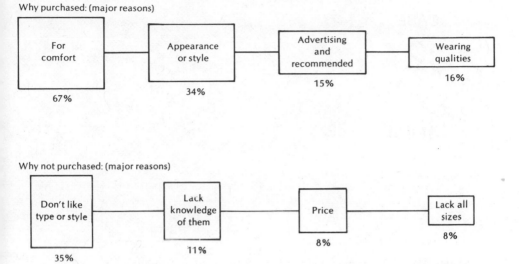

Why purchased: (major reasons)

For comfort	Appearance or style	Advertising and recommended	Wearing qualities
67%	34%	15%	16%

Why not purchased: (major reasons)

Don't like type or style	Lack knowledge of them	Price	Lack all sizes
35%	11%	8%	8%

strategy be changed, dropping the Sunday supplements, magazines, or both? Should the product itself be changed? In effect, the executives were wondering what changes in their marketing strategy were necessary in light of this new information.

12

Amtrak

In late 1975, the management of Amtrak faced a number of major decisions concerning their Detroit-Chicago route. They were considering purchasing a number of new Amfleet trains to put on this run. There were also questions about what services to offer on these trains if they were purchased.

HISTORY OF AMTRAK

Amtrak was established through federal legislation on April 30, 1971, as a last-ditch attempt to revitalize inter-city rail service in the United States. Railroads, during the previous ten years, had found it difficult to compete with other modes of transportation—in particular, the private automobile (and the new interstate highway system it used), and the jet aircraft in domestic service. Travel by rail in the United States had declined from 70 percent of all inter-city travel in 1947, to less than 5 percent in 1971.

Amtrak, a single nationwide passenger rail system, was designed to lure travelers back to the rails. In an era of increasing awareness of energy limitations, and of ever-growing numbers of people utilizing modes of transport other than the auto, revitalization of American rail service was viewed as a necessity. Amtrak's goal was increased ridership through refurbished equipment, modernization of terminal facilities, speed increases, and greater overall convenience.

At the time of the Amtrak takeover, no inter-city passenger rail cars had been built in ten years, and no passenger technology existed in the country to design and build modern cars. Stations were antiquated and without modern facilities of any kind in many cases. Equipment was in an almost constant state of malfunction, and was seldom cleaned. Connections were often impossible, or highly inconvenient. Rail service held little attraction for anyone except fearful flyers and train buffs. The National Railroad Passenger Corporation (Amtrak's official name) had its hands full.

For the purpose of service development, the various railroad lines and routes were divided into two categories: long-haul services and short- and medium-distance corridors. Long hauls were generally those routes of 700 or more miles, serviced by overnight or two day trains (e.g., The Broadway Limited, 900 miles, 17 hours, overnight between Chicago and New York). Corridors were lines over which several trains a day in each direction were operated. In particular, the corridors of less than 300 miles were thought to be ideally suited for high-quality, high-speed service, which could compete with the airlines. This style service if implemented, it was reasoned, could attract business travelers and others for whom travel time was of great importance. Amtrak had a good reason to believe this would work too: the New York–Washington corridor had offered such service since 1969—the Metroliners—and was very successful.

THE DETROIT-CHICAGO CORRIDOR

In the case of the Detroit-Chicago corridor (279 miles), Amtrak saw an opportunity to duplicate the fine operation between New York and Washington. As late as the early 1960s, the New York Central Railroad (which originally operated Amtrak's Detroit-Chicago line) had offered high-quality rail service on the route. Running times between the two cities were as fast as four and a half hours, and luxurious meal and parlor car service was offered. With the completion of Interstate 94 through to Detroit from Chicago, and the introduction of the 727 jet on "short-hop" flights, much of the market for this type of service disappeared. The train was no longer fast enough. As travel volume dwindled, services were cut.

First the parlor cars (first-class service aimed toward business travelers) came off, then the diners with their sitdown meal service. Coaches and snack bars remained. When Penn Central was formed in 1967 (via the merger of the Pennsylvania and New York Central Railroads), high losses were viewed as reason to further cut service quality. Car cleaning was minimized, maintenance became irregular. In 1969, running times were lengthened to five and a half hours. The Penn Central in its annual report served notice it wanted as few passenger trains as possible. Just prior to Amtrak's takeover of the route, Penn Central offered three trains in each direction a day over the route, one without food service at all, the other two with limited snack service. On-time performance was poor. Rats were once reported in the coaches. The service offered was as poor as it could possibly be.

On May 1, 1971, Amtrak took over this corridor. And as with many routes throughout the country, its first major step was to cut the frequency of service. Thereafter, two trains a day in each direction operated between the two cities. It was, according to Amtrak, a temporary economy move to limit the deficit. Further, said Amtrak in newspaper advertising, the remaining trains would be vastly improved.

Improvement was first accomplished by running the trains (the *Wolverine* and the *Saint Clair*) with cars from the C&O Railroad. Its equipment was in far better shape than the Penn Central's, which was immediately withdrawn from service to be rebuilt. The replacement equipment was more comfortable and better maintained, but meal service was still very limited. The schedule remained five and a half hours from endpoint to endpoint. Amtrak also began an advertising program in Detroit, basically just to tell people that the trains were there (many had forgotten or didn't know rail service existed to Chicago). As with other areas of the country, Amtrak promised refurbished cars within a year. The result was a stop in the decline of ridership, and a gradual turnaround by the end of the first year of operation. Unlike the original plans, refurbished cars began to arrive piecemeal—a car here or there, mixed in with older, untouched equipment. But this nonetheless showed good intentions. Schedules were adhered to better as well, and connections at Chicago were improved. This was aided by Amtrak's consolidation of all operations to one Chicago terminal—Union Station—and the elimination of across-town transfers.

But there were many problems with the initial effort as well. Amtrak operated its trains by contractual arrangement with the railroads—in this case, Penn Central. Because of this, they had only indirect control over on-board staff, and the dispatching and running of trains. Problems en route were handled by the railroad in the old manner—which often meant not handling them at all. Amtrak couldn't instruct attendants as to the way to deal with passengers, because the attendants still worked for the railroads. Amtrak, because of the situation, could say little about service quality or uniformity.

Equipment was also maintained by the railroad. Often, after individual cars had been rebuilt (at very high cost), they fell into disrepair because of continued poor maintenance. The age of the equipment was also a problem. The average car was 20 years old. While pleasant inside and comfortable to travel in, they were too old to be completely reliable. Air-conditioning failed or heating gave out while trains were en route. Since no passenger railroad cars had been built in the United States for almost ten years, no technology was immediately available to construct new equipment.

Stations along the route presented many problems. Without exception, they were run down, dirty, and without modern facilities. The Detroit station, once a busy rail center, was a decaying edifice, vast and frightening. Serving only four trains a day when Amtrak first took over, it was far too large for its task. Located on the west side of Detroit, it was inconvenient for persons from the east and north suburbs to get to it. The Niles, Michigan station had no heat, and in Battle Creek the main body of the station had been closed for several years. Conditions were so bad, several of Amtrak's advisory board recommended that three of the stations be ripped down rather than trying to fix them up, and new ones be built in their place.

THE ENERGY CRISIS

In 1973, after two years of operation, refurbished equipment ran on the corridor exclusively, stations were painted at last, and on-time operation (on the same slow schedule) became a reality. Then, in the fall of that year, the energy crunch descended on the nation. Gasoline prices and air fares went up substantially, and millions of Americans were forced onto public transportation. Suddenly, Amtrak had its hands full. Trains that were never more than half full were carrying three times their normal load. Overcrowding became commonplace. On the corridor, trains were unreserved (meaning that there was no limit on the number of tickets sold per train). Trains that could comfortably seat 300 people were carrying about 600. Food would run out almost before the trains left their originating stations. Passengers, due to the crowding, sometimes stood for four or five hours, or sat on suitcases in the aisles. Personnel became rude and discourteous. Fistfights broke out on occasion between conductors and irate passengers. The refurbished equipment in many cases couldn't take the abuse and wear it received from carrying this many people. The interiors became damaged and weren't repaired. Heating and air-conditioning were as erratic as ever. Malfunctioning equipment was allowed out on the line for the first time in Amtrak history, so that more cars were available to seat more people.

Amtrak received a ghastly black eye during the energy crunch. It was not able to adequately meet the hordes of people who suddenly came back to the rails. The Detroit-Chicago corridor in particular fared dismally in terms of service, with equipment, food service, and personnel getting more complaints than almost anywhere else in the system. But in two areas, things were positive. On-time performance remained good despite the crowds (which often slowed things down elsewhere) and ridership remained high into the summer of 1974.

THE TURBOLINERS

Based on these final two factors, Amtrak made a firm commitment to upgrade service on the route. In late 1973, the corporation leased two French Turboliner trains for experimental use on the St. Louis–Chicago corridor. Since no modern passenger equipment was yet available in the United States, Amtrak went to Europe where new trains could be acquired almost immediately. The Turbos' better schedules, improved food service, and high on-time reliability resulted in greatly improved ridership to and from St. Louis. Amtrak decided to purchase these two and four more sets of Turbo equipment, and to place some of them in service between Detroit and Chicago. In April of 1975, the Detroit-Chicago corridor became all turbo. As part of the service improvement program, an additional midday train was added, bringing the number of trains on the route to six daily; that is, in each direction, a morning, noon, and evening train. The new equipment was extremely sleek and modern. Its exterior was reminiscent of the Japanese "Bullet" train, and its interiors were plush, quiet and featured giant windows and automatic sliding glass doors between each car. Food service was provided cafeteria-style, with an area adjacent to the galley for eating and lounging, and fold-down trays available at each coach seat.

Because of the new technology that the equipment utilized, it was maintained at a special service facility in Chicago constructed specifically for this purpose. Service personnel were specially trained to work on board the new trains and thus the quality level of individual service was vastly improved. The introduction of the new service was accompanied by an innovative and clever advertising campaign on Detroit and Chicago television stations, and on local radio stations along the route. Perhaps because of the new trains themselves, or the extensive advertising, or the added service, or the coordination of the entire promotion, ridership on the corridor increased 72 percent the first month, and over 150 percent within three months. The trains ran regularly at their 300-passenger capacity. They were so successful, in fact, that a whole new set of problems arose.

Foremost among them was a problem related to their new technology. Because the equipment was foreign, it was constructed in a manner quite different from traditional American railway design. Hence, the maintenance people "out on the line" (that is, anywhere but at the service facility) didn't know how to work on the new trains. The troubleshooting manuals on board each train were no help to them either—they were in French.

As a result, if air-conditioning failed on a trip, it probably remained broken until the train returned to its Chicago maintenance facility. Sometimes that meant several trips if loads were heavy, and 300 . . . , 600 . . . , 900 uncomfortable passengers. More than once public address announce- ments were made asking anyone who could read French to come to the cockpit and translate the manual for the English-only maintenance per- sonnel.

The popularity of these trains led to another problem—overcrowding. Unlike conventional American equipment, cars couldn't be added or re- moved from the Turbos. They had a fixed number (five) and a standard carrying capacity of 300 people. They ran as unreserved trains however, meaning that Amtrak would sell tickets to as many people as wanted to ride, and often that was over 300. On weekends, some passengers stood for five and a half hours, all the way to Detroit, or Chicago. Even when there were no technical or capacity difficulties, the sleek, new Turbos still serviced stations in Michigan that were at least 50 years old, and which for the most part hadn't been renovated. Ann Arbor was the single ex- ception, but its refurbished station was far too small for the growing num- ber of passengers using the facility. These difficulties marred the generally good impression the turbotrains gave in advertising, and on the many good trips they made. The public failure resulted in a somewhat negative reputation. This was by no means pervasive though, and the trains con- tinued to do well on the route. On subsequent routes where Turbos were assigned, ridership increased as well, seemingly justifying the argument that if modern services were provided, the American public would travel by rail.

The success of this equipment also occurred, it should be pointed out, without great schedule improvement. Due to track conditions, the high- speed capabilities of the new trains could not initially be used, so it was the trains themselves, rather than their speed, that accounted for their popularity. With track improvement, it was reasoned they would be even more attractive to inter-city travelers.

Research data indicated that the average age of Detroit-Chicago train riders was 35 years old, with about 65 percent traveling on vacations, 25 percent on business, and 10 percent for other reasons.

THE DECISIONS TO BE MADE

In late 1975, the management of Amtrak faced a number of decisions with respect to the Detroit-Chicago route.

1. The first decision concerned the possibility of purchasing a number of Amfleet trains for the route. These trains were being built by the Budd Company of Philadelphia for use on a number of Amtrak routes. Amfleet

trains combined the modern aspects of the European Turboliners (speed, new interiors, standardized seating and food service) with the flexibility of old-style conventional equipment. On an Amfleet train, cars could be added or removed as load factors changed. Since they were American-built, the difficulty of foreign technology was eliminated. In addition, Amfleet trains offered the possibility of first-class, daytime accommodations featuring reserved seats and at-seat meal service.

In order to run three trains a day in each direction, Amtrak would have to purchase four locomotives and 24 Amfleet cars. The average Amfleet train on this run was thus expected to have one locomotive and six cars. Each locomotive would cost about $540,000. The price of cars varied depending on whether the car was a coach, first-class, parlor, dinette, and so on. On average the cars would cost Amtrak $425,000 each. A car would hold up to 84 passengers, with 60 in some cars. The useful life of this equipment was expected to be 20 years.

2. The second decision related to whether or not first-class accommodations should be available on the Detroit-Chicago Amfleet trains, if these trains were purchased. This service would include reserved seating and meal service at that seat. Reserved seats were spaced two together and a seat by itself, giving three seats across the car. About 10 percent of the seating capacity of an average six-car train could be available for first-class service. The incremental cost of meals and personnel to Amtrak of each first-class seat sold was estimated to be about $5.

3. A related decision here concerned the price of a first-class ticket, if such service were made available. The price of a coach ticket was $17.50 one way. This compared to $19.50 for the five-hour bus ride, and $39 for a coach seat, and $58 for a first-class seat for the one-hour plane ride.

4. At first, the Amfleet trains would continue to take five and a half hours to travel from downtown Detroit to downtown Chicago. They were capable of traveling much faster, but track conditions would not allow this. Amtrak was considering spending $3 million on track and signal improvements in the next year. This money and a great deal more to be put up by Conrail (the regional freight railway of the northeast) could improve the tracks such that travel could be cut to under four hours within a few years. The Amtrak funded improvements were expected to have about a ten-year useful life. The management of Amtrak was wondering whether or not they should spend this money, and aim for shorter run times.

5. There were five major stations on the Detroit-Chicago run. Amtrak was considering upgrading them. The cost to Amtrak would be $150,000 per station. The rest of the cost would be covered by the state of Michigan, and local cities. A 20-year useful life was expected on each improved station.

6. Amtrak's advertising agency was Needham, Harper, and Steers.

They had developed an advertising campaign for the Amfleet trains in general, and the Detroit-Chicago corridor more specifically. They planned to use a mix of television, radio, and newspapers. The media costs to Amtrak for the Detroit-Chicago run were proposed to be $300,000 per year.

The management of Amtrak wondered what decisions should be made with respect to the Detroit-Chicago corridor.

13

Marex Communications, Inc. —Telshop*

INTRODUCTION

At the beginning of October 1969, Mr. George Shine, managing director of Marex Communications, Inc., was preparing for a board meeting later that month. He had just received a marketing consultant's report, from which he had concluded that a grocery "Telephone Shop" should be considered by Marex as a spearhead for its computerized Telshop system.

Telshop, Marex's latest development, was a new automated order-entry system, which was designed to create a new dynamic "shopping center" for consumer purchasing by telephone and computer. The system would therefore benefit suppliers to whom Marex intended to sell the system, by enabling them to capitalize on a new market of "telephone shoppers" as well as providing them with an accurate and economical system of receiving and processing orders and of inventory control. In time, as more sophisticated communication devices were added, the method was designed to lead to a totally revolutionary marketing system.

Unfortunately, Mr. Shine had been unsuccessful in his attempts to sell Telshop to sufficient subscribers. They showed interest but felt that the market risks of this radical new service were too great to justify the investment involved. Others wanted exclusive rights to a much larger sales territory than Marex was prepared to assign them.

---

* Copyright by INSEAD—The European Institute of Business Administration, Fontainebleau, France. This case was written by Peter Mayer under the direction of Dr. David Weinstein, Assistant Professor of Marketing, INSEAD. Used with permission.

Mr. Shine, therefore, intended to recommend to the board that Marex itself run a demonstration of Telshop in one test area, to serve as a "shop window" to help sell the new system. He hoped that the success of this operating model would convince potential subscribers of a good return on their investment.

Marex was a successful participant in the growing market generated by the use of computer and telecommunications for data processing. Specifically, Marex specialized in creating systems that would provide data processing services to as yet noncomputerized businesses. These clients would use the Marex IBM 360/65 computer and personnel under service contracts with Marex.

The Telshop system was one application of the Marex method. It seemed particularly promising as retailing experts in numerous publications were forecasting that direct consumer shopping by telephone, eventually with the assistance of TV screens would be a future buoyant sector of the direct-selling industry.[1] Mail order was already an advanced branch of that industry.

Door-to-door selling was perhaps the oldest method of direct selling. With the development of communications and transport, other methods emerged. They included mail order and shopping by telephone. The former was comprised of many small- and a few medium-sized firms which specialized in novelty items such as gifts, books, and records; and larger firms which sold virtually everything. The "big five" (Sears, Wards, Spiegel, Aldens, and Penney) sent out 60 million catalogs annually, selling merchandise worth approximately $2.2 billion. Specialized mail-order houses for novelties, and so on were dominated by the "big six" (Breck's, Foster & Gallagher, Hanover House, Miles Kimball, Spencer Gifts and Sunset House), who, in 1967, had a total of 15.5 million customers and sales of about $100 million.

Both groups in the mail-order business reported an annual growth of about 10 percent. However, growth within mail-order houses selling every kind of merchandise was generated basically by the opening of new catalog-order centers and retail outlets. Direct mail sales of the "big five" represented only 20 percent of total catalog sales.

Telephone shopping was already widespread in many consumer and industrial markets. One basis for this was the personal acquaintance between buyer and seller (regular customers of local garages, spare-part stores, grocery stores, or drugstores). Another use was to meet the fast pickup and delivery needs, for example, in the fast-food and laundry businesses. A few department stores in major cities also used a telephone-sales system.

_____

[1] Particularly encouraging were A. F. Doody and W. P. Davidson, "The Next Revolution in Retailing," *Harvard Business Review,* May–June 1967.

It was generally used for special offers advertised in newspapers and was restricted to customers holding the store's credit card. The customer ordered the goods by telephone, his credit was verified and, upon delivery, he signed a credit slip to be included in his monthly bill. An alternative payment method in some stores was COD (cash on delivery). In this area, computers were sometimes used for sales statistics, accounting, and screening of target groups.

The new marketplace for consumer transactions planned by Telshop was to consist of suppliers grouped by region into entities capable of receiving and sending out orders for consumer goods. It was hoped that a maximum of five suppliers per region would be able to meet demands for all types of merchandise eventually offered by Telshop. These suppliers would probably be responsible for the buying of the merchandise, warehousing, and delivery of orders to consumers.

The Telshop computer system would be used for automatically processing those orders in a number of steps leading to a final order entry and processing. The steps would involve the following computer system:

1. Basic order processing and delivery instructions.
2. Credit evaluation.
3. Billing.
4. Inventory maintenance (updating of inventory stock position).
5. Accounts receivable handling.
6. Sales analysis.
7. Inventory control.
8. Production planning.
9. Management systems.

The consumers would be able to phone in their orders for merchandise which they would see advertised in newspapers, shopping newsletters, and catalogs. They would also hear about Telshop from TV and radio commercials. The option to receive mailed orders had been left open. In the initial stages, access by consumers, either by mail or telephone, would not be completely automated. Initially Telshop sales personnel would enter all orders upon receipt into the automated basic processing system.

Some of the advantages of the method to the consumers were seen as follows:

1. It was time saving.
2. One could shop at one's own convenience.
3. The consumer does not have to carry home the merchandise.
4. There is a clear choice of item.
5. The consumer is not "harassed" at the point of sale.
6. The consumer might benefit from lower prices by taking advantage of special sales offers.

The advantages to the suppliers were seen as follows:

1. The availability of a new untapped market.
2. The facility to sell goods via Telshop to consumers without having the expense of physical display at point of purchase.
3. Because of the limited number of suppliers per region, the supplier would have a competition-free market within the Telshop system.
4. A supplier could use a number of credit card systems and obtain cash periodically directly from them with no further administrative procedures.

It was anticipated that suppliers would not work under their own name, but instead that deliveries would be made under the Telshop name.

The decision to operate a demonstration model for Telshop involved running a warehouse of merchandise, a fleet of delivery trucks, and having sufficient personnel to fill and deliver orders. The Telshop computer system would serve as the communication and data processing part of the facility.

One of the areas the marketing consultant had been asked to report on was the line of merchandise most likely to be ordered by telephone. (Excerpts of the report are in Exhibit 1). From these findings, Mr. Shine concluded that target consumers would use telephone shopping most regularly and with maximum convenience for groceries, and that grocery merchandise was therefore the best fit to be used in the demonstration model.

He was also encouraged by the fact that according to a Bell Telephone Co. report (on a study carried out by National Family Opinion, Inc.), 36 percent of all shoppers were "locked in" (that is, they could not get out of the house to buy goods when required), and that 10 percent of the housewives in the United States would like to use telephone shopping on a regular basis for continuously needed items like groceries.

Industry sources disclosed that, in an average supermarket, a family's weekly shopping bill was about $30–$40. A medium-sized supermarket served approximately 1,200 families regularly and had annual sales of about $2 million. Its cost structure is shown in Table 1.[2]

Mr. Shine assumed his demonstration model would have an annual turnover similar to that of a medium-sized supermarket; i.e., approximately $2 million in annual sales. He further assumed a similar order size and geographical service area. He drew up his calculations as shown in Table 2. Mr. Shine realized that out of the final contribution, he would have to spend some money for advertising and promotion (see Exhibit 3). With respect to computer order processing, he figured the required sales volume would be generated by approximately 60,000 orders. Because Telshop

---

[2] For a breakdown of spendings, see Exhibit 2.

TABLE 1
Supermarket cost structure

Sales...................................		$2,000,000	100.0%
Cost of goods sold...................	$1,570,000		78.5
Gross margin........................		430,000	21.5
Warehouse and delivery expenses...	46,000		
Operating expenses and interest...........................	320,000		
Advertising and promotion..........	30,000		
Total expenses....................		$396,000	19.8
Net profit............................		34,000	1.7

offered substantial convenience to the consumer, he was considering charging customers a $1 fee per delivery to compensate for the processing costs. The costs to process 60,000 orders would be as shown in Table 3.

At the board meeting, Mr. Shine said:

> We can't sell our service. Nobody wants to be the first Telshop subscriber, and the few seriously considering Telshop requested unreasonably large exclusive territories.
>
> OK, then let's do the whole thing ourselves! We can hire consultants to solve the technical problems; we have cost figures on supermarkets, and we have data on shoppers. I am convinced that this system is more profitable than a conventional supermarket. Let's set up our own telephone shop! The idea seems even better if we take a look at convenience stores, offering the same kind of advantages as Telshop—quick shopping and convenience. Do you realize what this means? It means a lot of profit for us and, at the same time, proof of our success to all the suppliers we talked to during the last few months, who are afraid to subscribe.
>
> I already have some contacts with investors who are interested in helping substantially with financing this demonstration move. Now it's our turn to make up our minds where to start, how to attract the con-

TABLE 2
Cost estimate for a Telshop distribution facility

Sales..................................		$2,000,000	100.0%
Cost of goods sold...................	$1,570,000		78.5
Credit card billing costs..............	60,000		3.0
Gross margin........................		370,000	18.5
Delivery costs (12 trucks; $10,000 per truck with driver)..............	120,000		
Operating expenses and interest...........................	150,000		
Total expenses....................		270,000	13.5
Contribution before order processing and advertising costs.............................		100,000	5.0

TABLE 3
Costs to process 60,000 orders (estimates)*

CPU rental...	$24,000
Peripheral equipment rental............................	5,000
WATS lines for communications.........................	6,000
Personnel..	16,000
Rent..	4,500
Total processing costs for 60,000 orders.................	$55,500

* These costs were fixed for each block of 60,000 orders; that is, 70,000 orders would cost twice as much, as would 120,000 orders.

sumer and which market to aim at. In many markets, Telshop is a radically new service, and its implementation has to be planned very carefully. In order to acquire some know-how, I wouldn't object to putting up a joint venture with an experienced supermarket, or any other type of experienced merchandiser. We must move carefully and quickly because we now know that we aren't the first to think about such an operation.[3]

But I'm sure that when we've proved we can operate successfully, subscribers will rush to get in on the Telshop system. We'd better fix up now all the necessary subscription conditions. On the other hand, we must also look toward Europe, where the changeover from the around-the-corner grocery store to the modern supermarket has not yet fully taken place. Here we might well be able to attract customers away from the grocery store straight to our system, avoiding the transitory stages of grocery store/supermarket/Telshop.[4]

EXHIBIT 1
Consultant's report on Telshop and telephone shopping: Summary and conclusions

> There are difficulties in using a telephone-shopping system as a sales medium because of the risk, perceived by the customer, who does not have the conventional means of reducing his risk.
>
> On the other hand, the system offers convenience, which the shopper did not have before. The problem, in brief, is to match the particular array of products which project the least risk with the

[3] Mr. Shine was referring to the California "Telemart" which had just started up a system similar to Telshop in San Diego. This name had been used by Marex before, but had not been protected; and Marex was forced by a court order to use the name "Telshop" instead. An article describing the founding of Telemart is presented in Exhibit 4.

[4] See the "Telemart" article for a description of a telephone-shopping operation in Sweden.

EXHIBIT 1 (continued)

most convenience-seeking segment in the market. This coupling will produce the initial core of customers for the system.

Experience and word-of-mouth advertising will gradually promote the system to additional lines of merchandise and additional segments of customers in the market.

All this will be conditioned by superior service in terms of delivery pickups, well-trained telephone sales personnel, and satisfaction-enhancing on the part of the system.

The suburban homemaker who is under 40 with children living at home is suggested as the target customer, and several lines of products are suggested thereby.

On the supply side of the system, it is viewed that the system can either buy and resell the merchandise or be used by independent suppliers as an additional medium for sales. A primary consideration here is to have enough control of the suppliers of the goods so that all the servicing conditions mentioned before will be met.

Certain promotional and operational implications are also pointed out for further elaboration.

INTRODUCTION

The purpose of this report is to assess, on the basis of studies that were done in the past, the ideal posture or positioning of a telephone-shopping service. Regarding the crucial question of prospective merchandise, studies and investigations available were initially applied to a limited number of product lines. However, as will be shown, the emerging concept can be applied to a large variety of products and services.

In the projected business, the consumer will be able to shop at home by using his telephone. He will talk to a salesclerk backed up by a number of suppliers who will have merchandise ready for delivery at his order. At the same time, the system should serve the supplier with extra sales which otherwise would not have occurred via his marketing channels.

Positioning of the service will yield operational guides for the marketing of the system. This should be done by determining first the amount of information the system planners have to work with and which pieces of information carry most weight. This could be referred to as a "strategy of positioning."

I. STRATEGY OF POSITIONING

As a first step, a "target customer" of the system should be defined. By orienting the system towards this customer and tailoring it

EXHIBIT 1 (*continued*)

to his needs, the system's prospects for success will be increased. There are three alternative target customers to consider:

1. The shopper.
2. The supplier.
3. Both simultaneously.

Let us first consider the implication of starting with the supplier as our target customer. We might then save ourselves the search for information about the individual shopper as a target customer. Our role here would be to define and explain how the supplier would be entering another medium of marketing transactions. This would be especially applicable to the vast number of smaller specialty goods suppliers and stores who depend on orders and sidewalk shoppers.

The problem with this approach is the dependence of the system on the marketing and delivery methods and success of the supplier. The system could not and should not be a slave to the fluctuations of telephone orders to a particular supplier. By having a supplier as the target customer, we have no control over sales, and, further, it would be too risky to have the suppliers turn away from the system in the event that it did not live up their expectations.

Therefore, in order to retain maximum control and to roduco uncertainty to the minimum, we must have as target customers the ultimate users of the system. Once we have enough information about the ultimate users and can tailor the system, the products and the promotional tools to him, we then can turn to the supplier; and with our planning and information we have a much better position to negotiate and control the system. At that stage, we shall be able to assess whether a prospective supplier has a relevant line of products, whether he is able to supply prompt delivery and accept rejected merchandise, and whether his operating methods are adequate.

II. THE TARGET CUSTOMER

There are two major considerations which determine who is the prospective customer, how frequent his telephone shopping will be and to what extent (in terms of product and cost) he will shop by telephone:

1. Perceived risk.
2. Convenience.

EXHIBIT 1 (*continued*)

Perceived risk

The consumer might risk facing detrimental consequences because of making a decision to buy. These consist of:

1. Economic cost.
2. Time loss.
3. "Ego loss" and frustration.
4. Not achieving buying goals.

As far as we are concerned, these risks will either bar him from telephone shopping, or if he tries it once and either one or some of these consequences occur, he will not use the system anymore, and by word of mouth, may even hurt our efforts.

In order to make the transaction, the shopper must reduce his uncertainty regarding possible detrimental consequences. The consumer will reduce his uncertainty by collecting more information or imitating someone credible to him. The common uncertainty-reduction tools which are not available to the telephone shopper are:

1. Personal inspection of the merchandise.
2. Comparison.
3. Reference to sales personnel.

The uncertainty-reduction tools which are available are:

1. Reliance on past experience with product, brand, or store.
2. Reliance on advertising.
3. Reliance on someone else's experience.

In short, we can say that the less the number of decisions the shopper has to make, the less risk he will perceive. Studies and experience show that confidence was expressed in ordering particular kinds of merchandise by phone or mail in two cases:

1. When there was an ability to identify the items by brand, size, color, and other properties.
2. When standard reorder items were involved.

Convenience

Telephone shopping offers solutions to the following problems which the shopper may face:

1. Having to carry the merchandise.
2. Crowds, boredom, and fatigue.
3. Poor or confusing arrays of merchandise and difficulty in finding the wanted items.

EXHIBIT 1 (*continued*)

4. Traveling.
5. Spending time and money on traveling.
6. Inconveniences of making shopping-trip arrangements and then getting to the store.

This suggests that we should define our target customer as one who has to overcome these problems. We have to consider the following attributes:

1. Women with greater than average need for convenience in shopping.
2. Women with restricted mobility because of children at home.
3. Women residing in suburbs.
4. Women who are in possession of means to shop (income, possession of credit cards, and so on).
5. Customers temporarily tied down at home, or unable to get into town for special promotions.
6. Customers who may rely on newspapers and catalog advertising (as TV advertising has proved to be deficient in generating telephone orders).
7. Customers with intelligence and education who are aware of specific brands offered in a market which contains a number of different products.
8. Customers who are educated enough to compile a shopping list and assess shopping needs.
9. Customers who are enterprising enough to be willing to explore this new way of shopping.
10. Customers who are affiliated with formal and informal organizations.
11. Customers who are actively interested in leisure activities.

III. PROSPECTIVE PRODUCTS

A category of products with proven success in telephone shopping and mail ordering was packaged grocery products ordered on a weekly basis, to be complemented by the daily fresh foodstuffs bought in the local grocery.

Studies done on telephone shopping in department stores and mail-order houses have revealed a number of products appropriate to the target customer. As this new way of shopping spreads and is reinforced, other products and lines could be incorporated. The initial products could be:

1. Bed linens.
2. Women's stockings.

EXHIBIT 1 *(continued)*

3. Kitchen utensils.
4. Women's underwear and housecoats.
5. Toys and games.
6. Blankets.
7. Table linens.
8. Children's clothing.
9. Gifts (holidays and family events).
10. Branded small appliances.

It could not be stressed too strongly that telephone shopping involves a high degree of perceived risk which could be overcome in a learning process based upon shopping experience with those products mentioned and involving a minimum number of decisions. The consumer will learn to telephone-shop, and eventually will shop for other products by telephone as well.

IV. OPERATIONAL IMPLICATIONS

1. Advertising
   a. Informative.
   b. Facilitate ordering by brand, size, color, or code.
   c. Easy identification of items should be emphasized.
2. Service
   a. Well-informed telephone salesclerks.
   b. Well-trained salesclerks for suggestion and solicitation selling.
   c. Customer confidence and satisfaction should be increased by the manner in which telephone contacts are handled.
   d. Delivery and prompt pickup service are a major property of the system.
   e. Catalogs should be designed to be personal and of top quality.
   f. Service should be available after hours when stores usually close.
   g. Accurate filling of orders.
   h. An up-to-date inventory status information facility.

V. PROMOTION

1. Two promotional tools have to be used simultaneously at first until a certain momentum picks up. Specifically, we should reach the suburban homemaker, who has most of our target customer's attributes, by way of mail and meetings. The affiliation with formal and informal organizations should help stimu-

EXHIBIT 1 (*continued*)

late word-of-mouth advertising. By reaching wives of professional associations' members, we should increase the probability of reaching the opinion leaders among the women of
suburban communities. Simultaneously, newspaper and other
mass media advertising should be aimed at increasing the confidence in the system as a credible, well-known organization.
This tool could be dropped once repeat-purchases and word-
of-mouth advertising are dominant.

2. Catalogs should be updated periodically, with a sufficient visual
distinction between the issues.

3. The use of the system could be promoted as a sign of sophisti-
cation and a status symbol. For example, delivery should be
very distinctive in terms of delivery packages (boxes, bags,
etc.) and satisfaction should be enhanced with each delivery,
possibly through special courtesies.

4. Distinctive stationery and insignia should be used.

5. The system should have its own free membership card in addition to any credit cards accepted by the system.

6. Salesclerks should be very well trained in order to maintain
contacts in a personal and friendly atmosphere all the time.

VI. COMPETITION

By catering to this particular segment of customer, and taking
into account the target customer's prepurchase deliberations, gaining his purchase activities and postpurchase satisfaction in the
operation, a competitive advantage over conventional suppliers
should be achieved. This has to be coupled with a prompt delivery
and pickup service and rapid order processing. It is imperative to
use sophisticated communications equipment in order to maintain
the competitive edge.

VII. EXPERIENCE OF TELEPHONE SHOPPING

Studies report that telephone sales represent a substantial portion of the catalog operation of the two leading mail-order firms.
They operate separate organizations for telephone shopping and
work directly with the warehouses. Telephone sales of mail-order
firms have grown faster than any other phase of their operation.

The drawback a mail-order house has in this respect is its commitments to its own brand names. The new telephone-shopping system will work with nationally or locally accepted brand names.

In the supermarket-product category, as mentioned, telephone

EXHIBIT 1 (*continued*)

shopping has been tried by one firm, and its success was with that segment of the market which we have defined as our target customer. On the other hand, discount stores in the suburbs have not offered telephone-ordering facilities. This leaves our target customer only with the option of telephone-ordering from department stores, which do not operate as recommended here. This leaves the target customer, which we have defined, with real incentives to use our telephone-shopping system.

VIII. SUPPLIERS

It should not be a problem to convince a prospective supplier to use the system once a prospective customer is presented to him who otherwise would not have bought from him.

The operators of the system could either buy and resell the name brand or provide a tool to the various levels of suppliers to bypass, with additional sales, their wholesalers, distributors or other middlemen.

A possible problem with the second alternative may be the fact that a policy decision has to be made by the supplier which may alienate his middleman.

One solution to this problem is having the alienated middleman also participate in the system on a regional basis, compensating him for the additional sales made by the supplier. Again, the conditions of adequate service and personnel should be met, and this poses a problem of control over the delivery channels that should be maintained closely.

IX. CONCLUSION

The final recommendation of this report is that the proposed telephone shopping should be implemented with the defined target customer in mind, and the types of products provided which have a proven appeal to telephone and mail-order purchasers. The unique advantage of the proposed system is that it provides the customer with a wider range of brand-name products, more easily identified by code or designation, than a conventional department store normally provides, or any of the mail-order establishments have provided to date. Further advantage lies not only in unique ease of ordering, but also in special buying incentives such as clearly defined special sales prices and telephone and personal sales talks from individuals associated with the new system.

EXHIBIT 1 (*concluded*)

The logical approach to suppliers should take into account espe-cially the need for the new system to reduce the complexity of purchasing and packaging the foods purveyed therein. This should be accomplished by seeking a limited number of experienced re-gional suppliers capable of supplying that merchandise to be sold through our new system. These "participating suppliers" should provide goods at a wholesale price and take the responsibility of packaging for delivery. These participating suppliers should have the capability of arranging, through, say, no more than five such suppliers in a given sales region, the acquisition and preparation for delivery of all goods ordered in a designated region.

It remains to be decided precisely the manner of delivery, whether by the participating supplier, a third party, or the new sys-tem itself.

Finally, the new system should have adequate automated inven-tory, ordering, billing, credit checking, and communications con-trols.

EXHIBIT 2
Typical supermarket with an annual sales volume of $2 million—1968

	Net profit before tax	Gross margin (percent)	Percent of sales
Total store..	1.8%	21.5%	100%
Meat..		21.3	22.6
Produce (fresh vegetables, processed meat).................................		30.1	7.0
Dairy..		14.2	10.0
Bakery..		26.2	2.0
Frozen food..		25.2	5.2
Dry grocery (canned and bottled goods, detergents, cigarettes, etc.).................		20.8	47.7
Total nonfood...		27.9	5.5
Health and beauty aids....................................		29.2	3.1
Housewares..		24.5	1.2
Miscellaneous..		29.1	1.2

Notes: Total store margin 1.1 percent higher than in 1958, but meat and produce margins remained steady while health and beauty aids showed decline.

Margins on specific items range from 7.67 percent (cigarettes) to as high as 30 percent (instant milk).

Source: *Progressive Grocer*, 1969 and 1972.

EXHIBIT 3
Selecting advertising costs

Four-page newspaper supplements
   Color.. $10,000
     Black and white............................... 8,000
One 60-second regional TV spot.................. 2,000 (average)
One radio announcement........................ 500 (average)
One-page newspaper advertisement............. 2,000 (average)
Cost for 100,000, 40-page catalogs................ 30,000 (approximately)

EXHIBIT 4
Dialing for the groceries

In almost anybody's dream of the future, the harried housewife never undergoes the agony of dragging the kids through a supermarket. She shops by telephone and television, chatting briskly with a computer that totals her bill with flawless efficiency, and she is forever free from what A. G. Bailey calls a "nerve-wearing, time-wasting, fender-bending ordeal."

If 45-year-old "Bill" Bailey succeeds in his grandiose scheme, the San Diego housewife's dream future arrives late this summer. Telemart Enterprises, Inc., hopes to make grocery shopping by phone and computer a reality for some 3,000 women a day.

A former Beverly Hills advertising executive, now Telemart's chairman of the board, Bailey is busy setting up the company's first $1.1 million operation, with a distribution center that has a capacity equal to ten major supermarkets. And Bailey hopes that by opening day 40,000 women will have paid their $2 permanent membership fee.

Telemart shopping goes like this: A housewife makes up her grocery list from a shopper's guide that lists 3,000 food and nonfood items, each with a code number. Between 7 a.m. and 11 p.m. she phones one of 90 Telemart operators who hooks the call into an audio-response computer (dubbed "Clara"). The computer verifies the order, item by item, and quotes various quantity prices—for a single item, several items, or a case. The cost of the order is given, and a delivery time is scheduled—at least four hours later and within a two-hour target period.

When the housewife hangs up, the computer prints out an order sheet to be filled by warehouse clerks. Clara also figures out which of Telemart's 75 leased trucks should carry the order, over which route within the 415-square mile area the truck should go, and which orders should be loaded first to be delivered last. When the housewife gets her groceries, she pays $1 delivery charge (no tipping allowed) and pays for the order by check or is billed monthly.

"Telemart housewives," states Bailey with finality, "will more than make up the delivery charge by taking advantage of price breaks on quantity orders. Because we do the carrying, she can afford the case of soda or the 25-pound package of detergent."

EXHIBIT 4 (*continued*)

More than a year of research and development of the system has prepared him for almost every argument why the operation will not work. Replying to conventional grocers who say that shoppers like to pick such items as meat and produce personally, he points out that a woman can return any unsatisfactory merchandise at the time it is delivered.

Donald S. Perkins, president of Chicago-based Jewel Cos., doubts that the 3,000 items Telemart will list in its quarterly shopping guides are enough for profitable operation. He notes, too, that supermarkets operate with small staffs—primarily cashiers and clerks who restock the shelves. Telemart will take more people, more salaries, more equipment, he says.

Bailey counters with the claim that the items on his limited shopping list account for 80 percent of all grocery dollars spent in San Diego, and that the list will be expanded as time goes on. Costs of personnel and equipment will be more than offset by savings on the physical plan. "The biggest cost facing a supermarket is land and building. . . . Our one distribution facility is located on industrial land. We don't need a dozen branches to serve a population center."

"Telemart," says a skeptical spokesman for Safeway Stores, Inc., "appears a valid concept for a limited market. We'll keep an eye on it, but we have serious reservations about the feasibility of home delivery for a mass market." The president of one Southern California grocery chain is more direct: "The system is too error-prone. How are thousands of housewives going to get the code on the No. 10 can of corn correct?"

One of those most interested in Telemart is Rolf Millqvist, a balding Swede who founded a similar operation 16 years ago in Stockholm. Hemkoep (Home Shop) has virtually everything Telemart will have, except the computer. It grew from $50,000 in sales its first year to about $6 million in the mid-1960s. But volume has held steady since, and with prices rising about 4 percent annually, Hemkoep business actually has declined. One reason is that competitive supermarkets—and cars to get to them—have increased in recent years. To improve his cash flow, Millqvist now opens his warehouse to shopping-cart customers from 4:30 p.m. to 8 p.m.

Telemart, says Millqvist, is part of "the wave of the future," but he is not sure how far off that future is. He built his store with the idea that emancipated women of today had more important things to do than shop. "I'm afraid the development of the woman's role in society has not come as fast as I had hoped," he says. As for computers, they are too expensive, he says.

Hemkoep makes no charge for the 35,000 catalogs it sends out every two weeks, and delivery is free on orders of $15 or more.

Everyone connected with Telemart is aware of skepticism at home and abroad. But the youthful Bailey glibly talks of spending $20,000 or $30,000 a month for TV spots that will send housewives running to their phones to place "impulse buys."

EXHIBIT 4 (*concluded*)

"Though we rate Telemart as an extremely speculative investment, I've never seen a more thorough documentation behind a beginning operation," says W. C. Richardson, executive vice president of Birr, Wilson Co., Inc., the San Francisco investment banking firm that was going to handle Telemart's private placement to raise $1 million. Two weeks ago, Bailey decided instead to try to sell 250,000 shares of stock at $10 each to Californians—"so that we will have money for expansion." Present operating capital comes from officers of the company and from Food Baron, a San Diego fast-food franchiser.

Another supporter is Rohr Corp., the largest of the aerospace subcontractors which developed Telemart's computer system.

Bailey is scheduled to speak to women's groups over the next few months, introducing Telemart and asking housewives to try it for a month without paying the membership fee. "Our main challenge," he says, "is a marketing one. Our Wheaties are no different than anyone else's. What we've got to sell is service." To be successful, he estimates, he must capture 4 percent of the San Diego County grocery market. John Mabee, president of San Diego's Big Bear Supermarkets who has been watching Bailey in action, shakes his head, "If anyone can sell the housewife on Telemart, Bill Bailey can."

CASE

14

Southgate Shopping Center*

In April 1976, Mr. Dale Schlesinger, manager of Southgate Shopping Center in southeast suburban Cleveland, Ohio, pondered a formidable new competitor destined to open a bare eight tenths of a mile away by the following August. The new competitor was a gigantic shopping mall, Randall Park Mall, billed as the largest in the world. It had been under construction for well over a year. In April, one of the department store sites had been finished, and the Penney store at Southgate closed its doors and moved to the new shopping center. In so doing, the J. C. Penney Co. enlarged its store from 65,000 square feet to 200,000 square feet. The new mall when completely opened in August would have five other major department stores in addition to hundreds of smaller stores.

SOUTHGATE

Origin and facilities. The center is located on major traffic interceptors near an interstate highway. Southgate is presently the largest shopping center in Ohio and one of the largest in the United States. However, it is nothing like the behemoth soon to open. It consists of 135 stores and 1,350,000 square feet of building area; parking is available for 9,000 cars. However, it is old. It was opened in 1955 with 36 stores. Penney's was the first department store to come into Southgate, doing so in 1956 with the same 65,000 square foot store that it was leaving in 1976. Over the next several decades, Southgate experienced several expansions that brought it to its present sales of $150 million a year.

---

* This case was written by Robert F. Hartley, Professor of Marketing, and Donald W. Scotton, Professor and Chairperson, Department of Marketing, Cleveland State University. Used with permission.

187

EXHIBIT 1
Physical layout of Southgate

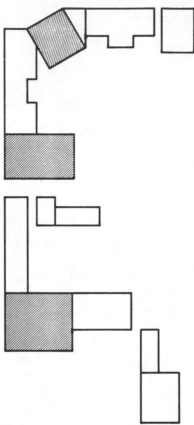

Southgate is not an enclosed mall for the all-weather comfort that is the mark of most new shopping centers constructed in the last decade. Furthermore, Southgate is not even a mall. (A mall center is the prototype for virtually all large centers today. Two or more department stores typically are placed at either end, with smaller specialty stores between. The major feature of a mall is a pedestrian walkway in the center. The entire complex can be enclosed or roofed to create all-weather shopping. Benches, trees, fountains, and "outdoor" restaurants are often placed in the mall. Parking typically is on all sides. The larger malls may have several floors of stores, each opening to the mall.) Rather, Southgate is a strip center that has grown in separate phases to accommodate the increase in consumer demand. Exhibit 1 shows the layout of Southgate.

The stores. There were three department stores: the Penney store of 65,000 square feet, and the May Company and Sears Roebuck stores, each having approximately 200,000 square feet. These stores are known as generator stores. That is, they pull people to them, sometimes from a considerable distance, and thereby contribute greatly to the traffic flow in their vicinity. Typically, in most shopping centers the greatest customer traffic is near the major department stores; these then become vital to the overall success of a shopping center. With the imminent opening of Randall Park Mall, Southgate is facing an erosion of its generator stores. As noted before, Penney's has already left, and as of June 1976, the 65,000 square foot former Penney store was standing vacant. Sears will be leaving Southgate in March; the May Company store intends to remain there, but May Company and Sears are both opening new units in the new mall, only eight-tenths of a mile away. Exhibit 2 shows the directory of stores in the Southgate Center prior to development of the Randall Park Mall.

Draw of Southgate. The major newspaper of Cleveland, *The Plain Dealer,* has for many years served its advertisers by conducting research as to the "draw" of the major shopping centers in the Cleveland metropolitan area. In this research, license plates of cars in the parking lots of their respective shopping centers are recorded and then traced to their home address. In 1975, a study was made about the Southgate shopping center: 6,631 cars were thus observed and their home locations geographically plotted. This study was done long before Randall Park Mall had opened, although it was under construction at the time.

It was found that 42.9 percent of the cars in attendance at Southgate came from more than five miles away. The survey also found that 48.9 percent of the cars were from the suburban communities of Maple Heights, Garfield Heights, and Bedford—these being located either contiguous to Southgate or south and southwest of it. The next highest percentage of cars was from east Cleveland, with 21.5 percent. An analysis of traffic by economic areas showed that 77.1 percent of the cars were from census tracts with median incomes of more than $11,000.[1]

EXHIBIT 2
Southgate store directory

DEPARTMENT STORES, GENERAL MERCHANDISE, AND VARIETY STORES	APPAREL STORES (MEN'S)	
F. W. Woolworth	Bond Clothes	Jerry Mills Clothes
J. C. Penney	Calvin's Specialty	Lyon Tailors
May Company	Shop	Parker's
Sears, Roebuck	Cleveland Tux Shop	Richman Brothers
	Diamond's Men's Shop	Southgate Custom
	Harry's Clothing	Tailor
		Tie Rack

[1] *Analysis of Customer Attendance, Southgate, 1975,* Marketing and Research Department, *The Plain Dealer,* Cleveland, Ohio.

EXHIBIT 2 *(continued)*

APPAREL STORES (WOMEN'S)
Bride & Formal
Klothes Line
Lane Bryant
Lerner Shop
Life Uniform
Motherhood Maternity
  Shop
Parklane Hosiery
Red Robin
Town & Country Shop
Ups & Downs
Winkelman's

SHOE STORES
Dr. Scholl's Foot
  Comfort Shoes
Faflik Shoes
Flagg Shoes
Hahn Shoes
Miles Shoes
Nobil Shoes
Thom McAn Shoes
The In Step

FOOD STORES AND RESTAURANTS
A&P
Arby's Beef House
American Harvest
  Health Food
Blue Grass Restaurant
Butcher Shop, The
Euclid Fish
Famous Recipe
  Restaurant
Fanny Farmer Candies
Fisher Fazio-Costa
Hough Bakery
International House
  of Pancakes
Lombardo's Pizza &
  Spaghetti
Maxson's Restaurant

New York Bakery
Oriental Terrace
  Restaurant
Pick-N-Pay
Teddi's Restaurant
York Steak House

SERVICE ESTABLISHMENTS
Allied Wigs
Andre Duval
Central National Bank
Cleveland Automobile
  Club
Cleveland Trust
  Company
Continental Bank
Cuyahoga Savings
D. O. Summers
Midland Guardian
  Loans
Mr. Angelo Wigs
National City Bank
Southgate Key &
  Shoe Repair
Southgate Laundromat
Southgate Patio
  Barbers
Southgate Village
  Barber Shop
Southgate Village
  Beauty Salon
Sun Finance
The Hair Dresser
Third Federal Savings
  & Loan Association
Travel Agent Tours
Union Commerce Bank
Union Savings & Loan
Universal CIT Credit
  Corporation
U.S. Life Credit
United States Post
  Office

MISCELLANEOUS
Agency Rent-A-Car
Alexander Flowers
A. M. Rose Tile
Bandstand Records
Bedrooms Unlimited
Big Auto Center
Blonder's
Burrow's
Candle Barn
Cleveland Typewriter
Fun City
Goodyear Service
  Center
Great Phone Company
Immerman's Craft
  Center
Industrial Electric
J. B. Robinson
  Jewelers
Jo Ann Fabrics
Kronheim's
Laurel Camera
Leader Personnel
Lemon Tree Cards &
  Gifts
Marlen Jewelers
Mr. Magic Car Wash
Olan Mills Studios
One-Hour Martinizing
Owl Optical
Pearl Carpet
Pet Kingdom
Pompelli Organs
Putt-Putt Golf Course
Radio Shack
Rayco Seat Covers
Regal Carpeting
R.H.P. Auto Centers
Sample House
Sherwin Williams Paint
  Store
Singer Sewing Center
Southgate Beverages
Southgate Cinema

EXHIBIT 2 *(concluded)*

MISCELLANEOUS *(continued)*	Sun Optical	DRUG STORES
Southgate Jewelry	Uniroyal Home & Tire Center	Cunningham Drug
Southgate Lanes	Furniture Land	Gray Drug
Southgate Music Center	Vision Center	Southgate Medical Pharmacy
State Liquor Store	Weight Watchers	

RANDALL PARK MALL

Randall Park Mall is located almost straight north of Southgate. It will have six major department stores for generators, and 260 other stores, altogether some 2.2 million square feet all under one roof. Exhibit 3 shows

EXHIBIT 3
Physical layout of Randall Park Mall

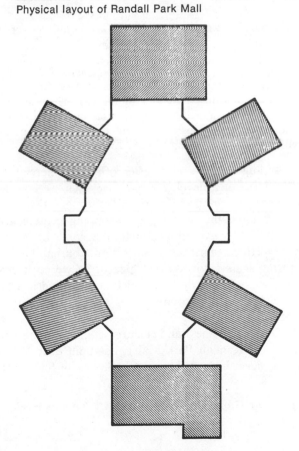

a physical diagram of the complex. Sales have been estimated "conservatively" at $200 million for the first year.

In typical mall fashion, parking in profusion will be on all sides of the complex. The enclosed mall will permit an array of amenities upon which one can only speculate before the grand opening. Two interstate highways are in close proximity to the new center.

TRENDS IN SHOPPING CENTER DEVELOPMENT

Mr. Dale Schlesinger, manager of Southgate, indicated that the trend in shopping centers is toward giantism. But as shopping centers become larger, it seems reasonable to expect that there must be an ultimate limit to size. How far is the average customer willing to walk? How many levels of stores can be piled up without confusing the customer? How many cars can be accommodated in a parking lot before the logistics of parking, finding one's car, and hiking to it will become too burdensome? And how about traffic congestion near a huge shopping center?

Despite these nagging worries, developers are building ever-bigger shopping complexes, and seemingly doing so successfully:

> Billed at the time as the world's largest enclosed multilevel shopping center, Woodfield opened 25 miles northwest of Chicago. It cost $90 million to construct, has 2 million square feet of space, 215 shops and services, and three major department stores, including the largest stores Sears and Penney have ever built and the largest suburban store that Marshall Field has ever put up.[2]

Along with these huge retail centers, often other commercial, recreational, and cultural facilities are developed nearby, such as hotels, apartment houses, office buildings, cultural centers, churches, and theaters. The result is that more and more the newer giant shopping centers are becoming miniature downtowns. A. Alfred Taubman, developer of Woodfield, says: "We are not competing against other centers or suburban business districts. We are competing against downtown Chicago. So we must come as close as we can to the strength and depth of selection you find in Chicago's core area. And if that kind of philosophy means building gigantic centers, then that's what we'll build."[3]

Edward J. DeBartolo, the nation's largest shopping center developer (who is building the Randall Park Mall), has built over 30 large ones in ten years. He has never had a failure and he knows of few. DeBartolo says,

---

[2] "Shopping Centers Grow into Shopping Cities," *Business Week,* September 4, 1971, p. 34.

[3] Ibid., p. 38.

". . . the national failure rate [of large shopping centers] over 25 years has been a fraction of 1 percent."[4]

What kind of a drawing power can a large center generate? Gene A. Robens, general manager of a southern California 1.2 million square foot mall, says: "When you talk about a shopping center as large as ours, you have to be sure you can draw from a 10- to 15-mile radius."[5] For the 2.2 million square foot facility of Randall Park Mall, conjecture is that it will draw from Akron, 30 miles to the south, from Youngstown, 50 miles to the southeast, and even from western Pennsylvania, 70 miles to the east.

REACTIONS OF SOUTHGATE

Mall manager. Despite the looming threat of unknown magnitude, and the actual or imminent departure of two of his major tenants, Penney's and Sears, Dale Schlesinger was not unduly worried. While he expected to lose some business initially, he thought this would be soon regained. He admitted that for the first three months of the Randall Park opening, it would be impossible to compete. The sheer volume of grand opening advertising —both on the part of the mall itself, and that of individual tenants—and the natural curiosity that the general public would have to visit this huge agglomeration of stores, would defeat any defensive efforts Southgate might take at this time. Schlesinger conceded that he was projecting a 10 percent loss of sales the first year after the Randall opening. He expected sales to be back to normal in the second year. "We think Southgate will remain viable, and will even have long term growth," Schlesinger stated.

While the loss of two of his major traffic generators might seem like a major blow to the center, Schlesinger was negotiating with both K-mart and Wards to replace Penneys and Sears. In the spring of 1976, there was still a waiting list of prospective tenants for the smaller stores and shops.

Strengths of Southgate relative to Randall Park Mall. In defense of his optimistic attitude regarding the new competition, Schlesinger noted a number of natural advantages that should accrue to Southgate.

First, he thought Southgate would benefit from a "spillover effect." By this, he expected that the sheer size and resulting volume of traffic drawn to the Randall Park Mall would result in such congestion, confusion, and shopping inconvenience that a goodly portion of shoppers would look around for a nearby and more convenient center to fill at least some of their shopping needs. Because Southgate was less than a mile away, it would be the primary beneficiary of this spillover business.

---

[4] As quoted in *Forbes,* "Why Shopping Centers Rode out the Storm," June 1, 1976, p. 35.

[5] "Shopping Centers Grow into Shopping Cities," p. 38.

Southgate presents its tenants with a definite rent advantage over the new mall. The range of rents per square foot are $2 to $8 at Southgate, versus $8 to $18 at Randall Park Mall. The difference in rents—which reflects the older center constructed at a time of much lower costs—could provide a major deterrent for any Southgate tenant contemplating a move to the new mall. More profit could be achieved at considerably less sales volume than would be the case at Randall. The lower cost structure also means that most tenants should be able to ride out the several lean months associated with the grand opening at the competing mall.

Southgate presumably offers its customers more ease and convenience of shopping. Being smaller and an attenuated strip type of center, customers can park close to the doors of those stores they want to visit; and they can get in and out faster than would be possible in a large mall. Furthermore, Southgate has three large supermarkets and these are big generators of customer traffic on a continuous basis. It is not expected that Randall Park Mall will have any supermarkets, and indeed an enclosed mall is not the ideal setting for such a store due to the inconvenience of handling bulky purchases. Therefore, Southgate is assured of considerable customer traffic regardless of Randall Park Mall.

Schlesinger also cited the probability that customer loyalty built up over 20 years with the "friendly merchants" of Southgate would not be quickly lost. "While customers may initially go to Randall Park Mall out of curiosity, many of them will come back here to buy, back to where they're known and appreciated."

Perhaps Southgate has another potential advantage vis-à-vis Randall. A major part of its customers come from the south. And the new Randall Mall is north of Southgate. This puts Southgate in the position of being an "interceptor." It is sited between a major source of customers and the new shopping mall. Many people may evince reluctance to pass by a shopping center—such as Southgate—to get exactly the same product at a greater distance. Of course, Randall Park Mall will act as an interceptor for customers coming from the north, and Southgate may get few of these customers. But according to the shopping center study of customer attendance conducted by the Cleveland *Plain Dealer,* Southgate was not getting much of this business before the opening of the Randall Park Mall.

Southgate merchant attitudes.   The attitudes of the mall management at Southgate are optimistic. But how about the attitudes of the individual store operators? Are they as optimistic, or are they running scared? In a research study conducted by students at Cleveland State University, 30 merchants at Southgate were interviewed. While part of the interviews are unstructured, one aspect was completely structured. The merchants were asked to check their attitudes and intentions to react on a series of scales numbered from 1 to 7, as shown in Exhibit 4.

EXHIBIT 4

1. What do you think will be the effect of Randall Park Mall on your shopping center?

Will affect severely		Will affect slightly		Will not affect	Will affect favorably	
1	2	3	4	5	6	7

Results: median of 30 responses, 3.5.

2. What do you think will be the effect of Randall Park Mall on your store here?

Will affect severely		Will affect slightly		Will not affect	Will affect favorably	
1	2	3	4	5	6	7

Results: median of 30 responses, 3.9.

3. What changes, if any, do you think you will make due to Randall Park Mall?

(a)

Much more advertising		Somewhat more advertising			No change in advertising	
1	2	3	4	5	6	7

Results: median of 30 responses, 5.3.

(b)

Much lower prices		Somewhat lower prices			No change in prices	
1	2	3	4	5	6	7

Results: median of 30 responses, 6.0.

(c)

Much more merchandise assortment		Somewhat more merchandise assortment			No change in merchandise assortment	
1	2	3	4	5	6	7

Results: median of 30 responses, 6.1.

(d)

Substantial remodeling		Some remodeling			No change in facilities	
1	2	3	4	5	6	7

Results: median of 30 responses, 6.5.

While the range of responses, particularly to questions 1 and 2 was wide, reflecting those who thought the new mall would affect Southgate and their business severely to those who thought the effect would be favorable, the median and the concentration of attitudes was that there would be no more than a slight effect. And the planned reactions to the new mall were generally "do nothing different." Thus the general optimism of Dale Schlesinger regarding the impact of Randall Park Mall on Southgate was supported by a majority of the merchants.

PLANNED CENTERWIDE PROMOTIONS AND MARKETING STRATEGY

The management of Southgate Center conceded that nothing could be done to combat or defend against the expected massive promotional thrust of the grand opening of Randall Park Mall. "Any advertising or other promoting we do for the first three months of the grand opening push of Randall would be simply money down the drain." But promotional efforts are being expanded, both for the period before this grand opening and for the time after the initial excitement of a grand opening has ebbed.

Starting April 12, 1976, more than three months before the scheduled opening of Randall, TV commercials (which are new for the shopping center industry in Cleveland) are planned for the three major TV channels. These will be narrated by Ted Knight of the "Mary Tyler Moore Show" and will stress the convenience and variety of stores and services available at Southgate. These TV commercials will be run over a two-year period, but with time out during the three months of the Randall grand opening.

Radio has been used regularly in the past 20 years to promote the entire shopping center, informing about special events, and in particular playing up the convenience of shopping at Southgate. It will continue to be used with newspapers, the traditional medium for retail advertising.

Southgate has had annual major shopping center promotions that have always attracted large crowds. A Christmas Parade and a Sidewalk Fair have been two of the most successful. It should be recognized, however, that an extended strip center such as Southgate has more difficulty in running overall shopping center promotions than mall-type shopping centers. Malls are more compact, less strung out, and the new enclosed center malls are adaptable to a variety of promotions. Auto shows, art exhibits, minicircuses, special exhibits of all kinds, and many types of entertainers such as rock 'n' roll bands and magician acts can readily be accommodated in the mall. These pull considerable customer traffic which benefits all tenants.

The Southgate management does not plan to permit the center to run down or deteriorate. Mr. Schlesinger responded that external repairs will be made as needed: "We certainly are not running scared." At the same time, there is no need to do extensive remodeling to make Southgate "more competitive." Eventually there may be some remodeling, especially in the area of lighting, but not until after Randall opens and the initial impact becomes more muted.

Admittedly the huge new mall cannot be entirely countered by Southgate. There is no way for it to remake itself into another colossal mall to match Randall. Its physical structure does not permit some of the "extra touches" that developers can throw into a mall, such as fountains and waterfalls; two- and three-story sculptures; trees, shrubs, and flowers; and colorful birds in huge cages. Nor can Southgate match the greatest amenity of all: an enclosed, climate-controlled mall for comfortable all-weather shopping, impervious to rain, sleet, snow, and summer heat.

But Dale Schlesinger is betting that Randall Park Mall is too big for its own good. "After all, a customer needs only so much variety of goods; after that, the additional variety simply becomes redundant." Southgate stands ready and conveniently nearby to catch the spillover of customers satiated with the sheer size of Randall.

15

Colonial Manor Hospital (A)*

In December 1975, Mr. Robert L. Kidd, the chief administrative officer of the Colonial Manor Hospital of Florence, Alabama, was engaged in reviewing the operations of the hospital and drafting a development plan to be submitted to the Administrative Board. Mr. Kidd felt several developments in the health-care field both nationally and locally made it necessary that the Colonial Manor intensify their marketing efforts in the future. According to him, a systematic marketing approach with a specific plan would be essential to maintain Colonial Manor's competitive position in the area and satisfactory level of earnings as a private hospital. He also felt that the hospital should develop both outpatient and inpatient business to fully utilize the hospital service capacity and increase the overall earnings of the hospital. First, he concentrated his attention on the problems of developing outpatient business for the Colonial Manor.

BACKGROUND

Colonial Manor Hospital was built in 1965 as a nursing home and converted to a 79-bed hospital. Humana purchased the facility in 1969, and a 21-bed wing was added, bringing the total bed count to 100. To date, the hospital is operating at 89 percent occupancy and is in the process of expanding to 155 beds.

There are several hospitals in the vicinity of Florence and the Tri-Cities

---

* This case was written by Gerald Crawford, Associate Professor of Marketing, University of North Alabama, and C. P. Rao, Associate Professor of Marketing, University of Arkansas at Fayetteville. Used with permission.

EXHIBIT 1
Geographic location of the hospital

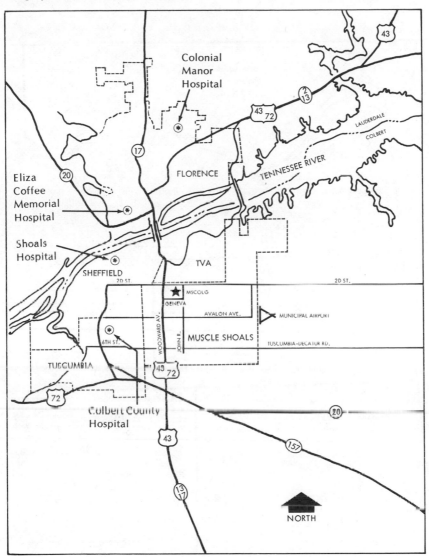

of Tuscumbia, Sheffield, and Muscle Shoals. The Eliza Coffee Memorial Hospital in Florence was the largest with 296 beds. Colbert County Hospital was undertaking an expansion program which would add 80 to 96 beds to its capacity. Coffee Memorial had a physical therapy wing which was affiliated with the Crippled Children's program, and the hospital served

EXHIBIT 2
Geographic admissions summary

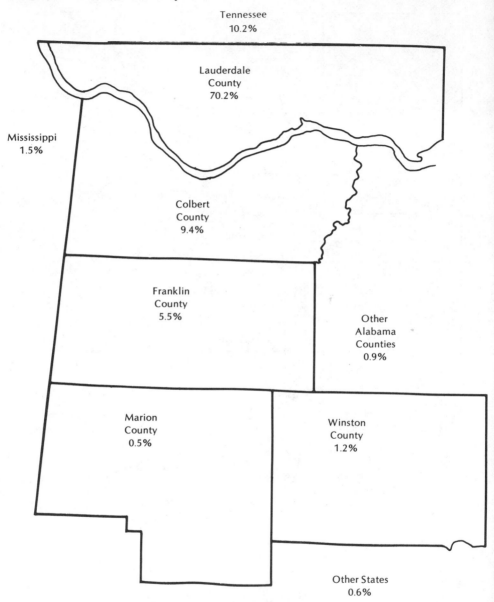

as a regional mental health center and was also the primary community emergency center.

Florence, Alabama, was a community of about 36,200 (1975 estimate) and the county seat of Lauderdale County, population 70,500. The Tri-Cities across the Tennessee River from Florence (Tuscumbia, Sheffield, and Muscle Shoals in Colbert County) had a total population of close to 70,000. Assuming a stable growth rate for this area, the population for Florence and Lauderdale Counties will be approximately 38,500 and 72,-900 by 1980. Analysis of the age distribution in Lauderdale and Colbert Counties in 1970 showed that 9 percent were 65 years or older and the median age was 28 years, compared to 27.1 for the state and 28.3 for the United States. The birth and death rates for Lauderdale County were 15.4 and 8.9, respectively, which were lower than the national averages—17.5 and 9.5. The area was considered a medium income area with 17.4 percent of families with incomes less than $3,000 and 10.9 percent above $15,000. Median family income was $7,608, which was higher than the state figure of $7,263. (See Exhibit 1.)

Florence served as the trade and service center of northwest Alabama extending into southern Tennessee and northeastern Mississippi. It was also an educational center for the region since it was the site of the University of North Alabama. It was considered the "bedroom" community for the executive level people employed by the industries located in the area south of the Tennessee River. Some of the industries in the area included

TABLE 1

Specialty	Active	Associate	Courtesy
Urology	1	1	1
Pathology	1		1
Surgery	3	1	5
Radiology	1	1	4
Opthalmology	1		3
Orthopedics	5		
General medicine	4	4	7
Internal medicine	1	1	5
Neurosurgery	2		
Anesthesiology	1		2
OB/GYN			3
EENT			1
OB			1
GYN			1
Psychiatry			1
Pediatrics			4
Dermatology			2
General practice and general surgery		1	6
ENT		2	
Total	20	11	47

TABLE 2

	1974	1975*
Admissions............................	3,925	3,960
Patient days..........................	31,437	29,724
Average length of stay (no. of days)..	8.0	7.5
Medical patient days..................	8,323	8,898
Surgical patient days.................	6,250	5,916
Gynecology patient days...............	1,074	939
Urology patient days..................	1,136	1,193
Orthopedic patient days...............	14,654	12,778
Pediatric patient days................	—	896

* Through July.

Reynolds Metal, TVA, Union Carbide, textile plants, Ford Motor Company, and fertilizer plants.

Florence was also the center for health care for the whole region including southern Tennessee and northeast Mississippi. (See Exhibit 2.) The medical staff had grown from 52 in 1969 to 78 in 1975 and represented many specialties which drew patients from the entire region. In 1975, two new physicians came to Florence to join the Colonial Manor staff—one was a urologist and the other an internist. Another physician

TABLE 3
Utilization by departments

Department	(1) Inpatient	(2) Outpatient	(3) Total	(col. 2 as percent of col. 3) Outpatient percent
Physical therapy				
7/73–6/74.........................	38,287	8,413	46,700	18.0%
7/74–6/75.........................	31,129	6,952	38,081	18.3
Respiratory therapy				
9/73–6/74.........................	11,123	24	11,147	0.2
7/74–6/75.........................	13,525	2	13,527	—
Emergency Room visits				
9/73–6/74.........................	640	2,222	2,862	77.6
7/74–6/75.........................	1,071	3,467	4,538	76.4
X-ray treatments				
7/73–6/74.........................	7,161	2,141	9,302	23.0
7/74–6/75.........................	7,955	2,913	10,868	26.8
Laboratory tests				
7/73–6/74.........................	83,652	2,940	86,592	3.4
7/74–6/75.........................	95,152	2,984	98,136	3.0
Surgery				
7/73–6/74.........................	1,828	19	1,847	1.0
7/74–6/75.........................	2,111	40	2,151	1.9

also expressed interest in coming to the area. The medical staff of the Colonial Manor and their activity status are given in Table 1.

Colonial Manor did most of the orthopedic work in the community, due to the concentration of orthopedic surgeons on the staff. Pediatric work was increasing especially with the addition of a specialist to the staff. Increased activity in this area was expected to continue with the impending arrival of the urologist who wanted to concentrate on pediatric urology. Eleven physicians had offices in the professional building next to the hospital, and construction of a second professional building near the hospital was under active consideration of the hospital management.

Utilization statistics for fiscal 1974 and fiscal 1975 (through July) are shown in Tables 2 and 3.

ENVIRONMENTAL ANALYSIS

Government-supported programs like Medicare, Medicaid, Crippled Children, indigent programs and others, pay hospitals on a cost basis. With new regulations limiting the number of days that a patient with a particular diagnosis can stay as an inpatient in the hospital, it is necessary that hospitals start a program of marketing outpatient services. (See Exhibit 3.)

EXHIBIT 3
Limits on inpatient costs by government regulations

On April 17, 1975, there was published in the *Federal Register* (40 FR 17190), a notice of proposed Schedule of Limits on Hospital Inpatient General Routine Service Costs for Hospitals with Cost-Reporting Periods Beginning on or after July 1, 1975. Section 1861 (v) (1) of the Social Security Act, as amended, permits the secretary of health, education, and welfare to set prospective limits on direct or indirect overall incurred costs of specific items or services or groups of items or services furnished by a provider, to be recognized as reasonable based on estimates of the cost necessary in the efficient delivery of needed health services.

1. The bulk of the comments dealt with the lowering of the limits to the 80th percentile. A number of commenters asserted that the limits were lowered to the 80th percentile only as a cost-cutting device, without consideration of the financial impact on providers or the possible reduction in the quality of care. Other commenters suggested that the lower limits based on the 80th percentile, with the accompanying lowering of the interim payment rate, would imperil the cash-flow position of many providers.

EXHIBIT 3 *(continued)*

2. Comments were made that the effects of such factors as educational programs, patient mix, or scope of service on the hospital's inpatient general routine service cost were ignored in the revised classification system. These factors were not ignored, but were carefully considered before the revised classification system was issued. It is true that institutions which have educational programs may incur higher costs than institutions without educational programs. However, the classification variables in the new system cause teaching hospitals to be grouped together. The regulations (see 405.460 (f) (2)) provide that, where a provider can demonstrate that its costs exceed the applicable limit by reason of educational activities or by the special needs of the patients treated, an exception can be made to the application of the limit, to the extent that the added costs flow from approved educational activities, to the extent they are atypical (although reasonable) for providers in the comparison group, or flow from the provision of special needs of patients treated and are necessary in the delivery of needed health care.

3. A number of commenters appeared to be under the impression that the limits apply to *total* hospital inpatient costs per day. It should be understood that the Schedule of Limits presented herein applies only to the hospital inpatient general *routine* service costs, but does not apply to the costs of services furnished in special-care units or to the costs of ancillary services.

4. Some parties expressed the view that they have a lower average length of stay than comparable hospitals, due to the more intense services that they provide, and this results in their having a higher routine service cost per day. They believe hospitals with shorter length of stays results from differences in case mix or from the provision of more intensive ancillary services. Since the published limits pertain to general routine service costs, the application of the limits does not more adversely affect hospitals with a lower average length of stay.

5. A number of parties commented that the classification system and Schedule of Limits does not distinguish between whether a hospital is an old or new one. Thus, a hospital with a new building and, therefore, with higher capital and interest costs, may have a higher routine cost per day than would other hospitals with older facilities.

Although a newer facility may have higher capital and interest costs than an older facility, a newer facility, generally, incorporates more advanced design concepts, which permit it to operate more efficiently than an older one and incur lower repair and maintenance costs. Thus, the different cost consequences of capital and interest costs, on one hand, and repair, maintenance, and operation of plant costs, on the other hand, are reasonably accounted for in the published limits.

Hospitals faced another problem in that the Emergency Room and out-patient services often resulted in increased bad debts. Most insurance companies did not cover for outpatient services and others only covered a percentage of the bill leaving a balance for the patients to pay. Hospitals had to strive hard to collect these small balances resulting in increased hospital costs.

Colonial Manor Hospital is also a private hospital liable for state and federal, sales and property taxes, competing with city and county hospitals, not liable to pay taxes. It is necessary for Colonial Manor's rates to be higher, as a result.

Colonial Manor Hospital was located in a better neighborhood than other hospitals in the area and had the room to expand if necessary.

COMPETITION

According to Mr. Kidd, Colonial Manor experienced keen competition mainly from the city and county hospital of Eliza Coffee Memorial. Eliza Memorial had 296 beds and offered the same number and types of services as the Colonial Manor. Eliza Memorial possessed certain medical equipment which the Colonial Manor made use of from time to time.

However, Colonial Manor was in the process of acquiring a new scanner. According to Mr. Kidd, this would enable them to perform brain scans, liver scans and other related tests in their hospital and this would not only increase the inpatient load, but would also attract some outpatients to the hospital.

Mr. Kidd felt that recruiting five to six more doctors should enable the Colonial Manor to compete effectively even after Eliza Memorial expanded their bed capacity. "It is our belief that patients go to where doctors will prefer to practice and we work toward a doctors-oriented policy rather than a patient-oriented one. If we can please the doctor, we have pleased the patient in the process."

ACTION PLAN TO INCREASE OUTPATIENT BUSINESS

A. Laboratory

The laboratory had been operating at a profit margin of 37.5 percent and outpatient revenues in July 1975 made up 4.4 percent of the total lab revenues.

Recommendations for the lab to increase its share of outpatient business were:

1. Request that a laboratory consultant study the current lab situation

and recommend action on some automated equipment for the hospital lab.

2. Pursue agreement with pathologist relative to hematology work to be possibly done in the hospital.
3. Assign a sales representative to approach the nursing homes in Tri-Cities area and surrounding areas about doing lab work, employee physicals, infection control tests, and cultures for them.
4. Meet with new physicians coming into the area to acquaint them with lab facilities and procedures in order to encourage them to use the hospital, rather than getting their own equipment and personnel.

B. Radiology Department

The Radiology Department faced competition primarily from the doctors, most of whom had their own equipment. There were four x-ray machines in the professional building adjacent to the hospital; most of the physicians had their own equipment when they moved into the professional building. The new physicians generally used the hospital radiology department.

The Radiology Department does about 200 procedures a month through the Emergency Room. The hospital had an agreement with the nearby nursing home and a new home under construction to do x-ray work.

The X-ray Department also did some industrial employee physicals for those whose physicians had no equipment.

As a result of the expansion program, the increased patient load was expected to increase the department work load by approximately one third, and the Radiology Department was being expanded accordingly.

The Radiology Department currently operated at a profit margin of 15.3 percent, and outpatient revenues comprised 19.3 percent of the total in July 1975.

Recommendations to increase outpatient business for the Radiology Department were:

1. Pursue construction of second professional building near the hospital for easier access to the hospital Radiology Department.
2. Approach physicians on a one-to-one basis regarding outpatient radiology work. The new physicians should be encouraged to use the hospital, rather than investing in their own equipment. Older physicians who already operated their equipment should be encouraged not to replace it when their equipment was no longer usable. This should not be too difficult in light of increasing costs and possible state legislation requiring inspection and use of x-ray technicians, not just nurses, to operate equipment.

C. Physical Therapy Department

The Physical Therapy Department was performing the largest number of procedures in the county, largely because of the concentration of orthopedic surgeons on the medical staff.

The Colonial Manor Physical Therapy Department did far more procedures than the separate physical therapy wing at the Eliza Coffee Memorial.

Local schools had their own equipment for therapy of athletic injuries. Industries in the area send their injured employees to Colonial Manor for their physical therapy needs.

The Physical Therapy Department currently operated at a profit margin of 54.3 percent and outpatient revenues comprised 13.1 percent of total revenues.

Recommendations to increase outpatient business for the Physical Therapy department were:

1. Contact nursing homes in the area to determine the market for physical therapy for their patients.
2. Contact area industries to determine interest in individual executive physical fitness programs developed by the physical and respiratory therapists. These programs would be developed with the cooperation of the physician who performed the annual physical examination.
3. Work with the Communications Department to develop outpatient brochures for physical therapy that would describe services and treatments and serve as prewritten prescriptions for the patients.

D. Respiratory Therapy Department

In the past, outpatient respiratory therapy work was not actively sought because it was felt that there were not adequate personnel to handle such an additional load. There was no commercial respiratory therapy service in the area, although some people did have their own home equipment. The nursing homes would be the prime places to start by offering respiratory therapy to patients in the nursing homes.

The Respiratory Therapy Department currently operated at a profit margin of 36.8 percent, but outpatient revenues have not been accurately recorded so it was not possible to measure the outpatient percentage.

Recommendations to increase outpatient business for the Respiratory Therapy Department were:

1. Contact nursing homes and extended care facilities to determine their present supplier of the service.
2. Analyze the feasibility, in line with the capabilities of the department,

of servicing nursing homes, and of providing service to homebound patients and of establishing a home equipment rental service.
3. Possibly conduct clinics on maintenance and calibration of home equipment.
4. Work with the Communications Department to adapt standardized brochures describing the services which can also serve as a prewritten prescription and instructions for the patients.

E. Outpatient surgery

Outpatient surgery at Colonial Manor was limited by the lack of space, especially for recovering surgery patients. In the current expansion program, the surgical suite was being expanded and one operating room was being equipped for outpatient surgery with a recovery area.

Physicians had a positive attitude toward outpatient surgery and these procedures would probably increase after completion of construction of expanded facilities. The new urologist indicated that he would want to do some cystoscopies on an outpatient basis and the new ENT men will also be able to use this capability. With the increasing concentration on malpractice liability, many of the procedures that were now performed in the doctors' offices may be moved to the hospital setting.

The high occupancy rate at Colonial Manor and the expected increase in the number of physicians were likely to increase the use of the outpatient surgery at Colonial Manor.

Specific recommendations to increase outpatient surgery at Colonial Manor were:

1. After discussions with the physicians, develop an organized program for outpatient surgery at Colonial Manor, including scheduling personnel, procedures to follow and separate charge structure, and so on.
2. Make a formal presentation to the medical staff on the potential of outpatient surgery, the benefits of the hospital setting over the office for minor procedures, and the program developed at Colonial Manor.

F. Central Supply

At present, there is no place in the area to buy medical supplies such as slings, collars, dressings, braces, and tennis elbow bands on an outpatient basis. There might be potential for setting up a separate outpatient services department which would sell these items including fitting by an ER nurse or attendant.

Other suggestions for increasing outpatient business were:

1. That efforts to secure commitments from one or two more physicians for space in a new professional building be intensified in order to secure Executive Committee approval to proceed with this project. Another professional building near the hospital will provide needed office space for physicians being recruited by Colonial Manor and a built-in market for the hospital lab and x-ray departments. Florence was a regional health center in the area and a second professional building could assist in making Colonial Manor the major regional health care facility.

2. Review the regional lab concept in relation to Colonial Manor and follow up on procuring automated equipment for the hospital lab, especially automated hematology equipment since the competing lab did not have the latter. The increased work load generated by the additional beds could not be accomplished entirely normally. Given the size of the hospital and its high occupancy rate, the lab would be able to generate enough inpatient and outpatient business to justify some automation. Outpatient business could start going directly to the competing lab showing no increase in revenue for the hospital if the lab was not automated.

3. Develop a total outpatient surgery program for Colonial Manor, including setting up a separate charge structure. Presently, there was no other outpatient surgery program in Florence and with the high rates of occupancy of the hospitals, the concentration of health-care specialties in Florence, the increase in the number of physicians in the area and the growing emphasis on utilization of outpatient services, this program will be highly successful.

4. On completing the construction of expanded facilities, encourage groups to hold meetings in the hospital; for example, Weight Watchers, Future Nurses, etc.

5. Sponsor public service clinics such as diabetes or cancer detection clinics; hypertension, obesity, and venereal disease clinics; and pulmonary function tests.

6. Participate in Career Week by having the director of nurses and other department heads make presentations to area schools.

7. Maintain contact with area industries and contact any new industries to determine their health service needs. Consider issuing VIP cards to industry employees with their insurance information which would allow them to be admitted without a cash deposit. Work with staff physicians to develop an "Executive Physical" package.

PART V

DISTRIBUTION DECISIONS

Marketers must make decisions on how to present the products they produce to their ultimate purchasers. Most producers do not present their products to end consumers themselves. They tend to make use of wholesalers and retailers.

The marketing decision maker has a number of decisions to make with respect to the distribution of a product. These include:

1. The types of wholesale and retail intermediaries to use.
2. The number of wholesale and retail intermediaries to use of each type.
3. The number of levels in the channel (degree of directness).
4. The ways to motivate existing channel members to perform effectively.

The first three cases in this section deal with these issues. Beyond these decisions are a series of decisions concerning the physical distribution of the product. These include: customer service level, inventory size, order quantities, reorder points, warehouse locations, and transportation. The last case in this section is concerned with physical distribution management.

The next section of this note is a short reminder of some of the concepts related to each of these decision points.

TYPES OF INTERMEDIARIES

There are many different types of wholesale and retail intermediaries. They vary on the types of products they carry and the services that they are able to perform. The decision on which types of intermediaries to utilize is related to the services that a firm desires to have performed. This is in turn related to the resources and skills of the firm and the needs and behavior of the ultimate consumer.

THE NUMBER OF INTERMEDIARIES

The firm must decide whether to have intensive, selective, or exclusive distribution at the wholesale and retail levels. This decision is related to the quality of support these intermediaries will give in each situation, the ability of the firm to service the intermediaries and the behavior of the ultimate consumer. For example, a wholesaler whom you want may only be willing to carry your products on an exclusive basis, or you may not be able to afford to contact all the retailers of a particular type. Alternatively, consumers may demand that your product be available at all outlets. This may force you into an intensive distribution situation.

NUMBER OF CHANNEL LEVELS

The decision on how direct a channel from producer to ultimate consumer should be is related to the cost of alternative channels, the service and control provided, the characteristics of the end consumer in terms of their numbers and geographic location, the perishability and bulkiness of the product, plus the characteristics of the firm, and competitive activity.

MOTIVATION

Once a channel is selected, motivating its members to perform effectively is an important activity. Motivating vehicles include: monetary things such as margins, allowances, cooperative programs; service activities such as training and technical advice, inventory taking, and display management; provision of physical items such as racks. Also important here are the interpersonal relationships among the people in the intermediaries and in your firm.

PHYSICAL DISTRIBUTION MANAGEMENT

Physical distribution management is a complex area where management science techniques have become important. In simple terms, the decision maker sets a customer service level (for example, deliver 95 percent of all orders within seven days) and then makes inventory, warehousing, and transportation decisions to reach this service level at minimum cost. The customer service level is set by considering costs, consumer behavior, and competitive activity.

CASE
16

Samahaiku Electronics

In May 1976, Mr. J. Akanu, overseas sales manager for Samahaiku Electronics of Japan, was attempting to define the best way to enter the U.S. market with the company's line of solid-state color and black and white televisions.

Samahaiku began in 1930 as a manufacturer of radios and sound equipment marketed in the Far East. In 1958, they expanded into television. Samahaiku distributed a full line of equipment to independent retail outlets who supplied their own service on warranties. Samahaiku equipment was noted for its reliability and high-quality amplification characteristics. Styling was not of major importance to the company. They relied mainly on their reputation for quality and in-store promotion by salespersons who could explain the finer features of the products in order to attract customers.

THE EUROPEAN ENTRY

In early 1958, Samahaiku was considering widening its distribution of radios and audio equipment to either Europe or the United States. At that time, they were a strong marketer in Japan, Taiwan, Australia, New Zealand, and scattered areas of Southeast Asia. In May 1958, the decision was made to enter into full distribution in Europe rather than the United States. This decision was based on two factors. First, many of their present customers had European ties (Australia and New Zealand to England; Vietnam to France, and so on) which they hoped to be able to use. Second, the U.S. market seemed flooded with the full range of radio and sound equipment from the high-priced, high-quality type to the mass distributed, low quality type. All segments had heavy U.S. and foreign competition.

By September 1958, Samahaiku was distributing their radio line in all the Western European and Scandinavian countries with the exception of Ireland and Finland. This rapid distribution had been achieved through the use of Janssen Imports, Ltd., a leading European importer-exporter headquartered in Denmark. Janssen had been able to obtain anywhere from one to ten outlets in each country, usually in the largest city or cities, and usually in the relatively new (for Europe) "department stores."

At the end of 1958, Samahaiku was distributing through 37 independent outlets. Only 28 of these were able to service units under the Samahaiku warranty, and the company was searching for service outlets which could supplement these distributors. In the nine nonservice stores, there was a replacement policy in effect.

Sales to European markets in the last four months of 1958 were 13,500 radios, totaling approximately $190,000 (in U.S. equivalents) at retail. Orders were running well above the sales figures, as Samahaiku was not able to supply the unexpectedly large increased volume demanded.

BLACK AND WHITE TELEVISION

The officers of Samahaiku had, for some time, thought that expansion was necessary if they were to reach the growth objectives of 15 percent per year that they had set for the company. With this expansion in mind, they had allocated money to the development of a black and white television set in 1954. By late 1958, the consensus was that they had a very marketable product which met the company's high standards of quality. Production and marketing had worked together in forecasting projected sales for the next three years for Samahaiku's primary markets. Based on production of three models at an average retail price of $460, sales for the last seven months of 1959 were estimated at 17,000 units and 1960 sales at 35,000 units. The 1961 sales of 42,000 units were based on an average retail price of $450. With the European market estimates added in, the sales figures were forecasted at 25,000, 80,000, and 95,000 units, respectively. The European market was felt to have much greater potential than the primary markets.

Samahaiku management then gave the go-ahead for the long-planned plant expansion which would give the company's two plants total capacity to produce 1 million radios and 250,000 television sets per year, in addition to approximately 50,000 other units of sound equipment. This construction was completed in May, giving seven months of full production in 1958.

Throughout the 1960s Samahaiku's sales increased steadily in all markets. In 1965, Samahaiku dropped Janssen as its distributor in Europe, in favor of a direct selling method in which Samahaiku maintained its own warehouses and sales force.

SITUATION IN 1970

In 1970, Samahaiku was using full capacity at the two plants. Television sales were better than expected as were sales of sound equipment units. Radio sales were down in units sold, but had increased in revenue, due to increased sales of the more expensive AM/FM and shortwave units. Comparative sales are shown in Exhibit 1.

EXHIBIT 1
A. Samahaiku sales 1961 and 1969

	1961	1969
Radio units..............................	675,000	890,000
Revenue from radio sales*..............	$ 6,075,000	$12,460,000
Television units..........................	120,000	250,000
Revenue from TV sales*.................	$13,200,000	$26,250,000
Other sound equipment units............	24,000	37,000
Revenue from sound equipment sales*...	$ 1,200,000	$ 2,590,000

* U.S. dollars.

B. Breakdown of sales geographically (percent)

	Far East	Europe
Radio units................................	70%	30%
Revenue...................................	55	45
Television units	33	67
Revenue...................................	30	70
Sound equipment units....................	28	72
Revenue...................................	20	80

By 1970, the R&D department had developed and tested their own solid-state technology and applied it to black and white and color television sets. The firm had actually produced a few hundred color sets in 1969 for test markets. These models were quickly accepted and the dealers were anxious to be able to sell in quantity. Again, the question of expansion and distribution arose. It was decided that if the firm was to be a successful full-line competitor in color television, a new, modern facility should be built. A new plant costing $2.4 million was scheduled to be completed in late 1972. This plant would be able to produce approximately 1.6 million color sets per year, depending on the product mix. Samahaiku estimated they could produce about 400,000 color sets using the old facilities between May

1970 and late 1972. Samahaiku management had been contemplating expanding their markets as well. They agreed that if acceptance of the new line in European markets met their expectations, their next step would be serious consideration of entering the U.S. market.

SITUATION IN 1975

The new Samahaiku plant was completed in January 1973. Production figures for 1970–74 are shown in the accompanying table.

	Television sets	
	Black and white	Color
1970...	780,000	60,000
1971...	820,000	130,000
1972...	800,000	140,000
1973...	600,000	400,000
1974...	570,000	615,000

Sales were made in all markets, but the European market accounted for 75 percent of the units sold.

The Samahaiku line consisted of four black and white models: 9-inch, 13-inch, 19-inch, and 21-inch portables. The color line had 13-inch, 19-inch, and 21-inch portables plus a 25-inch console model. The average factory price to retail accounts of a black and white portable (excluding freight) was $86. The average costs were direct materials $36, direct labor $8, factory overhead $2, and advertising $2.[1] Color sets were factory priced to retail accounts at $152 (average) for the portables and $300 for the console model. Costs were $68 for direct materials and $9.50 direct labor, plus $2.50 for factory overhead and $3 advertising.[2] Direct materials costs were $80 more for the console model. About 15 percent of the factory overhead and advertising costs were applicable to the U.S. market.

THE U.S. MARKET

The black and white market in the United States was highly price sensitive at this time, and Samahaiku was considering several options including cutting price, selling at a discount to large-volume dealers, paying freight on all orders over a certain amount, or offering special prices on certain models if ordered in quantity. The color market was not as price sensitive. Quality and reliability were of much greater concern.

---

[1] Based on a standard production volume of 600,000 units.
[2] Based on a standard production volume of 700,000 units.

EXHIBIT 2
Estimated market shares of television brands (percent)*

	First set	Second set
Zenith.............................	20.0%	7.3%
RCA Victor.........................	18.9	6.8
General Electric....................	7.4	5.1
Admiral............................	7.1	3.1
Sears (Silvertone)..................	6.8	3.3

* The five next largest manufacturers had a 21.5 percent share of first sets and 7.37 percent of second sets.

The U.S. market was a completely different one than the European or Far East markets. While Samahaiku had only two to five competitors in their Far East and European markets, there were over 25 in the United States. Data on the top five manufacturers are shown in Exhibit 2.

In 1974, portables had 98 percent of the black and white market and 67.8 percent of the color market. Console and combination models accounted for the balance. The 1975 estimates for portables were 98.5 percent and 66 percent, respectively (Exhibit 3).

Distribution outlets in the United States handling televisions were: furniture stores (38,732), household appliance stores (20,262), radio and TV stores (29,890), department stores (11,240), catalog showroom/mail-

EXHIBIT 3
Estimated U.S. television market (units and retail dollars)

	Unit sales	
	1974	1975*
Black and white...........	5,544,000	6,868,000
Color.....................	7,337,000	8,411,300
	12,881,000	15,279,300

Size	1975 dollar sales*	
(inches)	Black and white	Color
Under 12..................	$ 128,072,000	$ 821,800
12–15.....................	289,943,000	237,946,500
16–17.....................	47,232,000	302,280,000
18		49,920,000
19	163,903,500	1,179,920,000
21		44,000,000
23	20,630,500	391,500,000
25		1,201,785,000
Total.....................	$ 649,781,000	$3,408,173,300
Total black and white and color sets...............	$4,057,954,300	

* These are estimates.

order (7,671), discount stores (17,887), and other types (9,874). Sales by outlet type are shown in Exhibit 4.

The furniture stores usually handled larger models, especially consoles. The salespersons were well-informed about cabinetry and styling, but usually not too knowledgeable about electronics. The furniture stores usually sold at suggested retail price, yielding about a 55 percent margin on retail selling price, and offered no in-store service facilities.

Department stores were a large source of sales for both black and white and color sets. The salespersons were quite knowledgeable, and engaged in a fair amount of trying to get the customer to "trade up." Prices were sometimes discounted, particularly in larger chains. The department stores usually got about a 42 percent margin. In addition, they were eager to seek

EXHIBIT 4
Television sales by outlet type (percent)

	1974		1975*	
	Color	Black and white	Color	Black and white
Furniture stores......................	17%	5%	18%	5%
Department stores....................	20	18	20	18
Appliance/TV/radio...................	30	30	32	28
Catalog/mail-order...................	5	4	5	4
Discount chains......................	28	25	25	25
Others...............................		18		20

* Estimate.

"deals" on quantity buys, closeouts, and so on. Most of the large stores had their own service facilities, and carried their own private brands.

Appliance/radio/TV outlets consisted of two types: the discount appliance stores and the regular "retail" stores. The discount houses were high volume, low-price operations which, to obtain low overhead, often had no service facilities for TV. The salespersons were usually paid on commission and were aggressive in selling their higher margin models. Price-cutting was a necessity and dealers often bought in large quantity lots, watching for deals, damaged-model sales, and other ways to cut costs. The typical margin on both black and white and color sets was only about 22 percent in this type of outlet. Regular retail appliance/radio/TV outlets usually had knowledgeable salespersons and large service departments. Margins averaged about 35 percent.

Catalog showroom/mail-order sales were usually limited to a few smaller brands. Little selling at point-of-purchase could be done and no service was offered.

Discount chains, such as K-Mart stores, were a growing force in retailing televisions. Discounters had only lately begun handling TV and large ap-

pliances. They bought in large quantity at lowest possible cost. The manufacturers were usually willing to cut prices in order to obtain large volume
orders. Some of the larger chains were beginning to engage in private
branding, as well, from which they were able to gain very favorable terms
from manufacturers. For example, a U.S. manufacturer who engaged in
private branding for one of the large chains usually obtained a margin
(average) of 19 percent versus 34 percent for national brand sales.
Chains usually required the customer to contact the company or independent service facility for warranty service. Some stores supported "service centers" which would simply accept the set and send it on to the manufacturer for repairs. Selling at point of sale was almost nonexistent at the
chains. With low overhead and low margins (20 percent), the salespersons

EXHIBIT 5
Representative average retail price by type of television outlet for the size of
television sold by Samahaiku

Type of television	Furniture stores	Department stores	Appliance/ radio/TV discount stores	Appliance/ radio/TV regular stores	Discount chains
Black and white portable................	—	$150*	$115*	$130*	$115*
	—	120†	—	—	89†
Color portable............	—	270*	200*	240*	195*
	—	220†	—	—	160†
Color consoles............	$700*	600*	—	—	—

*Manufacturers' brands.
† Private brand.

were usually few in number and rarely informed about electronics or the
differences in major lines. These stores also carried very small lines of a
few manufacturers concentrating for the most part on the low end of the
model line. All the different outlets paid freight, as a rule, with the exception of the discount chains, who, if billed for freight, would simply de-
duct it from the invoice.

Exhibit 5 gives representative average retail prices of black and white,
and color television sets by type of retail outlet. These prices are for the
size of models that Samahaiku markets. Mr. Akanu wondered how many
and what type of accounts Samahaiku should try to obtain.

DISTRIBUTION ALTERNATIVES

In selling to the U.S. retail accounts they obtained, Samahaiku was considering two basic alternatives. The first alternative was to sell through

import/export-electronics wholesalers. These wholesalers would obtain and maintain retail accounts, plus provide warehousing services. Under this alternative, Samahaiku would have to provide its own service facilities. It was felt that two centers, one on the East Coast, and one on the West Coast would have to be established. These centers were designed to supplement retail account service departments. Rental on suitable property was estimated at $48,000 per year for each center. Margins for the import/ export-electronics wholesalers would be 11 percent of the factory price to retail accounts. This margin was given by Samahaiku lowering its factory price 11 percent below the standard factory price to retail accounts. It was expected that the wholesalers would sell to retail accounts at approximately the Samahaiku factory price to retail accounts.

The other distribution alternative that Samahaiku was considering was to sell direct to retail accounts using their own company salespersons. On the average, a salesperson could handle approximately 200 retail accounts. Their function was to obtain accounts, provide promotional displays, technical assistance, and serve as a liaison between retailers and the factory. They would be paid a straight salary ($14,000), plus expenses ($6,000). This alternative would require Samahaiku to obtain their own warehouse space in four locations in the United States. It was estimated that suitable facilities could be obtained at a total cost of $250,000 per year. Inventory carrying costs were expected to be about 15 percent of annual warehouse costs. Service facilities costs would be the same as under the distribution alternative.

Mr. Akanu wanted to begin shipping to the U.S. market as quickly as possible. He was anxious to select the appropriate retail selling structure for his product, and to select the best distribution alternative for his situation.

Pomona Products Company*

In July the officers of Pomona Products Company met to discuss the company's possible introduction of its line of southern vegetables into the New York market. The focus of the meeting was the strategy to be used for the introduction. They were particularly interested in the possible methods of promoting the products and in the channels of distribution to be used in distributing the southern vegetables.

COMPANY BACKGROUND

Pomona Products Company traces its beginnings to 1911, when a young man, George Riegel, saw a can of Spanish pimientos on a grocery shelf in Griffin, Georgia. (A pimiento is a red sweet pepper often used as a garnish, stuffing for green olives, or in relishes and salads.) He and his brother and father were commercial vegetable growers on a farm near Griffin, and together they had worked on improving the quality of vegetable crops, particularly peppers. Through the American Consul in Spain the Riegels secured six ounces of pimiento seed and in 1912 grew enough plants to set out one and one-half acres of pimiento plants on the Riegel farm.

Attempts to sell the pimientos on the fresh market met with no success because of the extreme toughness of the pimiento skins. George Riegel recalled that his interest in pimientos had stemmed from the canned Spanish product, so he decided to attempt the canning process himself. Skins were removed by immersing the pimientos in a lye solution, and after cleaning they were canned with salt and vinegar. The use of lye proved so

---

* This case was co-authored by John S. Wright, Professor of Marketing, Georgia State University.

tedious that the help of the Spanish Consul was again sought, and he reported that the skins in Spain were removed by roasting the pimientos for several minutes in a hot oven and wiping off charred skins with clean cloths.

The roasting operation proved far more satisfactory and by 1913 Mark Riegel perfected a mechanical roaster. It consisted of a coke-burning tunnel of fire brick, through which the cored pimientos passed, each placed over a steel spike fastened to an endless chain. The charred skins were then removed by sprinkler washers and brushes, with the final cleaning done by hand.

Finding the new roaster satisfactory, the Riegels continued their research on canning pimientos in a small shed on a farm near Pomona, Georgia, a few miles from Griffin. During the summer of 1914 they put up a small pack of pimientos in this little plant and the H. V. Kell Wholesale Grocery Company of Griffin marketed the entire pack.

An executive who was associated with the wholesaler became interested in the new pimiento cannery after his success in selling the first can of pimientos. He offered to provide financing for two additional roasters and a plant, to be built on his farm. Plans were made and the Pomona Products Company's first plant was built and equipped. The plant was an extremely large food-processing facility relative to the standards of that day.

Pimientos were first canned in the new plant in 1916 and sold under the Sunshine brand name. The total crop that year came from 75 acres, all located in Spalding County, of which Griffin is the county seat.

In 1920, the company was sold and the plant was moved several miles to Griffin where gas was available to provide fuel for the huge roasting ovens which charred the skins so they could be removed from the pimientos.

In spite of the problems faced by a new company processing a new product, Pomona Products Company grew and prospered. There were bleak years—when the pimiento crop was too short to produce a profitable pack. But the bad years were outnumbered by the good years and pimiento volume climbed steadily. Pomona's success led to the entry of other canners in the pimiento field, and over the years as many as 18 or 20 firms were in the business at one time. Growing of pimientos by farmers, once limited entirely to Georgia, now extends into several adjoining states and California.

To reduce its dependency on a single product, Pomona began processing and packing a number of southern fruits and vegetables which were also marketed under the Sunshine brand name. Currently, about 20 different fruits and vegetables are processed and canned including turnip greens, green beans, pickled peaches, potatoes, squash, rutabagas, and several varieties of peas and beans.

In 1955, Pomona Products Company became a subsidiary of Stokely-

Van Camp, Inc., of Indianapolis, Indiana. The Pomona Division is operated with a large degree of independence, but the relationship has given the firm greater resources for expanding their business. Stokely-Van Camp sales were over $200 million. Sales for the Pomona Products Company were approximately $5 million per year.

BACKGROUND OF THE PRODUCT LINE

The Pomona product line could be categorized into the following groups of products:

1. Pimientos.
2. Green beans.
3. Greens—turnip greens, collard greens, mustard greens, and so forth.
4. Potatoes.
5. Miscellaneous southern vegetables—field peas, squash, rutabagas, and so on.
6. Pickled peaches.

A list of products sold by Pomona, together with the share of company sales, is presented in Exhibit 1.

Data on the total market for the individual products was difficult to compile because the trade association, the National Canners Association, included most of Pomona's products in the "Miscellaneous Vegetables"

EXHIBIT 1
Sales breakdown by products

Commodity	Total case sales	Percent of total
Pimientos...........................	642,633	35.3%
Turnip greens......................	297,076	16.3
Green beans.......................	204,924	11.3
Pork and beans....................	175,766	9.6
Pickled peaches...................	110,284	6.0
Collard greens....................	60,709	3.3
White potatoes....................	58,049	3.2
Beans and potatoes................	51,761	2.8
Black-eyed peas...................	42,925	2.3
Mustard greens....................	30,902	1.7
Squash............................	30,248	1.7
Field peas........................	29,189	1.6
Spinach...........................	24,534	1.3
Rutabagas.........................	23,044	1.3
Mixed greens......................	12,758	0.7
Boiled peanuts....................	11,467	0.6
Lady peas.........................	6,910	0.3
Kale..............................	5,597	0.3
White acre peas...................	3,259	0.2
Kidney beans......................	2,413	0.1
Green and shelled beans...........	1,772	0.1
Total.........................	1,821,220	100.0%

EXHIBIT 2

Seasonal shipping index for Pomona Products retail size pimientos, greens, and green beans

	Pimientos	Greens	Green beans
Average month................	100	100	100
June.........................	87	63	64
July.........................	98	60	56
August.......................	148	102	95
September....................	82	128	93
October......................	125	137	122
November.....................	57	70	83
December.....................	82	72	68
January......................	134	142	132
February.....................	94	152	132
March........................	94	72	149
April........................	91	81	83
May..........................	113	114	78

category, which contained a wide variety of unrelated products. The director of marketing for Pomona estimated that the company had about 35 percent of the pimiento market, about one third of the leafy greens market, and less than 1 percent of the total market for green beans and Irish potatoes.

The product line contained a number of products which are very seasonal in nature. Exhibit 2 contains a seasonal shipping index by month for the company's three major product types.

EXHIBIT 3

Pomona Products sales by state, top ten states

Rank and state	Percent of total sales
1. Georgia................................	25%
2. Texas..................................	16*
3. Florida................................	14
4. North Carolina.........................	7
5. Alabama................................	7
6. South Carolina.........................	4
7. Tennessee..............................	3
8. Mississippi............................	2
9. Virginia...............................	2
10. Illinois...............................	1
Other states...........................	19
	100%

* Pimientos are 90 percent of the sales in Texas.

In addition to being concentrated in several seasons, the sales were concentrated by geographic area. Approximately 70 percent of Pomona's sales came from five states—Georgia, Texas, Florida, North Carolina, and Alabama. Exhibit 3 shows the sales breakdown by state.

Exhibit 4 contains an analysis, by product, of Pomona's strengths and weaknesses together with comments on the company's competitive position. Exhibit 5 presents information on each of the company's major competitors for pimientos and for southern vegetables.

EXHIBIT 4
Analysis of Pomona Products Company (PPC) market position

In terms of strength and weakness in sales, product, manufacturing, and marketing we rate our market position by category as follows:

	Category	Sales	Product	Manu-facturing	Marketing	Overall
1.	Pimientos	+	+	+	0	+
2.	Greens	+	+	+	0	+
3.	Spinach	−	0	+	0	0
4.	Green beans	−	−	+	0	−
5.	Green beans with potatoes	+	+	+	0	+
6.	Irish potatoes	−	0	−	0	−
7.	Miscellaneous seasonal vegetables	+	+	0	0	+
8.	Pickled peaches	+	+	+	+	++
9.	Nonseasonal vegetables	−	−	−	0	−

+ = strength; − = weakness; 0 = no special strength or weakness.

Most products suffer from a "commodity" image in the minds of retail and wholesale customers, and probably consumers. There are no apparent or significant differences in product quality or packaging of most items compared to major competition. Specific exceptions are turnip greens with diced turnips, green beans with potatoes, and pickled peaches. These specialty or combination items enjoy "brand" status and are among our leading volume and profit producers.

PPC is an unquestioned leader in the domestic pimiento industry.

PPC is probably the largest processor of leafy greens excluding spinach in the United States.

PPC has an exclusive product in pickled peaches, distinctive from spiced peaches. This item is extremely strong in the Southeast.

PPC was the first canner of turnip greens with diced turnips and has achieved strong distribution for the product.

Green beans with potatoes have responded to special sales effort in recent years and are in a fairly strong position.

In miscellaneous seasonal vegetables, rutabagas enjoy a unique position. Distribution is very good and volume is steadily increasing.

EXHIBIT 5
Pomona Products competition

I. *Pimientos*
   A. *National Biscuit Company,* Special Products Division, Woodbury, Ga. Dromedary brand. NBC is probably the largest domestic pimiento processor. National distribution. Strong franchise, sound pricing. An industry leader. Marketing headquarters in NYC.
   B. *Cherokee Products Co.,* Haddock, Ga. "O'Sage" brand and buyer's label. Strong regional competitor. Strength in Southeast especially with Winn-Dixie. Spotty distribution outside Southeast (New York City and Pacific Coast). A price follower.
   C. *King Pharr Canning Operations, Inc.,* Cullman, Ala. "King Pharr" and "Miss America" brands and buyer's label. Third or fourth largest Southeast processor. Follows industry pricing but makes exceptions through advertising rebates, promotion agreements, etc. A boat rocker.
   D. *Besco Products Co.,* Zebulon, Ga. "Miss Georgia" brand. Small packer. Price follower.
   E. *Monticello Canning Co.,* Crossville, Tenn. "Betty Ann" brand. Small packer. Follows industry pricing. Strong in Nashville, Chicago.
   F. *Heublein, Inc.,* Coastal Valley Canning Co. Division, Oxnard, Calif. "Ortega" brand. Largest Pacific Coast packer. Distribution generally west of Rocky Mountains and Houston. Marketing decisions made in East by Heublein.
II. *Southern vegetables*
   A. *Bush Bros.,* Dandridge, Tenn. "Bush's Best" and "Showboat" brands. A strong, multiline, reputable competitor. Very strong in green beans, greens, and dry packs. Stable pricing. Good trade reputation. Primary distribution in South and Midwest.
   B. *King Pharr Canning Operations, Inc.,* a multiline packer. Erratic pricing. Does not have a high-quality image with trade.
   C. *HLH Products, Inc.,* Dallas, Texas (plant in Sanford, Florida). Full-line packer of green beans, greens, and dry packs. Price-cutter and dealer. Not known as quality packer.
   D. *Miscellaneous other canners* include *Steel Canning Co.,* Springdale, Ark.; *Allen Canning Co.,* Siloam Springs, Ark.; *Besco Products Co.; Cherokee Products Co.* These are competitors on one or two items but not the full line of our products. The Arkansas packers are strong, low-price competitors on greens outside the Southeast.

POMONA PRODUCTS' MARKETING STRATEGY

The company defined its customers as retail and institutional grocery distributors and food manufacturers in the United States (excluding New Mexico, Arizona, Nevada, California, Oregon, Washington, and Alaska). Pimientos were marketed nationally, with the above exceptions, and the line of southern vegetables were marketed from Washington, D.C., to San Antonio. The products were not marketed on the West Coast because there was a strong competitor located there. With the high shipping costs, the price Pomona would have to charge would be too high for strong consumer acceptance.

Pomona's customers purchased regularly and frequently, usually at least once per month. Chains and large wholesalers purchased more often averaging twice per month. A typical chain would sell about 300 cases per year per store. No exclusive franchises were awarded, and all distributors were considered potential customers.

A network of about 70 food brokers was used as the company's sales organization. All Pomona's principal competitors also used food brokers except for the National Biscuit Company, which had company salesmen in some areas. The brokers were paid 3 percent of sales.

Pricing of pimientos was generally competitive, but stable. Vegetable prices varied more, but differences usually reflected freight advantages. Pomona's prices were competitive with major competition on pimientos, greens, green beans, other seasonal items, and nonseasonal products.

Very little advertising was done by Pomona or its competitors. Most of the promotion budget went into trade allowances. Several times a year an allowance of 50 cents per case would be offered on a few of the products.

The margins on the product line were approximately 20 percent for the retailer, 5 percent for the wholesaler, and 3 percent for the broker. The average case sales price to wholesalers and chains was $3.10 per case which is equivalent to approximately 17 cents per average can to the consumer.

Pomona Products Company had a reputation with the trade as a company with good- to high-quality products, excellent service, flexible promotions, and fair pricing. The company's brokers were well accepted by nearly all customers, and Pomona was considered a leader in the southern canning industry. The Sunshine brand label was used on all the company's products and private labels were utilized by a few of Pomona's customers.

The company had not conducted any research to determine the characteristics of the end consumers of their products. It was felt, however, that a significant proportion of the buyers were blacks, and the products sold well in predominately black areas.

THE DECISION CONCERNING ENTRY INTO
THE NEW YORK MARKET

In April, Mr. Ted Groth, who had been handling the company's sales for many years in the New York area, switched broker organizations and joined the Aris Brokerage Company. Pomona's sales in the New York market had been primarily pimiento sales, with only a small number of cases of southern vegetables. The new broker firm had a young, aggressive management who recognized the potential for the rest of the Pomona line in the New York market. Pimiento sales were approximately 7,000 cases and the new brokerage firm felt that with the addition of the line of southern vegetables they could sell at least 50,000 cases a year within a short period

EXHIBIT 6

Grocery store distribution, New York area stores

Chain	Number of stores in area	Percent of area volume
A&P.....................................	447	12.5%
Bohack.................................	175	5.5
Pathmark..............................	28	5.1
Walkbaum.............................	78	5.0
Hills.....................................	57	4.7
Grand Union..........................	107	3.9
Shoprite/Foodarama..................	50	3.1
Daitch Shopwell......................	90	3.0
First National.........................	73	2.8
Key Food Stores......................	139	2.6
Food Fair..............................	58	2.6
Met Foods*............................	996	2.4
King Kullen...........................	43	2.3
Associated Food Stores*..............	200	1.6
Gristede...............................	108	1.4
Dan's Supreme........................	19	0.8
Bozzuto*...............................	107	0.8
Royal Farms...........................	21	0.7
Sloan's.................................	23	0.7
Durso...................................	11	0.7
Handell................................	15	0.6
Krasdale Foods*.......................	900	0.5
E&B....................................	8	0.5
Mid Eastern Co-op.....................	12	0.5
Trunz...................................	56	0.4
Faith Supermarkets....................	5	0.4
7-Eleven...............................	30	0.4
D'Agostino Brothers...................	12	0.4
Fedco Foods...........................	14	0.4
Pick Quick.............................	11	0.4
Food Pageant.........................	8	0.3
Meats & Treats.......................	10	0.3
		67.3%

* Voluntary chain.

of time. There were more southern blacks in New York, for example, than were in the state of Georgia. There had been a large out-migration of people from the South into New York and other northern markets in the past two decades, and the executives felt that they would be very receptive to the Sunshine line of products. The key question was how to introduce the products into the market.

The brokerage firm prepared the list of grocery store distribution shown in Exhibit 6. There were a large number of chains in the New York market and the 32 chains on that list account for only two thirds of the food store volume in the area. Several of the Pomona and Aris executives felt that they should start with the A&P chain, try to get distribution in their stores, establish a successful sales record, and then seek distribution from the

EXHIBIT 7
Media rates for New York area

A. Radio (daytime rate, one-minute announcement)

Station	Rate
WABC	$170
WADO*	90
WCBS	270
WEVD	23
WHN	150
WHOM	70
WINS	225
WLIB	47
WMCA	175
WNBC	250
WNEW	235
WNJR†	50
WOR	150
WPAT	95
WPOW	18
WQXR	80
WRFM	95
WTFM	70
WVNJ	60
WWRL†	74

B. Newspapers (one 70-column inch ad—approximately 1,000 lines)

Paper	Rate	Circulation
El Diario–La Pensa‡	$ 980	66,900
New York Daily News	7,800	2,028,500
Post	3,580	598,512
New York Times	4,740	843,300

* Black and Spanish programming.
† All black programming.
‡ Spanish-language paper.

other chains. Other executives wanted to seek immediate distribution from as many chains as possible.

Another issue concerned which stores of a particular chain should stock the line of products. Should only the outlets in predominately black areas sell the products, or should Pomona strive for side distribution in the market?

The executives also wondered what promotional effort should be undertaken. Exhibit 7 contains a list of the various newspapers and radio stations available in the New York market, together with advertising rates. The company's gross margin was only about 25 percent of sales, so they wondered what promotional budget they could afford.

Although no canned southern vegetables were available in the market, frozen southern vegetables were. The executives felt that their pricing and margins would have to be the same as in other areas of the country to enable retailers to sell the products at a price competitive with the frozen products.

There would be virtually no additional fixed costs associated with the entry into the New York market. There was excess plant capacity for production, and the company had a warehouse in New York for pimientos, and there was plenty of space available for additional storage. Shipping costs would be about 50 cents per case, but this would be charged to the customers and passed on to the final consumers.

The marketing decisions had to be made soon to ensure that the plans could be executed before the slow end of the year season. If they were to enter the New York market, a total program would have to be developed in the next month.

CASE

18

Laramie Oil Company:
Retail Gasoline Division*

In April 1976, George Thomas, vice president in charge of domestic automotive gasoline distribution for the Laramie Oil Company, was considering what action he should take with regard to the company's 12,400 franchised and lessee-operated service stations. A number of developments that indicated discontent among franchisees and lessees had recently occurred. Although he was unsure as to what extent these developments indicated real widespread discontent, Mr. Thomas was wondering what might be causing it, and what action he should take at the present time, and in the long run.

COMPANY BACKGROUND

The Laramie Oil Company was a fully integrated petroleum company with operations in 21 countries. In 1975, domestic sales were $4.79 billion, and net income was $423.4 million. The Laramie product line included automotive gasoline, aviation fuels, distillates, lubricants, and assorted agricultural and industrial chemicals. Sales of automotive gasoline and related products accounted for 52 percent of revenues earned and 64 percent of net profit.

Both the international and domestic American Head Offices were situated in New York City. As distribution vice president, George Thomas

---

*This case was co-authored by C. Merle Crawford, Professor of Marketing, University of Michigan.

had responsibility for the overall maintenance of a strong network of retail outlets. This responsibility involved the setting of policies concerning lease terms, the selection of dealers, the training of dealers, the motivation of dealers, the dismissal of dealers, and any other factors involving the maintenance of dealer morale and overall effectiveness. Mr. Thomas only had responsibility for the company's Laramie brand stations. Laramie Oil also operated about 50 discount outlets and expected to open more in the near future. These outlets operated under a different brand name.

George Thomas described his objective as distribution vice president as follows:

> We've done a great deal of research to determine why gasoline purchasers use one brand of gasoline or another. In almost every instance, the consumer's perception of the gasoline retail outlet was a very significant determinant in brand selection. It appears that we're halfway to first base if we can keep our outlets modern and clean, plus provide the service that the consumer desires. By service, I mean more than just good, fast, competent pump island work. Service includes having outlets open when consumers need them, and making sure that outlets handle our national promotions. There is nothing more irritating to a customer who expects to receive a glass or coupon than to find that the station that he happens to be in isn't participating in the national promotion. That is one of the best ways to lose customers for good.
>
> Our whole retail distribution policy is directed toward providing a consistent type of physical outlet and service from one end of the country to the other. That's how gasoline is sold.

IMPLEMENTATION OF DISTRIBUTION POLICIES

George Thomas' control over the implementation of his department's policies was quite indirect. A general manager in each of five geographical divisions had responsibility for all marketing activities in his division, including retail distribution. Each division had a distribution manager whose responsibilities included the day-to-day implementation of corporate policies in regard to service station operations. The division distribution manager reported directly to the division general manager. The corporate and divisional distribution managers did, however, maintain informal contact with each other. Each divisional distribution manager had a number of district sales managers reporting directly to him. Direct contact with service station operators was maintained by company sales representatives, each of whom reported to a district sales manager. The sales representative was the final link in the chain of implementation between George Thomas' office and the service station operator. (See Exhibit 1 for a partial organization chart.)

EXHIBIT 1
Partial organization chart

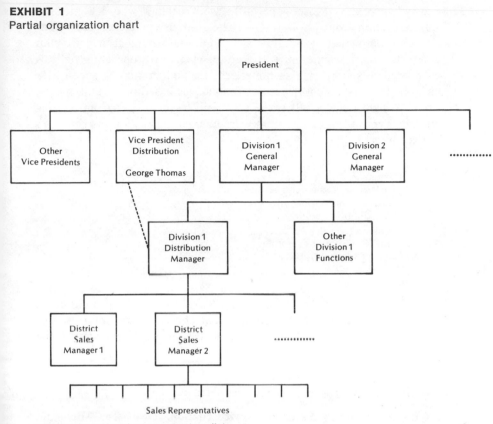

- - - - Indicates an informal communications link.

TYPE OF SERVICE STATIONS

Laramie Oil Company distributed its automotive products through three types of service stations:

1. *Company operated.* These stations were owned or leased by Laramie Oil who hired the service station personnel to operate them on a straight salary basis. Laramie controlled the retail price and all other aspects of all products sold through these stations. About 100 of Laramie's 12,400 stations were operated in this manner.

2. *Franchised dealers.* The station site and all physical facilities of franchised dealer operations were owned by the dealers themselves. Laramie did, however, provide financing, so that an individual dealer could commence operation by putting up as little as $2,000. The company, or local financial institutions, held mortgages on the land and physical facilities. About 500 outlets were in this category.

3. *Lessee operated.* Lessee operators were dealers who leased their service station from Laramie Oil. The stations, in these cases, continued to be owned by Laramie Oil. The lessee purchased petroleum products from Laramie but was free to set his own operating policies as related to such things as hours, prices, and brands of accessories carried. The lessee's cost price of gasoline was based on a "tank wagon price" which included all taxes and delivery charges to the lessee's station. Typical lessee operators were charged per gallon, as shown in the accompanying table.

Transport price (except tax)......................	$0.2130
Plus: State and federal taxes.....................	0.2500
Transport price (including tax)....................	$0.4630
Plus: Jobber margin.............................	0.0355
Tank wagon price...............................	$0.4985
Plus: Rent paid to Laramie......................	0.0315
Lessee's margin.................................	0.0500
Retail price.....................................	$0.5800

The cost price of gasoline to franchised dealers closely approximated the lessee cost arrangement, except that rent charges were not included. For most franchisees, interest charges on their mortgages tended to make up this cost difference.

A closer look at two Laramie lessee dealers

1. Jerry Williamson's Laramie Service Station, Dearborn, Michigan. Jerry Williamson's service station was located at one of the main intersections in the Detroit suburb of Dearborn. His customers were drawn mainly from local residents and commuters who drove through Dearborn on their way to and from their work in Detroit. Williamson was a class A automobile mechanic who had worked for a Ford dealership for eight years before becoming a Laramie dealer in 1964. He had put up $9,500 of his own money to obtain the right to be the Laramie lessee for his Dearborn location. Most of the $9,500 had been used to finance product inventories and tools, while some had been used to physically upgrade the station.

Williamson did a large automobile repair business. Over the years he had built up an excellent reputation among the residents of Dearborn for providing competent and reliable repair service. As a result of this business and his good location for attracting gasoline customers, he did an annual sales volume of slightly over $225,000. His profit statement for 1975 is presented in Exhibit 2.

Williamson took great pride in the fact that he had been able to build a very successful business operation. He thought of himself as being a part

EXHIBIT 2

Percentage profit statements for Jerry Williamson's and Fred Shaw's service stations for 1975

	Jerry Williamson	Fred Shaw
Sales.......................................	100.00%	100.00%
Cost of goods sold........................	75.36	75.24
Gross profit...............................	24.64	24.76
Expenses:		
Labor for outside work....................	0.46	0.29
Supplies...................................	0.75	0.79
Wages (excluding owner).................	8.38	8.69
Repairs and maintenance................	0.34	0.24
Advertising...............................	0.79	0.93
Delivery...................................	0.41	0.42
Bad debts.................................	0.02	0.02
Administrative............................	0.38	0.35
Miscellaneous............................	0.96	0.72
Rent.......................................	2.60	2.00
Insurance.................................	0.47	0.46
Utilities...................................	0.96	1.00
Taxes.....................................	0.74	0.66
Interest...................................	0.10	0.11
Depreciation.............................	0.60	0.65
Total expenses......................	17.96	17.33
Net profit.................................	6.68%	7.43%
Inventory turnover × 1 year..............	17.26	12.88

of the community as he took part in community work through his memberships in the Lion's Club, and the Chamber of Commerce. In the latter organization he had risen to the position of vice president, and was looking forward to being president at some time.

When he was asked if there were any negative aspects to being a Laramie dealer, Williamson replied as follows:

Well . . . not really; it's tough to complain a lot when you're making $33,000 a year. The only thing I really have to complain about is that Laramie pressures me to buy most of my repair parts and accessories from their own supply company or from company-approved jobbers. I think I could get slightly better margins from other jobbers, as the company takes a percentage rake-off from the approved jobbers. However, it's really a small complaint when you consider all the pluses that Laramie gives. Overall, I'm extremely pleased.

2. Fred Shaw's Laramie Service Station, Detroit, Michigan. Fred Shaw's service station was located in an industrial section of Detroit, with most of his customers being people who worked in the plants in the surrounding area. Prior to becoming the lessee of his current station, Shaw had worked as an employee in a suburban Laramie station. He had always wanted to be in business for himself and whenever he heard that a station was available, he would approach the sales representative involved to see if he could obtain the station. Most of the stations had required too much capital but finally he was able to obtain his current station by putting up $3,500 for the required inventories.

Although managing his station required long hours for Shaw, he preferred it to a very great extent over working for another dealer. It was in a very real sense to him the fulfillment of his dream of being his own boss.

Due to the nature of the surrounding environment, Shaw's station was quiet most of the day except when the shifts changed and then it was extremely busy. This constant changing from feast to famine made proper staffing extremely difficult, and required long hours to cover all shift changes.

Shaw's station was not as productive in either gasoline sales or repair service as was Jerry Williamson's. As a result, his 1975 sales volume was just under $95,000. Exhibit 2 presents his 1975 profit statement.

Hank Homes was the Laramie sales representative in Shaw's district, and on one of his weekly visits recently he asked Fred to take part in a special Bicentennial china giveaway promotion. Part of the conversation between the two men went as follows:

Hank: This looks to me to be one of the best promotions the company has ever put together. They're going to put about $2.5 million in advertising behind it. You should draw a pile of customers.

Fred: Come on, Hank. The type of customer who buys from my outlet isn't interested in bone china. It may be fine for other outlets, but I don't want in on this one. Besides, since the gasoline shortage of '73 and '74, I can't believe anyone wants to start these rotten giveaways again.

Hank: I disagree, Fred. I'm sure you'd do well with it. Why don't you let me sign you up. I think you'd be pleased with the results. We pretested this in Denver and it went well. Think about it for a few minutes while we discuss a few other things. It looks to me as if your station could use a new coat of paint this spring. If we let it go any longer, it will chase customers away.

Fred: I don't think I can afford to put out for the paint right now, Hank. You know what a problem I'm having making ends meet here.

Hank: Well, maybe I can help you out on that score. If I work on them at the regional office, they might let me absorb part or even all of the expense for you. . . . Think about the china promotion, Fred, and I'll drop back tomorrow.

Franchisee and lessee discontent

The following dealer comments were taken from meetings of several Laramie retail dealer associations in various parts of the United States. Laramie retail dealer associations were groups of Laramie dealers who had gotten together on their own for such purposes as: the discussion of mutual problems, the collective purchasing of products from independent suppliers, and the undertaking of various social activities. Not all Laramie dealers belonged to associations and the strength and activity level of the associations varied greatly.

Lessee 1: The company claims that we can set our own prices, but that damn sales rep comes into my place and tells me I can't sell at more than a four-cent markup. I can hardly scrape from one week to the next at that rate. . . . I know for sure he'll drop my lease if I don't set these prices. Our dealer association has had economists do studies that showed that on the average it takes a gross profit margin of nine cents a gallon to operate profitably. Margins today run from about three cents to eight cents with the average at about five and a half cents. That's just not enough.

Lessee 2: What really bugs me is those stupid games and contests I have to put up with. They advertise them like mad on TV, so I have to carry them or the customers start screaming. . . . I don't get any more business with them—all my competitors are running some game or another—all they do is add to my costs. It's really frustrating. I thought the oil crisis had finished these things. I guess I was wrong.

Lessee 3: I couldn't be more satisfied. I make a really good living. If some of you guys stopped complaining and started working, you could do the same.

Lessee 4: You know I'd really like to close my place down at night . . . the only reason I'm open nights is cause the sales rep said he wouldn't renew my lease if I didn't keep his hours   imagine that, I've worked for Laramie for 15 years as a dealer and they'd drop me just like that. I can't afford to lose my station but I'm losing money by staying open.

Lessee 5: What's really got me worried is that they are going to turn my station into a company-owned and -operated outlet. Where would I be then?

Lessee 6: The company is more interested in their gallonage than our profits, and those one-sided leases let them dictate what we'll charge and what products we'll sell. They also use the lease to ride herd on our prices.

Lessee 7: I had hoped that the Supreme Court rulings prohibiting forcing their TBA (tires, batteries, and accessories) brands on us would have helped; however, all it's done is to make their methods more subtle.

Franchisee 1: I thought when I put up my bucks I was going to be in business for myself—fat chance—that sales rep is in my place all the time suggesting what hours to work, how to work, what price to set. . . . If I object, he starts talking about revoking my franchise. I know the Laramie name draws customers but some of his suggestions are unreasonable.

Franchisee 2: This business of them running their own discount stations in competition with me has really got me bugged, too.

Comments of sales representatives (SR)

The following comments were taken from individual interviews with selected sales representatives:

SR 1: Sure, I set hours and prices and procedures; if I didn't, some of those dolts would be out of business tomorrow.

SR 2: To get the volume out of my territory that the district manager demands, I have to pressure the dealers. Talking about the lease is always effective. However, I've never actually threatened any of my dealers with the loss of the lease.

SR 3: If you're honest and friendly with your dealers and show them what they will gain from following what you suggest, then you don't have to threaten them to get cooperation.

SR 4: You can bet your life I'm out pushing our TBA line to dealers. That right hasn't been taken away from us. However, that doesn't mean we're going to club them over the head if they don't.

COMMENTS BY GEORGE THOMAS

(Made before a congressional committee.)

It isn't our policy to require dealers to maintain company directed hours or prices. The whole idea is that the dealer has the right to establish his own hours and prices.

I'd fire any sales representative found pressuring dealers on matters like prices or hours or contests.

It seems to me that what we have here is a situation completely analogous to the normal arrangement between the landlord and tenant. We have up to $200,000 invested in large stations, and if the dealers are mismanaging them we have a right and a duty to protect our investment.

DEVELOPMENTS IN 1975

A number of developments that concerned George Thomas took place in 1975.

1. A group of dealers in Chicago filed a suit against Laramie, alleging that Laramie violated the Sherman Act by using short-term leases to intimidate the dealers into following suggested retail prices. No decision had been handed down yet by the court.

2. A Laramie Marketing Research Staff report indicated that the turnover rate among Laramie dealers had increased significantly in the last few years. This problem of dealer turnover was common throughout the oil industry. Estimates indicated that approximately one third of all service stations in the United States change management every year. The Laramie turnover rate was below the national average, but was still very high. This high turnover was considered to be a very serious problem by George Thomas. Also disturbing was the fact that a significant number of long-service Laramie dealers had left to join

cut-rate chains who guaranteed station managers at least $1,500 income per month.

3. The Automotive Retail Trade Association had requested the Federal Trade Commission (FTC) to charge the seven major oil companies (including Laramie) with misrepresentation, breach of contract and promotion of price wars. The writ alleged misrepresentation of "exclusive" franchise agreements and breach of contract because the oil companies have opened "off-brand" stations near franchise service stations. The association charged that the off-brand stations sell at prices lower than the wholesale prices charged to the franchise dealers. The association wants an injunction to stop oil companies from creating subsidiary stations in direct competition with franchised dealers.

   The writ also criticized the oil companies for nondisclosure of fees or profits received by oil companies from firms which supply automobile products to the service stations. The association wanted to know this information since service station lessees are requested to buy the accessories only from designated dealers.

   Finally the writ criticized promotional gimmicks and giveaways as a financial burden to operators and alleged that oil companies "demanded" cooperation and participation under threat of nonrenewal of leases.

4. The Central States Automotive Retailers Association presented a brief to the governors of six states asking for legislation to prohibit gimmicks and giveaways connected with gasoline selling. The association alleged that an end to giveaways could reduce the selling price of gasoline by one or two cents a gallon. The brief also asked that oil companies be required to sell gasoline at one price to all customers. At present the wholesale price varies from customer to customer, with the highest being charged to leased gas stations.

Mr. Thomas reflected on these developments and wondered what alternative courses of action were available to him, and what action he should take both in the short run and in the long run. He also wondered what factors had caused the current problems.

Colonial Tire Corporation*

Colonial Tire Corporation (CTC) was a retail, wholesale, and mail-order distributor of automobile parts and accessories, hardware, sporting goods, and other related items. The company owned a number of retail outlets, but most sales were made through a chain of over 200 franchised dealers located in the New England states and New York. Financial information on the company is given in Exhibit 1.

Dealers operating under a Colonial Tire franchise agreed to sell merchandise obtained from Colonial Tire at prices not exceeding those published by the company and to follow various merchandising policies set out by the central organization. In return the associate store received a basic buying, merchandising and advertising service, and advice regarding facilities and financing. This arrangement, in the words of one company executive, "combines the advantages of chain store operation with the flexibility of an independent business."

Colonial Tire was aggressively expanding and developing its dealer organization and other retail operations. The company arranged financial assistance, for example, for proven dealers or those with exceptional potential, and encouraged progression of dealers to larger centers or locations having greater sales potential. A high proportion of the company's capital expenditures was allocated to the acquisition of retail locations. A recent development was the opening of a number of new catalog order stores operating as satellites to existing associate stores.

Expansion of sales and retail outlets was accompanied by a rapid in-

---

* This case was written by C. B. Johnston, Associate Dean and Professor of Marketing, University of Western Ontario. Used with permission.

EXHIBIT 1

Five-year financial and operating results

	1971	1972	1973	1974	1975
Number of stores	151	171	190	201	204
Working capital	$ 4,248,069	$ 5,269,275	$ 6,002,751	$ 3,172,258	$ 3,317,232
Capital expenditure	$ 1,263,437	$ 1,491,337	$ 2,163,766	$ 4,988,382	$ 3,299,130
Depreciation	$ 371,406	$ 400,236	$ 466,735	$ 765,891	$ 897,312
Fixed assets at net book value	$ 5,303,611	$ 7,397,291	$ 9,094,320	$13,316,811	$15,718,630
Earned surplus	$ 3,856,521	$10,451,899	$11,800,198	$12,713,094	$13,992,963
Net worth	$10,654,935	$12,633,712	$14,263,281	$15,698,137	$17,677,463
Net profit before income taxes	$ 3,144,119	$ 3,358,377	$ 3,529,001	$ 2,686,096	$ 2,612,170
Income taxes	$ 1,588,150	$ 1,735,907	$ 1,837,316	$ 1,367,810	$ 1,353,305
Net profit after income taxes	$ 1,555,969	$ 1,622,470	$ 1,691,685	$ 1,318,286	$ 1,258,865
Dividends	$ 127,570	$ 132,236	$ 279,103	$ 415,461	$ 427,079
Earnings reinvested in business	$ 1,428,399	$ 1,490,134	$ 1,412,582	$ 902,825	$ 831,786
Shares outstanding	529,680	551,370	584,569	596,402	614,677
Shareholders' equity per share	$ 20.12	$ 22.91	$ 24.40	$ 26.32	$ 28.75
Net profit per share*	$ 2.41	$ 2.51	$ 2.62	$ 2.04	$ 1.95

Note: Sales figures have not been released by the company.

* Adjusted for 5 for 1 split of June 30, 1960 and on the basis of 645,172 shares outstanding.

Source: Colonial Tire Corporation Annual Report, 1975.

crease and diversification in the merchandise lines handled. In 1955, CTC handled about 16,000 different items and this had increased to 18,000 items by 1975 representing an inventory investment of about $6 million. Most of the more important product lines were sold under private brands such as "Sure Safe" tires, "Maxi Power" batteries and spark plugs, and "Easy Flow" oils. The majority of the company's products were distributed from a central warehouse in Boston, built in 1958 and enlarged in 1972 to provide over 1 million square feet of space. A small part of the mail-order and wholesale warehouse business was carried on from another warehouse in Boston which provided about 88,000 square feet of selling space. The general office with an adjoining retail store and service station in which many new items and techniques were given trial, was located in downtown Boston.

EARLY ORDER PROCESSING AND INVENTORY MANAGEMENT

A unit record system was installed by CTC early in 1955 to facilitate invoicing of wholesale shipments and inventory management. Before this system was installed, procedures required a considerable amount of clerical work. Handwritten orders were received from the associate stores, were typed up, and priced out by head office clerical staff and then sent to the warehouse. Shipments were made if the goods were available and the order forms returned to the head office with the shipped goods checked off. Invoices for the associate stores were prepared from these returned forms. About 25 clerks were required to process the approximately 1,000 order/invoices per day. When parts of an order could not be filled, the buyers responsible for the items were notified and the associate store was notified that the items were on standing order.

Under the unit record system a "master card" was made up for each of the 16,000 items carried by CTC giving basic data on the product and specifying its location in the warehouse. Multiples of these cards were maintained in a central file in the head office. When handwritten orders came in a card was pulled from the file for each ordered item, the quantity was mark sensed on the card, and the bundle of cards representing an order was put into the card system to generate an invoice. The invoices were then sent to the warehouse for filling and shipping, then returned to the head office for customer statement billing, with goods not available checked off. As in the prior system, buyers and customers were notified of out-of-stock situations.

The inventory management process under the unit record system is outlined in Exhibit 2. Each of the company's 16,000 items was reviewed once a month. A control list determined which master item cards were

EXHIBIT 2
Manual inventory replenishment before 1960

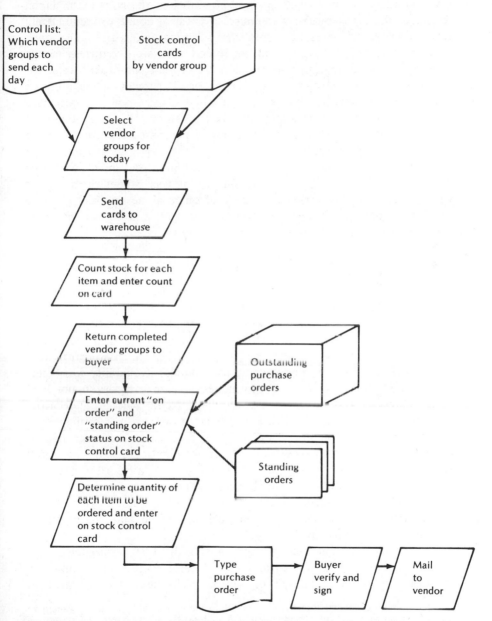

Note: Elapsed time up to two weeks: each item reviewed monthly.

to be sent to the warehouse each day of the month. The cards were batched by vendor groups—groups of suppliers providing similar products, whose products were stocked in close proximity in the warehouse. Upon receipt of the cards by the warehouse, a physical count was conducted. Four to six stockkeepers were employed full time at this task. The stock count was recorded on the item cards and they were returned to the appropriate buyer. With this information, the current "on-order" status for the item, and a set inventory requirement of 40 percent of the previous year's sales, the buyer could determine whether an order was necessary and in what quantities.[1] This quantity was entered on the master item card and served as a basis for the preparation of purchase orders which were later verified and signed by the buyer.

Although the unit record system represented an improvement over prior methods it had a number of disadvantages: it was expensive and costs were rising; order-processing time at head office alone required three to six days; 8 percent of the items ordered by dealers were out of stock; and inventory management was still very rudimentary.

THE FIRST COMPUTER SYSTEM

An International Business Machines (IBM) 1401 computer was installed at CTC in 1960 in response to growing volume problems with the unit record system and in line with CTC's philosophy of being on the forefront of new developments. Order processing started with the receipt by head office of mark sensed order cards from dealers. These cards were immediately converted to invoices and merchandise availability was determined by checking against the continuous inventory record maintained in the computer's random access memory file. Inventory updating occurred as each card was processed; if the merchandise ordered was available the inventory level in the computer memory was reduced by the order amount on the card, and an invoice went to the warehouse to ship the goods specified. If the merchandise ordered was out of stock, a record was entered into the computer memory, enabling the warehouse to assign and ship such merchandise immediately as it was received. Among other things, this system eliminated passing orders between office and warehouse to determine merchandise availability.

The inventory management system utilizing the 1401 computer is outlined in Exhibit 3. Stock control punched cards were sent to the data processing department instead of to the warehouse. This department

---

[1] The origin of this requirement was uncertain. Some thought that a top executive had once given it as a "guideline" and that it had slowly worked into the system as a rather firm decision rule. The performance of the rule was judged "not bad" at least in part because it provided for the large annual sales increase (about 20 percent) being realized.

EXHIBIT 3
Manual inventory replenishment 1960–1976

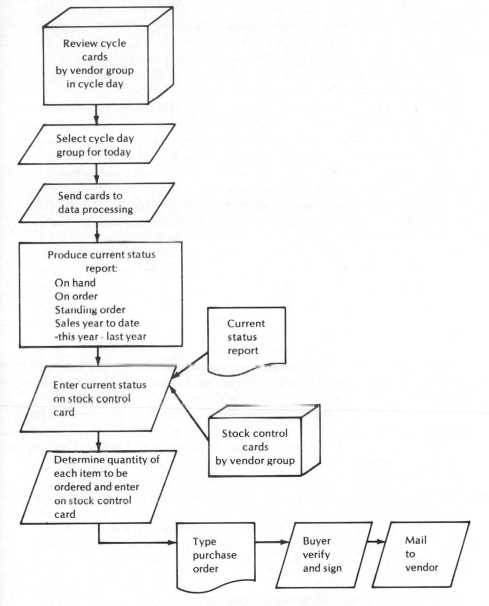

Note: Elapsed time up to three days; each item reviewed monthly.

produced a status report listing the stock on hand and on order and, in addition, sales figures for current and previous years. Another inventory report, called the "hot sheet," was generated daily by the data processing department listing items received, those getting low in stock (expedite condition) and those out of stock. This information was available to the buyer to aid his decisions on the quantity and timing for orders.

The installation of the 1401 system resulted in the provision of more accurate and timely information on inventory status. The time required to obtain the status of individual items was reduced from about two weeks to three days. Physical counts were reduced to once a year and it was discovered that the perpetual inventory on the random access file was usually within 0.50 percent of what was actually in stock. The number of stock-keepers to count inventory was reduced from six to one. Stock-out frequency dropped from 8 percent to 3 percent.

Despite these forward steps, management felt the buyers were still left with no clear idea of when and how much to order. Some rough guidelines of one-month minimum and three-month maximum inventory on hand were established to guide the buyers, but these rules of thumb did not necessarily correspond with prevailing economic order quantities. Thus, in many cases inventory levels were thought to be "too high," reducing stock turnover and tying up capital. In other cases stock-outs still occurred because of seasonal fluctuations, unreliable delivery times, and other reasons. A basic problem appeared to lie in the fact that few of the merchandise buyers appeared fully to understand and utilize the newly available information. For example, some buyers appeared to rely too extensively on the system, tending to wait for hot sheet reports to trigger orders without regard to varying lead-time requirements. Others appeared not to trust the new data and continued to order 40 percent of the previous year's sales. Management thought these problems were understandable, since, for a variety of reasons, a full effort had not been made to educate the buyers to utilize the new system and the buyers themselves were too busy with day-to-day business to spend much time working up a complete knowledge of the system. Steps were being taken so that these problems could be ironed out over time. In the meantime, management felt the buyers were much too tied up in expediting, preparation of purchase orders, and looking after special situations, to be as creative in their activities as desired.

THE PURCHASING ORGANIZATION

From the founding of CTC in 1932 through to his death in 1966, Mr. A. J. Labell was president of the firm and also took responsibility for the major part of the purchasing activities. He was, in fact, the only person in the firm in contact with all suppliers. He was assisted in the purchasing activities by four buyers who handled rebuying, stockkeeping and other clerical functions.

When Mr. Labell died quite suddenly there was virtually no one in CTC ready to take over the creative buying function. His son, Dave Labell, then 27, was asked to handle the buying operation. From 1966 to 1972, he was responsible for the development of the purchasing group at CTC. Mr. Dave Labell left CTC in 1972, and Mr. Jack Molloy was promoted to purchasing manager. Mr. Molloy had been with the company since the early 50s, starting in a clerical position and moving up through store management as well as being buyer for the electrical and auto accessory divisions.

In 1975, there were eight buyers reporting to Mr. Molloy, each responsible for a major line of merchandise (Exhibit 4). Each buyer was responsible for from 200 to 1,200 items. As a consequence, most of the buyer's time was consumed determining order quantities, talking to salesmen and reviewing the constant flow of new items, packs, and special promotions. A junior buyer was assigned to each buyer to assist him primarily by taking over clerical aspects of the job such as routine correspondence, documentation and filing, obtaining samples for tests, checking items in the stores, and handling minor complaints.

EXHIBIT 4
Organization chart

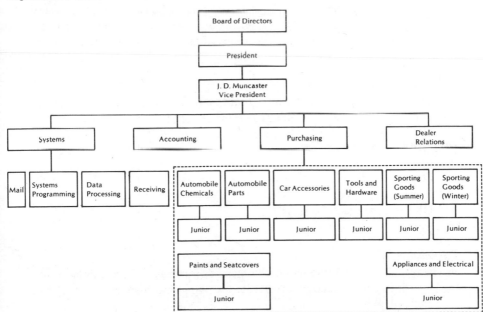

Expediting orders was a major and time-consuming task for the buyers and their juniors. For many merchandise lines more than one supplier was used to reduce dependence on any one source. In many cases this meant that the second or third source was a small supplier producing basically on order for CTC. The lead times quoted, particularly by these suppliers, were not very meaningful with the result that buyers spent up to 50 percent of their time tracing and expediting orders.

THE IMPACT SYSTEM

In an attempt to improve inventory levels and stock-out percentages, CTC management had for some time been encouraging the systems group to come up with an inventory replenishment system specifically designed for the company's requirements. In the fall of 1975, IBM suggested trial of their system called IMPACT—Inventory Management Programs and Control Techniques.

The stated objectives of the IMPACT system were to reduce inventory investment, fill orders as completely as possible (reduce stock-outs), minimize total inventory operating costs and free merchandisers of as much detail as possible. It consisted of three related but distinct subsystems:

1. Order quantity determination

This system provided an analysis of discount schedules, shipping rates, warehouse space, investment costs, etc., to determine the economic order quantity for each item or group of items. Basic data which management had to supply to this system included:

Supplier considerations
a. Discount structures, including quantity breaks and volume discounts.
b. Pack-size quantities or minimum quantity orders.

Inventory maintenance costs
a. Cost of capital.
b. Storage.
c. Taxes, insurance.
d. Obsolescence and depreciation.
e. Special handling.

Purchasing costs
a. Cost changes sustained with changes in order-rate in machine accounting, purchasing, accounts payable, receiving and inspection, freight or traffic departments.

Changes in the economic-order quantities due to changes in supplier or cost conditions could be handled readily by the system.

2. Forecasting

This subsystem prepared item-by-item forecasts using detailed sales records and exponential smoothing techniques. Forecast results, lead-time data, and specified safety-stock levels were reviewed to determine the stock level at which to order the quantity determined by the "ordering" subsystem. Each week or month the company could update forecasts on the basis of the most recent information. Data which the forecasting system required from management (in addition to a three-year span of monthly sales records) included:

a. Lead times, defined as the normal nonexpedited time the supplier would take from receipt of order to shipment.
b. Safety factors, which, when integrated with the forecast error for the item considered, would specify that item's safety stock.

3. Reviewing

This subsystem compared warehouse inventory levels, on-order information and the order-point specified by the forecasting subsystem to determine the time to order. With information from the ordering subsystem it also produced suggested order quantities. Review could be continuous (that is, after every transaction) but was commonly done on a weekly or biweekly basis.

The reviewing system could be used to print purchase orders automatically and to produce any desired merchandise reports.

As visualized for application at CTC the IMPACT system would review items weekly and prepare a suggested purchase order if one were necessary. The system would have the capability to adopt an independent or joint purchasing strategy for any supplier on specification by management.[2] (See Exhibit 5.) At this point the order would be reviewed by a buyer for approval or modification as dictated by any unusual circumstances at hand. The expected time lapse for the whole process from review through mailing an order was about three days.

The IMPACT system was a development of IBM's. A number of field trials of the IMPACT system had been undertaken, and IBM reported

---

[2] If purchase decisions for one item had little or no effect on supplier terms for other items or groups of items, an independent strategy would be specified. Joint replenishment was desirable in some cases, however, because of special supplier terms for aggregate (dollar, pounds, cubic feet) orders or because operating savings in clerical work could be realized.

EXHIBIT 5
Inventory replenishment using IMPACT

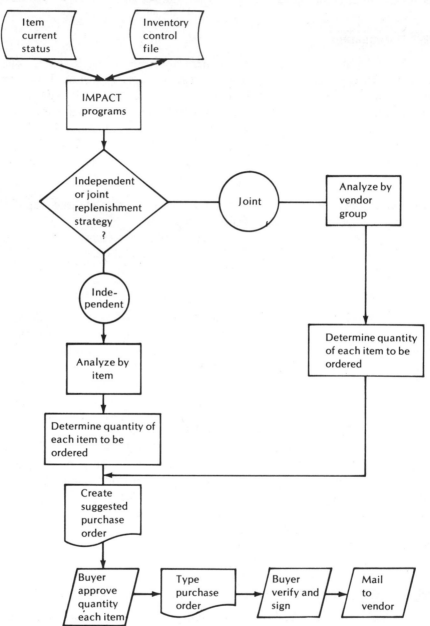

Note: Elapsed time up to three days: each item reviewed weekly.

favorable results from projects which had been in operation for more than a year, such as shown in the accompanying table:

Customer	Business	Inventory change	Service level*
S. S. Kresge.....................	Variety chain	Down 20%	Up 2.5%–98%
Fleming Company...............	Wholesale food	Down 15%	Up 2%–99.2%
Bowman Products Co............	Wholesale auto accessories	Down 26%	Up 2%–96%

* Service level was defined as the percentage of dollar demand which was filled routinely from goods on hand.

SYSTEMS GROUP CONSIDERATION OF THE IMPACT SYSTEM

Three members of CTC's systems group were involved in the consideration of IMPACT: Mr. K. G. Hand, the systems manager, and Messrs. J. Koab and R. Jackson, systems analysts (Exhibit 5). Mr. Hand had been trained as an IBM operator and had joined CTC in 1965 to work on the unit record system. By 1968 he had been appointed manager of the Systems Group. Mr. Koab had started with CTC in 1963 and after two years in the main Boston retail store became assistant to the warehouse manager. He had transferred into the Systems Group in 1970. Mr. Jackson had been with CTC since 1958, first in the retail store and then in purchasing. He had joined the Systems Group when plans were being made to install the 1401 system in 1959.

The Systems Group had spent a good deal of time with an IBM representative considering the applicability of IMPACT to the CTC operation. Since the company was considering switching from a 1401 to a System 3 computer under any circumstances, the hardware for implementing and experimenting with IMPACT would be available. They felt that the accumulated experience of the group in punched card and computer systems was quite substantial and would be equal to the demands of adapting IMPACT to the CTC operation. They also felt that their experience in other parts of the company would be of benefit in this process.

The Systems Group was aware that trial of the IMPACT system would involve some problems, particularly in the development of new data and reworking of available data. For example, the company had no systematic information at that time on the size of average purchases or on supplier lead times, and past sales data had been collected in a format that was not compatible with the demands of the IMPACT forecasting system. They felt the basic problem, however, was that of determining how the IMPACT system could be integrated into the existing CTC organization.

CONSIDERATION BY MANAGEMENT

Mr. R. B. Alexander was the member of management primarily in-volved in the consideration of the IMPACT system. Mr. Alexander had joined CTC after obtaining a B.A. in business administration in 1966 and an M.B.A. from Northwestern University in Chicago in 1967. From 1967 until 1970, he served as financial and operational analyst responsible for analysis of dealer operations. During these years he also spent part of his time in Hartford, Connecticut, operating a CTC Associate Store with his father. In 1970, Mr. Alexander was appointed vice president and general manager of Walter Alexander (Hartford) Inc., and spent his full time in Hartford. That same year he was elected to the board of directors of CTC and in the following year was appointed vice president of the company. It was not until April 1973, however, that he returned to Boston on a full-time basis as vice president with primary responsibility for marketing.

At a meeting with Mr. Alexander and Mr. Molloy early in 1975, Mr. Hand described the concept of IMPACT and the analytical techniques that IBM was prepared to make available on a trial study basis. Mr. Hand recommended a trial of the IMPACT system, giving the following reasons:

1. Based on the evidence available from other trials, IMPACT would result in lower inventories and higher service levels.
2. Buyers would be relieved of nonbuying functions such as reordering, providing time for the more creative parts of their job.
3. Reduced stock-outs would improve relations with associate stores and their customers.
4. The CTC Systems Group had the necessary skills and experience to implement the project.

In the ensuing discussion it was pointed out that about 30 percent of the company's merchandise was imported from Canada, Europe, and Japan, and that in these cases lead times might frequently be outside of the manufacturer's control. With respect to U.S. suppliers, which were the source of about two thirds of the merchandise, it was expected that fairly accurate lead times could be developed as the buyers had considerable experience with customs and shipping. In the case of European and Japanese suppliers the problem of specifying meaningful lead times would be quite complex because the suppliers had little experience in working to lead times and the increased possibility of customs and shipping problems.

Questions were also raised concerning the ability of IMPACT to handle seasonal items. Although the IBM representative stated that experience to date indicated most seasonal items could be handled without any problems, the prevailing opinion was that difficulties with seasonal items would depend in large part on the type of product. For luxury items such as swimming pools, forecasts based solely on prior sales would be subject to considerable error because sales were sensitive to weather and economic conditions. Other seasonal items which approached the necessity level such as snow shovels and garden tools could probably be forecast within the required limits of error.

A final point raised by Mr. Molloy was that the juniors were currently doing the bulk of the clerical work, so IMPACT would not create any major change in this area.

As the meeting drew to a close it became apparent that a decision was necessary on whether to pursue further the notion of introducing IMPACT to CTC at this time and if so, what specific steps should be taken.

PART VI

A. ADVERTISING DECISIONS

Advertising is the most visible and controversial activity carried on in marketing. The first five cases in this section focus their attention on this function.

Advertising is defined as all paid, non-personal forms of communication that are identified with a specific sponsor. It, therefore, includes expenditures on radio, television, newspaper, magazines, and outdoor billboards, plus the yellow pages. The largest absolute dollar spenders on advertising tend to be big consumer products companies, like Procter and Gamble, General Foods, and General Motors. The industries that spend the highest percentage of their sales on advertising are the drug and cosmetic companies, followed closely by packaged food products and soaps.

The marketing decision maker has a number of decisions to make with respect to advertising for a product. These include:

1. Setting advertising objectives.
2. Determining the advertising budget.
3. Deciding on what creative presentation should be used.
4. Selecting what media vehicles to use.
5. Selecting what scheduling pattern should be used.
6. Deciding how the advertising should be evaluated.

In the cases that follow in this section, the reader will work to make decisions in most of these areas. The next section of this note is a short reminder of some of the concepts related to each of these decision points.

PROMOTION DECISIONS

Advertising objectives

Advertising objectives should be stated in qualified terms with a specific time period designed for a specific market target. The objective may be in terms of profits, sales, or communications measures such as awareness, interest, and preference. The objective: "increase brand awareness" is obviously not as good a statement as "increase brand awareness to 85 percent of all women 18–40, in the next six months."

Advertising budgets

Advertising budgets are difficult to set. That is why companies have fallen into using rule of thumb methods such as (1) the "all we can afford" method; (2) the percentage of sales method; and (3) the matching competitors method. We would prefer decision makers to proceed by defining the task they hope to accomplish and then have them calculate the cost of doing this. This is called the task approach. To do this method the advertiser must understand the functional relationship between his or her task and advertising expenditures.

Creative development

Creative activity is usually done by an advertising agency. The final product is usually the result of much copy testing on dimensions such as attention getting and persuasiveness.

Media decision

Media decisions are of two types. The first is the selection of broad classes of media to be considered for future analysis. This is done by matching the media characteristics with the needs of the advertiser. For example, television allows for good visual demonstration. This may be a desired characteristic for the campaign at hand.

The second stage involves the selection of specific media vehicles, for example, the NFL football game versus "All in the Family" versus a page in *Fortune*. The procedures for doing this are complex. Simply stated, vehicles are compared on the basis of their cost per thousand (CPM) target audience persons reached. The vehicle with the lowest CPM is selected. Audience sizes are then adjusted to allow for duplication between vehicles and new CPMs are calculated. Then the lowest CPM vehicle at that point is selected. This process continues until the budget is used up. A number of computer algorithms have been developed to handle the many calculations made in this process.

Scheduling patterns

The advertisers must decide whether to (1) spend their budget continuously throughout the period; (2) concentrate it at a short interval or (3) spend it intermittently throughout the period. There are no good rules of thumb to answer this question. The advertisers must experiment to find out which pattern makes the most sense for their products.

Evaluating advertising

If the advertiser has specified quantitative objectives, one is then in a position to measure to see if the objectives were met. The procedure used should be specifically designed to fit the type of objective stated.

B. SALES MANAGEMENT DECISIONS

The last four cases in this section of the book deal with the management of the personal selling function. Personal selling is defined as all paid, personal forms of communication that are identified with a specific organization.

Organizations in the United States spend over one and one half times as much money on personal selling as they do on advertising. Effective management of personal selling activity is thus very important.

The marketing decision maker has a number of decisions to make with respect to personal selling for a product. These include:

1. Defining the selling job to be performed.
2. Establishing the desired characteristics of the salespersons who will do this job.
3. Determining the size of the sales force.
4. Recruiting and selecting salespersons.
5. Training salespersons.
6. Organizing the sales force.
7. Designing sales territories.
8. Assigning salespersons to territories.
9. Motivating salespersons.
10. Compensating salespersons.
11. Evaluating salespersons.

In the four sales management cases that are in this section, the reader will work to make decisions in most of these areas. Again, the next section of this note is a short reminder of some of the concepts related to each of these decisions.

Definition of the selling job

The beginning point of all sales management decisions is the definition of the selling job to be performed. For example, is the job basically just order taking or are there complex engineering presentations involved? In defining a particular selling job, one must keep in mind the role of personal selling in the overall marketing strategy and understand well the needs of the buyer or buyers involved. The competitive and physical environments of the job are also important considerations.

Desired characteristics for salespersons

Out of the definition of the selling job, the manager is able to establish a set of criteria for determining the type of person who should perform the selling job. One should list the personal background and individual skills and qualifications that are necessary to effectively perform the defined job. For example, in selling complex electrical equipment, the criteria might include the holding of a degree in electrical engineering, with strong oral communications skills to make presentations to customers.

Sales force size

Determining the necessary size of a sales force involves determining the effort level capabilities of an average salesperson and dividing that into a measure of the total selling job to be done. In doing so, judgments must be made on how many total accounts to serve, how often to call on them, and how many accounts an average salesperson can effectively handle.

Recruiting and selecting salespersons

The selection of the right salespersons basically involves generating a pool of prospects and evaluating those prospects using the criteria established for the selling job. Information is collected on prospects using application forms, personal interviews, and psychological tests.

Training

The basic objective of training is to bring a salesperson up to the required level of competence in those areas of the defined selling job that were deficient upon hiring. These might include product knowledge, oral presentation skills, field procedures, and so on. Decisions must be made as to who should do the training and where it should be done. Do we let current salespersons do the training in the field or have special people to do it at the office, or some combination?

Organizing the sales force

The sales force may be organized on a geographical, product, market, or some combination of these factors basis. If a salesperson can effectively handle all the company's products in a given geographic area then the geographical structure probably makes the most sense. Otherwise, the product or market basis seem appropriate. The selection between these two approaches depends on whether product or market knowledge is the most important.

Designing sales territories

No matter how a sales force is organized, each salesperson is assigned a product or market or geographic territory. The determination of the size of a territory involves the trade-off between equalizing the sales potential in each territory and equalizing the required salesperson effort in each territory. It is usually impossible to have all one's territories with equal potential and equal effort. Both potential and required effort change with time, requiring territories to be changed. The reaction of current salespersons must be considered in doing this.

Assigning salespersons to territories

Just who is assigned to a particular territory is a tough issue. The criteria necessary for success may vary by territory for a given company. Chicago is different from Provo, Utah. Individuals may be selected for a particular territory, requiring that the selection criteria reflect these differences,

Motivating salespersons

Many techniques are used to motivate salespersons. These include sales meetings, nonfinancial incentives, special recognition, and just the interpersonal style of the sales manager. However, these activities are not likely to be effective unless the selection, training, organization, territory designing, and assignment procedures are effective.

Compensation

Compensation is a key motivator that deserves special attention. The compensation plan (salary and/or commission, and/or bonuses for sales over quota) must fit the defined selling task, and the behavior one is trying to stimulate. For example, it would seem to make little sense to pay one's salespersons all on commission if the selling requires a great deal of new customer work with long purchase decision lead times.

Evaluating salespersons

Evaluation provides important feedback to the salespersons as to how they are performing against the standards that management holds to be important. These standards may include sales levels, sales versus quota, call frequencies, new accounts opened, work habits, and so on. Some subjective judgments are a necessity for some of these standards. The proper handling of this type of feedback is a strong motivator.

20

South-West Pharmaceutical Company*

In August of 1974, Frank Van Huesen, vice president of the New Orleans-based advertising agency, Advertising Associates, was sitting in his skyscraper office contemplating a meeting scheduled for the next week. At that time, he was to meet with Mr. Lewis Spring, president of South-West Pharmaceutical Company (S.W.P. Company), to discuss agency recommendations for Gentle Care advertising in 1975. Although advertising expenditures for Gentle Care, a skin conditioner for pregnant women, were relatively small, the client was an important account for Advertising Associates, with about $700,000 in billings. Even though the number of pregnant women had been declining, Gentle Care had been experiencing a sudden, unexpected surge in sales. Therefore, planning its future strategy posed a definite challenge to Van Huesen's marketing and advertising expertise. Before the meeting, he had to come up with sound answers to such questions as: "How much to spend for advertising?"; "What media mix to employ?"; and "What to say in messages for Gentle Care?"

COMPANY BACKGROUND

The S.W.P. Company of New Orleans, La., is the oldest manufacturer of proprietary medicine products in the United States. It all began in Iberville, La., in 1826 when Captain N. L. Denard obtained the "formula" for a tonic from the Choctaw Indians. Formulation took place on south

---

* This case was co-authored by John S. Wright, Professor of Marketing, Georgia State University.

Louisiana plantations for many years until 1860 when Charles Thomas Spring, a pharmacist, bought the formula for $25 and started making and selling bottles of the tonic for $5. The company was moved to New Orleans in 1874 because of the city's better transportation facilities, and growth continued in a sporadic way. In 1955, the Stanfield Company was absorbed and with it another unique product, Gentle Care, joined the S.W.P. product line.

The company now manufactures and sells three principal products: Spring's Tonic, Ease Eye Drops, and Gentle Care. Exhibit 1 shows a partial product list, which includes package sizes, prices charged to retailers per dozen items, suggested "list" prices to be charged customers by

EXHIBIT 1
Product and price list for S.W.P. Company

Wholesale discounts: 18 percent on net billing	Quantity: 150-pound minimum prepaid shipment. Any assortment of S.W.P. Company products in original case lots can be combined to meet these shipping requirements.	Resale to retailers. At list less applicable wholesaler's cash discount when earned. Terms: 2 percent if paid within 30 days from date of invoice. Net and due after discount period.

Product	Unit size	List dozen	List	Packed case	Case weight
Gentle Care liquid	3 oz.	$14.80	$1.85	3 doz.	9½ lbs.
Gentle Care cream	2 oz.	14.80	1.85	1 doz.	3 lbs.

retailers, as well as case sizes and weights. Wholesalers selling the products receive an 18 percent discount for performing their functions. Sales volume for the company was at an annual rate of less than $5 million in July 1974, and had been growing about 10 percent per year.

The firm's products have traditionally been sold in retail drug stores which received the merchandise through drug and specialty wholesalers. The company employs one salesman who calls upon present and prospective customers, primarily in the Southwest. Mr. Spring is active in several trade associations and spends much time traveling to cement trade relations. Management is keenly aware that customer buying patterns are changing and, therefore, efforts are being made to have company products stocked in discount stores, supermarkets, and chain drugstores. Consequently, many "direct" sales are made to large retailers and to rack jobbers. Of its 3,000 active accounts, 500 are large retail chains, and the remaining 2,500 are to a variety of middlemen including wholesale grocers, rack jobbers, and specialty jobbers.

THE PRODUCT AND ITS MARKET

Gentle Care is also very old as products go, having been first sold in 1869. The product, which is a skin conditioner especially formulated for use during pregnancy to relieve tight, dry skin, was originally provided in liquid form. When massaged on the skin, it has a very soothing and relaxing effect on the muscles. Gentle Care's basic ingredients include winter-pressed cottonseed oil, soft-liquid soap, camphor, and menthol.

EXHIBIT 2
Industry and pricing structure—body lotions and creams for use during pregnancy

Company	Product	Size	Retail price	Wholesale price per dozen
S.W.P. Company, Atlanta, Georgia..........	Gentle Care (liquid)	3 oz.	$1.85	$12.80
	Gentle Care (cream)	2 oz.	1.85	12.80
Leading Lady Foundations, Inc., Cleveland, Ohio......	Anne Alt Body Lotion	8 oz.	1.50	n.a.
Mothers Beautiful, Miami Beach, Fla...............	Mothers Beautiful Body Lotion	8 oz.	1.25	n.a.
Shannon Manufacturing Co., North Hollywood, Calif.....	Mary Jane Maternity Lotion	8 oz.	1.50	n.a.
Maternity Modes, Niles, Ill........................	Maternity Modes Protein Body Creme	4 oz.	1.50	n.a.

n.a. = not available.

In 1967, a line extension of the product was devised in the form of Gentle Care cream, whose ingredients include cottonseed oil, laury, myrestyl, cetyl, stearyl in absorption base, glycerin, sorbitol, perfume, and color. Currently the cream form comprises a small but growing percentage of Gentle Care sales.

Mr. Van Huesen describes the industry as "body lotions and creams for use during pregnancy." Exhibit 2 shows the few other companies in the industry, along with the pricing they employ. It should be noted that the other brands are very small in comparison to Gentle Care, are sold primarily through maternity shops, and have only regional or local distribution. None advertises, nor do the brands pose a competitive threat to Gentle Care, which is believed to have better distribution for its sales volume than any other drug product in the United States. By its very nature, the product is a "slow-mover" at the store level, and smaller outlets order the product in half-dozen lots. No deals have been made available to the middlemen in the past; however, an experiment was planned for the fall of 1974 when retailers would be offered a "one free in five" package deal.

Isolating the target market for Gentle Care may appear to be an obvious exercise—its consists of all pregnant women. Within that category of womankind, however, Mr. Van Huesen thought the prime target for such lotions and creams should be the first-time mother-to-be. If she decides to use such a product at that time, it is quite likely she will again use it during succeeding pregnancies. What role is played by "influencers" (the expectant mother's mother, older mothers in the neighborhood, aunts,

EXHIBIT 3
Birthrate by age of mother and color, United States, 1961–1971

Age (years)	Nonwhite			White		
	1961	1971	Percent change 1961–71	1961	1971	Percent change 1961–71
15–19.............	15.3%*	12.9%	−16%	7.9%	5.4%	−32%
20–24.............	29.3	18.5	−37	24.8	14.5	−42
25–29.............	22.2	13.6	−39	19.4	13.5	−30
30–34.............	13.6	8.0	−41	11.0	6.6	−45
35–39.............	7.5	4.0	−47	5.3	2.7	−49
40–44.............	2.2	1.2	−45	1.5	0.6	−60

* Table is read as follows: In 1961, of all nonwhite women between 15 and 19 years of age, 15.3 percent gave birth.

nurses, maternity shop personnel, and so forth) in the purchase and use decision is not known.

Birthrates in the United States have been declining precipitously, and the United States is approaching a state of Zero Population Growth, a point where deaths and births are in balance. Reference to Exhibit 3 shows, nevertheless, that one woman in seven in the 20–29 age range does have a baby in a given year. The declining number of women in the target market is further documented in an article which appeared in the July 13, 1974 issue of *Business Week,* which states:

. . . the total number of babies born in the U.S. last year [1973] dropped to 3.1 million, the lowest level since World War II. That compares with 4.2 million to 4.3 million births per year from 1956 through 1962, the peak of the postwar baby boom and 3.7 million as recently as 1970.[1]

[1] "The Baby Food Market," *Business Week,* July 13, 1974, p. 45

Little is known about the consumer decision to use these lotions and creams during pregnancy. How do women learn about such products? Are influencers important to the decision, or does advertising inform the expectant mother of the product's availability? In the absence of specific research into this area of consumer behavior, it was assumed by both Mr. Spring and Mr. Van Huesen that advertising plays a significant, if not *the* critical, role. The product recently had been experiencing large increases in sales, with 1974 sales expected to be about 50 percent greater than the 1972 level, in spite of a decline in the market potential for the

EXHIBIT 4

Gentle Care—Advertising to sales ratios, 1967–1974

	Sales	Advertising	A/S Ratio
1967	$ 94,789	$70,256	0.74
1968	97,832	41,046	0.42
1969	102,551	34,695	0.34
1970	125,157	34,525	0.28
1971	126,909	20,451	0.16
1972	132,143	34,088	0.26
1973	157,959	32,853	0.21
1974	200,000	37,500	0.19
	(projected)		

product category. Exhibit 4 gives the sales of Gentle Care from 1967 to 1974, as well as the advertising to sales ratio for that period. The large sales increases were being achieved by both the liquid and cream forms of Gentle Care.

MARKETING STRATEGY

The marketing strategies employed by S.W.P. Company are reflections of the marketing philosophy of its president, Lewis Spring. Before joining the firm in 1957, Spring worked in promotional jobs in the petroleum and entertainment industries and he views promotion as an important part of his job. Technical people are hired to handle the manufacturing and physical distribution sides of the business, while Spring concentrates on the marketing-sales-advertising operations.

This circumstance simplifies Van Huesen's job. There are no layers of bureaucratic approval of S.W.P. Company. Once Van Huesen and Spring agreed on a strategy to be followed, it was implemented. The process involved a combination of Spring's ideas on how proprietary drugs should be promoted and Van Huesen's understanding of how advertising can be used to achieve the company's goals.

For a long time, Spring has maintained great faith in the importance of package design to the sales success of the kind of products manufactured by his company. The company once changed advertising agencies over this issue; Spring thought the Gentle Care package needed changing, while agency personnel felt that such a change would destroy the product's "image with the consumer."

Another of Spring's marketing guidelines is that the smaller company "must find the one single most important use for the product" and build the promotional program around that point. Closely related is another philosophical belief, namely that the firm "should do what the competition is not doing," whether it is in the area of media selection, creative strategy, or other promotional concerns.

THE ADVERTISING BUDGET

The company management does not have any "cut-and-dried" formula for arriving at the advertising budget. Advertising's importance to the sales of company products is recognized by Lewis Spring; nevertheless, as Exhibit 4 reveals, the advertising-to-sales ratio has been declining over the past decade without a consequent decline in sales. The relatively large budget for 1967 was due to the simultaneous introduction of the cream and a change in package design, which was accompanied by an increased budget to help secure greater distribution. The drastic cutback in advertising expenditures for 1971 was due to an unsuccessful diversification into the cosmetic business which necessitated a recoupment of financial resources. The relative cutbacks in 1973 and 1974 were in response to tight money conditions at the time and to a management decision to "make 1974 a year of profit." Spring believes, however, that such cutbacks can be only a temporary phenomenon; in respect to advertising he holds that "you must be everlastingly at it."

MEDIA STRATEGY

As has been characteristic of the proprietary drug industry for generations, Gentle Care was traditionally advertised by means of small space ads placed in newspapers. Twenty years ago it was realized that for a product whose market is as highly segmented as that for Gentle Care, this media strategy resulted in a great deal of "wasted circulation" of the advertising message; thereafter, advertising for the product was concentrated solely in magazines.

As shown in Exhibit 5, there exists an appreciable number of magazines which can be characterized as "baby-oriented." Of course, within the category, those read during the prenatal stage are desired by the producers

EXHIBIT 5
Baby-oriented magazines

	Frequency of publication	Circulation	CPM (B/W)	Page rate (B/W) one insertion
American Baby....................	Monthly	1,108,700	8.92	$ 9,890
Baby Care........................	Quarterly	575,785	7.49	4,310
Baby Talk........................	Monthly	1,021,693	8.28	8,460
Congratulations..................	Annually	2,624,120*	n.a.†	20,670
Expecting........................	Quarterly	855,013	9.11	7,790
Good Housekeeping...............	Monthly	5,703,732	3.94	22,765
Modern Romances................	Monthly	752,339	3.48	2,645
Mothers' Manual..................	Bimonthly	913,085	8.77	8,010
Parents' Magazine and				
Better Family Living..............	Monthly	2,017,029	6.52	13,565
Redbook's Young Mother..........	Annually	1,519,888	4.77	19,345

* Distributed to specific places; CPM not determinable.
† n.a. = not available.
Source: SRDS *Consumer Magazines and Farm Publications,* vol. 56, no. 4 (April 26, 1974).

of pregnancy body skin conditioners. Once the child is born, the product is no longer needed, although it is possible that the woman will continue to use the product for other skin care purposes.

For many years, Gentle Care was featured in smaller-sized ads (one-sixth page to one-half page) in eight or ten magazines, one or two insertions per year. In other words, the emphasis was placed on the *reach* strategy—trying to get the message before as many different prospects as possible for a given expenditure of advertising dollars. This strategy was replaced with one aiming at greater *frequency;* fewer publications were used with more insertions in each magazine over the year. The rationale behind this change was based upon the fact that there is no seasonality in the product's use; women become pregnant throughout the 12 months.

The 1974 advertising schedule for Gentle Care is shown in Exhibit 6. One key change made in 1973 was switching out of *Redbook* where the product had been advertised every other month adjacent to the magazine's "expectant mother's" column. To ensure that position, larger space had to be purchased, so for the same amount of money, the entire McFadden Group of eight magazines was available, although for small-sized ads. The agency's media department felt that the McFadden Group would be a better match with the target market for Gentle Care than would *Redbook*. *Parents' Magazine* was included in the media schedule primarily to allow the company to use the seal of approval in Gentle Care advertising, even though its impact on sales was undetermined.

EXHIBIT 6
Gentle Care—1974 advertising plan

Magazine	Size ad	Cost per ad	Number ads	Total cost
Expecting...............	1/2 page	$3,310	2	$ 6,620
	(2 1/4 × 6 15/16 inches)			
	(71 lines)			
American Baby...........	1/2 col.	1,820	3	5,460
	(2 3/8 × 5 inches)			
	(71 lines)			
Mothers' Manual.........	1/3 page	1,800	2	3,600
	(4 9/16 × 5 inches)			
	(1 col.)			
Parents' Magazine.......	1/2 col.	2,665	2	5,330
	(2 1/4 × 5 inches)			
	(71 lines)			
McFadden's Group......	1/6 page	3,041	4	12,164
True Story.............	(2 1/4 × 5 1/16 inches)			
Photoplay..............	(1/4 col.)			
TV-Radio Mirror........				
True Confessions.......				
Motion Picture.........				
True Romance.........				
True Experience.......				
True Love.............				
Redbook				
Reserve for special				
regional				
availabilities.........				2,000
				$35,174
Estimated production				2,326
				$37,500

CREATIVE STRATEGY

Before Advertising Associates took over the account in 1969, Gentle Care was advertised through ads which featured the product jar. A typical ad, as created by the former agency, is shown in Exhibit 7. This ad shows an attractive woman's head with her hand apparently rubbing her shoulder. The headline is very general in content; it is not until the reader sees the subheading does she learn that Gentle Care is for use during pregnancy. Seals of approval from two well-known certification agencies were also featured, which meant that advertisements had to be placed in *Good Housekeeping* and *Parents' Magazine*. Exhibit 8 shows the first advertisement in company history which prominently displays that the product is for use during pregnancy.

The new campaign inaugurated by Advertising Associates in 1970, an

EXHIBIT 7
Pre-Advertising Associates ad for
Gentle Care

example of which is shown in Exhibit 9, was more direct; the reader could readily determine who used the product and for what purpose. One seal of approval, that of *Good Housekeeping* magazine, was dropped in the belief that the magazine's audience was much older than the target market for Gentle Care. The decision was discussed at length because the role of older women in the purchase and use of the product was not known.

Changing standards and values in our society are reflected in the 1974 campaign as shown in Exhibit 10. Here a nude model is seen actually applying the product as it would be done by the purchaser. Furthermore, the headline is direct and to the point. The *Parents' Magazine* seal is again featured, and the product package is illustrated in a subordinate position.

EXHIBIT 8
First Gentle Care ad prominently featuring
use during pregnancy

EXHIBIT 9
First ad in the Advertising Associates
campaign of 1970

Make Yourself Comfortable.

Treat your skin to a soothing beauty
massage with GENTLE CARE It's the
body skin conditioner that's especially
recommended during pregnancy. The rich,
lubricating liquid helps tight, dry
skin stay soft and supple. It
brings you ease and comfort
while you wait. Look for
GENTLE CARE
at your drug
counter.

Gentle
Care

EXHIBIT 10
Example of 1974 advertising for Gentle Care

Don't let your tummy get out of shape while you're pregnant.

Give your tight, dry skin a soothing massage with Gentle Care . Its special formula will help relieve the taut feeling and minimize itching. And it will help your skin stay soft and supple. So make yourself comfortable. Look for Gentle Care in cream or liquid form at your drug counter.

THE 1975 ADVERTISING PLAN

In mulling over the advertising history of his client, Van Huesen jotted down several questions which he felt needed answering before he could design the 1975 advertising plan for Gentle Care:

1. What level of advertising should be recommended for 1975?
2. What changes, if any, should be made in media strategy? Are specialized magazines the best media choice for Gentle Care? If so, are "baby-oriented" publications the best choice?
3. Is the frequency rather than the reach strategy to be continued for Gentle Care advertising in 1975?
4. Should the *Parents' Magazine* seal be retained?
5. What changes, if any, should Mr. Van Huesen recommend in the creative strategy for the product?

Once these questions were answered, Mr. Van Huesen felt he was ready to meet with Mr. Spring to present his recommendations for 1975 Gentle Care advertising. Van Huesen knew from past experience that he could anticipate some probing questions from Mr. Spring concerning how the effectiveness of the advertising for Gentle Care could be measured.

21

The Phoenix Suns*

On January 22, 1968, the board of governors of the National Basketball Association awarded a franchise to the city of Phoenix, Arizona. At the outset, the roster of the new team's owners read like a Hollywood "Who's Who," while the majority of players on the club's expansion roster had been prominently listed on the NBA's "Who Cares" list. The most famous of the owners were Andy Williams, Henry Mancini, Tony Curtis, Ed Ames, and Bobbi Gentry. But the most vital leadership of this new $2 million expansion team came from owners Richard Bloch of Los Angeles and Donald Diamond and Donald Pitt of Tucson.

THE SEARCH FOR THE WINNING COMBINATION

In March 1968, the Suns named Jerry Colangelo, a 28-year-old former University of Illinois basketball star and then executive assistant to the president of the Chicago Bulls, general manager. Colangelo promptly named John Kerr, one-time NBA Coach of the Year with the Bulls, as head coach of the newly formed club. Together, they set out to battle not only their NBA opponents, but also the large number of skeptics who termed Phoenix a "nonmajor league town" and who thought the franchise would not succeed.

---

*This case was written by John Murphy, Assistant Professor of Advertising, University of Texas, at Austin, and by Charles Patti, Associate Professor, Arizona State University. Used with permission.

The 1968–69 season saw the Suns suffer through their first season with a 16–66 record. Gail Goodrich, obtained in the expansion draft from the Los Angeles Lakers, led the team in scoring with 1,931 points, a 23.8 scoring average. Dick Van Arsdale, the Suns first choice in the expansion draft averaged 21 points per game. During this first season, the Suns sold 735 season tickets and drew a total of 160,565 (an average of 4,340 per game).

In December of that first season, Colangelo made the first of several moves that were to pay off in one of the most impressive building projects ever completed in the NBA without benefit of a superstar center. The Suns traded an unidentified draft choice and McCoy McLemore (originally selected from the Chicago Bulls) to Detroit for center Jim Fox. This was the first step in a journey that was to take the Suns from 16–66 to 48–34 in just two seasons.

But between steps one and two was the "Great Disappointment"—the loss of a coin flip with the Milwaukee Bucks for UCLA's Lew Alcindor (now Kareem Abdul-Jabbar). "Heads" had been called by Phoenix fans in a newspaper-sponsored contest.

"Through all the frustration of that first year," said Colangelo, "our one ray of hope was the coin flip and Alcindor. We had really built up our hopes when we lost the flip . . . well, I guess that has to be the low point of my life."

Indeed, Jabbar would have made a difference. From the 1970–71 season through the 1974–75 season, the Milwaukee Bucks won 317 games and lost only 140 for a league-leading .694 percentage. Jabbar contributed heavily to this impressive record.

Prior to the 1969–70 season, the Suns brought the controversial Connie Hawkins to the Suns after he jumped from the rival American Basketball Association. Hawkins had been banned from the NBA for alleged involvement with gamblers while a freshman at the University of Iowa, a charge later totally discredited.

During the Sun's second season, Hawkins led the team in scoring with a 24.6 average, earned a starting berth in the All-Star game and gained first team All-Pro honors. Van Arsdale also was named to the All-Star team for the second year. Midway through the season, John Kerr stepped down as head coach and General Manager Jerry Colangelo took over and guided the team to a 39–43 record and extended the Los Angeles Lakers to seven games before being eliminated in the play-offs.

In the 1970–71 season under the new coach, Cotton Fitzsimmons, the Suns posted the league's fourth best record (48–34). However, they failed to make the play-offs, finishing third in their division behind Milwaukee and Chicago. Van Arsdale led the club in scoring with a 21.9 average and

Paul Silas led in rebounding for the second straight season. Van Arsdale and Hawkins were again named to the All-Star team.

The next year was more of the same. The Suns met with even greater success on the court, this time winning 49 games, but again missed the play-offs because of nemeses Chicago and Milwaukee.[1]

Late in the 1971–72 season, the Suns signed Charlie Scott, the highest scoring player in ABA history. Scott, an All American at North Carolina and an Olympic star, quit the ABA Virginia Squires in a contract dispute. To get him, the Suns gave up future considerations to the Boston Celtics who held Scott's NBA rights. The future consideration later turned out to be Paul Silas.

After two seasons, Coach Fitzsimmons left the team to coach the Atlanta Hawks and Butch Van Breda Koff was named coach. Seven games into the 1972–73 season, Colangelo replaced Van Breda Koff as coach. That season, the Suns fell off to a 38–44 mark and again finished third in their division. Charlie Scott led the team in scoring with a record 25.3 average and along with Connie Hawkins was named to the All-Star team.

Prior to the 1973–74 season, Colangelo hired John MacLeod (head coach of the University of Oklahoma basketball team). Early in the season, Connie Hawkins was traded to Los Angeles for Keith Erickson who by season's end was named the Suns' Most Outstanding Player. Charlie Scott again led the club in scoring average with 25.4 points per game but missed the final 29 games with a broken arm. The Suns finished the season with a 30–52 record and finished fourth in their division.

Injuries and misfortune struck again during the 1974–75 season. The Suns' No. 1 draft choice, 1974 consensus All-American John Shumate, sat out the entire season because of a blood clotting disorder. Also, veteran forward-guard Keith Erickson was limited to only 49 games because of back problems. Although center Dennis Autrey established personal career highs in nearly every statistical category and forward Curtis Perry finished tenth among all NBA rebounders, the Suns again finished fourth in the Pacific Division with a 30–52 record.

MARKETING CONSIDERATIONS

The product. A professional sports team is, in many ways, no different than any other product or service. It is organized to make profits for the owners. The team hopefully possesses want-satisfying qualities— entertainment value—for which customers are willing to pay.

For the most part, the quality of sports products (teams) are evaluated

---

[1] Subsequently, the NBA rules were changed to provide for "wild card" play-off entries on the basis of win-loss percentage as well as standing in the league.

TABLE 1

Five-year cumulative NBA standings, 1970–1971 through 1974–1975 (includes both regular season and play-off competition)

Team	Won	Lost	Percent
1. Milwaukee Bucks...............	317	140	.694
2. Boston Celtics..................	314	150	.677
3. Chicago Bulls..................	277	175	.613
4. Los Angeles Lakers............	281	178	.612
5. New York Knicks...............	281	189	.598
6. Washington Bullets............	259	203	.561
7. Golden State Warriors.........	250	198	.558
8. Detroit Pistons................	208	212	.495
9. Phoenix Suns..................	197	213	.480
10. Seattle Supersonics...........	197	224	.468
11. Atlanta Hawks................	189	238	.443
12. Houston Rockets..............	183	235	.438
13. Kansas City Kings............	178	238	.428
14. Buffalo Braves................	161	262	.381
15. Philadelphia 76ers............	147	270	.353
16. Cleveland Cavaliers...........	139	271	.339
17. Portland Trail Blazers.........	133	277	.324
18. New Orleans Jazz.............	23	59	.280

on the basis of their success—the team's win and loss record. The Phoenix Suns' record between 1970 and 1974 is slightly below the .500 mark. Including both regular season and play-off competition, the Suns have won 197 games and lost 213 games. (See Table 1.) The Suns compete in what is considered to be the strongest division in the league. The Milwaukee Bucks (.694 win-loss percentage) and the Chicago Bulls (.613 win-loss percentage) are in the same division with the Suns.

The success of a professional sports team is affected by several variables including:

1. Injuries and illness to key players.
2. Ability to sign outstanding college players in the annual college draft.[2]
3. Personalities and motivations of individual players. Because most spectator sports are team games, the success of any team often depends on the willingness and abilities of team members to sacrifice individual stardom for the overall benefit of the team.

---

[2] At the end of each season, professional basketball teams take part in the annual college draft—the selection of the top college basketball players. The NBA team with the lowest win-loss percentage during the past season is allowed to draft first. The team with the highest win-loss percentage drafts last. Teams are allowed to trade their drafting positions for veteran players, for future draft selections, or for cash.

TABLE 2
Home attendance, 1968–1969 through 1974–1975

Year	Season ticket sales	Total attendance	Average	Paid attendance	Average	Dates
1968–69...........	735	160,565	4,340	120,396	3,254	37
1969–70...........	1,750	281,821	7,617	231,445	6,612	35
1970–71...........	3,200	332,945	8,120	293,748	7,344	40
1971–72...........	3,500	342,922	8,364	304,756	7,433	41
1972–73...........	4,400	342,177	8,344	312,006	7,609	41
1973–74...........	4,500	284,324	6,934	254,446	6,206	41
1974–75...........	3,910	253,096	6,173	213,221	5,201	41
Totals.......		1,997,850	7,242	1,730,018	6,268	276

The market. The potential of any sports market is a function of several variables including: its population size and demographic characteristics; amount, type, and quality of competition; degree of interest among the population in sports entertainment; amount of entertainment value supplied by the team; and ability of the market to purchase tickets.

The Phoenix Suns operate in the 31st largest Standard Metropolitan Statistical Area (SMSA) in the United States. Phoenix and the surrounding suburbs of Tempe, Scottsdale, and Mesa represent one of the fastest growing metropolitan areas in the United States.

The Suns view the market for basketball tickets in two categories: season ticket holders and individual game ticket buyers. The majority of the season tickets are sold to individual companies who purchase two–six tickets. About 500 season tickets are sold each year to large companies in the area. These tickets are sold largely on the basis of the merchandising and promotional potential for the purchasing company. Finally, individuals comprise the balance of the season ticket sales. Season ticket sales climbed from 735 for the Suns' first season and reached a high of 4,500 for the 1973–74 season. (See Table 2.)

Season ticket sales are very important to any sports franchise. They provide preseason operating income and form the base upon which additional attendance and profit can be added. As important as season ticket sales are, however, individual game sales still represent the majority of the paid attendance. Furthermore, attracting more individual game attendance will increase the likelihood of selling more season tickets for the succeeding season.

To learn more about the spectators of Suns basketball, a study was conducted toward the end of the 1974–75 season. Although the sample for this study was drawn from spectators who attended only one game, some interesting statistics were uncovered.

The study included interviews with 1,720 attendees at the Suns-Bulls game on April 4 in the Phoenix Coliseum. Over 31 percent of those interviewed held season tickets and also 27 percent of the respondents had their ticket given to them. Twenty-three percent said they attended games "once or twice" and 22 percent "all games." Slightly more than 35 percent said they would attend more games if the price of the tickets were lower and another 33 percent would attend more games if the team were better. (See Table 3 for complete results.)

In assessing the Phoenix market, General Manager Jerry Colangelo points out three factors which he feels tend to detract from the financial success of any major league sports franchise in the Phoenix area:

1. The lack of a large blue-collar market: typically, the blue-collar market makes up a sizable portion of most sports attendance. A study recently conducted for the Suns seems to support Colangelo's feelings. In attempting to define the audience for Suns' basketball, it was determined that 35.1 percent of the spectators were in the "professional" occupational category. The second largest category was "housewife" (15.7 percent). Colangelo feels that without the large base of support from the blue-collar market, the Suns' market is truly different than any of the other 16 NBA teams.

2. The success of any sports franchise depends on fans who will support the team during both winning and losing seasons. Because Phoenix has grown so fast and has attracted people from so many other regions of the country, there is difficulty in developing allegiance to a Phoenix team. Colangelo feels that "fair-and-foul-weather" allegiance is lacking partly because many of the new residents still feel loyalty to professional teams from their last place of residence. That is, migrants from Chicago or the Midwest, feel that the Chicago Bulls, Detroit Pistons, or Milwaukee Bucks are still "their team." Migrants from New York and other parts of the East Coast, feel strong allegiance to the Knickerbockers or Boston Celtics. In the same study mentioned above, over one third of the respondents selected a team other than the Suns as their favorite NBA team.

3. Finally, Colangelo feels that the year-round warm, dry climate of the Phoenix area works to detract from professional sports attendance. Because the weather is pleasant throughout the year, Phoenix area residents have the option to participate in a broad range of leisure activities, including year-round swimming, golf, tennis, boating, fishing, hiking, and camping.

Competition. The Phoenix area has long been known as a popular sports and recreation area. In addition to the availability of a large number of "nature-oriented" recreation activities (swimming, hiking, sightseeing, fishing, and so on), there are several excellent amateur and professional spectator sports teams in the area. In the spring, four major league baseball teams (Chicago Cubs, San Francisco Giants, Milwaukee Brewers, and

TABLE 3
Phoenix Suns Sports Quiz Survey*

Percent of respondents

1. How Ticket Obtained:
   Season ticket............. 31.2
   Ticket given............... 26.5
   Discount ticket............ 19.7
   Buy for game............. 12.6
   Other..................... 4.2
   No response............. 3.3
   Invalid................... 2.6

2. Recognize Players:
   Yes...................... 73.9
   No........................ 17.4
   No response............. 4.8
   Invalid................... 4.0

3. Reason for Attendance:
   Participate................ 10.2
   Professional entertainment 24.2
   Family entertainment..... 15.3
   Chance out............... 11.0
   Giveaways................. 1.3
   Team support............. 23.7
   Other..................... 6.3
   No response............. 4.9
   Invalid................... 3.0

4. Frequently Attended:
   All games................ 22.2
   Half of all 12.5
   1–4...................... 11.9
   Versus specific team...... 13.7
   Once or twice............. 23.0
   Other..................... 9.0
   No response............. 4.5
   Invalid................... 3.3

5. Reason to Attend More:
   Better team.............. 33.0
   Lower price.............. 35.3
   Superstar................. 5.1
   Giveaways................. 1.6
   Different division.......... 0.7
   Entertainment............ 2.6
   Other..................... 11.9
   No response............. 6.6
   Invalid................... 3.2

6. Read Sports Section:
   Yes—Sunday.............. 5.5
   Yes—daily................. 64.4
   Yes—once per week....... 7.0
   Yes—once per month..... 4.4
   No....................... 12.2
   No response............. 4.2
   Invaild................... 2.3

Percent of respondents

7. Ever Play Basketball:
   Yes—high school.......... 43.5
   Yes—college.............. 10.6
   No—playground........... 21.8
   Never..................... 15.8
   No response............. 5.0
   Invalid................... 3.3

8. Watch Suns on TV:
   Always................... 60.1
   Selected games........... 15.8
   Never..................... 6.6
   Infrequently............... 20.6
   No response............. 4.1
   Invalid................... 2.8

9. Listen to Suns on Radio:
   Always................... 24.5
   Selected games........... 16.1
   Never..................... 24.0
   Infrequently............... 26.5
   No response............. 6.2
   Invalid................... 2.7

10. Favorite NBA Team:
    Bucks.................... 2.5
    Bulls..................... 7.4
    Suns..................... 56.2
    Braves.................... 1.6
    Knicks.................... 3.8
    Celtics................... 13.7
    Lakers.................... 2.4
    Bullets................... 0.3
    Other..................... 2.7
    No response............. 6.5

11. What Sport Event Last Attended Other Than Pro Basketball:
    Baseball.................. 13.3
    Tennis.................... 5.2
    Golf...................... 8.5
    College basketball........ 14.7
    Hockey.................... 18.3
    High school basketball.... 9.3
    Other..................... 18.2
    No response............. 8.6
    Invalid................... 3.9

12. How Long in Phoenix:
    Less than two years....... 10.8
    Two–five years............. 16.3
    Five–ten years............. 13.7
    More than ten............. 43.7
    Visiting................... 5.0

TABLE 3 (*continued*)

Percent of respondents			*Percent of respondents*	
	Winters only	1.1	No response	8.8
	No response	5.9	Invalid	4.2
	Invalid	3.5	17. Occupation:	
13.	Where from:		Laborer—operator	2.1
	New York	5.3	Homemaker	15.7
	Chicago	12.7	Executive—professional	35.1
	South	5.7	Farmer	1.5
	California	7.7	Clerical—sales	7.9
	Southwest	4.5	Craft—skill	5.5
	East	9.1	Student	12.6
	Midwest	21.3	Other	8.4
	Arizona	12.4	No response	8.2
	Other	7.2	Invalid	3.0
	No response	8.1	18. Where Do You Live:	
	Invalid	5.9	South Phoenix	2.9
14.	What Sport Watched Most:		North Central Phoenix	26.0
	Baseball	7.6	East Phoenix	9.9
	Football	30.5	Scottsdale	9.0
	Basketball	39.2	West Phoenix	16.0
	Hockey	6.2	Glendale/Sun City	7.6
	Other	4.5	Tempe/Mesa	11.2
	No response	6.9	Buckeye/Tolleson	.6
	Invalid	5.1	Other	5.9
15.	What Sport Known Best:		No response	8.4
	Baseball	18.5	Invalid	2.3
	Football	16.0	19. Sex:	
	Basketball	37.8	Female	33.8
	Golf	6.9	Male	53.6
	Tennis	4.9	No response	7.1
	Other	2.8	Invalid	5.5
	No response	7.6	20. Age:	
	Invalid	5.3	Less than 15	4.9
16.	Discouraged from Attending:		16–20	8.6
	Parking	2.8	21–30	19.2
	Prices	33.8	31–35	12.6
	Ticket availability	3.9	36–40	10.2
	Team	20.6	41–45	9.6
	Time of game	4.5	46–55	13.4
	Location	3.6	More than 55	9.0
	Other	17.6	No response	8.7
			Invalid	3.7

* Compiled April 4, 1975; total sample size, 1,720.

the Oakland Athletics) hold spring training in the surrounding Phoenix suburbs. The Phoenix Giants (AAA minor league baseball team) play a 136 game schedule between April 10 and September 9. Arizona State University, located in adjacent Tempe, competes in the Western Athletic Conference in all major sports, and the annual football Fiesta Bowl is held in Tempe in December.

Until the 1974–75 season, the Phoenix Suns were the only "major league" sports franchise in the professional market. However, the Phoenix Roadrunners, members of the World Hockey Association, began play in Phoenix Coliseum in 1974. In January of 1975, the Denver Racquets, champions of the World Team Tennis League in 1974, were sold and moved to Phoenix. The Racquets, who also occupy the Coliseum, play a 44 match season (20 home dates) and during their first season in Phoenix drew approximately 86,000 fans. (See Exhibit 1.)

Promotion. The underlying objective of the promotional efforts of any sports team is to help increase attendance. The Suns have maintained two promotion campaigns—one directed toward increasing season ticket sales and the other toward increasing individual game ticket sales. Although major league sports franchises derive income from other sources, most of this revenue is dependent upon game attendance. For example, income from food and drink concessions; souvenir and program sales; and parking receipts all increase with increases in game attendance.

Season ticket promotions. The Suns promote season ticket sales primarily through their "Total Merchandising Package." This promotion consists of personally contacting a number of larger organizations in the Phoenix area and making available to them a variety of promotion ideas and programs—all related to Suns' season tickets. This "package" consists of coop advertising; package offers; traffic builders (via price discounting of tickets); and offering advertising messages at Suns' games through banners and messages announced on the public address system. The Suns' management feels that their "Total Merchandising Package" has been very successful because it sells season tickets while helping local companies accomplish their own promotion objectives.

In addition to the "Total Merchandising Package," the Suns also have used radio, television, and newspaper advertising as well as direct mail brochures, "leave-behind" pieces, and stuffers in Master Charge and BankAmericard monthly statements.

Individual game promotions. Because the target market for individual game tickets is much broader than the season ticket market, the Suns use a wider range of media to reach this market. The target markets for individual game tickets are (1) *anyone interested in sports entertainment, living in the Phoenix area, and capable of paying $3 for a general admission ticket.* Although the study mentioned earlier indicates that men are

EXHIBIT 1

The professional sports season in Phoenix

Team	Jan.–Feb.	March	April	May	June	July	Aug.	Sept.	Oct.	Nov.	Dec.	Average game attendance	Price of general admission*
Phoenix Suns (NBA)	← (41 home games) →											6,200	$1.50 3.00
Phoenix Racquets (World Team Tennis)		← (20 home matches) →										4,300	2.50 1.25
Phoenix Giants (Pacific Coast League)			← (68 home games) →									3,800	2.00 0.75
Phoenix Roadrunners (World Hockey Association)	← (40 home games) →												4.00 3.00
Major league baseball—spring training (Chicago Cubs, Milwaukee Brewers, Oakland Athletics, San Francisco Giants)	← (20–25 games for each team) →											1,000	2.00

* Higher price is for adult admission; lower price is for child admission.

perhaps more likely to attend games—the Suns believe that anyone, including children, professional homemakers, and working women are also excellent prospects; (2) *An important secondary market is visiting businessmen and conventioneers.* This is a rapidly growing market and can be reached efficiently through a number of advertising media, including newspapers, in-flight magazines, and hotel and motel lobby and room brochures.

The primary media used to promote individual game ticket sales are newspaper, radio, and television. (See Table 4.) In addition, schedule posters are placed in retail stores throughout the Phoenix area. Two direct mail pieces are also used:

1. Advance order mailer. This is a mailing piece sent during the first week of the regular season to the Suns' current mailing list of nonseason ticket holders. Prospects may order tickets for as many games in advance as they wish and be assured of having the same seat for each game.

TABLE 4
Phoenix Suns media expenditures

Medium	1972–73*	1973–74†	1974–75‡
Radio	$15,022	$15,412	$15,907
Newspaper	15,813	24,345	32,558
Television	1,810	1,054	0
Magazines	1,042	0	0
Totals	$33,687	$40,811	$48,465

* Represents only cash expended.
† Does not include $12,190 of media "purchased" by trading tickets for space and/or time.
‡ Does not include $41,555 of media "purchased" by trading tickets for space and/or time.

2. Group order mailer. This is a mailing piece sent to clubs in the Phoenix area and offers selected games at special rates for groups in minimum numbers. In addition, this same mailer is sent to chairmen of conventions known to be coming to Phoenix.

The Suns, like other professional sports franchises, also use a number of other promotions to help encourage attendance at individual games. These promotions include such activities as: "Family Night" (children admitted free when accompanied by paying adults); "2-for-1 Night" (two tickets for the price of one); "Ladies' Night" (women admitted free); and a number of giveaway Nights (free Suns' T-shirts, basketballs, athletic bags, seat cushions, and so on).

One of the Suns promotion objectives is to build support of the franchise by getting the entire family involved in basketball and the Suns team. Many of the promotions used by the Suns are, therefore, family-oriented. The Suns now start their home game at 7:30 P.M. (a half-hour earlier than before) so that youngsters can more conveniently attend games during a weekday school night. Also, some of the advertising is aimed directly at women.

CURRENT SITUATION

As the Phoenix Suns prepared for the 1975–76 season, General Manager Colangelo embarked on one of the most active trading and drafting programs in the seven-year history of the franchise.

Guard Paul Westphal arrived from the Boston Celtics in exchange for the talented, but enigmatic Charlie Scott. First-year center Earl Williams went to the Detroit Pistons for veteran forward Willie Norwood. Playmaker Phil Lumpkin was obtained from Portland for a future draft pick. Alvin Adams, three-time Big Eight Conference Player of the Year from Oklahoma, was the Club's No. 1 draft pick. Phoenix used one of its two first-round picks in 1976 to obtain Buffalo's No. 1 pick in 1975, and utilized the choice to select Ricky Sobers from the University of Nevada—Las Vegas. On a "look-see" basis, the Suns also signed free agent guard Duane Read of Portland State and former Suns guard Mo Layton.

As the Suns faced the 1975–76 season, several important factors would seem to affect the prospects for improvement in game attendance:

1. Attendance was down for the second year in 1974–75.
2. The team had just completed another disappointing season (32 games won; 50 games lost).
3. The player that drew the most fan interest, high-scoring guard, Charlie Scott had been traded.
4. The Suns faced increased major league competition from the Phoenix Roadrunners and the Phoenix Racquets.

At the same time, General Manager Colangelo felt the team had several items in its favor:

1. John Shumate, the Suns' first-round draft pick in 1974 and an All-American at Notre Dame, was healthy and ready to play the 1975–76 season.
2. The Suns had an excellent college draft in 1975. Their first-round selection was 6 foot, 9 inch center-forward Alvin Adams from the University of Oklahoma. Adams was expected to provide immediate help to the team.
3. In exchange for Charlie Scott, the Suns received guard Paul Westphall from the Boston Celtics. Westphall is a proven veteran and regarded as an excellent team player and therefore promised to make a substantial contribution to the Suns.

4.   Other key players (Erickson and Van Arsdale) who were injured part of the past season have recovered and should again provide the Suns with leadership and consistency.

In formulating the advertising and promotion plans for the 1975–76 season, General Manager Colangelo is hesitant to accept the advertising recommendations made by the Suns' advertising agency.

For the past several years, the Suns have been spending between $30,000–$50,000 for media advertising. The cost of giveaways, salaries, and production are not included in the above figure. To increase both season ticket sales and individual game ticket sales, the Suns' advertising agency has recommended a substantial increase in the 1975–76 advertising budget. The agency recommended a $110,000 advertising budget for the coming season. The agency points out that while the "Total Merchandising Package" has been successful, the value of the giveaway promotions is highly questionable. Furthermore, the agency felt that most of the past advertising campaigns aimed directly at increasing Suns' awareness and generating interest in the team was diluted. The agency also feels that a significant amount of attendance drop-off during the 1974–75 season was caused by the large advertising expenditures of the Phoenix Roadrunners. During the past season, the Roadrunners spent approximately $112,000 on advertising media ($140,000 including production). The Roadrunners had sold approximately 3,500 season tickets during the 1974–75 season for 40 home dates.

Mr. Colangelo was not convinced that the agency's advertising media budget recommendations were sound. It is his feeling that by far the most important factor in increasing attendance is the quality of the team. He felt this to be true for season ticket and individual game sales. He pointed out that during the 1970–71 and 1971–72 seasons, team attendance was growing rapidly without large advertising expenditures. During these two seasons, the team had excellent records and therefore generated spectator interest and support. The momentum of these two seasons and fan anticipation of an even stronger team brought about higher season ticket sales and total paid attendance during the 1973–74 season. However, after three consecutive losing seasons, Colangelo feels that potential spectators must now be convinced that the team is improved and can win consistently.

In addition, Colangelo felt that a 1973 study of sports fans' reactions to NBA basketball indicated that Phoenix fans have a comparatively strong liking for basketball and a high awareness of major professional sports leagues or associations. (See Table 5.) Therefore, he felt that heavy advertising expenditures were not required to build awareness and interest in the Suns.

TABLE 5
Awareness of major professional sports leagues or associations, by market (first and second mentions)

	Major league baseball	NFL	NBA	NHL	(Base)
Eastern Conference					
Atlantic:					
Boston............................	45%	32%	28%	37%	(101)
Buffalo............................	27	43	26	46	(95)
New York..........................	50	21	42	16	(98)
Philadelphia.......................	47	34	33	20	(100)
Central:					
Atlanta............................	48	51	31	11	(100)
Baltimore..........................	63	33	32	8	(98)
Cleveland..........................	50	41	33	7	(99)
Houston...........................	54	43	20	5	(101)
Western Conference					
Midwest:					
Chicago............................	58	23	22	20	(100)
Detroit.............................	53	32	26	12	(94)
Kansas City/Omaha................	56	51	19	8	(110)
Milwaukee.........................	36	52	52	14	(101)
Pacific:					
Golden State.......................	52	47	35	6	(97)
Los Angeles........................	52	40	32	7	(99)
Phoenix............................	39	41	30	8	(100)
Portland...........................	36	31	53	12	(98)
Seattle.............................	29	44	38	14	(104)
Total sample...................	47%	39%	32%	15%	(1,703)

EXHIBIT 2
1974–1975 Phoenix Suns promotion games

Date	Opposing team	Promotion
October 19.........	Kansas City—Omaha	Jack-in-the-Box 2-for-1/Mini Basketball
November 17......	Golden State	Valley West Mall 2-for-1
December 7.......	Los Angeles	Carnation Night
December 11......	Portland	Cobre Tire 2-for-1 Night
December 19......	Milwaukee	Metrocenter 2-for-1 Night
December 27......	Buffalo	Sears Plaque Night
January 11.........	New York	Carnation Campfire Girls Night
January 25.........	New Orleans	Sears 2-for-1 and Tote Bag
January 31.........	Los Angeles	KOY Radio Sock Night
February 14........	Boston	Jack-in-the-Box Team Picture Night
February 15........	Atlanta	Carnation Girl Scout Night
February 28........	Golden State	Carnation Boy Scout Night
March 8...........	Houston	Carnation Y-Indian Guide Night
March 19..........	New York	Chris-Town Mall Night
March 25..........	Milwaukee	Western Savings 2-for-1 Night
March 29..........	Kansas City—Omaha	Jack-in-the Box Flyer Night

CASE

22

Gulf Oil Company—U.S.*

In April 1974, Mr. Charles Swinson, advertising and sales promotion manager of Gulf Oil Company—U.S. was attempting to develop his recommendations to top management with respect to promotional activities of the firm during the coming fiscal year. Unprecedented developments in the energy market in the previous nine months had resulted in a complete turnabout in the promotional objectives and strategies of the entire oil industry. As a result of the "energy crisis," Mr. Swinson was under pressure to design a promotional communications plan to cope with a concerned and hostile public and sagging morale within the advertising department which had found it extremely difficult to adjust its thinking to the new environment.

BACKGROUND

The Gulf Oil Company—U.S., based in Houston, Texas, is a subsidiary of a diversified petroleum company, Gulf Oil Corporation, which was in its 73d year of operation. Gulf Oil—U.S. ranked as the fifth largest gasoline marketer in the United States, preceded by Texaco, Shell, Amoco, and Exxon, in that order. In recent years, Gulf had retained about a 6 percent share of market relative to its competitors. Table 1 presents data on total sales and advertising/media expenditures by the six largest oil company advertisers during 1972.

In addition to gasoline, motor oil, tires, automotive lubricants, and related automotive products produced by Gulf Oil—U.S., other divisions

---

*This case was written by John Murphy, Assistant Professor of Advertising, University of Texas, at Austin, and by Charles Patti, Associate Professor, Arizona State University. Used with permission.

TABLE 1
Sales and media expenditures, 1972: Six largest oil company advertisers

Company	Total sales ($ millions)	Total advertising expenditures ($ millions)	Percent of measured media*								
			General magazines	Farm publications	Business publications	Spot TV	Net TV	Spot radio	Net radio	Outdoor
Exxon Corp.	$22,438	$34	4.8%	0.9%	—	44.3%	20.3%	22.2%	—	7.5%
Shell Oil Corp.	4,817	31	7.9	4.8	1.5%	42.5	34.8	5.2	2.9%	0.4
Texaco Inc.	8,693	27	4.5	0.3	3.6	4.2	66.3	13.8	6.8	0.5
Standard (Indiana)	5,401	26	2.9	4.2	3.7	39.9	22.0	26.2	—	1.1
Mobil Oil Co.	10,295	24	5.3	4.1	2.7	17.2	40.9	22.9	6.4	0.4
Gulf Oil Corp.	7,624	23	1.9	—	4.0	13.8	66.3	10.6	2.1	1.3

* Media expenditures percentages are based on total expenditures in measured media only.

Source: *Advertising Age.*

and subsidiaries of Gulf were engaged in a wide variety of ventures. These ventures included a number of energy-related activities—coal mining, atomic power, petrochemicals, and other resource extraction. The parent corporation had enjoyed a lucrative 11-year alliance with Holiday Inns, Inc. Furthermore, the Gulf Oil Real Estate Development Co. was established in 1972 and among other projects was developing a residential, industrial and commercial complex on a 2,700-acre site in Orlando, Florida, near Disney World.

Consolidated net income of Gulf Oil Corporation for 1973 was $800 million compared with $447 million in 1972, an improvement of 79 percent (see Table 2). Higher earnings were attributed primarily to higher refined product prices and sales volume, a broadening plastics and chemicals market, elimination of marginal operations, and an expanded tanker fleet. Gulf worldwide profits were up 75 percent in the first quarter of 1974. The earnings from Gulf's U.S. petroleum operations increased 14 percent in 1973. This increase was attributed to increased prices for crude oil produced and to a 12.3 percent increase in refined product sales volume. Gulf maintained that product price increases received by the corporation reflected the recovery of increased costs as approved by the Cost of Living Council, and that by far the greatest increase in earnings was realized by overseas operations rather than by Gulf—U.S.

In the first quarter of 1973 the future looked extremely promising for Gulf, whose more than 20,000 service stations were servicing 6–8 million people *per week* in 35 states. Numerous factors were combining to create a record demand for gasoline (and other fuels as well). The 1971–72 car years were banner sales years. The average size and weight of the new cars was quite large. The new cars used 30 percent to 35 percent more gasoline, a fuel penalty resulting from strict federal auto emission standards. As the cars aged, the fuel penalties sometimes rose to 40 percent and 50 percent. The economy was such that it stimulated a maximum number of miles traveled—business was booming and income levels were high. Finally, research showed that 72 percent of the people who had bought a 1972 car had another car; 35 + percent became three-car families. Old cars weren't being retired and the demand for automobiles was growing at 8 percent–10 percent per year. Not only did all these statistics portend record sales of and demand for gasoline; more ominously, they portended an inevitable fuel crisis when this vast demand outstripped refining capacity of the oil companies. In the second quarter of 1973, talk of a fuel crisis or "energy crunch" began, and in the third and fourth quarters, the frightening effects of the energy crisis were initially felt. When it became clear that fuel oil would be in short supply in the United States that winter, the gasoline companies were allocated crude oil and their supply began to run short of demand by 2 percent–3 percent.

TABLE 2
Five-year-financial summary (in $ millions)

	1973	1972	1971	1970	1969
Statement of Income:					
Revenues:					
Sales and other operating revenues (includes consumer excise taxes)					
United States.....................	$ 4,626	$3,944	$3,841	$3,881	$3,703
Foreign...........................	5,217	3,680	3,364	2,716	2,407
	$ 9,843	$7,624	$7,205	$6,597	$6,110
Dividends, interest, equity earnings and other revenues..............	164	109	167	123	128
	$10,007	$7,733	$7,372	$6,720	$6,238
Deductions					
Purchased crude oil, products and merchandise......................	$ 2,833	$1,763	$1,651	$1,656	$1,431
Operating expenses................	1,618	1,447	1,330	1,182	1,089
Selling, general and administrative expenses........................	944	921	935	810	796
Consumer excise taxes.............	1,426	1,381	1,265	1,201	1,156
Sales, use, ad valorem, and other taxes............................	265	228	211	203	175
Income taxes					
United States....................	23	12	31	12	4
Foreign..........................	1,341	800	724	423	372
Deferred.........................	12	11	17	49	66
Depreciation, depletion, amortization and retirements...................	610	576	510	522	451
Interest on long-term debt.........	135	147	137	112	87
	$ 9,207	$7,286	$6,811	$6,170	$5,627
Income before extraordinary item.....	$ 800	$ 447	$ 561	$ 550	$ 611
Extraordinary item...................	—	(250)	—	—	—
Net income..........................	$ 800	$ 197	$ 561	$ 550	$ 611
Estimated losses from discontinued operations charged to net income					
Net (loss)........................	—	$ (27)	$ (32)	$ (26)	$ (19)
Per share........................	—	(.13)	(.15)	(.12)	(.09)
Per share data					
Income before extraordinary item...	$ 4.06	2.15	2.70	2.65	2.94
Extraordinary item.................	—	(1.20)	—	—	—
Net income........................	$ 4.06	$ .95	$ 2.70	$ 2.65	$ 2.94
Cash dividends....................	$ 1.50	$ 1.50	$ 1.50	$ 1.50	$ 1.50
Shareholders' equity...............	28.61	26.04	26.59	25.42	24.28

Source: *1973 Gulf Annual Report.*

PRODUCT ADVERTISING—GULFTANE

At the time the energy crunch hit, Gulf was undertaking a large-scale advertising campaign for its low-lead, medium-priced Gulftane gasoline. Normally product-specific advertising was not characteristic in the oil industry. Research had shown 95 percent awareness of the Gulf logo, and very high aided and unaided recall of Gulf advertising. Product-specific advertising had not been found to alter awareness—awareness resulted from point-of-sale promotions and transaction impressions. Advertising could have an effect on market share, however, and Gulftane was a 91-octane, low-lead product cheaper than competitors' low leads. Low leads were being specified in new car owners' manuals; the demand for such products had increased 50 percent to 60 percent in a year. All in all, Gulf felt Gulftane had tremendous competitive potential.

Unfortunately, with the onset of the energy crisis, intensive product advertising of Gulftane—in fact, *any* advertising campaign which would increase driveway traffic at Gulf service stations—was considered by Gulf management to be imprudent. Not only could Gulf *not* satisfy the additional demand, it was feared that intensive advertising for products in *very* finite supply would serve no purpose but to evoke hostility from the consuming public; it would be a needless expenditure of advertising dollars with possible negative consequences. Thus, in May of 1973, Gulf began phasing out Gulftane advertising (spot TV and radio plus newspapers) in the 75 markets where it was being marketed.

With the premature demise of the Gulftane campaign, Gulf was left with an advertising vacuum. Gulf executives and the subsidiary's ad agency Young & Rubicam felt they had to hit on new promotional tactics which would preserve the firm's market share and reputation without creating additional demand. The immediate strategy was no advertising at all. Studies showed that public opinion was beginning to run very strongly *against* the oil corporations who were advertising the most—namely, Exxon and Amoco. These firms were suggesting that consumers should drive slower, drive less, and use small cars in attempts to conserve fuel—tactics which some marketers call "demarketing," or attempting to manage a too-high level of demand for a scarce product.

Gallup polls and other studies indicated that 62 percent of the public did not really believe there was an energy crisis and 73 percent believed the oil companies were "rigging" the crisis so they could justify higher prices. By fall of 1973, Congress had picked up on the public discontent; certain members of Congress had accused the oil companies of conspiracy and the newly created Federal Energy Office was investigating the industry leaders. Gulf and the other oil companies stepped up their lobbying on Capitol Hill, because there was a growing fear that increasing consumer concern would result in a movement to nationalize the oil industry.

The fuel situation was worsened considerably in late fall of 1973 when the Arab oil countries embargoed oil shipments to the United States and drastically hiked the price of crude oil to *all* buyers. The fact that the embargo was visible proof of a real energy crisis could have helped the oil companies' credibility, except that published oil company profits were at a record high. Congress was talking of cutting oil company profits by

taxing, cutting oil depletion allowances, or putting price ceilings on gasoline. The oil industry was rapidly becoming everybody's scapegoat.

THE AGENCY'S POSITION

During the advertising hiatus which began with the demise of the Gulftane campaign, Gulf and Young & Rubicam developed a series of ad campaigns which were subjected to consumer panels and other tests of advertising effectiveness. These consumer education ads—which attempted a
logical, unemotional presentation of the facts on the energy crisis—were
tested, but fell through because viewers perceived them as self-serving
rather than objective. Ads suggesting that the consumer take measures to
conserve gasoline were perceived as an attempt by the oil companies to
shift the burden of responsibility to the consumers.

Young & Rubicam had come to the conclusion that an item-by-item
refutation by Gulf of all the charges made against Gulf and the industry
would do more harm than good. Consumer panel reaction to such "refutational" advertising had been quite negative. On the basis of their research,
Young & Rubicam concluded that the refutational ads apparently made
Gulf appear defensive and paranoid, and only added fuel to the fire by
focusing on controversial issues. Any facts invoked by Gulf in its own defense were immediately suspect. In addition, the creative talent at Young &
Rubicam felt that the educational but long-winded ads required in a consumer education or refutational campaign were an aesthetic washout. They
lacked eye appeal and the reader tended to lose interest halfway through.
Perhaps more important, the ad executives at Young & Rubicam were ap-
palled at the thought of writing off the large investments Gulf had made
over the years to increase driveway traffic and market share. Young &
Rubicam had worked hard to project an image of Gulf as a service-
oriented gasoline retailer marketing high-quality petroleum products. The
agency felt that Gulf could not afford to forfeit this image, even in and
especially in a time when oil companies were struggling for credibility and
public acceptance.

Young & Rubicam pointed out that although Gulf had drastically reduced their expenditures on advertising during 1973, in 1972 the subsidiary spent approximately $3.2 million to advertise Gulf dealer service.
Advertising expenditures during 1972 promoting gasoline for network and
spot TV were $1,597,000 and $1,578,000, respectively. During that year
Gulf auto tires advertising expenditures on network TV were $45,000.
The subsidiary also benefited from the parent corporation's general promotional expenditures of $3,735,000 during 1972.

Young & Rubicam was not opposed to all advertising. Indeed, they felt
that aggressive, large-scale product advertising was in order, particularly

since Gulf had developed a lead-free gasoline—Gulfcrest—with excellent market potential.

GULFCREST

Late in 1973, Gulf announced that Gulfcrest was ready for marketing. The product was to replace the popular Gulftane low lead. Gulfcrest was to be phased in gradually into all market areas in which Gulf operated with the product available in all areas by July 1, 1974. July 1 was the deadline set by the Environmental Protection Agency for the availability at most gasoline stations of a lead-free gasoline of at least 91-octane rating for use in the 1975 model automobiles.

During the final quarter of 1970, Gulf began making plans for the manufacturing and marketing of a no-lead gasoline to replace Gulftane. The firm had begun developing the new gasoline at that time after becoming convinced that it would eventually be necessary to produce a no-lead product to satisfy the Clean Air Act of 1970. Gulfcrest met or exceeded all EPA requirements for an unleaded product.

Consistent with their low profile promotional strategy, Gulfcrest was introduced without fanfare. Little publicity and no consumer advertising was utilized or planned to introduce the new gasoline.

Gulf's Marketing Department's research indicated that demand for Gulfcrest was 5 percent of the firm's total gasoline production, or about 1 million gallons a day. The firm's research projected demand growth to range from 7 to 10 percent per year, thus by 1980 Gulfcrest should account for 50 percent to 65 percent of total gasoline sales.

RESEARCH DEVELOPMENTS

In recent months, Gulf researchers had developed two promising items relevant to the gasoline shortage. The first was a catalyst that decomposes oxides of nitrogen in auto exhaust and thus may help make unleaded gasoline unnecessary. The catalyst had been sent to various automobile manufacturers and others for road testing. Gulf researchers had tested the unit on an engine test stand and found it effective for the equivalent of 50.000 miles of normal driving.

Second, through improvements in existing equipment and techniques, Gulf research had developed an easily portable device for checking and evaluating the efficiency of an automobile engine in only 30 seconds. The device was an infrared exhaust gas analyzer used to measure an engine's combustion as it relates to gasoline economy in two areas: hydrocarbon and carbon monoxide. Hydrocarbon parts per million are related to the engine's mechanical functions; for example, ignition, timing, spark plugs, and so on. The percentage of carbon monoxide in engine exhaust relates to the air/fuel mixture in the carburetor.

Two attendants are required for operation of the system. A long flexible tube connected to the device is attached to the exhaust pipe of the auto for a quick test which does not require raising the hood or asking the driver to get out from under the steering wheel. The test suggests if the engine is performing efficiently or if maintenance work is in order. If the test indicated an unsatisfactory condition on either or both of the readings a number of likely causes were identified to the motorist.

EXHIBIT 1
Newspaper advertising copy—Econo-Check Program

LOOK FOR GULF'S ECONO-CHECK

. . . at work in your neighborhood!

Find out in 30 seconds if you're getting
the most out of your gasoline!

These days you want to be sure you're getting your money's worth out of the gasoline you buy. And Gulf wants to help you do it.

So, we're bringing the Gulf ECONO-CHECK to you, right in your own neighborhood.

The Gulf ECONO-CHECK is a scientifically designed and specially equipped mobile van that will test your engine's performance—and tell you whether or not you're wasting gasoline through inefficient operation.

This is a test only. Not a tune-up. It'll only cost you $1.00 and our experts can give you a result in 30 seconds, without you raising the hood, or getting out from under the wheel.

What's more, if the test suggests you need maintenance work, and you have the work done, we'll give your car a post-maintenance check FREE, wherever our ECONO-CHECK van is at the time—regardless of where you have the maintenance performed.

So look for Gulf's ECONO-CHECK in your neighborhood soon. The little you spend in 30 seconds, can save you big money in the months ahead!

ECONO-CHECK SCHEDULE: November 26 to December 21— in front of Dillard's Department Store in Padre Staples Mall.

Gulf goes a little bit further

ECONO-CHECK PROGRAM

The second research development had led Gulf's marketing department to develop and test market a pilot project named the Econo-Check Program. The auto-exhaust analyzer was installed in Ford Econoline vans and two attendants performed the service for motorists in shopping center parking lots in two test markets—Corpus Christi, Texas, and Baton Rouge, Louisiana. In both test markets the program had been well publicized through advertising. Exhibit 1 presents the copy used in a 1,500-line newspaper ad promoting the service.

The Econo-Check Program was tested for three-week periods during November and December 1973 in both markets. In-depth consumer research was conducted immediately after performing the service and one-month later to explore consumer attitudes concerning the value of the program and their perception of the company providing the service. The results were extremely positive (see Table 3).

TABLE 3
Consumer attitudes toward Econo-Check Program

	Corpus Christi (n = 496)	Baton Rouge (n = 288)
How would you rate this Econo-Check service?		
Immediately after taking test		
Excellent	49%	44%
Very good	34	24
Good	13	23
Fair, poor	2	3
Don't know	2	6
Telephone survey—one month later		
Excellent	32	
Very good	36	
Good	26	
Fair, poor	1	
Don't know	2	
How do you feel about Econo-Check testing this car again or another car you might own? How likely are you to do this?		
Extremely likely	55	48
Very likely	25	24
Probably likely	13	19
Unlikely	6	9
Don't know	1	—
In general how do you feel about a major oil company furnishing this Econo-Check service?		
Extremely good idea	56	46
Very good idea	33	24
Good idea	9	28
Fair, poor, bad idea	2	2

On the basis of the test market results, the members of Gulf's marketing department responsible for evaluating the program recommended that Gulf:

1. Equip and staff six Econo-Check vans.
2. Conduct Econo-Check in 22 markets with a minimum of two vans per market for a minimum of two weeks each.
3. Offer the service to the consumer on a free basis.
4. Support the program with television and newspaper advertising.
5. Conduct consumer surveys on the Econo-Check and evaluate the program after four months.

Estimated costs to implement recommendations 1 through 4 are shown in the accompanying table.

Six Econo-Check vans	$ 60,000
Staff expense	99,200
Literature, maintenance, and miscellaneous	7,800
Advertising	275,000
	$442,000

OVERALL PROMOTIONAL OBJECTIVES: GULF OIL—U.S.

As a result of a series of task force meetings of the top management and planners of both Gulf Oil Corporation and Gulf—U.S. and their advertising agency a general statement of objectives and strategy for future promotional efforts had been developed. The objective of any proposed promotional effort would be to provide a positive consumer communication by offering an easily recognized consumer benefit which the public would perceive as having true value and would be competitively unique. Ideally the program would protect brand loyalty of current customers and strengthen Gulf's service image with potential customers without adding to service station problems where shortages existed. Further, the promotion should build a service capacity reputation and a favorable consumer attitude that would assist Gulf—U.S. and its dealers in capturing a larger share of the automotive service market on a continuing basis.

Finally, the promotional program should contribute to Gulf's credibility with the public and help foster renewed faith in the company as a responsible corporate citizen.

The major objectives and strategy guidelines were summarized as follows:

1. Offset customer's negative perception of Gulf and other oil companies.
2. Provide a positive consumer communication during the gasoline shortage.

3. Strengthen Gulf's service image without adding to service station problems where shortage situations exist.
4. Increase recognition of Gulf as a service-oriented company.

Although Young & Rubicam realized that promotion of a gasoline product was somewhat incompatible with Gulf's low-profile approach, the agency was in favor of promoting the introduction of Gulfcrest. In addition, at these meetings the agency reiterated their opposition to refutational advertising as an answer to Gulf's problems.

Set against this background Mr. Swinson had to develop his recommendations with respect first to the agency's position and the desirability of a refutational campaign. In addition, he had been asked to suggest alternative strategies for the firm's promotional activities during the coming fiscal year.

CASE

23

Rich's Department Store

The Executive Committee meeting had been a lengthy session, lasting through most of the morning, but Mr. Dick Mills, vice president and sales promotion director of Rich's Department Store, had returned to his office knowing that a major advertising decision was still not ready to be made. And Mr. Mills realized that it would be his responsibility to submit a final recommendation on media strategy at the next meeting.

Mr. Mills stared at the two neatly bound research reports that he had placed side-by-side on his desk. The pair of documents represented summaries of the two presentations that had been made to the Rich's Executive Committee that morning. These studies had been based on exactly the same data, drawn from the same in-store survey of Rich's customers. Each report had been prepared by an experienced and professional marketing researcher. Mr. Mills had expected the strong self-interests of the researchers to be reflected in their presentations and interpretations of the survey results, but he was confident that neither man would misrepresent the actual facts.

Mr. Mills had to admit to himself that he had been very surprised at the apparent major contradictions between the two presentations that he had heard earlier that morning. Mr. Mills and the research director of Rich's, who had also attended the morning presentations by the two outside researchers, had discussed the situation briefly after the meeting. The two men had decided to separately review the written reports and, then, to meet later in the afternoon to decide what additional steps to take.

Before re-reading the reports, Mr. Mills thought back over the events of the past three months that had eventually led to this situation.

Rich's Department Store was both the largest merchant and the largest single advertiser in Atlanta, Georgia. The store had been founded in 1867 and had grown to an annual sales volume of approximately $200 million through its downtown store and six branch stores located in major suburban shopping centers. The Rich's market share was 40 percent of department store sales in Atlanta and 25 percent of all general merchandise sales.

The Rich's advertising strategy in the past had been to emphasize newspaper advertising for specific sales items and to utilize broadcast media primarily for image purposes. Newspaper was also used for some image-oriented advertising, with occasional direct mailings used to promote specific sales items of merchandise. Rich's is the largest local advertiser in both print and broadcast media.

The two principal daily newspapers in Atlanta are *The Atlanta Journal* (evenings) and the *Atlanta Constitution* (mornings). These are two of the largest circulation newspapers in the South, and both have distinguished journalism traditions, including Pulitzer Prizes. Although both newspapers are owned by the same company, Atlanta Newspapers, Inc., there is little overlap of readership except for the combined Sunday morning edition.

There are 6 TV stations and 40 radio stations in the Atlanta market. However, broadcast media are dominated by WSB-TV and WSB Radio, both of which are owned by Cox Broadcasting Corporation.

Mr. Mills recalled that several months earlier, executives of Cox Broadcasting and of their two local stations had met with key executives of Rich's. One topic discussed at that meeting had been possible use of broadcast media to promote individual sales items. WSB had offered to participate with Rich's in a market test to determine the abilities of different media to sell specific items of merchandise.

As a result of these discussions, Mr. Miles had held a series of meetings with Mr. Jim Landon, research director of WSB-TV and Radio, and Mr. Ferguson Rood, research director of the Atlanta Newspapers, Inc., to design the market test. It was eventually decided to conduct the test during Rich's annual Harvest Sale, which has been the merchandising highlight of the year since 1925. This sale runs for two weeks each fall. The test was to center on ten specific items of merchandise which would be advertised in both print and broadcast media during the first three days of the sale. During this same period, in-store interviews would be conducted, by professional interviewers, with all purchasers of these ten items in three representative stores (see appendixes for detailed survey design, sample questionnaire, and media plan).

At the conclusion of the survey period, the Research Departments of both Atlanta Newspapers, Inc., and WSB were furnished duplicate computer card decks by Rich's containing survey data. It was this data that served as the basis for the presentations that Jim Landon and Ferguson

Rood had made to the Rich's Executive Committee. Excerpts from *The Atlanta Journal* and *Constitution* report are in Appendix A, and excerpts from the WSB report are presented in Appendix B.

These were the two presentations that Mr. Mills would have to reconcile to arrive at a decision about future media strategy for Rich's. Mr. Mills knew that a decision would have to be made quickly, in view of TV production lead times, if any change in media mix were to be considered for the upcoming Christmas sales season.

APPENDIX A

AN ANALYSIS OF A RICH'S IN-STORE STUDY OF ADVERTISING EFFECTIVENESS ON SPECIFIC PURCHASE DECISIONS*

FOREWORD

This report is the result of an innovative research study conducted by Rich's Department Store in partnership with Atlanta Newspapers, Inc. and Cox Broadcasting Corporation.

The study was designed to measure:

1. The relative performance of newspapers, television and radio as a source of influence on shoppers' decisions to purchase specific items.
2. Shoppers' exposure to specific item advertising messages.

The advertising period covered in this study consisted of three days (beginning Sunday, September 20) prior to Rich's annual Harvest Sale.

A total of 2,176 interviews were made on Monday and Tuesday, September 21 and 22. The interviews were made in three of Rich's seven stores —Downtown, Lenox Square, and Greenbriar, and focused on the ten departments in each store where the advertised items were sold.

An Atlanta interviewing firm was employed by Rich's to interview shoppers in each department immediately after they made their purchase. To qualify for the survey, shoppers had to purchase the specific advertised item or a directly related item.

---

* Presented by *The Atlanta Journal* and *Constitution* Research & Marketing Department.

SUMMARY AND INTERPRETATION

More than nine out of ten shoppers covered in this survey had the specific purchase in mind before going to Rich's, or knew it was *on special*.

Three fourths of all shoppers recalled being recently exposed to advertising messages for specific items.

More than half of all shoppers' decisions to purchase specific items were attributed to advertising.

Attributions to newspapers were more than twice those of television and radio combined in influencing specific item purchase decisions (71 percent versus 33 percent).

Dollar for dollar . . . newspapers delivered more than three times the influence on specific item purchase decisions than television and radio combined.

The advertising schedule placed in newspapers . . . was conspicuously more effective and more efficient . . . in influencing specific purchase decisions . . . than the saturation schedule placed in television and radio.

See Exhibits A–1 through A–16.

EXHIBIT A–1
Newspaper advertising schedule*

	Sunday Journal and Constitution (inches)	a.m. Constitution (inches)	p.m. Journal (inches)
Sunday..................	1,064		
Monday................		172	247
Tuesday...............		0	505
Total.............	1,064	172	752

* 1,989 column inches, the equivalent of 11.6 pages, made up the newspaper schedule covered in this survey.

EXHIBIT A–2
Broadcast schedule*

	Television			Radio		
	Sunday	Monday	Tuesday	Sunday	Monday	Tuesday
6 a.m.		X			X	X
7		X			X	X
8		X	X		X	X
9		X	X	X	X	X
10		X		X	X	X
11		X			X	X
12		X	X	X	X	X
1 p.m.	X	X	X	X	X	X
2	X	X	X	X	X	X
3	X	X	X	X	X	X
4	X	X	X	X	X	X
5	X	X	X	X	X	X
6	X	X		X	X	
7	X	X		X	X	
8	X	X				
9	X	X				
10	X	X				
11	X	X				
Total spots	42	86	49	53	121	87
Average number per schedule hour	3.8	4.8	6.1	5.3	8.6	7.2

* 438 30-second spots were scheduled to run on five television and five radio stations, for an average of eight spots per hour, between 6 a.m. and 11 p.m., over the three-day period.

EXHIBIT A-3

Comparison of advertising schedule and budget

	Broadcast spots			Newspaper space (inches)
	TV	Radio	Total	
Hard Goods:				
Mattress.....................	12	19	31	35
Carpeting...................	12	23	35	150
Draperies...................	16	26	42	407
Vacuum sweeper...........	15	22	37	172
Color television*...........	0	0	0	150
Soft Goods:				
Handbags..................	15	27	42	189
Girdles†.....................	15	27	42	0
Shoes.......................	15	27	42	398
Shirts*......................	56	64	120	86
Pant suits..................	21	26	47	400
Total ten departments:				
Sunday.....................	42	53	95	1,064
Monday.....................	86	121	207	420
Tuesday....................	49	87	136	505
Total..................	177	261	438	1,989
Budget......................			$27,158	$16,910

* The original broadcast schedule included 20 TV and 24 radio spots for the color television sets to run Tuesday. Since all the sets were sold on Monday, this commercial time was switched to shirts.

† While no Playtex girdle ads were scheduled to run in newspapers, other foundation advertising during the test period supported the influence.

EXHIBIT A–4
Interviews

	Number	Percent
Total	2,175	100%
Women	1,764	81
Men	380	18
Couples	31	1
Under 35	963	44
35–49	817	38
50 and older	394	18
White	1,966	90
Nonwhite	209	10
Hard goods	527	24
Mattress	71	3
Carpeting	45	2
Draperies	123	6
Vacuum sweeper	134	6
Color television	154	7
Soft goods	1,649	75
Handbags	284	13
Girdles	249	11
Shoes	393	18
Shirts	483	22
Pant suits	240	11
Distribution of interviews by store		
Downtown	683	31
Lenox Square	848	39
Greenbriar	645	30

EXHIBIT A–5

"Before coming to Rich's today, did you have in mind buying this specific brand/item, or did you decide after you came into the store?"

63 percent of all shoppers had the specific purchase in mind before going to Rich's.

These shoppers described the following as sources of influence on their buying decision when asked: "What was it that gave you the idea to buy this brand/item?"

Advertising	52%
Needed or wanted it	23
Past experience with it	16
Outside source suggestion	6
Other	7

EXHIBIT A–6

"Was the store having a special on this specific brand/item today, or were they selling at the regular price?"

84 percent of all shoppers said the brand/item was on special.

These shoppers gave the following sources when asked: "Where did you learn about that?"

Advertising...................................... 63%
Store display/crowds............................ 27
Outside source................................. 6
Other.. 4

EXHIBIT A–7
Advertising Influence

---

55 percent of all shoppers attributed their specific purchase decision to advertising. Of these 71 percent attributed their purchase to newspapers, 33 percent to broadcasts (28 percent to television and 9 percent to radio), and 9 percent to mail circulars.

Newspapers and broadcast accounted for 94 percent of all advertising influence. 61 percent of these influences were attributed to newspapers exclusive of broadcast, 23 percent were attributed to broadcast exclusive of newspapers, and 10 percent were attributed to both.

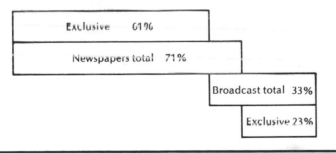

EXHIBIT A–8
Advertising influence

Newspapers and Television accounted for 90 percent of all advertising influence. 62 percent of these influences were attributed to newspapers exclusive of television. 19 percent were attributed to television exclusive of newspapers, and 9 percent were attributed to both.

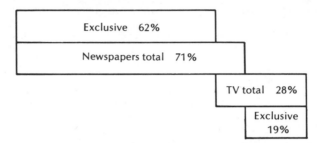

Newspapers and Radio accounted for 77 percent of all advertising influence. 68 percent of these influences were attributed to newspapers exclusive of radio. 6 percent were attributed to radio exclusive of newspapers, and 3 percent were attributed to both.

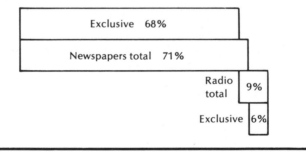

EXHIBIT A–9

Advertising influence—By shopper demographics (among the 55 percent of all shoppers who were influenced by advertising)

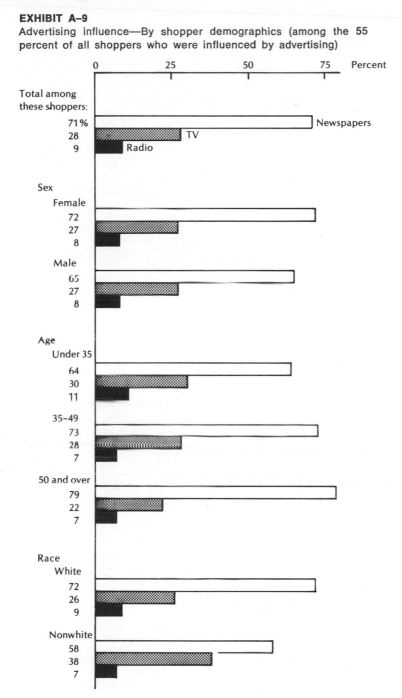

EXHIBIT A–10

Advertising influence—By shopping patterns (among the 55 percent of all shoppers who were influenced by advertising)

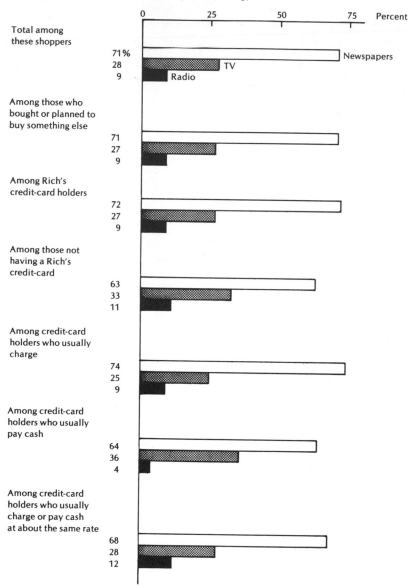

EXHIBIT A–11
Share of budget versus share of influence

EXHIBIT A–12
Newspapers/broadcast—Share of influence versus share of budget by departments

	Newspapers		Broadcast	
	Share of influence	Share of budget	Share of influence	Share of budget
Total............................	71%	38%	33%	62%
Hard goods.....................	77	45	30	55
Mattress......................	43	11	69	89
Carpeting.....................	83	39	23	61
Draperies.....................	83	56	22	44
Vacuum sweeper..............	70	25	45	75
Color TV......................	99	100	1	—
Soft goods......................	68	34	34	66
Handbags.....................	68	41	27	59
Girdles........................	28	—	74	100
Shoes.........................	87	54	25	46
Shirts.........................	63	12	36	88
Pant suits....................	82	53	16	47

EXHIBIT A–13

Comparison of advertising schedule/budget/shopper influence*

	Total 10 departments				
	Broadcast spots		Newspaper space		
	TV	Radio	Journal—Constitution	Constitution	Journal
Schedule					
Sunday...............	42	53	1,064		
Monday..............	86	121		172	248
Tuesday..............	49	87		0	505
	177	261	1,064	172	753

* 438 broadcast spots versus 1,989 inches; budget—$27,158 for broadcast spots versus $16,910 for newspaper space; and shopper influence—33 percent for broadcast spots versus 71 percent for newspaper space.

EXHIBIT A–14

Advertising exposure

74 percent of all shoppers recalled being exposed to specific advertising messages within the past day or two. Of these, 79 percent recalled newspapers, 53 percent recalled broadcasts (46 percent television, 18 percent radio), and 24 percent recalled mail circulars.

Newspapers and Broadcast accounted for 96 percent of all advertising messages. 43 percent recalled newspapers exclusive of broadcast. 17 percent recalled broadcast exclusive of newspapers, and 36 percent recalled both.

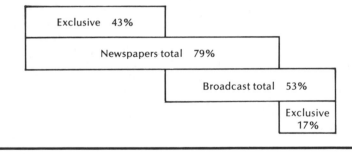

EXHIBIT A–15
Advertising exposure

Newspapers and Television accounted for 93 percent of all advertising messages. 47 percent recalled newspapers exclusive of television. 14 percent recalled television exclusive of newspapers, and 32 percent recalled both.

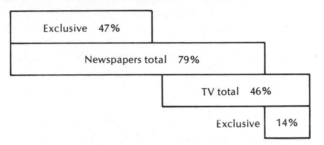

Newspapers and radio accounted for 85 percent of all advertising messages. 67 percent recalled newspapers exclusive of radio. 6 percent recalled radio exclusive of newspapers, and 12 percent recalled both.

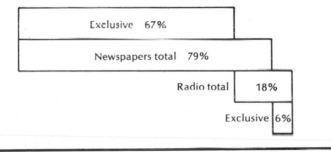

EXHIBIT A–16

                    HARVEST SALE IN-STORE CUSTOMER SURVEY

Interviewer Name: _____ (1-2) ____ STORE: . . . . . . .Downtown . . . . . Lenox . . . . . Greenbriar (3)

                                                                    1   2   3

DATE: M T W   TIME OF INTERVIEW: _____ DEPARTMENT: _____ (6)

        1   2   3 (4)   (5)

Hello. We're conducting a short survey among RICH'S customers:

1.   What did you happen to buy in this department today? _____

                                      (PROBE, BRAND, STYLE)

    _____ (7-8)

2.   Before coming to RICH'S today, did you have in mind buying this specific brand/item, or did you decide after you came into the store?

        HAD IN MIND. . . .(⬜)1   DECIDED IN STORE. . . . .(⬜)2 SKIP TO Q. #3 (9)

        What was it that gave you the

        idea to buy this brand/item? _____

        (IF APPROPRIATE, ASK: Where did you learn about that?) _____

        _____ (10-11)

3.   Was the store having a special on this specific brand/item today, or were they selling at the regular price?

        SPECIAL. . . . . . .(⬜)1   REGULAR PRICE. . . . . . .(⬜)2 SKIP TO Q. #4 (12)

        Where did you learn about that? _____

    _____ . (13-14)

4.   Do you recall seeing or hearing any advertising within the past day or two on radio or television or in the newspapers or in a mail circular that may have reminded you or helped you decide to buy this _____ today?

        YES. . . . .(⬜)1   NO. . . . .(⬜)2 SKIP TO Q. #5 (15)

        a. Where did you see or hear it? _____ (16)

	4a. UNAIDED RECALL	5. AIDED RECALL		
		YES	NO, DK	
RADIO.	1	1	2	(17)
NEWSPAPERS	2	1	2	(18)
TELEVISION.	3	1	2	(19)
MAIL CIRCULAR	4	1	2	(20)
OTHER, DON'T KNOW	5			

ASK FOR EACH MEDIUM NOT CHECKED IN Q. #4a.

5.   Did you happen to see or hear any of the following within the past day or two:

    A radio commercial for this specific _____? A newspaper ad for this specific _____? A television commercial for this specific _____? A mail circular for this specific _____?

6.   Have you bought anything else at RICH'S today, or do you plan to buy anything else at RICH'S today?

        YES. . . . .(⬜)1   NO. . . . .(⬜)2

7.   Do you (or your wife/husband) have a RICH'S credit card? (21)

        YES. . . . .(⬜)1   NO. . . . .(⬜)2 (22)

        a. Do you usually charge or pay cash for most of your purchases at RICH'S?

        CHARGE . . . .(⬜)1   CASH. . . . .(⬜)2   SAME. . . . .(⬜)3 (23)

8.   What is the name of the county where you live? _____ OUT-OF-STATE . .(⬜) (24-25-26)

    ESTIMATE AGE: UNDER 35 YEARS. .(⬜)1   SEX: FEMALE . . .(⬜)1   RACE: WHITE . . . . .(⬜)1 (27)

                        35 - 49 . . . .(⬜)2   MALE. . . . .(⬜)2   NON WHITE.(⬜)2 (28)

                        50+ . . . .(⬜)3 (29)

APPENDIX B ──────────────────────────────────

ANALYSIS OF RICH'S
IN-STORE SURVEY*

INTRODUCTION

First, we would like to state that WSB television and radio were pleased to have the opportunity to participate in this research effort with Rich's. We have one basic characteristic in common with Rich's—both WSB-TV and WSB Radio, like Rich's are dominant in the Atlanta market. Like Rich's, we are an Atlanta institution and have enjoyed dominance since our origination.

In this presentation, we will not attempt to interpret the results of your research from a marketing standpoint. You have your own market research department, and we are sure that they have done a capable job of analyzing and interpreting the results of the study from that aspect. Instead, we will concentrate on interpreting the results from a media standpoint, which is our particular area of experience.

The following pages contain our detailed analysis of this research for Rich's management.

PRE-HARVEST SALE ADVERTISING WEIGHT

Rich's Pre-Harvest Sale was heavily promoted with a "mix" of three media: radio, TV, and newspaper.

On the broadcast side, Rich's ran 261 radio spots on five stations and 177 TV spots on five stations promoting ten different items during a three-day period. It can be estimated that the total radio campaign reached about 90 percent of the Atlanta adult metro population, with the average listener exposed to seven commercial announcements (all products combined). The total television campaign also reached an estimated 90 percent of the Atlanta adult population, with the average viewer exposed to ten commercial announcements.

The newspaper campaign consisted of 13 ads for the specific items and 11 ads for related[1] items, or a total of 24 ads representing 1,987 inches of space in the *Journal* and *Constitution*. Rich's also ran 6,140 inches of other newspaper advertising during the three-day period. We have no way of estimating the reach and frequency of the newspaper ads.

───────────

* Presented by WSB-TV, WSB Radio, and Cox Broadcasting Research.
[1] Same item but different price than in the radio and TV commercial.

PRE-HARVEST SALE A SUCCESS

Rich's total advertising effort helped make the store's pre-Harvest Sale a tremendous success.

Monday, September 21, and Tuesday, September 22, were two of Rich's biggest days of the year according to traffic and sales volume. As far as we know, the departments participating in the test were all up considerably in sales volume compared to a year ago.

Unfortunately, sales results for the *specific items* tested were not available. However, it is our understanding that the departmentwide sales results reflected the success of the individual items in those departments that were tested.

The advertising effort for the pre-Harvest Sale represented one of the few times that Rich's has used a media-mix for *item selling*. Radio and TV have been used extensively by Rich's for institutional advertising and to announce sale events, but item selling has been limited in the past primarily to newspaper and direct mail. *The media-mix for item selling worked from a sales results standpoint.*

SUMMARY OF MEDIA RECALL FINDINGS

After analyzing the results of the survey, we found the following to be the most significant findings:

1. Because of the confusion and particularly the conditioning factor regarding newspaper, the three media cannot be completely compared in recall.
2. Recall for both radio and TV was significantly higher on Tuesday versus Monday, indicating that the broadcast media were building in impact on customers. Sales results were also generally better on Tuesday versus Monday.
3. Both radio and TV did *best* in recall (compared to newspaper) for items having the *least* amount of newspaper advertising. Radio and TV did *poorest* for items having the *greatest* amount of newspaper advertising.
4. In general, items where radio and TV did *best* in recall (compared to newspaper) had better sales results than items where radio and TV did poorest.
5. All three media performed better among high-priced items and for items where customers decided to buy before coming into the store.
6. Radio and TV balanced newspaper quite well by reaching younger adults than the print medium.

See Exhibits B–1 through B–3.

EXHIBIT B–1

Summary of newspaper recall

Item	Budget	Day/ads	Got idea	Learned of special	Direct recall
Draperies.............	$4,412	Sun.–2, Tues.–2	48%	68%	81%
Pant suits............	3,359	Sun.–2, Mon.–1, Tues.–3	50	56	63
Shoes.................	2,834	Sun.–1, Mon.–2, Tues.–1	48	55	72
Handbags............	1,670	Sun.–1, Tues.–1	30	30	60
Carpeting............	1,503	Sun.–1	61	63	80
Color TV..............	1,503	Sun.–1	62	68	66
Dress shirts..........	859	Sun.–1	40	40	54
Vacuum cleaner......	780	Mon.–4	36	62	64
Mattresses...........	260	Tues.–1	30	37	54
Career shirts.........	—	—	19	27	45
Girdles...............	—	—	12	15	16
Averages, all items*			42	51	64

* Excludes girdles (no ads), but includes career shirts because of ads for dress shirts, a related item.

EXHIBIT B–2

Summary of television recall

Item	Budget	Adult audience (000)	Got idea	Learned of special	Direct recall
Career shirts................	$2,998	1,373.4	15%	16%	27%
Draperies...................	2,714	776.5	11	15	37
Pant suits...................	2,494	885.4	8	9	39
Playtex girdles..............	2,364	752.1	25	34	32
Dress shirts.................	2,028	824.8	16	16	29
Handbags...................	1,922	649.2	10	10	34
Shoes.......................	1,909	724.7	11	14	41
Vacuum cleaner.............	1,867	627.4	19	36	42
Carpeting...................	1,790	624.5	8	12	29
Mattresses..................	1,627	691.9	40	48	49
Color TV.....................	—	—	0	0	5
Averages, all items*			16	21	36

* Excludes color TV (no commercials).

EXHIBIT B–3
Summary of radio recall

Item	Budget	Adult audience (000)	Got idea	Learned of special	Direct recall
Career shirts...................	$903	489.1	2%	6%	17%
Draperies......................	560	654.3	1	2	8
Shoes..........................	544	566.8	5	6	14
Pant suits.....................	539	633.9	1	2	12
Carpeting......................	513	590.9	8	7	24
Dress shirts...................	498	496.4	4	5	12
Girdles........................	482	553.0	6	9	11
Mattresses....................	477	527.6	11	23	29
Handbags.....................	476	475.1	2	3	20
Vacuum cleaner..............	453	482.1	7	8	10
Color TV......................	—	374.2	—	1	2
Averages, all items*			5	7	16

* Excludes color TV (no commercials).

THREE TYPES OF MEDIA RECALL IN THE STUDY

The questionnaire used in Rich's in-store survey obtained information about customers' recall of advertising media in three areas:

1. Idea to buy

For customers purchasing the item being tested, those that indicated having in mind buying that specific merchandise before coming to the store were asked *what gave them the idea to buy the item.* In this question, answers involving media came from top-of-mind recall (not aided). Non-media answers to this question, such as "needed" item, "wanted" item or "had past experience" with item were accepted.

2. Learned of special

Those customers who were aware of the store having a special on the specific item purchased were asked *where they learned about it.* In this question, answers involving media also came from top-of-mind recall and nonmedia responses such as "saw on display" or "friend told me" were accepted.

3. Direct recall

Customers were also asked if they recalled seeing or hearing any advertising that may have reminded them or helped them decide to buy the specific item. If they answered in the affirmative, they were then asked *where they saw or heard it.* If radio, newspaper, TV or mail circular were not mentioned by the respondent, they were also asked if they happened to hear a radio commercial, see a newspaper ad, and so on (aided recall). For purposes of analyzing the results, the unaided and aided answers to direct recall have been combined in this question.

EFFECT OF CONFUSION AND "CONDITIONING"

First, we would like to emphasize three points that should be taken into consideration when evaluating each advertising medium's performance based on the recall results of the study:

1. Because of the heavy amount of Rich's advertising activity in all media during the three-day period of interviewing, there was a certain amount of confusion that occurred among the customer-respondents regarding where they saw or heard advertising. This fact will be documented in the pages to follow.
2. Because Rich's traditionally has done the vast majority of its *item* advertising in newspaper, customers are "conditioned" to this particular medium; i.e., more inclined to think of Rich's merchandise being advertised in a newspaper.
3. During the three-day period of the study, *other department stores were also running newspaper* ads for items similar to Rich's items being tested. Some newspaper ad recall in this study could have been due to confusion with other stores' ads.

These points can all be substantiated by the following results:

Only slight confusion for radio commercials

There were *no* radio commercials for color TV sets, since the spots were canceled before they were scheduled to run on Tuesday afternoon.

<u>0%</u>	Claimed they got the idea to buy a color TV set from radio commercials.
<u>1%</u>	Thought they learned of color TV sets being on sale from radio commercials.
<u>2%</u>	Said they recalled hearing radio commercials for color TV sets.

Only slight confusion for TV commercials

There were *no* TV commercials for color TV sets, since the spots were canceled before they were scheduled to run on Tuesday afternoon.

<u>0%</u>   Claimed that they got the idea to buy a color TV set
from TV commercials.

<u>0%</u>   Thought they learned of color TV sets on sale from TV
commercials.

<u>5%</u>   Said they recalled seeing TV commercials for color TV
sets.

Some confusion and "conditioning" for mail circular

In the mail circular that Rich's distributed to its customers the week prior to the survey, there were *no* ads for any specific items, yet among the total sample of customer-respondents purchasing any of the 11 items tested:

<u>3%</u>   Claimed they got the idea to buy the specific item
from a mail circular.

<u>5%</u>   Thought they learned of the specific item being on
sale from a mail circular.

<u>18%</u> Said they recalled seeing a mail circular for the spe-
cific item.

Greater confusion and "conditioning" for newspaper ads

There were *no* Rich's newspaper ads for Playtex girdles, yet:

<u>12%</u> Claimed they got the idea to buy girdles from news-
paper ads.

<u>15%</u> Thought they learned of girdles being on sale from
newspaper ads.

<u>16%</u> Said they recalled seeing newspaper ads for girdles.

There were *no* Rich's newspaper ads for mattresses on either Sunday or Monday of the survey, yet among customers interviewed on Monday:

<u>27%</u> Claimed they got the idea to buy a mattress from
newspaper ads.

<u>30%</u> Thought they learned of the mattress being on sale
from newspaper ads.

<u>49%</u> Said they recalled seeing newspaper ads for
mattresses.

Caution in comparing media by recall!

As you can see, the extent of erroneous recall of newspaper advertising ranged from a low of 12 percent to a high of 49 percent. For this important reason, it is impossible to derive any accurate yardstick for measuring the separate value of each medium, dollar for dollar. In addition, these results cannot be converted to any type of advertising-to-sales ratio.

RADIO MAY HAVE BEEN HIGHER WITH MORE WSB SPOTS

Due to the problem created by trying to find enough availabilities on WSB only in morning and evening drive time (because of the agency's buying criteria) to handle commercials for 11 different items in three days, Atlanta's dominant radio station was not able to contribute as much weight as it should have to most of the media schedules. As a result, a higher proportion of spots ran on WQXI (primarily teens), WAOK (primarily ethnic) and WRNG (primarily 50+ listeners), and WPLO (lower socioeconomic level). A brief analysis of the number of radio commercials that ran for each item, showing the light proportion of WSB spots, is shown in the accompanying table.

	Total spots	WSB spots	WSB morning drive spots*
Career shirts	48	10	0
Carpeting	23	6	3
Color TV	—	—	—
Draperies	26	7	2
Dress shirts	15	6	2
Girdles	27	5	1
Handbags	27	5	1
Mattresses	19	6	2
Pant suits	26	8	2
Shoes	27	6	2
Vacuum cleaner	22	5	2
Total	260	64	17

* Monday or Tuesday.

TELEVISION VERSUS NEWSPAPER

While TV budgets were fairly even, newspaper budgets ranged from *$260* for mattresses up to *$4,412* for draperies. TV versus newspaper performance in all types of recall showed a good relationship to the amount of money spent in newspaper. The smaller the newspaper budget versus TV, the better TV performed versus newspaper in recall, and vice versa:

1. TV did *best* in all types of recall *compared to newspaper* for mattresses, career shirts and vacuum cleaners. These items had the *smallest amount* of advertising space in the newspaper compared to the others.
2. TV did *poorest* in all types of recall *compared to newspaper* for draperies, pant suits, shoes, and carpeting. These items had the *greater amount* of advertising space in the newspaper.

RADIO VERSUS NEWSPAPER

Again, radio budgets were fairly even compared to the wide range in newspaper budgets. Radio versus newspaper performance in all types of recall also showed a fairly strong relationship to the amount of money spent in newspaper. The smaller the newspaper budget versus radio, the better radio performed versus newspaper in recall, and vice versa:

1. Radio did *best* in all types of recall *compared to newspaper* for mattresses, vacuum cleaners, and career shirts. These items generally had the least newspaper space.
2. Radio did *poorest* in all types of recall *compared to newspaper* for draperies, pant suits, and handbags. These items generally had the greatest newspaper space.

LESS NEWSPAPER SPACE—NO HARM TO SALES VOLUME

We have just indicated that, as newspaper space was reduced, both radio and TV did better in recall.

How about Rich's sales volume?

There appeared to be little, if any, correlation between the amount of newspaper space and sales volume as measured by department sales increases. If anything, the reverse occurred:

	Monday	Tuesday
TV and radio did best		
(least newspaper space):		
Girdles..............................	+7%	+92%
Career shirts......................	+151	+349
Mattresses.........................	+43	+76
Vacuum cleaners..................	+98	+222
TV and radio did poorest		
(most newspaper space):		
Draperies..........................	−0	+9
Pant suits..........................	+17	+46
Shoes..............................	−19	+14
Carpeting..........................	−9	+526

IDEA TO BUY VERSUS DIRECT RECALL

One probable indication of the "conditioning" of Rich's customers to newspaper advertising comes from comparing initial "idea to buy" recall, where media responses came purely from top of mind, to the direct recall that came later in the interview, concentrating on each medium. All three media gained in regard to the proportion of customers recalling (from idea to buy to direct recall), but newspaper, having been recalled more from top of mind, gained the least, while TV and especially radio, in the background during top of mind "idea to buy," came to the surface more in the direct recall.

	Average recall, all items*		
	Idea to buy	Direct recall	Percent increase
Newspaper......................	42%	64%	+52%
TV...............................	16	36	+125
Radio...........................	5	16	+220

* Girdles were eliminated for newspaper and color TV sets for radio and TV because of no advertising.

FIRST DAY VERSUS SECOND DAY RECALL

Analysis of the direct recall results by day of interview produced an interesting fact. The impact of newspaper was initial, while both radio and TV performed significantly better on the second day. This is probably due to the nature of the broadcast media, which gain impact and effectiveness with *increased frequency* (as listeners and viewers are exposed to more commercials). In addition, sales results for all items were generally better on Tuesday than on Monday, compared to a year ago. This also indicates that, if spots had been spread more evenly over Sunday, Monday, and Tuesday (rather than concentrated on Sunday and Monday in most cases), and if interviewing had been extended through Wednesday, both radio and TV would have performed better in recall, at no increase in budget for either medium.

	Average recall, all items*		
	Monday	Tuesday	Tuesday percent difference
Newspaper......................	66%	62%	−6%
TV...............................	33	38	+15
Radio...........................	13	18	+38

* Mattresses were eliminated for newspaper as an invalid comparison, since there were no ads on Sunday or Monday. However, even though there were no radio or TV commercials for career shirts on Sunday or Monday, and no newspaper ads at all, this item was included in this comparison because there was advertising for dress shirts, a related item. Also girdles were eliminated for newspaper and color TV for radio and TV because of no advertising.

HIGH-PRICED VERSUS LOW-PRICED ITEMS

In order to analyze media performance by item *price range,* the items were divided into either a high-price (carpeting, color TV, draperies, mattresses, and vacuum cleaners) or a low-price (career shirts, dress shirts, girdles, handbags, pant suits, and shoes) group. All three media performed better among high-priced items compared to low-priced merchandise, especially radio and TV. However, the differences were greater regarding "idea to buy" recall and "learned of special" recall than with the direct recall. Customers who had made up their mind to buy a large ticket item were apparently more persuaded by advertising than those coming to Rich's for lower priced merchandise. However, whether in the market for high- or low-priced items, both type customers were exposed to advertising, as indicated in the direct recall.

	High-priced items	Low-priced items	High-priced percent difference
Idea to buy:			
Newspaper	47%	37%	+27%
TV	20	14	+43
Radio	7	3	+133
Learned of special:			
Newspaper	60	42	+43
TV	28	16	+75
Radio	10	5	+100
Direct recall:			
Newspaper	69	59	+17
TV	39	34	+15
Radio	18	14	+29

"HAD IN MIND" VERSUS "DECIDED IN STORE"

In order to analyze media performance by the extent to which customers had in mind to buy the item before coming to the store, the items were divided into two groups: "had in mind" and "decided in store," based on results to the question covering this aspect of purchasing. The four items where roughly half of the customers indicated deciding in the store (pant suits. dress shirts, career shirts, and handbags) were placed in the "decided in store" group. The other seven items, where significantly less customers indicated deciding in store, were placed in the "had in mind" group. All three media performed significantly better among items in the "had in mind" group, that is, for items where a greater proportion of customers made their decision in advance. The differences were greater regarding "idea to buy" and "learned of special" recall than with the direct recall.

	"Had in mind" items	"Decided in store" items	"Had in mind" percent difference
Idea to buy:			
Newspaper	48%	35%	+37%
TV	19	12	+58
Radio	6	2	+200
Learned of special:			
Newspaper	59	38	+55
TV	26	13	+100
Radio	9	4	+125
Direct recall:			
Newspaper	70	56	+25
TV	38	32	+19
Radio	16	15	+7

BROADCAST MEDIA RECALL REFLECTED YOUNGER ADULTS

By analyzing media recall by age of customer, it was determined that radio and TV balanced newspaper quite well by reaching younger adults. In all three types of recall, the under 35 age group was proportionately higher for broadcast, especially radio, than for newspaper. These figures are based on all items combined.

Age	Radio	TV	Newspaper
Got idea:			
Under 35	56%	44%	36%
35–49	31	38	44
50+	13	18	20
Learned of special:			
Under 35	50	43	36
35–49	34	41	41
50+	16	16	23
Direct recall:			
Under 35	50	44	41
35–49	33	38	41
50+	18	18	18

Note: Read Table. Of those customers indicating that they "got the idea" to buy an item from radio commercials, 56 percent were in the under 35 age group.

RICH'S DOMINANT POSITION IN ATLANTA

In concluding this presentation, we would like to announce the results of separate research that we have just completed that indicates the extent to which Rich's dominates the department store market in Atlanta, a domination that we feel is due to:

Outstanding management.

Quality of merchandise.

Attention to customer service and satisfaction.

Efficient use of advertising and promotion, *especially the use of a media-mix.*

PRESENTATION SUMMARY

1. With use of media-mix for item selling, the pre-Harvest Sale was a success. All departments participating in the test were up in sales volume.
2. Because of confusion and conditioning factors, recall results are not completely comparable between media.
3. In general, as the amount of newspaper space was reduced, the proportion of recall for both TV and radio was increased, and sales results were generally more favorable.
4. Sales volume was up significantly on Tuesday versus Monday in all departments, indicating a relationship with broadcast media recall, also up significantly on Tuesday as frequency increased.
5. All media had higher recall for higher priced items and items where customer generally decided in advance.
6. Separate research confirms Rich's dominance of the Atlanta market, especially versus Davison's. Rich's uses radio and TV effectively, Davison's uses very little broadcast media.

CASE
24

Exercise in Print Advertising Assessment

One of the most important and most difficult marketing decisions is the choice of creative executions in advertising. The purpose of this exercise is to help you develop skills in determining what is a good and a bad creative execution.

In preparation for your class session using this exercise, we would like you to spend time looking at *print* advertising (newspaper and magazine advertising). We would like you to select what you think is the "best ad" you have seen and the "worst ad" you have seen. To aid you in this task you might ask yourself the following questions:

1. What is the sponsor's apparent target segment(s)?
2. What are the objectives of the ad?
3. Is the basic appeal, theme, and copy approach appropriate for these purposes?

To the bottom of each ad you selected attach a small piece of paper containing the following information:

1. Sponsor of the ad.
2. Publication in which the ad appeared.
3. Publication date.
4. Your reason(s) for selecting that ad as the best or worse.
5. Your name.

Staple or tape this information to the bottom of the ad, but don't obscure any of the ad. Turn in your ads to your professor as required. In the class session you will get a chance to compare your choice of ads with your classmates.

25

Johnson-Murdock
Distillers, Inc.*

Dan Jenkins at age 32 was the youngest divisional manager at Johnson-Murdock Distillers, Inc. Hired by the firm from Seagrams Inc. in 1975, Jenkins had spent the past 18 months as a marketing assistant in the bourbon and rye whiskey division. Now, in 1977, as manager for the newly created imported wines group, he was faced with the problem of developing and implementing a marketing strategy for high-quality, white, red, and rosé wine from some of the finest vineyards in France.

When Jenkins accepted responsibility for the new wine division, he immediately asked for and received permission to hire an assistant. Because of his exclusive experience with whiskeys both at Seagrams and Johnson-Murdock, Jenkins wanted to hire a marketer from the wine industry. From Taylor Wines he hired Lorraine Barnes, a creative and accomplished young executive who was looking for a new career opportunity. While Jenkins and Barnes flew to Paris to finalize the purchase contract and the shipping schedule for 1977 and 1978, the Advertising and Promotion Department at Johnson-Murdock was preparing a promotional plan for presentation to the managers upon their return.

THE JOHNSON-MURDOCK CO.

Founded in 1892, Johnson-Murdock was a nationally known distiller of fine bonded whiskey, bourbon, and rye. Although not as large as Sea-

---

* This case was co-authored by Cynthia Rice, Graduate Student, University of Michigan.

grams, Heublein, or National Distillers, the firm was a major market factor in their specific products. Since the early 1960s, however, it had become apparent that industry growth areas were vodka, gin and imported tequila, rum, Canadian whiskey, and Scotch. Johnson-Murdock had hesitated to enter these new areas maintaining that their goal was to be number one in sales of their existing products. Meanwhile, the competition had aggressively entered these new segments of the liquor market, and almost all had added at least a vodka and gin to their product line. Some, like National Distillers had also diversified into other areas such as chemicals and mining or like Heublein into fast-food franchises. Johnson-Murdock remained fast to their original corporate strategy, and although they had tried a variety of promotional schemes over the past dozen years, their market shares were slowly but steadily declining.

In 1975, in response to increasingly irate and threatening stockholders, Johnson-Murdock Chairman Ernest Browne announced a plan to enter the growing wine market. It seemed pointless, he told the group, to try and catch up with the vodka, gin and imported liquor market eight–ten years late. However, marketing research showed that wine was coming on strong and promised a long and profitable future. Mr. Browne made the following statement at the 1976 shareholders meeting:

> There are great opportunities in the wine industry. Domestic wine consumption, including imports, grew at a compound annual rate of only 2.3 percent from 1948 to 1967. From 1967 to 1971, however, the compound annual growth rate was 8.3 percent and it's still expanding. Probably the most important thing for us at Johnson-Murdock to realize is that we are ready for a second wine revolution. The first revolution was in the late 1950s and 1960s when Gallo mass marketed low priced wines. Gallo is now a $250 million company. Of all the wine sold in the United States in 1973, 40 percent was from Gallo. Overall, the total retail value of wine (domestic and imported) sold in the United States is over $1.5 billion.
>
> But consumer tastes have changed—even in this very short period of time. There has been a decline in the demand for "pop" wines which are Gallo's specialty. Consumption of U.S. produced wines was up 7.8 percent in 1972, but imports were up 30.2 percent. People are ready to trade up to higher quality wines and the imports are very important here.
>
> We at Johnson-Murdock feel that consumers will associate existing producers with their present product quality level and when trading up make their selection from a new importer's or producer's line. We aim to be a major factor in this new area with our excellent marketing skills. The import market already provides a large base with more than 50 million gallons imported into the United States annually.
>
> Just to give you some established growth trends for imports listen to these statistics on U.S. consumption of imported wine:

	1971 (000 gallons)	1972 (000 gallons)	Percent change
France	9,480	12,486	+31.7%
Italy	9,820	11,278	+14.8
Spain	4,777	8,452	+76.9
Portugal	5,509	6,699	+21.6
Germany	3,708	4,662	+25.7
Total	33,294	43,577	+30.9

Preliminary data collected for the years since 1972 suggests that this growth pattern has continued.

We at Johnson-Murdock admit we have been too conservative in the past. Let me personally guarantee you, however, that we are now back on track. In our usual fashion we have carefully and thoroughly researched this area, and we are convinced that to maximize your welfare as stockholders this is the path of opportunity.

Now then, allow me to introduce to you our new divisional manager for imported wines, a man whom we are confident can make this operation a great success—Mr. Dan Jenkins.

THE WINE INDUSTRY

On the return flight from Paris, Jenkins and Barnes discussed their marketing strategy for the French wines. Both were very satisfied with the outcome of their negotiations. Judging from the quality of the product, the purchase price and probable promotional expenses, they estimated they could easily get the 15 percent profit margin customary for premium wines.

As of 1975, so-called premium wines retailed in the $3.25–$7.50 range for a 750 ml. or 25-ounce bottle. Although they still comprised less than 10 percent of the market, premium wines had the highest margins. The competition was typically from small, family-owned wineries or European imports. The mid-premium wines ranged from $2.00–$3.25 at retail and carried profit margins of 13 percent–15 percent. This segment accounted for about 20 percent of total U.S. wine sales. The competition was stiff, consisting mainly of Taylor, Christian Brothers, Almaden (owned by National Distillers), and Paul Masson (owned by Seagrams). The popularly priced wine segment was dominated by Gallo and Heublein-owned United Vintners, the two largest domestic wine producers. This segment accounted for two thirds of the total U.S. wine sales. Retailing at less than $2 per bottle the profit margins were a slim 7 percent–12.5 percent.

At this time, the typical distribution channels for wine included area wholesale distributors whose markups on cost varied from 10 percent–20 percent and package liquor dealers and/or supermarkets at the retail level. For supermarkets the typical wine markup was 35 percent–40 percent on cost as compared to 25 percent for beer and carbonated beverages and 20 percent–25 percent for general grocery products. Eager to carry wines, grocery stores had greatly expanded their shelf space allocations and in some cases had built wine "boutiques" within the store to add atmosphere. John Prinster, merchandising vice president for Safeway Inc., was quoted in the media as saying, the growth in wine sales from 1972–74 had been twice that of Safeway's overall supermarket business.

Although New York, Pennsylvania, and some other states still prohibited the sale of wine in food stores, most nationally distributed wines could be found on neighborhood supermarket shelves as well as in party stores and package liquor outlets. In supermarkets, however, wine was treated more as an impulse item. Here, there was a much greater burden on brand marketing strategies and merchandising than in liquor stores where personal sales assistance was available.

THE COMPETITION

The imported wine market in 1977 was highly fragmented with over 10,000 varieties from Europe, Australia, and South America. Although many of these wines had only regional distribution, some large grocery chains such as Safeway had also begun import operations. Neither the grocery store private label wines nor the regional imports seemed to present a serious threat to the nationally distributed premium wines such as Lancers, Mateus, and Blue Nun.

Schenley, a large national distiller, had become the largest U.S. wine importer by 1973. Mateus Rosé wine from Portugal was their largest selling premium wine with over 2.9 million gallons sold in 1972. Schenley's total imports for 1972 were around 4.7 million gallons. Heublein, the nation's largest vodka manufacturer with Smirnoff, Relska and Popov, and an aggressive marketer of distilled spirits, cordials and liquers, was responsible for importing Lancers red, white and rosé wines, also from Portugal. Lancers sold about 1 million gallons annually, but since being reformulated from a mildly effervescent to a still wine a few years previously, sales had begun to decline despite the very favorable overall demand trend. Blue Nun, a white wine, was imported by Schieffelin, also a distiller. This German white wine continues to be one of the fastest growing brands with sales of about 1.5 million gallons in 1972. Schieffelin supported the brand with a creative and humorous national radio campaign. They were rewarded with a brand name which was fast becoming a household word and had won several creative advertising awards.

Consumer education was still the major thrust of wine advertising in the early 1970s. Schenley sponsored a daily radio program on wines and

Schieffelin produced a video tape cassette, "A Complete Guide to Wines," which could be used as a supermarket display or for the many small groups of individuals who were forming neighborhood wine tasting clubs. Heublein, meanwhile, had gained an international reputation with highly publicized wine auctions. These annual sales of vintage wines selling for thousands of dollars per bottle gained wide press coverage, if only for a very limited period of time. In addition, all the major wine importers and domestic wineries published magazine supplements, sponsored seminars and wine tasting sessions, and distributed point of purchase materials to retail outlets.

Despite all these educational efforts consumers tended to get some conflicting information. While the classic serving rule of red wine with beef and white wine with fish and poultry continued to be promoted, Taylor put together an "anytime, anywhere" campaign that was very successful. A growing number of consumers now felt confident that they could "enjoy any wine with any food as long as they found them pleasant together." Also, packaging was taking on a different emphasis. Whereas a high-shouldered bottle used to signify a Bordeaux type wine and a sloping shouldered bottle implied a Burgundy, new carafe-styled bottles were becoming very popular and were heavily used by Paul Masson Vineyards for everything from a chablis to a Burgundy. The finer distinctions among wines were quickly disappearing.

All three premium wines that Jenkins and Barnes were concerned with were marketed in decidedly unconventional bottles. Lancers was in an opaque, jug-like bottle which was rose colored for their red and rosé and green for their white wine. Mateus Rosé was in a very dark green, antique-looking bottle which had a broad oval base and circular though not spherical face, and Blue Nun was bottled in an elongated slope-shouldered bottle of green glass with, of course, a nun in blue habit on the rather colorful label. The Johnson-Murdock contract with the French vineyards limited the packaging to traditional bottles of clear glass with conventional corks. The label style, however, could be embellished to suit the importer.

Media usage and budgets varied considerably in the wine industry. Jenkins estimated that the second largest importer, Monsieur Henri, a Pepsico subsidiary, had an advertising budget of about $60,000 in 1969 and over $5 million in 1975. Typically, popularly priced wines utilized mass appeals with television, radio, and general audience magazines. As the target markets became more specific, however, media usage also became far more specific. Individual segments of the market were being cultivated as brand images were carefully defined. Overall, Gallo supports its many brands with heavy network television support in the $4 million–$5 million range. As Gallo shifted its marketing strategy to build the image of its table wines, however, the firm placed much more emphasis on magazines. The premium table wines have been heavily advertised in *New Yorker, Money, Apartment Life, Psychology Today, People,* and *Cosmopolitan.*

Although packaging freedom was limited, Jenkins and Barnes were convinced there was a demand for a high-quality product such as theirs. The immediate problem was concentrating their limited promotional budget of $750,000 on the right market segment. They reasoned that once they had a foothold in the premium market they could expand not only their product line to include other fine wines but also their budget so they could then emphasize market penetration.

THE FRENCH WINE BUYER

Market research showed that imported French dinner or table wines were purchased at least on occasion by about 12 percent of all wine drinkers. Although French red and rosé wine purchases trailed those of German white, Italian red, and Portuguese red and white wines, executives at Johnson-Murdock saw this as an opportunity to establish their own nationally recognized brand. The consumer demographic profile developed by the Marketing Research Department at Johnson-Murdock and submitted to the Advertising Department resembled the following:

> The typical imported, premium priced, French wine drinker lives in urban or suburban areas. The major income earner holds a professional or managerial position and both men and women are predominately college graduates. Over 50 percent have annual incomes above $20,000 and a large share earn $25,000 or more. They are overwhelmingly young (24–45 years), white, married and have fewer than two children.
>
> These individuals seldom watch television other than the late night news and listen to radio infrequently other than when driving. For reaching this group, magazines are probably the media vehicle with the greatest potential for success. Specific publications that are either read or subscribed to by these individuals include: *Newsweek, Scientific American, Time, Playboy, Travel and Leisure, Smithsonian, Ms., Sports Illustrated, Business Week,* and *Esquire.*

THE PROMOTIONAL PLAN

The Advertising Department at Johnson-Murdock was known as one of the most creative in the liquor industry. Eye-catching outdoor advertising was their specialty. Since liquor was prohibited from being promoted on television, the department had limited experience in this medium. They were confident, however, that their skills would transfer. Gary Rombo, the media specialist assigned to the wine project, was particularly eager to go with late night television spots. "Certainly the sensuous image of French wines can be successfully portrayed. The glamour of Paris, the Riviera and the picturesque French countryside offer almost limitless opportunities."

Rombo had worked straight through the weekend in preparation for the presentation to Jenkins and Barnes. Almost ten days of concentrated effort had resulted in media schedules, elaborate storyboards, a new label design, and distinctive logo for the bottle, and studio photos to illustrate his proposed theme. Although bleary-eyed on Monday morning, Rombo was more excited about this project than any he had worked on in the previous two years since coming to Johnson-Murdock. He exuded confidence as he entered the conference room to meet his eager clients—Jenkins and Barnes.

Rombo began his presentation with the newly styled label and logo.

Rombo: Here's how I envision the label: Subdued shades of red and blue on a creamy white background . . . you'll recognize those as the French national colors as well as ours, of course . . . and this dignified yet ever-so-sensuous letter style for the logo—La Maison Rouge. It's French, but people can pronounce it . . . The Red House . . . regal yet sexy . . . easy to promote . . . easy to remember.

Jenkins: The logo and label are very good, Gary. Show us your promotional plan. How do you think we should distribute the budget? We've only got $750,000 to work with; Gallo spends that on magazines alone. What kinds of plans do you have for implementation?

Rombo: Don't worry. I've got this in enough detail so that with your approval we can start commercial production on Wednesday. I've notified our agency in general what to expect.

Rombo then unmasked his storyboards and projected slides of the illustrative studio photos on the conference room screen revealing: chic St. Tropez residents posed against the brilliant blue of the Mediterranean sky . . . shaded porticos . . . subtle melodies . . . seductive sips . . .

Rombo: Right between the late night news and Johnny Carson. All the stations have their rate schedule set up a little bit differently, but in New York City a 30-second spot would cost about $1,600 for the "Tonight Show" spot between 11:30 P.M. and 1:00 A.M. It's not so steep when you think of the coverage. In Chicago we could get the same thing for $1,000. For a 60-second spot in Detroit the price would run somewhere between $500–$800 depending on whether it is a single time only or more frequent airings. I don't recommend a national spot. I think we should concentrate on the big urban areas.

Barnes: How do the demographics for this spot hold up?

Rombo: As I recollect it's somewhat down scale in income and occupation overall. However, this is misleading, as the up scale audience we want is a segment of this viewing audience. We can reach them here. If you just looked at the averages you'd miss them as their incomes get averaged in with all the rest of the audience.

Barnes: Wait, Gary, we don't have that kind of budget, nor do I think that image is what we want. Your label was distinguished . . . almost conservative, why can't we carry a royalty theme instead of being quite so "swinging"?

Rombo: Jenkins, you agree with me don't you? This is eye-catching—almost breathtaking. Besides, impact is what we need initially . . . to get that toehold in the market . . .

(as he flipped through the slides again)

Jenkins: I do agree you have a sophisticated approach, but I'm afraid you're out of our price range, at least for the time being. What other possibilities did you look into?

Rombo: Well, I looked at what Research had to say, and as an alternative I thought we could do similar photo spreads in *Playboy* and *Travel and Leisure* and maybe some outdoor, resembling the Black Velvet ads.

Jenkins: That sounds much more feasible. Before we talk dollars, Lorraine, what do you think?"

Barnes: I think it's critical that we note the growing importance of women here. Trade data show 72 percent of the decisions to serve wine at dinner are made by women; 50 percent of the decisions of which specific wine to serve are made by women and 55 percent of the actual purchases of wine are made by women. I don't think our limited dollars are best spent in *Playboy* and *Travel and Leisure*. One bikini looks just like the next. Let me suggest something we used very successfully at Taylor.

The research network behind *Time* magazine has developed an interesting technique for reaching specific segments of the population. In addition to regional editions which just about every national magazine offers, *Time's* ZIP marketing approach allows an advertiser to purchase only specific zip code areas. They call this edition of *Time, Time Z*. *Time Z's* circulation goes to over 1,400 top income quintile ZIP code areas in 158 metro areas in the United States.

Let me explain how it works. In ZIP Marketing, all ZIPs in a market or group of markets are ranked in descending order by density of high-income families. Then households in these ZIPs are totaled in descending order and divided into equal fifths or quintiles. Time Z goes only to those ZIPs in metro areas which have the highest density of high income households.

As you may suspect, the top first and second quintile segments constitute a disproportionately large number of one's customers, particularly for wine and liquor products. We used this technique at Taylor for the Extra Dry Champagne. For the Philadelphia area, sales reports were collected from 200 state liquor stores in the metropolitan area. Stores were identified by ZIP code. All area ZIP codes were ranked in descending order based on U.S. Census data reporting the percentage of households within each ZIP area with annual incomes greater than $15,000. The households were then divided into quintiles and compared with retail champagne sales. The result was that 40 percent of those households (the top two quintiles) accounted for 68 percent of champagne purchases at retail. *Time* had enough distribution in that area so that we could reach our target market at a minimum of overcoverage.

I really believe this technique could be effectively utilized here. It's certainly not perfect, but I think we can have greater advertising frequency and build more awareness for the same dollars. Besides, if you want to continue the same campaign approach, the assortment of advertisers is more favorable in *Time*.

Rombo: ZIP codes aren't reliable, though. We'll miss pockets of people who buy in one zip code area but live across town in another zip area.

Barnes: The households are quintiled on the basis of number of upper income families first before looking at sales data. I'm confident the top quintiles include who we want, and we could have more repeat messages; a more concentrated effort.

Rombo: Maybe your *Playboy* criticism is right, but I'd rather overshoot the market a little and make sure my segment is covered than try and skimp like this crazy ZIP thing. The Post Office can't even make that system work. What are the cost figures on ZIP versus *Time*'s full coverage?"

Barnes: Yes, I have them in my files here. Let's see the cost figures were something like this:

Time top two quintiles—Rate base 1.2 million circulation
Black and white................	$15,940 full page	$13.28 CPM*
Four color......................	24,705 full page	20.59 CPM

Time regular coverage—Rate base 4.25 million circulation
Black and white................	$34,320 full page	$ 8.08 CPM
Four color......................	53,195 full page	12.52 CPM

---

* CPM = Cost per thousand.

Rombo: But, look at the CPMs, the regular *Time* has greater coverage and is significantly cheaper.

Barnes: Our target market is limited. We don't care about reaching individuals who aren't going to buy our product in the short run. Given what we have to work with, we can run far more ads at $15,000–$25,000 than $34,000–$53,000. Look at the economics of this situation.

Rombo: I am.

Jenkins: I think that this discussion is focused too much on selecting one particular television show or magazine. I guess I see *Time Z* as one magazine alternative we want to look at but not the only one. Also, I'm very concerned about taking CPMs on total circulation. Can't we do better than this?

Barnes: I suppose we ought to take a look at the CPMs of various magazines for the potential target audiences we want. Aren't we hooked into Simmons magazine readership data bank with our computer?

Rombo: Yes we are. I can do some runs right now if you're willing to wait ten minutes.

Rombo got up from his chair and went down to his office. The others had coffee and discussed the wine situation in France. Rombo made use of the computer terminal in his office to examine various media buys for a number of target audiences. He returned to the meeting in 15 minutes and presented all with a Xerox copy of the results of his computer runs (see Exhibit 2). All at the meeting examined the output and then Jenkins spoke.

Jenkins: If I may interject a comment here, I have another meeting to attend. Let us reconvene tomorrow at, say, 9:30, and firm up this media schedule. In the meantime, think hard on this data and on the rest of our discussion. We've got to get this project rolling to coincide with the product distribution schedule, but then again we can't afford to make a costly mistake.

EXHIBIT 1
JOHNSON-MURDOCK DISTILLERS, INC.
Consolidated income statement
1975
($000)

Net sales.............................		$348,316
Cost of goods sold......................	$243,232	
Selling expense........................	55,160	298,392
Operating Profit....................		$ 46,924
Other income.........................		678
Total Income......................		$ 47,602
Interest expense.......................	$ 6,591	
Income taxes.........................	20,340	26,931
Net Income........................		$ 20,671

Consolidated balance sheet
As of June 30, 1975
($000)

Assets		Liabilities		
Cash.....................	$ 5,919	Accounts payable........		$ 26,152
Net receivables..........	41,993	Notes payable............		4,875
Inventories*..............	153,175	Taxes payable............		6,055
Other current assets.....	1,405	Total Current........		$ 37,082
Total Current........	$202,492			
		Long-term notes..........		60,554
Net properties...........	38,840			
Goodwill.................	25,568	Stockholder's Equity:		
Other assets.............	11,909	Capital stock..............	$14,669	
Total Assets.........	$278,809	Capital surplus...........	87,597	
		Retained Earnings........	78,907	181,173
				$278,809

* At lower of average cost or market.

EXHIBIT 2
Results of computer run

Explanation of output

1. For each run a "target market" is defined by the user based on some demographic variable; for example, the first run specifies 18–34 year olds earning $15,000 and over as the target.
2. "Population" refers to the number of U.S. adults in this target; for example, there are 6,665,000 adults in the target market.
3. "Percent of base" refers to the ratio of population as defined in (2) to the total U.S. adult population; for example, 6,665,000 is 4.47 percent of the total U.S. adult population (over 18).
4. Cost refers to the four-color, full-page cost of a magazine.
5. "Reach (000)" refers to the number of target market readers of an average issue of a magazine in thousands.
6. Percent coverage (percent COVG) refers to the ratio of reach to population; for example, for *People* magazine it is 1,243,000/6,665,000 = 18.6 percent.
7. Percent composition (percent COMP) refers to the ratio of target audience readers of a magazine to total readers of a magazine; for example, 9.7 percent of *People* readers are in the 18–34—$15,000 and over target audience.
8. "CPM" refers to cost per thousand target audience readers.
9. Weighting (WGT) allows the user to adjust the audience figures for a magazine. A WGT of 100.0 means that the data on file are used as is in the calculations. *People* has been weighted up due to estimated expanded readership since the Simmons data were collected. Four different *Time* weights are presented. The 100.0 is the regular *Time* magazine. The other three weights for *Time* are for *Time Z*. This is so because Simmons surveys only measure readership on a national basis. Thus all special advertising editions of magazines (for example, *Time Z, Newsweek Executive, Business Week Industrial*) cannot be measured directly. What all publishers and users do in estimating readership is to simply take a percentage of the total readership when measuring demographic editions. *Time Z* is computed here by taking 50 percent, 55 percent, and 60 percent of regular *Time*. It was usual to use the 50 percent figure for $15,000 plus income and the 60 percent figure for $25,000 plus income.

TOTAL ADULTS 1976/1977 SIMMONS

TARGET MARKET:
  $15M+ AGE
18–34

POPULATION = 6665 (000)
PERCENT OF BASE = 4.47

RANK	COST	WGT	REACH (000)	% COVG	% COMP	CPM
1. PEOPLE	13475	111.20	1243	18.6	9.7	10.84
2. TIME	24705	60.00	1317	19.8	10.6	18.76
3. TIME	24705	55.00	1207	18.1	10.6	20.47
4. TIME	24705	50.00	1098	16.5	10.6	22.50
5. NEWSWEEK	38160	100.00	1687	25.3	9.5	22.62
6. PLAYBOY	40745	100.00	1684	25.3	10.6	24.20
7. TIME	53195	100.00	2196	32.9	10.6	24.22
8. SPORTS ILLUSTRATED	34010	100.00	1147	17.2	9.1	29.65
9. BUSINESS WEEK	18760	100.00	547	8.2	14.3	34.30
10. ESQUIRE	14000	100.00	408	6.1	8.8	34.31
11. US NEWS & WORLD REPORT	26420	100.00	691	10.4	8.2	38.23

TARGET MARKET:
  $15M+ AGE
35–49

POPULATION = 6635 (000)
PERCENT OF BASE = 4.45

RANK	COST	WGT	REACH (000)	% COVG	% COMP	CPM
1. TIME	24705	60.00	1162	17.5	9.4	21.26
2. TIME	24705	55.00	1065	16.1	9.4	23.20
3. PEOPLE	13475	111.20	571	8.6	4.4	23.60
4. BUSINESS WEEK	18760	100.00	750	11.3	19.6	24.91
5. TIME	24705	50.00	968	14.6	9.4	25.52
6. NEWSWEEK	38160	100.00	1438	21.7	8.1	26.54
7. TIME	53195	100.00	1937	29.2	9.4	27.46
8. SPORTS ILLUSTRATED	34010	100.00	1144	17.2	9.0	29.73
9. US NEWS & WORLD REPORT	26420	100.00	733	11.0	8.7	36.04
10. ESQUIRE	14000	100.00	287	4.3	6.2	48.78
11. PLAYBOY	40745	100.00	831	12.5	5.2	49.03

TARGET MARKET:
   $15M+ AGE
50–64

POPULATION = 4511 (000)
PERCENT OF BASE = 3.03

RANK		COST	WGT	REACH (000)	% COVG	% COMP	CPM
1.	US NEWS & WORLD REPORT	26420	100.00	775	17.2	9.2	34.09
2.	TIME	24705	60.00	695	15.4	5.6	35.55
3.	TIME	24705	55.00	637	14.1	5.6	38.78
4.	BUSINESS WEEK	18760	100.00	461	10.2	12.0	40.69
5.	NEWSWEEK	38160	100.00	927	20.5	5.2	41.17
6.	TIME	24705	50.00	579	12.8	5.6	42.67
7.	ESQUIRE	14000	100.00	315	7.0	6.8	44.44
8.	TIME	53195	100.00	1159	25.7	5.6	45.90
9.	PEOPLE	13475	111.20	285	6.3	2.2	47.28
10.	SPORTS ILLUSTRATED	34010	100.00	571	12.7	4.5	59.56
11.	PLAYBOY	40745	100.00	310	6.9	1.9	131.44

TARGET MARKET:
   $20M+ AGE
18–34

POPULATION = 4529 (000)
PERCENT OF BASE = 3.04

RANK		COST	WGT	REACH (000)	% COVG	% COMP	CPM
1.	PEOPLE	13475	111.20	895	19.8	6.9	15.06
2.	TIME	24705	60.00	978	21.6	7.9	25.26
3.	TIME	24705	55.00	896	19.8	7.9	27.57
4.	TIME	24705	50.00	815	18.0	7.9	30.31
5.	NEWSWEEK	38160	100.00	1225	27.0	6.9	31.15
6.	TIME	53195	100.00	1630	36.0	7.9	32.63
7.	PLAYBOY	40745	100.00	1108	24.5	7.0	36.77
8.	SPORTS ILLUSTRATED	34010	100.00	846	18.7	6.7	40.20
9.	ESQUIRE	14000	100.00	330	7.3	7.1	42.42
10.	BUSINESS WEEK	18760	100.00	404	8.9	10.5	46.44
11.	US NEWS & WORLD REPORT	26420	100.00	478	10.6	5.7	55.27

TARGET MARKET:
  $20M+ AGE
35–49

POPULATION = 5188 (000)
PERCENT OF BASE = 3.48

			REACH			
RANK	COST	WGT	(000)	% COVG	% COMP	CPM
1. PEOPLE	13475	111.20	535	10.3	4.2	25.19
2. TIME	24705	60.00	937	18.1	7.6	26.37
3. BUSINESS WEEK	18760	100.00	658	12.7	17.1	28.51
4. TIME	24705	55.00	859	16.6	7.6	28.76
5. TIME	24705	50.00	781	15.1	7.6	31.63
6. NEWSWEEK	38160	100.00	1150	22.2	6.4	33.18
7. TIME	53195	100.00	1563	30.1	7.6	34.03
8. SPORTS ILLUSTRATED	34010	100.00	950	18.3	7.6	35.80
9. US NEWS & WORLD REPORT	26420	100.00	633	12.2	7.5	41.74
10. ESQUIRE	14000	100.00	251	4.8	5.4	55.78
11. PLAYBOY	40745	100.00	686	13.2	4.3	59.40

TARGET MARKET:
  $20M+ AGE
50–64

POPULATION = 3634 (000)
PERCENT OF BASE = 2.44

			REACH			
RANK	COST	WGT	(000)	% COVG	% COMP	CPM
1. US NEWS & WORLD REPORT	26420	100.00	628	17.3	7.5	42.07
2. TIME	24705	60.00	582	16.0	4.7	42.45
3. BUSINESS WEEK	18760	100.00	409	11.3	10.7	45.87
4. TIME	24705	55.00	534	14.7	4.7	46.26
5. NEWSWEEK	38160	100.00	810	22.3	4.5	47.11
6. ESQUIRE	14000	100.00	285	7.8*	6.2	49.12
7. TIME	24705	50.00	485	13.3	4.7	50.94
8. TIME	53195	100.00	971	26.7	4.7	54.78
9. PEOPLE	13475	111.20	243	6.7	1.9	55.45
10. SPORTS ILLUSTRATED	34010	100.00	503	13.8	4.0	67.61
11. PLAYBOY	40745	100.00	266	7.3	1.7	153.18

TARGET MARKET:
  $25M+ AGE
18–34

POPULATION = 2694 (000)
PERCENT OF BASE = 1.81

RANK	COST	WGT	REACH (000)	% COVG	% COMP	CPM
1. PEOPLE	13475	111.20	560	20.8	4.3	24.06
2. TIME	24705	60.00	627	23.3	5.1	39.40
3. TIME	24705	55.00	574	21.3	5.1	43.04
4. TIME	24705	50.00	522	19.4	5.1	47.33
5. NEWSWEEK	38160	100.00	761	28.2	4.3	50.14
6. TIME	53195	100.00	1045	38.8	5.1	50.90
7. PLAYBOY	40745	100.00	715	26.5	4.5	56.99
8. ESQUIRE	14000	100.00	240	8.9*	5.2	58.33
9. SPORTS ILLUSTRATED	34010	100.00	514	19.1	4.1	66.17
10. US NEWS & WORLD REPORT	26420	100.00	357	13.3	4.2	74.01
11. BUSINESS WEEK	18760	100.00	247	9.2	6.4	75.95

TARGET MARKET:
  $25M+ AGE
35–49

POPULATION = 3437 (000)
PERCENT OF BASE = 2.31

RANK	COST	WGT	REACH (000)	% COVG	% COMP	CPM
1. PEOPLE	13475	111.20	356	10.4	2.8	37.85
2. TIME	24705	60.00	644	18.7	5.2	38.36
3. BUSINESS WEEK	18760	100.00	468	13.6	12.2	40.09
4. TIME	24705	55.00	590	17.2	5.2	41.87
5. TIME	24705	50.00	537	15.6	5.2	46.01
6. TIME	53195	100.00	1074	31.2	5.2	49.53
7. NEWSWEEK	38160	100.00	761	22.1	4.3	50.14
8. US NEWS & WORLD REPORT	26420	100.00	494	14.4	5.9	53.48
9. SPORTS ILLUSTRATED	34010	100.00	613	17.8	4.8	55.48
10. ESQUIRE	14000	100.00	177	5.1	3.8	79.10
11. PLAYBOY	40745	100.00	477	13.9	3.0	85.42

TARGET MARKET:
 $25M+ AGE
50–64

POPULATION = 2606 (000)
PERCENT OF BASE = 1.75

			REACH			
RANK	COST	WGT	(000)	% COVG	% COMP	CPM
1. TIME	24705	60.00	436	16.7	3.5	56.66
2. US NEWS & WORLD REPORT	26420	100.00	461	17.7	5.5	57.31
3. TIME	24705	55.00	399	15.3	3.5	61.92
4. NEWSWEEK	38160	100.00	596	22.9	3.3	64.03
5. BUSINESS WEEK	18760	100.00	289	11.1	7.5	64.91
6. PEOPLE	13475	111.20	205	7.9	1.6	65.73
7. TIME	24705	50.00	363	13.9	3.5	68.06
8. TIME	53195	100.00	727	27.9	3.5	73.17
9. ESQUIRE	14000	100.00	189	7.3*	4.1	74.07
10. SPORTS ILLUSTRATED	34010	100.00	362	13.9	2.9	93.95
11. PLAYBOY	40746	100.00	226	8.7	1.4	180.29

TARGET MARKET:
ATT/GRAD COLL+ (Attended or graduated from college)

POPULATION = 41285 (000)
PERCENT OF BASE = 27.70

			REACH			
RANK	COST	WGT	(000)	% COVG	% COMP	CPM
1. PEOPLE	13475	111.20	5760	14.0	44.7	2.34
2. TIME	24705	60.00	6784	16.4	54.8	3.64
3. TIME	24705	55.00	6219	15.1	54.8	3.97
4. NEWSWEEK	38160	100.00	9121	22.1	51.1	4.18
5. TIME	24705	50.00	5654	13.7	54.8	4.37
6. TIME	53195	100.00	11308	27.4	54.8	4.70
7. SPORTS ILLUSTRATED	34010	100.00	6131	14.9	48.4	5.55
8. US NEWS & WORLD REPORT	26420	100.00	4705	11.4	55.9	5.62
9. ESQUIRE	14000	100.00	2368	5.7	51.1	5.91
10. PLAYBOY	40746	100.00	6627	16.1	41.7	6.15
11. BUSINESS WEEK	18760	100.00	2757	6.7	71.9	6.80

TARGET MARKET:
ATT/GRAD COLL+
    $20M+

POPULATION = 18647 (000)
PERCENT OF BASE = 12.51

RANK	COST	WGT	REACH (000)	% COVG	% COMP	CPM
1. PEOPLE	13475	111.20	2595	13.9	20.1	5.19
2. TIME	24705	60.00	3632	19.5	29.3	6.80
3. TIME	24705	55.00	3329	17.9	29.3	7.42
4. TIME	24705	50.00	3027	16.2	29.3	8.16
5. NEWSWEEK	38160	100.00	4639	24.9	26.0	8.23
6. TIME	53195	100.00	6054	32.5	29.3	8.79
7. BUSINESS WEEK	18760	100.00	1911	10.2	49.8	9.82
8. US NEWS & WORLD REPORT	26420	100.00	2572	13.8	30.6	10.27
9. SPORTS ILLUSTRATED	34010	100.00	3227	17.3	25.5	10.54
10. ESQUIRE	14000	100.00	1133	6.1	24.4	12.36
11. PLAYBOY	40745	100.00	2657	14.2	16.7	15.33

TARGET MARKET:
PM ATT/GRAD COLL+ (PM = Professional or Managerial)
    $20M+

POPULATION = 10466 (000)
PERCENT OF BASE = 7.02

RANK	COST	WGT	REACH (000)	% COVG	% COMP	CPM
1. PEOPLE	13475	111.20	1327	12.7	10.3	10.15
2. TIME	24705	60.00	2242	21.4	18.1	11.02
3. TIME	24705	55.00	2055	19.6	18.1	12.02
4. TIME	24705	50.00	1868	17.8	18.1	13.23
5. BUSINESS WEEK	18760	100.00	1354	12.9	35.3	13.86
6. NEWSWEEK	38160	100.00	2723	26.0	15.3	14.01
7. TIME	53195	100.00	3737	35.7	18.1	14.23
8. US NEWS & WORLD REPORT	26420	100.00	1547	14.8	18.4	17.08
9. SPORTS ILLUSTRATED	34010	100.00	1882	18.0	14.9	18.07
10. ESQUIRE	14000	100.00	728	7.0	15.7	19.23
11. PLAYBOY	40745	100.00	1545	14.8	9.7	26.37

Allied Food Distributors

In April 1977, Ms. Elizabeth Ramsey, the district sales manager for the upper Midwest district of Allied Food Distributors, was preparing to hire a new salesperson for the southwest Indiana sales territory. The current salesperson in this territory was leaving the company at the end of June. Ms. Ramsey had narrowed the list of potential candidates to three. She wondered which of these applicants she should select.

COMPANY BACKGROUND

Allied Food Distributors was one of the largest food wholesalers in the United States. The company carried hundreds of different packaged food items (fruits, vegetables, cake mixes, cookies, powdered soft drinks, and so on) for sales to supermarkets and grocery stores. Allied carried items in two different circumstances. First, some small food companies had Allied carry their entire line in all areas of the United States. Allied was in essence their sales force. Second, some large food companies had Allied carry their lines in less populated parts of the country. These areas were not large enough to sustain a salesperson for each food company.

Allied operated in all 50 states. The country was divided into 20 sales districts. Ms. Ramsey's sales district included Michigan, Indiana, and Illinois. Each district was divided into a number of sales territories. A salesperson was assigned to each territory.

THE SOUTHWEST INDIANA TERRITORY

The sales territory for which Ms. Ramsey was seeking a salesperson was located in the southwest corner of Indiana. Exhibit 1 presents a map of the

EXHIBIT 1
A map of the southwest Indiana territory

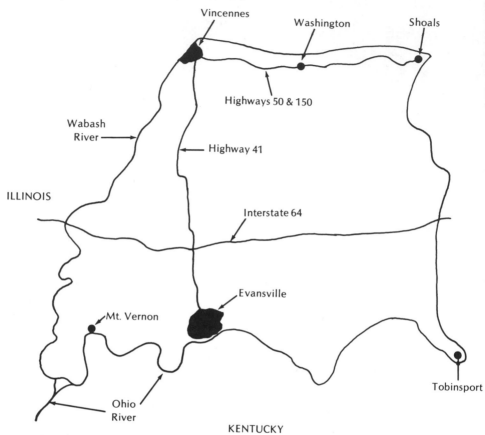

territory. It was bordered on the south by the Ohio River and the state of Kentucky, on the west by the Wabash River and the state of Illinois, and on the east by the Hoosier National Forest. The northern boundary ran a few miles north of Highways 50 and 150 that ran from Vincennes in the west through Washington to Shoals in the east. Evansville was the largest city in the area with a population of about 140,000. The salesperson for the territory was expected to live in Evansville, but would spend about three nights a week on the road. The only other reasonably large population concentration was in Vincennes with a population of about 20,000. Vincennes was located about 55 miles straight north of Evansville on Highway 41. Interstate Highway 64 ran the 80 miles east-west through the territory about 15 miles north of Evansville. Evansville was 165 miles southwest of Indianapolis, 170 east of St. Louis, Missouri, and 115 miles southwest of Louisville, Kentucky. The territory was very rural in character with agriculture being the dominant industry. The terrain was quite hilly, with poor soil. As a result, the farms in the area tended to be economically weak. There were many small towns and villages located throughout this basically rural environment.

THE SELLING TASK

Allied maintained 75 active retail accounts in the southwest Indiana territory. About ten of these accounts were medium- to large-sized independent supermarkets located in Evansville and Vincennes. The rest of the accounts were small, independent general food stores located throughout the territory.

The salesperson was expected to call on these accounts about every three weeks. The salesperson's duties included: checking displays and inventory levels for items already carried, obtaining orders on these items, informing retailers about new items, attempting to gain sales orders on these items, setting up special displays, and generally servicing the retailers' needs. Often, the salesperson would check the level of inventory on an item, make out an order, and present it to the retailer to be signed. The salesperson generally knew the store owner on a first name basis. The ordered goods were sent directly to the retailer from a warehouse located in Indianapolis.

THE SELECTION PROCESS

The responsibility for recruiting salespersons for the territories within a district was given to the district sales manager. The process consisted of the following steps:

1. An advertisement for the job was placed in newspapers in the state in question.
2. Those responding to the ad were sent job application forms.
3. The returned application forms were examined and certain applicants were asked to come to the district sales office for a full day of interviews.
4. The selection was then made by the district sales manager, or all applicants were rejected and the process started again.

TRAINING

Allied did all its salesperson training on-the-job. The salesperson on the territory that a new person would be assigned to, was given the task of training. Basically, this involved having the new person travel the territory to meet the retailers and to be shown how to obtain and send in orders. The district sales manager usually assisted in this process by traveling with the new salesperson for a few days.

COMPENSATION

The current salesperson on the southwest Indiana sales territory was earning a straight salary of about $16,000 per year plus fringe benefits. Ms. Ramsey indicated that she was willing to pay between $10,000 and $17,000 for a new person depending on the qualifications presented.

EXHIBIT 2
Information on Mr. Michael Gehringer

Personal information

Born July 15, 1935; married; three children ages 14, 16, and 19; height 5 feet, 10 inches; weight 205; excellent health; born and raised in Indianapolis.

Education

High school graduate; played football; no extracurricular activities of note.

Employment record

1. Currently employed by Allied Food Distributors in the warehouse in Indianapolis; two years with Allied; job responsibilities include processing orders from the field and expediting rush orders; current salary $650 per month.
2. In 1974–75 employed by Hoosier Van Lines in Indianapolis as a sales agent; terminating salary was $550 per month; left due to limits placed on salary and lack of challenge in the job.
3. In 1972–74 employed by Main Street Clothers of Indianapolis as a retail salesperson in the men's department; terminating salary $500 per month; left due to boring nature of this type of selling.
4. Between 1955 and 1972 held six other clerical and sales type jobs, all in Indianapolis.

Applicant's statement

I feel that my true employment interest lies in selling in a situation where I can be my own boss. This job seems just right.

Ms. Ramsey's comments

Seems very interested in job as a career.
Well recommended by his current boss.
Reasonably intelligent.
Good appearance.
Moderately aggressive.

THE CHOICES

On the basis of application forms and personal interviews, Ms. Ramsey had narrowed the field of applicants down to three. A summary of the information on their application forms along with the comments she had written to herself are contained in Exhibits 2, 3, and 4. She wondered which person she should select for the position.

EXHIBIT 3
Information on Mr. Carley Tobias

Personal information

Born February 12, 1947; married; two children ages 1 and 4; height 6 feet, 2 inches; weight 170; excellent health; born in San Francisco; raised in Cleveland, Ohio.

Education

High school and Community College graduate in business administration; student council president at Community College; plus belonged to a number of other clubs.

Employment record

1. Currently employed by The Drug Trading Company in Cincinnati as a salesperson; job responsibility Involves selling to retail drug stores; seven years with Drug Trading; current salary $1,100 per month.
2. In 1969–70 U.S. Army private; did one tour of duty in Vietnam.

Applicant's statement

I am seeking a new position because of the limited earning potential at Drug Trading, plus my family's desire to live in a less populated city.

Other information

He is very active in civic and church organizations in Cincinnati; he is currently president of the Sales and Marketing Executives of Cincinnati.

Ms. Ramsey's comments

Very personable.

Reasonably intelligent.

Good appearance.

He seems to like Cincinnati a lot.

Good experience.

EXHIBIT 4
Information on Mr. Arthur Woodhead

Personal information

Born May 26, 1955; single; height 6 feet; weight 180; excellent health; born and raised in Chicago.

Education

Will graduate in May 1977 from the University of Illinois, Chicago Circle with a B.B.A. Active in intramural athletics and student government.

Employment record

Summer jobs only; did house painting and gardening work for his own company. Earned $700 per month in summer of 1976.

Applicant's statement

I really like to run my own affairs, and selling seems like a good position to reach this objective.

Ms. Ramsey's comments

Well dressed and groomed.
Very intelligent.
Management potential, not career salesperson.
Not very aggressive.

Lawford Electric Company*

On February 3, 1969, Mr. Robert Allen, a field sales engineer for the Systems and Controls Division of the Lawford Electric Company, was notified by a letter from the Bayfield Milling Company that Bayfield had decided to purchase the drive system for a new shearing line from the AG Corporation. This news was a bitter disappointment to Mr. Allen because this sale, which he had been working on for over a year, would have resulted in a $871,000 order for him. He decided to review his call reports to see whether his failure to secure the order was caused by any flaw in his sales presentation to Bayfield personnel. He was sure the Lawford equipment was equal, if not superior, to the A G, Kennedy Electric, and Hamilton Electric products with which he had been in competition. He was just as certain that Bayfield personnel had been scrupulously fair in making their choice.

BACKGROUND INFORMATION

Lawford was one of the oldest, largest, and most respected firms in the electrical equipment industry. It manufactured a broad line of electric motors, generating equipment and control devices, and its products for service backup were widely regarded for quality and reliability. Lawford sales in 1968 were in excess of $100 million, second only to Kennedy Electric in this segment of the electrical equipment industry.

---

* This case was written by Derek A. Newton, Elis and Signe Olsson Professor of Business Administration, University of Virginia, Darden School of Business Administration. Copyright 1969 by the President and Fellows of Harvard College. Reproduced by permission.

Lawford sales executives considered Mr. Allen an above-average salesman. His background was similar to most of the other 37 Lawford field sales engineers. He held a Bachelor's degree in electrical engineering and was working on his Master's degree in a night program conducted by a local university. He had joined Lawford directly after college graduation in 1958 as an assistant sales engineer (handling routine telephone sales inquiries and processing and following up on customer orders) and had been promoted to his present position in 1960. A lifelong resident of Buffalo, Mr. Allen considered himself fortunate to be assigned the Buffalo sales territory, the site of his company's headquarters operations. He was married, the father of two young children and active in community affairs— Junior Chamber of Commerce, Rotary Club, and the local chapter of the Institute of Electrical and Electronic Engineers.

The Bayfield Milling Company was located in upstate New York, not far from the Lawford headquarters in Buffalo. Bayfield converted strip steel purchased from large steel producers into a variety of forms for sale to steel supply houses and end-users. The company also engaged in a limited steel supply business of its own. Bayfield sales in 1968 were in excess of $40 million.

Mr. Allen had been calling on Bayfield regularly during the past eight years. Given the size of his territory, which included the metropolitan areas of Albany, Syracuse, and Rochester, and the importance of Bayfield, whose annual purchases from Lawford occasionally totaled as much as $50,000, Mr. Allen attempted to call on Bayfield at least once a month. During this eight-year period Mr. Allen had formed close business friendships with Bayfield's purchasing agent, Mr. George Gibson, and with several of the company's engineers and operations personnel.

The shearing line recently ordered by Bayfield from Magna Machinery Corporation would add a new capability to Bayfield's mill operation, enabling the firm to convert rolled strips of steel into steel sheet of various dimensions. The shearing line would unroll strips of steel at high speed and by controlling the speed and tension of the strip at several points along the line would trim, flatten and shear the strip into sheets of precise dimensions, then convey the finished sheets into a stacking device and ultimately to a pallet for transfer to warehouse, truck or flat car. The cost of the mechanicals—including uncoiling rolls, pinch rolls, and drag rolls to control tension, side trimmers, shears, and conveyors, but excluding the drive system—was about $2 million.

ALLEN'S SALES ACTIVITY

From his call reports Mr. Allen reconstructed his activities during the period between January 15, 1968, when he learned of Bayfield's need for the new drive system, and February 3, 1969, when he learned that he had lost the sale.

January 15, 1968. Called on Gibson. Learned from him that Bayfield was soliciting bids on a drive system for a new shearing line. The line was to be purchased from Magna Machinery Corporation for delivery and installation in January 1970. Preliminary bids on the drive system for the line were due on July 15, 1968. Final bids were due on December 31, 1968, with the award announced on February 3, 1969. Gibson got very businesslike with me and said that *no* supplier sales personnel—including staff and management—were to contact Bayfield engineering personnel to discuss product specifications ("specs"). He said the operations vice president did not want them bothered since they would be too busy working on other problems connected with the new shearing line. Instead, all supplier personnel were to work through him [Gibson], although contact was to be permitted with operations personnel. Gibson gave me the name of the Magna engineer to contact for details of the new line. Gibson said that based on preliminary bids four or five suppliers would be chosen to submit final bids. The final decision would be a joint one made by Gibson, Lorenz, the chief engineer; Mainwaring, the plant superintendent; and Vogel, the operations vice president, who was also not to be contacted in person. Gibson suggested that Lawford would be a "cinch" to be one of the finalists, but Vogel and Lorenz would be "pretty hard-nosed" about the final decision. I took this to mean that cost would be an important factor.

Returned to the office and wrote the Magna engineer in Cleveland for the specs on the shearing line. Wrote to Albany Fabricators for a testimonial letter about the drive system I sold them last year for their slitting line. Told the boss [Fred Webster, Lawford regional sales manager] about the situation. "Anything I can do to help. . . ," he said. Took home for review our general specifications on various Lawford drive components.

January 23, 1968. Received specs from Magna (see Exhibit 1). Took them to Pollack [Lawford systems design engineer] and asked him to put together a tentative system for the Magna line. Called Mainwaring at Bayfield and made a luncheon date for next week.

February 2, 1968. Spent all morning with Gibson. Found out that operations and engineering were in a bad hassle over the drive system specs, but Gibson didn't understand the technicalities of the dispute. Showed him Pollack's tentative ideas. He seemed impressed. Spent about an hour going over the features of our variable voltage speed drives with stress on our static regulators for accurate speed control and our portable control panels. Left him a mountain of literature, including the Albany Fabricators' testimonial letter.

Spent $12 on lunch with Mainwaring and his assistant, Hughes. Told Hughes about a good place to buy a boat. Mainwaring denied that his people and engineering were having a hassle, the problem seemed to be

EXHIBIT 1
General description of Magna shearing line drive machinery requirements

Entry System, consists of:

Processor uncoiler, 100 kw. to operate as a drag generator. It is powered from a current-regulated static power supply. The motor field is controlled by a CEMF (counter electromotive force) regulator. The combination of the two regulator systems will ensure constant horsepower control over the full range of coil diameter.

Processor, 500 hp. motor powered from a voltage-regulated static power supply.

The No. 1 Loop regular controls processor speed.

No. 1 Pinch Roll, two 30 hp. motors powered from a current-regulated static power supply.

Side Trimmer, 250 hp. motor, and side trimmer Pinch Roll, 30 hp. powered from a voltage-regulated static power supply.

No. 2 Pinch Roll, two 30 hp. motors powered from a voltage-regulated static power supply.

The No. 2 Loop regulator controls the side trimmer and No. 2 Loop Pinch Roll speed.

Temper Mill System, consists of:

The No. 1 Bridle, three 120 hp., one 200 hp. motors to be powered from a current regulated static power supply. These motors are to operate as drag generators, with tachometer generator for speed indication.

Temper Mill, top—600 hp., bottom—600 hp. powered from a speed-regulated static power supply. One tachometer generator for speed indication and another for speed regulation.

No. 2 Bridle, one 200 hp., one 120 hp., two 250 hp., powered a static power supply which will be current regulated if the temper mill is used, and speed regulated when the temper mill is not used. A tachometer generator will provide the speed signal for regulation.

A voltage-regulated static power supply will be used to power No. 3 Loop Pinch Roll, two 20 hp. motors when shearing. It will also be used to power a deflector roll 7.5 hp. and an oiling machine, 20 hp. when the line is run for coiling.

The No. 3 Loop regulator, used only when shearing, controls the entire mill system speed.

The No. 1 Bridle is always used whether shearing or recoiling, and is current regulated for tension control.

The temper mill may be open or closed when either recoiling or shearing. If closed the No. 2 Bridle is current regulated. If mill is open, the rolls will not touch the strip and the No. 2 Bridle is speed regulated.

EXHIBIT 1 *(continued)*

If the mill is closed, it sets the speed of the mill system. If open, the No. 2 Bridle sets mill system speed.

Tension Reel—Hallden Shear System, consists of:

Tension Reel, 500 hp. motor, powered from a current-regulated static power supply. The motor field is controlled by a CEMF Regulator. The two regulator combination will regulate for constant horsepower, through the entire coil buildup.

Hallden Shear, 400 hp. motor is powered from the same static power supply as the tension reel except now it will be voltage regulated. The speed signal provided by a tachometer generator, driven by the shear leveler, will be the reference to the conveyor section.

The maximum line of speed when shearing is 350 f.p.m. (feet per minute) at a rated voltage.

When recoiling, the line speed can be increased by field weakening on some of the drives from 500 f.p.m. to 1,000 f.p.m. as outlined earlier. A selector switch on the main desk can preset the speed at 500 f.p.m. or 1,000 f.p.m. Interlocking will be provided to prevent change while the line is running.

When shearing, the Hallden Shear is the keynoter for the section beyond the shear. However, the line reference for the line as either a recoiling or shearing up to and through the shear is provided by the line reference motor-operated rheostat.

Conveyor and Leveler System, consists of:

The drives beyond the shear through Prime Pinch Roll (excluding the leveler) as shown on the single line are powered from a voltage-regulated semiconverter static power supply.

The strip leveler, 400 hp. motor is powered from a speed-regulated static power supply.

This section will have a fixed minimum speed of 75 f.p.m.

The drives are geared at 400 f.p.m. with field weakening to 450 f.p.m. on all those drives beyond the McKay Leveler.

---

that nobody had a clear understanding of what was needed. He added that "maybe the preliminary specs will give us a few ideas." He seemed to feel that engineering would draw up specs with whatever features his operations people wanted. Made a mental note to concentrate my sales efforts on Mainwaring.

After lunch I went over the same ground with Mainwaring and Hughes that I covered with Gibson, only in more detail. They both seemed concerned with reliability: "downtime kills you." I added that Lawford, being a neighbor so to speak, was in the best position to provide prompt and regular service. They agreed. Left them with the testimonial letter, a mountain of literature, and a copy of Pollack's proposal.

At home that evening I formulated my strategy. Decided to concentrate on Mainwaring at first, with emphasis on our service capability and product reliability. After Lawford had passed the preliminary bid stage I would shift my major effort to Lorenz in order to get a crack at influencing the final specs. Gibson would be "kept on board" throughout.

February 19, 1968. Stopped by to check progress with Gibson. Nothing new from him so I spent some time talking about our mutual activities in Rotary. Arranged a lunch with him, Lorenz, Mainwaring and my boss, Fred Webster, for middle of next month.

Went to see Mainwaring but he was out for the day. Hughes and I discussed some developments in systems design which improve reliability. Spent about an hour with the foreman on the cutting floor. He seemed to want a line which would allow fine tolerances in cutting accuracy. Talked to him about the advantages of the Lawford regulator systems as an aid to controlling tolerances due to their high-speed response capability. Discovered that two of their four slitting lines are powered by Lawford drive systems, one by a Kennedy system and one by an A G. The two Lawford systems were the oldest and the newest. Checked with several operators and they were unanimous in their praise of the Lawford machinery, although one man liked the A G because of the cast steel motor enclosure. When I pointed out that this feature made the motor bulky and harder to secure access to service, he remarked that he didn't have to service it but he "sure liked a big, heavy motor." Bought him a Coke and we parted friends.

March 14, 1968. Webster bought us all—Lorenz, Mainwaring, Gibson, Hughes, and myself—a magnificent lunch at the country club and made a great pitch about Lawford quality and service. This was the first time I had met Lorenz—he had joined Bayfield less than six months ago. He seemed a sour individual, but he loosened up after the second martini. After lunch I got Gibson aside and asked him about new developments. He now believed, as Mainwaring previously indicated, that the difficulty seemed to center on uncertainty as to what was needed in the drive system, and not on a dispute about features. He indicated that engineering had stopped working on the specs until after Bayfield had a chance to look over the preliminary bids.

April 10, 1968. Spent the morning with Mainwaring discussing the trade-off between the inertia in a heavy machine which provides for an even feed and the speed of response in a light machine which allows for more precise cutting tolerances. Left him with some additional literature describing Lawford's latest developments in regulator systems and a paperweight (a scale model of an experimental automobile powered by a Lawford electric motor). Stopped by to see Gibson and close a $2,500 order for circuit breakers.

May 20, 1968. Spent the day with Pollack working out the details of our tentative bid. His idea, based on my feedback, was a complete drive system which included d.c. adjustable voltage drive motors and control equipment, a.c. motors, a static d.c. constant potential power supply, and a static master regulator system. All components were Lawford made— a servicing advantage to Bayfield—and included a one-year warranty and service contract. Based on the Magna line specs, it seemed like a perfect compromise between even feed and cutting precision. Webster approved the pricing at $895,000 and I mailed out the bid later that week.

May 29, 1968. Checked with Gibson who grinned when I asked him how our bid looked. He said not to bother him until after July 15. We both laughed and I left for a brief visit on the cutting floor with the foreman. Found him grumbling about the regulator instability on the older Lawford slitting line drive system. Good-naturedly reminded him that regulators are temperature sensitive and a drive system of that age deserves congratulations, not criticism. He laughed and said that maybe we should replace it with another. I said that if he meant Bayfield should replace it with another Lawford, I would take it up immediately with Mainwaring. He laughed again and said the machine was O.K., he was only pulling my leg. On the way out I saw my old friend, the A G booster, and I bought him another Coke.

July 17, 1968. Gibson telephoned and said that a letter was in the mail inviting Lawford to bid on the final specifications. The other firms invited to bid were Kennedy, A G, and Hamilton. I dug up price lists and specs on our competitors' systems and took them home to study that evening.

The Kennedy product line was almost identical to Lawford's. Felt that Kennedy's had about a 5 percent price advantage over Lawford— item for item—but, on the other hand, their reputation for quality and service was not as good as Lawford's. Unlike both Kennedy and Lawford, A G and Hamilton did not manufacture all their own components. Lacking unit responsibility, I felt neither of these two companies could provide an extensively field tested integrated package. A G could offer more capacity in their regulator system than any of the other companies. This incremental capacity, however, would come at considerable additional cost to Bayfield. I felt that Bayfield would need add-on benefits only if they found themselves in the unlikely circumstance of buying another shearing line. Hamilton equipment I considered overpriced.

July 19, 1968. Stopped by to see Gibson. He suggested that our tentative bid was "a little high." Assured him that Lawford would be "rock bottom" once we had the final specs to bid on. Asked him about the committee's thinking on regulator capacity and he told me to go see Lorenz, but reminded me that supplier personnel could not bother anyone else in the engineering section. Lorenz could see me and I spent about an hour with him talking about our components. He did not seem as concerned about add-on capacity in the regulator system as he did about the system's stability. He said that the operating people were concerned about temperature sensitivity. Since this feature was one of Lawford's strong points,

I went into considerable detail with him about our temperature stability. Left him some additional literature of a highly technical nature to supplement the literature I had left with Gibson and Mainwaring which apparently had found its way to Lorenz's desk.

August 2, 1968.   Gibson told me over the phone that the committee had made no progress on the specs, nor did he expect any progress during August because of the vacation schedules. He suggested that I check back after Labor Day.

September 12, 1968.   Had lunch with Gibson and Lorenz. Both men agreed now that the committee had been in a bind over the specs. From the considerable experience Bayfield personnel had had with drive systems for smaller lines, such as the slitters, the committee had proceeded in the belief that this experience would be transferable, thus making a decision about a drive system for the shearing line relatively easy, despite the increase in size and complexity of the operation.

Apparently the problem had been a lack of criteria upon which the specs could be developed. Mainwaring had finally recognized this fact after the tentative bids had been opened. Implicit in all the tentative proposals were assumptions about criteria which were, in turn, manifested in a variety of špecs. Accordingly, Mainwaring had requested technical assistance from Magna engineers to develop criteria for Bayfield's installation. Mainwaring had just returned from a two-day visit to Magna headquarters with these criteria which Bayfield operating and engineering personnel were just beginning to study. Lorenz expected the final specs to be ready by early November.

This news elated me because I felt I was now in a position to go to work on Lorenz. I wanted to make sure that the specs included certain features standard with our constant potential power supply and our control panels. Incorporation of these features into the final specs I felt, would give Lawford a big price advantage in the bidding. Since Lorenz was busy that afternoon, I made an appointment to see him the following week.

September 20, 1968.   Had lunch with Lorenz and spent two more hours with him that afternoon. Covered thoroughly all aspects of our system with heavy emphasis on standard features in our power supply sets and control panels which reduce the incidence of generator breakdown and control component failure. He listened attentively throughout and asked very few additional questions. He seemed sold on the Lawford benefits.

October 4, 1968.   Had lunch with Hughes who told me that Mainwaring had left Bayfield for another job and that he had been promoted to Mainwaring's former position as plant superintendent. Neither Hughes, nor Gibson with whom I talked later that afternoon, cared to go into the details. Discussed with Hughes the reliability features I had discussed with Lorenz, only this time I stressed the benefits from the user point of view instead of the cost savings involved. Over dessert and coffee we discussed the merits of our respective boats. After lunch Gibson and I talked price but he managed to talk a lot without telling me much. Got the feeling that the operations vice president, Vogel, was upset about "some of the trimmings" the engineers wanted to write into the specs.

November 6, 1968.   Received final specs for drive system in the mail from Gibson. Also got an invitation to make a formal presentation on December 27 to Vogel, Lorenz, Hughes, and Gibson regarding our bid. The specs were a surprise. Bayfield had gone along with our power supply and control features, but also were specifying some special wiring—which was no problem—and a significant amount of additional capacity in the master regulator—which could be a problem. Put Pollack to work drawing up the final proposal and arranged for him and Webster to participate in the formal presentation.

November 8, 1968.   Called Gibson on the phone to verify the December 27 presentation date. Lawford, as were our three competitors, was to be given one hour for a presentation. The alphabet gave us a break; ours was to be the last presentation on that day. All four suppliers were expected to hand in their bids at the conclusion of their respective presentations. Asked him a few questions about the specs and he suggested that I see Lorenz.

November 11, 1968.   Spent two hours in the morning going over specs with Lorenz who, it turned out, was a stickler for attention to small details. Gave him a brief pitch on every detail and he seemed satisfied with my assurances that Lawford could deliver on all its promises. Stopped by to see Hughes who was quite busy, so I left after ten minutes. Neither he, Gibson, nor Lorenz was available for lunch.

December 27, 1968.   Our presentation went very well. Webster did a great job on Lawford's reliability and service. Pollack covered thoroughly the technical aspects of our proposed drive system, matching them with all Bayfield's specifications. I concluded with a summary and handed the sealed bid to Vogel. This latter, which Pollack, Webster and I had agonized over for hours previously, was priced at a "rock bottom" $871,000.

February 3, 1969.   After opening Gibson's letter and learning that A G had won the bid I called Gibson on the phone. He said that all bids had been in the "plus or minus $10,000 range" and that A G had just edged out Lawford. I asked him on what basis. He replied that Vogel, Lorenz and Hughes had felt the A G system "fitted in better" with the new shearing operation, but each gave different reasons for thinking so. He strongly suggested that holding a postmortem with the three men, either individually or collectively, would be a waste of time since all Bayfield personnel concerned in the purchase were relieved that the decision was over and done with. He congratulated me on Lawford's showing and expressed hope that I did not feel too bad about "coming in second."

CASE

28

Outdoor Sporting
Products, Inc.*

The annual sales volume of Outdoor Sporting Products, Inc., for the past six years had ranged between $1.6 million and $1.7 million. Although profits continued to be satisfactory, Mr. Hudson McDonald, president and chief operating officer, was concerned because sales had not increased appreciably from year to year. Consequently, he asked a consultant in New York City and the officers of the company to submit proposals for improving the salesmen's compensation plan, which he believed was the basic weakness in the firm's marketing operations.

Outdoor's factory and warehouse were located in Albany, New York, where the company manufactured and distributed sporting equipment, clothing, and accessories. Mr. Hudson McDonald, who managed the company, organized it in 1946 when he envisioned a growing market for sporting goods resulting from the predicted increase in leisure time and the rising levels of income in the United States.

Products of the company, numbering approximately 700 items, were grouped into three lines: (1) fishing supplies, (2) hunting supplies, and (3) accessories. The fishing supplies line, which accounted for approximately 40 percent of the company's annual sales, included nearly every item a fisherman would need such as fishing jackets, vests, caps, rods, and reels of all types, lines, flies, lures, landing nets, and creels. Thirty percent of annual sales were in the hunting supplies line which consisted of hunting clothing of all types including insulated and thermal underwear, safety

---

* Adapted from a case written by Zarrel V. Lambert, Auburn University, and Fred W. Kniffin, University of Connecticut, Stamford. Used with permission.

garments, shell holders, whistles, calls, and gun cases. The accessories line, which made up the balance of the company's annual sales volume, included items such as compasses, cooking kits, lanterns, hunting and fishing knives, hand warmers, and novelty gifts.

While the sales of the hunting and fishing lines were very seasonal, they tended to complement one another. The January–April period accounted for the bulk of the company's annual volume in fishing items, and most sales of hunting supplies were made during the months of May through August. Typically, the company's sales of all products reached their lows for the year during the month of December.

Outdoor's sales volume was $1.67 million in the current year with self-manufactured products accounting for 35 percent of this total. Fifty percent of the company's volume consisted of imported products which came principally from Japan. Items manufactured by other domestic producers and distributed by Outdoor accounted for the remaining 15 percent of total sales.

Mr. McDonald reported that wholesale prices to retailers were established by adding a markup of 50 to 100 percent to Outdoor's cost for the item. This rule was followed on self-manufactured products as well as for items purchased from other manufacturers. The resulting average markup across all products was 70 percent on cost.

Outdoor's market area consisted of the New England states, New York, Pennsylvania, Ohio, Michigan, Wisconsin, Indiana, Illinois, Kentucky, Tennessee, West Virginia, Virginia, Maryland, Delaware, and New Jersey. The area over which Outdoor could effectively compete was limited to some extent by shipping costs, since all orders were shipped from the factory and warehouse in Albany.

Outdoor's salesmen sold to approximately 6,000 retail stores in small- and medium-sized cities in its market area. Analysis of sales records showed that the firm's customer coverage was very poor in the large metropolitan areas. Typically, each account was a one- or two-store operation. Mr. McDonald stated that he knew for a fact that Outdoor's share of the market was very low, perhaps 2 to 3 percent; and for all practical purposes, he felt the company's sales potential was unlimited.

Mr. McDonald believed that with few exceptions, Outdoor's customers had little or no brand preference and in the vast majority of cases they bought hunting and fishing supplies from several suppliers.

It was McDonald's opinion that the pattern of retail distribution for hunting and fishing products had been changing during the past ten years as a result of the growth of discount stores. He thought that the proportion of retail sales for hunting and fishing supplies made by small- and medium-sized sporting goods outlets had been declining compared to the percent sold by discounters and chain stores. An analysis of company records revealed Outdoor had not developed business among the discounters with the exception of a few small discount stores. Some of Outdoor's executives felt that the lack of business with discounters might have been due in part to the company's pricing policy and in part to the pressures which current customers had exerted on company salesmen to keep them from calling on the discounters.

OUTDOOR'S SALES FORCE

The company's sales force played the major role in its marketing efforts since Outdoor did not use magazine, newspaper, or radio advertising to reach either the retail trade or consumers. One advertising piece that supplemented the work of the salesmen was Outdoor's merchandise catalog. It contained a complete listing of all the company's products and was mailed to all retailers who were either current accounts or prospective accounts. Typically, store buyers used the catalog for purposes of re-ordering.

Most accounts were contacted by a salesman two or three times a year. The salesmen planned their activities so that each store would be called upon at the beginning of the fishing season and again prior to the hunting season. Certain key accounts of some salesmen were contacted more often than two or three times a year.

Management believed that product knowledge was the major ingredient of a successful sales call. Consequently, Mr. McDonald had developed a "selling formula" which each salesman was required to learn before he took over a territory. The "formula" contained five parts: (1) the name and catalog number of each item sold by the company; (2) the sizes and colors in which each item was available; (3) the wholesale price of each item; (4) the suggested retail price of each item; and (5) the primary selling features of each item. After a new salesman had mastered the product knowledge specified by this "formula" he began working in his assigned territory and was usually accompanied by Mr. McDonald for several weeks.

Managing the sales force consumed approximately one third of Mr. McDonald's efforts. The remaining two thirds of his time was spent purchasing products for resale and in general administrative duties as the company's chief operating officer.

Mr. McDonald held semiannual sales meetings, had weekly telephone conversations with each salesman and had mimeographed bulletins containing information on products, prices, and special promotional deals mailed to all salesmen each week. Daily call reports and attendance at the semiannual sales meetings were required of all salesmen. One meeting was held the first week in January to introduce the spring line of fishing supplies. The hunting line was presented at the second meeting which was scheduled in May. Each of these sales meetings spanned four to five days

EXHIBIT 1

Salesmen: Age, years of service, territory, and sales

				Sales	
		Years of		Previous	Current
Salesmen	Age	service	Territory	year	year
Allen.......................	45	2	Illinois and Indiana	$ 82,566	$ 82,304
Campbell..................	62	10	Pennsylvania	298,048	345,060
Duvall.....................	23	1	New England	—	103,664
Edwards..................	39	1	Michigan	—	104,854
Gatewood.................	63	5	West Virginia	89,632	89,638
Hammond.................	54	2	Virginia	103,734	103,682
Logan.....................	37	1	Kentucky and Tennessee	—	141,930
Mason.....................	57	2	Delaware and Maryland	161,258	206,272
O'Bryan...................	59	4	Ohio	135,982	143,098
Samuels...................	42	3	New York and New Jersey	184,256	206,118
Wates.....................	67	5	Wisconsin	92,678	85,550
Salesmen terminated in previous year..........				457,204	—
House account............				64,346	61,120
Total.................				$1,669,704	$1,673,290

so the salesmen were able to study the new products being introduced and any changes in sales and company policies. The production manager and comptroller attended these sales meetings to answer questions and to discuss problems which the salesmen might have concerning deliveries and credit.

On a predetermined schedule each salesman telephoned Mr. McDonald every Monday morning to learn of changes in prices, special promotional offers, and delivery schedules of unshipped orders. At this time the salesman's activities for the week were discussed, and sometimes the salesman was asked by Mr. McDonald to collect past due accounts in his territory. In addition, the salesmen submitted daily call reports which listed the name of each account contacted and the results of the call. Generally, the salesmen planned their own itineraries in terms of the accounts and prospects that were to be contacted and the amount of time to be spent on each call.

Outdoor's sales force during the current year totaled 11 full-time men. Their ages ranged from 23 to 67 years and their tenure with the company from one to ten years. Salesmen, territories, and sales volumes for the previous year and the current year are shown in Exhibit 1.

COMPENSATION OF SALESMEN

The salesmen were paid straight commissions on their dollar sales volume for the calendar year. The commission rate was 5 percent on the first

$75,000, 6 percent on the next $25,000 in volume, and 7 percent on all sales over $100,000 for the year. Each week a salesman could draw all or a portion of his accumulated commissions. Mr. McDonald encouraged the salesmen to draw commissions as they accumulated since he felt the men were motivated to work harder when they had a very small or zero balance in their commission accounts. These accounts were closed at the end of the year so each salesman began the new year with nothing in his account.

The salesmen provided their own automobiles and paid their traveling expenses, of which all or a portion were reimbursed by per diem. Under the per diem plan, each salesman received $30 per day for Monday through Thursday and $14 for Friday, or a total of $134 for the normal workweek. No per diem was paid for Saturday, but a salesman received an additional $30 if he spent Saturday and Sunday nights in the territory.

In addition to the commission and per diem, a salesman could earn cash awards under two sales incentive plans that were installed two years ago. Under one which was called the Annual Sales Increase Awards Plan, a total of $5,200 was paid to the five salesmen having the largest percentage increase in dollar sales volume over the previous year. To be eligible for these awards, a salesman had to show a sales increase over the previous year. These awards were made at the January sales meeting, and the winners were determined by dividing the dollar amount of each salesman's increase by his volume for the previous year with the percentage increases ranked in descending order. The salesmen's earnings under this plan for the current year are shown in Exhibit 2.

EXHIBIT 2
Salesmen's earnings and incentive awards in the current year

Salesmen	Sales		Annual sales increase awards		Weekly sales increase awards (total accrued)	Earnings*
	Previous year	Current year	Increase in sales (percent)	Award		
Allen..............	$ 82,566	$ 82,304	(0.3%)	—	$ 506	$10,000†
Campbell..........	298,048	345,060	(15.8	$1,500 (2d)	1,122	22,404
Duvall.............	—	103,664	—	—	—	10,000†
Edwards...........	—	104,854	—	—	—	10,000†
Gatewood..........	89,632	89,638	(0.1)	200 (5th)	552	4,628
Hammond..........	103,734	103,682	—	—	210	10,000†
Logan.............	—	141,930	—	—	—	10,000†
Mason.............	161,258	206,272	27.9	2,000 (1st)	1,722	12,689
O'Bryan...........	135,982	143,098	5.2	500 (4th)	756	8,267
Samuels...........	184,256	206,118	11.9	1,000 (3d)	650	12,678
Wates.............	92,678	85,550	(7.7)	—	306	4,383

* Exclusive of incentive awards and per diem.
† Guarantee of $200 per week or $10,000 per year.

Under the second incentive plan, each salesman could win a Weekly Sales Increase Award for each week in which his dollar volume in the current year exceeded his sales for the corresponding week in the previous year. Beginning with an award of $2 for the first week, the amount of the award increased by $2 for each week in which the salesman surpassed his sales for the comparable week in the previous year. If a salesman produced higher sales during each of the 50 weeks in the current year, he received $2 for the 1st week, $4 for the 2d week, and $100 for the 50th week, or a total of $2,550 for the year. The salesman had to be employed by the company during the previous year to be eligible for these awards. A check for the total amount of the awards accrued during the year was presented to the salesmen at the sales meeting held in January. Earnings of the salesmen under this plan for the current year are shown in Exhibit 2.

The company frequently used "spiffs" to promote the sales of special items. The salesman was paid a "spiff," which usually was $2, for each order he obtained for the designated items in the promotion.

For the past three years in recruiting salesmen, Mr. McDonald had guaranteed the more qualified applicants a weekly income while they learned the business and developed their respective territories. During the current year, five salesmen, Allen, Duvall, Edwards, Hammond, and Logan, had a guarantee of $200 a week which they drew against their commissions. If the year's cumulative commissions for any of these salesmen were less than their cumulative weekly drawing accounts, they received no commissions. The commission and drawing accounts were closed on December 31 so each salesman began the new year with a zero balance in each account.

The company did not have a stated or written policy specifying the maximum length of time a salesman could receive a guarantee if his commissions continued to be less than his draw. Mr. McDonald held the opinion that the five salesmen who currently had guarantees would quit if these guarantees were withdrawn before their commissions reached $10,000 per year.

Mr. McDonald stated that he was convinced the annual earnings of Outdoor's salesmen had fallen behind earnings for comparable selling positions, particularly in the past six years. As a result, he felt that the company's ability to attract and hold high-caliber professional salesmen was being adversely affected. He strongly expressed the opinion that each salesman should be earning $20,000 annually.

COMPENSATION PLAN PROPOSALS

In December of the current year, Mr. McDonald met with his comptroller and production manager, who were the only other executives of the company and solicited their ideas concerning changes in the company's compensation plan for salesmen.

The comptroller pointed out that the salesmen having guarantees were not producing the sales that had been expected from their territories. He was concerned that the annual commissions earned by four of the five salesmen on guarantees were approximately half or less than their drawing accounts.

Furthermore, according to the comptroller, several of the salesmen who did not have guarantees were producing a relatively low volume of sales year after year. For example, annual sales remained at relatively low levels for Gatewood, O'Bryan, and Wates, who had been working four to five years in their respective territories.

The comptroller proposed that guarantees be reduced to $100 per week plus commissions at the regular rate on all sales. The $100 would not be drawn against commissions as was the case under the existing plan but would be in addition to any commissions earned. In the comptroller's opinion, this plan would motivate the salesmen to increase sales rapidly since their incomes would rise directly with their sales. The comptroller presented Exhibit 3 which showed the incomes of the five salesmen having guarantees in the current year as compared with the incomes they would have received under his plan.

From a sample check of recent shipments, the production manager had concluded that the salesmen tended to overwork accounts located within a 50-mile radius of their homes. Sales coverage was extremely light in a 60- to 100-mile radius of the salesmen's homes with somewhat better coverage beyond 100 miles. He argued that this pattern of sales coverage seemed to result from a desire by the salesmen to spend most evenings during the week at home with their families.

He proposed that the per diem be increased from $30 to $36 per day for Monday through Thursday, $14 for Friday, and $36 for Sunday if the

EXHIBIT 3

Comparison of earnings in current year under existing guarantee plan with earnings under the comptroller's plan*

Salesmen	Sales	Existing plan			Comptroller's plan		
		Com-missions	Guar-antee	Earnings	Com-missions	Guar-antee	Earnings
Allen................	$ 82,304	$4,188	$10,000	$10,000	$4,188	$5,000	$ 9,188
Duvall...............	103,664	5,506	10,000	10,000	5,506	5,000	10,506
Edwards.............	104,854	5,590	10,000	10,000	5,590	5,000	10,509
Hammond...........	103,682	5,508	10,000	10,000	5,508	5,000	10,508
Logan...............	141,930	8,185	10,000	10,000	8,185	5,000	13,185

* Exclusive of incentive awards and per diem.

salesman spent Sunday evening away from his home. He reasoned that the per diem of $36 for Sunday would act as a strong incentive for the salesmen to drive to the perimeters of their territories on Sunday evenings rather than use Monday morning for traveling. Further, he believed that the increase in per diem would encourage the salesmen to spend more evenings away from their homes which would result in a more uniform coverage of the sales territories and an overall increase in sales volume.

The consultant from New York City recommended that the guarantees and per diem be retained on the present basis and proposed that Outdoor adopt what he called a "Ten Percent Self-Improvement Plan." Under the consultant's plan each salesman would be paid, in addition to the regular commission, a monthly bonus commission of 10 percent on all dollar volume over his sales in the comparable month of the previous year. For example, if a salesman sold $20,000 worth of merchandise in January of the current year and $18,000 in January of the previous year, he would receive a $200 bonus check in February. For salesmen on guarantees, bonuses would be in addition to earnings. The consultant reasoned that the bonus commission would motivate the salesmen, both those with and without guarantees, to increase their sales.

He further recommended the discontinuation of the two sales incentive plans currently in effect. He felt the savings from these plans would nearly cover the costs of his proposal.

Following a discussion of these proposals with the management group, Mr. McDonald was undecided on which proposal to adopt, if any. Further, he wondered if any change in the compensation of salesmen would alleviate all of the present problems.

Pure Drug Company*

Mr. David Thomas had been transferred to the Syracuse, New York, Division of Pure Drug Company in the first week of May 1970. At this time he was appointed sales manager of the Syracuse wholesale drug division. Formerly he had been an assistant to the vice president in charge of sales at the company's headquarters in New York.

At the month-end sales meeting on the first Friday of June 1970, Mr. Harvey Brooks, a salesman in one of the division's rural territories, informed Mr. Thomas that he wished to retire at the end of July when he reached his 65th birthday. Mr. Thomas was surprised by Mr. Brooks' announcement because he had been informed by the division manager, Mr. Robert Jackson, that Mr. Brooks had requested and received a deferment of retirement until he reached his 66th birthday in July 1971. The only explanation offered by Mr. Brooks was that he had "changed his mind."

The retirement of Mr. Brooks posed a problem for Mr. Thomas, in that he had to decide what to do with Mr. Brooks' territory.

BACKGROUND OF THE SYRACUSE DIVISION

When Mr. Thomas became the divisional sales manager, he was 29 years old. He had joined Pure Drug (as the firm was known in trade circles) as a sales trainee after his graduation from Stanford University in 1964. During the next two years he worked as a salesman. In the fall of 1966, the sales

---

* This case was written by T. Levitt, Professor of Business Administration, Harvard University, R. Sorenson, President, Babson Institute, and U. Wiechman, Professor of Business Administration, Harvard University. Copyright 1972, the President and Fellows of Harvard College. Reproduced by permission.

manager of the company made Mr. Thomas one of his assistants. In this capacity Mr. Thomas helped the sales manager to arrange special sales promotions of the lines of different manufacturers.

Mr. Thomas' predecessor, Mr. Harry L. Schultz, had served as divisional sales manager for 15 years before his death in April. "H. L.," as Mr. Schultz had been known, worked as a salesman for the drug wholesale house that had been merged with Pure Drug to become its Syracuse Division. Although Mr. Thomas had made Mr. Schultz's acquaintance in the course of business, he did not know Mr. Schultz well. The salesmen often expressed their admiration and affection for Mr. Schultz to the new sales manager. Several salesmen, in fact, made a point of telling Mr. Thomas that "Old H. L." knew every druggist in 12 counties by his first name. Mr. Schultz had died of a heart attack while trout fishing with the president of the Syracuse Pharmacists' Association. The Syracuse Division manager said that most of the druggists in town attended Mr. Schultz's funeral.

The Syracuse Division of Pure Drug was one of 74 wholesale drug houses in the United States owned by the firm. Each division acted as a functionally autonomous unit having its own warehouse, sales department, buying department, and accounting department. The divisional manager was responsible for the performance of the unit he managed. There were, however, line functions performed by the regional and national offices that pertained directly to the individual departments. A district sales manager, for instance, was associated with a regional office in Albany for the purpose of implementing marketing policies established by the central office in New York.

As a service wholesaler, the Syracuse Division sold to the retail drug trade a broad line of approximately 18,000 items. The line might be described most conveniently as consisting of everything sold through drug stores except fresh food, tobacco products, newspapers, and magazines. In the trading area of Syracuse, Pure Drug competed with two other wholesalers; one of these carried substantially the same line of products; the other, a limited line of drug products.

The history of the Syracuse Division had been a profitable family-owned wholesale drug house before its merger with Pure Drug in 1950. The division had operated profitably since that date, although it had not shown a profit on sales equal to the average for the other wholesale drug divisions of Pure Drug. Since 1961, the annual net sales of the division had risen each year. Because the competitors did not announce their sales figures, it was impossible to ascertain, however, whether this increase in sales represented a change in the competitive situation or merely a general trend of business volume in the Syracuse trading area. Mr. Schultz had been of the opinion that the increase had been at the expense of competitors. The district drug sales manager, however, maintained that, since the trend of increase was less than that of other divisions in the northern New York region, the Syracuse Division may have actually lost ground competitively. A new measuring technique of calculating the potential wholesale purchasing power of retail drugstores, which had been adopted shortly before Mr. Thomas' transfer, indicated that the share of the wholesale drug market controlled by the Syracuse Division was below the median and below the mean for Pure Drug divisions.

Only a few of the present employees working in 1970 for the Syracuse Division had also been employed by the predecessor company. Mr. Schultz was the one remaining man of the executive echelon whose employment in the Syracuse Division antedated the merger. Most of the executives and salesmen currently active in the organization had been employed as executives or salesmen in the organization during the 1950s and 1960s. Two salesmen, however, Mr. Brooks and Mr. Clifford Nelson, had sold for the predecessor company before the merger.

Of the men who were employed as executives or salesmen before the 1960s, only Mr. Robert Jackson, the division manager, had a college degree which he had earned at a local YMCA night school. All the more recently employed young men were university or pharmacy college graduates. None of the younger men had been promoted when vacancies had occurred for the job of operations manager (who was in charge of the warehouse) and merchandise manager (who supervised buying) in the Syracuse Division; however, two of the younger men had been promoted to similar positions in other divisions when vacancies had occurred.

THE SYRACUSE DIVISION SALES FORCE

From the time when Mr. Thomas took over Mr. Schultz's duties he had devoted four days a week to the task of traveling through each sales territory with the salesmen who covered it. He had, however, made no changes in the practices or procedures of the sales force. The first occasion on which Mr. Thomas was required to make a decision of other than routine nature was when Mr. Brooks asked to be retired.

When Mr. Thomas took charge of the Syracuse Division sales force, it consisted of nine salesmen and four trainees. Four of the salesmen, Frederick Taylor, Edward Harrington, George Howard, and Larry Donnelly, had joined the company under the sales training program for college graduates initiated early in the 1960s. The other five salesmen had been with the company many years. Harvey Brooks and Clifford Nelson were senior in terms of service to the others. William Murray joined the company as a warehouse employee in 1946 when he was 19. He became a salesman in 1951. Walter Miller was employed as a salesman in 1951 when the wholesale drug firm that he had previously sold for went out of business. Mr. Miller, who was 48 years old, had been a wholesale drug salesman since he was 20. Albert Simpson came to Pure Drug after working as a missionary salesman for a manufacturer. Mr. Simpson, who was 26 when he joined the company in 1954, had served as an officer in the Army Medical Corps during the Korean War. He was discharged as a captain in hospital administration in 1958.

The four trainees were men who had graduated from colleges the preceding June. When Mr. Thomas arrived in Syracuse, these men were in the last phase of their 12-month training program. The trainees were spending much of their time traveling with the salesmen. Mr. Thomas, who now had the full responsibility for training these men, believed that Mr. Schultz had hired four trainees to cover anticipated turnover of salesmen, to cover anticipated turnover among the trainees themselves, and to implement the New York office's policy of getting more intensive coverage of each market area. The trainees, he understood, expected to receive territory assignments either in the Syracuse Division or elsewhere on the completion of their training period.

Mr. Thomas had not seen very much of the salesmen. His acquaintance with them had been formed at the sales meetings and while traveling with them through their territories.

Mr. Thomas was of the opinion that Walter Miller was a very easygoing, even-tempered person. He seemed to be very popular with the other salesmen and with his customers. Miller was very proud of his two sons, the younger one of whom was in high school while the other was the father of a son named after Mr. Miller. Mr. Thomas thought that the salesman liked him because Miller had commented to him several times that the suggestions offered by Mr. Thomas had been very helpful to him.

Harvey Brooks had not, in Mr. Thomas' opinion, been particularly friendly. Mr. Thomas had observed that Brooks was well-liked because of his good humor and friendly manner with everyone; however, Mr. Thomas had noticed that on a number of occasions Brooks had intimated that his age and experience should cause the sales manager to defer to his judgment. Mr. Brooks and his wife lived in the town of Oswego.

On June 4, 1970, Mr. Thomas had traveled with Mr. Brooks, and they had visited five of Mr. Brooks' accounts. On a routine form for sales managers reports on fieldwork with salesmen, which was filed with the district sales manager and New York sales manager, Mr. Thomas made the following comments about Mr. Brooks:

> *Points requiring attention.* Not using merchandising equipment; not following weekly sales plan. Pharmaceutical business going to com-

petitors because of lack of interest. Too much time spent on idle chatter. Only shows druggist what "he thinks they will buy." Tends to sell easy items instead of profitable ones.

Steps taken for correction.   Explained shortcomings and demonstrated how larger, more profitable orders could be obtained by following sales plan—did just that by getting the biggest order ever written for Carthage account.

Remarks.   Old-time "personality." Should do terrific volume if trained on new merchandising techniques.

On a similar form made out by Harry L. Schultz on the basis of working with Mr. Brooks on March 3, 1970, the following comments were made:

Points requiring attention.   Not getting pharmaceutical business. Not following promotion plans.

Steps taken for correction.   Told him about these things.

Remarks.   Brooks made this territory—can sell anything he sets his mind to—a real drummer—very popular with his customers.

George Howard, 29 years old, was the oldest of the group of salesmen who had passed through the formal sales training program. Mr. Thomas considered him earnest and conscientious. He had increased his sales each year. Although Mr. Thomas did not consider Howard to be the "salesman type," he noted that Howard had been quite successful in the use of the merchandising techniques which Mr. Thomas was seeking to implement.

William Murray handled a number of the big accounts in downtown Syracuse. Mr. Thomas believed that Murray was an excellent salesman who considered himself "very smooth." Mr. Thomas had been surprised at the affront Murray had taken when the sales manager had offered a few suggestions about the improvement of his selling technique. Mr. and Mrs. Murray were good friends of the Jacksons. The Murrays were social friends of the merchandise and operations managers and their wives. Mr. Thomas suspected that Murray had expected to be Mr. Schultz's successor.

Clifford Nelson seemed to Mr. Thomas to be an earnest and conscientious salesman. He had been amiable, though not cordial, toward Mr. Thomas. Mr. Thomas' report on calls on ten accounts on June 5, 1970, with Mr. Nelson contained the following statements:

Points requiring attention.   Rushing calls. Gets want book and tries to sell case lots on wanted items. Carries all merchandising equipment but doesn't use it.

Steps taken for correction.   Suggested change in routing; longer, better planned calls; conducted presentation demonstration.

Remarks.   Hardworking, conscientious, good salesman, but needs to be brought up to date on merchandising methods.

Mr. Schultz's comments on observations of Mr. Nelson on March 4, 1970, reported on the same form, were as follows:

Points requiring attention.   Uses the want book on the basis of most sales. Not pushing promotions.

Steps taken for correction.   Discussed shortcomings.

Remarks.   Nelson really knows how to sell—visits every customer each week. Hard worker—very loyal—even pushes goods with very low commission.

On the day Mr. Thomas had traveled with Nelson, the salesman suggested that Mr. Thomas have dinner at the Nelson's home. Mr. Thomas accepted the invitation, but at the end of the day Nelson took him to a restaurant in Watertown, explaining that he did not want to inconvenience his wife because his two daughters were home from college on vacation.

Albert Simpson had caused Mr. Thomas considerable concern. Simpson complained about sales management procedures, commission rates, the "lousy service of the warehouse people," and other such matters at sales meetings. Mr. Thomas believed that most of the complaints were founded in fact, but that the matters were usually trivial in that the other salesmen did not complain of these matters. Mr. Thomas mentioned his difficulties with Simpson to Mr. Jackson. Mr. Jackson's comment was that Simpson had been very friendly with Mr. Schultz. Simpson seemed to be quite popular with his customers.

Frederick Taylor was, in Mr. Thomas' opinion, the most ambitious, aggressive, and argumentative salesman in the Syracuse Division. He had been employed by the company since his graduation from the University of Rochester in 1966, first as a trainee and then as a salesman. Taylor had substantially increased the sales volume of the territory assigned to him. He had persuaded Mr. Schultz to assign him six inactive hospital accounts in July of 1968. In six months, Taylor made sales to these accounts in excess of $50,000. The other salesmen considered him "cocky" and a "big spender." Mr. Thomas thought his attitude was one of independence. If Taylor agreed with a sales plan, he worked hard to achieve its objectives, but if he did not agree, he did not cooperate at all. Mr. Thomas thought that he had been very successful in working with Taylor.

Larry Donnelly impressed Mr. Thomas as being unsure of himself. Donnelly seemed to be confused and overworked. Mr. Thomas attributed this difficulty to Donnelly's trying to serve too many accounts in too large an area. Donnelly was very solicitous about Mr. Thomas's suggestions on improvement of his work. Donnelly was 24 years old. Mr. Thomas believed that he would improve in time with proper help. Donnelly had raised his sales to the point where he was on commission instead of salary in March of 1970.

Edward Harrington was the only salesman who worked on a salary. His sales volume was not sufficient to sustain an income of $600 a month which was the company minimum for salesmen with more than one year's experience. Harrington was very apologetic about being on a salary. Mr. Thomas believed that Harrington's determination to "make good" would be realized because of the latter's conscientiousness. The salesman was 25. When he had been assigned the territory two years before, it had consisted largely of uncontacted accounts. The volume of sales had tripled in the meantime. Mr. Thomas felt that Harrington appreciated all the help he was given and that in time Harrington would be an excellent salesman.

Sales commission rates were as follows:

	Percent
Brooks and Nelson......................	2.375%
Miller and Donnelly......................	2.25
Murray and Simpson.....................	2.125
Howard and Taylor......................	2

Mr. Thomas said that expense accounts amounted to about 0.75 percent of sales for both city and country salesmen. The differences in percentage rates of commissions were explained by Mr. Thomas in terms of the differential commissions set by the company. Higher commission rates were given on items the company wished to "push," such as pharmaceuticals and calendar promotion items.

The trainees were something of an unknown quantity to Mr. Thomas. He had training conferences with them in which he had thought they had performed rather poorly. He believed that Mr. Schultz had neglected the training of the new men. All four of them seemed to be good prospects. They were eager to be assigned territories, as they informed Mr. Thomas as often as possible.

The turnover of the Syracuse Division sales force has been very low among the senior salesmen. Six of the sales training program men had left the division since 1965. Two had been promoted to department heads in other divisions. Four had left to work for manufacturers. Because manufacturers valued salesmen with wholesaling experience and competing wholesalers did not have training programs for young men, there were many opportunities for a salesman who desired to leave.

SALES MANAGEMENT

Since Mr. Thomas had replaced Mr. Schultz, he had devoted considerable thought to the problem of improving the sales performance of the Syracuse Division. He had accepted a transfer to the new job at the urging of Mr. Richard Topping, the vice president in charge of sales. Mr. Thomas was one of a dozen young men whom Mr. Topping had brought into the New York office to work as assistants to the top sales executives. None of the young assistants had remained in the New York office for more than three years, for Mr. Topping made a policy of offering the young men field assignments so that they could "show their stuff." Mr. Thomas believed that the sales performance of the Syracuse Division could be bettered by an improved plan of sales management. He knew that the share of the Syracuse market for wholesale purchases of retail drugstores[1] held by Pure Drug was only 20.05 percent as against a 48 percent share for some of the other divisions.

Mr. Topping, for whom Mr. Thomas worked immediately before his transfer, had focused his staff's attention upon the qualitative aspects of sales policy. Mr. Thomas had assisted Mr. Topping in implementing merchandising plans intended to utilize the salesmen's selling efforts in such a way as to minimize the handling cost of sales and maximize the gross margin.

The company encouraged the salesmen to use a threefold plan for increasing profitability:

1. Sales of larger average value per line of the order were encouraged because the cost of processing and filling each line of an order was practically constant.
2. Sales of larger total value were encouraged because the delivery cost for orders having a total weight between 20 and 100 pounds was practically constant.
3. Because some manufacturers offered margins considerably larger than others, sales of products carrying higher margins were encouraged. Salesmen's commissions varied with the margins available to Pure Drug on the products they sold.

The executives of the company also sought to increase the effectiveness of Pure Drug promotions by setting up a sales calendar. The sales calendar coordinated the activities of all Pure Drug divisions so that during a given calendar period every account would be solicited for the sale of particular items yielding satisfactory profits. The type of activity represented by the

---

[1] The potential wholesale sales for retail drugstores were calculated by the New York office market analysis section. This market estimate, called the PWPP (potential wholesale purchasing power) was calculated for each county by adjusting retail drugstore sales to an estimate of the purchases of goods from wholesalers.

sales calendar required that the salesmen in each division follow a pattern in selling to every individual account. The sales manager was responsible for coordinating the activities of his salesmen.

The matter of selling patterns was largely the responsibility of the division sales manager. Mr. Thomas believed that his predecessor had never really accepted the changes that had taken place in the merchandising policy of the New York office.

EXHIBIT 1
Syracuse Division trading area

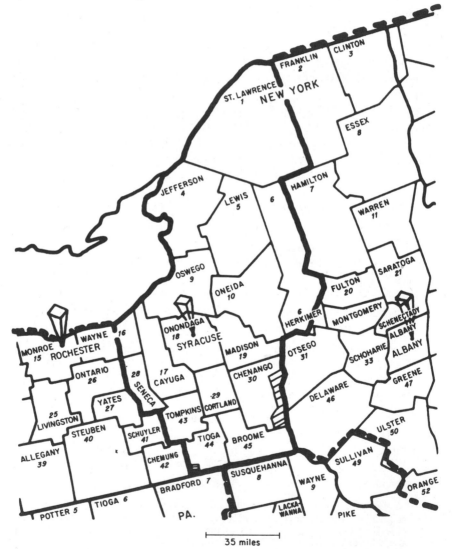

35 miles

Mr. Thomas had inherited from his predecessor a system of sales department records which had been carefully maintained. The national offices required each division to keep uniform sales and market analysis records. During the period of Mr. Thomas's work in the New York office, he had developed a familiarity with the uses of these records.

The basis of the sales and market analysis record was the division trading area. The limits of the trading area were determined by the economics of selling costs, and the factors on which the costs were based were transportation costs of delivery and salesmen's traveling expenses. Mr. Thomas knew from his own experience that delineation of trading areas was influenced by tradition, geographic conditions, the number of salesmen, the number of calls a salesman could make, the estimated market potential, competition, and agreements with adjacent Pure Drug divisions. The Syracuse Division was bordered by the trading areas of Pure Drug divisions located in Rochester and Albany on the east, south, and west; to the north was the Canadian border. A map of this division is included here in Exhibit 1.

Exhibit 2 gives information on sales and sales potential by county. Exhibits 3 and 4 show selected data on salesmen's territory assignments and performance. During the time since his arrival, Mr. Thomas had formed the opinion that the present salesmen's territories had been established without careful regard for the number of stores in the area, the sales potential, or the amount of traveling involved. Although Mr. Thomas had not yet studied any one territory carefully, he suspected all his salesmen of skimming the cream from many of their accounts because they did not have adequate time to do a thorough selling job in each store.

Mr. Thomas had been able to observe the performance records of other divisional sales managers while he worked in New York. He knew that some sales managers had achieved substantial improvements on the past performances of their divisions.

SALES TERRITORIES OF BROOKS AND NELSON

The territory that Mr. Brooks covered included accounts scattered through small towns in four counties of the rural area northeast of Syracuse (see Exhibit 5). Mr. Brooks had originally developed the accounts in the four-county area for the predecessor company. At the time he undertook this task the competing service wholesaler already had established a mail-order business with the rural druggists in this area. Mr. Brooks had taken to the road in 1940 to build up the sales in all four counties. He had been hired specifically for this job because he was a native of the area and an experienced "drummer."

Five years later Mr. Clifford Nelson, a friend of Mr. Brooks, became

EXHIBIT 2

Selected data on sales and sales potentials, by counties

County	Code	Popu-lation (000)	Per cent	Retailers Sold	Inactive accounts	Accounts not sold	Total	Potential wholesale purchasing power* (000)	Per cent area PWPP	Sales† (000)	Sales per cent PWPP	Hospitals Sold	Hospitals Not sold	Hospitals Sales (000)	Miscella-neous sales (000)
St. Lawrence	1	117.2	6.3%	23	1	2	26	$1,090	4.4%	$408	26.9%	2	4	$ 8	$ 6
Jefferson	4	90.2	4.9	34	—	—	34	1,306	5.3	367	28.2	2	2	4	—
Lewis	5	24.8	1.3	8	—	—	8	261	1.0	86	32.2	—	1	—	3
Herkimer	6	69.3	3.7	10	6	1	17	624	2.5	98	15.7	—	2	—	—
Oswego	9	97.8	5.3	25	1	—	26	1,340	5.5	373	27.1	1	2	—	10
Oneida	10	285.4	15.5	46	14	12	72	3,480	14.2	375	10.5	—	13	—	7
Wayne	16	76.6	4.1	4	—	1	5	247	1.0	55	22.3	—	—	—	—
Cayuga	17	75.6	4.1	12	4	—	16	561	2.3	101	18.0	2	—	4	27
Onondaga	18	474.8	25.8	98	9	13	120	7,647	31.2	2,166	28.7	6	9	108	192
Madison	19	59.7	3.2	12	2	3	17	1,250	5.1	261	20.9	—	2	—	—
Seneca	28	34.4	1.9	6	1	3	10	558	2.3	84	15.0	2	1	6	24
Cortland	29	45.4	2.5	6	2	1	9	510	2.1	161	31.5	—	2	—	—
Chenango	30	48.2	2.6	4	2	6	12	568	2.3	63	11.1	—	3	—	—
Tompkins	43	75.7	4.1	9	1	4	14	815	3.3	132	16.2	—	5	—	—
Tioga	44	46.2	2.5	4	—	7	11	322	1.3	80	24.8	—	—	—	—
Broome	45	225.3	12.2	22	2	13	37	3,970	16.2	253	6.4	—	8	—	18
		1,846.6	100.0%	323	45	66	434	$24,549	100.0%	$5,063	20.5%	15	54	$130	$287

* Includes miscellaneous but not hospital or house sales.
† Excludes miscellaneous sales, sales to hospitals, and house sales.

EXHIBIT 3
Selected data on salesmen's territory assignments by county

Salesman	County	Sales, 1969*	Active† accounts	Esti-mated‡ poten-tial (000)	As-signed† accounts
Miller....................	Chenango	$ 61,902	4	$ 567	15
	Tompkins	132,900	9	815	19
	Tioga	79,678	4	322	11
	Broome	270,300	22	3,971	45
	Total	544,780	39	5,675	90
Brooks..................	Jefferson	146,034	16	906	18
	Lewis	86,394	8	261	9
	Oswego	369,860	25	1,070	28
	Total	602,288	49	2,237	55
Howard..................	Onondaga	229,017	14	910	14
	Madison	260,850	12	1,250	19
	Cortland	161,000	6	510	11
	Total	650,867	32	2,670	44
Murray..................	Onondaga	756,153	33	2,225	44
	Total	756,153	33	2,225	44
Nelson..................	St. Lawrence	408,176	25	1,090	32
	Jefferson	222,519	20	400	20
	Oswego	2,780	1	270	1
	Total	633,475	46	1,760	53
Simpson.................	Onondaga	733,926	29	3,008	48
	Total	733,926	29	3,008	48
Taylor...................	Onondaga	638,073	29	1,504	29
	Total	638,073	28	1,504	29
Donnelly................	Herkimer	97,060	10	624	19
	Oneida	375,000	46	3,480	85
	Total	472,060	56	4,104	104
Harrington..............	Wayne	54,400	4	247	5
	Cayuga	127,000	14	561	18
	Seneca	108,780	8	558	13
	Total	290,180	26	1,366	36
Hospitals................	Taylor-Syracuse	108,000			
	All others	22,000			
House accounts.........		$ 529,012			
Total Division sales......		$5,980,764			

* The figures by salesmen include sales to chain and independent drugstores, and to miscel-laneous accounts, but do not include sales to hospitals or house accounts indicated at the foot of the table.

† Includes hospitals and other recognized drug outlets in the territory.

‡ No potential is calculated for hospitals or miscellaneous sales. However, where a county is divided among several salesmen, the potential sales figure for each salesman is obtained by allocating the county potential in proportion to the total number of potential drugstore and miscellaneous accounts in that county assigned to that salesman.

EXHIBIT 4

Summary data on salesmen's performance

	1969 sales (000s)	Per-cent	1969 Potential† (000s)	Per-cent	Sales percent of potential	1969 active accounts‡ No.	Percent	1969 assigned accounts‡ No.	Percent	Active accounts percent of assigned	1969 sales per account	Potential per assigned account§
I:												
Miller..........	$ 545	10.2%	5,675	23.2%	9.6%	39	11.5%	90	17.9%	43.4%	$14,000	$63,100
Brooks..........	602	11.3	2,237	9.1	27.0	49	14.5	55	10.9	89.0	12,300	40,600
Murray..........	756	14.2	2,225	9.1	34.0	33	9.8	44	8.8	75.0	22,900	50,500
Nelson..........	634*	11.9	1,760	7.2	36.0	46	13.6	53	10.5	85.0	13,800	33,200
Simpson..........	734	13.8	3,008	12.2	24.5	29	8.6	48	9.5	60.5	25,350	62,700
Subtotal.........	$3,271	61.4%	14,905	60.8%	22.0	196	58.0%	290	57.6%	67.2	16,700	51,400
II:												
Howard..........	651	12.2	2,670	10.9	24.4	32	9.5	44	8.7	72.7	20,360	60,600
Taylor..........	638*	12.0	1,504	6.1	42.4	28	8.3	29	5.8	96.5	26,700	51,800
Donnelly..........	472	8.9	4,104	16.7	11.5	56	16.5	104	20.7	53.8	8,420	39,500
Harrington..........	290*	5.5	1,366	5.5	21.3	26	7.7	36	7.2	72.3	11,150	38,000
Subtotal.........	$2,051	38.6%	9,644	39.2%	21.3	142	42.0%	213	42.4%	66.7	14,470	45,300
Total.........	$5,322*	100.0%	24,549	100.0%	21.7	338	100.0%	503	100.0%	67.0	15,730	48,800
Hospital sales by:												
Taylor..........	108											
Nelson..........	12											
Harrington..........	10											
House sales:	529											
Grand total........	$5,981											

* Excluding hospital sales.

† No potential is calculated for hospital or miscellaneous sales. However, where a county is divided among several salesmen, the potential sales figure for each salesman is obtained by allocating the county potential in proportion to the total *number* of potential drugstore and miscellaneous accounts in that county assigned to that salesman.

‡ Includes hospitals and other recognized drug outlets in the territory.

§ Understated since hospitals and miscellaneous accounts are included in the assigned accounts listed but not in the potential.

2/ Exhibit 6. Mr. Brooks' accounts that Mr. Nelson wants total $417,985 (87.7 percent of Mr. Brooks's sales in Jefferson County, 80 percent in Oswego County, or 69.4 percent of the territory total. Added to Nelson's 1969 sales, would increase his volume 65 percent to $1,063,207. Brooks' old territory would be left with $184,303 in sales.

3/ Using commission rates as given, earnings are: Miller, $12,270; Brooks, $14,290; Murray, $16,080; Nelson, $15,400; Simpson, $15,600; Howard, $13,020; Taylor, $12,760; Donnelly, $10,620; Harrington, $7,200.

EXHIBIT 5
Counties sold By Messrs. Brooks and Nelson

a division salesman, and, at the suggestion of Mr. Brooks, covered other accounts in the same four-county area. Mr. Nelson had been a salesman for a proprietary medicine firm before he joined the wholesale drug house. He was seven years younger than Mr. Brooks. Since that time Mr. Brooks had serviced a number of accounts in the four-county area. The list of accounts that each of these men handled appears in Exhibit 6 and 7. Mr. Thomas noticed that the incomes which Messrs. Brooks and Nelson had received from commissions were very stable over the years.

EXHIBIT 6. Accounts sold by Harvey Brooks, by counties, with 1969 purchases

Jefferson County:

Adams Center	D	$ 3,570
(Alexandria Bay	D	18,300)
(Alexandria Bay	D	15,790)
Bellville	D	2,100
(Carthage	D	61,000)
Chaumont	D	604
(Clayton	D	10,630)
(Clayton	D	16,400)
Deferiet	D	369
Dexter	D	11,670
Ellisburg	D	236
LaFargeville	D	522
Plessis	D	880
Redwood	M	108
Rodman	D	3,210
Sackets Harbor	D	645
County total		$146,034

Lewis County:

Beaver Falls	D	$ 3,810
Croghan	D	24,597
Harrisville	D	18,516
Lowville	D	23,688
Lowville	D	4,314
Lyons Falls	D	6,024
Port Leydon	D	2,325
Turin	M	3,120
County total		$86,394

Oswego County:

Calosse	D	$ 1,709
Central Square	D	1,857
Constantia	M	72
Cleveland	M	390
(Fulton	D	15,120)
(Fulton	D	24,510)
(Fulton	D	27,800)
(Fulton	D	38,400)
Hannibal	D	3,890
Hastings	M	3,840
Lacona	M	462
Mexico	D	15,900
Oswego	D	12,075
(Oswego	D	20,760)
(Oswego	D	24,100)
(Oswego	D	41,000)
(Oswego	D	43,900)
(Oswego	D	22,430)
Oswego	H	15
Parish	M	5,160
Phoenix	D	9,730
(Pulaski	D	8,750)
(Pulaski	D	29,080)
Sandy Creek	D	14,130
West Monroe	D	4,780
County total		$369,860
Territory total		$602,288

Code: D = independent drugstore; C = chain drugstore; M = miscellaneous account; H = Hospital. **Note:** Accounts in parentheses are those wanted by Mr. Nelson.

EXHIBIT 7. Accounts sold by Clifford Nelson, by counties, with 1969 purchases

St. Lawrence County:		
Canton...........................	D	$ 39,240
Edwards..........................	D	2,016
Edwards..........................	M	5,655
Gouverneur.......................	D	678
Gouverneur.......................	D	28,149
Gouverneur.......................	D	49,559
Heuvelton........................	D	324
Messena..........................	D	33,777
Messena..........................	D	10,191
Messena..........................	C	7,344
Messena..........................	C	6,675
Messena..........................	H	114
Madrid...........................	D	4,296
Morristown.......................	D	8,193
Norfolk..........................	D	8,985
Norwood..........................	D	9,417
Ogdensburg.......................	D	24,270
Ogdensburg.......................	D	67,665
Ogdensburg.......................	D	21,609
Ogdensburg.......................	D	10,140
Ogdensburg.......................	M	447
Ogdensburg.......................	H	7,959
Potsdam..........................	D	46,332
Potsdam..........................	C	22,113
Potsdam Falls....................	D	1,101
County total....................		$416,249
Jefferson County:		
Adams............................	C	$ 1,885
Carthage.........................	C	2,130
Evans Mills......................	D	2,210
Philadelphia.....................	D	3,780
Watertown........................	D	30,200
Watertown........................	D	4,740
Watertown........................	D	8,800
Watertown........................	D	30,680
Watertown........................	D	18,440
Watertown........................	D	26,300
Watertown........................	D	38,200
Watertown........................	D	23,000
Watertown........................	D	9,700
Watertown........................	D	854
Watertown........................	D	11,320
Watertown........................	C	3,630
Watertown........................	C	5,970
Watertown........................	M	680
Watertown........................	H	126
Watertown........................	H	3,600
County total....................		$226,245
Oswego County:		
Pulaski..........................	C	2,730
Territorial total...............		$645,224

Code: D = independent drugstore; C = chain drugstore; M = miscellaneous account; H = hospital.

A VISIT FROM MR. NELSON

On the Wednesday morning following the June sales meeting, Mr. Thomas saw Mr. Nelson come in the front door of the Syracuse Division offices. Although the salesman passed within 30 feet of Mr. Thomas's desk, he did not appear to notice the sales manager. Mr. Nelson walked through the office area to the partitioned space where Mr. Jackson's private office was located. Twenty minutes later Mr. Nelson emerged from the division manager's office and made his way to Mr. Thomas's desk.

"Hi there, young fellah!" he shouted as he approached.

"Howdy, Cliff. Sit down and chat awhile," Mr. Thomas replied. "What got you out of bed so early?" he asked, knowing that the salesman must have risen at 6 o'clock to make the drive to Syracuse from his home in Watertown.

Mr. Nelson squeezed his bulky frame into the armchair next to the desk. "It's a shame Harvey is retiring," he said. "I never thought he could stand to give it up. I never knew anyone who enjoyed selling as much as Harvey —'cept, maybe me." Mr. Nelson continued praising Mr. Brooks and telling anecdotes which illustrated his point until Mr. Thomas began to wonder whether Mr. Nelson thought that the sales manager was biased in some way against the retiring salesman. Mr. Thomas recalled that he had made some critical remarks about Mr. Brooks to Mr. Jackson, but he could not recall any discussion of Mr. Brooks' shortcomings with the man himself or any of the other salesmen. Mr. Nelson ended his remarks by saying "Old 'H. L.,' God rest his soul, always said that Harvey was the best damn wholesale drug salesman we'd ever known."

There was a brief silence as Mr. Thomas did not realize that Mr. Nelson was finished. Finally Mr. Thomas said, "You know, Cliff, I think we ought to have a testimonial dinner for Harvey at the July sales meeting."

Mr. Nelson made no comment on Mr. Thomas's suggestion; instead, he went on to say, "None of these green trainees will ever be able to take Harvey's place. Those druggists there are old-timers. They would resent being high pressured by some kid blown up to twice his size with college degrees. No sir! You've got to sell 'em right in those country stores."

Mr. Thomas did not believe that Mr. Nelson's opinion about the adaptability of the younger, college educated salesmen was justified by the evidence available. He recalled that several of these men in country territories had done better on their May sales quotas than either Mr. Brooks or Mr. Nelson. He was proud of his self-restraint when he commented, "Selling in a country territory is certainly different."

"That's right, Dave, I wanted to make sure you understood these things before I told you." Mr. Nelson was nervously massaging his double chin between his thumb and forefinger.

Mr. Thomas looked at him with a quizzical expression. "Told me what."

"I have just been talking to Mr. Jackson. Well, I was talking to him about an understanding between Harvey and me. We always agreed that if anything should happen to the other, or he should retire, or something—well, we agreed that the one who remained should get to take over his choice of the other's accounts. We told 'H. L.' about this and he said, 'Boys, what's O.K. by you is O.K. by me. You two developed that territory and you deserve to be rewarded for it.' Well, yes sir, that's the way it was."

Without pausing, Mr. Nelson went on, "I just told Mr. Jackson about it. He said that he remembered talking about the whole thing with 'H. L.' 'Yes,' he said, 'Tell Thomas about it,' he said, 'Tell Thomas about it.' Harvey and I went over his accounts on Sunday. I went over his list of accounts with him and checked the ones that I want. Here is the list with the accounts all checked off.[2] I already know nearly all the proprietors. You'll see that—"

"Wait a minute, Cliff! Wait a minute!" Mr. Thomas interrupted. "You've lost me completely. In the first place, if there is any assignment of accounts to be made I'll do it. It will be done on a basis that is fair to the salesmen concerned and profitable to the company. You know that."

"Dave, I'm only asking for what is fair." Mr. Nelson's face was flushed. Mr. Thomas noticed that the man he had always believed to be deliberately confident and self-possessed was now so agitated that it was difficult for him to speak. "I don't want my territory chopped up and handed to some green kid!"

Mr. Thomas noticed that everybody in the office was now watching Mr. Nelson. "Calm down, Cliff," he whispered to the salesman, indicating with a nod of his head that others were watching.

"Don't talk to me that way, you young squirt!" replied Mr. Nelson. "I don't care. A man with 25 years' service deserves some consideration."

"You're absolutely right, Cliff. You're absolutely right." As Mr. Thomas repeated his words, Mr. Nelson settled back in his chair. The typewriters started clattering again.

"Now, first of all, Cliff," queried Mr. Thomas, as he tried to return the conversation to a friendly basis, "where did you get the idea that your territory was going to be 'chopped up'?"

"You said so yourself. You said it at the very first sales meeting when you made that speech about how you were going to boost sales in Syracuse." Mr. Nelson emphasized his words by pounding on the side of the desk with his Masonic ring.

Mr. Thomas reflected for a moment. He recalled giving a talk at his first sales meeting at the end of May called, "How we can do a better job

---

[2] Mr. Nelson's selected accounts are the accounts in parentheses in Exhibit 6.

for Pure Drug." The speech was a restatement of the merchandising policy of the New York office. He had mentioned that getting more profitable business would require that a larger percentage of the purchases of each account would have to come to Pure Drug; that receiving a larger share of the business from each store would require more selling time in each store; and that greater concentration on each account would require reorganization of the sales territories. He realized that his future plans did entail reorganization of the territories; he had not anticipated, however, any such reaction as Mr. Nelson's.

Finally, Mr. Thomas said, "I do plan to make some territorial changes—not right away—at least not until I have looked things over pretty darn carefully. Of course, you understand that our first duty is to make greater profits for the company. Some of our territories would be a great deal more profitable if they were organized and handled in a different manner."

"What are you going to do about Harvey's territory?" asked Mr. Nelson.

"Well, I just haven't had a chance to study the situation yet," he replied. "If I could make the territory more profitable by reorganizing it, I guess that is what they would expect me to do." Since Mr. Thomas had not yet looked over the information about the territory, he was anxious not to commit himself to any course of action relating to it.

"What about the promises the company made to me about letting me choose the accounts I want?" the salesman asked.

"You don't mean the company's promise; you mean Mr. Schultz's promise," Mr. Thomas corrected him.

"Well, if Mr. Schultz wasn't 'the company,' I don't see how you figure that you are!" Mr. Nelson's face resumed its flush.

"OK, Cliff. How about giving me a chance to look over the situation. You know that I want to do the right thing. Let me go over your list of the accounts you want. In a few days I can talk intelligently about the matter." Mr. Thomas felt that there was no point in carrying on the discussion.

"All right, Dave," said Mr. Nelson, rising. The two men walked towards the front entrance of the office. As they reached the top of the steps leading to the front door, Mr. Nelson turned to the sales manager and offered his hand. "Look, Dave. I'm sorry I got so mad. You just can't imagine what this means to me. I know you'll see it my way when you know the whole story." Mr. Nelson's voice sounded strained.

Mr. Thomas watched the older man leave. He felt embarrassed at the realization that Mr. Nelson's parting words had been overheard by several manufacturers' representatives standing nearby.

A CONVERSATION WITH THE DIVISION MANAGER

Mr. Thomas decided to talk at once to Mr. Jackson about his conversation with Mr. Nelson. He walked over to Mr. Jackson's office. He hesitated in the doorway; Mr. Jackson looked up and then indicated with a gesture that Mr. Thomas was to take a seat.

The sales manager sat down. He waited for Mr. Jackson to speak. Mr. Jackson was occupied for the moment with the problem of unwrapping a cigar. Mr. Thomas opened the conversation by saying, "Clifford Nelson just stopped by to speak to me."

"Yeah?" said Mr. Jackson, removing bitten flakes of tobacco from the end of his tongue.

"He said something about getting some of Harvey Brooks's accounts when Harvey retired," Mr. Thomas said in a deliberately questioning manner.

"Yeah."

The sales manager continued, "Well, this idea of his was based on a promise that he said 'H. T.' had made."

"Yeah. He told me that, too."

"Did Schultz make such a promise?" Mr. Thomas inquired.

"Hell, I don't know. It sounds like him." He tilted back in his swivel chair.

"What shall I do about it?"

"Don't ask me; you're the sales manager." Mr. Jackson paused, holding his cigar away from his lips as if he were about to speak. Just as Mr. Thomas was about to say something, Mr. Jackson lurched forward to flick the ashes from his cigar into his ashtray. "Look here, Dave. I don't want any morale problems around here. You're the first of the 'wonder boys' to be put in charge of a department in this division. I don't want you to do anything to mess up the morale. We never had any morale problems when Schultz was alive. We don't want anything like that in this division."

Mr. Thomas was momentarily bewildered. He knew by the way that Mr. Jackson used the phrase "wonder boys" that he was referring to the college men who had been brought into the organization by Mr. Topping, the vice president in charge of sales.

Mr. Jackson went on, "Why the devil did you tell the men that you were going to reassign the sales territories without even telling me?"

"But you were there when I said it."

"Said what?"

"Well, at my first sales meeting, that one of the ways we were going to get more business was to reorganize the sales territory," Mr. Thomas replied.

"I certainly don't remember anything like that. Dave, you gave a good inspirational talk; but I sure can't remember anything about reassigning territories."

"Actually, I just mentioned the reorganization of territories in passing," the sales manager smiled.

"I'll be damned. That sort of thing is always happening. Here everybody is frothing at the mouth about something that they think we are going to do and we haven't the slightest idea why they think we're going to do it. You know, the real reason Harvey Brooks asked to be retired instead of staying on as he planned was probably this fear of having his territory reorganized. Both he and Nelson know that their pension on retirement is based on their earnings in the last five years of active employment. Now that I think of it, three or four of the other salesmen have stopped in during the last couple of weeks to tell me what a fine job they were doing. They probably had this territory reassignment bogey on their minds."

Mr. Jackson's cigar was no longer burning. He began groping under the papers on his desk for a match.

Mr. Thomas took advantage of this pause in the conversation. "Mr. Jackson, I think there are some real advantages to be won by an adjustment of the sales territories. I think—"

"You still think that after today?" the division manager asked in a sarcastic tone.

"Why, yes! The profit we make on sales to an individual account is related closely to delivery expense. The larger the total proportion of the account's business we get, the more profit we make because the delivery expense remains more or less constant."

"Look, Dave. You college men always have everything all figured out with slide rules, but sometimes that doesn't count. Morale is the important thing. The salesmen won't stand for having their territories changed. I know that you have four trainees that you'd like to put out on territories. You put them out on parts of the territories belonging to some of the more experienced men—bam! God knows how many of our good salesmen would be left. Now, I've never had any trouble with sales force morale since I've been manager of this division. Old Schultz, bless his soul, never let me down. He wasn't any damn Ph.D., but, by golly, he could handle men. Don't get off on the wrong foot with the boys, Dave. With the labor situation in the warehouse being what it is, I've just got too much on my mind. I don't want you to be creating more problems than I can handle. How 'bout it, boy!"

Mr. Jackson ground out his half-smoked cigar, looking steadily at Mr. Thomas.

Mr. Thomas was upset because the division manager had imputed to him a lack of concern for morale problems. He had always thought of himself as being very considerate of the thoughts and feelings of others. He realized that at the moment his foremost desire was to get away from Mr. Jackson.

Mr. Thomas rose from his chair saying, "Mr. Jackson, you can count on me. I know you are right about this morale business."

"Atta boy," said the division manager. "It does us a lot of good to talk like this once in a while. Now, you see if you can make peace with the salesmen. I want you to handle everything yourself."

"Well, thanks a lot," said the sales manager, as he backed out of the office door.

As he walked through the office after talking with Mr. Jackson, he saw two manufacturers' representatives with whom he had appointments already seated near the receptionist's desk. His schedule of appointments that day did not permit him to do more than gather the material pertaining to the Nelson and Brooks territories.

MR. THOMAS GOES HOME

Mr. Thomas left the office shortly after five o'clock to drive to his home in a suburb of Syracuse. It was a particularly hot and humid day. Pre-Fourth-of-July traffic lengthened the drive by nearly 20 minutes. When he finally turned into his own driveway, he felt as though his skin were caked with grime and perspiration. He got out of the car and walked around the house to the terrace in the rear. Betsy, his wife, was sewing in a deck chair under the awning.

"Hello, Dave. You're late," she said, looking up with a smile.

"I know it. Even the traffic was bad today." He dropped his coat on a glass-topped table and sprawled out full length on the glider. "Honestly, I'm so exhausted and dirty that I am disgusted with myself."

"Bad day?"

"Awful. You just can't imagine how discouraging it is trying to get this job organized. You would think that it would be obvious to everybody that what ails the Syracuse Division is the organization of the sales force," said Mr. Thomas, arranging a pillow under his head.

"I didn't realize that you thought anything was wrong with the Syracuse Division."

"Well, what I mean is that we get only 20 percent of the potential wholesale business. If I could organize the sales force my way—well, God knows, maybe we could get 40 percent of the business. That is what the New York office watches for. The sales manager who increases his division's share of the market gets the promotions when they come along. I know Mr. Topping transferred me to this division because he knew these possibilities existed."

"I don't understand. Is Mr. Topping still your boss, or is Mr. Jackson?" asked his wife.

"Betsy, it's terribly discouraging. Mr. Jackson is my boss, but I'll never get anywhere with Pure Drug unless Mr. Topping and the other people in New York promote me."

"Don't you like Mr. Jackson?"

"I had a run-in with him today."

"You didn't!" she said crossly as she laid her sewing aside.

Mr. Thomas had not anticipated this reaction. He gazed up at the awning as if he did not notice his wife's intent expression. "We didn't argue particularly. He just—well, he doesn't know too much about sales management. He put his foot down on my plans to reorganize the territories."

"I can't understand why you would go and get yourself into a fight with your boss when you haven't been here even two months. We should never have bought this house!"

"Honestly, honey, I didn't have any fight. Everything is OK. He just —well, do you want me to be a divisional sales manager all my life?"

She smiled and said nothing.

He continued, "I'm sorry you married such a grouch, but I just get plain mad when somebody calls me a wonder boy."

"You're tired," she said sympathetically. "Why don't you go up and take a shower while I feed the children. We can have a drink and then eat our dinner whenever we feel like it. It's only meat loaf, anyway."

"That sounds wonderful," he said, raising himself from his prone position.

AN UNEXPECTED CALLER

Mr. Thomas had just stepped out of the shower when he heard his wife calling to him. "Dave, Fred Taylor is here to see you."

"Tell him I'll be down in just a minute. Give him a drink, Betsy."

As he dressed, Mr. Thomas wondered why the salesman had chosen the dinner hour to call. During the month since he had moved into his new home, no salesman had ever dropped in uninvited.

When Mr. Thomas came downstairs, he found Mr. Taylor on the living room couch with a gin and tonic in his hand.

"Hello, Fred," said Mr. Thomas crossing the room with his right hand extended. "You look as if you had a hot day. Why don't you take off your coat? If we go out to the terrace, you may get a chance to cool off."

"Thanks, Dave," the visitor said as he moved out to the terrace. "I'm sorry to come barging in this way, but I thought it was important."

"Well, what's on your mind?" said Mr. Thomas as he sat down.

Mr. Taylor started to speak but hesitated as Mrs. Thomas came out of the door with two glasses in her hand. She handed one glass to Mr. Thomas, then excused herself saying, "I think I better see if the children are all right."

After she had disappeared into the house, Mr. Taylor said, "I heard about what happened at the office today, so I thought I'd come over to tell you that we stand 100 percent behind you."

Mr. Thomas was perplexed by Mr. Taylor's words. He realized that the incident to which the salesman referred was probably his meeting with Mr. Nelson. Mr. Thomas said, "I'm not sure what you mean, Fred."

"I heard that you and Nelson had it out this morning about changing the sales territories," Mr. Taylor replied.

Mr. Thomas smiled. Two thoughts entered his mind. He was amused at the proportions that the brief conversation of that morning had assumed in the minds of so many people; but, at the same time, he was curious as to how Mr. Taylor, who had presumably been in the field selling, had heard about the incident so soon. Without hesitation he asked, "Where did you hear about this, Fred?"

"Bill Murray told me! He was down at the warehouse with Walter Miller when I stopped off to pick up a special narcotics order for a customer. They are all excited about this territory business. Murray said Nelson came out to his house at lunch time and told him about it. Everybody figured that you were going to change the territories when you started traveling around with each of the boys, especially after what you said at your first sales meeting."

"Well, the reason I went on the road with each of the men, Fred," said Mr. Thomas, "was so that I could learn more about their selling problems and, at the same time, meet the customers."

Mr. Taylor smiled, "Sure, but when you started filling out a rating sheet on each account, I couldn't help thinking you had some reason for it."

Mr. Thomas realized that the salesman had spoken with irony in his voice, but he thought it was better to let the matter pass as if he had not noticed it. Since he was planning to use the information that he gathered for reorganization of the sales territories, he decided that he would be frank with Mr. Taylor in order to find out what the young salesman's reaction might be on the question of territorial changes. He said, "Fred, I've thought a lot about making some changes in the territories.—"

Mr. Taylor interrupted him. "That's terrific. I'm sure glad to hear that. I don't like to speak ill of the dead, but old Schultz really gave the trainees the short end of the stick when he put us on territories. He either gave a man a territory of uncontacted accounts so he beat his head against a stone wall until he finally quit, and that is just what happened to two guys who trained with me, or else he gave him a territory where somebody had to be replaced and where some of the best accounts had been handed over to one of the older salesmen. Well, I know for a fact that when I took over my territory from Mike Green, Bill Murray and Albert Simpson got 12 of Green's best accounts. And, damn it, I got more sales out of what was left than Green ever did, but Murray and Simpson's total sales didn't go up at all. It took me a while, but, by golly, I had the laugh at every sales meeting when our monthly sales figures were announced."

"Is that right?" said Mr. Thomas.

"Damn right! And I wasn't the only one. That's why those old duffers are so down on the four of us that have come with the division since the mid-1960s. We've beaten them at their own game."

"Do you think that Harrington and Howard and Donnelly feel the same way?" asked Mr. Thomas.

"Think, hell! I know it! That's all we ever talk about. If you reorganize those territories and give us back the accounts that Schultz took away, you'll see some real sales records. Take, for example, the Medical Arts Pharmacy out by Mercy Hospital. Bill Murray got that one away from my territory and he calls there only once a week. If I could get that one back, I'd get in there three times a week and get five times as much business."

Mr. Thomas had to raise his hands in a gesture of protest. "Don't you have enough accounts already, Fred, to keep you busy?"

"Dave, I spend 50 hours a week on the road and I love it; but I know damn well that if I put some of the time I spend in 'two-by-four' stores into some of those big juicy accounts like Medical Arts Pharmacy, I'd do even more business."

Mr. Thomas commented, "I'm not particularly anxious to argue the point now, but if you start putting your time into Medical Arts Pharmacy, what's going to happen to your sales to the 'two-by-four' stores?"

The salesman replied, "Those druggists all know me. They'd go right on buying."

Mr. Thomas did not agree with Mr. Taylor, and he thought that the salesman realized this.

After a moment of silence Mr. Taylor rose from his chair saying, "I'd better scoot home. My wife will be waiting for me with a rolling pin for being late so I'd better get out before your wife gets at me with a skillet," Mr. Taylor laughed heartily at his own joke.

The two men walked around the house to Mr. Taylor's car. As the salesman climbed into the car, he said, "Dave, don't forget what I said, Harrington, Howard, Donnelly and I stand 100 percent behind you. You won't ever hear us talk about going over to a competitor!"

"Who's talking about that?" asked Mr. Thomas.

"Well," said Mr. Taylor as he started the motor and shifted into gear, "I don't want to tell tales out of school."

"Sure," Mr. Thomas said quickly. "I'm sorry I asked. So long, Fred. I'll see you soon."

Mr. Thomas watched the salesman back out of the driveway and drive away.

PART VII

The cases in the pricing section of this book involve several different kinds of decisions. A firm's pricing strategy is extremely important because of the quickness with which a change can be implemented, because of the importance of price to consumers in their purchase decisions, and because of the direct impact of prices on profits.

The first important consideration in establishing a price for a product is the firm's pricing objectives. A firm striving for growth may utilize a totally different strategy from one who is seeking to discourage others from cutting prices or to desensitize consumers to price. Firms with objectives oriented around maximizing long-run profits may utilize different strategies than firms who are seeking to maximize short-run profits. Thus, the first step in establishing a price should be to clearly identify what the objectives are.

Two alternative strategies often utilized are skimming and penetration. A skimming strategy is one in which a high initial price is set, and the product is sold to all those consumers willing to pay this price. The price is then lowered somewhat, and the product is sold to those consumers willing to pay that price. This process continues for some time, "skimming the cream" off the top of the market with each price change. For example, when electronic calculators were first introduced, they were priced at more than $300. A number of scientific and engineering related organizations were willing to purchase the product at this price. The price was then lowered to the neighborhood of $150 to $200, and a

PRICING DECISIONS

number of other organizations were willing to purchase the product. Later, the price was reduced to the $50 to $100 range and very many more buyers entered the market. Eventually, the price was lowered still further and many more consumers entered the market.

A skimming strategy is appropriate when there are no close substitutes for the product and the demand is inelastic with respect to price. It is a very conservative policy allowing the marketer to recover as much of the costs as possible quickly in the event that demand is not that great. It also allows the marketer to accumulate money for aggressive penetration later when competition enters the market. A skimming strategy is an effective way to segment the market, as in the calculator example and in the case of the book market where a skimming strategy is used for hardcover books, and the paperback edition is later introduced using a penetration strategy.

A penetration strategy utilizes a low initial price in the hopes of penetrating a large proportion of the market in a short period of time. This strategy would be used when one or more of the following conditions existed:

a.   High short-run price elasticity [for example, the low price of the Model-T Ford allowed many people to purchase a car for the first time].
b.   Large economies of scale in production.
c.   The probability of quick public acceptance.
d.   The probability of quick competitive imitation.

The specific pricing decisions that have to be made include the price level to set, price variation including discount structures and geographic price differences, margins to be given to various intermediaries in the channels of distribution, and the determination of when to change the price structure.

A number of different pricing methods are utilized by organizations. Some use the cost-plus method, whereby a certain percentage is added to the firm's costs to establish their pricing. This method is often used by industrial marketers and by wholesalers and retailers. Other organizations use break-even analysis, marginal cost analysis, and/or marginal revenue analysis to determine their pricing structure. Still other organizations are price followers and use a strategy of meeting the prices of competitors.

The ideal way to determine the price that should be charged involves analyzing a number of variables before actually setting the price. Included would be:

1.   *Consumer buying patterns.*   What price would consumers expect to pay for this type of product? What are the important price points or price lines that different segments of the market desire?
2.   *Product differentiation.*   In what ways is the company's product different from the others on the market? What advantages does the product offer the consumer?
3.   *What is the competitive structure* of the industry, and what stage of the product life cycle is the product in?
4.   *How price sensitive* is total industry demand, and how price sensitive is demand for the individual firm's product? What is the size of the total market and what is the likelihood of economies of scale?

5. *What is the economic climate forecast,* and how sensitive is the demand of the product to changes in the economic climate?
6. *Legal and social considerations.*   New interpretations of the Robinson-Patman Act (prohibiting price discrimination) and various state laws governing pricing must be taken into consideration.
7. *Cost structure of the firm.*   The relationship between fixed costs and variable costs are extremely important in pricing decisions, as is the cost structure of the firm compared to competitors' pricing structure. Pricing strategy for a hotel, with a very low variable cost ratio, will of necessity be quite different than pricing strategy for a clothing manufacturer which has a very high variable cost ratio.
8. *The overall marketing strategy for the product.*   It is important to recognize that the pricing strategy must be consistent with all the other elements of the firm's marketing strategy.

30

Twin Peaks National Bank*

On February 2, 1976, Mr. James Clark, vice president in charge of marketing, Twin Peaks National Bank, received a telephone call from the president of the bank, Mr. Frank Horman, regarding the bank's All-in-One Account. Mr. Horman mentioned that he had been looking at the different services that the bank offered. Mr. Horman indicated that he was contemplating changes in pricing policies for the bank's services that would increase the bank's profitability without jeopardizing its market share. Mr. Horman felt that since Twin Peaks National Bank had the lowest price of all competitors for the All-in-One type account that he would like a review of the All-in-One account to determine if a change in pricing or service should be made.

After the telephone conversation with Mr. Horman, Mr. Clark met with the product manager, Mr. Joe Will, who was in charge of the All-in-One Account and the marketing research manager, Mr. Steve Hale, to explain Mr. Horman's concern regarding the pricing policy for the All-in-One Account. Mr. Will had worked with the account since its inception in July 1973. Mr. Hale had started with the bank in 1974 and had formulated some data on the All-in-One Account.

Mr. Will felt that Mr. Hale should conduct further research on the customer demographics in order to evaluate the service since its inception to determine if the All-in-One Account had met the objectives that were initially set up for the program. The three managers decided to meet again

---

* This case was written by Subhash C. Jain, Associate Professor of Marketing, University of Connecticut and Iqbal Mathur, Associate Professor of Marketing, University of Pittsburgh. Used with permission.

at a later date to make a recommendation on any change that could be made to the account to increase the bank's profitability without affecting Twin Peaks' market share.

BACKGROUND

The Twin Peaks National Bank was the lead bank in the Twin Peaks Holding Corporation which had 12 other banks located in the state of Ohio. The Holding Company was the eighth largest in the state with total assets of $1.4 billion. Twin Peaks National Bank was the second largest in Frank County which had a population of 900,000. Twin Peaks had been primarily a wholesale bank serving commercial customers and correspondent banks throughout the state. However in 1960, management recognized the opportunity in the retail market and the bank opened its first branch and then proceeded to its present level of 33 branches located in prime market areas in the county. In keeping with the changing needs of the retail customer, Twin Peaks was the first bank in the community to introduce a package account. This was called the All-in-One Account which consisted of seven banking services with a single charge per month.

The package included the following:

Write all the checks you want for a $2 monthly fee.

Free personalized checks.

A Passbook Savings Account with $1 deposited by the bank.

Ten percent rebate of the finance charge on qualifying installment loans.

Free traveler's checks.

A 24-hour bank at the automated banking machines.

Overdraft protection with checking reserve. Lets you write a check for more money than you have in your checking account, up to your credit line.

The exclusiveness of the All-in-One Account lasted for six months until other banks in town introduced their package accounts. Exhibit 1 shows the services and charges of the various banks in the community.

ALL-IN-ONE ACCOUNT GROWTH

When the All-in-One Account was introduced in July, 1973, it was projected that by the end of the third year there would be 10,000 All-in-One Accounts. This projection was based on a review of the previous three years and the highest percentage rate change was used. Regular savings account growth was projected at 160 percent of the regular demand

EXHIBIT 1
Package comparison

	Twin Peaks	Bank 1	Bank 2	Bank 3	Bank 4
Price.............................	$2.00	$2.50	$2.75	$2.25	Free*
Checks included....................	Yes	Yes	Yes	Yes	No
Charge card........................	Yes	Yes	Yes	Yes	No
24-hour banking....................	Yes	Yes	Yes	Yes	No
Identification card.................	Yes	Yes	Yes	Yes	No
Savings............................	$1.00	$2.50	0	$1.00	No
Installment loan rebate.............	10%	0.50% add†	Average month‡	0.50% add†	No§
Safe deposit box included..........	No	Yes	No	No	No
Overdraft demand deposit..........	Yes	Yes	Yes	Yes	No
Official checks.....................	No	Yes	No	No	No
Travelers checks...................	Yes	Yes	No	Yes	No
Check cashing......................	Yes	Yes	Yes	Yes	No
Money orders......................	No	Yes	No	Yes	Yes
Budget............................	No	Yes	No	No	No

* $100 minimum deposit required.
† The regular add-on interest rate is reduced by 0.50 percent (from 6 percent add-on to 5.50 percent, for example).
‡ The rebate is equal to the average interest paid per month during the time period of the loan.
§ Regular rates are comparable to rates of the other banks after deducting their rebates.
Source: Company records.

deposit accounts outstanding at year-end. Checking reserve accounts were projected at 15 percent annual growth which compared to a growth of 14.3 percent in the prior year.

The success of the All-in-One Account is shown in Exhibit 2, which illustrates the actual growth of the All-in-One Account and related accounts as compared with the growth without the All-in-One Account and related accounts using the above assumptions.

ALL-IN-ONE ACCOUNT IMPACT ON MARKET SHARE

Using weekly Federal Reserve Bank data and averaging weeks into months, Twin Peaks' market share was compared with the other two major banks within Frank County. The figures were available for regular savings, Master Charge, and checking reserve. Exhibits 3, 4, and 5 indicate that the bank's market share increased each year since the inception of the All-in-One Account. Exhibit 6 was developed by utilizing a survey taken by the bank's Research Department to show the impact of the All-in-One Account on the total demand deposit accounts as well as the new demand deposit accounts market.

EXHIBIT 2

Number growth of All-in-One—Related accounts

	Year-end number of accounts					Number change				Percent change			
	1971	1972	1973	1974	1975	71-72	72-73	73-74	74-75	71-72	72-73	73-74	74-75
Scenario 1— With All-in-One													
All-in-One	0	0	6,180	18,931	30,500	n.a.*	6,180	12,751	11,569	n.a.	0 %	206.3%	61.1%
Regular DDA†	54,082	57,321	63,344	72,118	82,427	3,239	6,023	8,774	10,309	6.0%	10.5	13.9	14.3
Regular savings	80,475	90,311	102,557	116,566	133,244	9,336	12,246	14,009	16,678	12.2	13.6	13.7	14.3
Master Charge	46,264	47,150	58,063	63,158	70,000	886	10,913	5,095	6,842	1.9	23.1	8.8	10.8
Checking reserve	6,900	7,884	14,028	27,417	40,000	984	6,144	13,389	12,583	14.3	77.9	95.4	45.9
Scenario 2—Without All-in-One (control)													
All-in-One													
Regular DDA	54,082	57,321	62,193	67,479	73,215	3,239	4,872	5,286	5,736	6.0	8.5	8.5	8.5
Regular savings	80,475	90,311	99,509	107,966	117,114	9,836	9,198	3,457	9,148	12.2	10.2	8.5	8.5
Master Charge	46,264	47,150	52,864	57,357	62,233	886	5,714	4,493	4,876	1.9	12.1	8.5	8.5
Checking reserve	6,900	7,884	9,067	10,427	11,991	984	1,183	1,360	1,564	14.3	15.0	15.0	15.0

Note: Regular DDA control projected based on review of 1969–70, 1970–71, and 1971–72 percent changes of 7.2, 8.5, and 6, respectively. Then arbitrarily selected highest of the three (8.5 percent). Regular savings control projected by assuming that it would run 160 percent of regular DDA numbers outstanding. Master Charge control projected by assuming that it would run 85 percent of regular DDA numbers outstanding. Checking reserve control projected by arbitrarily selecting an annual percent charge of 15 percent which is slightly higher than the 14.3 percent rate experienced one year prior to All-in-One.

* n.a.—Not applicable.

† DDA—Demand deposit account (checking).

Source: Company records.

EXHIBIT 3

Market shares: Regular savings

	Share of market				Share of market increase			
	1972	1973	1974	1975	1972	1973	1974	1975
Twin Peaks.......	28.9	29.2	29.5	30.3	33.1	33.6	34.0	34.3
Other............	71.1	70.8	70.5	69.7	66.9	66.4	66.0	65.7

Source: Federal Reserve Bank data.

EXHIBIT 4

Market shares: Frank County Master Charge Cards

	Share of market				Share of market increase			
	1972	1973	1974	1975	1972	1973	1974	1975
Twin Peaks..........	20.92	21.99	22.68	23.68	23.7	25.8	24.1	44.6
Other...............	79.08	78.01	77.32	76.32	76.3	74.2	75.9	55.4

Source: Federal Reserve Bank data.

EXHIBIT 5

Market shares: Overdraft checking

	Share of market			Share of market increase	
	1972	1973	1974	1973	1974
Twin Peaks.........	29.3	27.7	34.3	11.8	67.8
Bank 1.............	31.6	34.0	32.7	57.4	25.9
Bank 2.............	39.0	38.0	33.0	30.8	6.3

Source: Federal Reserve Bank data.

EXHIBIT 6

Market shares: Demand deposit accounts

	New account market		General market	
	3/73	3/75	11/73	2/75
Twin Peaks..............	27.9	38.8	29.1	35.4
Bank 1...................	34.9	37.6	29.1	31.7
Bank 2...................	37.2	23.5	41.8	32.9

Source: Company records.

RETENTION OF ACCOUNTS

A major objective of the All-in-One Account was the cross-selling of bank services. The assumption was that the more services a bank customer had, the harder it would be for him to leave the bank. Net growth was determined as follows: acquisition − attrition = net growth. The bank's

EXHIBIT 7
Attrition rate for selected product lines, 1971–1975

	Regular demand deposit accounts				Regular savings accounts			
	Opened	Closed	Accounts out- standing	Attri- tion rate*	Opened	Closed	Accounts out- standing	Attrition rate*
1971...............			54,082				80,475	
1972...............	14,654	11,415	57,321	21.1	28,314	18,478	90,311	23.0
1973...............	18,347	12,324	63,344	21.5	31,977	19,731	102,557	21.8
1974...............	20,771	11,997	72,118	18.9	35,964	21,955	116,566	21.4
1975...............	22,298	11,989	82,427	16.6	37,910	21,232	133,244	18.2

* Calculated as a percentage of previous year's outstanding.
Source: Company records.

performance in reducing the number of closed accounts increased its net growth.

Exhibit 7 shows the attrition rate for demand deposit and savings accounts since 1972. Their retention performance had allowed Twin Peaks to have a positive increase (14.3 percent versus 13.9 percent) in overall acquisition rate in 1975 even though the percentage of open rate decreased from 1974.

CUSTOMER SURVEY

A survey of 3,997 All-in-One Accounts was made in order to determine the customer demographics and evaluate the service and its components. This was accomplished through the mailing of a questionnaire and the investigating of the account activity through the Central Information File for these customers. A total of 2,278 replied for a 57 percent return which represented 11.3 percent of the total All-in-One Accounts.

The All-in-One Account service had attracted the young, highly educated white-collar worker with above average income. Specifically the predominant characteristics were:

41 percent are 25–34 years of age.

19 percent are 35–44 years of age.

49 percent have a college degree.

67 percent are white-collar workers.

47 percent have income of $15,000 or more.

59 percent were Twin Peak conversions.

The mail-out survey indicated that 59 percent of the All-in-One Account customers were conversions from existing Twin Peaks checking account holders.

EXHIBIT 8
All-in-One—Most important features

Attribute	Percent mentioned
Price	62%
Checking reserve	59
Free checks	46
24-hour banking	32
Unlimited checking	31
10% loan rebate	22
Traveler's checks	20
No minimum balance DDA	10
Master Charge	8
Convenience	2
Savings account dollars deposited	2
Easy to understand	1
No answer/no opinion	13

Source: Company records.

An additional 18 percent of the customers switched from other Frank County banks. This was followed by 13 percent new moves, 6 percent change in marital status, 4 percent other, and 3 percent additional account and first account. Analysis was done on the 18 percent of the customers who switched banks. Of these respondents, 25 percent switched for convenient location, 24 percent due to dissatisfaction at another bank, 24 percent based on the $2 price, and 21 percent due to the All-in-One package.

The participants in the survey were asked to give their opinions on the four most important features of the All-in-One Account. The most important feature turned out to be the price followed by checking reserve. The results of this open-end question are shown in Exhibit 8.

ACCOUNT PROFITABILITY

The All-in-One Account study included the measurement of account activity through the CIF (Central Information File). Based on this measurement, the average All-in-One Account customer was then analyzed for profit/loss. This income and expense analysis (Exhibit 9) shows that the average All-in-One Account customer contributed $19.09 before tax, profits and indirect overhead. If this analysis were applied to the 30,500 All-in-One Account customers the operating profit contributed from these accounts would be $582,245.00, which is $0.238 per share.

A review of this information showed that the All-in-One Account had tremendous impact on the growth of the bank's market share. It had accomplished all of the objectives set up in July 1973 when the service

EXHIBIT 9
Income and expense analysis (account customer average for All-in-One)

Income	
All-in-One fee	$ 24.00
Installment loan	131.47
Master Charge	24.34
Checking reserve	12.45
	$192.26
Expense	
Travelers checks	$ 0.27
DDA*	
Operation cost	38.27
Personal checks	4.29
Savings:	
Operation cost	4.59
Interest	34.59
Installment:	
Operation cost	37.48
Rebate	12.85
Master Charge—operation cost	10.88
Checking reserve—operation cost	1.56
Cost of borrowed funds	13.78
Bad debt:	
Installment (1%)	9.37
Master Charge (2%)	3.58
Checking reserve (2%)	1.66
	$173.17
Net contribution before tax to profit and indirect overhead	19.09

* DDA—Demand deposit account.
Source: Company records.

was first introduced. It had increased the cross-selling of the bank's services. It had proved to be a checking account that was unique to other competitors. It reduced the attrition rate of Twin Peaks' customers and it was a marketable service which reflected an aggressive retail-oriented corporate image that Twin Peaks desired to project.

Mr. Will and Mr. Hale agreed that the fee charged for the All-in-One Account was inelastic and since the service was still in its growth stage that a small change in price and/or service would not affect the demand for the All-in-One Account. They also felt that if a substantial change in price were made, a service should also be added to somewhat offset the price change. They recommended to Mr. Clark that he present the following proposals to Mr. Horman:

1. The All-in-One Account fee may be increased to $3 per month and a safe deposit box included.

2.   The All-in-One Account fee may be increased to $2.50 per month with no additional service.
3.   The All-in-One Account fee may be increased to $2.50 per month and the installment loan rebate reduced to 5 percent.
4.   The All-in-One Account charge may be left at $2 with the installment loan rebate reduced to 5 percent.

United Techtronics

In June 1977, United Techtronics faced a major pricing decision with respect to its new video screen television system. "We're really excited here at United Techtronics," exclaimed Mr. Roy Cowing, the founder and president of United Techtronics. "We've made a most significant technological breakthrough in large screen, video television systems." He went on to explain that the marketing plan for 1978 for this product was now his major area of concern, and that what price to charge was the marketing question that was giving him the most difficulty.

COMPANY HISTORY

United Techtronics (UT) was founded in Boston in 1959 by Mr. Cowing. Prior to that time Mr. Cowing had been an associate professor of electrical engineering at M.I.T. Mr. Cowing founded UT to manufacture and market products making use of some of the electronic inventions he had developed while at M.I.T. Sales were made mostly to the space program and the military. Sales grew from $100,000 in 1960 to $27 million in 1976. Profits in 1976 were $3.2 million.

THE VIDEO SCREEN PROJECT

For a number of years beginning in the late 1960s, Mr. Cowing had been looking to reduce the company's dependency on government sales. One of the diversification projects that he had committed research and development monies to was the so-called video screen project. The objective of this project was to develop a system whereby a television picture could be displayed on a screen as big as 8 to 10 feet diagonally. In late 1976, one of UT's engineers made the necessary breakthrough. The rest of 1976 and the first few months of 1977 were spent producing working prototypes. Up until June 1977, UT had invested $600,000 in the project.

VIDEO SCREEN TELEVISION

Extra large-screen television systems were not new. There were a number of companies who sold such systems both to the consumer and commercial (taverns, restaurants, and so on) markets. Most current systems made use of special magnifying lens that projected a regular small television picture onto a special screen. The result of this process is that the final picture lacked much of the brightness of the original small screen. As a result, the picture had to be viewed in a darkened room. There were some other video systems that did not use the magnifying process. These systems used special tubes, but also suffered from a lack of brightness.

UT had developed a system that was bright enough to be viewed in regular daylight on a screen up to 10 feet diagonally. Mr. Cowing was unwilling to discuss how this was accomplished. He would only say that the process was protected by patent, and that he thought it would take at least two to three years for any competitor to duplicate the results of the system.

A number of large and small companies were active in this area. Admiral, General Electric, RCA, Zenith, and Sony were all thought to be working on developing large-screen systems directed at the consumer market. Sony was rumored to be ready to introduce a 60-inch diagonal screen system that would retail for about $2,500. A number of small companies were already producing systems. Advent Corporation, a small New England company, claimed to have sold 4,000, 84-inch diagonal units in two years at a $4,000 price. Muntz Manufacturing claimed one-year sales of 5,000, 50-inch diagonal units at prices from $1,500 to $2,500. Mr. Cowing was adamant that none of these systems gave as bright a picture as UT's. He estimated that about 10,000 large-screen systems were sold in 1976.

COST STRUCTURE

Mr. Cowing expected about 50 percent of the suggested retail selling price to go for wholesaler and retailer margins. He expected that UT's direct manufacturing costs would vary depending on the volume produced. Exhibit 1 presents these estimates. He expected direct labor costs to fall at higher production volumes due to the increased automation of the

EXHIBIT 1
Estimated production costs of UT's video screen system

		Volume	
	0–5,000	5,001– 10,000	10,001– 20,000
Raw materials................	$ 480	$460	$410
Direct labor..................	540	320	115
Total direct costs............	$1,020	$780	$525

process and improved worker skills. Material costs were expected to fall due to less waste due to automation. The equipment costs necessary to automate the product process were $70,000 to produce in the 0–5,000 unit range, an additional $50,000 to produce in the 5,001–10,000 unit range, and an additional $40,000 to produce in the 10,001–20,000 unit range. The useful life of this equipment was put at five years. Mr. Cowing was sure that production costs were substantially below those of current competitors including Sony. Such was the magnitude of UT's technological breakthrough. Mr. Cowing was unwilling to produce over 20,000 units a year in the first few years due to the limited cash resources of the company to support inventories, and so on.

MARKET STUDIES

Mr. Cowing wanted to establish a position in the consumer market for his product. He felt that the long-run potential was greater there than in the commercial market. With this end in mind he hired a small economic research consulting firm to undertake a consumer study to determine the likely reaction to alternative retail prices for the system. These consultants undertook extensive interviews with potential television purchasers, plus examined the sales and pricing histories of competitive products. They concluded that: "UT's video screen system would be highly price elastic across a range of prices from $500 to $5,000, both in a primary and secondary demand sense." They went on to estimate the price elasticity of demand in this range to be between 4.0 and 6.5.

THE PRICING DIVISION

Mr. Cowing was considering a number of alternative suggested retail prices. "I can see arguments for pricing anywhere from above Advent's to substantially below Muntz's lowest price," he said.

JRV Industries

Steven O'Connor was the manager of the pricing department of JRV Industries. In April 1977, he was evaluating possible pricing moves in three distinct divisions of the company. He knew that the president of JRV Industries was expecting him to make insightful recommendations to each of the three divisions. He wanted to be able to present well-reasoned arguments for his recommendations.

BACKGROUND

JRV Industries was a very large, American-based conglomerate. It ranked high on *Fortune*'s 500 list of companies. Divisions of the corporation included chemicals, paper products, automobile parts, aerospace, steel, insurance, and fertilizer. Like many other large conglomerates JRV had been considered a glamour company in the 1960s, but had fallen on some difficult times in the 1970s.

The divisions of the company had all at one time been separate companies. They had all been acquired by JRV for various combinations of debt and stock. These acquisitions had resulted in a continuous increase in JRV's earnings throughout the 1960s. The acquired companies were made divisions of JRV, but were allowed to completely manage their own affairs as if they were still independent companies. In most cases, the management personnel of these companies were allowed to remain in the same positions as before they were acquired.

With the advent of energy problems, inflation and recession in the

1970s, JRV's earnings growth slowed down and even declined in 1974 and 1975. As a result of this, JRV's share price fell dramatically making further acquisitions more difficult.

In late 1974, Frank Hughes, JRV's president, decided that the parent company needed to take a more active role in the management of its divisions. The format he selected for doing this was to set up departments at the parent company whose function it was to advise the divisions how to handle specific problems. The Pricing Department was one such department. Its function was to make recommendations to the divisions as to what strategic pricing moves the divisions should make. It did not involve itself in day-to-day price setting, but only those pricing decisions of a strategic nature. Steven O'Connor was appointed manager of the Pricing Department in January 1977, to replace Nancy Duff, who had been named assistant to the president.

The head office departments had a lot of influence with the divisions. A division manager knew he would have to discuss his rejection of a head office recommendation with Mr. Hughes. It was in this setting that Steve O'Connor turned his attention to one of the first sets of recommendations he would have to make as manager. There were three separate divisions that required a pricing strategy recommendation from him.

THE FERTILIZER DIVISION

JRV's "Nitro Plus" brand of fertilizer was the nation's best selling brand of farm fertilizer. It was extensively used in the growing of wheat and other grain crops. Its name was used generically by many farmers to represent its product category. This reputation had been built on the basis of continuous product improvements, and a strong advertising campaign to farmers over many years. It was sold by JRV to farm products wholesalers who in turn sold it to farmer supply dealers, farm cooperatives, and other types of farm-oriented retail outlets.

The farm fertilizer market was subject to supply and demand imbalances. In the period 1973 to late 1975, the demand had exceeded the industry's ability to produce. As a result, the price of fertilizer had risen substantially and some farmers had been unable to buy all the fertilizer they desired. With the coming on stream of a number of new fertilizer plants in early 1976, the situation had reversed itself. Excess capacity became available in mid-1976.

JRV held 56 percent of the farm fertilizer market in January 1975. The next largest competitor held 20 percent, while all other competitors held less than 10 percent of the market. It had long been JRV's pricing policy to lead the market up, but never down. It would, however, follow the market down if it thought that the lower price would stand for a reasonably long time. JRV had led the market up for all the price increases during 1973 to 1975.

Beginning in July 1975, some of JRV's competitors began what turned out to be a series of price cuts. In the following 18 months the manufacturers' selling price for farm fertilizer had been lowered 3 percent on each of five different occasions. In each instance JRV had matched the price decrease after a waiting period of a few months. JRV's January 1977 market share was 43 percent. Rumors of new price decreases were persistent as Steven O'Connor considered what course of action he should recommend to the fertilizer division.

THE AUTOMOBILE PARTS DIVISION

JRV's automobile parts division sold a wide range of original equipment parts to the domestic American automobile manufacturers. One of its major parts was shock absorbers. In 1974, JRV held about 30 percent of the original equipment manufacturers (OEM) market for shock absorbers. Two other large manufacturers supplied another 50 percent, with the rest shared by a group of smaller manufacturers. The profit margin on shock absorbers sold to OEMs was very small, but volume levels tended to be such that JRV usually made a reasonable ROI (return on investment) on this item. The exception to this was when automobile sales were depressed.

In 1975, Vimi Enterprises, a French-based manufacturer of automobile parts, entered the U.S. OEM market in shock absorbers. Vimi built a large shock absorber plant in Flint, Michigan, as a base to supply the OEMs. Steve O'Connor estimated that this plant could supply about 20 percent of the OEM's needs in shock absorbers in a good automobile sales year. Almost immediately Vimi began taking market share away from other shock absorber suppliers. By January 1977, Vimi held about 18 percent of the OEM market in shock absorbers. JRV's share had fallen to 25 percent, and the other two major competitors had lost about 3 percent each. The other 6 percent gain by Vimi had been at the expense of the small suppliers.

Vimi's main weapon in entering the market had been a very low price. Their listed price to OEMs was substantially below JRV's total production costs. JRV had not matched this price but had been forced to lower prices somewhat. As a result, the division was in the red on this product. It seemed to Steven O'Connor that Vimi could not possibly be making a profit on shock absorbers. He thought that the division was quite late in requesting assistance on this matter. He hoped it wasn't too late to take meaningful action.

STEEL PRODUCTS DIVISION

JRV competed in the specialty steel alloy part of the steel market. The alloys that JRV manufactured were used mainly in the manufacturing of both large commercial jets and military planes. In 1975, JRV ranked fifth among steel producers who supplied this market, with a 10 percent market share. The two largest producers held about 30 percent each with the third largest having about 15 percent and the fourth largest 12 percent.

In early 1976, one of the two largest producers began an aggressive marketing campaign to gain more sales. They had increased the size of their sales force, upped their advertising budget in trade journals, and had substantially lowered prices. This campaign was very successful. By January 1977, their market share was over 40 percent. The second largest supplier's share had fallen to 25 percent and JRV's was down to 7 percent.

In later 1976, the second largest supplier undertook an aggressive campaign of its own. Prices were lowered even more as a result. Steven O'Connor knew that some of JRV's other competitors were considering leaving this business. JRV's profit on this product was almost zero in January 1977. He wondered what he should recommend to this division.

33

Consolidated-Bathurst Pulp and Paper Limited*

On the morning of September 28, 1973, Mr. John Andrew, president of Consolidated-Bathurst Pulp and Paper Limited, was evaluating the current price charged for newsprint to U.S. customers. A number of recent developments in the newsprint market had provoked this evaluation. Newsprint was in much shorter supply than in previous years due to a large increase in demand in the last two years. This increase had not been matched by increased industry capacity to produce. Also, a number of competitors' newsprint mills were shut down by strikes. Mr. Andrew was considering a change from Consolidated-Bathurst's current price of U.S. $175 per ton. He was aware that he would have to carefully consider both the customers' reactions and the competitions' reactions to any changes that he might make.

COMPANY BACKGROUND

Consolidated-Bathurst Pulp and Paper Limited was a wholly owned subsidiary of Consolidated-Bathurst Limited, a fully integrated, multiproduct paper company. Mr. Andrew was a senior vice president of the parent company, besides holding the operating responsibility for the newsprint division.

In 1972, Consolidated-Bathurst Limited had sales of $348 million and had assets of $430 million. The company's sales and earnings performance record for the period 1966–72 is shown in Exhibit 1. In 1970 and 1971, the company operated at a loss. Throughout this period the newsprint operation, the firm's major product line, had remained profitable, but with

---

* Copyright 1974, the University of Western Ontario. Reproduced with permission.

insufficient return on investment to warrant the investment of additional capital to purchase a new newsprint machine. These machines cost about $120,000 per daily ton, if built at an existing mill site with wood handling facilities available. At a new site, the costs of developing this wood handling capacity would raise the cost to about $150,000 per daily ton. Thus, a machine that could produce 500 tons per day would cost about $75 million. Consolidated-Bathurst had made some capital investments in the last few years and as a result anticipated that their capacity would increase by 70,000 tons per year at the end of 1973. This increase in capacity would come from an extension of their Belgo Division Mill in Shawinigan, Quebec. An old newsprint machine had been purchased and modified at a cost of $11 million to give this increase in capacity.

Governments, particularly provincial, had frequently distorted the industry's normal growth pattern. By means of grants and tax incentives, they had promoted expansion when it was not needed, sometimes in a locale which was not and never could be economic. Many of these ventures had proven to be disastrous. (Developments in Newfoundland and Manitoba were outstanding examples of this.)

Mr. Andrew was concerned that increased prices would be an incentive for competitors to develop new mills. The risks were that expansion by competitors would decrease Consolidated-Bathurst's share of the market and also that rapid expansion by many companies could result in significant overcapacity such as had existed some few years before.

In 1972, Consolidated-Bathurst recorded a newsprint sales volume of 912,000 tons, of which about two thirds was sold in U.S. markets. About 10 percent was sold overseas and the rest in Canada. Other Consolidated-Bathurst products included pulp, container board, kraft paper, boxboard, lumber, and packaging products. Overall, the company's total business was 56 percent basic mill products, 41 percent packaging, and 3 percent lumber.

THE NEWSPRINT INDUSTRY

Consolidated-Bathurst ranked fifth in newsprint capacity in Canada with 9.2 percent of the total capacity. Exhibit 2 shows the capacity and shares of the other Canada-based competitors in the industry. Operating capacity rates for the past nine years as shown in Exhibit 3, were a major element in pricing decisions by members of the industry. There were also a number of significant U.S. producers of newsprint. Exhibit 4 shows their estimated capacities. The U.S. companies were very important in the pricing process for newsprint. Consolidated-Bathurst sales personnel felt that American publishers attached a higher degree of legitimacy to price increases originating with U.S.-based producers. At the present time, only Great Northern,

Crown Zellerbach, and Publishers Paper of the U.S. producers were placing their major sales emphasis in the prime market areas of the Canadian producers.

Most pulp and paper companies were experiencing increasing production costs. As shown in Exhibit 5, manufacturing costs as a percentage of sales were higher in 1972 than most of the previous seven years. Consolidated-Bathurst's manufacturing costs as a percentage of sales had risen sharply in the previous three years and in 1973 were above the industry average. An increase in the cost of labour in 1974 was expected to increase production costs even more. Although Consolidated-Bathurst did not have any workers on strike, the demands of wage parity with other firms that were on strike would certainly be a major factor in future negotiating sessions. The current industry labour position is shown in Exhibit 6. The seriousness of the situation was reported in the *Globe and Mail* on Friday, September 28, 1973:

> Despite recent settlements in Ontario, strikes in the Quebec pulp and paper industry continue to present a bleak contrast to an otherwise rosy prospect for that key Quebec industry.
>
> No end is in sight to strikes involving about 5,000 workers that began several weeks ago at five mills, three of them in Quebec, owned by Canadian International Paper Co. of Montreal, nor to strikes by about 1,800 employees that began in August at two Quebec mills of Price Co. Limited of Quebec City.
>
> Meanwhile, the UPIU (United Paperworkers International Union) has resumed contract negotiations with the Eastern Canada Newsprint Group, which is bargaining on behalf of five mills owned by four Quebec companies and one in Nova Scotia. Negotiations involving several other Quebec mills remain in abeyance in their preliminary stages.
>
> These strikes come at a time when sales have generally been "Terrific" for pulp and paper producers, says Paul E. Lachance, President of the Council of Pulp and Paper Producers of Quebec.
>
> He considers the strikes particularly unfortunate because the industry could have been selling so much. He estimates that between CIP and Price, about $1 million a day of sales are being lost.
>
> Dr. Lachance expects strong markets to continue in 1974.

THE MARKET FOR NEWSPRINT

About 50 percent of newsprint in the United States was consumed by major metropolitan papers and the rest by much smaller dailies and weeklies. Papers like the *New York Times* and the *Detroit News,* for example, would consume about 400,000 tons and 100,000 tons of newsprint every year, respectively. Consolidated-Bathurst sold mostly to larger papers or groups of papers. Their yearly contracts with the larger papers or groups of papers ranged from 20,000 tons to over 100,000 tons with an average of about 50,000 tons. Consolidated-Bathurst had a total of about 170 accounts with 10 percent of these accounting for almost 70 percent of sales and 25 percent accounting for over 90 percent of sales. In the United States some of the larger contracts were held with the *Baltimore Sun,* The Newhouse Group (including *Long Island Daily* and *Cleveland Plain Dealer*), the Knight Newspapers (including *Miami Herald, Beacon Journal,* Akron, Ohio, *Detroit Free Press*), the *Detroit News, Philadelphia Bulletin, Boston Globe, The Wall Street Journal* and the *New York Daily News.* Major Canadian customers included *La Presse Trans-Canada Newspapers,* the *Montreal Star* and the *Toronto Star.* For large accounts, newsprint contracts were negotiated by Mr. Andrew and his immediate subordinates. The publisher and financial vice president usually represented the newspaper in these negotiations. Most other newsprint producers had about the same amount of account concentration as Consolidated-Bathurst.

In determining which newsprint producer received a particular volume of newsprint contract, publishers considered the printability and runability (amount of breakage in the press), delivery time, sales terms, and customer technical service to correct any problems. Personal relationship among negotiators was also considered to be very important. Almost all publishers had two or three sources of supply. Also, they quite often purchased some cut-price newsprint from smaller suppliers in Scandinavia or the United States.

About 85 percent of Canadian newsprint was produced in eastern Canada with the remaining 15 percent being produced in British Columbia. The major western producers were MacMillan-Bloedel Limited, Crown Zellerbach, and B. C. Forest Products. These producers sold mainly in the western United States and the Orient. MacMillan-Bloedel also had about 25 percent of its total capacity at Rothesay in eastern Canada and so competed directly with the eastern producers. The eastern producers sold mainly in the Northeast and Midwest United States, the United Kingdom, South America, and Canada.

Personnel at Consolidated-Bathurst estimated that in 1974, U.S. production would be 3.4 million tons out of a capacity of 3.6 million tons, and that Canadian production would be 9.8 million tons out of a capacity of 10.6 million tons. U.S. exports were expected to be about 100,000 tons while Canadian overseas exports were expected to be about 1.7 million tons. Scandinavian imports into the United States were expected to be about 300,000 tons. Total U.S. demand for 1974 was estimated at 10.5 million tons, while Canadian demand was expected to be 900,000 tons. Another 200,000 tons were expected to be sold for inventory.

Mr. Andrew knew that a few competitors had started marketing a 30-pound grade of newsprint. An important factor was that the thinner sheet produced a 6 percent saving in wood consumption. This saving was important as the pulp and paper industry was quickly approaching the limit of low-cost, accessible wood resources. The impact of this thinner paper on publishers was not yet known.

Consolidated-Bathurst also made higher quality newsprint grades which sold at a 3 percent to 10 percent premium over the standard price.

HISTORY OF PRICE CHANGES

Because of the competitiveness in the newsprint market, any price changes were made after much deliberation and with full anticipation of possible competitive moves. An outline of pricing activity in the U.S. newsprint market in recent years is shown in Exhibit 7. This exhibit only lists those firms that were in the first group of firms to act on any price change. After a sorting out period following a price change most firms sold at the established market price within a particular geographic market. Usually a change was made effective from a future date which allowed both competitors and purchasers time to analyze and react to the change. The North-South distinction in the exhibit refers to the fact that major publishers in the southeastern states had bargained one firm against another to get a lower market price than existed in the northeastern states. This difference existed despite the increased distance and transportation costs.

Most sales contracts were for five to ten years but provisions for price increases were outlined in clauses tying them to "general although not necessarily universal" industry prices. In relation to these contracts, members of the sales staff generally felt that the customer was not bound if the conditions under which the contract was signed should change.

Newsprint represented about 30 percent of the total costs to newspaper publishers, and consequently, newsprint price increases had to be passed on by the publisher, usually to advertisers, if he was to maintain his profitability. Timing of a price increase therefore was critical—if it came just after the publisher had revised his advertising rates (which were usually fixed for a certain period) then he would have no means of recouping the extra cost. Rate cards for major publishers were set at many different times throughout the year.

Newspaper publishers had in the past reacted in several ways to the announcement of a price increase for newsprint. The first reaction was sometimes emotional. Heated telephone calls, letters pleading for reconsideration or speeches castigating the Canadian newsprint "cartel" were not uncommon.

Publishers could also take direct action by threatening to cancel their contracts. Some contracts actually had been cancelled using the price increase as an excuse, but the real reason might have been something else. More often, customers used the threat of cancellation to extract discounts from suppliers. This pressure was particularly effective when either of the following conditions existed:

a. The market was soft; that is, the industry was in a general state of oversupply. In this case, the customer would likely be able to find supply elsewhere, often at a reduced price.

b. The customer had more than one supplier. If one supplier was willing to grant a discount, the customer could use this as leverage to obtain concessions from the others. A prime example of this type of situation existed in the southern United States where a publisher-controlled newsprint company had influenced the establishment of a market price $2 less than the rest of the eastern United States. Because of this, Canadian mills charged a lower price to southern customers than to those in the North.

In August 1971, President Nixon imposed universal wage and price controls in the United States for 90 days. As of September 1973, the newsprint industry was operating under voluntary restraint on prices. Price increases were allowed, but were subject to review by the Cost of Living Council. If this council considered a price increase to be unreasonable, it could order the price rolled back.

THE FUTURE

Mr. Andrew was anxious to avoid any losses in the future especially in view of Consolidated-Bathurst's performance in previous years. In evaluating all the factors, Mr. Andrew knew that he would have to decide what the new price should be and when the change was to be made if he decided to make any price change at all. He also wondered if now was the time to make the investment in a new newsprint machine, and if so, what size of machine. He expected that production costs for newsprint on a new machine would be about 10 percent less than the current average total cost. Mr. Andrew knew that he was operating in a basically conservative commodity business. He was anxious to make good decisions both for his company and for his industry.

EXHIBIT 1
Sales and earnings results ($000)

	1972	1971	1970	1969	1968	1967	1966
Net sales..............	$348,055	$343,362	$353,944	$348,087	$295,472	$242,198	$234,485
Earnings (before extraordinary items).	6,496	442	589	10,554	13,126	17,788	21,108
Per common share*....	0.55	(0.45)	(0.42)	1.23	1.69	2.48	3.05
Net earnings (loss) per share after extraordinary items*.........	0.56	(8.70)	(2.30)	1.40	1.36	2:40	3.00

* Per common share earnings are stated after deducting application of preferred dividend requirements.

EXHIBIT 2

Canadian newsprint producers (>200,000 tons) in order of size, by capacity and residual total (<200,000 tons) lumped

Producer	Capacity (tons)	Share of industry (percent)
1. MacMillan-Bloedel Ltd........................	1,364,100	13.4%
2. Canadian International Paper..................	1,154,100	11.3
3. The Price Company Ltd........................	1,058,400	10.4
4. Abitibi Paper Co. Ltd...........................	1,044,200	10.2
5. Consolidated-Bathurst Ltd.....................	936,600	9.2
6. Ontario Paper Co. Ltd..........................	765,000	7.5
7. Bowaters Canadian Corp. Ltd..................	546,200	5.4
8. Domtar Newsprint Ltd..........................	540,300	5.3
9. Great Lakes Paper Co. Ltd.....................	432,200	4.2
10. Anglo-Canadian Pulp & Paper.................	336,800	3.3
11. Spruce Falls Power & Paper Co................	332,100	3.3
12. Ontario-Minnesota Pulp & Paper Co...........	322,200	3.2
13. Donohue Co. Ltd...............................	257,000	2.5
14. Crown Zellerbach Can. Ltd.....................	254,100	2.5
15. B. C. Forest Products Ltd......................	242,700	2.4
Balance of producers (<200,000 ton producers).......................	607,600	5.9
	10,193,600	100.0

EXHIBIT 3

Canadian newsprint industry: Capacity, operating ratio, production, reserve capacity (1965 through 8 months 1973)

Year	Official capacity*	Indicated operating ratio	Production	Indicated reserve capacity
1965......................	8,420,800	91.7	7,719,700	701,100
1966......................	8,878,100	94.8	8,418,800	459,300
1967......................	9,293,900	86.6	8,051,500	1,242,400
1968......................	9,655,400	83.2	8,031,300	1,624,100
1969......................	9,611,500	91.1	8,758,400	853,100
1970......................	9,718,900	88.6	8,607,500	1,111,400
1971......................	10,050,400	82.6	8,297,000	1,753,400
1972......................	10,117,900	85.6	8,660,800	1,457,100
8 months—1973...........	6,795,100	90.5	6,130,100	665,000
12 months—1973..........	10,193,600†			

* Capacity figures shown are official, theoretically possible amounts. An approximate 95 percent is considered practically possible. Note also that these figures represent nondutiable (U.S. tariff) grades only and do not incorporate Groundwood Printing and Specialty Grades (dutiable) of which some 500,000 tons per annum are produced. Detailed capacities of the latter are not published and, indeed, some part of the above capacities can be shifted to produce dutiable grades as market demand dictates and profit incentives exist.

† Estimated.

EXHIBIT 4

Major U.S. newsprint producers

Producer	Capacity (tons)
Southland Paper...................	470,000
Kimberly-Clark.....................	420,000
Publishers Paper..................	360,000
Great Northern....................	360,000
Boise Cascade.....................	135,000
Boise Price.......................	150,000
Others............................	<100,000

EXHIBIT 5

Ratio of manufacturing costs to gross sales: Index 1965 = 100

Year	Industry
1972............................	108
1971............................	107
1970............................	103
1969............................	106
1968............................	108
1967............................	106
1966............................	102
1965............................	100

EXHIBIT 6

Eastern Canadian newsprint mills—Strikes situation as of September 28, 1973

Company	Date strike began	Status
MacMillan Rothesay Ltd. (MacMillan-Bloedel Mill at Rothesay, Quebec)..................................	September 9	Still out
E. B. Eddy......................................	August 29	Ratified Sept. 14
Canadian Cellulose...........................	August 1	Settled Aug. 5
C.I.P.—Gatineau, LaTuque, Trois Rivieres....................................	July 27	Still out
C.I.P.—Hawkesbury..........................	August 3	Still out
New Brunswick International Paper...........	August 8	Still out
Ontario and Minnesota Pulp and Paper—Fort Frances........................	July 3	Still out
—Kenora.............................	July 9	Still out
Price Company—Alma and Kenogami.........	August 10	Still out

EXHIBIT 7
Outline of U.S. newsprint price changes (1965–1973) in U.S. dollars per ton

Date	Company (in order of announcement)	Announced increase or decrease	Effective price	Effective date	
March 1, 1966 (est.)	Domtar......	$10	$145	April 1, 1966	
	Bowater Sales Corp......	10	145	April 1, 1966	
	Consolidated Paper (Consolidated-Bathurst's 1966 name)......	10	145	April 1, 1966	
March 23, 1966	Domtar announces rollback......	(5)	140	May 16, 1966	
	Bowater Sales Corp......	(5)	140	May 16, 1966	
	Great Lakes Paper......	(5)	140	May 16, 1966	
April 20, 1966	All firms change effective date......	(5)	140	June 1, 1966	
September 26, 1966	Crown Zellerbach Corp......	4	138	June 1, 1967	West Coast
October 25, 1966	MacMillan Bloedel......	(3)	137	June 1, 1967	United States only
November 1, 1966	Crown Zellerbach......	3	140	June 1, 1967	
March 15, 1967	Consolidated Paper......	3	143	July 1, 1967	
March 17, 1967	International Paper Sales Co......	3	143	July 1, 1967	
September 27, 1968	International Paper Sales Co......	5	148	January 1, 1969 North	
		4	147	January 1, 1969 South*	
	All others follow immediately after				
September 24, 1969	Bowater Sales Co......	4–5	152	January 1, 1970	Wipes out all price differential—universal price
November 20, 1969	(Consolidated-Bathurst is 4th company to announce price increase) $1 price differential to South reinstated......	(1)	152	January 1, 1970 North	
			151	January 1, 1970 South	
September 8, 1970	Anglo-Canadian......	10	162	January 1, 1971	
	Consolidated-Bathurst......	10	162	January 1, 1971	
	International Paper......	10	162	January 1, 1971	

Date	Company				
September 22, 1970	Boise-Cascade	10	162	January 1, 1971	South only
November 3, 1970	Boise-Cascade	8	160	January 1, 1971	All markets
November 4, 1970	Abitibi	8	160	January 1, 1971	South
November 15, 1970	Southland Paper	7	159	January 1, 1971	South
November 15, 1970	All majors	8	160	November 15, 1970	Canada only
December 6, 1970	All majors	8	160	April 1, 1971	
August 12, 1971	MacMillan-Bloedel	8	168	November 1, 1971	
	Price Company	8	168	November 1, 1971	
	(Consolidated-Bathurst s 5th company to announce price increase)				
August 15, 1971	Nixon imposes wage-price freeze. Price increase dropped.				
December 10, 1971 (Est.)	International Paper Sales Co.	8	168	December 1971	North
	(3.4%, or $5.25 price increase approved by U.S. Price Commission)	5.25	164.25	December 1971	South
	Consolidated-Bathurst	8	168	December 1971	North
December 1, 1972	Great Northern Paper Co.	5	170	February 1, 1973	
	Southland Paper Co.	5	170	February 1, 1973	
	(Consolidated-Bathurst is 4th company to announce price increase (December 19)).				
April 12, 1973	Bowater Sales Co.	5	175	July 1, 1973	
	Kruger Pulp and Paper	5	175	July 1, 1973	
	Consolidated-Bathurst	5	175	July 1, 1973	

* South includes Texas, Oklahoma, Louisianna, Arkansas, Missouri, and Kansas.

34

Limestone Electronics, Inc.*

In January 1977, Limestone Electronics, Inc., a large producer of military and industrial electronics equipment, was facing a decision concerning its bid in the latest round of competition to supply the U.S. Air Force with a recently developed airborne radar system, the electronically agile radar (EAR). This was the second round of bidding in the past 18 months. Limestone had participated in preliminary development studies of EAR as well as in the initial contract competition. Limestone's executives considered success in the current bidding to be crucial to gaining a long-term lucrative relationship with the Air Force as the principal supplier of the radar system.

ELECTRONICALLY AGILE RADAR

In the early 1970s, advances in electronics technology occurred which for the first time raised the possibility of an operational airborne phased-array multimode radar that could also be cost-efficient. This new radar (EAR), mounted in the nose of the aircraft, offered clear advantages over conventional airborne radar systems in that it combined functions which previously had required three separate radar units. Specifically, EAR simultaneously provided three different types of aircraft navigation: forward-looking (including ground-mapping and air surveillance), terrain-following, and Doppler-type navigation (relationship to other moving objects). A major deterrent to the development of EAR systems had been prohibitively high costs, which had been largely overcome in the current

---

* This case was co-authored by Duncan LaBay, Graduate Student, University of Michigan.

state-of-the-art form through the incorporation of a high-speed steerable radar beam.

By 1974, Air Force officials felt that advances in technology and resultant cost reductions clearly warranted the serious consideration of adoption of EAR as standard equipment in future aircraft requirements, and began planning for preliminary studies to be carried out by a small number of private contractors under the sponsorship of the USAF Avionics Laboratory.

LIMESTONE ELECTRONICS

Limestone Electronics began operations in the 1950s, and rapidly became known in industrial markets for the quality and reliability of its products, which included electronics, communications and navigational devices. The firm remained exclusively in the industrial segment until 1969, when management created a separate division, the Division of Military Services (DMS), to handle military contracts, which were seen as an attractive opportunity to expand sales and profits. Over the following five years, DMS continued to expand to the point that, in 1974, it accounted for 40 percent of Limestone's sales and revenues. DMS actively undertook research and development contracts with various military agencies, in addition to contracting for ongoing military requirements and subcontracting with other industrial companies involved in government bidding.

PRELIMINARY STUDIES

In April 1974, the USAF Avionics Laboratory selected five firms to build prototype models of the agile radar system from a group of some 25 contractors originally considered as potential suppliers. This selection was made following visits by a USAF team to each of the contractor's facilities and briefings by the company representatives as to their resources, organizations, and product capabilities. Limestone received notification that it was one of the five chosen.

Under the terms established by Avionics, the preliminary study phase was to cover eight months, during which time each firm was to design and produce a prototype EAR system. These prototype studies were to be funded on a cost-plus-incentive-fee basis. Under this contract method, a target cost for the project is negotiated in advance along with a profit level allowing the firm a given return on investment. Additionally, a profit formula is established to be used in allocating excess cost or profit between the government and the contractor in the event the actual cost exceeds or is below the target cost. Thus, the firm has an incentive to keep costs below the target cost. At the end of the period, the Avionics Laboratory would perform extensive testing and evaluation of the prototypes, and make a recommendation to the Air Force as to which design should be accepted and placed for competitive bidding for large-scale production.

Limestone Electronics completed work on the prototype in December 1974 and submitted it to the Avionics Laboratory along with blueprints and a comprehensive technical background report compiled by the EAR project manager at DMS. The project manager was confident that Limestone's would be the prototype eventually selected by the USAF, although probably not without some modification. His project engineers had been in close contact with officials from Avionics throughout the period, making cost-effective design trade-offs. DMS felt that as a result, they had designed a system which met the original specification requirements but at a substantially reduced cost from what the competitive designs were anticipated to be.

INITIAL CONTRACT COMPETITION

By May 1975, the Air Force had completed its testing and evaluation. The outcome came as a surprise to members of Limestone's DMS: one of the other firms, Melrose Electronics, had submitted a design which the Air Force felt was technologically superior to Limestone's entry, and which could be produced at a similar (although slightly higher) initial cost. The major advantage of the Melrose unit was the incorporation of a testing mechanism in the radar which would allow fault-tracing and isolation of defective components within the unit in the case of malfunction. Given their modular construction of the EAR, the faulty internal component could be found and replaced with a spare plug-in module, rather than having to tear down the entire EAR unit.

Considerable cost savings would result over the life of the units, since the USAF would stock merely the replaceable modules, shipping defective ones back to the manufacturer for rebuilding as required, rather than stocking and returning spare EAR line-replaceable units. Melrose estimated the plug-in modules at $2,000, while the complete EAR was expected to cost approximately $50,000. Analysis of the Melrose EAR determined that the built-in testing device was effective in at least 95 percent of the cases in finding the faulty component. For the other 5 percent of the time, the entire unit would have to be returned for repair. The initial cost was approximately 4 percent higher than comparable units without the testing circuitry (that is, Limestone), but life cycle costs were estimated to be reduced 40 percent as a result, thus more than justifying the additional initial outlay.

The USAF initial requirements were for 50 EAR systems, to be produced under a firm fixed price contract with no progress payments. With this contract method, the bid accepted by the government is a firm price (not subject to renegotiation or overruns) which will be paid upon completion of the contract. This stipulation of payment on completion is in contrast with some other contracts which provide for periodic progress payments of some percentage of the supplier's costs by the government. Blueprints as supplied by Melrose Electronics were available for inspection, in addition to the detailed specifications released by the USAF. Bids were to be submitted on a unit price basis, with the entire contract going to the low bidder.

It was expected that the contractor would be able to produce these 50 units within 18 months, with production capacity capable of being increased at a later date to meet eventual production requirements of subsequent contracts. Consistent with the life cycle costing approach adopted in considering the additional fault-tracing circuitry, the USAF required a service warranty included in the initial bid covering repair of defective units and/or modules.

Potentially, eight to ten firms might submit bids for the project, although the three main competitors were expected to be Melrose, Limestone, and a third firm, H-T-R Instruments, all of which had been involved in the preliminary studies.

In considering its bid for the project, the Limestone DMS team was aware of the initial advantageous position held by Melrose Electronics, since their prototype had been accepted largely without changes. DMS still felt it could meet or better the production capabilities and efficiency of Melrose, and decided to shave its costs to a minimum in an attempt to

EXHIBIT 1

Initial contract competition—Cost estimates and bid price per unit, 50 EAR systems

Labor		
Manufacturing	$ 2,426	
Assembly	3,596	
Quality control, testing	1,527	
	$ 7,549	
Overhead on labor (175%)	13,211	
Total labor costs		$20,760
Material		18,788
Total labor and material		$39,548
Engineering	$ 2,013	
Overhead on engineering (145%)	2,919	
Total engineering		4,932
Service contract (4% of labor, materials)		1,582
Manufacturing costs		$46,062
Administrative costs (10%)		4,606
Total cost		$50,668
Profit (5%)		2,533
Bid		$53,201

win the initial contract. By landing this contract, the experience gained in production would give a substantial competitive advantage for future contracts.

A bid of $53,201 per unit was ultimately submitted by Limestone Electronics for 50 Electronically Agile Radar systems. The breakdown of their various cost components is given in Exhibit 1. A profit figure of 5 percent was included, which was considerably below the normal required rate of return, but which was justified by future expected returns.

The Air Force received four bids on the initial contract, with the results as follows:

	Per unit
Limestone Electronics	$53,201
Melrose Electronics	53,396
H-T-R Instruments	56,085
Holden Company	57,827

The contract was awarded to Limestone, which began production operations in July 1975 with a targeted completion date of December 1976.

PRODUCTION EXPERIENCE

As of December 1975, only a handful of EAR units had been completed, owing largely to extensive start-up difficulties. A major problem had been encountered with the blueprints and specifications as provided by Melrose. Parts did not fit; tolerances were found to be exceedingly tight. As a result a great deal of individual component-testing was required rather than random batch examination as was originally intended. Problems with other suppliers of component parts also arose which further delayed the production schedule. Costs were higher than anticipated due in part to unexpected price rises and in part because of a strike at the plant of a crucial supplier which forced Limestone to contract with another (higher priced) source. Engineering costs were likewise underestimated. More engineering design and development was required than had been budgeted. By midsummer 1976, many of the difficulties had been resolved and progress toward more automated production had been made. There was increasing optimism at Limestone that the time schedule of 50 units by December 1976 could be met.

SECOND CONTRACT COMPETITION

In late December 1976, the USAF announced a second contract competition for an additional 200 EAR units. Further, the Air Force announced that bids for this contract would be accepted in increments of 25 (that is, each firm was required to submit bids for quantities of 25, 50, 75, . . . , 200 units). The other terms of the contract were as in the initial bidding, with a time requirement for completion of 24 months. By calling for incremental bidding, the Air Force hoped to accomplish two purposes: (1) keep its procurement costs at a minimum, and (2) establish alternate sources of supply of its requirements, in keeping with long-standing tradition in military contract policy. At the time of this announcement, Limestone had supplied 45 of the original 50 EAR systems contracted in June 1975. The remaining five were scheduled for delivery by January 15, 1976.

Early in January, the Limestone DMS team compiled summary cost data (see Exhibit 2) concerning the production of the first 40 EAR sys-

EXHIBIT 2

Cost experience per unit—40 EAR systems manufactured under initial contract

Labor		
Manufacturing.....................................	$ 1,205	
Assembly..	3,741	
Quality control, testing..........................	2,951	
	$ 7,897	
Overhead on labor (160%).......................	12,635	
Total labor costs...................................		$20,532
Material..		26,531
Total labor and material...........................		$47,063
Engineering.......................................	$ 2,305	
Overhead on engineering (145%).................	3,342	
Total engineering..................................		5,647
Service contract (4% of labor, materials)..........		1,883
Manufacturing costs...............................		$54,593
Administrative costs (8%).........................		4,367
Total cost..		$58,960

tems from the original contract. Full cost data for the entire 50 units would not be available until after the submission date for bids on the second round. The team also drew together cost estimates for the second contract bidding (see Exhibit 3).

The problem confronting the DMS project manager was to determine Limestone's bid on the second contract. He was aware of the rather substantial cost overruns which had occurred in the initial production. He realized that some of the problems encountered had been satisfactorily resolved, but that difficulties with testing, quality control, and automated production still remained. Additionally there was skepticism from certain

EXHIBIT 3
Second contract competition—Cost estimates per unit, 100 EAR systems (50% of total contract)*

Labor		
Manufacturing..................................	$ 385	
Assembly..	2,843	
Quality control, testing...........................	1,527	
	$ 4,755	
Overhead on labor (160%).......................	7,608	
Total labor costs..................................		$12,363
Material...		20,340
Total labor and material..........................		$32,703
Engineering.......................................	$ 2,013	
Overhead on engineering (135%).................	2,718	
Total engineering.................................		4,731
Service contract (4% of labor, materials)...........		1,308
Manufacturing costs..............................		$38,742
Administrative costs (8%).........................		3,099
Total cost..		$41,841

* Costs were estimated to average 5 percent lower per unit than the given figures if 150 units were produced, 9 percent lower for production of 200 units, and 6 percent higher if 50 units were produced.

members within the DMS team as to whether the second contract cost estimates as submitted were realistic given these problems.

It was also known that Melrose Electronics had been following events at Limestone over the past 18 months with great interest. Clearly Melrose was eager to remain in competition for future EAR contracts. Word had been passed from Limestone's headquarters to the DMS group that reliable industry sources indicated H-T-R Instruments was also very interested in the latest contract opportunity. Representatives of H-T-R had apparently held rather lengthy discussions about the EAR system with the USAF recently. Also sources had indicated that expanded production experience within the past 12 months on a related electronic navigational device put H-T-R in a substantially improved competitive position.

The most recent long-range planning forecast released by the Air Force (January 1976) placed their estimated requirements for further EAR systems (beyond those contracts already announced) at over 500 units within the next five years.

PART VIII

MARKETING AND PUBLIC POLICY

The current environment of the marketing manager is one undergoing rapid change and transition. Probably the most noteworthy of these developments, whether for better or for worse, is the increasing pervasiveness of "public" influences on marketing institutions and decision making. In this context, public influences are generally defined to include different levels of government (acting through legislation, regulation, or moral suasion), organized public groups (the consumerism movement, for example), individual advocates of change, and the force of changing public attitudes and opinion.

The cases in this section seek to develop an improved understanding of some of these trends and developments, and to provide practice for students in rendering decisions in a contemporary environment. The specific objectives of the cases are as follows:

1. To improve capacity for marketing decision making in situations where public influences are involved.
2. To explore the nature and extent of public influences on marketing institutions and decision making.
3. To develop conceptual foundations leading to an improved understanding of contemporary developments in marketing.

Approaches to decision making in the area of marketing and public policy are

This note draws heavily on the work of Professor Michael Pearce of the University of Western Ontario.

429

not well established. One possible approach makes three assumptions. They are as follows:

1. Marketing and public policy decisions are made in a bargaining arena containing many interest groups.
2. Either explicit or implicit bargaining takes place among the interest groups in this arena whenever a marketing decision involves public influences.
3. Better decisions will be made if the objectives, motivations and behaviors of each interest group are understood.

   With the assumptions in mind, we now shall present an approach to decision making in this area:

1. List and/or diagram the interest groups involved in a particular decision context. Note the interrelationships among them.
2. Identify the behavior of each group.
3. Attempt to explain this behavior by examining the objectives, motivations, values of the people comprising the groups.
4. Identify what each group stands to lose or gain in the bargaining.
5. Identify what each group might be most willing to give up. What would they most want in return?
6. Based upon this analysis, predict the likely strategies of each group.
7. Make a decision based upon the anticipated reaction of each group to the alternatives you are considering. Be sure to have a contingency in case their reactions are not as you anticipated.

CASE

35

F&F Sales Company

Tom Frolik leaned back in his chair and reflected upon the events that had taken place earlier that day. His first day back to work after a long weekend over New Year's had really been hectic. Apparently while he had been on his skiing vacation, an article had appeared in the morning newspaper indicating that the Georgia State Troopers were upset about the effectiveness of radar detectors such as the Fuzzbusters that he marketed, and had encouraged several legislators to introduce a bill for the upcoming General Assembly outlawing these devices in Georgia. The phone had been ringing all day with many people calling to order a Fuzzbuster before their sale became illegal. Recognizing the potential consequences of this act for his company, he decided to develop a complete plan of action in the next few days.

BACKGROUND ON RADAR DETECTORS

The first radar detectors were marketed in the early 1960s. Typically, the units were not very high quality and sold for a price between $19.95 and $29.95. These units clipped onto the visor and would emit a beep when police radar was detected, allowing the driver to slow down before being caught in a radar trap. Although these units were relatively unsophisticated, several companies were somewhat successful in marketing them through mail-order advertising. With speed limits of 70 or 75 m.p.h. on most highways, however, most people did not have a need for these units.

Things changed dramatically beginning in 1973 with the fuel crisis and

431

oil embargo. Speed limits were reduced nationally to 55 m.p.h. and were often enforced. The first response to this development was a dramatic increase in the sale of Citizens Band (CB) radios, which had been in existence for a number of years, but had experienced a very low level of sales. Many truckers purchased these units, and soon thereafter salesmen and other individuals who had to drive a great deal began purchasing CB units. By 1975, the general public started buying CB radios in great numbers.

There were several problems with the CB radios as a means of avoiding speeding tickets. First, as more and more amateurs started using their radios, the channels became very cluttered. Often it was hard to hear what people were saying, as many people tried to use the same channel. Second, the CB radio became less and less reliable as the police (Smokey the Bear) put CB radios in their cars also. Thus, they could receive the same messages that truckers and other drivers were sending to each other. Third, the CB radio became much less reliable at night with the users' inability to see the police speed trap in the dark.

In addition to the problems with the effectiveness of CB radios, the

EXHIBIT 1

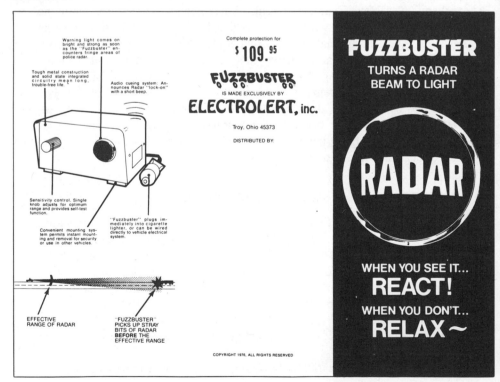

EXHIBIT 1 (continued)

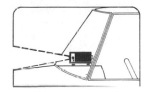
state of the art on radar increased substantially about this time. With the old police radar units, about all they could do was set up a radar trap. New mobile radar units were developed that allowed the policemen to get a radar reading on a speeding car while the police car was moving. Another dramatic development was the ability of police radar to determine the speed of a car even though the police car was going in the opposite direction. Thus, a police officer could detect a speeding car going in the other direction, make a U-turn and arrest the speeder, something that was unheard of previously.

It was in this environment of reduced speed limits, increased enforcement, reduced effectiveness of CB radios, and increased effectiveness of police radar that the Fuzzbuster was introduced by the Electrolert Company in 1975. The Fuzzbuster, a military-type, parametric radar receiver, is sensitive to one/one hundredth of one-millionth of one watt, approximately the strength of radar at three miles if not blocked or otherwise attenuated. The Fuzzbuster receives in the 10.5 GHz Amateur (ham microwave) Band.

Drawing less than one quarter of a watt power, the Fuzzbuster can be left on indefinitely. It is installed on the dash of the car and has a self-contained antenna. The unit plugs into the cigarette lighter. When radar is picked up by the receiver, a warning light goes on and at the same time, a high-pitched tone is generated. The tone cuts off after two to three seconds, but the lamp remains bright until the radar signal ceases. The Fuzzbuster provides this identification of radar up to three miles distant. A pamphlet describing the Fuzzbuster is reproduced in Exhibit 1.

BACKGROUND ON TOM FROLIK AND
F&F SALES COMPANY

Tom Frolik first became aware of Fuzzbusters in January 1976, when he was working as a consultant to a large truck stop on Interstate 75 in Georgia. At that time Fuzzbusters had a suggested retail price of $99.95 and were sold to the retailer for $75. The truck stop ordered one dozen and sold them. They then ordered another dozen, and these also sold quite rapidly. Mr. Frolik then contacted the Electrolert Company and worked out an arrangement to become a distributor. The truck stop had a warehouse distribution subsidiary which bought replacement parts for trucks, and this subsidiary became an Electrolert distributor. About this time some product improvements were made, the most important being the introduction of a flashing light in addition to the beep when radar was detected, and the retail price was increased to $109.95. The wholesale price was $79.

The price to the distributor was $59 per unit, but they had to order in gross (a gross is 144 units). The manufacturer provided sample advertising mats and allowed $3 per unit for coop advertising allowances. In March 1976, the truck stop ordered its first gross and at the same time, reduced the retail price to $84.95. Mr. Frolik recalled that they sold like hotcakes at this price, but because of complaints from those who had paid $109.95, and a feeling that a higher price would not hurt sales, they decided to raise the price to $89.95.

The truck stop distributor subsidiary made no attempt to sell Fuzzbusters through any other outlets, but did sell them through a second truck stop which they had recently purchased.

By October they had sold five gross (720 units) and were told that they had a big backup on the coop advertising allowance. At the same time, the owner of the truck stop began to have some guilt feelings about marketing the product and decided he did not want to advertise it using his company name.

In late October, Tom Frolik announced that he was leaving the truck stop company to move to Atlanta to establish his own consulting firm

EXHIBIT 2

and start several entrepreneurial enterprises. The owner of the truck stop suggested that Frolik market in the Atlanta area some of the products that the truck stop's distributor subsidiary handled. Frolik suggested that he be given the use of the advertising allowance credit for the Fuzzbuster, that he put in the time on the project, and that the truck stop owner and he split the profits on an equal basis. His proposal was accepted by the truck stop owner, and thus F&F Sales Company was created.

In November when Frolik came to Atlanta, the advertising allowance was up to $2,200. The Electrolert Company would pay 50 percent of all advertising expenditures for the Fuzzbuster up to this amount, but they would pay 100 percent of the expenses for newspaper advertising. Because of this provision, Frolik decided to take out some ads in *The Atlanta Journal* and *Constitution*. Exhibit 2 contains the ad that was approved by Electrolert. Mr. Frolik decided to run the ad four times—Sunday, December 12, the evening of December 16, the morning of December 17, and Sunday, December 19. These four ads, at an average of approximately $550 each, would utilize the full coop advertising allowance available.

After the December 12 ad ran, with minimal response, Mr. Frolik changed the ad by inserting the telephone number of his office where people could call for further information or to place an order which would be charged to a bank credit card (using the truck stop's bank credit card mechanism). The four ads resulted in the immediate sale of 60 Fuzzbusters, with approximately half the people calling in for information before sending in their order. Mr. Frolik indicated that most of these buyers were salesmen, rather than truckers.

Three other outlets in Atlanta were advertising Fuzzbusters at this time. Two of these were retailers which took out small ads at a price of $99.95 and $109.95, with both stores requiring the consumer to come to the retail outlet to purchase the Fuzzbuster. The third source was a firm in Alabama that offered a toll free number together with a coupon in the ad for ordering. This firm, which accepted credit cards, charged $89.95 plus tax and handling ($3.50 for the tax and handling, the same as F&F Sales charged).

Although there were several other companies which marketed similar kinds of products, Mr. Frolik felt that the Fuzzbuster was the best radar detector available on the market. In the Atlanta area, these competitors had virtually no distribution.

CURRENT SITUATION

As a result of the four ads in the middle of December, Mr. Frolik had been quite optimistic about sales of the Fuzzbuster. He had a number of ideas which he was planning to implement to increase sales, including taking out some classified advertising in the CB radio section of the classified ads. He also knew that Radio Shack stores did not stock Fuzz-busters or competitors, so he planned to write to the 43 Radio Shack store managers in his area and ask them to send any customers who requested this product to him.

Thus, all was very rosy for F&F Sales Company and Mr. Frolik when he left on Friday, December 24 for a ten-day skiing vacation. By the time he returned to the office on January 3, things were quite different. Ex-

EXHIBIT 3
Fuzzbuster newspaper article

FUZZ BUSTERS REALLY WORK
Troopers Want Radar Detectors Outlawed

By Keeler McCartney

Georgia state troopers are up in arms over the latest gadgets some motorists are using to detect highway radar speed timers, and they want the upcoming General Assembly to do something about it.

Bill Wilson, information officer of the state Department of Public Safety, said the gadgets in question detect the presence of radar machines and warn drivers before the troopers have a chance to detect speeders.

"It just isn't fair," Wilson said.

He said the warning devices, usually mounted on the dashboards of autos and trucks, can be purchased for $99.95 under the suggestive trade names of "Fuzz Busters," "Bear Finders" and "Trooper Snoopers."

As they approach radar stations, drivers equipped with the devices are alerted by a variety of noises ranging from the wail of an upended talking doll to the buzz of an angry bee and the beep of a telephone answering service.

The safety department has prepared a bill to submit to the next General Assembly which would make it a misdemeanor to possess, manufacture or sell the devices in Georgia.

Troopers have checked the devices and found that they do, indeed, give the driver ample warning to slow down to the legal 55-mile limit before he enters a radar field, Wilson declared.

State Patrol Capt. R. C. Womack, who conducted a series of the tests in the Thomson and Savannah areas, concluded his findings this way:

"These devices are very demoralizing to the trooper who works the road day after day attempting to enforce the national speed limit. It is also a pathetic situation when a $100 device can counteract a $2,000 piece of equipment being used by law enforcement officers."

The troopers may be down because of the radar warning detectors, but they definitely are not out. They've worked up a trick or two of their own to beat the gadgets.

One of their favorites is to keep the radar speed timer turned off until the driver is well within range and then flick it on.

EXHIBIT 3 (*continued*)

"The warning device will sound, all right," Wilson grinned. "But it's too late. The driver has already been caught."

And troopers have figured out the Citizens' Band (CB) lingo that goes with the use of radar detectors.

A favorite among truck drivers is, "My bird dogs are barking."

While awaiting legislative action, the troopers are collecting advertisements of the warning gadgets.

"Put a ——— on your dash and you can drive relaxed again," one ad suggests.

"No watching for radar lurking in the bushes or trying to make sense out of the CB radio chatter," says another. "And you don't have to put up with squeaky bleeps that warn you too late. Now you can enjoy the drive."

Wilson said legislation which the safety department is seeking is similar to laws already passed in the states of Virginia and Connecticut and the cities of Denver, Colo., and Washington, D.C.

Reprinted with permission from the *Atlanta Constitution*, December 31, 1976, p. 1.

hibit 3 contains the article which ran in the morning *Atlanta Constitution* on Friday, December 31 describing the plan by the Georgia State Troopers to outlaw Fuzzbusters. Exhibit 4 contains the proposed legislation that would be introduced in the Georgia legislature. Mr. Frolik had read that the Virginia legislature had banned the devices several years earlier, but that the public outcry against such action had been so strong that legislation lifting the ban on radar detectors was under consideration in that state, and had a high likelihood of passing.

EXHIBIT 4
Proposed legislation

H. B. No. 545
By: Representatives Milford of the 13th, Coleman of the 118th, Smith of the 42nd, McDonald of the 12th and Childs of the 51st

A BILL TO BE ENTITLED

AN ACT

To prohibit the use of devices on motor vehicles used to detect the presence of radar upon highways; to prohibit the operation of motor vehicles so equipped; to prohibit the sale of such devices; to provide for penalties; to provide an effective date; to repeal conflicting laws; and for other purposes.

EXHIBIT 4 (*continued*)

BE IT ENACTED BY THE GENERAL ASSEMBLY OF GEORGIA:

Section 1. Prohibiting use of devices on motor vehicles to detect presence of radar upon highways or operation of motor vehicles so equipped or sale of such devices. It shall be unlawful for any person to operate a motor vehicle upon the highways of this State when such vehicle is equipped with any device or mechanism to detect the emission of radio microwaves in the electromagnetic spectrum, which microwaves are employed by police to measure the speed of motor vehicles upon the highways of this State for law enforcement purposes; it shall be unlawful to use any such device or mechanism upon any such motor vehicle upon the highways; it shall be unlawful to sell any such device or mechanism in this State. Provided, however, that the provisions of this section shall not apply to any receiver of radio waves of any frequency lawfully licensed by any State or federal agency.

Section 2. Any person, firm, or corporation violating the provision of this Act shall be guilty of a misdemeanor and, upon conviction thereof, shall be punished as for a misdemeanor, and any such prohibited device or mechanism shall be forfeited to the court trying the case.

Section 3. The presence of any such prohibited device or mechanism in or upon a motor vehicle upon the highways of this State shall constitute prima facie evidence of the violation of this section. The State need not prove that the device in question was in an operative condition or being operated.

Section 4. This section shall not apply to motor vehicles owned by the State or any political subdivision thereof and which are used by the police of any such government nor to law enforcement officers in their official duties, nor to the sale of any such device or mechanism to law enforcement agencies for use in their official duties.

Section 5. This Act shall become effective upon its approval by the Governor or upon its becoming a law without his approval.

Section 6. All laws and parts of laws in conflict with this Act are hereby repealed.

Mr. Frolik realized that his vacation was over and that he would have to develop a plan of action for the next few weeks. His first thought was that none of the cases he had studied during his M.B.A. program at a well-known eastern business school had dealt with this type of problem.

CASE

36

Zerex Anti-Leak Antifreeze*

Zerex Anti-Leak Antifreeze was introduced to the market in 1969 and was subsequently the target of charges by the Federal Trade Commission (FTC). This case presents a description of the events surrounding Du Pont's initial development of Zerex Anti-Leak Antifreeze, testing and marketing of Zerex, the initial FTC charges against Zerex, and the bargaining between Du Pont and the FTC to resolve these charges. Finally, the negotiations relative to the formal FTC charges are described.

BACKGROUND ON THE DU PONT COMPANY

The Du Pont Company was founded in 1802 by Éleuthère Irénée Du Pont de Nemours to manufacture gunpowder. From this beginning, the company grew and expanded until today, Du Pont has 122 domestic plants in 31 states, over 1,700 products, and total worldwide employment of over 132,000 people. The company has a history of product innovation. For example, Du Pont introduced cellophane in the United States, "Duco" nitrocellulose lacquer paint, neoprene synthetic rubber, nylon, and a number of other products.

The success of the company has been helped by three major strategies: (1) to develop new products; (2) to improve existing ones; and (3) to increase return on overseas investment. The development of new products was an important part of the strategy and Zerex Anti-Leak Antifreeze was one of the outputs.

---

* This case was co-authored by William Bohan, the Ford Motor Company.

HISTORY OF ZEREX ANTI-LEAK ANTIFREEZE

Zerex antifreeze has been on the market for over 30 years. The product consists of ethylene glycol, and various rust and corrosion inhibiters. Beginning in the early 1960s, Du Pont began investigating the possibility of adding an anti-leak agent to Zerex. While there were a number of stop-leak products on the market at the time, they were all temporary cures. The types of materials used for stopping leaks included rice hulls, peanut shells, pepper, oatmeal, and wheat. These products would stop a leak existing at the time of installation, but did not form a permanent seal. They would not stay dispersed in solution, and they would not stop a leak occurring at a later time.

Du Pont began development of a product which would seal small holes in the radiator, would form a permanent seal, would offer continuing protection against small leaks, and would not clog or adversely affect the operation of the cooling system in any way. The product finally introduced into Zerex consisted of a stabilized polystyrene in the form of small spheres ranging in size from less than 1 mil to a maximum of 20 mils in diameter. The polystyrene spheres would not settle out and when a leak occurred, the pressure of the cooling system forced the small spheres through the hole. The larger spheres bridged the hole and the small spheres would gather behind and around it. Because of the heat and pressure of the cooling system and a special coating on the spheres, the spheres locked together forming a solid, permanent seal. Holes larger than 20 mils still had to be sealed mechanically, but a Du Pont study indicated that 80 percent of all leaks could be sealed by these anti-leak spheres.

A test program was initiated in 1967 to confirm the anti-leak properties and to ensure that the spheres would not adversely affect cooling systems. Three different test series were conducted by Du Pont. First, anti-leak Zerex was installed in cars operated by employees in Philadelphia. Second, 329 taxicabs in Philadelphia were tested with the anti-leak spheres. Third, cars were tested in San Antonio, Texas, by Southwest Research Institute. No problems were reported in any of the tests.

MARKETING ZEREX ANTI-LEAK ANTIFREEZE

Test markets

Once the series of product use tests was successfully completed in 1967, test markets in two cities were conducted. Over 75,000 gallons of Zerex Anti-Leak Antifreeze were sold in Green Bay, Wisconsin, and Peoria, Illinois, in 1968. In the estimated 50,000 cars in which Zerex was installed, no problems were reported. Sales in the two test markets were considered to be successful and the decision was made to introduce anti-leak Zerex nationally in 1969. The addition of anti-leak Zerex resulted in a total of four antifreezes marketed by Du Pont at the time.

Advertising

With the decision to go national, Du Pont's automotive products advertising agency, Batten, Barton, Durstine, and Osborn, Inc., (BBDO) began developing an advertising theme for anti-leak Zerex. By June 1969, a proposed ad had been developed which showed a can of anti-leak Zerex being punctured. The antifreeze shot out for a few seconds, then abruptly ceased to flow.

In June 1969, the proposed national television commercial was shown, in storyboard form, to the Federal Trade Commission. Some minor revisions were suggested by the FTC which were incorporated when the commercial was produced. Early in August 1969, a copy of the finished commercial was mailed to the FTC with a request that any further comments be forwarded before the initial airing of the commercial over Labor Day weekend, 1969. No comments were received and the campaign was launched. The advertising campaign was placed on national television and continued virtually unchanged from 1969 through 1970. Sales of anti-leak Zerex were estimated to be about $23 million in 1970.

Potential problems surface

In April 1970, a consumer-oriented magazine, *Consumer Bulletin,* suggested that new car owners with anti-leak Zerex installed would be well advised to replace it with some other antifreeze because of a "considerable" number of failures in auto-cooling systems with the anti-leak Zerex. These cooling system failures were reported by experienced radiator men who attributed plugged cooling systems to anti-leak Zerex. Du Pont, concerned with this adverse publicity regarding its product, began action to correct the trouble, particularly with members of the National Automotive Radiator Service Association (NARSA) which had withdrawn its guarantee on radiators serviced and then filled with anti-leak Zerex. An investigation was launched and Du Pont was able to convince the NARSA by August 1970 that dirty cooling systems and not Zerex were the primary causes of problems, except for problems caused from some early production of anti-leak Zerex. Reports had been circulating that some early problems with anti-leak Zerex were due to "early production difficulties" and a batch of material that had been improperly mixed by independent canners who had mixed in too many polystyrene spheres.

The first FTC action

On November 25, 1970, apparently in response to consumer complaints that anti-leak Zerex caused cooling systems to clog, the FTC called a press conference and announced its intention to issue a complaint against Du Pont and BBDO. Specifically, the FTC charged that:

1. The firm's "can stabbing" demonstration for its Zerex Anti-Leak Antifreeze was invalid.
2. It had not disclosed that Zerex may damage the car's cooling system although it knew or had reason to know this.
3. Du Pont had advertised Zerex for use in the cooling system without having conducted scientific tests that were adequate to establish whether it would or could cause damage.

"Can stabbing" demonstration

The FTC took exception to the TV commercial because it claimed the demonstration was unlike actual operating conditions within an automobile cooling system. In the "can stabbing" demonstration, a 50–50 solution of Zerex and water was circulated through a Zerex can by means of a pump. The can was punctured releasing a steady stream which stopped within seconds. Meanwhile a voice off camera stated, "We're going to drive home a point about new Anti-Leak Zerex Antifreeze. It stops most common radiator leaks . . . just like that." The can was then punctured three more times in rapid succession, causing three more leaks which stopped within seconds. During the puncturing sequence the phrase "50 percent Zerex solution circulating under pressure" was superimposed on the screen. At the end of the demonstration the phrase "Guaranteed not to run out on you" was superimposed on the screen.

The FTC contended that this demonstration was false, misleading, and deceptive because it was not, as represented, evidence which actually proved that Zerex will stop leaks which actually occur in automotive cooling systems under normal operating conditions. In automotive cooling systems, (1) the pressure varies within a wide range from zero up to the design pressure of the system—approximately 12 to 15 pounds per square inch; (2) the solution circulates at a rate of approximately 35 gallons per minute; and (3) leaks usually occur in areas where the solution flows toward or surges around the opening. In contrast, in the demonstration, (1) a pressure of four pounds per square inch was used; (2) the circulation rate was one gallon per minute; and (3) the solution flows past the leaks.

Cooling system damage

Next, the FTC charged that Du Pont had represented in advertisements and on its labels that Zerex was effective in sealing leaks in automotive cooling systems, without disclosing the fact it may cause damage to the system or components. According to the FTC, Du Pont had received information from various sources by which it knew or had reason to believe, that using Zerex under normal operating conditions could or might cause damage to various parts or components of automotive cooling systems. In spite of this, Du Pont continued to market and advertise Zerex without disclosing this possibility in its advertisements and on its labels.

Lack of scientific tests

Finally, the FTC accused Du Pont of introducing anti-leak Zerex without having conducted adequate scientific tests to determine whether or not it would or could cause damage to automobile cooling systems under ordinary conditions of use.

National publicity

The FTC announcement received wide publicity. A national TV network news show reproduced the whole commercial in the context of its being "faked." Also, *The New York Times* printed a two-column illustration of the "faked commercial." *Business Week* reported the proposed complaint on December 5, 1970, and quoted Du Pont as having tested 6 million cars during the 1968 and 1969 winters. These cars produced only 600 complaints of clogging which Du Pont said were caused by rusted, corroded radiators.[1] A national telephone survey revealed that approximately 49 percent of all U.S. car owners were aware of the FTC release, and about half of them accepted the charges as entirely or partially true.

INITIAL BARGAINING

This section describes the important interactions between the FTC, Du Pont, and BBDO. The bargaining is given in chronological order.

1970 actions

On November 30, a copy of the notice to issue a complaint by the FTC was received by Du Pont. Du Pont contacted the FTC to determine if a

---

[1] "FTC Ties a Can to a Zerex Ad," *Business Week,* December 5, 1970, p. 30.

consent order could be negotiated. The FTC indicated willingness to negotiate.

On December 8, the FTC was officially advised by Du Pont and BBDO that they were interested in negotiating a consent agreement.

On December 23, Du Pont met with a representative of the FTC staff to discuss terms of a consent agreement. This informal discussion revealed that the FTC was willing to view a demonstration to resolve the questions on effect of pressure and circulation rates, as well as the issue involving the location of leaks in a real-world cooling system. It was clarified that the FTC claimed Zerex may cause damage by plugging heater cores, coating radiator caps which could cause them to stay slightly open, and causing thermostats to remain slightly open. No claims of damage were being made for radiator cores. The FTC claimed damage may occur with dirty cooling systems—not clean cooling systems. The FTC staff representative indicated that the following had to be included in any consent agreement:

1. Label directions to advise users of Zerex of what could happen if it were added to a dirty cooling system.
2. Label directions on how to clean a dirty cooling system.
3. Advertising copy which stated that label directions should be followed to avoid possible damage.

Du Pont also requested the FTC to extend the hearing date by 30 days to attempt to resolve the issues by a consent agreement.

In the last of December, the FTC began to obtain more data on Zerex field testing. The taxicab company in Philadelphia, which was included in the earlier Zerex tests, was contacted by the FTC and certain information regarding test procedure used, maintenance procedures, and description of the vehicles tested, was requested.

1971 actions

In early January, the Philadelphia taxicab company answered the FTC inquiry with information on vehicle makes, years, and mileage, and a statement that the normal maintenance for cooling systems was to check for fluid levels, leaks, and loose hoses, and a copy of Du Pont's test procedure which did not include back flushing, but did suggest flushing with another Du Pont product.

On January 21, a representative of the FTC staff agreed to visit a Du Pont laboratory to witness a Zerex anti-leak demonstration.

The next day, Du Pont gave the FTC staff representative its proposed consent order. The major points included:

1. Product coverage of the order would be limited to automotive antifreeze.

2. Agreement not to advertise antifreeze which when used under ordinary conditions of use could cause operational problems unless it was clearly and conspicuously disclosed that such problems could occur, and that the procedures which could be employed to prevent such problems would be set forth on antifreeze labels.

This agreement not to advertise antifreeze which could cause problems implied that pretesting would be conducted to determine if, in fact, any problems might arise.

On January 29, a group from the FTC staff visited DuPont to observe a Zerex demonstration. For the demonstration, a standard Plymouth radiator was used which contained a 50 percent solution of Zerex purchased at a retail outlet. The solution was circulated at a pressure of 7½ psi and a rate of 30 gallons per minute. The television can-stabber was used to puncture the radiator. Six of nine holes sealed in 5 seconds or less, while the other three holes sealed in 42, 27, and 17 seconds. This demonstration was similar in nature to the can-stabbing commercial, except it used an automotive radiator.

On February 1, members of the FTC staff indicated that a consent order must include at least, "automotive antifreeze or any other automotive product." Discussions were also held on specific wording.

On February 3, a proposed consent order was agreed to between Du Pont and a representative of the FTC staff. It included the following:

1. All allegations that the can-stabbing commercial was false would be dropped.
2. Product coverage included automotive antifreeze or any other automotive product.
3. Labels would say, "Putting anti-leak antifreeze in a dirty cooling system can lead to operational problems."
4. TV ads would say, "Just dumping antifreeze into dirty cooling systems can lead to problems. Follow directions on the container."

On February 12, the head of the FTC's Bureau of Consumer Protection, Mr. Robert Pitofsky, rejected the proposed consent agreement for the following reasons:

1. It would allow comparison advertising which could result in statements like, "Zerex, like other anti-leak antifreezes can cause operational problems." It was felt by Mr. Pitofsky that Zerex caused more problems than its competitors.
2. It did not include a provision on product testing.

On February 25, a meeting was held between Du Pont and members of the FTC staff to determine if there was any basis for further negotiations. The FTC staff indicated that there was no evidence to support the contention that Zerex caused more problems than its competitors (in contrast to the contention by Mr. Pitofsky), and Du Pont should be able to make a comparative statement. The FTC staff offered to work up proposed wording for the testing portion of the agreement.

In early March, several meetings were held to discuss proposed wording between members of the FTC staff and Du Pont. Du Pont upheld its desire to include a comparative statement about Zerex and other anti-leak antifreezes and planned to use scientific tests to identify potential problems under the normal operation mode of use. The FTC staff preferred broader language which would cover reasonably foreseeable conditions of use. No agreements were reached.

On March 5, Du Pont contacted A. D. Little, Inc., to determine costs and timing for a study at radiator repair shops to gain information on causes of heater and radiator failures.

On March 8, members of the FTC staff visited the studio where the television demonstration was filmed. A re-creation of the can-stabbing demonstration was conducted and worked perfectly.

Another negotiation session was held March 10. The FTC staff members wanted wording like, "Zerex causes operational problems in some vehicles in which it is used." Du Pont didn't agree and another meeting was set up.

On March 12, a second agreement for a consent order was reached between members of the FTC staff and Du Pont. The order included:

1. Wording which said, "Zerex causes problems in some dirty cooling systems."
2. If the FTC could show Zerex causes problems with radiator caps and thermostats, that would be disclosed.
3. Product testing must be adequate to determine if problems were caused in a significant number of vehicles.
4. Can labels would comply with the order within 60 days of the effective date.

On March 17, the proposed consent agreement was signed by Du Pont executives and submitted to the FTC.

The rest of March was spent agreeing with members of the FTC staff on specific details related to implementation of the proposed consent order.

On April 7, can labels complying with the wording contained in the proposed consent decree were ordered.

A letter was sent to the FTC staff on April 21, which stated that Du Pont need not include the wording about problems if it can be shown in the future by scientific tests that no problems occur.

On April 21, a representative of the FTC staff informed Du Pont that the consent order had been signed and forwarded to the head of the Bureau of Consumer Protection, Mr. Pitofsky.

On May 10, Mr. Pitofsky advised Du Pont that while he would forward the proposed agreement to the FTC commissioners, he would recommend against acceptance of the consent order for three reasons:

1. No consumer thinks he has a dirty cooling system, so a disclosure limited to dirty systems will have no effect.
2. Product testing should be conducted to ensure that problems occur in only a minimum number of vehicles.
3. Sixty days is too long a time period to get labels into compliance.

Negotiations were conducted between Du Pont and the FTC on specific wording up until the proposed order was reviewed by the commissioners. On May 19, the commissioners rejected the proposed order. The commissioners wanted wording on labels which stated, "This antifreeze can cause damage in all cars except new ones and those with specially maintained cooling systems." If this wording was not incorporated, litigation was threatened.

On May 20, Du Pont met with the FTC to review the situation. It was reported that the Commission would not accept an order which applied to only dirty cooling systems. Du Pont would not agree that Zerex caused "damage." Du Pont suggested wording which said Zerex may cause problems in some cars that did not have clean cooling systems.

On May 21, the Commission contacted Du Pont with two proposed wordings, either of which would be acceptable.

1. "Zerex . . . can cause damage in some cars that do not have clean cooling systems."
2. "Zerex can cause costly operational problems in some cars that do not have clean cooling systems."

About this time, the results of the A. D. Little study of radiator repair shops became available which indicated that Zerex was not a factor in cooling problems—even in dirty systems.

On June 2, Du Pont met with the FTC to review its technical position on Zerex. Only 1 percent of car owners experienced plugging, which indicated no evidence of plugging by Zerex. The manufacturing tests were reviewed which indicated that the anti-leak spheres could not cause clogging. Du Pont took the position that words such as "harmful," "damage," or "costly operational problems" were not acceptable, and that Du Pont was prepared for litigation.

On June 6, a technical position paper was delivered to the FTC which said that Zerex didn't cause or contribute in any significant way to plugging. Some early production problems were admitted.

On June 25, NBC approved the can-stabbing commercial for 1971 showing, provided the guarantee statement was revised to a one-year satisfaction guarantee or money back.

The negotiations with the FTC had broken down completely by the end of June. The FTC staff advised Du Pont that some form of corrective advertising may be in the formal complaint, but asked if Du Pont would be willing to accept the consent order agreed to in March which included: (1) the wording, "Zerex causes problems in some dirty cooling systems," (2) any use problems would be disclosed, (3) product testing to determine existence of problems, and (4) complying can labels within 60 days of the order. Du Pont agreed to accept the March version of the consent order, provided it would become effective January 1, 1972. The FTC did not respond.

Since nothing was heard from the FTC, the affirmative disclosure of possible problems was dropped from the Zerex labels on July 2.

On July 20, a member of the FTC staff informed Du Pont that a formal complaint would be issued shortly. The new complaint was similar to the proposed complaint except for allegations against the can-stabbing demonstration.

On August 19, Du Pont issued a press release which outlined its technical position on Zerex (Exhibit 1). The results of the study at radiator

EXHIBIT 1
Statement by Dr. Wallace E. Gordon, vice president, the Du Pont Company, in response to a Federal Trade Commission complaint about Anti-Leak "Zerex" Antifreeze

> Du Pont will contest the Federal Trade Commission's complaint in the strongest possible way, while continuing to vigorously market and advertise "Zerex." The FTC admitted its error in the case of the "can-stabbing" demonstration, and we are confident that the Commission will be found wrong again. The threat to ban the product is totally without foundation in fact or in law.
>
> The heart of the Commission's original allegation was that the "can-stabbing" demonstration used to advertise "Zerex" on television was "false, misleading and deceptive." After viewing the commercial demonstration in person and seeing a demonstration in which an actual operating radiator was used, the FTC vindicated the demonstration, saying that it was true and nondeceptive. In the circumstances, Du Pont is at a loss to understand the factual basis of the FTC's continuing complaint, and therefore, is contesting the Commission's action.
>
> Anti-leak "Zerex" cannot and does not cause damage to cooling systems under normal conditions of use. In plugged radiators and

EXHIBIT 1 (*continued*)

heaters analyzed by the company, the polymer in "Zerex," if present at all, was found to constitute only 1 to 5 percent of the plugging material. Ninety-five to 99 percent (a ratio of at least 20 to 1) was the other material—core sand (resulting from the casting of the block), rust and scale, high lead solder corrosion products, bits of rubber and aluminum, stop-leak materials installed by the car manufacturer (ginger root), consumer-type stop leaks (asbestos fiber and a variety of organic materials), grease, and so forth.

Moreover, the particles of the other material were at least twice the size of the largest particles of polymer. Most of the sealer in "Zerex"—about 95 percent—is less than 0.0015 of an inch in diameter. Five percent have diameters from 0.0015 to 0.0020 of an inch. The minimum width of the opening of one slot in a heater core —the smallest passage in a cooling system—is 0.0040 of an inch.

Only four grams of polymer are contained in two gallons of "Zerex," the amount used to protect a normal cooling system. By contrast, other anti-leak materials contain one half to four times as much sealer by volume, with maximum particle size two to four times as large as the largest polymer particle. The polymer in "Zerex" is stabilized and does not bond either to itself or to corrosion products in the cooling system. Thus, the contribution of the polymer in "Zerex" to cooling system damage is nonexistent.

Anti-leak "Zerex" was thoroughly tested before commercialization. In addition to two years of laboratory work, the product was road tested in hundreds of vehicles. These included 458 cars, trucks, and taxicabs prior to national sale, then test marketing during which the product was installed in an estimated 30,000 vehicles. No reports of operational problems were encountered in this experience.

Since national sale started, additional controlled tests have been regularly run, including 14 instrumented test cars at Southwest Research Co. in Houston, Texas. No problems were encountered in these tests. The other test cars were taxicabs, in which "Zerex" was compared with another anti-leak antifreeze product. Two instances of clogged cooling systems were reported for each material and all four cases were found to be highly contaminated systems which would have failed without anti-leak antifreeze.

As with most Du Pont products, research and development programs to improve performance and economics are a continuous effort, and improvements have been made in "Zerex" over the last two years. Our confidence in this value and safety of the product applies to both the original and subsequent formulations.

Du Pont was confident enough in the ability of anti-leak "Zerex" to perform as advertised that it sold the product with an uncondi-

EXHIBIT 1 (*concluded*)

tional moneyback guarantee. In 21 months of commercial sale, the complaint rate for operational problems ran about 0.0001 percent of the 15 million motorists who used the product—amazingly low in the circumstances. All of these problems were found to be caused by excessive dirt, rust, or corrosion, not by "Zerex."

repair shops were given which showed that only 1 percent to 5 percent of the material responsible for plugged radiators was the polymer in Zerex. Ninety-five percent to 99 percent was found to be other materials. The release also said that the FTC had vindicated the can-stabbing demonstration, and Du Pont could not understand the reason for the FTC's continuing complaint.

There was little contact between the FTC and Du Pont from this time until November 1971.

The formal FTC complaint

On November 12, 1971, after almost a year from the initial notification of its intent to issue a complaint, the FTC issued a formal complaint against Du Pont. Specific charges in the complaint were that:

1. Du Pont had advertised that Zerex was effective in sealing leaks without stating or disclosing the fact that it could cause damage to automotive cooling systems or component parts.
2. Du Pont had received information from various sources by which it knew or had reason to believe that use of Zerex could cause damage; and Du Pont continued to market and advertise Zerex without disclosing this to the purchasing public.
3. Du Pont had introduced Zerex onto the market without adequate scientific tests to establish whether or not it would or could cause damage to automotive cooling systems under ordinary conditions of use.

The FTC alleged that by marketing and advertising Zerex, Du Pont represented directly or indirectly that Zerex would not damage cooling systems under ordinary use. The FTC believed that scientific tests had not been used to establish the existence of damage potential. The FTC charged that the Zerex ads were false and misleading and constituted unfair and deceptive acts and practices in violation of Section 5 of the Federal Trade Commission Act.

A hearing was set for January 11, 1972, at which time Du Pont was invited to appear and show cause why an order should not be entered requiring Du Pont to cease and desist from the alleged violation.

The complaint further stated that if the charges in the complaint were found to be true, then the following relief would be ordered:

1. Du Pont shall cease and desist from advertising, offering for sale, selling or distributing a product which causes damage under normal conditions unless Du Pont makes a clear and conspicuous disclosure in all advertisements and on all labels that such damage can occur and further, the type of damage that can occur and any procedure which could be used to prevent the damage.
2. Du Pont shall cease and desist from advertising, offering for sale, selling or distributing a product which has not been the subject of scientific tests, before being placed on the market, to establish that the product will not cause damage under ordinary conditions of use.

Absent from the FTC complaint was any mention of the "can-stabbing" commercial. In fact, in its press release, the Commission stated that, "the demonstration was accurate and not deceptive." The Associated Press released a story on November 17, 1972, and quoted the FTC as saying, "The demonstration was accurate and not deceptive." But the AP went on to report that the FTC had complained that anti-leak Zerex is being marketed while it can damage automobile radiators. The FTC complaint and a subsequent news release had been interpreted to mean that current Zerex could damage cooling systems. In fact, the FTC complaint was based on the 1970 anti-leak Zerex formula which had been revised. A revised AP story was released on November 19, 1972, which correctly reported that it was the early Zerex formulation that caused problems—not the current formulation.

More bargaining

Immediately after the formal FTC complaint was announced, the president of BBDO issued a press release which stated that the can-stabbing demonstration in the Zerex ad had been dropped from the complaint. The release went on to say, "the adverse publicity could have been avoided had the commission [FTC] given us the opportunity to prove the truth and accuracy of the demonstration before making a public announcement."

On November 23, 1971, BBDO sent letters to 13 Michigan members of the Congress, Representatives Marvin L. Esch, Garry Brown, Edward Hutchinson, Gerald R. Ford, Charles E. Chamberlain, Donald W. Riegle, Jr., James Harvey, Guy VanderJagt, Elford A. Cederberg, Phillip E. Ruppe, William S. Broomfield, Jack McDonald, and Senator Robert P.

Griffin. The letters mentioned that the FTC admitted it has "insufficient evidence at the present time," that Zerex as currently formulated can damage cooling systems. The letter stated that "The FTC is blatantly guilty of the same improprieties it so indiscriminately and so often unfairly levels at advertisers and advertising agencies—making unsubstantiated and misleading statements." (See Exhibit 2.)

EXHIBIT 2
Example of a letter sent to a member of Congress by BBDO

November 23, 1971

Dear _____:

You may recall that last December I wrote to you regarding charges made by the FTC against Du Pont de Nemours & Company and my company, BBDO, Inc., for alleged false and misleading advertising of the product Zerex antifreeze.

November 16, 1971, the FTC formally announced it had dropped these charges. Naturally, we are pleased to have received this belated exoneration from the FTC, although its action is unlikely to rectify damage to the reputation of Du Pont, the product, and BBDO.

I have enclosed copies of a statement by Tom Dillon, president of BBDO, which acknowledge the reversal of the FTC position but which also reveals that the FTC is renewing an unproved previous allegation against Du Pont Zerex. In its revised charge, the FTC admits it has "insufficient evidence at the present time" that Zerex as currently formulated can damage cooling systems. In view of the total lack of data to support the latest accusation, one must conclude this new statement is a ploy designed to divert attention from the FTC's admission of error concerning the TV commercial. Indeed, the attached *Detroit Free Press* article, which inaccurately reports the FTC positions, supports our contention that the Commission intentionally tried to confuse the public and the press.

Thus, in both the original charge and the renunciation, the FTC is blatantly guilty of the same improprieties it so indiscriminately and so often unfairly levels at advertisers and advertising agencies —making unsubstantiated and misleading statements.

There is no question that the FTC's "shoot from the hip," "accuse now—research later" approach unnecessarily magnifies consumer discontent with business. It seems to me that the long-term interest of the consumer will not be served by repetition of these questionable FTC practices. It is vital that zealousness by regulatory agencies in protecting the consumer does not turn into an antibusiness vendetta.

EXHIBIT 2 (continued)

I believe that all leaders—governmental and business—who desire a robust, flourishing economy based on our capitalistic system must be alert to excesses and abuses whether they are performed by the regulated or the regulators.

I sincerely hope you will take a few moments to read these brief attachments because this case is an example of FTC policies and attitudes which, if left unchecked, can cause irreparable damage to the foundations of our economic process.

I'd appreciate any comments you might have on this issue.

Warm regards,

John A. Gibbs
Vice President

JAG:dk
Attachments

In a few days, a meeting was arranged by Senator Griffin between BBDO and several FTC commissioners. At that meeting, the procedure which allowed the FTC to publicize an intention to issue a complaint was discussed. The situation at the time was that the FTC could issue a press release announcing its intention to issue a complaint when it had reason to believe that the law had been violated. The thrust of the BBDO discussion was to require the FTC to begin meetings with the manufacturers and advertising agencies of the product and resolve the problem before any public announcement was made. It was decided that a letter would be sent to the FTC chairman by BBDO to formally request that the policy on publicity and press releases be reviewed. In this way, it was hoped that future problems between business and the FTC could be negotiated and solved before they became unnecessarily damaging to consumers, business, or the FTC.

Responses from the congressmen who received the November 23, 1971 letter began to be received. Congressman Gerald R. Ford (R., Mich.) said, "I very much appreciate your views and it does seem to me that the FTC should be slapped down, and hard. . . . Too much irreparable damage is done by FTC when it takes action which must later be revised." Congressman Phillip E. Ruppe (R., Mich.) replied, "your experience would indicate that the administration of consumer protection laws is only as good as the people who must decide how and where changes will be filed."

Congressman Garry VanderJagt (R., Mich.) wrote to the FTC requesting information on the complaint. The FTC responded to him on December 30, 1971 reinforcing the points in the formal complaint. But it stated that the FTC now "seeks an order which would prevent any similar future conduct on Du Pont's part in the marketing of automotive products."

On December 22, 1971, Du Pont officially answered the complaint. Du Pont stated that it was without knowledge and information that Zerex could cause damage, denied that Zerex could cause damage to cooling systems or component parts, denied the allegation that scientific tests had not been conducted or obtained, and denied that its advertising was false, misleading, deceptive, or unfair. Du Pont demanded that the complaint be dismissed.

At this same time, Du Pont requested that the January 11, 1972, hearing date be changed to on or after January 18, 1972, to allow time for a pre-hearing conference to discuss the issues. The rescheduled hearing was set for January 18, 1972, but was subsequently rescheduled for late March 1972.

During January and February 1972, one pre-hearing conference was held at which time the hearing examiner reaffirmed that the "can-stabbing" commercial was absolved, and the complaint was concerned with past production of Zerex. The meeting resulted in a motion from the FTC attorneys to withdraw the Du Pont matter from adjudication to allow disposition by consent order. Because of the motion to proceed with a consent order, the pre-hearing conference which was to precede the original January 11 hearing was postponed indefinitely.

On March 29, the FTC attorneys recommended that the Du Pont matter be withdrawn from adjudication to allow proceeding with a consent order. Du Pont also requested the entire matter be kept on a nonpublic basis until an agreement could be worked out.

On March 17, 1972, the president of BBDO sent a letter to FTC Chairman Miles W. Kirkpatrick. The letter included the chronology of events surrounding the Zerex case. It was suggested that the FTC discontinue the practice of publicizing the issuance of proposed complaints except in cases involving a clear and present danger to health or safety. Further, it was suggested that an order not be part of the complaint. It was suggested that negotiations between the FTC and business could be improved if premature publicity could be eliminated. The letter was an attempt to achieve procedural changes at the FTC. By eliminating early publicity which surrounded the current practice of announcing an intent to file a complaint, the respondent could negotiate with the FTC to resolve the issues. Premature publicity could be very damaging as was experienced in the case of Zerex antifreeze.

Mr. Robert Pitofsky, chief, Bureau of Consumer Protection, Federal

Trade Commission stated during a panel discussion before the American Advertising Federation that the FTC "probably didn't have enough information about Du Pont's side of the issue when it issued a proposed complaint challenging the validity of the demonstration for Zerex." A new procedure had been recently implemented which provided that the commission staff no longer recommends a complaint to the commission until the other side has been afforded the opportunity to argue its side at the staff level. This includes the submission of written materials to the commission so that both arguments are before the commission before a decision is made to proceed with a proposed argument.

On April 14, 1972, the hearing examiner for the case agreed with the recommendation to withdraw from adjudication because Du Pont and the FTC had executed an agreement which contained an order to cease and desist. On April 28, 1972, the FTC issued an order withdrawing the Du Pont Zerex antifreeze matter from adjudication.

The consent order

On June 16, 1972, the FTC announced it had provisionally accepted a consent order which would require Du Pont to disclose any damage potential of its retail automotive products, and not market any retail automotive products in the future unless the product had been tested and it had been determined that no damage would occur under ordinary conditions of use.

Potential damage disclosure

Du Pont was ordered to cease and desist from advertising, offering for sale, selling, or distributing any retail consumer automotive product which under normal use conditions damaged automotive vehicles unless a clear disclosure was placed in all advertising which:

1. Identifies that damage can or might occur.
2. Identifies the make and model in which damage can or might occur.
3. Identifies any procedures which can be used to prevent such damage.

Three defenses were allowed: (1) if Du Pont could establish that it neither knew nor had reason to know that the product was used under the specified condition damage would occur; (2) if Du Pont could show the damage was isolated or unique in nature and it could not be reasonably expected that a large number of vehicles would experience damage; and (3) if Du Pont ceased disseminating any product with any label within 60 days of learning that damage from a product would occur.

Product testing

Du Pont was also ordered to cease and desist from advertising, offering for sale, selling, or distributing any such product unless it has been tested to determine if the product, when used in its intended manner and under ordinary conditions will cause damage to vehicles in which it is used.

On July 24, 1972, the final consent order was published which was the same as the agreement announced June 16, 1972.

Effect on Du Pont

The consent order had no effect on the promotion, advertising, or production of Zerex because all requirements of the consent order had already been incorporated from the beginning by Du Pont.

Breakfast Cereal Industry and the FTC*

On April 26, 1972, the Federal Trade Commission (FTC) issued a complaint against the four largest ready-to-eat cereal companies. This complaint charged that Kellogg, General Mills, General Foods, and Quaker had developed a "shared monopoly" position in the market for ready-to-eat (RTE) breakfast cereals. The complaint further charged that this "shared monopoly" resulted in inflated prices, excess profits and return on investment, suppression of product innovation, and blocking of new competitors from entering the industry. This was deemed to be in violation of Section 5 of the Federal Trade Commission Act. The four companies named in the complaint were asked to respond to the specifics of the complaint.

THE INDUSTRY

Exhibit 1 presents a summary of key facts about the ready-to-eat cereal industry as contained in the FTC complaint. In summary the industry is highly concentrated. The largest four firms hold about 90 percent of industry sales with the largest six companies holding about 98 percent of industry sales. The FTC complaint charged that the four firm concentration ratio (percentage of sales held by the largest four firms) had increased from 84 percent in 1950 to over 90 percent in 1970. The specific actions that resulted in this alleged illegal "shared monopoly" are outlined in the complaint in Exhibit 2.

---

* This case was prepared from public documents based on a suggestion by Professor Michael Pearce of the University of Western Ontario.

THE FEDERAL TRADE COMMISSION (FTC)

The Federal Trade Commission Act of 1914 established a five-person commission to administer the FTC Act. The most important provision of the FTC Act was section 5. It originally read that: "unfair methods of competition in commerce are hereby declared unlawful." Early interpretations of this section did not allow for injury to consumers. It was only injury to competition that was covered. In 1938, section 5 was amended by the *Whealer-Lea Act* to read that: "unfair methods of competition in commerce and unfair or deceptive acts or practices in commerce are hereby declared unlawful."

Section 5 had been successfully used to attack such things as price-fixing, boycotts, exclusive dealing and tying agreements, price discrimination, mergers, bribery, misrepresentation in advertising and promotion, and many other practices.

The FTC was made up of a chairperson and four other commissioners appointed by the president to staggered seven-year terms. The president designated the chairperson. The FTC staff consisted of about 400 lawyers and 200 economists and other professionals. Usually the staff prepared complaints for presentation to a hearing examiner who would also hear the charged parties defense and then render a decision. This decision could be appealed to the five commissioners by either the staff or the defendant. If the commissioners voted to uphold the complaint, they would then order a remedy. Exhibit 3 gives the proposed remedy in the ready-to-eat cereal industry case. At this point the decision of the commissioners could be appealed to the federal courts. It was not uncommon for the Supreme Court to decide whether or not a particular practice was "unfair" and thus illegal.

It was a common practice of the FTC to try and reach agreements with charged parties without going through the formal hearing process. They were hoping to do this in the cereal industry case.

Cases in marketing management

EXHIBIT 1
Key facts on the ready-to-eat cereal industry, as contained in the FTC complaint

Company	Products	Assets 1970	Sales 1970	Rank in sales in United States	Ready-to-eat cereal sales 1970	Percent cereal market	Cereal advertising 1970
Kellogg	RTE cereals, tea, soup, gelatin, pudding	$347 million	$614 million	191	$300 million	45%	$36 million
General Mills	RTE cereals, flour, toys, chemicals, clothes, jewelry	$665 million	Over $1 billion	116	$141 million	21	$19 million
General Foods	RTE cereals, coffee, beverages, frozen food, pet food, desserts	$1.3 billion	Over $2 billion	45	$92 million	16	$9 million
Quaker	RTE cereals, frozen foods, cookies, pet food, chemicals	$391 million	$597 million	195	$56 million	9	$9 million
Nabisco†	RTE cereals, cookies, candy, snack food	$503 million	$868 million	140	$26 million	4	$3 million
Ralston Purina†	RTE cereals, pet food, animal food, snack food, frozen food	$775 million	$1.5 billion	71	Over $20 million*	3	Over $4 million*

* 1969 data.
† Not a party to FTC's complaint.

EXHIBIT 2
Complaint

> The Federal Trade Commission has reason to believe that the party respondents named in the caption hereof, and hereinafter more particularly designated and described, have violated and are now violating the provisions of Section 5 of the Federal Trade Commission Act (Title 15, U.S.C. § 45). Accordingly, the Commission hereby issues this Complaint stating its charges with respect thereto as follows:
>
>   *   *   *   *   *
>
> For at least the past 30 years, and continuing to the present, respondents, and each of them, have engaged in acts or have practiced fore-

EXHIBIT 2 (*continued*)

bearance with respect to the acts of other respondents, the effect of which has been to maintain a highly concentrated, noncompetitive market structure in the production and sale of RTE cereal.

During this period respondents, in maintaining the aforesaid market structure, have been, and are now engaged in, among others, the following acts and practices:

A. BRAND PROLIFERATION, PRODUCT DIFFERENTIATION AND TRADEMARK PROMOTION

Respondents have introduced to the market a profusion of RTE cereal brands. During the period 1950 through 1970 approximately 150 brands, mostly trademarked, were marketed by respondents. Over half of these brands were introduced after 1960. In introducing and promoting these new brands respondents have employed intensive advertising directed particularly to children. Respondents have used advertising to promote trademarks that conceal the true nature of the product.

Respondents artificially differentiate their RTE cereals. Respondents produce basically similar RTE cereals, and then emphasize and exaggerate trivial variations such as color and shape. Respondents employ trademarks to conceal such basic similarities and to differentiate cereal brands. Respondents also use premiums to induce purchases of RTE cereals.

Respondents have steadily increased the level of advertising expenditures for RTE cereals. During the period 1950 through 1970, respondents' aggregate annual advertising expenditures for RTE cereals tripled from $26 million to $81 million. In 1970, respondent's advertising-to-sales ratio for RTE cereals averaged 13 percent.

These practices of proliferating brands, differentiating similar products and promoting trademarks through intensive advertising result in high barriers to entry into the RTE cereal market.

B. UNFAIR METHODS OF COMPETITION IN ADVERTISING AND PRODUCT PROMOTION

1. By means of statements and representations contained in their advertisements, respondents:

In advertisements aimed at children, represent directly or by implication, that their RTE cereals without any other foods enable children to perform the physical activities represented or implied in their advertisements.

In truth and in fact:

Respondents' RTE cereals do not enable children to perform the physical activities represented or implied in their advertisements. A child's ability to perform such physical activities depends on many other factors,

EXHIBIT 2 (*continued*)

including but not limited to general body build, exercise, rest, a balanced diet and age.

2.   By means of statements and representations contained in their advertisements respondents Kellogg, General Mills, and General Foods represent, directly or by implication, that consuming RTE cereal at breakfast:

a.   Will result in loss of body weight without vigorous adherence to a reduced calorie diet.
b.   Will result in maintenance of present body weight even if total caloric intake increases.
c.   Will result in loss or maintenance of body weight without adherence to regular physical exercise.

   In truth and in fact:

a.   Consuming RTE cereal at breakfast will not result in loss of body weight without vigorous adherence to a reduced calorie diet.
b.   Consuming RTE cereal at breakfast will not result in maintenance of body weight even if total caloric intake increases.
c.   Consuming RTE cereal at breakfast will not result in loss or maintenance of body weight without adherence to regular physical exercise.

3.   By means of statements and representations contained in their advertisements respondents General Mills and Kellogg:

a.   Represent, directly or by implication, that failure to eat one of their RTE cereals results in the failure of athletes or others to perform to their full capabilities.
b.   Represent, directly or by implication, that the ingestion of one of their RTE cereals by athletes or others enables them to perform better in their respective activities.

   In truth and in fact:

a.   Failure to eat one of the RTE cereals of such respondents will not result in the failure of athletes or others to perform to their full capabilities.
b.   The ingestion of one of the RTE cereals of such respondents will not enable athletes or others to perform better in their respective activities.

4.   The use by respondents of the aforesaid unfair methods of competition in advertising and product promotion has the capacity and tendency to mislead consumers, particularly children, into the mistaken belief that respondents' RTE cereals are different from other RTE cereals, thereby facilitating artificial differentiation and brand proliferation. These unfair methods of competition have contributed to and enhanced respondents'

EXHIBIT 2 (*continued*)

ability to obtain and maintain monopoly prices and to exclude competitors from the manufacture and sale of RTE cereal.

C. CONTROL OF SHELF SPACE

Kellogg is the principal supplier of shelf space services for the RTE cereal sections of retail grocery outlets. Such services include the selection, placement and removal of RTE cereals and allocation of shelf space for RTE cereals to each respondent and to other RTE cereal producers.

Through such services respondents have interfered with and now interfere with the marketing efforts of other producers of RTE and other breakfast cereals and producers of other breakfast foods. Through such services respondents restrict the shelf positions and the number of facings for Nabisco and Ralston RTE cereals, and remove the RTE cereals of small regional producers.

All respondents acquiesce in and benefit from the Kellogg shelf space program which protects and perpetuates their respective market shares through the removal or controlled exposure of other breakfast food products including, but not limited to, RTE cereal products.

D. ACQUISITION OF COMPETITORS

During the past 70 years numerous acquisitions have occurred in the breakfast cereal industry. One of the effects of these acquisitions was the elimination of significant sources of private label RTE cereal. Among them are the following:

In 1943, General Foods acquired Jersey Cereal Company, a Pennsylvania corporation. Before acquisition by General Foods, Jersey Cereal Company was a substantial competitor in the sale of private label and other RTE cereal.

In 1943, Kellogg leased and controlled the manufacturing facilities of Miller Cereal Company, Omaha, Nebraska, a substantial competitor in the sale of private label and other RTE cereal. In 1958, upon termination of the said leasing agreement, Kellogg purchased the assets of Miller.

In 1946, General Foods acquired the RTE manufacturing facilities of Campbell Cereal Company, Minneapolis, Minnesota, a substantial competitor in the sale of RTE cereal. Following this acquisition, General Foods dismantled the RTE facilities of Campbell and shipped said facilities to South Africa.

The aforesaid acquisitions have enhanced the shared monopoly structure of the RTE cereal industry.

5. Respondents, and each of them, have exercised monopoly power in the RTE cereal market by engaging in the following price and sales promotion practices, among others:

EXHIBIT 2 *(concluded)*

a.   Refrained from challenging each other's decisions to increase prices for RTE cereals, and, in general, acquiesced in or followed the price increases of each of them.
b.   Restricted the use of trade deals and trade-directed promotions for RTE cereals.
c.   Limited the use of consumer-directed promotions for RTE cereals, such as coupons, cents-off deals, and premiums.

   6.   Respondents' acts and practices aforesaid have had the following effects, among others:

a.   Respondents have, individually and collectively, established and maintained artificially inflated prices for RTE cereals.
b.   Respondents have obtained profits and returns on investment substantially in excess of those that they would have obtained in a competitively structured market.
c.   Product innovation has been largely supplanted by product imitation.
d.   Actual and potential competition in the manufacture and sale of RTE cereals has been hindered, lessened, eliminated and foreclosed.
e.   Significant entry in the RTE cereal market has been blockaded for over 30 years.
f.   Meaningful price competition does not exist in the RTE cereal market.
g.   American consumers have been forced to pay substantially higher prices for RTE cereals than they would have had to pay in a competitively structured market.

   7.   Through the aforesaid acts and practices:

a.   Respondents individually and in combination have maintained, and now maintain, a highly concentrated, noncompetitive market structure in the production and sale of RTE cereal, in violation of Section 5 of the Federal Trade Commission Act.
b.   Respondents, individually and collectively, have obtained, shared and exercised, and now share and exercise, monopoly power in, and have monopolized, the production and sale of RTE cereal, in violation of Section 5 of the Federal Trade Commission Act.
c.   Respondents, and each of them, have erected, maintained and raised barriers to entry to the RTE cereal market through unfair methods of competition, in violation of Section 5 of the Federal Trade Commission Act.

   Wherefore, the Premises Considered, the Federal Trade Commission on this 26th day of April, A.D., 1972, issues its complaint against said respondents.

*   *   *   *   *

EXHIBIT 3
Proposed order

Should the Commission conclude from the record developed in any adjudicative proceeding in this matter that the respondents are in violation of Section 5 of the Federal Trade Commission Act as alleged in the Complaint, the Commission may order such relief as is supported by the record and is necessary and appropriate including, but not limited to:

1. Divestiture of assets, including plants and other facilities, for the formation of new corporate entities to engage in the manufacture, distribution and sale of RTE cereals, and such trademarks, brand names and know-how as may be required for, or useful in, such manufacture, distribution, and sale.
2. Licensing of existing brands or trademarks and future brands or trademarks on a royalty-free basis for a specified period of time.
3. Prohibition of acquisitions of stock or assets of firms engaged in the business of manufacturing or selling RTE cereals for a specified period of time.
4. Prohibition of any practices found to be anticompetitive, including but not limited to shelf space services or use of particular methods of selling or advertising acts or practices, and other provisions appropriate to correct or remedy the effects of such anticompetitive practices.
5. Periodic review of the provisions of any order that may be entered.

CASE

38

Sears, Roebuck and Company and the FTC*

In the summer of 1974, the Federal Trade Commission (FTC) charged Sears, Roebuck and Company with deceptive merchandising of its more expensive home appliances. The agency accused the nation's largest retailer of using bait and switch tactics: using a non–bona fide offer for a service or product to draw in a potential buyer who could then be switched to a higher priced service or product. Sears denied the charges and a formal complaint was issued by the FTC.

The rest of this case will provide background on the Sears company and the basis on which the FTC's charges were filed.

HISTORY OF SEARS

Richard Warren Sears entered the mail-order business in 1886 with the founding of the R. W. Sears Watch Company in Minneapolis. By buying discontinued or overstocked lines, the 23-year-old Sears was able to sell profitably for just slightly more than the retail jewelers' cost. As the business grew, Sears moved to Chicago and established a mail-order plant. He was soon joined by a watchmaker named Alvah C. Roebuck. In 1893, the corporate name of the firm became Sears, Roebuck and Company.

In 1925, Sears' business activities were directed toward the retail field by General Robert E. Wood. Wood, as president of Sears, identified the

---

* This case was prepared from Public Documents, from library information, and from interviews with people knowledgeable in the appliance field.

466

trend toward urbanization in the United States. As a result of his theory that neither the downtown department stores nor the mail-order houses were serving the newly developing areas adequately, Sears began opening retail stores. From these beginnings, Sears has grown to a company with sales exceeding $13 billion annually, with more than 840 retail stores.

ORGANIZATION

In terms of merchandising, there are 51 national merchandising managers who report to the merchandising vice president. Each manager is responsible for a given group of products and have reporting to them a retail sales manager, a catalog sales manager, a merchandising controller, and from 6 to 25 buyers. Each buyer is a profit center and determines the source of the product, the purchase price, product design, product research and development, retail price, service, and basically sales and profits. Each buyer receives a bonus based entirely on his annual sales and margin growth.

At the retail level, each store has department heads responsible for the various product groups within the store and they are evaluated as profit centers. These department heads, with the store manager's approval, set the product policies for the store. Since the buyers are evaluated on the basis of the profits these divisions earn, it is reasonable to assume that they have strong incentives to develop a product policy that would maximize the division heads' profits and bonus. From the store manager down to the salespersons, the bonus based on profits is a large part of the total compensation. Many in the industry felt that the heavy bonuses available to the sales force were crucial to Sears' success in the area of appliances.

SEARS' APPLIANCE STRATEGY

It should be noted that appliance sales play an important role in the success of Sears. About one sixth of Sears revenue comes from appliances. Because of the overall importance of the big ticket items, Sears' appliance strategy is an integral part of Sears' corporate strategy. This strategy is based on volume. The higher the volume, the lower the price Sears can demand from its suppliers and the greater the economies of scale (that is, distribution costs). Volume determines costs and margins. The Sears' buyers concentrate on two significant areas in order to get the sales volume and profit growth expected from appliances. First, getting traffic into the stores, and second, selling the middle- and top-of-the-line models. The product development, product line structure, advertising, and sales training and compensation are all geared along these two points and will be described in greater detail below. The FTC began its investigation with these policies.

PRODUCT DEVELOPMENT

The buyers work with just one source for a product line, and try to keep the manufacturers' cost to a minimum in order to control Sears' costs. The buyers and manufacturers engage in two types of research. The first is developing new features or designs for existing products and the second is exploring for totally new processes. The Sears appliance buyers are placed in a dilemma. In order to be competitive, Sears needs the new best selling features. But, every change in the product line increases production costs. The unit costs fall the longer a specific model is produced. With a greater number of models the inventory costs also increase.

With this situation, Sears doesn't take any risks by introducing major new features. Instead, they are satisfied with copying the competitors' best selling features. Although Sears places a heavy emphasis on product development, the research is done to maintain a competitive position rather than to be a leader in technological innovations.

PRODUCT LINE STRUCTURE

The Sears national merchandising manager for home laundry described the product line structure as follows:

> In structuring our product line we pay close attention to the selling strategy used in the stores. We begin with the top of the line, the very best product we can make, with all the most advanced features. We then build a low-priced machine of the same quality as the top-of-the-line, but with fewer features.
>
> After we have established the top-of-the-line and the bottom-of-the-line (our opening price point) we ask, "How many models do we need to fill the gap?" On the one hand, each price point must give the consumer real benefits as compared to the price point immediately below it. On the other hand, the jump between price points must not be so great that the consumer will be unwilling to move up. And we do not want to have too many price points, since every increase in stock keeping units increases inventories. On automatic washing machines, we have six basic price points: $119, $149, $169, $189, $219, and $239. Approximately 60 percent of our sales are between $189 and $219.[1]

This method for determining the product line contains the two key elements of buyer concern—generating traffic and selling the top models. Set-

---

[1] E. R. Corey, and S. H. Star, *Organization Strategy: A Marketing Approach* (Boston: Harvard Business School, Division of Research, Harvard University Press, 1971), p. 302.

ting the bottom-of-the-line model price below the competition provides a means of drawing customers into the stores and the specific price points facilitate trading up to a higher priced model.

ADVERTISING POLICY

Advertisements are usually on the lowest priced model of a line to attract shoppers into the stores. Additionally, Sears frequently runs heavily advertised sales. It was not uncommon for Sears to run over ten sales per year on the low-priced items in an appliance line.

SALES TRAINING AND COMPENSATION

The training process at Sears utilizes workbooks, filmstrips, and quizzes to ensure that each salesperson has a full understanding of the job. The National Headquarters in Chicago provides each store with current training materials. There are five stages of retail training at Sears:

1. Induction. A simple introduction to Sears and the particular store where the person will be working.
2. Basic. An introduction to the particular department where the person will be working and training in various sales techniques.
3. Advanced. Advanced training of sales techniques and the selling of specialized products and services.
4 Current sales training. Keeping the sales force up to date on new products and policies.
5. Management training. Training for divisional management.

The most important area for the purpose of this case is the basic training. This is where the appliance sales force learns the key to being successful—trading up. The main emphasis of the training program is that trading up is the best sales technique for adding to the salesperson's commission and that by trading up, the customers are best satisfied. Part of the rational behind trading up is that the customers really don't know what they want without knowing what is available. Therefore, they should be exposed to the very best. If that model is overdesigned for their needs, the salesperson can start trading down by subtracting features on each lower priced model.

If a customer comes into the store for a special advertised appliance, the salesperson is instructed to take the customer first to the advertised model. However, before closing the sale the salesperson would try to show the best available model.

The sales force at the time of the FTC's investigation was compensated by a base salary and a bonus based on sales quotas and commissions. The commissions varied from department to department but were at least 9 percent for all sewing machines and some other appliances. The sales quotas were for the higher priced models in each line.

BAIT AND SWITCH ADVERTISING

Bait and switch advertising falls under Section 5 of the Federal Trade Commission Act. This section prohibits unfair methods of competition and unfair and deceptive acts and practices in commerce.

The FTC Trade Rule Guide defines bait advertising as:

> . . . an alluring but insincere offer to sell a product or service which the advertiser in truth does not intend or want to sell. Its purpose is to switch consumers from buying the advertised merchandise, in order to sell something else, usually at a higher price. . . . The primary aim of a bait advertisement is to obtain leads as to persons interested in buying merchandise of the type so advertised.

Exhibit 1 contains the full presentation.

EXHIBIT 1
FTC bait-and-switch guidelines

BAIT ADVERTISING DEFINED

Bait advertising is an alluring but insincere offer to sell a product or service which the advertiser in truth does not intend or want to sell. Its purpose is to switch consumers from buying the advertised merchandise, in order to sell something else, usually at a higher price or on a basis more advantageous to the advertiser. The primary aim of a bait advertisement is to obtain leads as to persons interested in buying merchandise of the type so advertised.

BAIT ADVERTISEMENT

No advertisement containing an offer to sell a product should be published when the offer is not a bona fide effort to sell the advertised product.

INITIAL OFFER

a. No statement or illustration should be used in any advertisement which creates a false impression of the grade, quality, make, value, currency of model, size, color, usability, or origin of the product offered, or which may otherwise misrepresent the product in such a manner that later, on disclosure of the true facts, the purchaser may be switched from the advertised product to another.

b. Even though the true facts are subsequently made known to the buyer, the law is violated if the first contact or interview is secured by deception.

EXHIBIT 1 *(continued)*

DISCOURAGEMENT OF PURCHASE OF ADVERTISED MERCHANDISE

No act or practice should be engaged in by an advertiser to discourage the purchase of the advertised merchandise as part of a bait scheme to sell other merchandise.

Among acts or practices which will be considered in determining if an advertisement is a bona fide offer are:

a.   The refusal to show, demonstrate, or sell the product offered in accordance with the terms of the offer.
b.   The disparagement by acts or words of the advertised product or the disparagement of the guarantee, credit terms, availability of service, repairs or parts, or in any other respect, in connection with it.
c.   The failure to have available at all outlets listed in the advertisement a sufficient quantity of the advertised product to meet reasonably anticipated demands, unless the advertisement clearly and adequately discloses that supply is limited and/or the merchandise is available only at designated outlets.
d.   The refusal to take orders for the advertised merchandise to be delivered within a reasonable period of time.
e.   The showing or demonstrating of a product which is defective, unusable or impractical for the purpose represented or implied in the advertisement.
f.   Use of a sales plan or method of compensation for salesmen or penalizing salesmen, designed to prevent or discourage them from selling the advertised product.

SWITCH AFTER SALE

No practice should be pursued by an advertiser, in the event of sale of the advertised product, or "unselling" with the intent and purpose of selling other merchandise in its stead.

Among acts or practices which will be considered in determining if the initial sale was in good faith, and not a stratagem to sell other merchandise, are:

a.   Accepting a deposit for the advertised product, then switching the purchaser to a higher priced product.
b.   Failure to make delivery of the advertised product within a reasonable time or to make a refund.
c.   Disparagement by acts or words of the advertised product, or the disparagement of the guarantee, credit terms, availability of service, repairs, or in any other respect, in connection with it.
d.   The delivery of the advertised product which is defective, unusable or impractical for the purpose represented or implied in the advertisement.

Bait and switch schemes are evidenced by such practices as refusal to show the advertised product, disparagement of the product, failure to have reasonable quantity available for sale, refusal to take orders for delivery within a reasonable time, demonstration or delivery of a defective product, discouraging salespersons from selling advertised products, attempts to switch the customer to another product after accepting a deposit, or failure to make delivery within a reasonable time.

Before the FTC can prosecute a case, it must appear to the commission that an unfair or deceptive act or practice has occurred and that a proceeding to stop the violation "would be to the interest of the public."

FTC ALLEGATIONS

The FTC's complaint charged Sears with misleading sales practices that arose from the retailer's commission schedule for sales personnel. Specifically, Sears was charged with using bait and switch advertising tactics in the selling of sewing machines and laundry appliances.

The example provided by the FTC pertained to the low-priced sewing machines. Allegedly, Sears advertised the $58 machines to attract customers, but the salespersons later made disparaging statements about the advertised model in an effort to sell more expensive sewing machines.

In addition to seeking an order requiring Sears to halt the deceptive practices, the FTC sought an unusual remedy that would require a change in the compensation system for salespersons. Exhibit 2 presents a copy of key sections of the complaint.

The Sears senior vice president for merchandising, James W. Button, immediately denied the charges and countered the specific example by stating that Sears sold 80,000 of its $58 sewing machines during the period under investigation by the FTC. Additionally, he said the $58 machine was the third best seller of more than 20 different models in Sears' line. Button concluded, "the facts in this case are so totally different from the facts of bait and switch cases brought by the commission in the past that Sears can only conclude that the commission is seeking to get a new and previously unannounced theory of law."[2]

One of the five FTC commissioners, Mayo J. Thompson, cast a dissenting vote. Thompson felt that the complaint failed to address the question of whether the products the customers were switched to were themselves good or bad buys and therefore there had been no showing of probable consumer injury.

In February 1976, the case was presented to the FTC hearing board.

---

[2] K. Bacon and D. Elsner, "FTC Charges Sears with a Sales Ruse, Urges New System for Paying Salesmen," *The Wall Street Journal,* July 11, 1974, p. 3.

EXHIBIT 2
Key sections of the complaint

Paragraph three. In the course and conduct of its business as afore-said, respondent ships, and causes to be shipped, sewing machines, washers and dryers, and other major home appliances to said retail department stores for sale to the purchasing public. Advertising and promotional material is prepared or caused to be prepared by respondent in Chicago, Illinois, and transmitted to respondent's retail department stores for their use. In the course and conduct of its business as aforesaid, respondent now causes and for some time past has caused, the publication of said advertising, concerning sewing machines, washers and dryers, and other major home appliances in newspapers of general circulation. Respondent further engages in business, in commerce, consisting of the transmission and receipt of letters, invoices, reports, contracts and other documents of a commercial nature between respondent's headquarters and its retail department stores in the various states, and at all times mentioned herein has maintained, a substantial course of trade in said merchandise in commerce, as "commerce" is defined in the Federal Trade Commission Act.

Paragraph four. Typical and illustrative, but not all inclusive, of the major home appliances advertised and the statements made in such advertisements are the following:

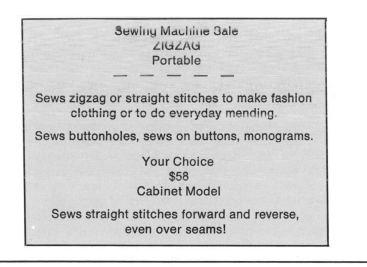

Sewing Machine Sale
ZIGZAG
Portable

— — — — —

Sews zigzag or straight stitches to make fashion clothing or to do everyday mending.

Sews buttonholes, sews on buttons, monograms.

Your Choice
$58
Cabinet Model

Sews straight stitches forward and reverse, even over seams!

EXHIBIT 2 *(continued)*

Portable Zigzag Sewing Machine
from Sears

$58

Sews on buttons, sews buttonholes;
does zigzag or straight stitching.

Monograms, appliques, other fancy work
for household linens, gifts.

Sews forward and reverse for her
convenience.

Paragraph five. Through the use of the aforesaid statements and others not specifically set out herein, respondent has represented, directly and by implication, that the offers set forth in said advertisements are bona fide offers to sell the advertised sewing machines, washers and dryers, and other major home appliances at the prices mentioned in said advertisements.

Paragraph six. In truth and in fact, said offers were not, and are not bona fide offers to sell respondent's sewing machines, washers and dryers, and other major home appliances at the advertised prices, but, to the contrary were, and are, made to induce prospective purchasers to visit respondent's retail department stores.

Therefore, the statements and representations as set forth in paragraphs four and five were, and are, false, misleading and deceptive.

Paragraph seven. When prospective purchasers visit respondent's retail department stores in response to respondent's aforesaid advertisements and attempt to purchase the advertised sewing machines, washers and dryers, and other major home appliances at the advertised prices, respondent's salesmen make no effort to sell the advertised major home appliances, but, in fact, disparage the advertised sewing machines, washers and dryers, and other major home appliances in a manner calculated to discourage the purchase thereof, and attempt to, and often do, sell other sewing machines, washers and dryers, and other major home appliances to said prospective purchasers at higher prices. By way of disparaging said major home appliances, respondent's salesmen point out certain features that the advertised major home appliances are lacking without disclosing the absence of these features in respondent's aforesaid advertising. Among and typical, but not all inclusive of the disparaging statements and representations made by respondent's salesmen are the following:

EXHIBIT 2 (*continued*)

1. The advertised sewing machines are noisy and not quiet running.
2. Certain of the aforesaid sewing machines will not sew straight stitch, zigzag stitch, or in reverse.
3. The advertised sewing machines do not have respondent's standard sewing machine guarantee and are not guaranteed for as long a period of time as respondent's more expensive sewing machine models.
4. Prospective purchasers will find it difficult to adjust the advertised sewing machines to sew over seams in material on different thicknesses of material.
5. The advertised sewing machine will not sew buttonholes.
6. None of the advertised sewing machines are available for sale; and if the advertised machines are ordered, there will be long delays in delivery.

Paragraph eight.   In truth and in fact, the aforesaid disparaging statements and representations made by respondent's salesmen have the effect of discouraging prospective purchasers from purchasing the advertised sewing machines, washers and dryers, and other major home appliances and inducing said prospective purchasers to purchase other sewing machines, washers and dryers, and other major home appliances at higher prices.

Paragraph nine.   Respondent has advertised certain of its lower priced models of sewing machines, washers and dryers, and other major home appliances with the intention that respondent's salesmen will be able to make misleading comparisons between the lower priced models and higher priced models of said appliances.

Paragraph ten.   Respondent uses a method of compensating its salesmen of sewing machines, washers and dryers, and other major home appliances that rewards said salesmen for selling higher priced sewing machines, washers and dryers, and other major home appliances. At the same time respondent deters said salesmen from selling the advertised sewing machines, washers and dryers, and other major home appliances. This combination of circumstances has forced or encouraged respondent's salesmen of sewing machines, washers and dryers, and other major home appliances to use bait and switch sales tactics such as those described in paragraphs seven, eight, and nine.

Paragraph eleven.   In the course and conduct of their aforesaid business, and at all times mentioned herein, respondent has been, and now is, in substantial competition in commerce, with corporations, firms and individuals, engaged in the sale and distribution of sewing machines, washers and dryers, and other major home appliances of the same general kind and nature as those sold by respondent.

Paragraph twelve.   The use by respondent of the aforesaid false, misleading and deceptive statements, representations, acts and practices has

EXHIBIT 2 (continued)

had, and now has the tendency and capacity to mislead and deceive a substantial portion of the purchasing public into the erroneous and mistaken belief that said statements and representations were and are true, and to induce a substantial number thereof to purchase respondent's said sewing machines, washers and dryers, and other major home appliances at higher prices than said members of the purchasing public had intended to pay by reasons of said erroneous and mistaken belief.

Paragraph thirteen. The aforesaid acts and practices of respondent, as herein alleged, were and are all to the prejudice and injury of the public and of respondent's competitors, unfair methods of competition in commerce and unfair and deceptive acts and practices in commerce, in violation of Section 5 of the Federal Trade Commission Act.

NOTICE OF CONTEMPLATED RELIEF

Should the Commission conclude from the record developed in any adjudicative proceeding in this matter that the respondent, Sears, Roebuck & Co., is in violation of Section 5 of the Federal Trade Commission Act, as alleged in the Complaint, the Commission may order such relief as is supported by the record and is necessary and appropriate, including, but not limited to:

1. Prohibition of offering to sell any product or service when such offer is not a bona fide offer to sell such product or service at the stated price.
2. Prohibition of disparagement or refusal to sell any sewing machine, washer and dryer, or other major home appliance advertised by respondent.
3. Prohibition of the utilization of any demonstration or display of any advertised sewing machine, washer and dryer, or other major home appliance in which the advertised major home appliance is made to appear defective in some way.
4. Prohibition of the failure to have available at all outlets listed in advertisements for sewing machines, washers and dryers, or other major home appliances a sufficient quantity of the advertised major home appliances to meet reasonably anticipated demands.
5. Prohibition of refusal to take orders for advertised sewing machines, washers and dryers, and other major home appliances.
6. Prohibition of the making, directly or by implication, orally or in writing, any false, misleading or deceptive comparisons between the advertised sewing machines, washers and dryers, and other major home appliances and other more expensive major home appliances of the same type.
7. Prohibition of the failure to disclose, clearly and conspicuously, within the text of each advertisement for sewing machines, washers

EXHIBIT 2 (concluded)

and dryers, and other major home appliances that respondent is the subject of a Federal Trade Commission cease and desist order relating to bait and switch sales tactics.

8. Prohibition of the utilization of any system of compensation for salesmen of sewing machines, washers and dryers, and other major home appliances that is linked in any way to or coordinated with any of the following:

   a. Product sales quotas which discriminate against low margin, advertised items.

   b. Employee discipline or retention programs which discriminate against sales of advertised merchandise.

   c. Use of bait and switch tactics.

9. Requirement that each purchaser of a "Major home appliance" (as defined in the complaint accompanying this Notice of Contemplated Relief) other than the lowest priced advertised major home appliance, be given notice and the right to cancel such purchase in accordance with the provisions of the Trade Regulation Rule concerning a Cooling-Off Period for Door-to-Door Sales, 37 Fed. Reg. 22934, October 18, 1972. This requirement applies to all "sale" advertising for the duration of the "sale" and for three (3) business days after any other advertisement is published.

10. Any other provisions appropriate to correct or remedy the effects of anticompetitive practices engaged in by respondent.

11. Requirement that appropriate persons be notified of the terms of the Order and that periodic compliance reports to be filed with the Commission.

PART IX

This section contains five cases which are comprehensive in nature, requiring the student to make a number of decisions in several different marketing decision areas. Thus, a great deal of integration is necessary. A decision in one of the marketing areas may have a significant impact on the other decisions which must be made to complete the marketing program.

In developing a complete marketing program for a product, one must start with the firm's overall goals and objectives. Then all the environmental factors such as demand, competition, marketing laws, distribution alternatives, and cost structure must be analyzed. At this point, a number of opportunities as well as potential problems will have been identified, and specific marketing objectives can be established.

The marketer must make a clear definition of the target market(s) to be served. This can be determined only after a thorough evaluation of all the alternative segments of the market, their needs, wants, attitudes and behavior, the strengths and weaknesses of the firm's products and those of competitors, and the potential profitability of various alternatives.

The next step in developing the marketing program is to search for the optimal marketing mix; that is, what is the best combination of product strategy, pricing strategy, promotion strategy, and distribution strategy? Typically, there will be a number of possible alternatives for each of these, so the marketer must determine the interrelationships among

MARKETING PROGRAMS

479

them and choose the optimal combination based upon a complete situation analysis.

The last step in the development of a marketing program is to create a plan for implementing the program. Without adequate implementation, even the best designed plans will fail.

CASE

39

A&W Drive-Ins (Fundy) Limited*

"It is all psychological—when he picks up that burger it feels pretty good. The merchandising appeal of that larger hamburger and the weight in comparison to McDonald's is significant—it is noticed by the customer. A&W isn't strong enough in the market that we can afford to tinker with the portioning, which is definitely one of our strong points." These thoughts passed through Mr. Ed Drayson's mind in 1973 as he sat preparing a set of recommendations for the company's board of directors. The company was facing rapidly rising food and operating costs in its A&W outlets in the Atlantic Provinces of Canada. These rising costs were threatening to drastically cut the contribution these outlets made to company overhead and profit.

The cost pressures were particularly severe in A&W's hamburger line, where meat costs were expected to be 40 percent higher in the summer of 1973 than they had been in the fall of 1972. The company's problems were compounded by the increasing competition posed by McDonald's and other fast-food operators, who were aggressively expanding in the A&W (Fundy) market area.

THE COMPANY

Mr. Drayson was the president of A&W Drive-Ins (Fundy) Limited, and was directly responsible for the firm's A&W operations. Mr. Drayson's

---

* This case was written by Adrian B. Ryans, Assistant Professor of Marketing, Stanford University. Used with permission of the author and the University of Western Ontario.

office was located in Moncton, New Brunswick, although the company's head office staff, whose main function was to provide accounting services for the company, was located in Toronto. All the managers of A&W outlets in the Atlantic Provinces reported directly to Mr. Drayson. The company was also involved in a number of non-A&W activities. Mr. Harry Brathwaite, the chairman of the board, spent much of his time supervising these activities.

A&W Drive-Ins (Fundy) was a franchisee of A&W Food Services of Canada Limited which held the A&W franchise for Canada. A&W (Fundy) operated eight A&W outlets in the Atlantic Provinces, and five outlets in Ontario. There were also a number of other A&W operators in the Atlantic Provinces, but none had franchises in the cities served by A&W (Fundy). The locations of the eight outlets in New Brunswick, Nova Scotia, and Prince Edward Island are shown in Exhibit 1. Monthly sales by outlet for 1971, 1972, and the first three months of 1973 are shown in Exhibit 2. All outlets in the Atlantic Provinces, except Oromocto, were

EXHIBIT 1
Location of A&W (Fundy) units

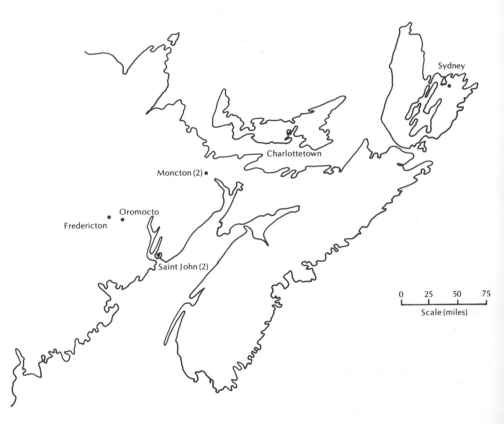

drive-in restaurants. The Oromocto restaurant provided inside seating in a shopping centre.

For each unit A&W (Fundy) had opened it had entered into a license agreement with A&W Food Services of Canada. Basically each franchise agreement granted the franchisee a license to operate a drive-in restaurant and to use the A&W trademarks in advertising and on menus, packaging and signs in the preparation and sale of A&W beverages, products, and approved menu items. The license agreement remained in effect for a 20-year term, provided the franchisee met the terms of the agreement— the major ones being:

The franchisee was to pay an initial fee of $2,500 and an annual service fee of approximately 1 percent of gross sales.

The restaurant was to be constructed, at the franchisee's expense, in accordance with plans and specifications provided by A&W Food Services of Canada.

The equipment for the restaurant had to be purchased from the franchisor.

The operator of the restaurant was required to attend an A&W restaurant management training course.

The franchisee was required to purchase all uniforms, packaging materials and special A&W concentrates, syrups, bases, and spices from the franchisor.

The recent agreements required the franchisee to contribute 1.50 percent of his gross sales to a national advertising and promotional fund. Some of the agreements required contributions to a regional advertising fund. Most agreements also specified a minimum percentage of gross sales that must be spent on local promotion and advertising.

Unlike a number of other fast-food franchisors, A&W Food Services of Canada did allow the franchisee some latitude in the selection of his menu. He was required to serve certain products, such as the "Burger Family," but he was also allowed to select items from a list of optional products, and he could, if authorized by A&W Food Services of Canada, offer specialty items. "Fried clams" was one such item on the menu of the A&W (Fundy) outlets. The menu in use in the A&W (Fundy) outlets in April 1973 is shown in Exhibit 3.

Commenting on the terms of the franchise agreement, Mr. Drayson noted that the costs of supplies, while marked up by the franchisor, were not greatly different from the prices A&W (Fundy) would have to pay in the market, given its smaller purchasing power. With regards to the requirements for local advertising and promotion Mr. Drayson noted that it was not constraining, since A&W (Fundy) typically allocated a much

EXHIBIT 2
Monthly sales by unit—1971–1973

1971 Sales

	Jan.	Feb.	March	April	May
Charlottetown....................	$ 17,503	$ 18,740	$ 21,594	$ 27,139	$ 29,235
Fredericton......................	20,405	18,706	24,182	32,027	36,675
Sydney..........................	22,196	21,594	26,534	31,785	34,851
Saint John No. 1................	20,157	19,928	24,548	28,563	31,432
Saint John No. 2................	—	—	—	—	—
Moncton No. 1..................	11,787	12,268	13,782	18,096	21,074
Moncton No. 2..................	9,380	9,956	11,573	15,006	17,959
Oromocto.......................	16,408	14,006	15,886	16,182	16,710
	$117,836	$115,198	$138,099	$168,798	$187,936

1972 Sales

	Jan.	Feb.	March	April	May
Charlottetown....................	$ 20,702	$ 21,728	$ 25,690	$ 34,638	$ 34,776
Fredericton......................	19,091	18,890	23,569	35,592	36,048
Sydney..........................	21,176	17,739	25,025	30,202	35,998
Saint John No. 1................	21,067	19,975	24,655	33,339	36,497
Saint John No. 2................	22,523	19,712	24,090	32,407	35,245
Moncton No. 1..................	14,942	13,559	16,764	24,350	26,673
Moncton No. 2..................	12,572	11,246	14,197	20,314	22,611
Oromocto.......................	13,875	13,399	15,950	16,255	16,953
	$145,948	$136,248	$169,940	$227,097	$244,801

1973 Sales

	Jan.	Feb.	March
Charlottetown....................	$ 30,390	$ 28,243	$ 42,264
Fredericton......................	21,754	23,534	34,311
Sydney..........................	26,636	20,719	30,095
Saint John No. 1................	24,860	23,245	28,031
Saint John No. 2................	23,473	22,369	29,970
Moncton No. 1..................	17,737	16,878	23,578
Moncton No. 2..................	15,898	14,257	22,830
Oromocto.......................	14,825	14,528	19,482
	$175,573	$163,773	$230,561

higher percentage of sales to local advertising and promotion. In summarizing, Mr. Drayson pointed out that the value of a franchise and the reasonableness of the terms depend ultimately on the attention to, and the skill of the national firm in, building the A&W image, creating effective national advertising and promotion, and providing operating and menu suggestions. He indicated that he felt that the national advertising and promotion programme of A&W Food Services of Canada could be improved.

THE COMPETITION

Most of the A&W outlets operated in a highly competitive environment, with competition ranging from local takeouts to such national chains as

June	July	Aug.	Sept.	Oct.	Nov.	Dec.	Total
$ 28,806	$ 43,320	$ 43,435	$ 31,357	$ 31,965	$ 29,879	$ 23,387	$ 346,360
29,639	38,810	38,230	35,954	37,354	37,144	25,553	374,679
34,709	36,242	35,535	29,139	29,923	29,244	24,853	356,605
30,338	34,766	34,562	31,062	34,545	34,390	24,836	349,127
—	—	—	—	—	—	26,295	26,295
20,433	24,587	24,895	21,757	22,366	20,635	17,074	228,754
18,267	24,518	24,164	19,634	20,095	18,926	14,818	204,296
18,042	25,307	23,465	17,665	21,212	16,818	16,833	218,534
$180,234	$227,550	$224,286	$186,568	$197,460	$187,036	$173,649	$2,104,650

June	July	Aug.	Sept.	Oct.	Nov.	Dec.	Total
$ 40,496	$ 61,649	$ 58,361	$ 38,499	$ 36,301	$ 33,877	$ 33,707	$ 440,424
38,181	43,070	40,555	38,478	33,413	28,789	24,639	380,315
39,186	43,082	43,353	33,848	30,096	31,167	31,329	382,201
35,001	40,783	37,660	31,339	31,543	28,687	25,957	366,503
34,725	36,994	36,164	30,128	28,956	27,123	25,384	353,451
28,319	32,738	31,598	27,013	24,540	21,266	19,620	281,382
25,765	31,822	31,520	24,857	21,693	18,864	16,976	252,437
20,531	24,951	22,573	17,253	17,224	16,903	16,424	212,291
$262,204	$315,089	$301,784	$241,415	$223,766	$206,676	$194,036	$2,669,004

McDonald's, Harvey's, and Kentucky Fried Chicken. Some of the local chains such as Deluxe French Fries in Moncton were well established with good local reputations.

The toughest competitive environment existed in Moncton, where there were two A&W's, two McDonald's, one Harvey's, two Kentucky Fried Chicken stores and three Deluxe French Fries outlets. A&W (Fundy) had opened its first drive-in in the Atlantic Provinces in Moncton in July 1965. Harvey's had been the first national competitor to follow A&W into Moncton, which it did in 1968. The second A&W drive-in was opened in 1969 and was located about two miles from the first one. The opening of the second outlet had a significant impact on the sales of the first one. McDonald's entered Moncton with two outlets in 1970. The McDonald's were

EXHIBIT 3
April 1973 menu

BURGERS

PAPA BURGER 64
2 Patties Meat

MAMA BURGER .44
Single Patty

BABY BURGER .24
(Cheese on above 5¢, Bacon 5¢)

TEEN BURGER .59
SINGLE PATTY · LETTUCE · TOMATO
BACON · MAYONNAISE · CHEESE ·
TOASTED SESAME SEED BUN

**ALL SERVED WITH YOUR CHOICE OF
MUSTARD, KETCHUP, PICKLES
and ONIONS**

BEVERAGES

A & W ROOT BEER . . . . .20 .15
Baby Root Beer free to children under 6

A & W ORANGE . . . . .20 .15

ICE CREAM FLOAT . . . . .10 extra

MILK SHAKES .35

MILK . . . . .30 .20

COFFEE 15

TEA 15

HOT CHOCOLATE 15

	Gal.	½ Gal.	Qt.
Root Beer	.95	.60	.35
Orange	1.00	.80	.50
	Plus Deposit		

SIDE ORDERS

COLE SLAW, side order 15

HOT DOG 34

WHISTLE DOG .49
With bacon, cheese & relish

FRENCH FRIES, side order . . . . .19 .29

ONION RINGS 35

FISH & CHIPS 65

FRIED CLAMS (When available) 75

FRIED CLAMS & CHIPS 95

**CONEY SAUCE, on Hot Dogs
Burgers and Fries** 15

STRAWBERRY SHORTCAKE 39

APPLE TURNOVER 20

SUNDAE 25
Chocolate or Strawberry

ICE CREAM 15

CHICKEN

CHUBBY DINNER 1.19
3 Pcs. Chicken, French Fries

CHUBBY JUNIOR 89
2 Pcs. Chicken, French Fries

CHUBBY "6" 1.79
6 Pcs. Chicken

CHUBBY "12" 2.99
12 Pcs. Chicken

CHUBBY "18" 4.49
18 Pcs. Chicken

FAMILY PAK FRENCH FRIES 95

COLE SLAW
½ pint 30   1 pint 50

**ALL ORDERS CAN BE PREPARED
FOR TAKE OUT**

A & W DRIVE-INS (FUNDY) LIMITED

(See List of Maritime Locations on Back)

both located within one-quarter mile of the two A&W outlets. In fact every major competitor in Moncton had a store located within about one-half mile of A&W's Moncton No. 1 drive-in. Until McDonald's entered Moncton, the sales in the two A&W drive-ins had been expanding steadily. After the opening, A&W's sales in Moncton dropped and then gradually began to rise again. The impact of the opening was such that A&W's sales in the year following the opening were about equal to those in the previous year.

In April 1973, there were approximately 300 A&W outlets in Canada. By comparison there were less that 100 McDonald's units, although McDonald's had announced that by the end of 1973 they planned to have 140 units in operation. Mr. Drayson knew that the McDonald's operation was in many ways different from his own A&W operation. He felt that some of these differences were reflected in two McDonald's pro forma income statements shown in Exhibit 4. These income statements were from 1972 material provided by McDonald's to prospective franchisees, and

EXHIBIT 4

McDonald's typical Canadian pro forma statement

		Percent		Percent
Net Sales...........................	$400,000	100.0%	$600,000	100.0%
Food.................................	134,000	33.5	201,000	33.5
Paper................................	20,000	5.0	30,000	5.0
Total Cost.......................	$154,000	38.5%	$231,000	38.5%
Gross Profit.....................	246,000	61.5	369,000	61.5
Controllable Expenses:				
Crew labor.........................	69,200	17.3	94,200	15.7
Management labor...................	19,200	4.8	19,200	3.2
Payroll deductions.................	5,500	1.4	6,500	1.1
Travel expenses....................	750	0.2	750	0.1
Advertising........................	16,000	4.0	24,000	4.0
Promotion..........................	4,000	1.0	6,000	1.0
Outside services...................	2,800	0.7	2,900	0.5
Linen..............................	2,000	0.5	2,200	0.4
Operating supplies.................	3,500	0.9	4,000	0.7
Maintenance and repairs............	4,000	1.0	4,500	0.7
Utilities..........................	8,000	2.0	8,500	1.4
Office and telephone expenses......	900	0.2	1,000	0.2
Miscellaneous......................	750	0.2	850	0.1
Total Controllables..............	$136,600	34.2%	$174,600	29.1%
Noncontrollable Expenses				
Rent*..............................	34,000	8.5	51,000	8.5
Service fee........................	12,000	3.0	18,000	3.0
Legal and accounting...............	700	0.2	700	0.1
Insurance..........................	1,600	0.4	1,600	0.3
Taxes and licenses.................	4,800	1.2	4,800	0.8
Equipment lease....................	720	0.2	720	0.1
Depreciation and amortization†.....	9,625	2.4	9,625	1.6
Total Noncontrollables..........	$ 63,445	15.9%	$ 86,445	14.4%
Total Operating Expenses........	200,045	50.0	261,045	43.5
Net Operating Income............	45,955	11.5	107,955	18.0
Cash Flow........................	$ 55,580	13.9%	$117,580	19.6%

All the above figures are estimates and can change due to many factors.

* Note that McDonald's owns the land and building.

† Based over 10 years on assets, 20 years on fees.

were said to represent typical pro forma statements for McDonald's units in Canada.

In April 1973, McDonald's had one outlet in Fredericton which had opened in June 1971 and one in Saint John that had only been open about two weeks. The McDonald's unit in Saint John was located within a quarter mile of A&W's Saint John No. 1 drive-in. In the two weeks since the McDonald's unit had opened sales in the Saint John No. 1 outlet had been about 20 percent lower than in the corresponding period in 1972. Mr. Drayson had heard rumours that a second McDonald's was soon to be built in Saint John. Mr. Drayson had also just learned that McDonald's had purchased a site in Sydney directly across the street from the A&W drive-in. This store was expected to open in October 1973. McDonald's was also reported to be looking for a site in Charlottetown. Again, it seemed quite likely that the McDonald's would be close to the A&W.

McDonald's April 1973 prices and those for the most nearly comparable A&W products were as shown in the accompanying table:

McDonald's		A&W	
Hamburger.................. 0.25		Happy Burger.............. 0.24	
(1 $\frac{1}{10}$ lb. patty)*		(1 $\frac{1}{10}$ lb. patty)	
Cheeseburger.............. 0.30		Happy Burger with cheese.. 0.29	
(1 $\frac{1}{10}$ lb. patty)		(1 $\frac{1}{10}$ lb. patty)	
¼ lb. Burger............... 0.60		Papa Burger............... 0.64	
(1 $\frac{1}{4}$ lb. patty)		(2 $\frac{1}{5}$ lb. patties)	
¼ lb. Cheeseburger........ 0.70		Papa Burger with cheese.... 0.69	
($\frac{1}{4}$ lb. patty)		(2 $\frac{1}{5}$ lb. patties)	
Big Mac................... 0.65		Teenburger................ 0.59	
(2 $\frac{1}{10}$ lb. patties)		(1 $\frac{1}{5}$ lb. patty)	
Fries...................... 0.23 & 0.39		Fries...................... 0.19 & 0.29	
Milk shakes............... 0.30		Milk shakes............... 0.35	
Drinks..................... 0.15 & 0.20		Drinks..................... 0.15 & 0.20	

* All weights are uncooked weight.

The competitive situation in each of the six cities is summarized in Exhibit 5.

Mr. Drayson had received in 1971 a report conducted for A&W's national advertising agency by a firm of consultants. A total of 1,200 people had been interviewed by telephone, with equal sample sizes in Moncton, Montreal, Toronto, Edmonton, Kamloops, and Vancouver. Quota sampling had been used in each city to ensure that 50 married adult males, 50 married adult females, 50 males 16–20 years old and 50 females 16–20 years old would be interviewed. The research had been undertaken to determine the awareness, trial, and usage of various drive-in eating places. Some results from this study are reported in Exhibit 6 on page 490.

EXHIBIT 5
Major A&W competitors (in operation and expected—
March 31, 1973)

Moncton, N.B.
McDonald's—two units (1970)
Harvey's (1968)
Kentucky Fried Chicken—two units
Deluxe French Fries—three units
Independents

Saint John, N.B.
McDonald's (March 1973, second unit expected)
Deluxe French Fries—two units
Kentucky Fried Chicken—two units
Independents

Fredericton, N.B.
McDonald's (June 1971)
Kentucky Fried Chicken—two units
Dixie Lee Fried Chicken
Independents

Sydney
Kentucky Fried Chicken
Independents
McDonald's (expected October 1972)

Charlottetown
Kentucky Fried Chicken
Independents
McDonald's (expected)

Oromocto
None

A&W (Fundy) and other A&W operators in the Maritimes spent over $150,000 in media advertising in the Maritimes, using materials produced and made available by A&W's national advertising agency. The advertising featured two fictional characters, Albert and Walter, who were used to promote the high quality of A&W's products and particular items on the A&W menu. The overall theme was "Two great ideas are better than one" —which referred to the root beer and burger combinations. Little was known about McDonald's spending plans except that they provided heavy advertising support when they opened new units. McDonald's advertising and promotion was generally regarded by those in the fast-food trade as

EXHIBIT 6

Excerpts from consultant's report: A. Reasons for preferring favourite eating place

	A&W	Deluxe	Mc Donald's	Harvey's	All other burgers	All chicken	All pizza	All other	Total
Number of respondents.......	451	46	118	78	209	111	38	87	1,138
Food:									
Quantity of..................	6%	11%	3%	4%	3%	5%	3%	3%	5%
Variety of...................	5	4	1	5	5	—	8	2	4
Type of.....................	15	—	8	8	4	10	21	7	10
Quality/taste of.............	54	28	20	42	42	34	26	56	44
Other specific..............	2	—	—	1	1	5	3	1	2
Other nonspecific...........	—	—	10	—	10	1	—	3	3
Service:									
Speed of....................	6	13	19	9	10	13	13	14	10
Efficiency...................	16	7	8	4	4	10	5	6	10
Other specific..............	1	—	2	—	3	2	—	2	2
Other nonspecific...........	*	—	3	—	4	2	—	—	1
Premises:									
Clean.......................	4	2	3	3	7	5	—	6	4
Decor/atmosphere..........	2	—	1	3	8	2	8	5	3
Facilities/seating/									
fixtures, etc..............	13	—	2	3	9	2	16	5	8
Parking/parking lot..........	1	—	2	1	*	3	—	1	1
Other specific..............	1	—	1	—	*	1	3	1	1
Other nonspecific...........	—	—	—	—	*	2	—	1	*
Location:									
Convenience of/no. of/									
location..................	28	33	36	31	35	41	24	44	33
Other specific..............	1	—	—	—	—	—	—	—	*
Other nonspecific...........	*	—	—	—	—	—	—	—	*
Price/value, etc./all mentions..	6	30	52	10	15	13	5	15	15
Other:									
Opportunity.................	*	—	2	—	—	2	—	—	1
Desire......................	*	—	—	—	—	—	—	—	*
Availability of transportation.	1	—	—	—	*	1	8	2	1
Usual spot/place............	6	2	3	1	1	—	—	1	3
Where friends go............	15	7	10	14	8	1	11	8	11
Staff of eating place.........	6	—	3	—	4	—	5	8	4
Other comments............	5	—	5	4	3	5	—	8	4
Nothing.....................	*	—	—	—	—	—	—	—	*
Don't know.................	1	—	1	3	—	—	—	—	1
No answer..................	3	2	2	5	2	2	3	5	3

* Less than 0.5 percent.

Note: Column percentages may add up to more than 100 percent due to multiple responses by some respondents.

being of the highest quality, with its varied emphasis on children's promotions and the overall theme of "You deserve a break today."

Each A&W (Fundy) outlet completed a daily report of operations. Hour-by-hour sales and customer count were two of the items included in these reports. Summaries of two of these forms for different outlets and different days are included in Exhibit 7 on page 493.

EXHIBIT 6 (*continued*)

B. Things disliked about A&W by those who do not visit A&W most frequently by municipality

	Monc-ton	Mon-treal	To-ronto	Edmon-ton	Kam-loops	Van-couver
Number of respondents.....	121	117	142	69	72	166
Food:						
Quantity of................	4%	2%	1%	—	8%	4%
Variety of.................	3	3	2	—	3	5
Type of...................	2	5	—	10%	1	3
Quality/taste of...........	15	8	15	22	18	16
Other specific.............	—	2	1	—	—	5
Other nonspecific	—	—	—	—	—	3
Service:						
Speed of..................	3	—	10	14	17	13
Efficiency.................	7	—	2	7	3	5
Other specific.............	1	1	1	3	—	4
Other nonspecific.........	—	—	—	—	—	1
Premises:						
Clean.....................	—	—	1	1	—	2
Decor/atmosphere........	1	2	1	3	4	1
Facilities/seating/						
fixtures, etc.............	5	3	12	6	6	10
Parking/parking lot.......	2	1	—	3	1	1
Other specific.............	—	—	3	1	—	—
Other nonspecific.........	—	—	—	—	—	—
Location:						
Convenience of/no. of/						
location.................	4	20	8	10	1	2
Other specific.............		—	—	—	—	—
Other nonspecific.........		—	—	—	—	—
Price/value, etc./all						
mentions.................	31	4	12	7	29	20
Other:						
Opportunity...............	—	—	—	—	—	—
Desire....................	—	3	—	—	—	—
Availability of						
transportation...........	4	2	2	6	1	—
Usual spot/place..........	—	2	1	—	—	1
Where friends go..........	—	—	—	—	4	—
Staff of eating place.......	—	3	2	1	1	5
Other comments..........	1	3	3	16	1	2
Nothing...................	25	24	25	22	13	14
Don't know...............	2	10	19	1	—	11
No answer................	7	15	5	6	12	3

Note: Percentages may add to more than 100 percent as some respondents gave more than one answer.

"We feel that we have done the best job of any A&W operator in competing with McDonald's," Mr. Drayson had remarked. "We reduced our prices substantially in 1971 and we were successful in building volume." He noted that other A&W operators had retained their historical pricing policies which resulted in April 1973 with many units charging 75 cents for a Teenburger, versus the 59 cents charged by A&W (Fundy).

EXHIBIT 6 (concluded)

C. Things liked about A&W by those who do not visit A&W most frequently by municipality

	Monc-ton	Mon-treal	To-ronto	Edmon-ton	Kam-loops	Van-couver
Number of respondents.....	121	117	142	69	72	166
Food:						
Quantity of................	2%	—	—	6%	1%	1%
Variety of.................	2	4%	5%	4	6	2
Type of....................	—	8	13	9	4	25
Quality/taste of...........	45	18	19	49	54	23
Other specific.............	1	3	4	4	1	11
Other nonspecific.........	—	—	—	—	—	—
Service:						
Speed of..................	19	4	4	10	15	6
Efficiency.................	7	11	8	25	11	4
Other specific.............	1	3	1	—	—	5
Other nonspecific.........	1	—	—	—	—	2
Premises:						
Clean.....................	6	—	3	3	3	2
Decor/atmosphere........	—	—	1	1	3	—
Facilities/seating/						
fixtures.................	17	23	8	4	6	3
Parking/parking lot.......	—	4	1	3	3	1
Other specific.............	—	—	—	1	1	—
Other nonspecific.........	—	—	—	—	—	—
Location:						
Convenience of/no. of/						
location.................	4	—	4	4	8	4
Other specific.............	—	—	—	—	—	—
Other nonspecific.........	—	—	—	—	—	—
Price/value, etc./all						
mentions.................	2	1	2	7	8	1
Other:						
Opportunity...............	—	—	—	—	1	—
Desire....................	—	—	—	—	—	—
Availability of trans-						
portation................	2	—	—	—	—	—
Usual spot/place..........	—	—	—	—	—	—
Where friends go..........	1	—	—	3	—	—
Staff of eating place.......	10	1	2	10	13	4
Other comments..........	1	4	3	4	—	4
Nothing...................	10	3	18	10	4	12
Don't know...............	5	9	21	9	—	9
No answer................	9	32	11	1	8	5

Note: Percentages may add to more than 100 percent as some respondents gave more than one answer.

A&W (Fundy) had extensively publicized its price reductions in 1971. The publicity had included a small card which had been distributed to customers. A sample is included as Exhibit 8 on page 494. In Mr. Drayson's opinion, A&W (Fundy) had not been entirely successful in dispelling the high-price image.

EXHIBIT 7
Summary of selected data from daily operations reports

Ending hour	Unit A (Sunday)		Unit B (Friday)	
	Hourly sales	Hourly customer count	Hourly sales	Hourly customer count
Noon...................	$ 23.92	13	$ 10.19	6
1 p.m.................	92.02	34	84.94	41
2 p.m.................	71.63	27	26.65	15
3 p.m.................	64.15	33	16.75	12
4 p.m.................	100.10	41	19.33	20
5 p.m.................	137.72	51	20.53	13
6 p.m.................	220.57	70	91.38	34
7 p.m.................	221.68	77	86.80	33
8 p.m.................	127.67	47	55.78	25
9 p.m.................	125.71	50	34.96	17
10 p.m................	174.70	70	52.46	34
11 p.m................	155.03	60	76.85	40
Midnight..............	139.13	57	92.98	50
1 a.m.................	83.56	32	104.36	57
2 a.m.................	56.68	28	105.08	53
Totals...........	$1,794.27	690	$879.04	450

Prices had stayed relatively constant from 1971 to late in 1972. In September 1972, the company had conducted an extensive cost of sales study for each item on its menu for each outlet to estimate the theoretical food and packaging cost as a percentage of sales. Portions of this report for the Saint John's drive-ins are shown in Exhibit 9 on page 495.

In late 1972 prices, especially meat prices, began to rise across Canada, and a number of A&W franchisees in Canada began to lobby for a move to smaller hamburger patties. A&W had always had a standard of six hamburger patties to the pound (uncooked weight) in Canada. By January 1973, however, several of the largest A&W operators in Canada, including A&W (Fundy), had moved to seven patties to the pound.

THE SITUATION IN APRIL 1973

By March 1973, the cost situation had deteriorated further. In a March 21 memo to senior executives in the company and members of the board of directors, Mr. Drayson noted: "Our meat prices from suppliers have increased from approximately 61 cents per pound last September to the current 70 cents in New Brunswick and 81½ cents in Charlottetown. Sydney is the only unit with any kind of a break at the present time and is paying 61 cents per pound, but I am sure this will not last long. All indications are that beef will cost us 85 cents per pound in all units before the

EXHIBIT 8
1971 price reduction announcement

A & W's New Look of "Total Value" for 1971!

At first glance, our new menu may not seem much diferent. But take a second look, because there's a story to tell. Many of our prices are down. Why have we done this? Well, some people think when costs go up the only thing to do is raise prices. Sometimes that's true but at A & W we think the best way to overcome our own rising costs is to do more business and we think the best way to do more business is to increase the value to our customer. We refuse to compromise on quality, the size of our portions or our service. So, as you look over the menu on the reverse side you will note we have lowered some of our prices — at first glance they may not appear large but when your bill is totalled you will be pleasantly surprised. So that's the story, the same high standards of quality and service but greater value to you.

A & W DRIVE-INS (FUNDY) LIMITED

The BURGER FAMILY

PAPA BURGER 64
           2 Patties Meat
MAMA BURGER 44
           Single Patty
BABY BURGER 24
    (Cheese on above 5¢, Bacon 5¢)
TEEN BURGER 59
(Single Patty with Cheese, Bacon, Lettuce, Tomato, Mayonnaise, Toasted Sesame Seed Bun)
All served with your choice of Mustard, Ketchup, Pickles and Onions

CHUBBY CHICKEN

CHUBBY DINNER 1.35
   3 Pcs. Chicken, French Fries, Cole Slaw
CHUBBY JUNIOR. 90
   2 Pcs. Chicken, French Fries
CHUBBY NINE 2.75
      9 Pcs. Chicken
CHUBBY FIFTEEN. 3.75
      15 Pcs. Chicken
CHUBBY TWENTY-ONE. 4.95
      21 Pcs. Chicken
FAMILY PAK FRENCH FRIES 1.00
Cole Slaw,   4 oz. 15¢, ½ pint 30¢, 1 pint 50¢

OTHER A & W FEATURES

Hot Dog 34
Whistle Dog, Bacon, Cheese & Relish 49
French Fries. 25
Onion Rings. 35
Fish and Chips 65
Fish on a Bun 15
Fried Clams (When Available). 75
Fried Clams and Chips 1.00

BEVERAGES — DESSERTS

A & W ROOT BEER. . . . . .25 - .15
A & W ORANGE . . . . .25 - .15
   Baby root beer free to children under 6
ICE CREAM FLOAT . . . . .35 - .25
MILKSHAKES 35
MILK. . . . . .30 - .20
COFFEE 15
TEA. 15
HOT CHOCOLATE .15
APPLE TURNOVER 25
   (With cheese or ice cream 10¢ extra)
SUNDAE
   Chocolate or Strawberry 20
ICE CREAM 10

EXHIBIT 9

Cost of sales (Saint John), September 1972

Teen Burger—59¢

Meat	10.33
Bun	3.25
Seasoning	0.10
Onion	1.46
Mustard	0.15
Ketchup	0.33
Pickles (2)	0.66
Bacon	1.76
Cheese	2.00
Mayonnaise	0.86
Lettuce	0.60
Tomato	0.90
Bag	1.71
	24.11¢—40.8%

Chubby Dinner—$1.19

3 pcs. chicken	42.90
3 oz. fries	5.22
Ketchup	0.66
Portion cup	0.20
Plastic fork	0.35
Salt	0.01
Grease-proof paper	0.41
Box	4.47
	54.22¢—45.6%

Jumbo root beer—Mug .... 3.72¢—18.6%
Jumbo root beer—Take out .... 6.21¢—31.0%

Baby Burger—24¢

Meat	6.20
Bun	2.83
Seasoning	0.02
Mustard	0.08
Ketchup	0.17
Pickle	0.33
Onion	0.73
Bag	1.24
	11.60¢ 48.3%

---

summer is over. Therefore, I feel any changes we make should be based on the assumption we will be paying 85 cents per pound shortly and this will probably not decrease very much by the end of the year. If we are to meet our profit objectives I feel we must move our cost of sales percentages back to last September's level. To do this, there appear to be at least three options: (1) raise prices, (2) decrease the patty size by moving to eight patties per pound, or (3) decrease the patty size as well as increasing prices."

EXHIBIT 10
Past and planned minimum hourly wage rate in New Brunswick, Nova Scotia, and Prince Edward Island

	New Bruns- wick	Nova Scotia	Prince Edward Island
April 1, 1972...............	$1.40	$1.35 ($1.20)*	$1.25 ($0.95)
April 1, 1973...............	1.50	1.55	1.24 ($1.10)
July 1, 1973................	1.50	1.65	1.65 ($1.40)
January 1, 1974 (planned)..	1.75	1.65	1.65

* Hourly rate in parentheses is for females, where this differs from the male hourly rate.

Later in the memo Mr. Drayson added: "I think we must also bear in mind the fact that we have had to absorb increases not only in food costs, but also in all other operating costs." Mr. Drayson was particularly conscious of the rise in labor costs. He had pointed out: "If you look back to 1965, when we first opened up, wages in our stores on an annual basis

EXHIBIT 11
Analysis of sales Moncton No. 1, March 1973 (Saturday)

Item	Selling price	Units	Sales
Pa......................	$0.64	107	$ 68.48
Pa Ch*..................	0.69	17	11.73
Grandpa................	0.94	4	3.76
Pa Ch Bac†............	0.79	6	4.74
Ma.....................	0.44	77	33.88
Ma Ch..................	0.49	20	9.80
Ma Ch Bac.............	0.59	2	1.18
Teen...................	0.59	312	184.08
Pa Teen................	0.89	5	4.45
Grandpa Teen..........	1.19	1	1.19
Happy..................	0.25	135	33.75
Happy Ch..............	0.30	9	2.70
Hot Dog................	0.39	17	6.63
Whistle Dog............	0.49	34	16.66
French fries............	0.19 & 0.29	115	30.16
Onion rings............	0.39	118	46.02
Fish & Chips...........	0.69	40	27.60
Fried clams............	0.85	14	11.90
Fried clams & F.F.......	1.05	17	17.85
Burger Platters‡........	Various	139	116.91
Chicken................	Various	—	82.38
Drinks.................	Various	—	176.83
Other..................	Various	—	18.25
			$910.93

* Ch—with cheese.
† Bac—with bacon.
‡ Consists of a burger, fries, and coleslaw.

amounted to 17 to 18 percent of gross sales, exclusive of the manager's salary. Today we are looking at wage percentages anywhere from 20 to 24 percent, with the average being 22 to 23 percent." He remarked that the increases were mainly due to increases in the minimum wage. The 1973 and the planned 1974 minimum wages in the Atlantic Provinces are noted in Exhibit 10. A&W (Fundy) paid on the average about 30 cents per hour higher than the minimum wage.

Mr. Drayson also attached to the memo a photocopy of a sales mix study done on one of the Moncton A&W drive-ins on a Saturday earlier in March. A copy of the study is contained in Exhibit 11. Mr. Drayson felt that the sales mix was quite representative of the sales mix in the company as a whole.

Mr. Drayson had already discussed the options at some length with Mr. Brathwaite, and he knew that Mr. Brathwaite had some strong opinions about what should be done. Mr. Brathwaite believed A&W (Fundy) should try to position itself very close to McDonald's, by reducing the portions, if this was necessary to keep prices roughly comparable. Mr. Brathwaite felt that the customer didn't notice small differences in hamburger sizes. He pointed out, for example, that no customer appeared to have noticed

EXHIBIT 12
1973 profit plan—Saint John No. 1

Net sales.....................................	$330,000
Food (including paper)....................	123,100
Gross Profit............................	$206,900
Controllable Expenses:	
Wages and fringe benefits.................	83,900
Management salaries......................	10,000
Advertising and promotion	
National (1.5%)..........................	5,000
Local...................................	19,800
Uniforms................................	1,200
Utilities.................................	4,400
Miscellaneous unit expenses*............	17,100
TOTAL CONTROLLABLES............	$148,000
Noncontrollable Expenses:	
Lease of land and building................	18,800
Franchise fee (1.5%)......................	5,000
Accounting services......................	3,000
Insurance and taxes......................	1,400
Equipment depreciation...................	5,400
Administration†..........................	8,900
Total Noncontrollables...............	42,500
Total Operating Expenses...........	190,500
Unit Contribution....................	16,400

* Includes cleaning supplies, maintenance, snow removal, refuse collection, telephone, and so on.
† Allocated by head office.

A&W's switch from six to the pound to seven to the pound. Mr. Brathwaite felt that A&W could move quite easily to eight to the pound without the customer knowing, since it was a common practice in the fast-food trade to scale down the bun size by a proportional amount. Mr. Drayson disagreed with this. He felt that eight patties to the pound would be sufficiently different from six patties to the pound that many customers would notice.

As he once again reviewed the options, Mr. Drayson turned to the 1973 profit plan for one of the Saint John's units (Exhibit 12) which had been prepared in November 1972, based on the food cost data prepared in September 1972. He knew that it was a reasonably representative outlet and he realized that if the company were to meet its profit objectives for 1973, he would have to obtain approximately the same contribution from this outlet irrespective of the rising costs. He realized the board of directors would expect him to have a concrete set of recommendations.

Dutch Food Industries
Company (A)*

In early September, Jan de Vries, product manager for Dutch Food Industries' new salad dressing product, was wondering what strategy to follow with respect to this new product. His assistant had prepared information concerning alternative promotional methods to use to introduce the new product, and he was concerned with exactly which of these he should recommend for the product's introduction. He also wondered what price the new product should retail for and when the company should introduce the new product. Mr. de Vries had to decide these issues in the next couple of days, as his report containing his recommendations on the introduction of the new salad dressing was due on the desk of the director of marketing the following Monday.

COMPANY BACKGROUND

The Netherlands Oil Factory of Delft, The Netherlands, was founded in 1884. This firm, which supplied edible oils to the growing margarine industry, merged in 1900 with a French milling company. The new firm then operated under the name Dutch Food Industries Company (DFI).

From this origin, the brand name DFI became increasingly strong and was eventually given to all of the company's branded products. More recently, the name was registered for use internationally.

In the course of the 1920s, DFI became an important factor in the

---

* The authors were assisted in writing this case by Jos Viehoff, Graduate Student, Netherlands School of Economics.

margarine market. The company was a troublesome competitor for the Margarine Union, the company formed by the merger in 1927 of the two margarine giants, Van den Bergh and Jurgens. In 1928, an agreement was reached by which DFI joined the Margarine Union.

In 1930, the interests of the Margarine Union were merged with those of International Industries Corporation—a large, diversified, and international organization. It was in this way that DFI became a part of the International Industries complex of companies.

International Industries Corporation (IIC) is a worldwide organization with major interests in the production of margarine, other edible fats and oils, soups, ice cream, frozen foods, meats, cheeses, soaps, and detergents.

The total sales of IIC were more than $1 billion.[1] Profits before taxes were $56 million.

Within IIC, DFI proceeded with its original activities after its margarine factory was closed, namely developing its exports of oils and fats, its trade in bakery products, as well as a number of branded food products. The following list indicates the range of consumer products which the company marketed: table oil, household fats, mayonnaise, salad dressing (several varieties), tomato ketchup, peanut butter, and peanuts.

DFI's total annual sales were between $14 million–$28 million. Profits before taxes were between $1.4 million–$2.8 million.

BACKGROUND ON THE DRESSING MARKET

A large and growing percentage of Holland's population eats lettuce, usually with salad dressing, with their meals. Estimates indicated that 82 percent of the people ate lettuce with salad dressing regularly. The salad dressing market has extreme seasonal demand as shown in Exhibit 1. This seasonal pattern coincides with the periods of greatest production of lettuce in Holland. Thus, 50 percent of the total year's volume for the salad dressing market occurs in the four months beginning in April. During this period, lettuce is plentiful and sells for approximately $0.06 per head.

The total salad dressing market was growing at approximately 7 percent per year. DFI's share of the market had declined from 20.7 percent to 16.6 percent over the last five years. The total market for salad dressings at manufacturer's level was currently estimated at between $7 million and $8.4 million. The company was looking for ways to halt the decline in market share and, in fact, increase DFI's share of the growing market.

Historically, the salad dressing market was composed of two segments. The first was a 25 percent oil-based salad dressing, which comprised 90 percent of the total market. The other 10 percent of the market consisted

---

[1] All financial data in this case are presented in U.S. dollars.

EXHIBIT 1
Seasonal analysis of salad dressing market (percentage of annual
total market sales—bimonthly periods)

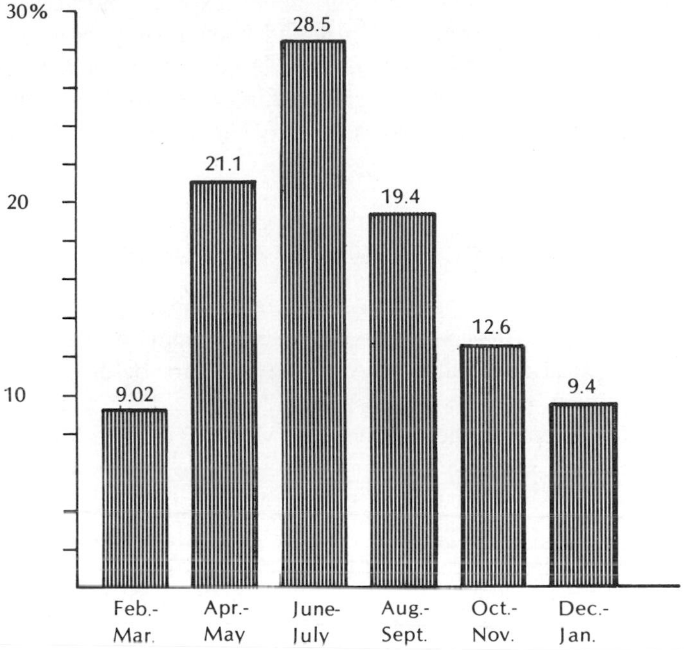

of 50 percent oil-based salad dressing, a slightly creamier product. Previously, DFI, in an effort to increase its market share, had introduced a new product which was 50 percent oil based. Up to that time, DFI sold only 25 percent oil-based salad dressing. The product, called Delfine, was not successful in obtaining the desired volume and profit. While DFI still marketed Delfine, almost all of DFI's volume came from its 25 percent oil-based product, Slasaus.

A research study was conducted to help the DFI marketing executives determine why Delfine was not successful. Several reasons emerged:

1. The potential of the 50 percent oil-based market was much smaller than originally anticipated, and only a small percentage of the total population was even interested in this product.
2. The consumers could detect only a small difference between the 25 percent oil-based and the 50 percent oil-based varieties when blind-tested. The difference was not noticeable enough for the consumers to prefer the 50 percent oil-based product.
3. The 50 percent oil-based salad dressing was more expensive, and the

consumer was not willing to pay the difference for an apparently almost imperceptible difference.

Because the Delfine sales were well below expectations, DFI removed the heavy promotion support which it had been giving the product. The executives decided to wait for a significant breakthrough of a product with unique advantages. The Delfine experience indicated to them that it would take a totally new type of product for DFI to increase its market share significantly.

BACKGROUND AND DEVELOPMENT OF SLAMIX

Every two years, the company conducted a housewives' habits study in which a panel of 700 consumers was asked about their household and their food preparation habits. In August two years before, the company received the most recent study, called PMC-11. The housewives were asked how they prepared their lettuce and what ingredients they used. The results showed that an extremely large percentage of the housewives added not only salad dressing to lettuce, but also added other ingredients such as salt, pepper, eggs, onion, gherkins, and so on. Thus DFI executives got the idea that putting some of these ingredients in the salad dressing would result in a real convenience for the housewife, and DFI would have the significant new product for which they had been searching. The laboratory, in August of the same year, began developing a "dressed" salad dressing which included some of the ingredients which many housewives were accustomed to adding.

Early in the next year, a committee called the Slamix Committee,[2] was formed to make sure that every part of the company was involved in the development of this new product. The committee, which was headed up by the product manager, had representatives from various parts of the company, including development, production, and marketing. The committee studied production problems, laboratory findings, and in general, was charged with the responsibility of seeing that the development progressed as scheduled. The committee did not have decision-making powers but either invited decision makers to important meetings or wrote reports to the people who were in a position to make the required decisions.

After several product tests concerned with taste and keeping properties were conducted at the factory, the company, one year after laboratory work began, undertook its first consumer test of the new "dressed" salad dressing. A panel of housewives was shown a bottle of the new product

---

[2] Literally translated, Slasaus means "lettuce sauce," and Slamix is literally "lettuce mix."

which was a salad dressing containing pieces of gherkins, onions, and paprika. Several conclusions emerged from this study:

1. The "dressed" salad dressing was seen by the housewives as more than a salad dressing with ingredients. It was seen as a completely new product.
2. There were two sides to this newness:
    a.   By looking at the product, they thought that it had a new taste.
    b.   The convenience aspect was strongly stressed by the housewives.
3. The housewives thought that the new product would be good for decorating the lettuce. With its new color (light red with colorful ingredients), they thought that they could decorate the lettuce much better than with present salad dressings which were creme-colored and very similar to mayonnaise.
4. When asked about the ingredients, one half of the housewives were favorable toward paprika, and half were against it. This apparently was a troublesome ingredient. However, because of the convenience aspect, gherkins and onions were favored by the housewives.

Later, a second consumer study was conducted by the Institute of Household Research in Rotterdam. A sample of 140 housewives who actually used salad dressing on lettuce was given a bottle of the new product to take home. Then, they were visited in their homes. Much useful information emerged from this study. After looking at the product, but before trying it, the housewives said that it looked like a fun product, it made them happy, and they thought that it would taste good. When asked what they thought the product contained, they said tomatoes, red paprika, celery, gherkins, and green paprika.

However, the company was disappointed with the housewives' overall evaluation of the product. Only 20 percent of the housewives said that they thought the product was very good, 11 percent did not like the product, and 69 percent of the housewives said that there were some favorable and some unfavorable aspects of the product. The main reason for the 80 percent unfavorable reaction was the consistency of the new salad dressing. It was too thin. The housewives could pour it too easily and it rapidly went to the bottom of the bowl. Because it fell to the bottom, the housewives said that it was much harder to decorate their salad. It was also uneconomical because they felt that they would put too much on if the product was that thin. There were also problems with taste. Many of the housewives thought it was too sour or too sharp. The paprika was the main reason for the dissatisfaction.

In spite of the above problems, there were several aspects of the study which encouraged the company to proceed with the development of this new product. When asked how they would change the ingredients in the

EXHIBIT 2
Preference test: Slasaus versus "dressed" salad dressing

Prefer	Taste	Appear-ance	Decoration aspects	Con-sistency	Con-venience
"Dressed" salad dressing........	59%	73%	46%	18%	50%
Slasaus.........................	38	20	44	65	20
No preference/no difference......	3	7	10	17	30
	100%	100%	100%	100%	100%

"dressed" salad dressing, only 47 percent of the housewives suggested changes. Most recommended that more onions be added. The housewives were asked for their preference between DFI's Slasaus and the new "dressed" salad dressing. As shown in Exhibit 2, the housewives preferred the new product, except for its consistency. Sixty percent of the housewives said that they would buy the product if it were possible to buy it in the store. Since this was a very high positive response, the company was very encouraged.

The marketing, production, and development groups, coordinated by the Slamix Committee, began work on incorporating the required changes made evident by this consumer study. DFI's development group experimented with changes in the consistency, taste, and ingredients. The production group experimented with a new production process. DFI had intended to introduce the new "dressed" salad dressing in a few months. However, the top corporate executives decided that, before the new product could be introduced, an extensive test of its keeping properties (vulnerability to deterioration) would have to be conducted.

The keeping-properties test showed that after several months the light red-colored product changed to a pink color. The difference in color was only slight, but DFI executives thought that the consumer reaction to this change should be tested. They decided that at the same time they would conduct a consumer test to find a name for this new product. A sample of 180 housewives from the Institute of Household Research was used to get at these questions. Only 2 out of the 180 housewives saw that there was a difference in color between the two bottles of the new product. When they were told that there was a slight difference and were shown the two bottles together, most of the housewives could not see the color change, and those that could were not unhappy about it.

The housewives were then asked what the name for this product should be. The phrase "mixed salad dressing" kept coming up. The housewives were then asked what they thought of two names which the company had screened, "Slamix" (lettuce mix) and "Spikkeltjessaus" (sauce with little spots). Eighty-one percent thought that Slamix was a very good name.

Only 26 percent thought that Spikkeltjessaus was a good name. The name Slamix was chosen for the new product. Interestingly, that was the name that the company had used internally for the new product when it was first being developed.

A short time later, DFI had solved the color-change problem. The company now thought that it had a product ready to be marketed, so a final consumer test was undertaken to test the effect of all of the changes that had been made during the previous year.

Two versions of Slamix, a white one and a pink one, were tested at the Institute for Household Research. One hundred eighty housewives were asked what they thought of the product and whether they would buy it or not. The negative reactions to the product were minimal. Almost no negative comments were voiced. The problems of consistency, color, taste, and ingredients had apparently been solved. When asked if they would buy the product, 76 percent of those shown the pink product, and 70 percent of those shown the white product responded in a positive manner. After tasting the two versions of Slamix, the housewives revealed a strong preference for the pink Slamix. The DFI executives felt that the product was now ready to be marketed.

DFI executives next reviewed the financial projections prepared by Mr. de Vries, the product manager. Almost no capital investment would be required as the Slamix would be produced by using present production facilities. Only a few machines, at a total cost of $11,000, would be required.

At an early stage in the development of the product, Slamix sales had been forecasted at 3.7 percent of the total market at the end of the first year. Encouraged by the results of the consumer tests, DFI executives revised their estimate of sales. The new forecast was for approximately 6.7 percent of the market. (See Exhibit 3.)

The directors of the company thought that they finally had the product for which they had been waiting. The consumer tests were complete, and the product had found very high favor with the consumers. There was significant technological development involved in the product, and DFI

EXHIBIT 3
Forecasted sales of Slamix

Year	Share of market (percent)
Original estimates	
Year 1.................................	3.7%
Year 2.................................	3.9
Year 3.................................	4.4
Revised estimates	
Year 1.................................	6.7
Year 2.................................	11.7

executives thought that it would take considerable time for the competition to duplicate the product. The product manager's projected sales seemed reasonable. Mr. de Vries was asked to prepare a comprehensive report concerning the introductory marketing strategy to be used to introduce the new product.

PRICING STRATEGY

The first problem that the product manager had to resolve concerned the suggested retail price that the company should charge for Slamix. To help Mr. de Vries make his recommendation, the assistant product manager had made a list of the following considerations:

1. The company's total cost for a 0.30-liter sized bottle of Slamix was $0.20. This was 20 percent higher than DFI's regular salad dressing, Slasaus.

2. The gross margin for Slasaus was 22 percent. Because of the unique qualities of Slamix, large development costs, and possible substitution with Slasaus, a higher gross margin for Slamix might be considered.

3. DFI gave the wholesalers a 7.9 percent margin and retailers a 14.6 percent margin for Slasaus. Possibly these should be increased for Slamix to encourage greater acceptance and promotion by the trade channels of distribution.

4. The two leading salad dressings, Salata by Duyvis and Slasaus, both had a retail price of $0.28 for the 0.30-liter bottle. The retail price for the .60-liter bottle was $.48. Private label salad dressings were $0.22 for a .30-liter bottle. The average price for all salad dressings was approximately $0.26.

5. DFI had conducted some research on the optimal price of Slamix. After using a sample of the product, 140 housewives were asked what price they would be willing to pay for Slamix. Their responses, by percent, were:

	Percent
$0.31 or less............................	45%
Between $0.31 and $0.40...............	41
$0.40 or more..........................	14
Total............................	100%

The average price mentioned was $0.34.

The assistant product manager also prepared the table shown in Ex-

EXHIBIT 4
Alternative prices for Slamix*

		Slamix					
	Slasaus	1	2	3	4	5	6
Retail price.................	$0.28	$0.32	$0.34	$0.34	$0.36	$0.37	$0.38
Price to retailer.............	0.24	0.28	0.28	0.29	0.295	0.31	0.316
Price to wholesaler.........	0.21	0.25	0.25	0.26	0.26	0.28	0.28
Cost.......................	0.165	0.20	0.20	0.20	0.20	0.20	0.20

* Selected figures in this table have been disguised.

hibit 4. The first column shows the retail price, and gives data that allows one to calculate trade margins and gross margin for Slasaus. The remaining six columns show alternative retail prices for Slamix, resulting from different trade margins and gross margins. Mr. de Vries wondered which of these prices he should recommend to the board of directors.

PROMOTION ALTERNATIVES

The board of directors told the product manager that he had $203,000 for his promotion budget. Of this, $7,000 was to be allocated as Slamix's share of the general corporate advertising which aided all DFI products. The $203,000 was determined by using a percentage of the "expected gross profit of the first year" for Slamix.[3] DFI's policy was to break even in the third year of the new product, attaining a total payback within five years. The company was generally willing to spend the gross profit for the first year as part of the total investment.

The company had already given considerable thought to the sales message and the brand image desired for Slamix. The information below was sent to the advertising agency to help in planning the promotional program of the company:

Sales message. It is now possible, in a completely new way, to make delicious salad. Sla + Slamix = Sla Klaar. (Lettuce + Slamix = Lettuce Ready)

Supporting message. Slamix is a salad dressing with pieces of onion, gherkins, and paprika.

Desired brand image. With Slamix you can make, very easily and very

---

[3] It was possible that the percentage could be greater than 100 percent. This would mean that the company was willing to spend more than the first year's gross profit for initial promotion.

quickly, a delicious salad that also looks nice. Slamix is a complete, good, handy product. DFI is a modern firm with up-to-date ideas.

Thus, the company wanted to get across three principal points. They are (1) that Slamix is a completely new product, (2) that it is convenient, and (3) that it is a salad dressing with ingredients making it a complete salad dressing.

The product manager was undecided as to how to divide the $196,000 among the following alternatives:

1. Television.
2. Radio.
3. Newspaper advertising.
4. Magazines.
5. Sampling.
6. Coupons.
7. Price-off promotion.
8. Key chain premiums.
9. Trade allowances.

Television

The product manager thought that television would be advantageous because of the ability to show the product in actual use—a housewife pouring Slamix onto the lettuce. The cost of using the television medium is shown in Exhibit 5. The company did not have a choice among the seven blocks of time, but had to take whatever was available. For planning, however, they figured an average cost of a 30-second ad would be $1,800. Mr. de Vries felt that at least 25 advertisements were necessary before the TV advertising would have maximum impact.

EXHIBIT 5
Data on Dutch television media

Station	Block number	Time	Cost of 30-second ad
Nederland 1	1	Before early news	$2,300
Nederland 1	2	After early news	2,300
Nederland 1	3	Before late news	2,950
Nederland 1	4	After late news	2,950
Nederland 2	5	After early news	500
Nederland 2	6	Before late news	840
Nederland 2	7	After late news	840
Average cost per 30-second TV ad			$1,800
Production cost for a TV ad			7,000

TV coverage per 1,000 households = 850 or 85 percent.
Only about one half of the homes can receive Nederland 2.

Radio

The chief attraction of radio was its extremely low price. Each 30-second radio ad cost $126 on Radio Veronica, a popular station during the daytime. Production costs for a radio ad were approximately $840. Only 60 percent of the households could receive Radio Veronica, mainly in the western part of the country. Mr. de Vries felt that if radio were used, a minimum of 100 spots should be purchased.

Newspapers

Mr. de Vries thought the main advantages of newspapers would be the announcement effect and its influence with the local trade. Nationally, the cost of each half-page insertion would be $14,000.

Magazines

Magazines would be a desirable addition to the promotional program for several reasons. Due to the ability to use color, the company could show the product as it actually looked on the shelf. By using several women's magazines, the company could reach a select audience of people reading the magazine at its leisure. Data on selected Dutch magazines are shown in Exhibit 6. Mr. de Vries thought that if they were to use a magazine campaign, at least ten insertions would be necessary before the advertising would be very effective. Of the possibilities in Exhibit 6, the agency thought that the combination of *Eva, Margriet,* and *AVRO-Televizier* would be most effective for DFI, since the combination would reach a large number of people at a relatively low cost.

Sampling

Although he realized that it was very expensive, Mr. de Vries considered the use of direct-mail sampling. A small 12 cm. by 18 cm. (approximately 5 x 7 inches) folder could be mailed to Holland's 3.7 million households for $20,000. The cost, however, would increase substantially if a small bottle of the product were to be included in the direct mailing. This cost would be 20 cents for handling, plus 75 cents for the actual sample. Thus, it would cost $980,000 to sample the whole country.

Coupon

Mr. de Vries was considering whether or not to include a coupon good for $0.04 off the purchase of Slamix with one of the other DFI products—

EXHIBIT 6

Data on selected Dutch magazines

| Magazines | Type | Circulation | Frequency | Price for full-page ad | | Cost per 1,000 circulation* |
				Black and white	Color	
Eva.................	Women's	375,000	Weekly	$ 770	$1,408	$3.75
Margriet............	Women's	825,000	Weekly	2,100	3,440	4.15
Libelle.............	Women's	570,000	Weekly	1,416	2,340	4.10
Prinses............	Women's	213,000	Weekly	660	1,175	5.55
Panorama..........	General	403,000	Weekly	1,300	2,150	5.40
Nieuwe Revu.......	General	261,000	Weekly	920	1,540	5.90
Spiegel............	General	175,000	Weekly	710	1,325	7.55
Het Beste..........	Digest	325,000	Monthly	965	1,615	4.90
Studio.............	TV guide	575,000	Weekly	1,525	2,420	4.20
NCRV-gids..........	TV guide	482,000	Weekly	1,420	2,290	4.75
Vara-gids..........	TV guide	504,000	Weekly	1,500	2,370	4.70
AVRO-Televizier.....	TV guide	950,000	Weekly	2,600	3,870	4.05
Combination of Eva, Margriet, and AVRO-Televizier.........				4,900	7,785	3.65

* Cost of one-page color ad, divided by circulation in thousands. With Eva as an example, cost per 1,000 circulation = $1,408/375 = $3.75.

mayonnaise, for example. He estimated that 900,000 coupons would be distributed. At a redemption rate of 5 percent, the cost would, thus, be approximately $1,700.

Price-off

DFI made use of a reduced retail price for most of its new product introductions. Thus, the product manager thought it quite normal to consider the use of reducing the retail price by U.S. $0.07 per bottle and identifying this price reduction on the label of the product. It was felt that this reduced price would encourage the housewives to try Slamix. It was also quite normal to follow up this sales promotion with a similar price reduction approximately five months after the product was introduced. This would encourage those who had still not tried the product to purchase a bottle and would encourage those who had already bought one bottle to continue purchasing the new product. The cost of this price-off promotion is shown in Exhibit 7.

EXHIBIT 7

Introduction:
720,000 bottles at 25 cents (U.S. $0.07) off each...... $50,400
Handling and display materials..................... 2,800
     Total... $53,200
Follow-up five months later:
600,000 bottles at 25 cents (U.S. $0.07) off each...... $42,000
Handling and display materials..................... 2,800
     Total... $44,800

Key chain premium

It was very unusual to use a free premium to introduce a new product, but Mr. de Vries was considering this alternative for several reasons. Many products in Holland at this time were using key chains as a premium. As shown in Exhibit 8, an extremely large percentage of the people in Holland were collecting key chains. The details of the research showed that mothers

EXHIBIT 8
Percentage of households collecting key chains

	June	July	September
Households with children.............	45	n.a.	n.a.
Households without children..........	5	n.a.	n.a.
Total (weighted average)........	34	37	41

n.a. = not available.

EXHIBIT 9

Introduction:
  720,000 bottles = about 220 metric tons
    750,000 key chains at $0.056...................... $42,000
    Handling costs and display materials............... 16,800
      Total... $58,800
Follow-up five months later:
  600,000 bottles = about 180 tons
    625,000 key chains at $0.056...................... $35,000
    Handling costs and display materials............... 14,000
      Total... $49,000

---

and daughters were more likely to collect key chains, especially if the children were between 8 and 11 years of age. Mr. de Vries felt that if he used key chains as premiums for the introduction of Slamix he could have a follow-up promotion five months later using either key chains or price-off deals. Selected cost information on the key chain promotion is shown in Exhibit 9.

Trade allowances

The product manager also considered the use of trade allowances to encourage the retailers to accept and promote the new product. The company traditionally offered $0.28 per case of 12 bottles. Thus, if it was decided that trade allowances were desirable, the cost would be $16,800 for the initial introduction and an additional $14,000 used during the follow-up promotion five months later. Trade allowances could be used together with either the price-off promotion or the key chain promotion. The product manager felt that trade allowances would not be very effective without one of the two consumer sales promotions.

DISTRIBUTION

Outside of the question of what trade margins to use and whether or not to use trade allowances during the consumer sales promotions discussed above, Mr. de Vries did not see any problems with distribution. DFI had a sales force of approximately 50 persons who regularly called on 10,000 outlets in Holland. It was felt that the sales force could handle the introduction of the new product with no problem.

The last problem the product manager faced concerned the timing of the introduction of Slamix. The product would be ready for introduction in October. Mr. de Vries wondered whether the seasonal nature of the demand for the product would make it more desirable to hold off the introduction until March of the next year.

The *Michiganensian*

INTRODUCTION

The 1976 *Michiganensian* (or *Ensian* as it was known), the yearbook of the University of Michigan, was in the opinion of its editor, "on most business counts, not very successful at all." Editor Gordon Martin felt that sales were poor despite publication of a high-quality book. Sales had declined from a peak of approximately 3,800 annually in the late 1960s to 1,500 books in 1976 on the campus of 33,800 students. The low volume of sales and increasing publication costs had seriously threatened the existence of the publication. In May of 1976, Martin faced the problem of developing a marketing plan before work started on the 1977 *Michiganensian*.

HISTORY

The first of the annuals published by student editors was a four-page pamphlet, *The University Register,* issued in June 1857. This publication contained the names of regents, faculty, graduates, students, and members of the literary and secret societies. During the school year 1858–59 the first issue of *The .Palladium* was published. *The Palladium* was published semiannually by a group of seven secret societies, or fraternities, as they are now called. *The Palladium* gradually increased in size and improved in content until in 1896 it was a book illustrated with cuts and drawings and containing a considerable amount of literary material. Eventually 15 different fraternities cooperated on its editorial board.

Dissatisfied with their treatment in *The Palladium,* a group of anti-secret society independents published the first issue of *The University Castalia* in the 1870s. In 1890 it was renamed *The Castalian.* It contained literary material and illustrations. In 1894, the senior class of the Law School published an annual devoted to the fraternities, societies, and activities of the law students. In 1894, the book was called *To Wit,* and the last two issues, in 1895 and 1896 were called *Res Gestae.*

In April 1897, the first issue of the *Michiganensian* appeared, the result of a consolidation of *The Palladium, The Castalian,* and *Res Gestae.* It represented senior literary, engineering, and law classes. It has remained ever since the official student yearbook of the University of Michigan. Control of the *Michiganensian* was vested in the Board in Control of Student Publications in 1908, and since that time all of the editors and business managers of the publication have been chosen annually by the board. It was suggested in 1900, that the *Michiganensian* "should be given more the character of a yearbook, should be paged and indexed, and made the Michigan reference book of the year, giving the names of winners of various University contests, lists of society members, etc." These suggestions have been generally followed by the editors. The history of the *Michiganensian* has been one of slow evolution, rather than of any marked alterations from year to year.

By 1958, the *Michiganensian* was a book of 500 pages. Today the book is smaller by some 200 pages but continues to include articles and photographs on various aspects of U of M's 19 schools and colleges, on the various campus activities, sections recounting the athletic achievements of Michigan teams and features on the Ann Arbor area. Each graduating student may have his picture in the book and group pictures of fraternities, sororities, and other campus organizations are also included (see Exhibit 1 for information on enrollment and campus organizations). The *Michiganensian* is now considered the comprehensive Michigan yearbook.

THE BOARD FOR STUDENT PUBLICATIONS

At a meeting of the University Senate on June 2, 1903, a report by a special committee on nonathletic student organizations recommended that a board be created to regulate student publications. The board was to acquire the stock, property and goodwill of the publications and have full control of all questions pertaining to publication. The board was to consist of seven members, four appointed by the president of the university from the University Senate and three elected by the students from the student body. These recommendations were adopted creating the Board in Control of Student Publications. In 1919, the board was incorporated as a nonprofit corporation. Later, the name was changed to The Board for Student Publications.

By 1915, the board had retained earnings of $14,000 which were earmarked for construction of a student publications building. The board petitioned the Regents of the university for permission to turn over its funds for investment and safekeeping to the treasurer of the university. Today the board has a reserve account of approximately $750,000 which is invested in the university's portfolio. In 1932, construction was completed on the Student Publications Building which has office space for the *Michigan Daily* (student newspaper), *Generation* (student literary magazine), the *Gargoyle* (student humor magazine), and the *Michiganensian*.

At the time the board took over control of the various publications, they were owned and operated by students, many of whom derived considerable income from that source. At first the board allowed managing editors and business managers a percentage of the net profits of the publications. Later, a system of salaries was adopted.

In the opinion of Professor Larry Berlin, current chairperson of the board: "The Board for Student Publications exists to protect the University from tort liability and to safeguard the fiscal integrity of the various student publications. We are a completely autonomous body."

THE *MICHIGANENSIAN*

Product

The book itself has always been a fairly traditional yearbook. In photographs and copy it undertakes to relate the events of the school year. The following is a statement by the editor that appeared in the front of the 1976 *Michiganensian*, describing the book:

Where did this book come from?

It came from the typewriters and cameras of a score of students who, like you, want to remember what it was like to be a student at the University of Michigan in 1975–1976. We can't give you the times that happened then, they're gone. No one has slowed or saved time since it began an eternity ago and no one is likely to slow its pace in the eons waiting to unfold.

We've tried to freeze images of that time in pictures and print so that we, you and others might recall the events that defined the personality of that year. Realizing the limitations of printed pages, we've tried to document that year as best we can in a photojournalistic capacity.

Just as it is impossible to save time and live it a second time, it is impossible to truly describe a year's events in any number of printed pages.

> We have but one volume, an inch or so thick, in which we must describe
> hundreds of days in the lives of thousands of individuals.
>   We've done the best we can to fulfill our obligation by freezing images
> of the events, people and feelings that we feel characterized this time and
> this place. Our report is more than a general sampling, we hope, for
> we've tried to go beyond the obvious surface images. We've tried to
> probe, to feel the pulse of the university and to communicate the vitality
> which the passage of time will never let us experience again.

During the late 1950s and through the 1960s, the yearbook usually contained about 500 pages. Increased printing costs caused that number to be reduced in the 1970s until the 1975 edition had only 224 pages. The 1976 volume had 295 pages.

Within the framework of a traditional yearbook, each year the *Ensian* reflects the particular tastes of the staff. The editor is free to lay out the book in whatever way he or she chooses. The 1974 book emphasized printed copy because the editor was an English major. The 1976 book is largely photographic because Gordon Martin is interested in photography.

The book is usually divided into sections covering Academics, Campus Life, Sports, Arts, Organizations, and Seniors. The end of the book is reserved for pictures of seniors. The 1976 *Ensian* contained 50 pages with 1,269 senior pictures, out of about 5,000 seniors on campus. There are also eight pages of color photography; the remainder are black and white. The book is hard bound with end sheets of 65-pound cover stock, using four-color processes. Work on the book must be completed by December 30 to meet the April delivery date.

Price

The 1976 *Michiganensian* sold for $9 which represented a $1 increase over the previous year. Students who order the book before the end of October are given a $1 discount. The discount is usually offered in a letter sent to seniors announcing the appointment schedule for senior pictures.

In addition to the price of the yearbook, seniors who want their pictures to appear in the book must pay a $3 sitting fee to the yearbook. Some yearbooks, notably that of Michigan State University, have dropped the sitting fee altogether in order to entice more seniors into the book. The sitting fee and price of the book are felt by the publisher's representative to be "about average" for collegiate books in Michigan. Former Editor Marty Schwartz stated, "The price of the book is determined more from the budgetary considerations of the book than from consideration of the impact the price will have on sales."

Promotion

Exhibits 2–6 summarize the promotional tools employed by the *Michiganensian* business staff. Although there had never been any attempt to measure the effectiveness of the various promotions, Editor Martin felt that direct mailings worked best. In 1975, however, the mid-August mailing was not sent out because of an error in the photographer's scheduling.

Distribution

Distribution of the *Michiganensian* is essentially a one-step process. The complete yearbooks are sent by the publisher to the *Michiganensian* office in the Student Publications Building in April. Students can then come in and buy a book or pick up the one that they had ordered.

Other outlets for books are occasionally used but account for only a small number of sales. The two largest bookstores in Ann Arbor are given several books on consignment, keeping $1 on consignment sales. In 1975, two salespersons sold 53 books in five hours during Commencement Exercises. The following is a breakdown of typical sales resulting from various promotional or distribution techniques (see also Exhibit 2):

	Percent
Salespersons	7.59%
Organizations*	6.85
Senior letter	31.56
Frosh letter	2.24
Ensian office	13.82
Booth sales	24.23
Christmas letter	13.71

* Sales of books as part of full page contracts to student organizations on campus.

Each year approximately 100 books are earmarked for free distribution. The books are given to staff members, members of the Board for Student Publications and various libraries on campus. These free books are counted into the sales totals quoted by the *Ensian* staff.

ORGANIZATION

As is apparent from Exhibits 7 and 8, the organization of the *Michiganensian* staff varies greatly from year to year. This annual change in organization is reflective of the lack of continuity on the *Ensian* staff. It also reflects the interests of the editor. In 1975, the editor was primarily concerned with improving the financial position of the publication, thus, the business manager occupied the second highest organizational rung with the associate editor. The 1976 organization is much less hierarchical. The position of associate editor has been eliminated and replaced by the photo editor, reflecting the editor's desire to upgrade the photo-journalistic aspect of the book.

As was stated earlier, the book is divided into several topical areas. The task of assembling each of these areas is assigned to a section editor. The section editors can draw from the photo staff and the copy staff for assistance, but have no line authority over them. It is vitally important that the staff cooperate well as a cohesive unit.

Most staff members count the learning experience, enjoyment, and personal satisfaction as their primary compensation. The size of the staff has an indirect bearing on how well staff members feel they have been compensated. If the staff is small, the work load tends to become burdensome. In the past, many staff members have worked only one year and refused reemployment because their job entailed "too much work and too little pay." The economic benefits of staff positions are slight, as the accompanying table shows:

Salaries for *Michiganensian* Staff

	1975 staff (per year)	*1976 staff (per year)*
Editor-in-chief	$1,000	$1,000
Associate editor	275	
Business manager	400	440
Sales manager	260	320
Section editors	200	150
Staff	100	
Darkroom technician	30*	30*
Publicity director		200
Copy editor		125
Photo editor		125

* This salary is figured weekly instead of annually.

FINANCIAL

The financial standing of the *Michiganensian* could at best be characterized as precarious. Unit sales have dropped 60.5 percent from the peak 1968 level. In this same time period, total revenues and total expenses fell by only approximately 47 percent each, demonstrating the impact of inflation on the yearbook industry. This impact is seen as worse when it is remembered that the *Michiganensian* of 1976 is some 200 pages smaller than the 1968 book. Exhibit 9 displays the budgets (1968–76) approved by the Board for Control of Student Publications and the performance relative to those budgets. Only total revenue and expense figures are available for the years prior to 1973. Exhibit 10 shows budget projections and the income statements for the years 1973–75, plus the budget projections for 1976. Exhibit 10 shows that the major sources of revenues are book sales, senior pictures, and organizations. The Organizations account is revenue from the sale of full pages to campus organizations. (See Exhibit 11 for a copy of the *Michiganensian* Page Contract which explains pricing and discounts.) The account called Nonoperating and Miscellaneous is used for sales of past year's books and some photographic work (Exhibit 10B).

On the expense side the major contribution is the Publication account. Each year the editor draws up specifications for the books and receives at least three bids from yearbook publishers. The size of the publication expense will vary widely depending on several factors: The number of pages in the book; the size of the pages; the quality of the paper, ink, and cover; the photographic techniques or special effects used; and so on.

The contract for the 1976 *Michiganensian* called for 1,500 books of 200 pages. Because of the layout and typesetting involved, the cost per book is high for the initial production run. Once the initial run has been completed the charge per book drops dramatically. The publisher (Worthington of Michigan) will charge the *Ensian* only $3.53 per book beyond the initial contract run of 1,500 books.

COMPETITION

There are no longer the campuswide rivalries that marked the early student publications. The *Michiganensian* is the only campuswide student yearbook. However, several schools put out their own yearbooks, some regularly, others only from time to time. The most notable of the regular competition is the Medical School's yearbook, the *Acquimenitas*. Despite the fact that the *Acquimenitas* is hurriedly put together and priced as high as the *Michiganensian,* it sells 375 copies each year. Despite low overhead and a relatively high price, the *Acquimenitas* is also in financial difficulty because of its low volume.

After reviewing the situation of the *Michiganensian,* Gordon Martin was searching for solid solutions. He was looking for a way to make the *Michiganensian* successful without significantly increasing costs. He wondered what changes in procedure and strategy were necessary to accomplish the goal. In effect, he pondered what changes in the marketing plan were necessary to promote the success of the *Michiganensian* in the future.

EXHIBIT 1
Enrollment statistics*

Enrollment by class:	
Freshpersons	5,241
Sophomores........................	5,151
Juniors............................	5,638
Seniors............................	4,736
Graduate..........................	13,039
Enrollment by school or college:	
Architecture and Urban Planning....	348
Art................................	409
Business Administration............	1,070
Dentistry..........................	767
Education.........................	1,076
Engineering........................	3,373
Rackham (Graduate)................	7,455
Law................................	1,093
Library Science.....................	285
Literature, Science and Arts.........	12,893
Medical School.....................	948
Music..............................	791
Natural Resources..................	718
Nursing............................	942
Pharmacy..........................	489
Public Health......................	598
Social Work........................	550
Total...........................	33,805

* Excluded are the 2,535 students enrolled in
special programs, night school, or the Flint or
Dearborn Campuses. Organizations: There are
over 300 student organizations registered with
the Michigan Student Assembly Office. Membership ranges from 3 to 250 members.

EXHIBIT 2
Promotional tools

Mailings

Second week of August. Letter to the permanent address of seniors,
advertising both senior pictures and yearbook sales. This letter offers a
$1 discount for ordering the book before the end of October. (See Exhibit
3 for an example of this letter.)

First week of September. Letter to freshpersons inviting them to
work on the *Michiganensian* staff or to buy the book. (See Exhibit 4 for an
example of this letter.)

Third week of September. Letter to Ann Arbor address of seniors
informing them that senior pictures are being taken. (See Exhibit 5 for an
example of this letter.)

Christmas. Letter to the parents of seniors suggesting a *Michiganen-*

EXHIBIT 2 (*continued*)

sian as a Christmas present for their son or daughter. (See Exhibit 6 for an example of this letter.)

Newspaper

Ads are run in the *Michigan Daily* as space permits. The *Michiganensian* does not pay for ads but reciprocates by devoting several pages of the yearbook to coverage of the *Daily.*

Radio

Spots are run on WCBN, the student-operated radio station on the campus. The *Michiganensian* does not pay for the ads but reciprocates by devoting several pages of the yearbook to coverage of the radio station.

Posters

Both the photographer (of senior pictures) and the publisher provide printed posters to promote the yearbook. The posters are displayed throughout the campus near busy thoroughfares.

Miscellaneous

Flyers. The starting lineup and *Michiganensian* ads are printed on flyers that are distributed free at U of M football games.

Booth on the Diag. A booth is erected on the central square of campus to serve as a place to make appointments for senior picture sittings and take orders for purchase of the book.

Telephone campaign. Telephone calls are made to seniors to remind them to have their pictures taken.

EXHIBIT 3
August letter to seniors

Dear Senior:

You probably do not need any reminders that this will be your last year as an undergraduate at the University of Michigan. This letter is to remind you that it is time to make an appointment to have your senior picture taken. Before I give you the facts, let me give you my feelings. I too will be a senior and I too have wondered at times whether I wanted to have my picture taken. After thinking it over I did come up with quite a few positive reasons. First of all, pictures come in quite handy when you're job hunting. When was the last time you had your picture taken? When you were a senior in high school, right? You've probably gone through transitions since then

EXHIBIT 3 (*continued*)

and do not have that 17- or 18-year-old look any longer. We also have a new photographer—Toot Photographers, Inc. of Chicago (yea, Toot)—so no excuses about that. As far as buying the yearbook, perhaps you have many friends who are grad students—we'll be including them too this year. (This more complete coverage will be throughout the book.) And believe it or not, I do have one more reason. My years at school have been and will be remembered as some of my best times ever and I know I'll want a 1976 *Michiganensian*.

Now the facts:

1. There will be a $3.00 fee paid at the time of sitting which includes having your picture in the yearbook with your name, degree, and major. There will be an opportunity to purchase additional pictures.
2. Pictures will be taken in natural color. At least six proofs will be sent to you; double exposures and other special effects are available.
3. Pictures will be taken beginning September 29th. Yearbooks will be available for $8.00 before October 30th ($9.00 after) with the coupon at the bottom of this letter.
4. Appointments are *important.* So why not return the enclosed appointment card to the *Michiganensian* office? Otherwise watch the *Daily* for more details on our appointment booths or call the *Michiganensian* office.

Yearbooks will be sold during this period too, but you can order your yearbook now (before you have a chance to misplace this letter) by sending the coupon along with a check or money order for $8.00 made out to the *Michiganensian* and sending it to the Ensian office.

Sincerely,

Marketing Manager

Enclosed is a check or money order for $8.00. Please reserve one *Michiganensian* in my name. I understand that I will receive a receipt within one week.

NAME_____
ANN ARBOR ADDRESS_____ ZIP CODE_____
MAILING INSTRUCTIONS: ($1.00 charge for mailing book)_____
_____
_____

EXHIBIT 4
Letter to freshpersons

Dear Freshperson:

On behalf of the staff of the *Michiganensian,* I would like to take this opportunity to welcome you to the University of Michigan. We, at the *Ensian,* feel that first-year students have much to offer to our organization and hope that you will stop by and see what we have to offer in the way of campus activity.

The *Ensian,* Michigan's yearbook, covers all facets of life at the university and will be a valuable remembrance of your first year at Michigan. Campus life-styles, activities, and sports are all represented in this comprehensive annual. As with your high school yearbook, you'll want to have your *Michiganensian* to review in future years.

By sending the enclosed coupon with your check or money order you can reserve your *Michiganensian* (which comes out in the spring) for $8.00, a dollar off the $9.00 price.

Sincerely,

Sales Manager

Enclosed is a check or money order made out to the *Michiganensian* for $8.00. Please reserve one copy in my name. I understand that I will receive a receipt in the fall.

NAME _____
ANN ARBOR ADDRESS_____
MAILING INSTRUCTIONS: ($1.00 charge for mailing book)_____
_____
_____

EXHIBIT 5
September letter to seniors

Dear Senior:

Congratulations on your upcoming graduation! Currently the preparations for the 1976 *Michiganensian, your* yearbook, are in full swing. We would like to have *all* seniors included in the '76 *Ensian, but we can't do it without your help.*

For your convenience, Toot Photographers, Inc., of Chicago will be at the university starting October 13, 1975. Pictures will be taken on the first floor of the Student Publications Building by appointment to ensure that you will not have to wait. Only these pictures can be used—we retain the right to refuse any pictures not taken by Toot.

The only cost to you is a $3.00 sitting fee, unless of course, you decide to purchase additional prints for your personal use.

A fine selection of six poses will be taken of you in beautiful natural color. Natural color proofs will be mailed directly to you for your selection. You will select the pose to be included in the *Ensian.*

To make arrangements to have your picture taken, please do the following without delay:

Make an appointment at the booth on the Diag, Wednesday, October 6 to Friday, October 15—10:00 a.m. to 4:00 p.m.

After October 15, call 764–0561 or drop by the first floor of the Student Publications Building, 10:00 a.m. to 4:00 p.m.

If unable to do the above, please call 764–0561 any evening 7:00 p.m. to 8:00 p.m. for an appointment starting on October 4.

Please take five minutes to make an appointment. This will be your only opportunity to be included in the 1976 *Michiganensian.*

Enclosed is a check or money order for a yearbook at the senior rate of $8.00. (Offer expires October 30.) Please reserve a yearbook in my name.

NAME_____ LOCAL ADDRESS_____
                                                        ZIP_____

MAILING INSTRUCTIONS: (add $1.00 for mailing)
ADDRESS_____
CITY_____ STATE_____ ZIP_____
After October 30, yearbooks cost $9.00. Present or send this coupon at the Student Publications Building, 420 Maynard before October 30 to save $1.00.

EXHIBIT 6
Christmas letter to parents of seniors

Dear Parents,

   Soon your son or daughter will be graduating from the University of Michigan. While a diploma is awarded for academic achievement, certainly the college experience represents much more. A yearbook captures all the highlights of that experience. Academics is an important section of our book, but we also include campus life, sports, arts, organizations, and a special section on seniors.
   We feel a yearbook complements a diploma. Therefore we're providing you with this opportunity to purchase a *Michiganensian* for your son or daughter. The books will come out at the beginning of April and can be picked up at our office. It is possible for us to mail them. To order a book simply fill out the form below and send it to the *Ensian* office along with a check or money order for $9.00.

Sincerely,

The *Ensian* Staff

Enclosed is a check or money order for $9.00. Please reserve one *Michiganensian* in my name. (Unfortunately we cannot bill you later.)

NAME:_____
Mailing instructions: (add $1.00 for postage)
ADDRESS:_____
STATE_____ ZIP_____

EXHIBIT 7

Organization chart, 1975 *Michiganensian* staff, Martin A. Schwartz, editor-in-chief*

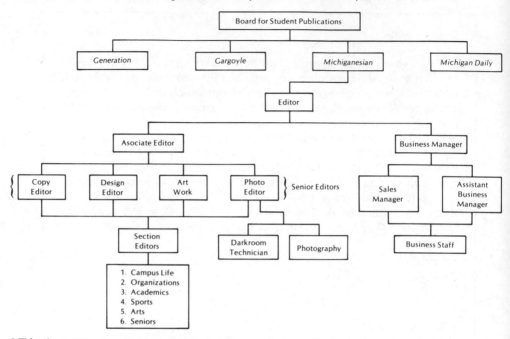

* This chart appears as drawn by Martin A. Schwartz, former editor-in-chief, without alterations.

EXHIBIT 8

Organization chart, 1976 *Michiganensian* staff, Gordon Martin, editor-in-chief

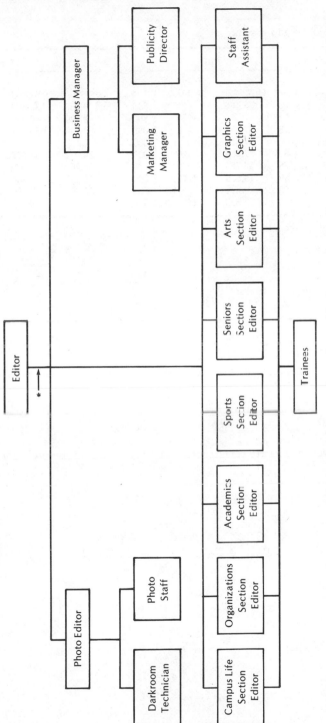

Note: The section editors are on the same organizational level as the photo editor and business manager and are shown below only for ease of display. This chart appears as drawn by Gordon Martin, editor-in-chief, without alterations.

* For 1977 the position of associate editor will be inserted at this point to groom an editor for 1978.

EXHIBIT 9
Financial budgeting and results

	Budget				Actual			
Year	Revenue	Expense	Profit (loss)	Units	Revenue	Expense	Profit (loss)	Units
1967–1968	$37,000	$36,580	$ 420	3,800	$38,160	$38,392	$ (232)	n.a.
1968–1969	43,951	42,965	986	3,800	42,800	40,549	2,251	n.a.
1969–1970	38,178	37,003	1,175	3,000	34,740	39,377	(4,637)	n.a.
1970–1971	n.a.	n.a.	n.a.	2,000	n.a.	n.a.	(3,440)	n.a.
1971–1972	27,660	27,465	195	2,000	24,972	31,067	(6,095)	n.a.
1972–1973	23,325	22,755	570	1,500	16,760	19,025	(2,265)	n.a.
1973–1974	19,685	19,865	(185)	1,500	21,186	21,884	(698)	1,500
1974–1975	20,100	20,471	(371)	1,500	20,398	20,196	202	1,453
1975–1976	22,150	22,350	(200)	1,500	n.a.	n.a.	n.a.	1,500

n.a. = not available.

EXHIBIT 10A

Financial budgets and results by account

	1972–73 actual	1973–74 Budget	1973–74 Actual	1974–75 Budget	1974–75 Actual	1975–76 budget
Revenue						
Book sales................	$ 7,555.00	$ 9,200.00	$ 9,968.00	$ 9,200.00	$ 8,721.50	$ 9,600.00
Organizations............	1,380.00	1,380.00	1,327.00	1,350.00	1,245.00	1,350.00
Senior pictures..........	7,423.80	8,150.00	9,070.50	9,000.00	9,853.00	10,700.00
Nonoperating and miscellaneous......	401.27	350.00	560.50	550.00	578.27	500.00
Advertising..............	0	600.00	260.00	0	0	0
	$16,760.07	$19,680.00	$21,186.00	$20,100.00	$20,397.77	$22,150.00
Expenses						
Publication..............	$ 8,826.41	$ 8,800.00	$ 8,728.86	$ 8,400.00	$ 8,437.15	$10,700.00
Student payroll..........	2,680.00	3,235.00	3,138.00	3,575.00	3,560.00	3,265.00
Delivery expense........	117.67	125.00	289.71	150.00	132.22	150.00
Advertising and publicity....	490.49	500.00	696.87	700.00	826.08	825.00
Telephone and telegraph..	164.95	200.00	189.36	165.00	168.61	175.00
Photo expenses..........	1,715.75	1,800.00	1,656.07	1,800.00	2,012.89	1,450.00
Art expenses............	13.42	50.00	115.00	50.00	13.28	25.00
Office expenses.........	210.84	200.00	157.10	200.00	116.20	125.00
Miscellaneous...........	10.74	50.00	210.35	50.00	79.27	50.00
Sales tax...............	179.19	300.00	385.06	350.00	312.28	350.00
Bad debt................	0	0	0	0	0	0
Commissions.............	76.50	700.00	31.00	0	55.00	0
	$14,485.96	$15,960.00	$15,607.38	$15,440.00	$15,712.98	$17,115.00
Net before General Administrative......	$ 2,274.11	$ 3,720.00	$ 5,578.62	$ 4,660.00	$ 4,684.79	$ 5,035.00
General Administrative Allocation........	4,539.24	4,905.00	4,880.34	4,950.00	4,591.96	5,235.00
Net Income or (Loss)...	$(2,265.13)	$(1,135.00)	$ 698.28	$ (290.00)	$ 92.83	$ (200.00)

EXHIBIT 10B
Notes on the budgets 1973–1976

Revenue

Booksales Account. Will not yield the number of books sold when divided by the price since some of the books are sold at discount.

Organizations Account. Revenue from the sale of pages of coverage to student organizations.

Senior Pictures Account. $3 sitting fee and $4.75 payment from the photographer for each picture taken.

Nonoperating and Miscellaneous Account. Includes the sale of *Ensians* from previous years and the sale of copies of individual photographs.

Advertising Account. At one time the back of the book was reserved for pages of advertising (usually sold to local Ann Arbor merchants). Advertising was dropped in 1975.

Expense

Publication Account. The cost of the contract with the publishing company.

Student Payroll Account. Salaries to student employees.

Delivery Expense Account. Postage for books that are mailed.

Advertising and Publicity Account. See Exhibit 3 for details of the promotional program.

Telephone and Telegraph Account. Self-explanatory.

Photo Expense Account. Includes the cost of some photographic supplies, but most supplies are provided by the senior picture photographer as part of the contract. This account also includes $2 payment to student photographers for each photographic assignment. Each assignment yields on the average three pictures that are printed in the *Ensian.*

Art Expense Account. Artwork for the cover and section dividers of the book.

Office Expense Account. Office supplies.

Miscellaneous Account. Includes $119 of travel expense for 1973–74 actual.

Sales Tax Account. Self-explanatory.

Bad Debt Account. Self-explanatory.

Commissions Account. Commissions to student salespersons and bookstores.

Net before general and administrative

Must break even here to be considered a going concern by the Board in Control of Student Publications.

General and administrative allocation

Charged by the Board in Control of Student Publications. It is not supposed to be rent, but is allocated based on the amount of office space and clerical time that the publication uses.

EXHIBIT 11

MICHIGANENSIAN PAGE CONTRACT

Date_____

The *MICHIGANENSIAN* agrees to insert_____full pages

for _____
                    (name of organization)

_____
                    (billing address)

1. We agree to pay the *Michiganensian* for space at the following
    rates: (please check one)

Number of pages	Without discount	With both discounts	With book discount
_____1	$60.00	$50.00	$1 × number of *Michiganensians* ordered
_____2	$100.00	$90.00	_____

    a. All additional pages will be at the rate of $40.00 per page.
    b. This contract must be returned to the Business Manager,
        Michiganensian, 420 Maynard, Ann Arbor.
    c. The discounts that are available:
        (1) $5.00 if this contract is returned by _____.
        (2) $5.00 if payment is made by _____.
        (3) $1.00 × the number of *Michiganensians* ordered
             and paid for with the return of the contract.

2. The *Michiganensian* reserves the right to make changes in
    any copy submitted.

For the *Michiganensian*   For _____
                                                    (organization)
_____
(Business Manager)   _____
Phone: 764–0561   (signature)

                                      _____
                                           (office held)

                                      _____
                                              (phone)

CASE

42

Atlanta-Tucker
Industrial Park*

Bill Hare sat at his desk studying the large map of Atlanta which hung on the wall. His attention was focused on a region to the northeast of the city in the Tucker-Stone Mountain area. As he studied the map, he reviewed once again the problems now facing him and the alternatives available.

The area which so engrossed Mr. Hare was a new industrial park development known as Atlanta-Tucker Industrial Park. The project was owned by Royal Palm Beach Colony, Inc., a real estate company in Miami, Florida. Royal Palm had acquired the 300 acres of raw industrial land in the summer of 1973 and had invested $1.4 million over the next 15 months grading the land, cutting in roads, and preparing the sites. Although the land preparation had been completed by August 1974, no lots had been sold in November of 1975 when Royal Palm offered Mr. Hare the exclusive right to market the development. Mr. Hare was now faced with determining a complete marketing program for the property, including the type of clients to seek, financial arrangements to offer, prices of lots, as well as advertising and promotional strategy.

BACKGROUND OF ROYAL PALM BEACH COLONY, INC.

Royal Palm Beach Colony, Inc., was a large real estate development firm in southern Florida. In April 1974, the company had total assets of $92,162,000 with earnings for the fiscal year of $1,881,000. With the ex-

---

* This case was co-authored by Peggy Lipsey, Graduate Student, Georgia State University.

ception of Atlanta-Tucker Industrial Park, the company dealt exclusively in residential property, offering fully developed land and housing in planned communities in southern and western Florida. Atlanta-Tucker represented their only venture into commercial and industrial real estate, and their only project outside Florida.

Since 1974, the generally poor economic condition in the country had been paralleled by a severe depression in the real estate and construction industries. Royal Palm's earnings dropped to $228,000 in 1975 while their interest expense on revolving credits alone had amounted to $4,020,000. The company had been granted a $15 million revolving credit by a group of banks in 1972 which was extended to $30 million in 1973. The economic downturn made it impossible for the company to begin amortizing this $30 million credit with quarterly payments of $2.5 million as scheduled in April 1975. After lengthy negotiations, bank lenders agreed to restructure the loan in November 1975 under terms which management considered highly favorable.

The loan negotiations concluded above did not include a $7.1 million loan on the property in Atlanta, however. At the present time, the company was engaged in ongoing negotiations in an attempt to restructure this loan. If unsuccessful, they would not be able to meet the payments as now arranged and the lender could declare a default. Under certain circumstances, a default on this loan could result in a default on the $30 million loan. The primary condition placed upon the company by the lender for restructure was that 25 of the available acres in the Atlanta-Tucker develop-

EXHIBIT 1
Picture of Atlanta-Tucker Industrial Park

ment must be sold by June 1976. Management believed, however, that the sale of any of the property would be accepted by the lender as evidence of a viable concern and enable them to restructure the loan. A picture of the property is shown in Exhibit 1.

BACKGROUND OF WILLIAM D. HARE

Bill Hare had graduated from Georgia Institute of Technology in Atlanta, Georgia, in 1965 with a B.S. in Industrial Management. His involvement with industrial development began in 1967 when he was employed by Clayton McLendon, Inc., a small industrial real estate firm. His experience with industrial land included investigation, analysis, selection, and acquisition of sites for clients; structuring build-lease transactions for industrial and commercial clients; and the assembly and sale of tracts of land with industrial potential for investors and developers. Mr. Hare felt that the main impact of his experiences during this period was an in-depth exposure to the industrial and commercial real estate business and to the Society of Industrial Realtors, a professional organization which enabled him to meet industry leaders on both the local and national level and to develop the contacts so necessary in the brokerage business.

After leaving Clayton McLendon, Inc., in 1972, Mr. Hare continued in all phases of commercial and industrial brokerage, first on his own and later with a partner. During this period, he was active in site acquisitions for several national and local firms, handling all phases of negotiations and sales. His most recent activity included two major studies of Atlanta real estate for national firms. The first was for Kaiser-Aetna, which was seeking 200 acres to develop, and the second was for S. S. Kresge Company, which was looking for a site for a 2-million-square-foot warehouse under one roof.

CONTRACT BETWEEN MR. HARE AND ROYAL PALM

Mr. Hare first became aware of the Atlanta-Tucker development in early 1975 when seeking property for a client who wished to locate in that area. He realized at the time that the project had no strong marketing program and decided to make an initial contact with Herbert Kaplan, the president of Royal Palm, through a mutual acquaintance. The following year, Royal Palm decided to actively seek a broker in the Atlanta area for the project and, after interviewing several prospects, offered a contract for the exclusive right to sell to Mr. Hare. The only exceptions to this contract were clients generated directly by Royal Palm's own activities.

In accepting the contract, Mr. Hare recognized that the property had several problems which he would have to overcome. First, in any project of this type, access to highways was a critical consideration by industries considering locating in the area. Although all internal roads had been completed, the highway connecting the project with the Stone Mountain Industrial Boulevard, a major link with the interstate system, was not completed. Current access to the site was limited to the Lawrenceville Highway, a narrow, two-lane road in relatively poor condition. Although Mr. Hare and Royal Palm had recently sold the right-of-way to the highway department for $280,000, negotiations were not complete for the property rights on each side of Atlanta-Tucker. Highway officials estimated that the initial contract would be let in July 1976, but felt that it would be three years before the connection was completed. Mr. Hare felt that unless support of local politicians could be acquired to move the completion date to one year, it would be difficult to sell the lots. He felt that this would take some of his time, but could be accomplished.

Despite the severity of the transportation situation, Mr. Hare viewed the second major problem of Atlanta-Tucker as even more difficult to overcome. The project had existed for two years in a state of inertia, and it was now crucial to break this pattern and generate an initial sale. Mr. Hare realized that a careful review of the pricing strategy would be necessary in order to meet the short-range goal of an immediate sale while preserving the long-range pricing standards. In addition, he considered the possibility of erecting a speculative building on one lot. His experience had indicated that many clients were initially interested in seeing only completed buildings although they later often bought the land and had their own buildings erected. Thus, he felt if he had any type of building with which to draw the prospects out to look at the project, he might be able to sell them the land.

A final problem had recently been brought to Mr. Hare's attention. Although all utilities had been installed in the initial development stage, a countywide moratorium had been in effect on sewage additions at that time. The result was that the current sewer availability was limited to 42,000 gallons per day. When installed, county officials had assured the developers that this was a temporary problem, but to date no additions had been undertaken. Unless an immediate improvement was made, a serious limitation was placed on the types of industries that could be serviced. In fact, Mr. Hare felt he would be primarily restricted to distribution facilities until this problem was corrected.

Despite the severe problems facing the development, Mr. Hare was confident that his own background in industrial real estate and his personal contacts with Atlanta brokers, politicians, utility companies, and railroads would enable him to succeed in developing the project. He felt he needed a single project with a well-defined goal on which to concentrate his effort. Further, he had found that working on a specific project usually generated other business, and his contract with Royal Palm did not prevent him from selling or leasing to prospects in other industrial parks if Atlanta-Tucker could not meet the client's needs. Finally, although concerned about the current financial position of Royal Palm, he was convinced that the project would eventually be developed, and if Royal Palm were not successful in their financial negotiations, he felt the contacts he was now establishing with First National City Bank, the lender, could be of value in the future.

The contract between Mr. Hare and Royal Palm went into effect in November 1975 and was to expire in June 1976. It provided that Mr. Hare would receive a 5 percent commission on the total sales price in cash at the time of closing for any property which he sold where neither another broker nor Royal Palm was involved. In any cooperative deals with another broker, the broker would receive 5 percent and Mr. Hare would receive 3 percent. This policy was competitive with the commissions offered by the majority of the industrial parks in the Atlanta area, although one park had recently increased the rate from 5 percent to 10 percent in an effort to generate more sales.

BACKGROUND OF THE ATLANTA MARKET

In determining the marketing strategy he wished to follow, Mr. Hare felt it might be helpful to review the historical development of other industrial parks in Atlanta and the different approaches which had been employed, both successfully and unsuccessfully, by other developers. In addition, he knew that the current demand for industrial property and the practices of his major competitors would have a great impact on his price and the amenities he offered.

Originally, industrial development in Atlanta had been primarily an activity of the railroads who would buy large tracts of land to develop or to sell raw. This land was sold to industries which used the rails, and the railroad had high freight revenue requirements which a firm must meet in order to qualify to buy the land. Only about 25 percent of all firms were able to meet these requirements so that a large market was open to the private developer.

In 1948, Scott Candler, the one-man county commission for DeKalb County, negotiated with General Motors to locate on a site of land in his county in return for a road being built to the location. This road became Peachtree Industrial Boulevard and eventually attracted a large number of other industries to the area.

This development pattern was to be repeated at numerous other locations throughout the five-county metropolitan area. The developers would negotiate with the political structure to obtain roads and with the power companies for utilities, and then use those amenities to draw industry into the area. In the early 1960s, the Atlanta and State Chambers of Commerce also played significant roles in attracting new firms. Most of these early developments used a "no frills" concept. The user got exactly what he needed in terms of square feet of space and few additional amenities were provided.

In 1961, the Great Southwest Corporation built the Atlanta Gateway Park Industrial Center and with it introduced several new concepts into the industrial development of Atlanta. First, they deviated from the earlier "no frills" idea by adding landscaping, sculpture, and other such amenities, while initially offering the lots at the same price as other developers. This action forced other industrial park developers to upgrade their parks, but different developers continued to place varying amounts of emphasis on this area. Second, they were the first developer interested in selling just the sites. While previous promoters had been concerned with selling land in order to construct a building on it, Great Southwest was willing to sell sites to independent builders who would then locate the ultimate user and construct the building. This led to a number of builders who owned individual lots in several different places and who could offer their clients a choice of locations.

In contrast to the strategy of Great Southwest, other successful parks did not attempt to sell the land at all. Rather, the developer sought to find firms interested in build-lease agreements so that they retained control of the entire development. Still other industrial park districts offered a variety of terms so that both sales and build-lease arrangements were available.

The proliferation of industrial parks continued throughout the 1960s and the early 1970s so that by 1975, there were approximately 50 parks in the metropolitan area. Exhibit 2 shows the location and basic characteristics of some of the larger industrial districts at that time. Despite the large number, Mr. Hare did not feel that he was in direct competition with most of them. He based this conclusion on the fact that rail facilities were available on 75 percent of all the sites in Atlanta-Tucker Industrial Park. Although 80 percent of all industrial firms did not use rails, the remaining 20 percent represented some of the larger national firms. This caused Mr. Hare to perceive his direct competition as those parks offering comparable rail services.

In viewing demand for industrial real estate, Mr. Hare considered the following facts about land usage as important in formulating his plans. First, he knew that the average industrial building covered about 50 percent of the acreage of the lot. The bulk of the lots sold, representing roughly one half of the total sales, were for 5 to 15 acres. Speculative

EXHIBIT 2
Industrial parks in Atlanta

Name and address of industrial park	Developer (D) Owner (O)	Agent & Phone		Acreage and/or sq. ft. completed 1/1/75	Do you have speculative building on this site?	Does park have a railroad siding?
		BARTOW COUNTY				
1. Interstate 75 Industrial Area (2 mi. S. of Cartersville)	LaVista Corp. (O & D)	Don Perry 934-1800	400 acres	0	No	Yes
		CLAYTON COUNTY				
2. Airport Plaza 400-510 Plaza Dr.	Stonehenge Properties Inc. (D) RGI (O)	J.H. Ewing & Sons 256-9001	10 acres	3 acres	Yes	No
3. Atlanta/Clayton District Lee's Mill Rd.	Shaheen & Co. (O & D)	Shaneen & Co. 681-1234	8 acres	144,390 sq. ft.	Yes	No
4. Atlanta-Southern Industrial Park Ga. 54 near I-75	Winston Ent. (D) Jack Rooker (O)	Jack Rooker 961-4880	310 acres	160,000 sq. ft.	plans for speculative building	Yes
5. Central Industrial District Forest Park, Ga.	Southern Railway System (O & D)	J.C. Cook 688-0800	50 acres remaining	35 acres	No. (others do)	Yes
6. Morrow Business Park Ga. 54 near I-75	Winston Ent (D) Jack Rooker (O)	Jack Rooker 961-4880	105 acres	850,000 sq. ft.	plans for speculative building	Yes
8. 75/54 Industrial Park (nr. I-75 South & Ga. 54 intersection)	Dr. William Flynn (O)	J.H. Ewing & Sons 256-9001	50 acres		No	No
		COBB COUNTY				
9. Acworth Industrial Park 1902 Leland Dr. Marietta, Ga.	Jack W. Chancey & C.A. Overcash (O & D)	None	33 acres	5,000 sq. ft.	No	Yes
10. Cobb-Marietta Industrial Park 1095 Marietta Ind. Dr. NE Marietta, Ga.	Georgia Marietta Co. Inc. (O & D)	R. Glenn Reed, Bill Little 422-9900	375 acres	1,000,000 sq. ft.	Yes	Yes
11. Franklin Park Delk & Franklin Rds. Marietta, Ga.	M & M Investment Co. (O & D)	458-9441	435,000 sq. ft.	325,000 sq. ft.	Yes	No
12. North Cobb Industrial Park 1130 Shallowford Rd. NE (approx. 4½ miles North of Canton Hwy. & I-75 Intersection)	Hobart Early (O & D)	Walter Boden 351-6813	66 acres	0	No	Yes
13. Windy Hill Industrial Park McCoba Dr. Smyrna, Ga.	McCoba Corp. (O & D)	McDaniell Ins. & Realty Co. 435-9023	16 acres	92,000 sq. ft. (6 bldgs.)	No.	No.
		COWETA COUNTY				
14. Shenandoah Industrial Park Amlajack Blvd. Shenandoah, Ga. (I-85 Newnan Exit)	Shenandoah Dev. Inc. (O & D)	A.A. Simon 577-4820	1,000 acres	0	Planned	Planned

buildings were usually erected on lots of this size. There was also a tendency for firms to buy more land than needed for their immediate purposes in order to have expansion capacity.

Mr. Hare felt some concern about the current demand for industrial property in the Atlanta area. Demand in the industrial real estate market

EXHIBIT 2 (*continued*)

Name and address of industrial park	Developer (D) Owner (O)	Agent & Phone	Acreage	and/or sq. ft. completed 1/1/75	Do you have speculative building on this site?	Does park have a railroad siding?
DeKALB COUNTY						
15 Atlanta Tucker Commercial-Industrial Park 4571 Lawrenceville Hwy. Tucker, Ga.	Royal Atlanta Dev. Corp. (O & D)	William B. Hare Jr. 688-1273	350 acres (156 acres developed)	Land development just completed	No	Yes
16. Chamblee Industrial District New Peachtree Rd.	Shaheen & Co. (O & D)	Shaheen & Co. 681-1234	11 acres	203,480 sq. ft.	Yes	No
17. Cherokee Industrial Park Bonsal Rd. & Koppers Rd. (btwn. Cedar Grove & Henrico Rds.)	Cherokee Ind. Park Inc. (O & D)	R.L. Rothberg 522-1114	85 acres	50 acres	No	Yes
18. East Ponce de Leon Industrial Park Laredo Dr. & Dekalb Ind. Way Decatur, Ga.	Pattillo Construction Co. Inc. (O & D)	Jim Topple 377-0124	75 acres	418,700 sq. ft.	No	Yes
19. Mountain Interchange Industrial Park Mountain Ind. Blvd. & Stone Mtn. Frwy. Tucker, Ga.	Stone & Webster Inc. (O & D)	Harry E. Hopper 448-7408	100 acres	60%	No	NO
20. North Park I-285 & Buford Hwy.	M&M Investment Co. (O & D)	458-9441	1,600,000 sq. ft.	All	No	No
21. Northeast Atlanta Industrial Park Peachtree Ind. Blvd. at Winters Chapel Rd.	Kay Developers (O & D)	I.L. Kunian 691-6987 Max L. Kuniansky 355-6000	169 acres	1,000,000 sq. ft.	Yes	
22. Oakcliff Center 3400 Oakcliff Rd. Doraville, Ga.	Oakcliff Ltd. (O & D)	Greg Gregory 261-2323	22 acres	175,000 sq. ft.	Yes	No
23. Oakcliff Industrial Park Oakcliff Ind. St.	Shaheen (O & D)	Shaheen & Co. 681-1234	25 acres	389,541 sq. ft.	Yes	No
24. Panola Industrial Park Minola Dr. Lithonia, Ga.	Pattillo Construction Co. Inc. (O & D)	Jim Topple 377-0124	275 acres	379,000 sq. ft.	Yes	No
25. Pleasantdale Industrial Park Pleasantdale Rd.	Stone & Webster Inc. (O & D)	Harry E. Hopper 448-7408	120 acres	None	No	No
26. Stone Mountain Industrial District Kelton Dr.	Shaheen & Co. (O & D)	Shaheen & Co. 681-1234	36 acres	100,904 sq. ft.	Yes	Can be constructed
27. Stone Mountain Industrial Park Stone Mtn. Blvd. Tucker, Ga.	Pattillo Construction Co. Inc. (O & D)	Jim Topple 377-0124	2,000 acres	5,265,000 sq. ft.	Yes	Yes
28. Tucker Northeast Industrial Park 2090 Tucker Ind. Blvd.	William H. Benton (O & D)	Greg Gregory 261-2323	32 acres	138,000 sq. ft.	Yes	No
FAYETTE COUNTY						
28-A. Peachtree City Industrial Park Peachtree City, Ga.	Garden Cities Corp. (O & D)	Andy McGregor 487-8585	3,500 acres	316 acres	Yes	Yes

is measured by the absorption rate at which land is actually taken off the market by the final user. Previously the absorption rate had been approximately 500 to 600 acres per year in the Atlanta metropolitan area. During the past year, this rate had dropped to approximately 300 acres. The total acreage sold in 1974 had been primarily in three developments: Snapfinger Industrial Park with 94 acres; Atlanta Gateway Industrial

EXHIBIT 2 (*continued*)

Name and address of industrial park	Developer (D) Owner (O)	Agent & Phone	Acreage and/or sq. ft. completed 1/1/75	Do you have speculative building on this site?	Does park have a railroad siding?
		FULTON COUNTY			
29. Apollo Properties Fulton Ind. Blvd. (N. of Campbellton Rd.)	Apollo Partnerships Ltd.	Open 432-4151	500 acres	Undeveloped land	No	No
30. Armour-Ottley Industrial Park Monroe Dr.	Southern Railway System (O & D)	J.C. Cook 688-0800	10 acres remaining	5 acres	No	Yes
31. Atlanta Air Center 1149 Central Ave. East Point, Ga.	Atlanta Air Center (D)	Rena K. Rider 761-3151	60 acres	389.116 sq. ft.	Yes	Yes
32. Atlanta Gateway Park Fulton Ind. Blvd.	Kunian Enterprises (O & D); MGIC Equities (O)	Kunian Enterprises 691-6987	3.000 acres	1,800 acres	Yes	Yes
33. Checkerboard Atlanta Industrial Park I-85 South at Jonesboro Rd.	Ralston-Purina Co. (O); Cauble & Co. (D)	Nick Schiltz 577-7332	100 acres	400,000 sq. ft.	No	Yes
34. Fulton County Industrial District Fulton Ind. Blvd.	Fulton County (O)	Henry Robinson 522-5477	2,480 acres	2,242 acres	Yes	Yes
35. Fulton Industrial District Shirley Dr.	Shaheen & Co. (O & D)	Shaheen & Co. 681-1234	8 acres	128.180 sq. ft.	Yes	No
36. Interpark I-85 & US 29 (approx. 1 mi. S. of Fairburn)	Interpark Assoc. (O & D)	William B. Hare Jr. 688-1273	320 acres	0	No	Yes
37. M.D. Hodges Ent. Inc. Business Park Fulton Ind. Blvd. at Cascade Rd.	M.D. Hodges Ent. Inc. (O & D)	691-4007	242 acres		Preliminary plans	Yes
38. M.D. Hodges Ent. Inc. Fulton Industrial District Fulton Ind. Blvd.	M.D. Hodges Ent. Inc. (O & D)	691-4007	24 acres		Yes	No
39. M.D. Hodges Ent. Inc. Fulton Industrial District I-20 West	M.D. Hodges Ent. Inc. (O & D)	691-4007	13 acres		Preliminary plans	Yes
40. M.D. Hodges Ent. Inc. Industrial Area I-75 South	M.D. Hodges Ent. Inc. (O & D)	691-4007	7 acres	71.000 sq. ft.	Yes	No
41. Metrolanta Park Fulton Ind. Blvd. & Bucknell Dr.	Southwest Fulton Minipark (O)	Tommy James 351-6813	32 acres (1,393.920 sq. ft.)	72.000 sq. ft.	Yes	Yes
42. Northwest Industrial Park McArthur Blvd. & Chattahoochee Ave.	Jobade Corp. (O); W. Armstrong Smith (D)	W.A. Smith 767-0564	80 acres	40 acres	Yes	Yes
43. South Perimeter Industrial Park Sullivan Rd.	Shaheen & Co. (O & D)	Shaheen & Co. 681-1234	25 acres	169.200 sq. ft.	Yes	No
44. Unnamed Jefferson St.	Southern Railway System (O & D)	J.C. Cook 688-0800	24 acres		No	Yes

Park with 92 acres; and Kaiser-Aetna with 60 acres. Industry leaders were undecided as to the ultimate effect the current recession might have on long-term absorption rates, but most experts agreed that 1976 would show some improvement.

ALTERNATIVE MARKETING STRATEGIES

In determining an overall marketing strategy, Mr. Hare felt there were seven distinct decision areas. These included:

EXHIBIT 2 (*continued*)

Name and address of industrial park	Developer (D) Owner (O)	Agent & Phone	Acreage and/or sq. ft. completed 1/1/75	Do you have speculative building on this site?	Does park have a railroad siding?
GWINNETT COUNTY					
45. Duluth-Southern Industrial District Pleasanthill Rd. Duluth, Ga.	Southern Railway System (O & D)	J.C. Cook 688-0800	1,300 acres remaining	20 acres	No	Yes
46. I-85 Norcross/Tucker Industrial Area Norcross-Tucker Rd. & I-85	LaVista Corp. (O & D)	Don Perry 934-1800	20 acres	0	No	No
47. Interstate Industrial Park I-85 & Beaver Ruin Rd. Norcross, Ga.	Harry Weeks, Lou Robinson & A. Weeks (D); W.R.W. (O)	Lou Robinson 633-5115	164 acres	575,000 sq. ft.	Yes	No
47-A. Norcross/85 Center I-85 & Norcross Tucker Rd. Norcross, Ga.	Norcross 85 Park Inc. (O & D)	Bob Jones 872-6611	140 acres	400,000 sq. ft.	Yes	No
48. Norcross Industrial Park Buford Hwy.	Winston Ent. (D); Jack Rooker (O)	Jack Rooker 961-4880	42 acres	0	Plans for speculative bldg.	Yes
49. Norcross-Southern Industrial District I-85 & Pleasantdale Rd. Doraville, Ga.	Southern Railway System (O & D)	J.C. Cook 688-0800	809 acres remaining	75 acres	No (others do)	Yes
50. North 85 Park	Land Concepts (O)	Watt Neal 352-1882	12 acres	40,000 sq. ft.	50,000 sq. ft. (Spring, 1976)	Yes
51. Peachtree Corners Atlantic Blvd. & Adriatic Ct.	Shaheen & Co. (O & D)	Shaheen & Co. 681-1234	16 acres	187,844 sq. ft.	Yes	No
52. Peachtree Corners Business Park Peachtree Corners	Kaiser Aetna (O & D)	R.E. Williams Jr. 659-7906	345 acres	970,000 sq. ft.	Yes	Yes
ROCKDALE COUNTY					
53. Conyers Industrial Area I-20 at West Ave. Exit	LaVista Corp. (O & D)	Don Perry 934-1800	200 acres	0	No	No
54. Rockdale Industrial Plaza Old Conyers Hwy. 12 Conyers, Ga.	Pattillo Construction Co. Inc. (O & D)	Jim Tonnie 977-0104	400 acres	1,030,000 sq. ft.	No	Yes
WALTON COUNTY					
55. Circle Industrial Park Ga. Hwy. 229 Social Circle, Ga.	Robert Bick	256-3395	226 acres	0	No	Yes

1. To select a name for the park.
2. To establish the prices to charge.
3. To determine the most effective sales force.
4. To determine the type of clients he wished to attract and the type of district (mixed or specialized) he wished to establish.
5. To determine the amenities he wished to offer including what, if any, additional services such as ongoing property management should be included.

EXHIBIT 2 (*concluded*)

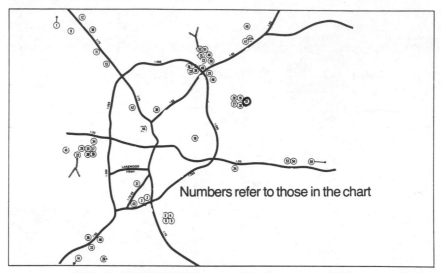

Numbers refer to those in the chart

Note: Data for this chart of Metro Atlanta industrial parks and warehouses were obtained from the responses to hundreds of questionnaires sent by *Atlanta Magazine* to real estate firms, developers, agents and known industrial park offices. Numbers shown at the outset of each listing refer to the same digits on the locator map indicating approximate site of parks.

Source: Adapted from "Zoning: Industrial Occupancy: Rising," by Bruce Galphin, *Atlanta Magazine* (Atlanta Chamber of Commerce, February 1976), pp. 43–56. Copyright 1976, *Atlanta Magazine*. Reprinted with permission.

6. To set the level and mix of advertising, promotion, and publicity.
7. To choose the best financing alternatives to offer.

He recognized that each of these factors could have a large independent impact and could also interact with the other decision variables.

Name of the district

Mr. Hare felt one of the most pressing decisions facing him was the selection of a name for the development. He thought Atlanta-Tucker Industrial District was too long and that a shorter, "catchy" name would be better. Since the name "Royal" had been used in other projects owned by Royal Palm Colony, he considered calling it Royal Atlanta.

Pricing

A second major area where immediate attention was needed was in determining the pricing strategy for the development. Royal Palm had recognized that their original prices of $36,000–$43,000 per acre were too high and had agreed they should be cut 20 percent when Mr. Hare took over the project. Mr. Hare wondered, however, if more drastic cuts might be wise to generate a few quick sales. He had even considered a sales price below the $17,500 actual investment per acre which Royal Palm had in the land. He had not determined how low he would be willing to go or how many acres he would sell at a reduced price. He realized that he must balance the immediate need for tenants against the long-range impact that too many concessions would have on the ultimate profits.

In addition to the goals of the developer and the investment cost involved, the competitive advantages and disadvantages of the project in comparison to similar developments would be an important determinant of the pricing policy. Mr. Hare had checked the prices of several other developments and had found the following price ranges:

Snapfinger Industrial Park..................	$30,000–$35,000 per acre
Peachtree Corners (Kaiser-Aetna)...........	$25,000 for raw land
	$35,000 lots with poor slope
	$45,000–$55,000 choice
	developed lots
Tucker-Stone Mountain....................	$30,000–$35,000 per acre

Mr. Hare realized that the different parks offered vastly different facilities and services, and knew that additions he made in these areas would have an impact on his price. He also noted that some of the higher priced projects were not under any real pressure to sell the lots at the present time and felt it would be more profitable to hold the land until demand reached their price.

Sales force

The third decision in determining how to market Atlanta-Tucker was selecting the most effective sales force to employ. Although many industrial parks sold strictly through independent brokers, a few hired their own sales force.

There were approximately 18 industrial brokerage firms in Atlanta, most having two brokers. If Mr. Hare chose to market the project through these professional industrial real estate brokers, he would probably achieve the broadest initial exposure. Sales made by brokers would reduce his own commission from 5 percent to 3 percent, however. If he chose to hire his own sales force, there were two alternatives available. Under the first he could hire a number of salespersons on a salaried basis to make cold calls and attempt to generate interest directly from the potential user. He estimated it would cost approximately $25,000 to hire an experienced sales representative, although an inexperienced person could probably be found for $10,000. The cost of this sales force would have to be paid by Mr. Hare since there were no agreements with Royal Palm to cover this contingency. A second approach might be to hire a salesperson on commission. Under this plan, the salesperson would be provided with a desk and telephone, and would receive 60 percent of all revenues he or she generated. Mr. Hare currently had one employee who worked for him on this basis.

Type of park

In deciding what type of tenants to seek, Mr. Hare felt there was a strong conflict between the short- and long-range goals. In the short run, it was vital to attract one or more initial tenants in order to satisfy the loan requirements and to generate activity. In the long range, however, it was vital that the early tenants not compromise either the ultimate use of the complex or destroy the pricing structure.

Mr. Hare was currently negotiating seriously with three vastly different prospects. The first was a metal plating company which needed three acres and was willing to purchase it for $15,000 per acre and begin construction immediately with plans to be in the new facilities within six months. Financing presented no problems with this prospect, but a serious limitation was imposed by the available sewage facilities. If the metal plating company did purchase the land, it would exceed the total sewage capacity now available. Mr. Hare thought he could solve the sewage problem by spending $15,000 for additional capacity, but he wondered how the sale might influence the future prices he could charge. He was sure that other potential buyers would learn about the price the metal plating company had paid and was afraid they would be reluctant to pay more than this.

The second prospect was a Panasonic distributor which needed five acres for a warehouse. They were offering $50,000 for the land and also planned to be in residence within six months. In addition, Mr. Hare knew there was a possibility that he might be able to negotiate the construction of their building with a local builder. He felt, however, they wanted a building that would cost $10 per square foot, but they really only wanted to pay about $8 per square foot. The final prospect was a lumber company which wanted a site for a retail operation, but they were purchasing the land with plans to build in about three years. They were discussing a price of $30,000 per acre and would need approximately five acres.

Several prospects of a different type were also under consideration at this time. All involved the creation of recreational facilities such as a tennis club or an ice rink in the complex. Mr. Hare felt this would be an added attraction to industry and that a venture of this type could easily be supported by the surrounding residential area. A recent survey indicated that there were 120,000 people within ten minutes of the property.

The creation of a tennis club would cost approximately $500,000 and would be composed of 12 outdoor courts and a clubhouse. The cost involved would include $10,000 for each court, $25,000 an acre for the land, and $100,000 for the clubhouse which would include lockers, sauna, pro shop, and a sandwich shop. In order to be profitable, such a tennis club would need to have 600 members with initiation fees of $250 and monthly dues of $25. Mr. Hare was currently in touch with a professional organizer who had completed a feasibility study and would oversee the construction, hire the operating staff, and manage the club during the first year. Preliminary surveys had indicated high potential in the project. It was undecided at this time whether Royal Palm would undertake the project itself or bring in an outside promoter to handle the development.

Also under consideration was a double ice rink. This sport had recently been gaining in popularity and some experimentation had been done in converting the rinks into four tennis courts during slack periods.

Finally, Royal Palm had considered donating some land to be used as a site for athletic activities. This might be used by industrial leagues or as a community practice field for Little League players.

It was hoped that each of these ventures would perform the joint functions of generating activity in the park and increasing the public awareness of its existence as well as offering an additional attraction to industry in weighing location decisions.

Advertising and promotional alternatives

Mr. Hare also faced several alternative decisions concerning advertising and promotional activities. The terms of his contract with Royal Palm specified that he would be given $30,000 for use during the eight month period between November 1975 and June 1976 for advertising and promoting Atlanta-Tucker. The only restraint placed upon Mr. Hare was that he must submit written justification for all expenditures made.

Prior to this time, advertising had been handled exclusively by the in-house advertising personnel in Miami. Although the people responsible had never seen the Atlanta-Tucker development, they prepared all copy and selected the media to be used. They had employed primarily trade magazines such as *Site Selection Handbook, Area Development Magazine,* and *Real Estate Atlanta.* A sample of the copy used appears in Exhibit 3. This ad had been run in *Real Estate Atlanta* every month for the past year.

Mr. Hare was currently considering whether the best use of his $30,000 would be in personal contact (including travel to meet clients, entertaining, and so on), direct mail, advertising, or publicity. If he decided to employ more than one method, he would also need to determine what proportion of his funds to allocate to each.

Mr. Hare felt that the most effective advertising tool in industrial real

EXHIBIT 3
Ad for Atlanta-Tucker Industrial Park

estate was personal contacts, but he knew there were two approaches he might take in this area. Under the first, he would attempt to contact directly the real estate executives of individual companies who might be considering locating in Atlanta. One approach might be to call on firms currently located in nearby industrial complexes in hopes of obtaining information about companies which were considering expansions or moves. He realized that he probably would not be talking with the person directly involved in making this decision in the local office, but hoped it might provide some leads. He had recently agreed to head up the Heart Fund Drive in the Tucker area and thought this might give him an "in" with the firms involved. While he knew this personal contact might be the best approach, he had to weigh the possible advantages of such canvassing against the demand which it would make on his time.

In addition to cold calls in the Tucker area, Mr. Hare also had the complete files of the prospects that had been identified before he took over the marketing of the park and felt that one possibility was to rework these old leads. A review of the old records revealed that there were approximately 20 major files which he might investigate as well as a number of responses to past advertising. He estimated that about 70 percent of these files were worthless, but still considered them one of the best sources for prospects available.

A second approach to the personal contact was to work through the real estate brokers both in Atlanta and in other major cities. Mr. Hare had already made private appointments for lunch and a personal visit to the project with 10 to 12 of the most prominent real estate brokers in Atlanta. He hoped that this one-on-one consideration might generate some special interest. In addition, he was considering a group presentation in the form of a party on the site for all local brokers. He would like to have some unique approach which might distinguish the showing from other projects. Possibilities included having a railroad car, complete with a band and beer, pick up the brokers downtown and carry them to the site. Also under consideration was having a helicopter or hot air balloon for an aerial view. The practical implications and cost of these ventures had not been fully evaluated, but Mr. Hare felt the trick was to get some other interested party involved so that the cost could be shared.

In addition to local brokers, Mr. Hare had considered going to New York and a few other major cities and calling on prominent brokers who might have clients interested in the Atlanta area. He had not decided whether to contact these brokers through a formal interview in their offices or to have a series of parties where five to ten brokers were invited on a more informal basis. He estimated that each of these parties would cost from $200–$500.

In addition to public contact, Mr. Hare viewed direct mail as an effective advertising tool. He was currently investigating the cost of preparing and mailing a brochure to a selected list of prospects although he had not determined his exact mailing list. One possibility was to send the brochures to a published list of 3,000 corporate real estate executives across the country. A second possibility was to use a private list of 600 firms which he knew had expressed interest in locating in Georgia. A final possible mailing list could be compiled from a book of manufacturers currently located in Georgia which was published by the state. Mr. Hare estimated that the brochures would cost approximately $1.25–$1.50 each including printing, handling, and postage. Since the mailing would be done by part-time secretarial help, the order in which the mailing was done could also be a factor.

Mr. Hare also felt that some consideration must be given to media advertising. He had considered placing ads in several local magazines including *Atlanta Magazine,* a monthly publication of the Chamber of Commerce, *Real Estate Atlanta,* a local trade magazine, and *Plant Location,* a trade publication that was mailed to all corporate real estate executives. He had also considered advertising in some less traditional sources such as *Southern Living* magazine, but was concerned with the expense involved here. He had not considered using the Atlanta issue of such national magazines as *Newsweek* and *Time* because he did not feel they reached his target market. A summary of the rates, circulation, and publication dates of these magazines is included in Exhibit 4.

In addition to selecting the media, Mr. Hare was faced with a decision on the copy to use. Preliminary talks with the advertising people at Royal Palm indicated they were willing to assist, but Mr. Hare wondered if he wanted to use this source. He knew that if he decided to do the copy on his own he could obtain assistance from the advertising staff of *Real Estate Atlanta* for a nominal fee.

A final promotional device which Mr. Hare thought might be effective in generating activity was the use of publicity. He was considering several diverse activities which he hoped would stimulate some media response. One such idea was to sponsor a kite festival in conjunction with a local kite specialty shop. Such an event would be open to the public, and would include demonstrations, free kites, and refreshments. Although he would need to purchase some of the kites as promotional gifts, he hoped to include a local bottling company in the promotion and have them provide the refreshments. He also considered inviting several charity functions such as the Heart Fund to set up a booth so that free public service announcements on radio and television would be possible. In addition, he considered some type of go-cart or marathon race as possible publicity stunts. By involving other groups in these projects he felt the cost would be less than $500 for each event. He hoped that the media

EXHIBIT 4

Advertising rates of selected publications

	Black and white		Color	
Magazine	Full page	One-third page	Full page	One-third page
Southern Living (Ga. edition)..........	$1,390	$ 610	$ 2,405	$1,035
Southern Living (complete)............	7,850	2,720	11,110	4,880
Atlanta Magazine.....................	865	345	1,095	575
Plant Location.......................	1,600	620	—	—
Site Selection Handbook...............	1,150	570	1,725	1,145
Time (Atlanta edition)................	850	—	1,325	—
Newsweek (Atlanta edition)...........	810	—	1,265	—
Real Estate Atlanta...................	475	250	650	425

Southern Living (Ga. edition)..........	Circulation 100,000; monthly.
Southern Living (complete edition).....	Circulation 1,147,000; monthly.
Atlanta Magazine.....................	Circulation 22,000; published by Chamber of Commerce; monthly.
Plant Location.......................	Circulation 41,000; single copy $15; published annually.
Site Selection Handbook...............	Circulation 23,500; published January, June, September.
Time (Atlanta edition)................	Circulation 40,000.
Newsweek (Atlanta edition)...........	Circulation 30,000.
Real Estate Atlanta...................	Circulation 10,000 except for two special issues with circulation of 20,000 each (with rates 50 percent higher for these issues); monthly.

coverage generated would stimulate awareness of the project, but was not sure how best to involve the media (for example, one station as a sponsor versus more general, but less complete, coverage on all stations) nor how effective such measures would really be.

A final consideration was to select a logo and have it printed on T-shirts or golf shirts to give to potential customers and to brokers. The price of these shirts would vary with the quality from $2.98 up.

ALTERNATIVE FINANCING METHODS

In reviewing the operation of other developments in both the Atlanta area and nationwide, Mr. Hare realized that there were several different financial approaches he might take in developing Atlanta-Tucker Industrial Park. Since Royal Palm had no experience in industrial real estate, they had not previously given consideration to any of the numerous plans available to a developer.

In addition to the conventional purchase of land for the construction of a building by the owner/tenant, several leasing arrangements had become popular during the past few years, and Mr. Hare was considering how to employ these methods in Atlanta-Tucker Industrial Park. The first involved a straight or conventional lease in which the building was leased directly from the owner. The second type involved a build-lease agreement whereby the owner of the property built the structure to the exact specifications of the lessee who then signed a long-term lease. A variation of this alternative would be industrial revenue bond financing where the owner would be the DeKalb County Industrial Authority. A third alternative currently employed was the ground lease. Under this plan, the owner of the property subjected the land to a long-term ground or land lease whereby the site was leased, but the lessee constructed his own building on the property. The second and third alternatives had proved especially effective in reducing the initial investment outlay involved for the company seeking new facilities and had thus reduced buyer resistance in some cases.

In addition to lease arrangements, Mr. Hare also considered the possibility of selling sites on terms where the client would pay 25 percent down with the rest of the payment due over the next three to four years. This plan offered the client who had no immediate plans to build the opportunity to purchase the lot and have it paid off by the time he was ready to construct a building. A variation of this plan would involve selling a very small lot with the option to purchase the surrounding area over the next few years. The company could thus go ahead and start the building with a minimum outlay for the property and still be assured that they would have the additional space they anticipated needing in the long run.

A final financial arrangement which appealed to Mr. Hare was working with a builder on build-lease deals where he and the builder would actually finance the construction of the building. In this way, he would be a part owner and could hope to make substantial long-range profits.

Mr. Hare had observed that there was a growing interest in shorter terms for leases by both tenants and owners and felt this might have some impact on his arrangements. The short lease of three to five years provided the owner the opportunity to adjust his rates as rising interest rates and inflation cut into his profit while offering the firm the flexibility to change as future growth affected his needs.

Since all of these financing plans depended in part upon the credit of the clients, Mr. Hare realized that extensive negotiations with lenders might be involved.

CASE

43

Mirco Games*

Mirco Games, a division of Mirco, Inc., designs, develops, and markets table soccer, electronic video, and pinball games for the coin-operated and home entertainment industries. Located in Phoenix, Arizona, the firm has experienced rapid growth in the sales of its games. Although Mirco Games was enjoying an increase in demand for its product lines, John Walsh, chairman of the board of Mirco, Inc., was concerned about what strategies the Games Division should employ over the next few years.

HISTORY OF MIRCO, INC.

Mirco, Inc. (the company) was incorporated in Arizona on November 11, 1971, to succeed and to acquire the assets of a partnership known as John L. Walsh & Associates, which was composed of Messrs. John L. Walsh, Bruce E. Kinkner, and Robert M. Kessler, who are the founders of the company. As of January 1, 1976, the company consisted of the parent company, Mirco, Inc., and five divisions: (1) Mirco Electronic Distributors, (2) Mirco Systems, (3) Mirco Games, (4) Mirco Games Australia Pty., Ltd., and (5) Mirco Games of Europe.

At its founding, the company's business was to design, develop, and market computer software for automatic testing systems used in high-volume production maintenance, depot, and field testing facilities for

---

* This case was written by Robert B. Kaiser, Director of Marketing, Mirco Games, Lonnie L. Ostrom, Associate Professor of Marketing, Arizona State University, and William E. Rief, Professor of Management, Arizona State University. Used with permission.

electronic equipment. The Mirco Electronic Distributors division was established on December 15, 1972, to engage in business as a distributor of component parts to electronic equipment manufacturers. On December 18, 1973, another division, Mirco Systems, was formed to carry on the electronic test business through the continued design and marketing of the company's software and to design and market test equipment. On December 26, 1973, the company acquired the assets and business of Arizona Automation, Inc., which was merged into another division called Mirco Games. The business of Mirco Games is to design, manufacture, and market table soccer, pinball, and electronic video games. Each segment of the company's business is more fully described below.

Generally, the parent company provides planning, accounting, legal, and financial services to each of the divisions. As of March 1976, corporate headquarters had 35 employees: the chairman of the board, president, vice president—operations, vice president—controller, an accountant, an

EXHIBIT 1
MIRCO, INC. AND SUBSIDIARIES
Consolidated Statement of Income
For the years ended January 31, 1973–1976

	1976	1975	1974	1973 (unaudited)
Net sales	$9,394,397	$5,033,717	$2,078,266	$1,156,319
Cost of sales	6,045,170	3,286,400	1,383,670	601,782
Gross Profit	$3,349,227	$1,747,317	$ 694,596	$ 554,537
Operating Expenses:				
Engineering	$ 897,407	$ 268,207	$ 255,130	$ 85,924
Selling	1,218,905	775,188	164,411	54,934
General and administrative	891,822	525,256	327,723	293,988
	$3,008,134	$1,568,651	$ 747,264	$ 434,846
Income from operations	$ 341,093	$ 178,666	$ (52,668)	$ 119,691
Interest expense	84,995	68,390	17,648	4,168
Income before income taxes and extraordinary item	$ 256,098	$ 110,276	$ (70,316)	$ 115,523
Provision for income taxes	123,000	48,625	31,048	55,145
Income before extraordinary item	$ 133,098	$ 61,651	$ (101,364)	$ 60,378
Extraordinary item—Income tax reduction resulting from loss carry-forward benefits	—	48,625	—	15,708
Net Income	$ 133,098	$ 110,276	$ (101,364)	$ 76,086
Income per Capital and Equivalent Share:				
Before extraordinary item	$ 0.08	$ 0.04	$ (0.08)	$ 0.05
Extraordinary item	—	0.04	—	0.02
	$ 0.08	$ 0.08	$ (0.08)	$ 0.07
Average Number of Capital and Equivalent Shares Outstanding during the Year	$1,575,939	$1,450,112	$1,232,623	$1,114,173

office manager, 4 bookkeepers, 2 secretaries, 1 personnel specialist, and 22 purchasing, maintenance, quality control, and warehouse personnel.

In fiscal year 1976, ending January 31, 1976, the company achieved sales of more than $9 million, which represented an outstanding record of growth. Exhibit 1 contains consolidated income statements for the years 1973–76, and Exhibit 2 consolidated balance sheets for 1975 and 1976.

EXHIBIT 2
MIRCO, INC. AND SUBSIDIARIES

Consolidated Balance Sheet
For the Years Ended January 31, 1976 and 1975

Assets	1976	1975
Current Assets:		
Cash and certificates of deposit.....................	$ 129,556	$ 17,700
Accounts receivable, less allowance of $45,000 at January 31, 1976, and $181,500 at January 31, 1975, for doubtful accounts.............................	839,730	813,473
Account receivable from Membrain, Inc. (a stockholder)...................................	27,148	—
Notes receivable....................................	14,586	—
Inventories..	1,573,684	1,223,169
Prepaid expenses and other assets.................	27,497	5,986
Total Current Assets...........................	$2,612,201	$2,060,328
Leasehold improvements............................	$ 47,812	$ 38,117
Machinery and equipment..........................	300,197	178,902
Automobiles.......................................	13,028	14,324
Furniture and fixtures.............................	56,627	26,579
Total Leasehold Improvements and Equipment	$ 417,664	$ 257,922
Less: Accumulated depreciation..................	112,782	53,603
	$ 304,882	$ 204,319
	$2,917,083	$2,264,647

Liabilities and Stockholders' Investment		
Current Liabilities:		
Notes payable.....................................	$ 610,000	$ 445,503
Current portion of long-term debt..................	15,213	12,923
Accounts payable.................................	709,032	713,102
Accrued payroll...................................	37,570	6,221
Accrued interest..................................	6,702	8,727
Other accrued expenses...........................	73,113	23,790
Income taxes currently payable....................	104,000	—
Total Current Liabilities.......................	$1,555,630	$1,210,266
Long-Term Debt, Less Current Portion..............	$ 33,838	$ 49,051
Stockholders' Investment:		
Capital stock; no par value; 5,000,000 shares authorized; 1,607,423 shares outstanding at January 31, 1976, and 1,391,880 shares outstanding at January 31, 1975...	$1,270,037	$ 947,863
Note receivable taken as consideration on sale of capital stock..................................	(132,987)	—
Retained earnings.............................	190,565	57,467
	$1,327,615	$1,005,330
	$2,917,083	$2,264,647

The distribution business

Mirco Electronic Distributors supplies component parts such as semi-conductors, capacitors, connectors, and resistors to (1) manufacturers of electronic equipment and (2) users of the equipment for modification, replacement, or spare parts. This division performs an economic role by purchasing components from manufacturers (and sometimes from other distributors), maintaining an inventory, filling orders on demand, and providing quick delivery. In addition, it complements the other Mirco divisions by providing them with accurate information about the status of parts and equipment in the industry and supplying them with component parts and equipment at a reduced cost.

The distribution business is highly competitive. To meet competition, one must be able to obtain representation of lines of components, anticipate customers' future needs, and maintain inventories accordingly. If Mirco Electronic Distributors stocks components for which demand fails to develop, it will tie up working capital in unprofitable inventories that may have to be disposed of at or below cost.

Mirco Electronic Distributors is a regional distributor. Its market area includes Arizona; the Albuquerque, Las Cruces, and Roswell areas of New Mexico; the Denver and Henderson areas of Colorado; Los Angeles, California; Las Vegas, Nevada; and Salt Lake City, Utah.

The test business

Mirco Systems designs, develops, manufactures, and markets hardware and computer software for the automatic testing of commercial and military digital electronic equipment. "Software" is a term generally used to describe computer programs; that is, a set of instructions which cause a computer to perform desired operations. The term "hardware" is used to describe the actual equipment.

Electronic equipment generally consists of numerous integrated circuit boards. Each circuit board contains approximately 10 to 300 components. These boards are tested for defects by the manufacturer at the completion of the manufacturing and assembly process. Boards also are tested after the equipment has been put into use as part of preventive or remedial maintenance programs.

Recent advances in technology have led to the development of computer systems to perform such testing automatically. These automatic test systems determine and identify faulty components in circuit boards. Automatic test systems are used primarily in high-volume production and maintenance testing facilities. The users of such systems include both the manufacturers and the owners of equipment using semiconductor components. It is possible to test circuit boards manually but it is becoming increasingly more difficult and costly to do so because of advanced technology and the time required to test the more complex boards.

At present, Mirco Systems markets its proprietary Fault Logic and Simulation Hybrid (FLASH) program. The FLASH program aids in the development of software for logic card testers, including the simulation of complex test patterns and the generation of a fault directory for logic components on printed circuit boards. It also is used to develop testing programs for specific circuit boards.

Mirco Systems also manufactures and markets automatic test equipment (hardware). In addition, it purchases test equipment from Membrain Limited, a United Kingdom corporation, for sale in the United States. Such equipment is usually sold in conjunction with the sale of software products generated by Mirco Systems. Although FLASH is considered a proprietary product, in reality the program has little protection from competition. Because there is a constant risk of obsolescence in the test business, the firm's long-run success may ultimately depend on the success of its research and development program.

Test Programming Services is a group that creates software and specific test programs for customers. It functions primarily in support of hardware sales. This capability is considered to be critical to the test business as it enables Mirco Systems to offer complete test systems. Mirco Systems has had no difficulty in recruiting suitable people to write test programs and expects to have no difficulty in the future.

Management believes that competition in the test business is based on quality, product performance, price, and postdelivery support. There are several other companies in the test business, most of whom are larger, well-financed, diversified electronics firms. Each competitor has its own systems.

The games business

On December 26, 1973, Mirco, Inc., acquired the business of Arizona Automation, Inc., which had existed since 1970. The company issued 174,000 shares of its capital stock, without par value, to Richard N. Raymond and Virginia A. Raymond, his wife, who were the sole shareholders of Arizona Automation. The shares were valued, for the purposes of that transaction, at $3.50 per share. Arizona Automation was merged into Mirco, Inc. and became Mirco Games. Of the 174,000 shares, 30,000 shares were escrowed for a period of one year. The escrowed shares were to be available to the company in case any claims were to arise against the former shareholders in Arizona Automation on account of any breach of warranty made in connection with the transaction. The purpose of

EXHIBIT 3

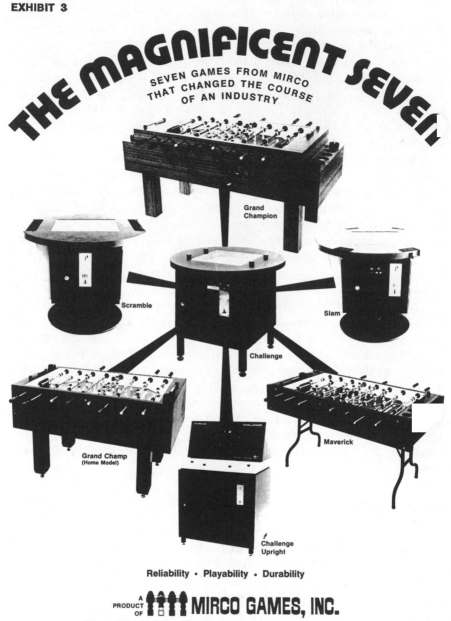

THE MAGNIFICENT SEVEN

SEVEN GAMES FROM MIRCO
THAT CHANGED THE COURSE
OF AN INDUSTRY

Grand Champion

Scramble

Slam

Challenge

Grand Champ
(Home Model)

Maverick

Challenge Upright

Reliability • Playability • Durability

A PRODUCT OF **MIRCO GAMES, INC.**

Phone (602) 944-5578 • 1960 W. North Lane • Phoenix, Arizona 85021 the acquisition was to acquire an existing marketing organization for the distribution of electronic games and to acquire the "know-how" in the games business possessed by Mr. Raymond.

Of approximately 150 employees in Mirco, Inc., about half of them are in the Games Division. The company has two main product lines: (1) table soccer, marketed under the name "Champion Soccer," which comes in a variety of models, and (2) video games, which consist of two versions of electronic ping-pong and come in either an upright cabinet or a cocktail table cabinet. Exhibit 3 provides a display of the basic models offered by Mirco Games.

Of the $9.4 million total sales in fiscal year 1976, about $7.3 million were from the Games Division. Of the $7.3 million games sales, $1.2 million were from table soccer and $6.1 million from video games. The breakdown geographically was: $6.5 million in U.S. game sales, $200,000 in German and $600,000 in Australian games sales. This compares with games sales of just under $1 million in both fiscal years 1973 and 1974.

The company believed that competition in the games business was based upon playability, price, and quality. Contrary to soccer games, which have been marketed in Europe for over 50 years and have more recently established a strong market in the United States, it is difficult to predict whether electronic games will continue over time to have consumer appeal.

Mirco Games has several competitors in soccer and video games. The major competitors in soccer are Dynamo, Tournament Soccer, Garlando, and Deutsch Meister, while in video games they are Atari and Ramtek. There is also a risk that a major, well-financed firm will enter the video games market in which case the industry would be faced with much stiffer competition.

Australia and Europe were perceived to be good potential markets for video games. In order to avoid high import duties, Mirco began to assemble video games in Australia in April 1975 and in Germany in September 1975.

AMUSEMENT GAMES INDUSTRY

The term "coin-industry" is often applied to the manufacturers and distributors of coin-operated equipment for consumer use. The two main segments in this industry are vending machines (food, drink, cigarettes, and so on) and amusement machines.

Amusement machines consist of coin-operated phonographs (juke boxes) and amusement games, such as pool tables, pinball machines, table soccer, and video games. The principal manufacturers of pinball machines were Gottlieb, Balley, Chicago Coin, and Williams. Coin-operated phonographs are manufactured by Seeburg, Rock-ola, and Rowe. The newest development, video games, has been spawned by new companies outside of the traditional industry network.

Sales are seasonal in nature. New products are introduced in the fall and generally available in the following first quarter (February, March, and April). New product introductions are geared to the Music Operators of America trade show which is held annually in late October or early November.

The present structure of the amusement games industry was developed in the 1930s. At that time, the need for the distributor came into being with the introduction of coin-operated phonograph and pinball machines. The primary purpose of the distributor was to provide electrical and mechanical servicing. Distributors were either owned by the manufacturers or were independent. They, in turn, helped set up the operator, who was responsible for locating the game equipment and sharing revenues with the location owner. This distribution network remains virtually intact today.

The operator is the owner of the equipment. In addition to seeking out new locations, he is responsible for routine servicing. The operator typically has a route which he maintains, making periodic collections from the cash

EXHIBIT 4
Channels of distribution for the amusement games industry

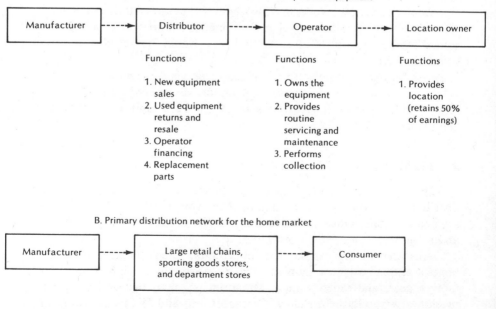

A. Conventional distribution network for coin-operated equipment

Manufacturer	Distributor	Operator	Location owner

	Functions	Functions	Functions
	1. New equipment sales 2. Used equipment returns and resale 3. Operator financing 4. Replacement parts	1. Owns the equipment 2. Provides routine servicing and maintenance 3. Performs collection	1. Provides location (retains 50% of earnings)

B. Primary distribution network for the home market

Manufacturer	Large retail chains, sporting goods stores, and department stores	Consumer

boxes attached to the equipment and dividing the earnings with the location owner (typically 50–50). The specific functions associated with each member of the conventional channel are identified in Exhibit 4.

TABLE SOCCER

Table soccer appears to have originated in Germany in the late 1920s or early 1930s. Soccer is known as football in many European countries, and the German word for football, fussball, is the alternative name used for table soccer in the United States (under a variety of spellings). Presently, European versions of the game are manufactured in West Germany, France, and Italy.

The first soccer games that were exported to the United States in the mid-1950s were not readily accepted. In 1962, L. T. Patterson Distributors of Cincinnati made the first major commitment to distribute a German-produced table called "Foosball." Because it was a relatively unknown sport in America and required a high skill level, the acceptance was slow for many years and it was not until the late 1960s that table soccer became a significant factor in the games industry. One of the contributing factors to its growth in popularity in the United States was the demand created by servicemen who had been introduced to the game while stationed in Europe.

In 1967, Dick Raymond and John Walsh, while working for General Electric in Germany, became interested in table soccer. Soccer tables were found in many of the bars and taverns of France, Germany, and Italy and were avidly played by Europeans as well as by American servicemen and businessmen. Raymond and Walsh saw the potential for such a game and made plans to export tables to the United States.

When Raymond and Walsh returned to Phoenix in 1970, they formed Arizona Automation. Within a year following incorporation, Raymond purchased Walsh's share and became sole owner of Arizona Automation. In 1971, Arizona Automation began building a soccer table known as Champion Soccer. In four years, annual sales climbed from $15,000 to approximately $1 million.

Manufacturing

The component parts for Champion Soccer are purchased from outside vendors and the game is assembled by Mirco Games. There are presently alternate sources for all of the components except the figurines. Should that source fail, it is estimated that production would be delayed for approximately two months while a new source was found.

Patents, trademarks, and licensing

The company has registered Champion Soccer as a trademark in the United States and in Canada. An application for trademark registration has been filed with respect to the design of figurines for the soccer game, and a patent has been granted for the "two point ball control" figurine. There are no other patents or other protection for the table soccer products.

Competition

Due to the high quality of its soccer tables, Mirco has been a dominant force in the United States market with about $1.2 million in sales out of an industry total of $12 million. Recently, however, Mirco has experienced increased competition from a number of firms that have entered the market, especially Dynamo and Tournament Soccer. In order to maintain its leadership in the soccer table market, Mirco was forced to significantly redesign its soccer tables to improve their appearance, playability, and durability. Dynamo's approach to the market is similar to Mirco's in that they cultivate a high-quality image and have introduced several technical innovations into their product; among them are the textured tempered glass playfield, the massive table to prevent table movement during play, the balanced figurine, and precision ground steel rods. Mirco subsequently incorporated some of these innovations to maintain their market position. Tournament Soccer has pursued the market through an active and expensive program utilizing table soccer tournaments throughout the United States. Their current tournament program offers prize money in excess of $250,000 per year.

Marketing

Mirco markets its coin-operated soccer games through approximately 50 distributors that are located for the most part in the United States and Canada (see Exhibit 4). As is typical of the industry, there are no binding contractual arrangements with any of these distributors. They are free to deal in competitive products or to discontinue to distribute Mirco's products at any time. Home table soccer games are distributed through major retail chains, sporting goods and department stores, and the American Express catalog. In addition, a small amount of government business is handled via the Government Services Administration.

Pricing.   Pricing is consistent with Mirco's image as a quality producer of soccer games. There is only one distributor price regardless of quantity. A typical selling price to the operator for a high quality coin-operated table soccer game is around $675. The channel markup is approximately 35 percent.

Promotion. Mirco Games advertises in the coin-operated equipment trade journals, such as *Cashbox, Playmeter, Replay,* and in sporting goods magazines. It also promotes its products at trade shows like the National Sporting Goods Association and the Music Operators of America. Bob Seagren, Olympic gold medal winner and superstar champion, is used extensively in advertisements and trade show displays.

Mirco also has engaged in a series of promotional events, mainly in the form of statewide tournaments in key metropolitan cities. In 1973 and 1974, they sponsored the Louisiana State Soccer Tournaments, both of which were $2,000 events. In 1975, Mirco tournaments were held in Detroit, Minneapolis, Omaha, and Kansas City, with total prize money exceeding $16,000. The 1976 schedule includes St. Louis, Rochester, and Detroit.

Market research. Market information is obtained from three principal sources: the distributors, operators, and location owners. At times, games are "test marketed" by placing them in selected locations and analyzing their earning power over a given period of time.

ELECTRONIC (VIDEO AND PINBALL) GAMES

Atari was the first company to successfully market a video game. It was called "Pong" and was a two-player tennis-type game operated with electronic paddles and a ball. The acceptance of this product was phenomenal and before long more than 30 producers of video games were in the market, from the large established companies to the newly formed "garage-type" operations. Although it is relatively easy for a new company to enter the video games market, the failure rate of new entrants is extremely high, due primarily to a lack of adequate testing capability, poor service, high operating costs, limited financing, and little marketing expertise. According to one financial analyst who observed 24 games companies during 1974, 20 went out of business, 2 were marginal in nature, and the remaining 2 were Mirco and Atari.

Mirco Games entered the market in 1973 with its two-player video game, Champion Ping Pong, at a time when competitors were introducing a great variety of more sophisticated games. It was felt that the company's expertise in the area of electronic testing equipment would provide them with two immediate advantages over their major competitors: quick turnaround in servicing (24 hours) and a more reliable product. Unfortunately, these two advantages were not sufficient to offset Champion Ping Pong's lack of playability, which is the primary competitive factor in video games. The urgent need to develop new products was recognized by Mirco at that time; however, an extremely tight cash-flow position prevented major R&D expenditures for video games. In 1973, the Mirco Systems Division had invested heavily in R&D to develop its computer-controlled test equipment, which was not yet ready for production, and it had severely drained the company's finances.

In March 1974, Mirco Games introduced the Challenge upright four-player video game which featured one free game in the event that one or two players beat the machine in the player versus machine mode. Unfortunately, this innovative feature was not sufficient to offset the fact that competition had introduced four-player games 12 months earlier and the market was now saturated. In July 1974, the "Challenge" cocktail table version was introduced. The major advantage of this game was its appeal to sophisticated locations, such as Holiday Inns, Playboy Clubs, and country clubs, which previously had not been a viable market for video games. Unfortunately, the conventional distribution network was ill-equipped to implement a marketing strategy to take advantage of this new and rapidly expanding market.

Distributor. In order to exploit this new market for cocktail table models, Bob Kaiser, marketing manager, decided to set up an entirely new channel of distribution, which became known as the nonconventional distribution network (see Exhibit 5). He sought out individual entrepreneurs, such as real estate people and stocks and bonds salespersons, who, due to the recession, were without a product to market but had sufficient capital to invest in a new venture. This strategy proved to be very successful and, in fact, helped stimulate sales of the tabletop video game through conventional distributors and operators. One major advantage of the nonconventional channel is that terms are cash, whereas in the conventional channel they are net 30 and the manufacturer is frequently forced to extend credit for 60 to 90 days.

Innovation. Innovation is a requirement for survival in the games industry. Mirco's achievements in this area have not been spectacular. However, a Mirco processor pinball machine, which was a first in the industry, was introduced in late 1975. Management felt that this product would successfully lead Mirco into a new segment of the coin-operated market.

Pricing. Two pricing constraints are active in the marketplace. In the segment of the market dominated by innovative games, particularly video, pricing is determined primarily by the earning power of the machine, that is, its ability to sit in a location and, without being promoted, attract players. (The location life of a video game is less than 90 days as a rule.) In that segment of the market where the products are stable and have a long life in a specific location, such as pool tables and table soccer, pricing is solely a function of competition.

EXHIBIT 5
Nonconventional distribution network for video games

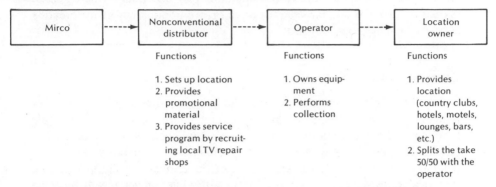

Manufacturing

With respect to electronic games, Mirco purchases all components, such as television monitors and subassemblies, from outside vendors and assembles the games itself. At the present time, the sole source for television monitors is Motorola. Although no difficulties are anticipated in obtaining sufficient quantities of monitors from Motorola, significant production delays and expenses probably would be encountered in changing to another vendor.

Home video games market

Along with coin-operated electronic games, video and pinball games for the home promise to have a great future: projections go as high as $1 billion by 1980. In 1972, Magnavox brought out the first home video game, "Odyssey," for the price of over $100. Several new entrants are now active in this area, including Atari which introduced their home model version of "Pong" in 1975. One of the obstacles in this new market is that FCC approval is required for any games that hook up to a TV antenna.

Brisk sales were reported by both Magnavox and Atari during the 1975 Christmas season. Atari's version of "Pong" was sold by Sears, which stated that it could sell all it could get. Magnavox, which had introduced an improved version of Odyssey a few months earlier, marketed its products through its vast network of approximately 2,500 dealers throughout the United States.

It is anticipated that home video games will soon be available for $30–$40 retail. Most products will include multiple games, color, sound, and remote controls. On-screen score display and variable difficulty are possible features.

In January 1976, Mirco entered into an agreement with Fairchild Camera and Instrument to jointly develop and produce home video games. Christmas of 1976 was targeted for a major promotional effort for creating a new consumer mass market.

Computerized pinball

In 1975, Mirco was the first on the market with a micro-computer pinball machine in which one printed circuit board handles all electronic functions. The game featured an electronic semiconductor memory, LED (digital display) readouts, and a self-diagnostic capability for quick troubleshooting. Although it was the hit of the annual Music Operators of America trade show, it was too early to tell what impact it will have on the traditional coin-operated pinball market. One concern is that because of Mirco's lack of expertise in backglass and playfield design, both strong competitive features in pinball machines because of their association with playability in the minds of players, it may not be able to take full advantage of being first in the microcomputer pinball market.

THE FUTURE OF THE GAMES BUSINESS

In 1976, the electronic games market was still in its infancy. Atari was the leader in video sales, with about $18 million in 1975, and "close to $30 million" projected for 1976. Although sales information is difficult to obtain about other firms in this industry, it was believed that Mirco Games was number two. Whereas Atari produces many different types of video games, Mirco has concentrated its efforts in producing a few models of one basic game. During the period in which Mirco successfully marketed the "Challenge" table top video game, Atari introduced 50 new game designs.

It is expected that semiconductor companies will play a major role in the games business. In early 1976, research was under way at General Instrument, Texas Instruments, and National Semiconductor to develop video products. With the possibility of many companies invading the territory of the traditional manufacturer of coin-operated games, the long-run outcome is somewhat uncertain. The traditional companies are likely to react strongly to protect their existing markets.

Table soccer appears to have a good 15 to 20 percent per year growth potential. In contrast to the video market, this market appears to be extremely stable.

Another uncertainty is the extent to which the expanding home game market will affect the sales of coin-operated games. The traditional companies feel that home games will stimulate rather than take away from their business, and they predict a steady growth in the next few years.

Home games market

Strategies in the home games market are difficult to determine because of rapid technological changes. Games with their own video displays are likely to evolve and they may be tied in with the computer terminal that one day will be installed in most homes. One definite advantage for new companies entering this market is that because home electronics games (video and pinball) are so new, no strong brand loyalty currently exists.

INDEX OF CASES

Index of cases